DIGITAL SYSTEMS

HARDWARE ORGANIZATION AND DESIGN

DIGITAL SYSTEMS

HARDWARE ORGANIZATION AND DESIGN

THIRD EDITION

Fredrick J. Hill
Professor of Electrical Engineering
University of Arizona

Gerald R. Peterson
Professor of Electrical Engineering
University of Arizona

John Wiley & Sons
New York   Chichester   Brisbane   Toronto   Singapore

Library of Congress Cataloging-in-Publication Data

Hill, Fredrick J.
    Digital systems.

    1. Computer engineering.   2. Computer architecture.
I. Peterson, Gerald R. II. Title.
TK7888.3.H5 1987   621.39   86-34027
ISBN 0-471-80806-7

Printed in the United States of America

10 9 8 7 6 5 4 3 2 1

Preface

The need for a book on digital computer hardware design that is really an engineering textbook was evident at the time of the writing of the first edition. Traditionally, engineering textbooks are concerned with imparting a skill—with teaching the student how to do something. By contrast, most books on computer design are little more than descriptive surveys of existing computer hardware. In reading such books, the student is an observer rather than a participant.

In this book, we involve the student in the design process rather than just describe the end product. The principal vehicle for this involvement is a register transfer level hardware description language. Various languages of this kind have been proposed, but none have met with general acceptance. The authors have developed, in the course of writing the three editions of this book, A Hardware Programming Language (AHPL), some of whose operators resemble those of APL. Now, when the designer writes an AHPL expression, he or she is able to picture clearly the hardware that will eventually result. Using this language, we explore the design of a wide variety of digital hardware systems and present concrete design examples as liberally as possible throughout the book.

This book is written for the computer scientist and systems programmer, as well as for the electrical engineer. Undoubtedly, many users of this book will never be responsible for actual hardware design, but the design point of view is a fascinating one even for the student whose primary objective is to become familiar with hardware organization and system architecture. We have used this text in classes divided almost equally between computer science students with no engineering background and electrical engineering students with prior courses in switching theory and electronics. The responses from both groups have been positive and most gratifying.

The only topics specifically prerequisite to this book are programming in a high-level language, the binary number system, Boolean algebra, and Karnaugh maps. We assume that the instructor will have no difficulty presenting a brief introduction to these topics if necessary. In addition to this material, the only prerequisites for a course based on this book would be programming experience, a certain degree of intellectual maturity, and a serious interest in computers. Electrical engineers who hope to design digital hardware should master switching theory and sequential circuits, as well as the material presented in this book. For these students, a prior course covering material similar in scope to the first 15 chapters of our switching theory book is highly desirable.

A primary objective in writing the second edition of the book was improving, formalizing, and firming up the hardware correspondence of AHPL. In this third edition, AHPL remains the same, but most treatments of subject matter have been substantially revised. Much has happened in the field of digital hardware since this book first appeared in 1973. The word length of almost every computer is now a multiple of 8-bits. We have, thus, replaced the 18-bit SIC with a 32-bit machine, RIC. RIC is more powerful than SIC; but, in order that it remain a convenient teaching vehicle, RIC has a somewhat less extensive instruction set than most 16- and 32-bit microprocessors.

Currently, almost all computer input-output is memory mapped I/O. We have completely rewritten Chapters 9, 10, 11, and 12 to incorporate this approach to input-output almost exclusively. Serial data communications has been expanded and has replaced the presentation of the 6800 microprocessor in Chapter 12. We now expect most students using this book to have some previous exposure to 8-bit microprocessors.

Although Chapter 8 of the previous edition remained relevant, this chapter was also revised and expanded to reflect the 32-bit architecture. Similarly, the treatment of associative and virtual memory in Chapter 13, a previous strong point, has been expanded.

Chapter 6, in which the AHPL description of RIC is developed, remains the focal point of the book. In preparation, Chapter 2 defines the architecture of RIC and Chapters 4 and 5 define AHPL. Following Chapter 6, the instructor can continue in the order of the book or go directly to Chapter 8 on microprogramming or to Chapters 9 through 12 on input-output. Likewise, Chapters 7 and 8 are not prerequisite to Chapter 13.

Our objective remains to introduce system into the design process. However, it has not been our intention to reduce the process to a cookbook procedure. A premium is placed on the imagination of the designer. This is evident in the problem sets that have themselves been updated and expanded to reflect the new material.

Since about 1980, many users of the book have been able to take advantage of HPSIM2, a function-level simulator for the clock-mode language AHPL. HPSIM2 remains applicable to AHPL as used in this third edition. Versions are available for personal computers using MS-DOS, for the VAX, and for IBM and CDC mainframes. For information, write the authors through the University of Arizona Engineering Experiment Station.

Contents

1. INTRODUCTION

2. ARCHITECTURE OF A REPRESENTATIVE 32-BIT PROCESSOR

3. SYSTEM BUILDING BLOCKS

4. DESIGN CONVENTIONS

5. INTRODUCTION TO A HARDWARE PROGRAMMING LANGUAGE (AHPL)

6. MACHINE ORGANIZATION AND HARDWARE PROGRAMS

7. HARDWARE REALIZATIONS

8. MICROPROGRAMMING

9. INTERSYSTEM COMMUNICATIONS

10. INTERRUPT AND MEMORY-MAPPED I/O

11. PERIPHERALS AND INTERFACING

12. SERIAL COMMUNICATIONS AND ERROR CONTROL IMPLEMENTATION

13. MEMORY APPROACHES FOR LARGE SYSTEMS

14. HIGH-SPEED ADDITION

15. MULTIPLICATION AND DIVISION

16. FLOATING-POINT ARITHMETIC

17. INCREASING CPU CAPABILITY

APPENDIX

Index   595

DIGITAL SYSTEMS
HARDWARE ORGANIZATION AND DESIGN

Introduction

1.1 Objective of the Book

The objective of this book is, quite simply, to teach you how to design complex digital systems. There is certainly no shortage of books on digital systems, but few deal directly with the problem of systems design. Books on digital systems fall primarily into three categories: (1) largely software, (2) primarily switching theory, and (3) computer architecture from a descriptive point of view. It is our contention that the first two categories deal with subjects quite distinct from, although related to, digital systems design. Books in the third category, although useful as an introduction to digital systems, fail to involve the reader in the design process.

Our primary resolve in writing this book has been to avoid merely describing computer hardware. Wherever possible, we have tried to emphasize the designer's point of view, starting with a problem to be solved and then considering possible means of solution. Our primary vehicle for involving you in the design experience is a *hardware description language* for specifying the *control sequence,* a step-by-step description of the functioning of the digital system. The control sequences are easily translated into control unit hardware. Once this is accomplished, the *digital system,* except for electronic circuit details, is designed.

We have used the term *digital system* without providing a definition. In the broadest sense, *digital* simply means that information is represented by signals that take on a limited number of discrete values and is processed by devices that normally function only in a limited number of discrete states. Further, the lack of practical devices capable of functioning reliably in more than two discrete states has resulted in the vast majority of digital devices being binary; that is, having signals and states limited to two discrete values. Any structure of physical devices assembled to process or transmit digital information may be termed a *digital system*. This includes, for example, teletypes, dial telephone switching exchanges, telemetering systems, tape transports and other peripheral equipments, and, of course, computers. Often, the word *system* is thought of as implying a *large* or *complex* system. For the present, our definition will be the broader one, presented first. In later chapters, large or complex may find its way into our meaning of *system* as we seek to distinguish a complete computing facility from its various components, such as a memory unit.

The characteristics of digital systems vary, and the approach to their design sometimes varies as well. Consider the very general model of a digital system shown in Fig. 1.1. Although in practice the distinction may not always be apparent, we shall arbitrarily separate the information that enters and leaves a digital system into two categories: (1) information to be processed or transmitted, and (2) control information. Information in the first category usually occurs in the form of a time-sequence of information vectors. A vector might be a *byte,* 8 binary bits; it might be a word of 16 to 64 bits; or it might be several words. In any case, a large number of wires are required to handle a vector in a physical system. Usually, the bits of a vector are treated within the system in some uniform manner, rather than each bit being treated in a separate way.

The second category, control information, usually occurs in smaller quantities, involving physically a range of one to a very small number of wires. Control information is self-defining. It is information that guides the digital system in performing its functions. Sometimes, the control information is received only. In other cases, control pulses are sent out to control the functions of some other equipment.

Certain digital systems handle only control information. The controller for an elevator is a good example. Systems of this type may be designed as *sequential circuits*. The procedures for sequential circuits design are well defined and are discussed in a number of introductory textbooks. See, for example, reference [3]. Classical sequential circuit techniques have not proved satisfactory for designing systems to process vectors of information. Consequently, computers have never been designed that way. The control portion of a more general digital system is, however, a sequential circuit and may be treated as such. For more complex systems, particularly computers, the portion that may be treated effectively as a classical sequential circuit is a relatively small part of the whole.

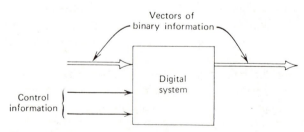

Figure 1.1. Types of digital information.

Digital computers certainly form the most important class of digital systems. Nearly every day we are reminded of the ways in which computers have basically altered our society, and the case for their importance can hardly be overstated. In this book, we shall be primarily concerned with digital computers and their peripheral equipment for two reasons. First, computers are the most important type of digital system. Second, virtually every aspect of digital design is encountered in computer design, so that the person well-versed in computer design should be capable of designing any type of digital system.

For the computer scientist whose primary interest is software, this book may stand alone as an engaging (we hope) introduction to the philosophy of hardware design. With more imaginative use of microprogramming, the overlap of hardware and software functions becomes increasingly apparent. A familiarity with hardware at the level of details presented herein will be increasingly required of persons going into the area of systems programming. Further, the steadily increasing importance of the microprocessor creates a real need for designers with competence in both the hardware and software aspects of digital systems design.

For the computer engineer, it is certainly not our intention to minimize the importance of companion courses in switching theory and digital circuit design. As contrasted with the computer scientist, the computer engineer has the responsibility of making the hardware work. Particular circuit technologies give rise to special problems that occupy ever-increasing amounts of engineering effort.

1.2   Evolution of the Computer

The history of mechanical aids to computation goes back many centuries. The development of the abacus apparently predates recorded history. In the 17th century, Pascal and Leibniz developed mechanical calculators, the ancestors through hundreds of years of development of today's desk calculators. The first device that was a computer in the modern sense was proposed about 1830 by Charles Babbage.

Babbage, an eccentric English mathematician, was one of the most fascinating characters in the history of science. He was concerned with improving the methods of computing mathematical tables. Until the advent of digital computers, mathematical tables were computed by teams of mathematicians, grinding away endlessly at desk calculators, performing the same calculations over and over to produce the thousands of entries in tables of logarithms, trigonometric functions, and the like. Babbage was working on some improved log tables and so despaired at ever getting the job done that he resolved to build a machine to do it.

The result of his first efforts was the Difference Engine, the first description of which he published in 1822. The Difference Engine carried out a fixed sequence of calculations, specified by mechanical settings of levers, cams, gears, and other devices. Even data had to be entered mechanically. The results were printed out immediately on computation. The Difference Engine was funded by the British government and was partially completed when Babbage conceived the idea of using punched cards, invented by Jacquard in 1801, to provide the input and storage of results. He proposed that instructions be read from one set of cards and data from another set, with the results stored on still another set. The proposed machine, which he called the Analytical Engine, even had a primitive decision capability. Although instructions had to be executed in the order read from the cards, an instruction could specify alternative actions, based on a test of previous results.

Babbage first started work on the Analytical Engine about 1830; the remainder of his life (he died in 1871) was spent in a fruitless effort to get the machine built. His ideas were a hundred years ahead of technology. The mechanical technology of the day was inadequate to meet the requirements of his designs. Indeed, it is doubtful if the Analytical Engine could be realized by mechanical means even today. The realization of Charles Babbage's dreams had to await the development of electronics.

In 1937, Howard Aiken, of Harvard University, proposed the Automatic Sequence Controlled Calculator, based on a combination of Babbage's ideas and the technology of the electromechanical calculators then being produced by IBM. Construction of this machine, more generally known as Mark I, was started in 1939, sponsored jointly by Harvard and IBM. The completed machine was dedicated August 7, 1944, a date considered by many to mark the start of the computer era.

Mark I was primarily electromechanical, being constructed mostly of switches and relays, a factor that severely limited its speed. Scientists at the Aberdeen Proving Ground, concerned with the development of ballistic tables for new weapons systems, recognized the need for a faster computer than Mark I. As a result, a contract was awarded in 1943 to the University of Pennsylvania to develop a digital computer using vacuum tubes instead of relays. The result was ENIAC, the world's first electronic digital computer. The ENIAC development team was led by J. P. Eckert and J. W. Mauchly. The mathematical consultant to the group was John von Neumann, one of the most creative mathematicians of this century. As the development of the digital computer involved the efforts of many brilliant individuals, no one person can be said to have invented the computer. Nevertheless, many people consider von Neumann to be the single most important figure in the history of the computer.

Although Mark I is generally considered to be the first digital computer, its structure was very little like that of present-day computers. It essentially consisted of many electromechanical calculators, working in parallel on a common problem, under the direction of a single control unit. This paralleling of many calculating units was made necessary by the slow speed of the electromechanical devices. The control unit read the instructions from a paper tape and, like the Analytical Engine, could execute them only in the sequence received.

ENIAC was essentially an electronic version of Mark I, with many parallel calculating elements and a sequential control unit. During the development of ENIAC, two new concepts emerged. The first was the realization that the great speed of electronic devices made it unnecessary to have many parallel calculating elements. The second was the idea that storing the program in memory, in much the same manner as data are stored, would make it possible to branch to alternate sequences of instructions, rather than being tied to a fixed sequence. These two concepts, together with some new developments in electronics, led to the proposal for a new machine, the EDVAC computer.

The development of the EDVAC proposal was a team effort, so it is difficult to assign credit for specific ideas to specific persons. Nevertheless, it was von Neumann who tied all the ideas together for the first time, in the *First Draft for a Report on EDVAC,* issued in June 1945. In this document, von Neumann set forth the basic logical structure of the *stored-program computer*. The following five criteria essentially define the computer, in terms of the capabilities it must have.

1. It must have an *input* medium, by means of which an essentially unlimited number of operands or instructions may be entered.
2. It must have a *store,* from which operands or instructions may be obtained and into which results may be entered, *in any desired order*.
3. It must have a *calculating* section, capable of carrying out arithmetic or logical operations on any operands taken from the store.
4. It must have an *output* medium, by means of which an essentially unlimited number of results may be delivered to the user.
5. It must have a *control unit,* capable of interpreting instructions obtained from memory, and capable of choosing between alternative courses of action on the basis of computed results.

The basic structure resulting from these criteria is known as the *von Neumann structure,* and virtually all computers built since that time have used this structure.

The ENIAC/EDVAC team broke up in 1946, Eckert and Mauchly leaving to found their own company, and von Neumann going to the Institute for Advanced Study at Princeton. The departure of many key people seriously slowed development of EDVAC, and it was not finally completed until 1950. Building on the basic structure of EDVAC, Eckert and Mauchly developed the first commercially produced computer, UNIVAC I, the first unit of which was delivered in 1951. At Princeton, von Neumann led the development of the IAS computer, which was also completed in 1951. During the course of this project, von Neumann contributed another basic idea, that of allowing a program to modify the address portion of instructions. This was the first approach to executing a single set of instructions over a range of data, a feature that is now facilitated through *indexing* and *indirect addressing*.

In succeeding years, the power and speed of computers have increased many orders of magnitude while the costs have decreased to a similar extent. Computers now influence every part of society. The recent development of the microcomputer has brought almost every citizen of the industrialized world into direct contact with these machines.

1.3 Basic Organization of Digital Computers

Any computer meeting the criteria set forth in the previous section will be basically organized as shown in Fig. 1.2. The exact nature of the components making up the five sections of the computer may vary widely, and the sections may overlap or share components, but the five functions associated with the five sections may be clearly identified in any digital computer.

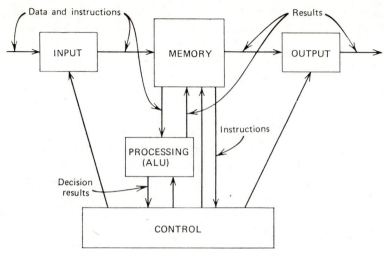

Figure 1.2. Basic computer organization.

The memory is the source or destination of all the information flowing to or from the other four sections of the computer. The memory may be regarded as a collection of storage locations for information; with each location is associated an *address*, by means of which that location may be accessed by the other sections of the computer. The amount of information that can be stored in an individually addressable location, expressed in terms of the number of bits (binary digits), is known as the *word length* of the memory. Word lengths in modern computers typically range from 8 bits to 64 bits.

A great variety of devices are used for memory, ranging from fast, low-capacity devices with a high cost per bit, to slow, high-capacity devices with a low cost per bit. A single computer may employ a hierarchy of memory devices of varying speed/ capacity ratios. The main memory—that portion of memory in the most direct communications with the control and processing sections—is usually a high-speed random access memory with a capacity ranging upward from 64K bytes (1K = 1024). This may be backed up by any number of slower devices, such as disk drives or tape transports, which may make bulk transfers of large numbers of words to or from main memory.

The primary functions of the input and output sections are as their names imply; but they have two subsidiary functions, buffering and data conversion, which are not quite so obvious. The buffering function provides the interface between the very fast processing section and the comparatively slow "outside world." For example, a human operator may type a file at a rate of a few characters per second. This file may then be transferred between a disk drive and main memory at a rate of 100,000 characters per second, and main memory can communicate with the processing unit at the rate of a million words per second.

The processing section, which we shall refer to as the *arithmetic-logical unit* (ALU), implements the various arithmetic and logical operations on operands obtained from memory. ALUs vary considerably in the number of different operations implemented. The minimum possible set of operations for a general purpose computer is a subject of some theoretical interest; as few as two may be sufficient, but even microcomputer ALUs have a repertory of up to 256 commands.

The control section receives instruction words from memory, decodes them, and issues the appropriate control signals to the other sections to cause the desired operations to take place. It also receives the results of various tests on data made by the ALU, on the basis of which it may choose between alternative courses of action. The combination of the ALU and the control unit is often known as the *central processing unit* (CPU).

Although all computers conform to the basic organization discussed here, computers vary greatly in complexity, size, and capability, and various classifications have been used over the years. When computers first appeared in the 1950s, it was common to classify them as *business* or *scientific,* depending on the type of application for which they were primarily intended. Later, as more models appeared, computers began to be classified as small, medium, or large, depending on their complexity, size, and cost. In the 1960s, *minicomputers* appeared, the most popular of which was the PDP/8, which used 12-bit words and had only 4096 words of memory in its standard form. The 1970s saw the introduction of the *microprocessor* and the *microcomputer.* A microprocessor is basically a CPU on a single integrated circuit chip. A microcomputer is a complete computer system consisting of a microprocessor, memory, input/output electronics, and a variable number of I/O devices—usually a keyboard, a monitor, and one or two disks, all in a compact package that will fit on a desk.

As advances in technology, particularly in *microelectronics,* have increased the power and complexity of computers, the meaning of these various categories has shifted. Some microcomputers available today are more powerful than most large computers of the 1950s, and even the smallest *micro* of today is more powerful than most of the *minis* of the 1960s. At this writing, it is common to classify machines as microcomputers or *mainframe* computers. Mainframe computers are too big to fit on a desk top and are packaged in one or more stand-alone cabinets. In terms of organizational complexity, the CPUs of mainframes may not differ greatly from those of the larger micros, but they will often be faster and have longer word lengths. Probably the most important difference between micros and mainframes is that mainframes will have more powerful peripherals, such as high-speed tape drives and line printers. Mainframes are in turn categorized as *minicomputers, maxicomputers,* or *supercomputers,* but just where the boundaries are between mini and maxi will usually depend on who is talking about whose computer. About all we can say for sure is that a maxicomputer is bigger than a minicomputer. Supercomputers are usually defined in terms of execution speed, as computers capable of executing in excess of 100 MIPS (million instructions per second).

1.4   Instruction Formats

You can get an idea of what information must be included in an instruction word by considering how you might give instructions to a person who is to do computations manually. That person will be provided with a ledger sheet of data and a sheet of instructions. Then a typical instruction might read, "Take a number from column 1, add it to a number in column 2, enter the sum in 3, and proceed to line 4 of the instruction sheet for the next step." In computer terms, this is a *four-address* instruction.

An instruction word, which is simply a string of 0's and 1's, is divided into several sections (fields), each of which is interpreted to have some specific significance by the control unit. The format of a four-address instruction is shown in Fig. 1.3a. The *opcode* is the numeric code, typically 4 to 8 bits, indicating the operation—add, subtract, shift, or such—to be performed. The remainder of the word provides the four addresses in the memory required for the two *operands,* the result, and the next instruction.

The main problem with the four-address instructions is the length of instruction required to accommodate four addresses. Because accessing instructions takes time, it is highly desirable that only one memory access be required to obtain an instruction. Thus the pressure is strong to limit the complexity of the instructions, so they may fit into a single memory word. The length of an address determines the size of the memory *address space,* that is, the number of words that can be addressed by an instruction. Because addresses are binary numbers, the number of words in the address space will be a power of two. It is conventional to express the size of the address space in terms of "K" or "M"—where K stands for 1024, the power of two nearest to one thousand, and M stands for 1,048,576, the power of two nearest to one million. The more words in the address space, the more bits will be required to specify a location. For example, a 64K address space, a popular size in microprocessors, will require 16-bit addresses, so that a four-address instruction will require 64 bits just for addresses. Only the very largest machines will have words this long.

The number of addresses in the instruction word can be reduced by letting some of the information be "understood." Most of the time, computer programs proceed in a fixed sequence, *branching* to an alternate path only occasionally. We therefore specify that the instructions shall be stored in sequentially numbered locations, and the next instruction will be taken from the next sequential location, unless otherwise specified.

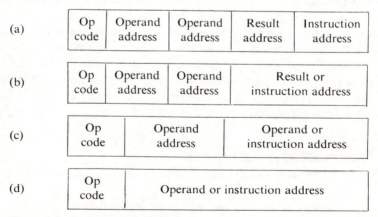

Figure 1.3. Typical instruction formats.

This concept leads to the three-address instruction (Fig. 1.3b), which will typically have the meaning, "Take the operands from the first two addresses, store the result at the third address, and take the next instruction from the next sequential location." Deviation from the fixed sequence requires a branch instruction, which could have the meaning, "Compare the operands taken from the first two addresses; if they are equal, take the next instruction from the third address; if not, take the next instruction from the next sequential location."

The number of required addresses can be further reduced by allowing the destination of the result to be "understood." The two-address instruction (Fig. 1.3c) takes on two standard forms.

The *replacement* instruction typically has the meaning, "Take the operands from the two addresses, store the result at the second address (replacing the second operand), and take the next instruction from the next sequential location." This type of instruction is inconvenient if both operands need to be preserved for further operations. The problem can be avoided by specifying a standard register in the CPU, usually known as the *accumulator,* as the destination for results. Then a typical two-address instruction will have the meaning, "Take the operands from the two addresses, place the result in the accumulator, and take the next instruction from the next sequential location." With this form, we must also have a store instruction, of the form, "Store the contents of the accumulator in one of the two specified addresses." In either case, the branch instruction might take the form, "Compare the contents of the first address with the contents of the accumulator; if they are equal, take the next instruction from the second address; if not, take the next instruction from the next sequential location."

In Fig. 1.3d, we show the single-address format, which allows the source of the second operand to be "understood." Now the typical instruction will have the meaning, "Take the first operand from the addressed location, the second from the accumulator, place the result in the accumulator, and take the next instruction from the next sequential location." A typical branch instruction might take the form, "Test the contents of the accumulator; if they are zero, take the next instruction from the addressed location; if not, continue in sequence."

Finally, although not shown in Fig. 1.3, there is the "addressless" or *inferred address* format in which the opcode specifies (infers) the location to be modified. An example is CLEAR ACCUMULATOR, which sets the accumulator to all 0's. One might consider the accumulator to be the addressed location, but the important point is that there is no section of the instruction that specifies the address of a location in memory. The entire instruction is considered to be an opcode.

The choice of an instruction format is a difficult one, requiring the balancing of a number of conflicting factors. The single-address is obviously the most efficient in terms of the amount of memory space required for each instruction. However, a program written in single-address instructions will certainly have more instructions than will a corresponding one written in multiple-address instructions. The more information included in each instruction, the fewer instructions required to accomplish a given task. Even this is not a simple relationship; even if fields are allocated for two addresses, not all instructions need two addresses. Thus, if we make the word length long enough to accommodate two addresses, space will be wasted in some instructions.

Prior to about 1970, most computers had only a single accumulator, and the addresses always referred to locations in memory. The number of bits required to address a reasonable amount of memory usually restricted designers to the single-address format, unless the machine had a very long word length. As the cost of electronic realization has decreased, however, the use of a set of *general-purpose registers* instead of a single accumulator has become the rule. This makes it possible to carry out many operations without referencing the main memory, with the address portion of the instruction specifying the registers to be used. If the machine has eight registers, for example, only 9 bits are required to specify three different registers, for both operands and the result. Two-address and three-address instructions thus become practical, even preferable, for instructions involving only registers. However, it will always be necessary to reference memory using some instructions in the single-address format. Today, except for a few 8-bit micros with a single accumulator, most computers include zero-, one- and two-address formats. The three-address format is still relatively uncommon, and we know of no machines using the four-address format.

A problem with multiple-formats is that it may be difficult to determine a single word length that is appropriate. In 8-bit and 16-bit micros, instructions are commonly spread over one, two, or three words. In mainframes with long words, a single word may contain one or more instructions. These and other options and variations, touched on here, will be considered in more detail in Chapter 6.

1.5 Software

Programs written in the form of instructions discussed in the previous section, strings of binary 1's and 0's, are known as *machine-language* programs. All programs must be ultimately placed in this form, since these are the only kind of instructions the control unit can interpret. Writing programs in machine code is, at least, unpleasant. First, binary strings are cumbersome, inconvenient, and downright unnatural to human beings. Second, the programmer must assign binary addresses to all the data and instructions, and, even worse, keep track of all these addresses.

In the early days of computers, programmers had to work in machine language. Many despaired of computers ever being of much use because getting a really useful program running was virtually impossible. As we know, the problem was solved by writing programs to get the computers to do most of the drudgery of programming. Those programs that process programs are called *system software*. System software is so important that the success of a particular computer model is often determined more by the quality of the software than by the quality of the hardware. Many of the developments in computer organization have come about in response to the need for efficient processing of the system software.

The first system program, suggested by von Neumann in 1945, merely converted instructions from octal form on punched cards to binary strings. Once it was recognized that the computer could modify the representation of instructions, it was quite natural to replace the numeric opcodes with mnemonic names, such as ADD, MULT, and DIV, and write a program to enable the computer to convert these names to the equivalent codes. Next, it was established that a program could assign symbolic variables to memory locations. The program that accomplished these functions became known as an *assembler,* with its input called *assembly language.*

Assembly language is an immense improvement over machine language, but each computer has its own assembly language. Knowledge of how to program one computer in its assembly language will be of little value in programming any other computer. Preferable are languages in which we can write programs that will execute on virtually any computer. This leads us to the concept of *high-level languages,* such as PASCAL, C, and FORTRAN. These high-level languages permit us to write programs in forms as close as possible to the natural, human-oriented, languages. Thus, a mathematical formula such as

$$s = \frac{-b \pm \sqrt{b^2 - 4ac}}{2a}$$

may be evaluated by a single, similar appearing program statement.

The evaluation of a formula such as the foregoing will obviously require many machine-language instructions. There are two distinct methods for processing high-level language programs. In one method, as the program is executed, each statement is converted into a corresponding set of machine-language instructions, which are immediately executed before proceeding to the next statement of the high-level language program. A system functioning in this manner is known as an *interpreter.*

Interpreters are inefficient for programs with repetitive loops. An interpreter must translate the instructions in the loop on every pass through the loop. This is clearly wasteful, because the translation is the same on every pass. This drawback of interpreters is avoided by another class of programs called *compilers.* A compiler translates the complete program into a machine-language program that is executed only after the compiling process is complete. Although a compiler for a given language must be written separately for each computer, this can be accomplished for any machine having adequate memory capacity to hold the software. Thus, in theory, a program written in a popular high-level language can be run on any computer.

Another important piece of system software is the *operating system* program (e.g., CPM, MS-DOS, UNIX, VMS). In the early days of computers, every program run had to be loaded, started, and terminated by an operator using switches on more than one piece of equipment. With modern computers capable of executing programs for multiple users in a fraction of a second, such human intervention is obviously impractical. Thus operating systems control the actual running of the computer. For a larger machine, the operating system will schedule execution of user programs. A microcomputer operating system simply makes user control of the computer more convenient.

We have not discussed many specialized types of software. Although the hardware and software of a computer make up an integral and inseparable whole, system software represents a complete area of study in itself. In this book we are concerned with software only to the extent that some understanding of software is essential to good hardware design. A knowledge of programming, at least in a problem-oriented language, is a prerequisite to this book; anyone seriously interested in computer design must also study software design.

1.6   Hardware Descriptions

In the next chapter, we shall define a computer, RIC, which will serve as our primary example throughout the remainder of the book. Chapter 3 will provide some background on computer components for those readers who have not encountered them elsewhere. The remainder of the book will approach the systematic design of all aspects of digital hardware systems.

As in the first two editions of this book, our approach will use the hardware description language AHPL. The relationship of this language to hardware will be developed in Chapter 4, and the language will be formally defined in Chapter 5. Is a hardware description language first published in 1973 still the proper vehicle for this book? Our affirmative answer is justified as follows. AHPL has been successfully tested on a broad spectrum of design problems and tuned gradually since its inception. The language was revised most extensively and the hardware correspondence made precise in preparation for the second edition. AHPL is still supported by the *function level simulator* HPSIM, which is now available to many users of the second edition. The only major change in the language for this edition is the adoption of structured notation for combinational logic unit descriptions, as will be discussed in Chapter 5. This change will have no impact on HPSIM.

The only alternative to AHPL that might be given serious consideration is VHDL (VHSIC hardware description language), a language supported by the U.S. Department of Defense. VHDL is intended for use over all levels of hardware description, from the digital circuit to the abstract algorithm. For this reason, it could not be tailored for clock-mode description as was AHPL. The more cumbersome VHDL can have an important positive impact on the electronics industry, but it is ill-suited for use in a textbook. For the reader who will eventually come to grips with VHDL, this book and AHPL will provide a proper stepping-stone.

References

1. P. Morrison, and E. Morrison, eds., *Charles Babbage and His Calculating Engines,* Dover, New York, 1961.
2. B. V. Bowden, *Faster than Thought,* Putnam, London, 1953.
3. F. J. Hill, and G. R. Peterson, *Introduction to Switching Theory and Logical Design,* 3rd ed., Wiley, New York, 1981.
4. H. H. Aiken, "Proposed Automatic Calculating Machine," *IEEE Spectrum,* Vol. 1, Aug. 1964, pp. 62–69.
5. R. Serrell, et al., "The Evolution of Computing Machines and Systems," *Proc. I.R.E.,* Vol. 50, May 1962, pp. 1040–1058.

6. F. Y. Dill, "Battle of the Giant Brains," *Popular Electronics,* Vol. 34, April 1971, pp. 39–43.

7. H. H. Goldstine, *The Computer from Pascal to von Neumann,* Princeton University Press, Princeton, N.J., 1972.

8. H. Tropp, "The Effervescent Years: A Retrospective," *IEEE Spectrum,* Vol. 11, Feb. 1974, pp. 70–79.

9. *VHDL Version 7.2 Users Manual,* Intermetrics, Bethesda, Md., 1985.

10. *VHDL Version 7.2 Language Reference Manual,* Intermetrics, Bethesda, Md., 1985.

2 Architecture of a Representative 32-Bit Processor

2.1 Levels of Description

In this chapter, we will present the initial description of a 32-bit processor that will be the principal design example through much of the book. Having said that, an immediate question is, "At what level should we describe this processor?" To answer this question in a meaningful manner, we need to consider the general problem of computer description. Computers are such enormously complex devices that there can be no one way of describing them or representing them. One way to describe a computer is to describe the hardware. Many people would probably say that hardware is the actual physical "stuff" that comprises the system. That is true, but hardware can be described at several levels, and with different languages. That is, a different form of description is appropriate at each level. In addition, it is helpful to divide the hardware into the elements and the values. The elements are the physical things that do the processing, which you can put your hands on; the values are what is being processed.

The lowest hardware level is the *circuit level,* where the elements are things such as resistors, transistors, and switches and the values are usually voltages and currents. The forms of description are schematic diagrams and circuit equations. The next level is the *logic level,* where the elements are gates and flip-flops and the values are 1s or 0s, that is, single units of information. The forms of description are Boolean equations and logic diagrams. Next comes the *register transfer level,* where the elements are registers and logic units, buses and control units, and the values are bytes or words, that is, sets of bits that are treated together as single items of information. The forms of description are register transfer languages, block diagrams, and flowcharts. Just above and closely related to the register transfer level is the *micropro-*

gramming level, the lowest level of machine-dependent description. Here we are concerned with special forms of programs (sometimes called *firmware*) that control the basic register transfer operations of the processor. Finally, there is the *system level,* where the elements are processors, memories, disk drives, and the like, and the values may still be words, but will often be files, records, and programs. The forms of description include PMS notation (to be introduced in Chapter 9), Kiviat graphs, and natural language.

Register transfer and microprogramming-level languages are capable of describing both function and structure of a digital system. Above this level, structure and function must be described by different media. Block diagrams and PMS diagrams describe the system structure, and, in the latter case, quantitative characteristics of systems, but do not describe function. At the user level, a function is described in terms of the machine language instructions, that is, coded vectors of binary values entered into the computer by the user to instruct it to carry out the basic operations of the computer, such as ADD, AND, and SHIFT. The complete set of such operations that the machine can carry out is known as the *instruction set.* Clearly, the instruction set of any computer is one of its most important specifications. Close to the instruction set level is the assembly language level, and here we have entered the realm of *software,* as discussed in Section 1.5.

All these levels and types of descriptions are important; different people will use different ones, depending on their interests. An applications programmer might be interested only in the high-level languages available on the machine. An engineer responsible for circuit board layout might be interested only in a description at the logic level. In this book, we are primarily interested in design at levels that involve both hardware and programming considerations. Therefore, our description will be primarily at the register transfer level. Alas, how are you to know in advance something about what we are trying to describe at this level? Computers and other digital equipment are not conceived at the register transfer level. As we progress through the book, you will notice that we will often proceed to design (write a register transfer level description of) a miscellaneous piece of digital equipment based on only a natural language description. For a computer, we can do much better.

In a classic 1964 paper, Amdahl, Blaauw, and Brooks [1] proposed dividing the design description of a computer into three levels: architecture, implementation, and realization. *Architecture* refers to the attributes of the computer as seen by the machine language programmer, that is, the conceptual structure and functional behavior. This definition includes the instruction set and format, memory word length and size, and all registers that are accessible to the programmer. On my shelf at this writing are paperback volumes labelled user manuals or programming manuals of machines such as the Motorola 68020, the NS 16000, and the Intel 80286. These manuals describe architecture. *Implementation* is defined as the actual hardware organization, including data paths, logic units, and control units. We will think of an implementation as a register transfer level description. Many implementations of a single architecture are possible. These implementations may execute programs on slightly different hardware configurations at different speeds, but they must execute the same programs, and, of course, obtain the same results. *Realization* refers to the actual physical structure, including logic technologies, board layouts, interconnections, and power supplies.

This is a book about the implementation of digital systems including computers. In this chapter, we present the architecture of the primary computer example for implementation. We assume that you already have experience in assembly language programming. Although a routine example or two will be presented to demand your attention, this chapter will not teach programming. It will appear very much like a user manual, like an architecture manual.

2.2   Registers and Memory

In this and the following sections of this chapter, we will present the architecture of a computer that we shall call RIC, standing for representative instructional computer.[1] RIC is a 32-bit machine that is not identical to any real computer, but incorporates features of several popular machines, such as VAX, Motorola 68020, and National 16032. The whole business of specifying the word length of a computer is a lot more complicated now than it once was, since most modern machines work with more than one word length. For example, many popular microprocessors today are considered dual length and are sometimes referred to as 8/16-bit or 16/32-bit processors. RIC is a "pure" 32-bit machine in the sense that its main data paths are 32 bits wide, it reads or writes 32 bits at a time when accessing memory, and its primary commands manipulate 32-bit data. RIC uses 24-bit memory addresses, giving it an address space of 16M (16,777,216) 32-bit words. It is important to note that *each address points at a 32-bit word, the nominal word length of RIC*, even though we shall find that some instructions occupy only 16 bits or one halfword.

Nearly all computers now have word lengths that are multiples of 8 bits, the standard unit of storage for an alphanumeric character. We are quite naturally following that convention in this third edition. Our choice of the 32-bit word length allows us to avoid the complication of multiword instructions in our first example of a computer organization. This feature, which must be used in 8- and 16-bit computers, will be introduced at the end of Chapter 6.

There are four registers that are accessible to the programmer; that is, there are instructions by means of which these registers can be directly accessed. The *accumulator* is the main data register of the machine. In two-operand instructions, such as ADD, it is the source of one operand and the destination of the result. It is a 32-bit register. The *index register* is an address register used for modifying memory addresses in a manner to be discussed later. The *stack pointer* is an address register used for controlling a special memory structure known as the *stack*. Because they handle only

---

[1]We suggest you not worry about what RIC stands for. The custom of using acronyms as computer names is hard to ignore, but the only important thing about a computer name is that it be short and easy to remember.

addresses, the index register and stack pointer are 24-bit registers. The *status register* is an 8-bit register made up of eight single-bit flags indicating the status of various parts of the computer. This is not a register in the usual sense that its contents represent some single unit of information, such as a numeric operand. The 8 bits are logically independent of one another for most purposes, but it is convenient to think of them as a single register for ease of reference and manipulation in some operations. Because we shall be referring to them frequently, we shall assign two-letter symbols to these registers as follows: *AC* for accumulator, *IX* for index register, *SP* for stack pointer, and *SR* for status register.

There is one more register that, although not directly accessible, is used in so many different commands that it is usually considered part of the main register set. This is the *program counter, PC*. In Section 1.4 we noted that, except in four-address instructions, it is assumed that instructions are normally stored in sequential locations in memory. The computer will fetch instructions from successive locations unless a branch or a jump is executed. Such a procedure clearly implies some means of keeping

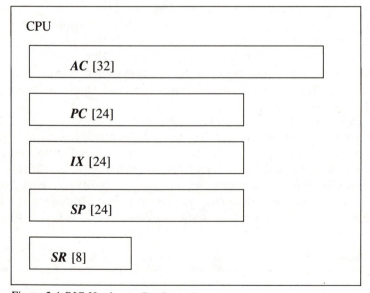

Figure 2.1 RIC Hardware Configuration

track of the location of the instructions. This function is carried out by the program counter. Each time a new instruction is to be fetched from memory, the address of the instruction is obtained from the program counter. If the instruction is not a branch or a jump, the program counter will be incremented to provide the address of the next instruction. A branch or a jump instruction will place the address of the next instruction in the program counter. The symbol for the program counter will be *PC*. The five registers just discussed are included in the central processing unit (CPU), depicted with the memory configuration in Fig. 2.1.

Several other registers in RIC are "transparent" to the programmer, in the sense that there is no need for the programmer to know their contents or even to be aware of their existence. These registers are important to the implementation of the machine and will be discussed in Chapter 6, but they do not form a part of the architecture as defined in Section 2.1. The situation is somewhat analogous to mailing a letter from San Francisco to London. The letter may go through New York, but you do not need to know that.

2.3   Single-Address Instructions

We noted in Section 1.4 that most modern computers use more than one instruction format, and that is the case with RIC. RIC will use two instruction lengths, 32-bit and 16-bit. In each length, there will be several formats. To keep things from getting too complicated, we shall consider the various formats separately in this chapter. First we shall consider the "classic" single-address format, in which the most common type of instruction is one in which the address refers to a location in memory that provides one operand, with the second operand coming from the accumulator and the result being left in the accumulator. This format has probably been used in more different computers than any other, and, even today, there are probably no computers that do not include this format in their instruction sets.

The format for single-address instructions in RIC is shown in Fig. 2.2. The first 8 bits correspond to the opcode in Fig. 1.3d, but here the opcode section has been divided into separate sections. All 8 bits are opcode in the sense of specifying what the computer is to do, but the complexity of modern computers makes it desirable to divide the opcode into sections having different functions. When there is more than one instruction format, one or more bits will often be used to indicate which format is being used. This is the case here, with bit 4 = 1 indicating a 32-bit instruction. Bits 0 through 3 are the "proper" opcode specifying the operation to be carried out. With 4 bits available, 16 operations could be specified. Fifteen operations will be

Figure 2.2 Single-Address Instruction Format for RIC

specified, as shown in Fig. 2.3, with the remaining opcode used for branch instructions to have a different format. Consistent with the notation that the assembly language defines the architecture, the corresponding 4-bit opcodes are not shown. These will be tabulated in Chapter 6, where the implementation of RIC is considered. In this figure, each instruction is identified by its *mnemonic,* the three-letter assembly language symbol for the instruction.

ADD, ADC, SUB, and SBC are the arithmetic operations, providing for addition and subtraction. The distinction between add and subtract with or without carry will be discussed later. AND, OR, and XOR are the logical operations, providing for bit-by-bit Boolean operations between the two operands. INC and DEC will increment and decrement, respectively, the addressed location in memory. MVT loads the *AC* with the contents of the addressed location in memory. MVF stores the contents of *AC* in the addressed location. For JMP, the address contained in the instruction becomes the address of the next instruction. Discussion of CMP, BIT, and JSR will be deferred to later sections.

The AM section of the instruction (bits 5–7 in Fig. 2.2) specifies the *addressing mode,* which determines how the 24 address bits are used. There are five addressing modes for the single-address instructions for RIC, as shown in Fig. 2.4. The three unused codes will be reserved for future expansion. The assembly language mnemonic for each addressing mode is also shown in Fig. 2.4. This notation is illustrated for the MVT instruction. Except for immediate addressing, for which some of the opcodes do not apply, any of the mnemonics listed in Fig. 2.3 could have been used. The last 24 bits or the address portion of the instruction is represented by ADDR.

The *direct mode* is the mode described in Section 1.4; that is, the 24-bit address refers directly to a location in memory. In the *indirect mode,* the 24-bit address in

Mnemonic	Operation
SBC	Subtract operands with carry, result to *AC*
SUB	Subtract operands, result to *AC*
ADC	Add operands with carry, result to *AC*
ADD	Add operands, result to *AC*
ORA	Logical OR of operands, result to *AC*
AND	Logical AND of operands, result to *AC*
XOR	Exclusive OR of operands, result to *AC*
MVT	Move to *AC* (load *AC*)
MVF	Move from *AC* (store *AC*)
CMP	Arithmetic compare
BIT	Logical compare
INC	Increment memory location
DEC	Decrement memory location
JSR	Jump to subroutine
JMP	Jump to addressed location for next instruction

Figure 2.3 Single-Address Instructions in RIC

AM bits 5–7	Addressing Mode	Mnemonic
000	Direct	MVT ADDR
001	Indirect	MVT (ADDR)
010	Indexed	MVT ADDR, X
011	Indirect Indexed	MVT (ADDR), X
100	Immediate	MVT #ADDR

Figure 2.4 Addressing Modes in RIC

memory is the address of a location in memory that contains the address of the operand in its lower 24 bits. This addressing mode is illustrated in Fig. 2.5. Hexadecimal notation is used for the various words and addresses. In this case, we assume that location 014613 contains the instruction (in standard assembly language form)

ADD (246A7B)

Assuming the opcode for ADD is 0101 in binary, the hex code for the instruction would be

59246A7B

The address portion of this instruction is the indirect address, pointing to location

246A7B

which we assume contains

8439F641

The lower 24 bits of this word form the *effective address,* pointing to location

39F641

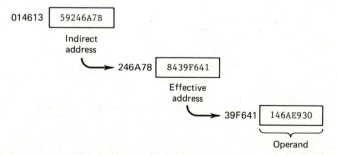

Figure 2.5. Indirect addressing in RIC.

The contents of this location will be used as the operand, to be added to the contents of **AC**.

For *indexed addressing*, the contents of the index register, **IX,** are added to the address in the instruction to obtain the effective address. As an example, assume the location 014613 now contains the instruction

    ADD 246A7B, X

(5A246A7B in hex) and **IX** contains 000008. The addressing process is shown in Fig. 2.6.

Indirect indexed addressing combines the two modes of addressing, first obtaining an address indirectly and then adding it to the index register, **IX**. Assume we have the command

    ADD (246A7B), X

(5B246A7B in hex) and **IX** again contains 000008. The addressing process is illustrated in Fig. 2.7.

Immediate addressing is not really an addressing mode at all, since the 24-bit address from the instruction does not refer to a location in memory, but is itself the *sign-extended* operand. Whenever an operand is not full-length, there are two important questions: (1) Where is the operand placed in the full-length word? and (2) What happens to the other bits? With sign-extension, the operand is right-justified, that is, moved all the way to the right in the word, and the leftmost bit (sign bit) is copied into the remaining bit positions. For example,

010100010000100001111000

will sign-extend to

00000000010100010000100001111000

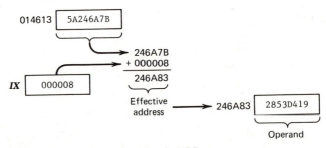

Figure 2.6. Indexed addressing in RIC.

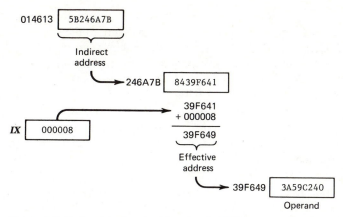

Figure 2.7. Indirect indexed addressing in RIC.

while

$$110100010000100001111000$$

will sign-extend to

$$111111111101000100001000001111000$$

Sign-extension will be used in RIC whenever operands that are not full-length are encountered.

Because names for addressing modes are not completely standardized, we have explained their functions in RIC in some detail, to be sure that there are no misunderstandings. However, we assume that readers of this book are competent assembly language programmers, familiar with the operation and use of these addressing modes. For readers lacking such background, we recommend Chapters 11 and 12 of Ref. 2.

2.4 Two-Address Instructions

If bit 4 = 0 in the instruction, it is a 16-bit instruction. Many of the operations specified by the 15 single-address opcodes remain meaningful where the two operands are both the contents of registers in the CPU instead of the accumulator and a memory location. In this case, no 24-bit address is necessary in the instruction. Instead, the two register operands can be identified by short bit fields (addresses), in this case, 4 bits each. Each of the instructions ADD, ADC, SUB, SBC, AND, ORA, XOR, MVT, CMP, and BIT is meaningful for a two-address format. The binary codes for these two-address instructions will be the same as for the corresponding single-address instructions. As in the single-address case, the opcode will occupy the first 4 bits of a two-address instruction. The six binary codes corresponding to the single-address instructions INC, DEC, JMP, MVF, branch, and JSR, which are not meaningful two-address instructions, will be used to specify other 16-bit instruction formats.

As noted in Section 1.4, formats with more than one address become more practical when the addresses select operands from a limited number of registers, so that only a few address bits are needed. This is the case with RIC, where the two-address format is used for instructions that manipulate registers. The format for these instructions is shown in Fig. 2.8. Since this is a 16-bit instruction, we can have two instructions in a memory word, thus conserving memory space and reducing access time for fetching instructions.

The opcode is in the usual position (bits 0–3) and must be for one of the 10 operations noted previously. Bit 4 = 0 indicates a 16-bit instruction. Bit 5 could be left unspecified for future expansion if the opcodes for the 10 valid two-address instructions are avoided in all other two-address instructions. AD1 specifies one of the three registers that is to serve as the destination of the result of the operation. If there are two source operands, the initial contents of this register will also be one of these operands. The MODE bits specify how AD2 is to be used. If MODE = 00, AD2 specifies a source register. If MODE = 01, the four bits of AD2 are used as a 4-bit immediate operand, sign-extended.

With this format, a remarkable variety of operations can be specified. For example, the instruction

$$\begin{array}{llll} \text{0010} & \text{01 1111 00} & \text{0000} & \text{(27C0 hex)} \\ \textbf{\textit{MVT}} & \textbf{\textit{SP}} \quad \text{RM} & \textbf{\textit{AC}} & \end{array}$$

transfers the rightmost 24 bits of *AC* to *SP,* that is, loads the stack pointer. Note that transfers from a larger register to a smaller one and vice-versa are always right-justified. Clearing the accumulator is accomplished by

$$\begin{array}{llll} \text{0010} & \text{01 0000 10 0000} & & \text{(2420 hex)} \\ \textbf{\textit{MVT}} & \textbf{\textit{AC}} \quad \text{IMQ} \ 0 & & \end{array}$$

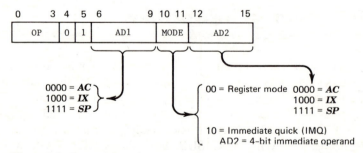

Figure 2.8. Two-address format.

while the index register is incremented by

$$0000 \ 01 \ 1000 \ 10 \ 0001 \qquad\qquad (0611 \text{ hex})$$
$$\text{ADD} \quad \textit{IX} \quad \text{IMQ} \quad 1$$

It will certainly have occurred to you that we have used more bits than necessary in some parts of this format. For example, there are only three possible choices for AD1, so that two bits would be enough, but we have used four. We have similarly used more bits than needed for MODE and AD2. This format has been carefully designed to facilitate future expansion of RIC through the addition of more registers. At later points in the book we shall add considerably to the power and complexity of RIC. We feel it better to keep the machine fairly simple at first, lest the main concepts be lost in a welter of detail. For those who would like to see a more complicated design, just be patient!

We shall see in the next section that branch and jump operations must always be to an instruction that begins at a *word boundary,* and therefore, 32-bit instructions must fit in the 32-bit word spaces in memory (they cannot be offset 16 bits). Thus, 16-bit instructions must occur in pairs. In some cases it may be necessary to incorporate a 16-bit NOP (no operation) instruction to fill a slot. As we use RIC assembly language in this chapter, we need only refer to such instructions with NOP. As we shall see in Chapter 6, there will be numerous unused 16-bit instruction codes that can be treated as NOPs.

2.5 Branch Instructions

In Section 1.4, we discussed the need for instructions that will cause the next instruction to be fetched from some location other than the next sequential location in memory. The JMP instruction listed in Fig. 2.3 is one such instruction. RIC will also have branch instructions. The distinction between jump instructions and branch instructions lies in the way the next address is determined. Jump instructions use *absolute addressing,* that is, the address specified by the instruction, by either direct or indirect addressing, is independent of where the jump instruction itself happens to be located. If the instruction is

    JMP 046924

then the next instruction will be fetched from location 046924, no matter where that jump instruction is located.

By contrast, branch instructions use *relative addressing.* The "address" portion of the branch instruction is not an address at all but a *displacement,* a numeric value that is added to the address of the next sequential location to obtain the address of the *next* instruction. For example, assume we have the instruction

    BRA   0006

(BRA stands for "branch always"). If this instruction is located at 014811, the next instruction will be fetched from 014818 (014812 + 0006), but if this instruction is located at 026186, the next instruction will be fetched from 02618D (026187 + 0006).

Relative addressing is important because it is necessary in writing *position-independent* codes, that is, programs that will run properly no matter where they are located in memory. There are many reasons why it may be necessary to load a program into different areas of memory at different times, but this cannot be done if the program contains jumps. If the program includes the jump instruction

    JMP   046924

then the correct next instruction had better be at 046924. But if we have

    BRA   0008

all that is required is that the next instruction be eight ahead of the next word. Thus, the program can be moved around at will, as long as the whole program is moved the same amount. This consideration is so important that many programmers consider it a serious error to use a jump instruction. (There is more to position-independent coding than just avoiding jumps, but relative addressing is critically important.)

The JMP and BRA commands are unconditional. We also need conditional jumps or branches that allow the programmer to make decisions between two possible courses of action at appropriate points in the program. In RIC, only branches will be conditional, because jump instructions require full-length addresses, which do not leave any bits available to specify the conditions to be tested. This is another advantage of relative addressing, that the displacement does not have to be as long as a full address. It is usually sufficient to be able to branch within a certain limited area of memory around the current instruction. The format for branch instructions is shown in Fig. 2.9. The opcode of 0111, together with bit 4 = 1 (32-bit instruction) indicates a branch instruction.

The displacement of 16-bits is treated as a signed 2's complement number, permitting a branch range of 32K forward or backward. The remaining 11 bits (5–15) will specify the conditions to be tested. The basic meaning of the branch instruction will be: "IF the branch conditions are satisfied, THEN add the displacement to the next sequential address to obtain the address of the next instruction; ELSE, the next sequential address will be the address of the next instruction." Note the classic "IF-THEN-ELSE" form familiar to programmers.

0 3	4 5	15 16	31
0111	1	CONDITIONS	DISPLACEMENT

Figure 2.9 Branch Format in RIC

In Section 1.4, we suggested that conditional branch instructions might test the accumulator for specified conditions, such as all 0's or a negative number. This was the pattern in early computers, in which the accumulator was the main operating register and there was little need to test anything else. As more registers were added, however, it became impractical to have enough branch instructions for all the registers that might be tested. This problem led to the introduction of condition code flags (or just flags), individual flip-flops that may be set or cleared by any operations that affect the contents in any of the operating registers, or in some cases, memory locations. In RIC, we have four such flags, the *carry flag,* C, the *negative flag,* N, the *zero flag,* Z, and the *overflow flag,* V. These four flags, together with others to be specified later, make up the status register mentioned in Section 2.2.

The carry flag will be affected only by the four addition and subtraction commands and by INC and DEC. This C flag will be set if any of these operations produce a result that is too large to fit in the destination register. For example, if we increment a location that contains FFFFFFFF (hex for all 1's), the result should be 100000000 (hex), but that will not fit in a 32-bit location, so we have a carry. The C will be cleared (or left 0) if any of these operations produce a result that is not too large for the destination location.

The negative flag will be set when any operation produces a result in which the leftmost bit is 1, and cleared when the leftmost bit is 0. To put it another way, the N flag copies the leftmost bit of the result. The name of the flag refers to the fact that a 1 in the leftmost bit indicates a negative number if the operand is a signed number. Note that the operand may not be a number at all, in which case the leftmost bit is not a sign bit. The N flag will still copy that bit, and it is up to the programmer to interpret the significance of the flag.

The zero flag is set when the result of any operation is all 0's, and cleared when it is not. This is sometimes confusing to novice programmers, since Z = 1 indicates a zero result, but that is the standard convention.

The overflow flag indicates overflow from addition and subtraction of 2's complement numbers. For purposes of overflow, all arithmetic operations in RIC assume 2's complement operands. An operand is taken as the 2's complement representative of a negative number if the leftmost bit is 1. If the leftmost bit is 0, the number is taken as positive. If two numbers with the same sign are added, the result must also have this same sign (same leftmost bit) or overflow has occurred. The situation is similar for subtraction. For more discussion of overflow, see Chapter 6 of Ref. 2.

The basic branch instructions in RIC are listed in Fig. 2.10. We have branches on each possible condition of the four flags plus an unconditional branch and a branch to subroutine. The branch to subroutine bears the same relationship to JSR as BRA does to JMP, that is, the branch uses relative addressing and the jump uses absolute addressing. We will not discuss the CONDITIONS section of the branch instruction at this time. This section will be coded in such a way that it will be possible to specify branches on many combinations of flags, not just individual flags, but we will defer discussion of this until Chapter 6.

In Section 2.2 we mentioned the CMP and BIT commands, but deferred the discussion, because we could not describe the functioning of these commands until

Mnemonic	Meaning	Flag Condition
BEQ	Branch on equal to zero	Z = 1
BNE	Branch on not equal to zero	Z = 0
BPL	Branch on plus	N = 0
BMI	Branch on minus	N = 1
BCS	Branch on carry set	C = 1
BCC	Branch on carry clear	C = 0
BVS	Branch on overflow	V = 1
BVC	Branch on no overflow	V = 0
BRA	Branch always	Any
BSR	Branch to subroutine	Any

Figure 2.10 Branch Instructions in RIC

we had discussed the flags. A common operation in programming is arithmetic comparison of two numbers to determine which is larger or if they are equal. The standard way to do this is to subtract one number from the other and then test the flags. However, if we use the SUB command, the operand in *AC* is lost, replaced by the difference. We could save the number in memory before subtracting and then restore it, but that requires extra steps. Furthermore, we are not interested in the actual difference, the flags provide all the information we need. The CMP command subtracts the addressed operand from *AC* and sets the flags accordingly, but it does not put the result into the accumulator. This is especially useful when we want to make successive comparisons of an operand in *AC* to several numbers in memory. The BIT command works in the same way except that it performs the logical AND of the two operands, to facilitate logical comparisons without losing the operand in *AC*.

Example 2.1

Write in RIC assembly language a short routine that will determine whether or not all words in one 32-word array are identical to the corresponding words in another 32-word array. Each array will consist of 32 consecutive memory locations. The location of the arrays within RIC memory is arbitrary. When the routine is called, a pointer to the location of the first array is found in a memory location labelled by AA. The pointer to the second array is found in location BB. At the end of the routine, *AC* is to contain 0 if all 32 words match, and FFFFFFFF (hex) if there is one or more mismatches. All constants are to be written in hexadecimal form.

Solution

The problem is a natural for indirect indexed addressing. As shown in Fig. 2.11, the indirect indexed steps MVT (AA),X and XOR (BB),X are executed for each of the 32 pairs of words or until the result of one such pair of operations is nonzero. There arc four 16-bit instructions in the program, none of which occurs consecutively. Therefore, each is followed by a NOP so that all instructions will begin on a word boundary.

```
                         MVT    IX    #0
                         NOP
         LOC1            MVT    #20
                         CMP    AC    IX
                         NOP
                         BEQ    +7                    "to LOC3"
                         MVT    (AA) , X
                         XOR    (BB) , X
                         BEQ    +2                    "to LOC2"
                         MVT    #FFFFFF
                         BRA    +3                    "to END"
         LOC2            ADD    IX    #01
                         NOP
                         BRA    −A                    "to LOC1"
         LOC3            MVT    #0
         END             HLT
```

Figure 2.11 Routine to Compare Two Arrays

Four relative branch instructions are included in the program. In this case, the relative addresses are shown explicitly. Some assemblers may provide assistance in computing these numbers. Two observations must be made concerning this computation. First, the number is relative to the address after that of the branch instruction itself. (We shall see in Chapter 6 that this is because the program counter is incremented prior to adding the relative address.) Second, each pair of 16-bit instructions is counted as a single address. Consider, for example, the BRA + 3. After this instruction has been fetched, the program counter will contain the address LOC2. This address points at a word that contains two 16-bit instructions. Thus END = LOC2 + 3.

2.6   Stacks and Subroutines

Stacks are a recent development in computer architecture compared to most of the features we have discussed to this point, but they are now virtually standard. In Section 1.4, we mentioned the concept of zero-address instructions, in which the location of the operand is inferred by the opcode. In most zero-address instructions, the inferred location is a register, but the use of the stack pointer enables us to access memory with zero-address instructions. This is done through a new addressing mode, *referred addressing,* in which the instruction refers to a register that contains the address of the location in memory to be accessed. This mode is similar to indirect addressing, but the fact that the address is in a register rather than in memory is significant. Indirect addressing requires two accesses to memory—one to fetch the address, one to access the operand location. Referred addressing gets the address from a register, which is much faster than getting it from memory, and makes only one access to memory, to access the operand location.

A *stack,* in a programming sense, is just a reserved area in memory that can be accessed through the stack pointer, *SP,* and the zero-address stack commands PSH (for push) and POP (or PULL in some machines). The operation of a stack is illustrated in Fig. 2.12. In Fig. 2.12a, *SP* initially contains the address 124000 and we assume that *AC* contains the operand ABLE. If we now execute a PSH command, *SP* is decremented to 123FFF and the operand ABLE is pushed onto the stack at that address in memory. The situation after execution of this first push is shown in Fig. 2.12b. Now assume that we load a new operand, BAKER, into *AC* and execute another PSH. *SP* is now decremented to 123FFE and BAKER is pushed onto the stack (Fig. 2.12c). At all times, the location pointed to by *SP* is known as the *top of the stack.* Thus, ABLE is at the top of the stack in Fig. 2.12b, whereas BAKER is at the top of the stack in Fig. 2.12c.

Now let us assume that we execute some arbitrary series of operations that do not affect the stack but change *AC* to some new value, DELTA (Fig. 2.12d). If we

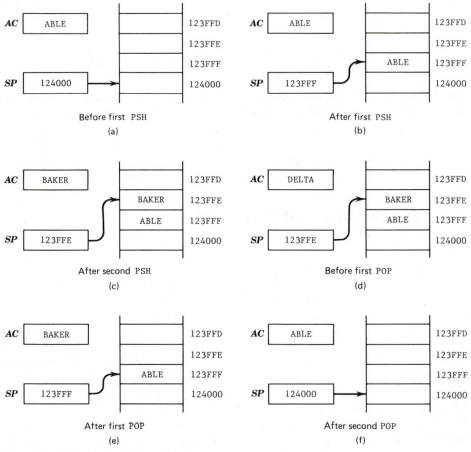

Figure 2.12. Stack operations in RIC.

now execute a POP, BAKER is moved from the top of the stack to *AC* and *SP* is then incremented to 123FFF, so that ABLE is now at the top of the stack (Fig. 2.12e). Another POP will move ABLE to *AC,* increment *SP* to 124000, leaving the stack empty (Fig. 2.12f). As we shall see in the next chapter, no memory location is ever "empty" in the physical sense, there is always something there. In this case, even after the two POPs, locations 123FFF and 123FFE still contain the operands ABLE and BAKER. The stack is considered empty in the programming sense, that is, the locations are now available for other uses as the programmer chooses.

Important factors in the use of a stack are the location and extent of the stack. In Fig. 2.12, how did the stack pointer get set to 124000 in the first place? And how many pushes are allowed before the addresses start repeating, overwriting words that were pushed earlier? In some cases, these factors are controlled by the hardware; in other cases, they are left entirely to the discretion of the programmer. In either situation, the programmer must have direct access to the stack pointer in order to control it properly. In RIC, this is provided by the two-address format, which permits the programmer to manipulate the stack pointer in any way that may be desirable. We will not discuss the format of the PSH and POP instructions in RIC at this time, but you may assume that these commands do exist, functioning as just described.

The uses of stacks are many and varied. The programming aspects of stacks are quite beyond the scope of this book. However, there is one use of stacks that forms a part of the architecture of RIC. That is the use of the stack in handling subroutines. The usual subroutine is just a short program that a programmer can use repeatedly to perform some task that may occur many times in the course of a larger main program. For example, a process control program might call for reading a command from a keyboard at several points in the program. The programmer will write a subroutine to read in a command string from a keyboard. At any point in the main program where a new command is needed, the subroutine will be called.

That is the basic idea, and we assume that all our readers have used subroutines. But how does it work at the machine level? Getting to the subroutine is no problem. Presumably, we know where it is, so all we have to do is jump to it. But how do we get back to the main program? The subroutine is going to be called from many places in the main program, so it cannot end with a jump back to some fixed location. When a new instruction is fetched, the address of the instruction is obtained from the program counter. During the fetch of the instruction, *PC* is incremented, to point to the next sequential location. Execution of a jump or branch simply requires changing the address in *PC* to the address of the next instruction. JMP loads the address from the instruction into *PC,* while a branch adds a number (the displacement) to *PC.*

If the instruction being fetched is a jump or branch to a subroutine, the next sequential address obtained by incrementing *PC* during the fetch cycle is the address of the instruction we want to come back to after completion of the subroutine. Therefore, that address must be saved before changing *PC* to the address of the subroutine. Both JSR and BSR push the contents of *PC* onto the stack before changing *PC* to the address of the subroutine. To complete the process, we add a new instruction, RTS, return from subroutine. RTS will be the final instruction in any subroutine. It pops the return address off the stack and loads it into *PC.* The next fetch then goes to the next instruction in the main program. Note that the push on JSR or BSR and the pop on RTS are automatic, the programmer does not have to put in PSH or POP instructions. But the programmer must exercise some care. The JSR or BSR will push the return address onto the top of the stack, wherever that may be. The RTS will pick up whatever is on top of the stack. If the subroutine uses the stack, care must be taken to see that the return address does not get lost. We will not consider the format of RTS for the present.

2.7 Shifts and Miscellaneous Instructions

Shifts and rotates form another important group of data-handling instructions. These instructions move the bits of an operand right or left within a register or memory location. In a shift, the bits shifted out of one end of the register are just dropped and 0's are shifted into the vacant positions at the other end. In a rotate, the bits shifted out of one end are shifted back into the other end. Usually, all these instructions have a common format and four different things have to be specified: (1) shift or rotate, (2) address of the operand, (3) direction of shift or rotate, right or left, (4) distance of the shift, in bits. Simpler machines usually shift or rotate only 1 bit at a time, so that multiple instructions are needed for multiple shifts. More complex machines provide for multiple shifts in a single instruction.

The shift/rotate instruction is a register-only instruction, but the instruction format differs from those considered previously because no address is needed, shifting and rotating being available only in *AC*. The format for this instruction is given in Fig. 2.13. Bits 0:4 = 0110, which is not a two-address opcode, establishes that this is the 16-bit shift/rotate instruction. It is a shift if bit 5 = 0, a rotate if bit 5 = 1. Bit 10 indicates the direction of shift or rotate, and bits 11:15 specify the shift/rotate distance as a 5-bit number.

The meaning of bit 6 depends on whether the operation is shift or rotate. For rotate, bit 6 indicates whether or not the carry flag will be included in the rotation. The carry flag will always be used in shifts, to receive the bit shifted out, and bit 6 will indicate whether the shift will be *arithmetic* or *logical*. A logical shift is the

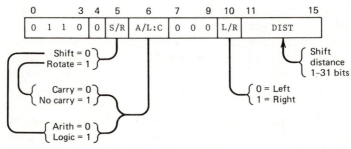

Figure 2.13. Shift/rotate instruction.

20	00010100	11101100	-20
10	00001010	11110110	-10
5	00000101	11111011	-5

| (a) | (b) |

Figure 2.14 Multiplying and Dividing by Shifting

"standard" shift, in which zeros are shifted into the vacated positions. The need for the arithmetic shift arises from the fact that shifts are commonly used to multiply or divide numbers by powers of two. Figure 2.14a shows the numbers 5, 10, and 20 as 8-bit binary numbers. When 10 is shifted left, the result is 20 (multiply by 2), and when 10 is shifted right, the result is 5 (divide by 2). In either case, we note that zeros have been shifted into the vacated positions, so that this seems to be the same as a logical shift.

Figure 2.14b shows the 8-bit binary representations of -20, -10, and -5 in signed 2's complement form. Again we see that a left shift multiplies by 2, a right shift divides by 2, with one important difference. For the left shifts, from -5 to -10 to -20, the case is the same as for logical shifts—0 is shifted into the vacated positions. However, for the right shifts from -20 to -10 to -5, we see that a 1 must be shifted into the vacant positions. The explanation is simple, the sign bit is not a numeric bit and must be retained for signed numbers. For arithmetic shifts, the sign bit is held constant and is copied into the most significant numeric bits for right shifts.

With these considerations, there are seven distinct shift/rotate operations.

LSR	Logical shift right
ASR	Arithmetic shift right
SHL	Shift left
ROR	Rotate right
RRC	Rotate right with carry
ROL	Rotate left
RLC	Rotate left with carry

These seven operations are shown pictorially in Fig. 2.15, together with a register transfer level description for each operation for a 1-bit shift. The implementation of these seven operations is quite similar. We shall see them accomplished in a single short sequence of register transfer level steps in Chapter 6.

A number of other instructions in RIC are very important for efficient programming, but they do not fit into any particular category. Some of them are listed in Fig. 2.16. PSH, POP, NOP, and RTS were discussed earlier. In addition to providing for even numbers of 16-bit instructions, one or more successive NOPs have other important applications, such as in waiting loops. The HLT instructions does just what it says; it stops the computer. The CLC and SEC instructions are useful in connection with the shift/rotate instructions, as they permit the programmer to set the carry flag bit to 0 or 1 and then shift it into a register. There is no need to present the 16-bit binary

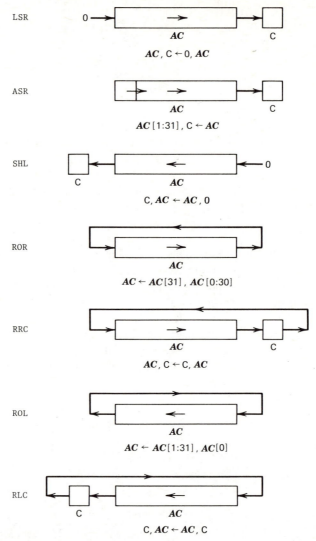

Figure 2.15. Shift/rotate operations in RIC.

codes that specify these instructions at this point. The codes will be specified in Chapter 6 when their implementation is considered.

The CLC and SEC instructions are also useful in connections with the ADC and SBC instructions. The ADD and SUB instructions simply add or subtract two 32-bit numbers, producing a 32-bit result with possible carry-out or overflow. The ADC and SBC instructions do the same except they include the contents of C as a 1-bit input to the least significant (rightmost) bit position. This permits concatenation of words for addition or subtraction of numbers too large to fit in 32 bits. Suppose we have some very large number, such as the federal deficit, too large to fit into 32

Mnemonic	Operation
PSH	Push *AC* on stack
POP	Pop stack to *AC*
RTS	Return from subroutine
NOP	No operation
HLT	Halt
CLC	Clear carry flag
SEC	Set carry flag

Figure 2.16 Miscellaneous 16-bit Instructions in RIC

bits, and we wish to add it to some other similarly large number. The two numbers would each be spread over two or more words in memory. To add them, we bring the least significant word of one operand into *AC*, set C to 0 with CLC, and add the least significant word of the other operand with ADC. The 32-bit sum forms the least significant word of the sum, and the carry, if any, is then added in with the next significant words of the two operands, using ADC. This capability is obviously essential in machines with short word lengths, such as 8 bits or 16 bits, but it is surprising how often operands are encountered that will not even fit into 32 bits.

We have not exhausted the instruction set of RIC. In particular, we have not considered the instructions associated with the input/output and interrupt systems. But, there is a limit to how much we can consider at one time. It is most convenient to consider all the issues associated with input and output of information to and from RIC at one place in the book. This will be accomplished in Chapter 10. RIC as defined here is a powerful and sophisticated machine, quite adequate to serve as a design example for a good part of the book. We will get to additional complexities in due time, but let us walk before we try to run.

Problems

2.1 Suppose that additional addressing modes were to be added to a modified version of RIC so that only 3 bits were available to specify the opcode. Make a list of the subset of eight of the single-address instructions from Fig. 2.3 that are most important to include for the sake of convenient programming.

2.2 Why are the two-address (16-bit) versions of the instructions INC and DEC not included in the RIC architecture? Why is a two-address MVF not included?

2.3 What would be the primary disadvantage of letting 32-bit instructions overlap word boundaries? If we ignored this disadvantage, would it be possible to implement a version of RIC that would allow branching to any 32-bit or 16-bit instruction even at a halfword boundary? Discuss in one or two sentences how this might be accomplished.

2.4 Suppose that the arrays in Example 2.1 were only six words long. Would this make it possible to use quick immediate two-address instructions to reduce the number of memory words occupied by the routine? Rewrite the routine accordingly. Will the execution time of the new routine be less? Why or why not?

2.5 Write a RIC assembly language program that will use indexing in implementing a DO loop for the addition of a one-dimensional array of 16 positive 32-bit numbers. Assume that there will be no overflow.

2.6 Write a RIC assembly language routine that will reorder the bits of a 32-bit word as shown here.

16–19, 0–3, 20–23, 4–7, 24–27, 8–11, 28–31, 12–15

As a preliminary part of your solution, define your own assembly language notation for the rotate instructions that you will employ.

2.7 Write a subroutine, in RIC assembly language, to convert all the characters in an ASCII string of eight decimal digits into binary-coded-decimal (BCD) form. All eight 4-bit BCD characters are to be packed into a single word. The 8 ASCII bytes are packed into two consecutive memory words. The address of the string is passed via the stack, and the result is left in *AC*.

2.8 Write a RIC assembly language program that might be generated by a RIC compiler from the following FORTRAN code. All variables are integers. Assume the address of X array is at location XADDR.

```
SUM = 0
DO 20 I = 1, 10
SUM = SUM + (X(I) + 18)
X(I) = X(I) - 3
20    CONTINUE
```

2.9 Write a subroutine, in RIC assembly language, to transport an N × N matrix stored in a sequential memory array with row major ordering. The starting address of the array is passed on the stack and N in *IX*. Clean up the stack before returning from the subroutine.

2.10 Write a RIC assembly language subroutine that generates a pseudorandom integer between 0 and $2^{31} - 1$. It must take the contents of the accumulator as the seed in the following algorithm and return the random number in the accumulator.

    (a)   Rotate the seed right 3 bits.

    (b)   If the end bits (lowest- and highest-order bits) are both 0 or both 1, set 2 middle bits that are 6 bits apart to 0 and the low-order bit to 1. Otherwise, set them in the opposite way.

    (c)   Clear the sign bit to 0.

References

1. G. M. Amdahl, G. A. Blaauw, and F. P. Brooks, "Architecture of the IBM System/360," *IBM J. Research Development,* Vol. 2, 1964.
2. F. J. Hill and G. R. Peterson, *Digital Logic and Microprocessors,* Wiley, New York, 1984.
3. *The NS16000 Data Book,* National Semiconductor Corp., Santa Clara, Calif., 1983.
4. *The 16-Bit Microprocessor User Manual: Motorola Edition,* 3rd ed., Prentice–Hall, Englewood Cliffs, N.J., 1982.
5. R. Rector and G. Alexy, *The 8086 Book,* Osborne/McGraw–Hill, Berkeley, Calif., 1980.
6. *VAX Architecture Handbook,* Digital Equipment Corp., Maynard, Mass., 1981.

3 System Building Blocks

3.1 Introduction

In this chapter, we shall present a brief and rather general discussion of some of the basic types of logic and memory devices used in digital computers. The actual design of these devices is not the concern of the system designer, who generally regards them as "black boxes" with certain known characteristics. On the other hand, intelligent selection and application of these devices does require some understanding of their operation and an appreciation of their limitations. In addition, without some physical interpretation of registers, memory, and the like, much of the material in following chapters may seem too abstract to many readers. Readers who are already familiar with digital hardware may skip the majority of the topics in this chapter without loss of continuity.

Logic circuits are implemented in a tremendous variety of technologies. There are, for example, transistor-transistor logic (TTL), MOS logic, and emitter-coupled logic (ECL). These various types differ in matters of speed, cost, power consumption, physical dimensions, immunity to environmental influences, and other factors; but they all accomplish the same basic purpose, and from the point of view of this book, the differences are of little importance. All of them accept input signals in which the voltage levels represent the values of certain logical (binary) variables and produce output signals in which the voltage levels correspond to logical functions of the input variables.

The purpose of logic circuits, then, is to process signals and produce outputs that are functions of the inputs. The outputs are available only during the duration of the input signals. The purpose of memory devices is to store information for later use, generally returning it without alteration, in the same form in which it was originally stored. The definition of memory is elusive. We shall simply settle for the intuitive idea that a memory device is any device that we place in a specific, identifiable physical state for the specific purpose of preserving information, without alteration, until a later time. The terms *memory* and *storage* are often used interchangeably, but many authors make a distinction between *main memory* and *secondary storage*. In main memory, the storage medium is a permanent physical component of the computer system. The information stored cannot be removed from the system except by reading it out of the main memory. In secondary storage systems, the storage media, for example, magnetic tape, can be physically removed from the system, with the information stored therein available for later use when the storage media are put back into the system.

Memory or storage devices may be classified in a number of different ways. First, most may be classified as being either magnetic or electronic. Magnetic devices use ferromagnetic materials, which can be placed in a specific magnetic state by the passage of electric currents through them or near them, and which then maintain these states indefinitely until interrogated. The chief types of magnetic memory are tape, disk, and core. Electronic memory devices are primarily transistor circuits in which the outputs can be set to certain voltage levels by the application of certain input signals and will be maintained even when the input signals are removed. A common electronic memory device is the bistable latch, or flip-flop, which can be used to construct *register memories* (RM).

Memories may also be classified by the type of access to the stored information. In *random access memories* (RAM), all stored information is equally accessible, in the sense that any given piece of information may be retrieved in exactly the same length of time as any other piece of information. Semiconductor memories are usually classified as RAM. Tape, by contrast, is *sequential access storage* (SAS), in which information can be retrieved only in the same order in which it was stored. When you want a particular piece of information off tape, you simply start running the tape until the desired information comes into position to be read. The access time is thus dependent on where the desired information is located relative to the starting point.

Between these two categories is disk memory, which is classified as *direct access storage* (DAS). Disks store information in the same sequential manner as tapes, but the total storage area is divided into segments that can be accessed directly, without reading through all the information between the current and desired segment. Once the desired segment has been accessed, information will then be read out sequentially in the same manner as with tape.

A final special category, which resembles logic as well as memory, is the *read-only memory* (ROM). The stored information is actually built into the structure of the device. The stored information can then be read out electronically but can be changed only by alteration of the structure of the device.

The foregoing classification and listing is quite broad and general and is not intended to be complete. There are many other specialized memory devices, some fitting into the preceding categories, some not really fitting into any category.

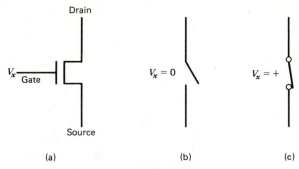

Figure 3.1. Operation of a MOS transistor.

3.2 Logic Elements

In this section, we shall present what will be to many of you a review of fundamental logic elements. We shall briefly introduce the circuits that implement the combinational logic operations AND, OR, NOT, NAND, and NOR, which will be used freely in subsequent chapters. There are several families of logic elements, each with its unique circuit properties. We shall introduce one such family that is easily described and is used extensively in the design of very-large-scale integrated circuits (VLSI) such as microprocessors.

The MOS (metal oxide semiconductor) logic family is based almost entirely on a single device, a MOS field effect transistor, that very closely approximates an ideal switch. Shown in Fig. 3.1a is the standard symbol for the MOS transistor with the accepted names for its three terminals.[1] Actually, the device is symmetric, and the source and drain can be readily interchanged. The gate may be regarded as the input line. As shown in Fig. 3.1b, the device is a close approximation of an open switch when the gate voltage V_x is close to 0. When V_x is a positive voltage, typically 1 to 5 volts, the switch is closed and behaves as a very small electrical resistance. This situation is depicted in Fig. 3.1c. In the logic circuits to be described following, we shall let 0 volts represent logical 0 and the positive voltage represent logical 1. To be consistent with the prior edition, we shall let the nominal positive voltage be +5 volts.

The fundamental MOS logic element is the inverter shown in Fig. 3.2a. The upper (pull-up) device is actually a depletion mode transistor designed to function as a relatively large resistor when connected as given and when the lower transistor switch is closed. For purposes of this simplified discussion, you should simply regard it as a large resistor, as shown in Fig. 3.2b. When x is logical 0 and V_x is 0 volts, as in Fig. 3.2c, the lower transistor (pull-down) switch is open. Because no current is present in the resistor R_D, the output voltage is +5 volts and the logical output, z, is 1. When

---

[1]More specifically, NMOS. There are actually two types of MOS elements that are excited by gate voltages of opposite polarity.

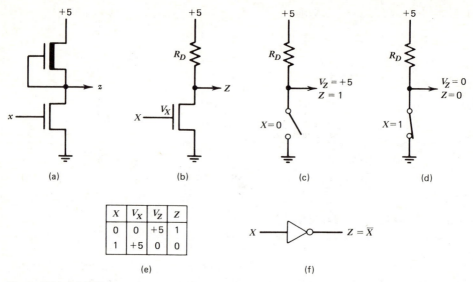

Figure 3.2. A MOS inverter.

$x = 1$ and V_x is positive, the lower transistor switch is closed, as depicted in Fig. 3.2d. Now the output is connected to 0 volts; and $z = 0$. These values are tabulated in Fig. 3.2e. We observe from this table that the circuit of Fig. 3.2a implements the logical NOT operation and is indeed an inverter, as asserted at the beginning of the paragraph. The standard symbol for the inverter is given in Fig. 3.2f.

Next consider the circuit of Fig. 3.3a, in which a second pull-down transistor has been added in series. Now both inputs must be logical 1 if the output is to be

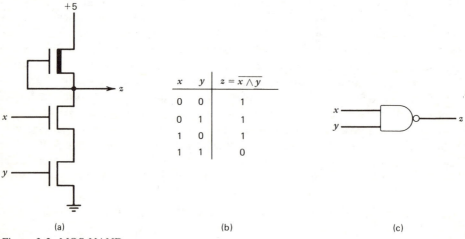

Figure 3.3. MOS NAND gate.

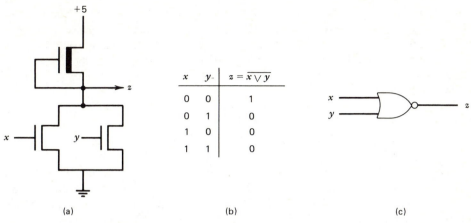

(a)   (b)   (c)

Figure 3.4. MOS NOR gate.

pulled down to 0 volts. If either or both devices has a 0 input, the output will be $+5$ volts or logical 1. The tabulation of these values in Fig. 3.3b describes a device that is called a logical NAND (NOT AND) gate. The standard symbol for this device is given in Fig. 3.3c. Figure 3.4 shows a similar device in which the two pull-down transistors are connected in parallel. Now the output, z, will be 0 if either input is 1. It will be logical 1 if both inputs are 0. This device is a NOR (NOT OR) gate.

As we shall see shortly, it is possible to represent any logical function using only NAND gates; and this is often done in practice. In this book, we shall find it convenient to express designs in terms of AND, OR, and NOT gates rather than in terms of NAND gates only or NOR gates only. An AND gate may be realized by adding an inverter to the output of a NAND gate ($\bar{\bar{z}} = z$), as shown in Fig. 3.5. The standard symbol for an AND gate is given in Fig. 3.5c. Adding an inverter to the NOR yields an OR gate, the standard symbol for which is given in Fig. 3.5d.

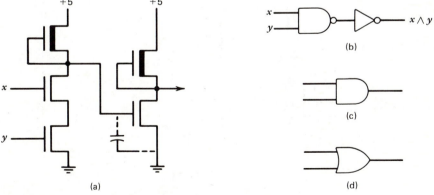

(a)   (b)   (c)   (d)

Figure 3.5. MOS AND and OR gates.

Looking again at Fig. 3.5a will reveal a capacitor depicted at the gate input of the second inverter. This capacitor is not a separate component but instead represents an inherent property of the MOS device. The gate of a MOS transistor will draw no steady-state current. The input resistance is infinite. However, when the value of the line connected to the device input changes, time is required for the charging or discharging of the capacitor to the new value.

Space will not permit the detailed analysis of all logic families in use. A second family of considerable importance is bipolar TTL (transistor-transistor logic). Usually, TTL gates can change values at higher speeds than can MOS but require a larger area on the integrated circuit chip to implement. For this reason, TTL is used where relatively less complex digital networks are implemented within an integrated circuit package. TTL is the most widely used technology where only a few individually accessible gates or memory elements are included in a package. A TTL NAND gate is shown in Fig. 3.6.

The logical inversion noted in MOS occurs in most types of electronic logic, so that NAND and NOR are often cheaper and more convenient to realize than are AND and OR. In this book, we shall find it convenient to rely on the AND and OR functions. This does not present a problem, since networks of AND, OR, and NOT gates can always be converted to NAND or NOR networks.

Consider the simple logical circuit of Fig. 3.7a, which consists of three NAND gates driving another NAND gate. From De Morgan's law,

$$\overline{X \wedge Y \wedge Z} = \overline{X} \vee \overline{Y} \vee \overline{Z}$$

we see that the final NAND gate can be replaced by an OR gate with inversion on the inputs (Fig. 3.7b). Next,

$$\overline{\overline{X}} = X$$

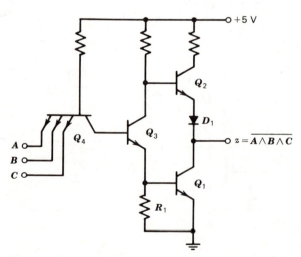

Figure 3.6. TTL NAND gate.

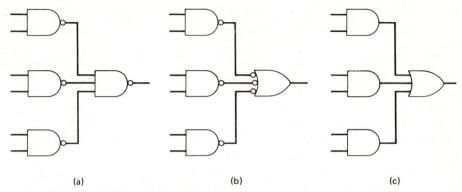

(a)   (b)   (c)

Figure 3.7. Conversion of NAND-NAND to AND-OR circuit.

so that the two successive inversions on the lines between the input and output gates cancel, giving the circuit of Fig. 3.7c. Thus we see that a two-level NAND circuit is equivalent to a two-level AND-OR circuit. In a similar fashion, we can show that a two-level NOR circuit is equivalent to a two-level OR-AND circuit.

Until about 1970, gate circuits such as those discussed in this section were commonly realized from discrete components—resistors, transistors, diodes—mounted on plastic cards and wired together. Today, logic circuits are almost invariably realized in integrated circuit form. An *integrated circuit* is a complete electronic circuit implanted by electrochemical methods on a single chip of silicon. The earliest integrated circuits typically realized a few gates on a single chip. As the technology advanced, the circuit density steadily increased, until today complete computers, comprising tens of thousands of components, can be placed on $\frac{1}{4}$-in. square chips.

Integrated circuits can be classified in a variety of ways. One classification is in terms of the type of electronic technology used. Currently popular technologies include TTL, ECL, CMOS, NMOS, and PMOS. NMOS and PMOS are two slightly different physical realizations of the MOS model discussed in this section. These five technologies differ in such characteristics as speed, power consumption, and packing density. ECL is very fast but consumes a lot of power. CMOS is slower but consumes so little power that it is suitable for battery-powered applications, such as electronic watches. NMOS has the highest packing density and is used in very complex circuits, such as microprocessors. TTL, which falls about in the middle in all characteristics, is by far the most popular technology and is available in more different circuits than all the others put together.

Integrated circuits can also be classified in terms of circuit complexity. *Small-scale integration* (SSI) encompasses circuits with up to 10 gates per chip. *Medium-scale integration* (MSI) includes circuits with from 10 to 100 gates per chip. From 100 to about 5000 gates per chip we have *large-scale integration* (LSI), and above this we have *very-large-scale integration* (VLSI). In SSI chips, we have individual gates and flip-flops. MSI chips realize more complex logic functions, such as code conversion and arithmetic operations. LSI and VLSI chips realize complete digital systems, such as memory units and microprocessors.

3.3 Speed, Delay, and Fanout in Logic Circuits

As suggested by Fig. 3.5a, all digital circuits contain intrinsic capacitance, which requires time to charge or discharge. These capacitive effects, together with device and connection resistance, determine the speed at which a digital system will operate. At the level of the individual logic element, the speed limitation is defined in terms of *gate delay*. The precise delay mechanisms and their relative importance will vary with the logic family. For MOS LSI circuits, the delay of an inverter is largely a function of the number and location of devices it must drive. This situation is suggested by Fig. 3.8a, where the inverter drives three devices, the gate capacitances of which are shown. Each path resistance shown is effectively in series with the resistance of the pull-up or pull-down device itself.

Shown in Figure 3.8b is the typical response of an inverter to an ideal input signal. Notice that two effects are present on both transitions. A delay occurs before the output begins to change value followed by a rise or fall time during which the output voltage actually changes. The system designer will usually not be concerned with the distinction between rise and fall times and delay. The two effects will usually be lumped together and represented by an ideal delay, as illustrated in Fig. 3.9. In this book, we shall assume that the change in a gate output will always follow a change in the gate input by a period of time t_d.

The delay associated with closing the pull-down switch is called the *turn-on delay* while the delay associated with opening the switch is the *turn-off delay*. For the MOS circuit of Figure 3.8a, the turn-off delay associated with the inverter is a function of the physical dimensions of the pull-up device, the number of paths driven, and the length and, therefore, the resistance of each path. Driving more gates with the output of the inverter will increase its delay. Therefore, specification of a maximum tolerable delay will establish a limit on the number of devices that can be driven. This limit is called the *fan-out limit*. Because the inputs to MOS devices draw negligible current

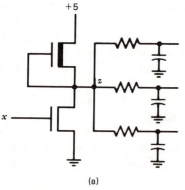
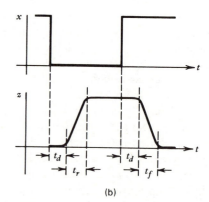

(a)   (b)

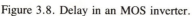

Figure 3.8. Delay in an MOS inverter.

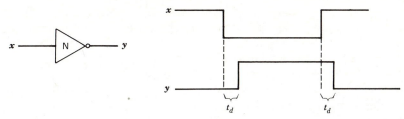

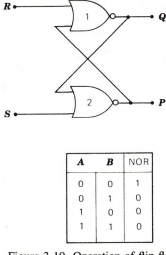

Figure 3.9. Ideal gate delay.

in the steady state, the fan-out limit is dictated by delay considerations. For other logic families, static characteristics may play a role in establishing this fan-out limit.

3.4 Flip-Flops and Register Memory (RM)

As we have seen, memory, the ability to store information, is essential in a digital system. The most common type of electronic memory device is the *flip-flop*. Figure 3.10 shows the circuit for a flip-flop constructed from two NOR gates and the timing diagram for a typical operating sequence. We have also repeated the truth table for NOR for convenience in explaining the operation.

At the start, both inputs are at 0, the Q output is at 0, and the P output at 1. Since the outputs are fed back to the inputs of the gates, we must check to see that the assumed conditions are consistent. Gate 1 has inputs of $R = 0$ and $P = 1$, giving

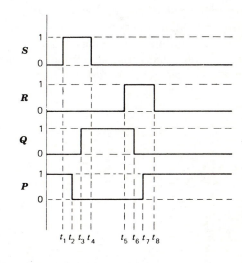

A	B	NOR
0	0	1
0	1	0
1	0	0
1	1	0

Figure 3.10. Operation of flip-flop.

an output $Q = 0$, which checks. Similarly, at gate 2 we have $S = 0$ and $Q = 0$, giving $P = 1$. At time t_1, input S goes to 1. The inputs of gate 2 are thus changing from 00 to 01. After a delay (as discussed in the last section), P changes from 1 to 0 at time t_2. This changes the inputs of gate 1 from 01 to 00, so Q changes from 0 to 1 at t_3. This changes the inputs of gate 2 from 01 to 11, but has no effect on the outputs. Similarly, the change of S from 1 to 0 at t_4 has no effect. When R goes to 1, Q goes to 0, driving P to 1, thus *locking-in Q,* so that the return of R to 0 has no further effect.

Note that it is the change of an input (S or R) from 0 to 1 that initiates the change of state of the flip-flop. The return of the signal to 0 has no effect; therefore, it could occur at any time after the output change has stabilized. In Fig. 3.10, if S returned to 0 before time t_3, the input to gate 2 would again be 0, tending to cause P to return to 1. In this situation, the operation of the circuit would be unpredictable.

Clearly, the timing of signals applied to the S and R inputs of the cross-coupled gates is critical. Most digital systems are *clocked*. This means that a periodic external signal (the clock) is supplied to the digital system and some circuit mechanism is incorporated to ensure that all memory elements in the circuit can only change values at one specific point in the clock period. This implies that memory elements that will change values during a given period will change in unison. The new values of the outputs of memory elements after the *triggering point* in the clock period will be functions only of the old values (values before the triggering point) of the various memory elements and the circuit inputs. Most of you will be familiar with this statement as the definition of a clock-mode sequential circuit, a definition to which the remainder of this book will conform.

In bipolar logic circuits (e.g., TTL), satisfaction of the clock-mode definition is usually assured by adding circuitry to each individual memory element such that all memory element output changes are triggered by a particular edge of each pulse of the periodic clock signal. This approach is illustrated in Fig. 3.11 for a falling-edge-triggered D-type flip-flop.

A D flip-flop has a single data input (D) and a clock input. At the time of the specific clock transition, the flip-flop output takes on the value of the D input at that same time. Note that this definition implies that the value at D must be stable at the

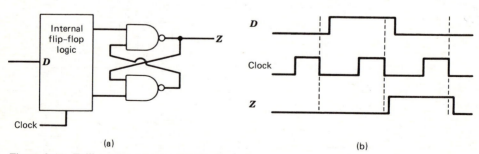

Figure 3.11. Falling-edge-triggered D flip-flop.

time of the transition. If D is changing during the transition, it should be intuitively obvious that we cannot be sure what the flip-flop will do. As will be discussed in some detail in the next chapter, it is also assumed that, if the output value changes, it will do so immediately following the completion of the triggering transition.

The D flip-flop will be almost universally used throughout this book. Notice that the cross-coupled pair of gates remains the mechanism for storing the output value. For more details on the box in Fig. 3.11a labelled "Internal flip-flop logic," refer to any of the many books on logic design such as Ref. 1. Most important is the timing diagram of Fig. 3.11b, which specifies that every change in the memory element output occurs immediately following a falling transition on the clock input.

In MOS circuits, the clock-mode definition is enforced somewhat differently. Such circuits are typically driven by a *two-phase* clock, the second phase being approximately the complement of the first phase, as depicted in Fig. 3.12c. The simplest MOS memory element is given in Fig. 3.12a. The memory element value is actually stored for a short time by the input capacitance of the MOS gate. When phase $\Phi 2$ is active, the stored value is refreshed. When phase $\Phi 1$ is active, a new value is gated into the flip-flop. No edge-triggering mechanism is present in Fig. 3.12a. Instead, phase $\Phi 1$ will remain on for approximately half the clock period. In order that the memory element value not change more than once while phase $\Phi 1$ is on, a gate controlled by phase $\Phi 2$ must be placed between the memory element and any external logic feeding back to the input of the element. This is depicted in Fig. 3.12b. It can be seen that once phase $\Phi 1$ has gated a new value into the memory element, that this value will not change again until after the next phase $\Phi 2$ occurs. Therefore, the circuit behaves just as if each change of flip-flop value is triggered by the falling edge of phase $\Phi 2$ or the rising edge of phase $\Phi 1$.

MOS IC parts may be connected to the same clock-mode sequential circuit with bipolar parts, provided that the nominal clocking edges in the two circuits are synchronized. Shown in Fig. 3.12d is the nominal falling-edge-triggering clock equivalent of the two-phase clock of Fig. 3.12c. With the exception of treatments of dynamic memories in Sections 3.6 and 5.8, a clock of the form of Fig. 3.12d will always be assumed in subsequent discussions where reference to a clock is needed. It will always be possible to translate directly the resulting circuits to corresponding two-phase MOS implementations.

Flip-flops may be used individually to store single bits, in which case they are often referred to as *flags,* or they may be used to construct *registers*. A register is simply a set of n flip-flops, used to store n-bit words, where n may range from 2 to 100 or more. For example, in RIC, the accumulator is a 32-bit register, the program counter is a 24-bit register, and so on. Registers may be constructed with any type of flip-flop; we shall use D flip-flops in this book. The nomenclature here is not completely standard. Some manufacturers used the word *register* to signify any storage location permanently assigned to the processing unit for some specific purpose and not addressable in the same sense as ordinary memory locations. Thus, they may speak of a computer as having several hundred registers, when, in fact, these "registers" are simply reserved locations in random access memory. There is nothing wrong with this

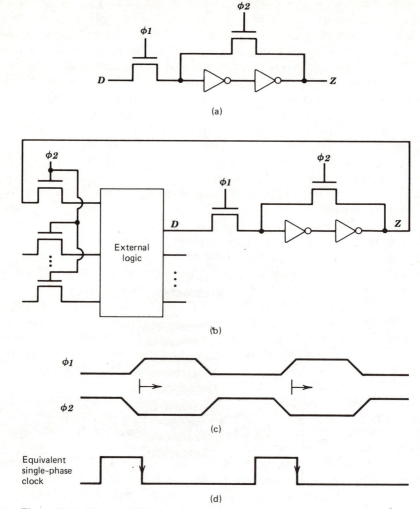

Figure 3.12. Clocked MOS memory element.

practice, and it may reflect a tendency for the functions of memory and processing to merge in some designs. However, we shall use the term *register memory* (RM) exclusively to denote independent vectors of flip-flops.

3.5 Random Access Memory (RAM)

Flip-flop registers are the fastest memory devices available, but they are too expensive to be used for main memory. Until the 1970s, main memory systems were usually based on some type of magnetic technology, with magnetic core memory being the dominant form of main memory. With the advent of integrated circuits, however, the cost of electronic memories has steadily decreased while the performance has steadily increased, to the point where they are now the standard form of main memory. Even today, core memories are occasionally used because they are *nonvolatile,* that is, they retain stored information even when the power goes off.

When we talk of the *main* memory of a computer, we generally refer to a relatively large store in which we can place entire programs or operating systems. Also, the main memory should feature *random access;* that is, the access time to any given location in memory should be the same as to any other location. If access is not random, then the programmer must carefully specify storage locations for data and instructions so as to minimize access times, a requirement that makes programming more difficult. Electronic random access memories are available in two basic types, *static* (SRAM), and *dynamic* (DRAM). Although there are exceptions, SRAMs are usually characterized as *synchronous,* whereas DRAMs are usually *asynchronous.*

A model of a typical SRAM is depicted in Fig. 3.13. Associated with this memory is an address register. Except for a short time delay following the change of contents of the address register and during a *write in memory* operation, the word in memory specified by the binary number in the address register appears continuously on lines **DATAOUT**. If a control pulse appears on the line **write,** the word currently represented on lines **DATAIN** will be stored in the memory location specified by the number in the address register. For small memories, this storage operation can be completed with the new word appearing on lines **DATAOUT,** within one clock period following the start of the pulse on line **write.**

The *decoder* illustrated in Fig. 3.13, is an essential component of every random access memory. The decoder has n input lines and 2^n output lines. One and only one output line will have the value logical 1 for each combination of input values. A simple implementation of a 3 to 2^3 or 3-bit decoder is illustrated in Fig. 3.14a. Notice that the output of the top AND gate, for example, will be 1 if and only if $a_3 = a_2 = a_1 = 0$.

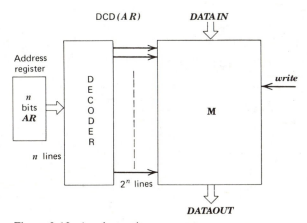

Figure 3.13. An electronic memory.

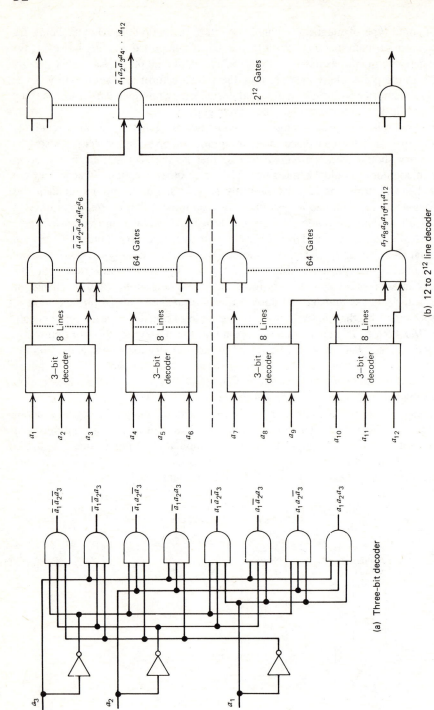

Figure 3.14. Decoders.

In theory, the networks of 3.14a could be extended directly to any number, n, inputs using 2^n gates with n inputs each. In practice, a fan-in limitation will eventually be reached in any technology. Thus, some type of multilevel network must be employed in large decoders. An example of a 12 to 2^{12} line decoder based on four 3-bit decoders is shown in Fig. 3.14b.

To keep the diagram readable, only a few connections are actually shown. The 3-bit decoders may be considered to be copies of the circuit of Fig. 3.14a in integrated circuit form. There are 64 pairs of output lines, one from each of the upper two 3-bit decoders. These pairs form the inputs to the upper 64 second-level AND gates. The outputs of these gates are the 64 possible minterms of the variables a_1, a_2, a_3, a_4, a_5 and a_6. The lower 64 second-level gate outputs are the minterms of a_7, a_8, a_9, a_{10}, a_{11}, and a_{12}. The 2^{12} twelve-bit minterms are formed by using all possible pairs of outputs of the second-level gates (one from the upper 64 and one from the lower 64) to form inputs to the final 2^{12} AND gates. The total cost of the network is almost entirely reflected in the 2^{12} gates in the final level of the network. Hence the network is arranged so that these gates are two-input gates. Also, we may conclude that the cost of the network is approximately proportional to the number of output lines rather than the number of input lines. As an example, a 12 to 2^{12} line decoder would be much more expensive than a 6 to 2^6 line decoder.

A segment of a clocked memory implemented using D flip-flops is illustrated in Fig. 3.15. Only words $i - 1$, i, and $i + 1$ out of 2^n words and only the first 3 bits of each word are shown. Each bit is stored in a D flip-flop. Notice that only the bits of one word will be gated through the AND gates at the output of the flip-flops of that word. This will be the word corresponding to the number in the address register. The word line from the decoder for this word will carry a logical 1. All other word lines will be 0. The addressed word will propagate through the chains of OR gates to **DATAOUT**. In practice the ORing function may be organized using multi-input gates or a wired NOR configuration to significantly reduce the number of logic levels and hence the time delay following a change in the contents of the address register.

A pulse on line **write** will pass through only one of the 2^n gates to which it is connected. This will be the gate that is connected to the word line carrying a logical 1 and corresponding to the number in the address register. Thus this pulse will reach only the clock inputs of the flip-flops in the addressed word. This pulse will cause the vector **DATAIN** to be clocked into the flip-flops of that data word. We see that the memory of Fig. 3.15 functions in the manner prescribed for the model of Fig. 3.13 for both read and write operations.

If the memory just discussed were composed of clocked D flip-flops of the type shown in Fig. 3.11, it would function like a bank of fast registers, in which a previously stored word could be read at the same time that a new word was being written. The ability to read and write separately in a RAM is of limited value, since read and write are usually separate operations at the programming level. The cost of a memory device is mostly determined by the complexity of the individual memory cells, and the cost of a memory device constructed of clocked D flip-flops could seldom be justified.

Fig. 3.16 shows a more economical form of bipolar memory cell. The functioning of this example circuit may be explained as follows. In the cell's normal state when

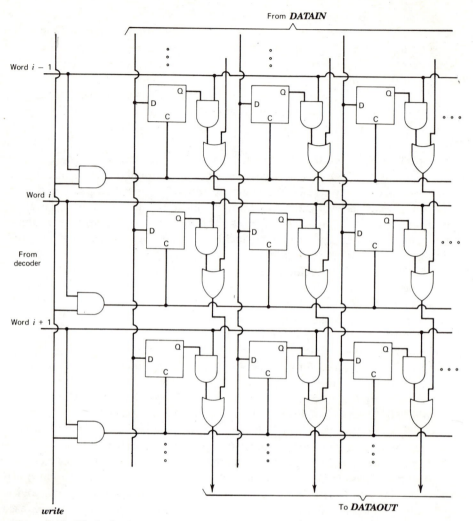

From **DATAIN**

Word $i - 1$

Word i

From
decoder

Word $i + 1$

write   To **DATAOUT**

Figure 3.15. Clocked memory.

not selected for a read or write operation, the **word select** line is at a potential of 0.3 volts and the emitter labelled b is held at about 0.5 volts. In this situation, either transistor T_1 or transistor T_2 will be cutoff and the other turned on. If T_1 is turned on, a 1 is stored in the memory element. If T_2 is on, a 0 is stored. When the value stored in this memory element is to be read, the **word select** line is raised to 3 volts. This prevents current from flowing from the emitter labelled a. If T_1 were turned on, the current in this transistor would necessarily flow from emitter b onto the "bit" line where it would be detected by a *sense amplifier*. If T_1 had been turned off, no current would have flowed from either a or b and none would have been detected by the sense

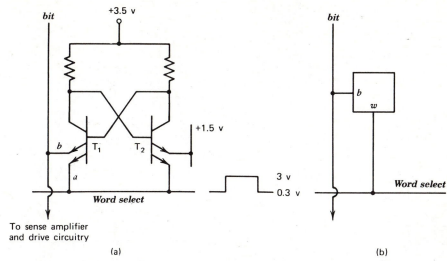

Figure 3.16. Bipolar random access memory element.

amplifier. Thus the output of the sense amplifier will equal the value stored in the memory element as long as the word select is held at 3 volts.

No voltage is externally imposed on line **bit** during a read operation, so that the cell returns to its former operating condition when **word select** returns to 0.3 volts. To write in the cell, a voltage is imposed on line **bit** and then **word select** is raised to 3 volts. If b is held at 0 volts, T_1 will be turned on and T_2 turned off. If b is held above 1.5 volts, T_1 is turned off and T_2 on. The circuit remains in its new state after **word select** is returned to 0.3 volt.

A simplified representation of the RAM memory element is given in Fig. 3.16b. Making b serve as both an input and an output for the cell requires some special circuitry in each integrated circuit memory package. This includes sense amplifiers and circuitry that can impose three separate voltages on the bit lines. This may, nonetheless, be the most efficient approach to the design of a bipolar LSI memory.

A 64-bit RAM package composed of sixteen 4-bit words complete with decoder is depicted in Fig. 3.17. For a longer word length, it is only necessary to connect several such packages in parallel. The **chip select** line makes it possible to use additional packages to increase the number of words in a complete memory. This line will be 1 only when it is desired to address a word in the particular package. If **write enable** is 0 (and **chip select** = 1), the addressed 4-bit word will appear on the output lines S_0, S_1, S_2, and S_3. A **write enable** = 1 will cause the input data word on D_0, D_1, D_2, and D_3 to be written into the addressed location. The output of the sense amplifiers is not meaningful while **write enable** = 1.

Bipolar RAM packages are available containing as many as $16K^2$ or more bits.

---

[2]In referring to computer memories, 1Kb has been defined as 1024 bits.

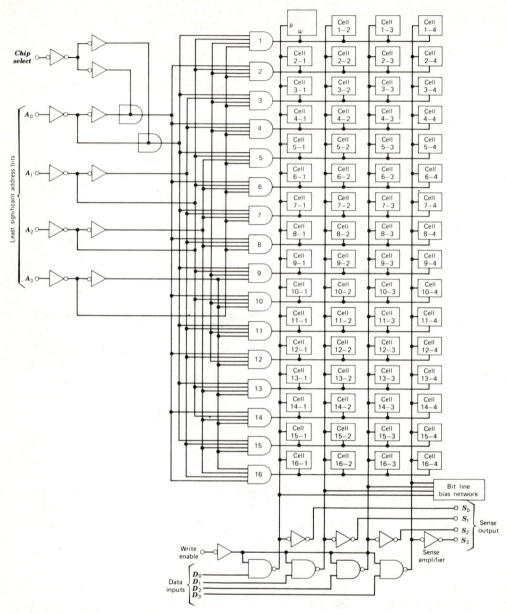

Figure 3.17. A 16 × 4 RAM.

To best take advantage of available output pins, this type of memory might be organized as 16K one-bit words. Another approach to efficient pin use is to let the data input and data output share a common set of pins. This is made possible by using an internal busing network. In this case, an additional control line, which might be called **read** (**read** = 1 for READ and **read** = 0 for WRITE), would be required to switch the data bus between input and output.

Memory devices, such as described in the preceding section, are termed *static* RAMs because stored values will be retained as long as power is applied to the device. In MOS technology, there is available an even simpler memory element than the two-transistor device of Fig. 3.16. As shown in Fig. 3.18, this cell consists of a capacitor and a MOS switch. This switch represents a very high resistance, almost an open circuit, when the value connected to the gate on line **select** is 0. When a positive voltage is placed on **select,** the switch is closed and the capacitor is charged to whatever value has been connected to line **in/out.** After the switch has opened, the desired charge will remain on the capacitor until it is read or for several milliseconds, but not indefinitely. Therefore, the value of each cell must be refreshed periodically, that is, the value must be sensed and the capacitor recharged to that value. The cell must also be recharged after it is read. For this reason, this type of memory is called *dynamic* memory.

Figure 3.19 depicts a vastly scaled down version of a dynamic MOS memory consisting of only eight words of 1-bit each. Three address bits are required to address the eight 1-bit data words. Notice that the address bits are divided into a row address consisting of the high-order bits and a column address that are decoded separately. Whenever a new address is placed on the **ADBUS** for a read operation, the output of the row decoder corresponding to that row address goes to 1. The two bits in the row selected by that line are connected to the 2-bit **IDBUS**. While clock phase $\Phi 2$ is active, the amplified voltage from one of these two lines, as selected by the decoded column address bit, is routed to the data output by one of the switches labelled S1. After the end of each read operation, while phase $\Phi 1$ is active, switch S2 is closed to cause the two capacitors on the row just read to be recharged to their original values. The timing relationships required of the signals involved in the read operation are shown in Fig. 3.20a.

To write in the dynamic memory, *datain* is routed through one of the switches labelled S3, as selected by the column address, to the corresponding **IDBUS** line. The cell selected by the row address is then charged from the active **IDBUS** line.

During refresh, all rows must be read and then rewritten with the same values.

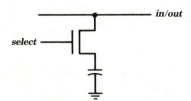

Figure 3.18. Dynamic memory cell.

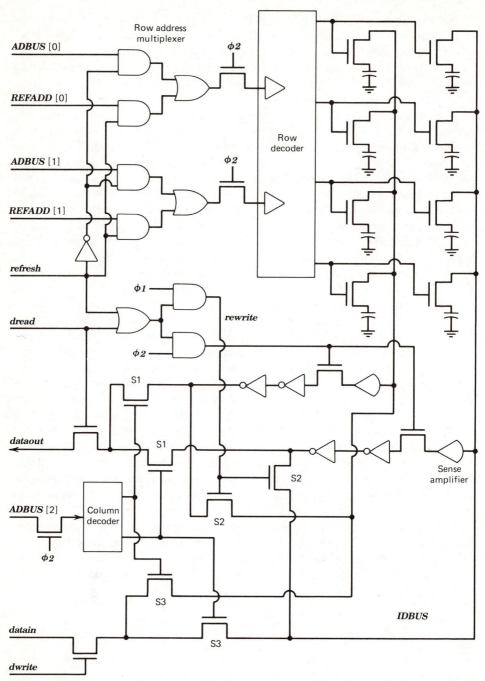

Figure 3.19. 8 × 1 MOS dynamic memory.

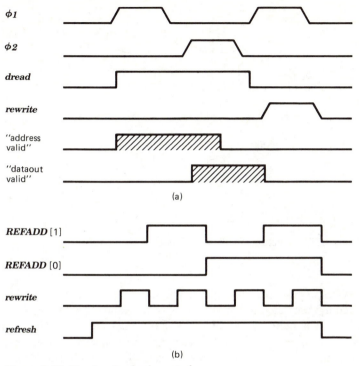

Figure 3.20. Read and refresh control.

When the line **refresh** = 1, the external address bus is disconnected and a local refresh address is connected to address bits 0 and 1. A controller, which is not shown, must cause **REFADD** to count through all four row addresses. These addresses are routed through the multiplexer to select each decoder output in order. As shown in Fig. 3.20b, at the end of each refresh address cycle during phase $\Phi 1$, **rewrite** goes to 1 to connect the values just read back through the **IDBUS** to recharge the same cells.

The read, write, and refresh mechanisms just discussed are common to all dynamic memories. The designated control lines, however, are simplifications of those used in practice. Available dynamic memory chips have many more than 8 bits. Chips of 256K × 1 bit and 1 megabit capacity are available. The division of the address into the row address and column address is standard. The 64K bit memory, for example, has 128 rows and 128 columns in each of four quadrants. Each of the 128 rows must be refreshed once every 2 msec.

Memory packages of 1 bit per word are organized into units of eight packages and provided with a memory controller. Extra packages may be included to provide for error control. The overall memory control lines as seen by the CPU are not necessarily the same as those on the individual packages. A memory controller must be provided to control refresh and to manage the interface of the memory to the computer address and data buses.

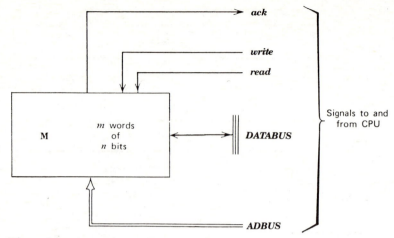

Figure 3.21. Asynchronous memory model.

The refresh operations in dynamic memories will take place at fixed intervals that may be quite unrelated to the clock rate of the central processor. As a result, the response time to a memory request cannot be predicted, and such memories are classified as *asynchronous*. A typical asynchronous memory model is depicted in Fig. 3.21. For a read, the central processor will place the address of the desired word on **ADBUS** and issue a control signal on line, **read.** When the desired data word has been placed on the **DATABUS,** the memory will return a signal on line **ack** (acknowledge). If a memory refresh is ongoing when a read request occurs, no acknowledge signal will appear until the refresh is complete.

For a write operation, the CPU will put the address on **ADBUS** and the data on the **DATABUS** and then issue a signal on line **write.** An acknowledge will appear when the data has been written in memory. In Section 5.8, we shall be in a position to describe the controller for a typical dynamic RAM.

3.6   Direct Access Storage (DAS)

Random access memory is simply too expensive to provide the only means of storing information in computer systems. Virtually all computer systems provide one or more types of secondary storage. Secondary storage does more than provide a large storage capacity at low cost. It also usually provides a means of physically removing the stored information from the computer, for off-line storage or for convenient transfer of information to other computers. If you have used microcomputers, you are aware that they are totally useless without software that you purchase stored on a floppy disk. By far the most common types of secondary storage are disk and tape.

In terms of access, disk units are classified as *direct access storage* (DAS)

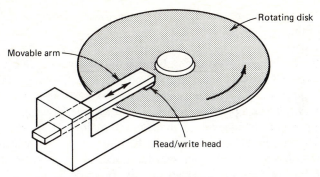

Figure 3.22. Basic structure of single-disk memory.

devices. The basic structure of a small disk memory is shown in Fig. 3.22. A metal disk coated with a ferromagnetic material rotates under a read/write head mounted on a movable arm that positions the head radially over the disk. The speed of rotation is typically 1800 to 3600 rpm. The manner in which information is stored or recovered is indicated in Fig. 3.23, in which we show a cross section of a read/write head and the disk passing under it. To write information, we pass a current through the coil of the read/write head, which in turn sets up a magnetic flux in the armature (Fig. 3.23a). When the flux crosses the gap in the armature, it passes through the magnetic coating of the disk, thus magnetizing a small area on the disk. The size of the magnetized area depends on the speed of the disk and the duration of the write current. Bit density on disks runs from several hundred to several thousand bits per inch. For reading, the coil is used as a sense winding. As the magnetized area passes under the head, the motion of the flux field relative to the head causes a flux change ($d\phi/dt$) in the gap, which induces a voltage in the sense winding (Fig. 3.23b). This voltage is detected by a sense amplifier and used to set a register. This reading process is nondestructive, since there is no current flowing to alter the stored flux pattern. There are a number of different ways of coding the information on the disk. Different directions of magnetization may be used for 0's and 1's, or 1's may be indicated by a change of flux

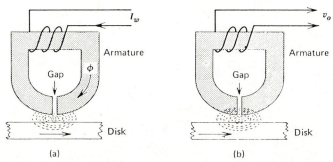

Figure 3.23. Write and read operations on a magnetic disk.

direction and 0's by no change of flux, and so on. See this chapter's References for details on recording processes.

The arrangement shown in Fig. 3.22, with a single disk and a single head on a movable arm is by far the most common, but other arrangements are used. There may be a large number of heads mounted in fixed positions distributed radially across the surfaces (both sides are used) of the disk. This is known as a one-head-per-track system, where a *track* is simply the circular pattern recorded by a single head. Larger storage capacities can be obtained through the use of multiple disks arranged in a stack on a single shaft. The heads are mounted on the arms of a *comb,* which moves in or out radially to position the heads over selected tracks (Fig. 3.24). Both sides of the disks are used, but we have shown heads on only one side for clarity.

Data transfer in disk memories is sequential in that data are transferred 1 bit at a time as the disks move by the heads. However, access in a disk memory is termed *direct* because the head can move across the disk directly to a desired track, or the track can be directly selected electronically in a multiple-head system. Once the desired track has been accessed, it is necessary to wait for the desired location (sector) to move into position under the head. In a fully sequential memory, such as tape, it is necessary to wait for all information between the present location and the desired location to move under the head. Although it is possible to select any track randomly, access in a disk system is not random in the same sense as in RAM, since the time for access is dependent on the location of the desired information. Once the desired track has been accessed, it is necessary to wait for the desired information to move under the head. The average waiting time, the *latency time,* is the time for half a revolution, 16.7 msec for an 1800 rpm disk. To this time must be added the time to select the track, which, for a movable head system, obviously depends on how far the head has to move from the initial track to the final track. In a movable head system,

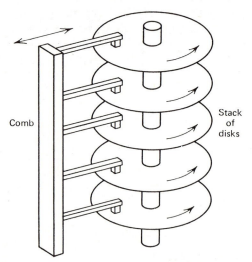

Figure 3.24. Basic structure of multidisk memory.

the head-positioning time is dominant, whereas in a multiple-head system, the latency time is dominant.

There are probably as many different ways of arranging data on a disk as there are different models of disk memories, but a typical arrangement is that shown in Fig. 3.25. The index gap is used to reset the timing circuits once each revolution. A timing track, sometimes incorporated onto the disk during manufacturing, may be used to provide synchronizing pulses for read and write operations. Data are usually stored in bytes (groups of 8 bits). A track address register is provided into which the address of the desired track will be placed. In the case of a multiple-disk system, the track address register will have sufficient bits to specify any track on any disk.

Within a track, information is organized into sectors, with sectors separated by gaps, that is, short segments with no information recorded, or some repetitive pattern, such as all 0's, recorded. In theory, it would be possible to locate a sector by counting gaps from the index gap. (Note that this implies that there must be a way of distinguishing the index gap from sector gaps.) This is rarely done, however, with identification of sectors being provided by identifier blocks at the start of each sector (see Fig. 3.25b). The nature of the identifier information varies from one system to another, but the basic process is always the same. The system moves from gap to gap and then compares the *stored address information* for a match to the address of the desired sector. This use of stored address information is another key distinction between random access systems and direct or sequential access systems. The address in a random access system is uniquely identified with a specific physical location, totally independent of the information stored. Locations in direct access and sequential access systems are not physically unique, and stored addressing information is invariably used to identify a desired unit of stored data wholly or partially.

Note that the circumference of a track obviously depends on its radial location. If we record at maximum bit density on the innermost track, the outer tracks will be recorded at lower densities, thus "wasting" space. This problem can be alleviated by

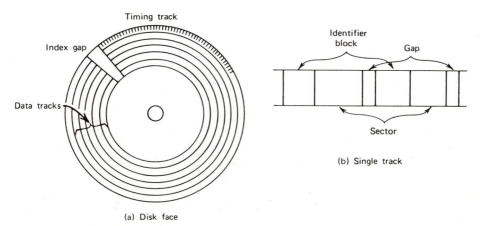

(a) Disk face

Figure 3.25. Typical arrangement of data on disk memory.

dividing the disk radially into zones, each zone having its own timing and word-mark tracks, with the number of words per track decreasing as we move toward the center of the disk.

Several different types of disks are used. Large-capacity disk systems in main-frame computers are most commonly multiple-disk systems using rigid metal disks, which may be fixed or removable in the form of *disk-packs*. Such systems typically provide storage capacities in the range 100 to 1000 megabytes, with access times from 1 to 100 msec. Smaller systems usually use single-disk systems, either rigid or floppy. Single fixed, rigid disk systems, often called *Winchester systems,* provide storage capacities of 5 to 20 megabytes and access times in the range of 100 to 1000 msec. Floppy disk systems use removable flexible plastic disks that provide storage capacities up to 1 megabyte per disk and access times of several seconds. All the figures just given are typical for systems available as of the time this is written but will change rapidly as the technology develops.

Because of the long access time, data are nearly always transferred in and out of DAS systems in large blocks of hundreds or thousands of bytes, which will be stored in sequential locations. Thus, it may take anywhere from 5 to 2000 msec to access a particular block of data; once accessed, and providing no further head move-ment is required, data can be transferred at rates up to 10 Mbytes/sec. The typical model of a disk system, shown in Figure 3.26, is based on the assumption that data will be transferred in large blocks.

When a logical 1 is observed on line *seek,* the lines labelled *INPUT* are treated as the address of the track that must be accessed. Once the disk has located a read head on the desired track, it will indicate with a signal on *ready.* The controlling system will respond with a signal on line *read.* Each data byte appearing on the eight lines *DATAOUT* will be signalled by a pulse on line *time.* Successive bytes will be examined until the desired record description is encountered. If information is to be read from the disk, the reading continues with the data bytes routed to the CPU. No

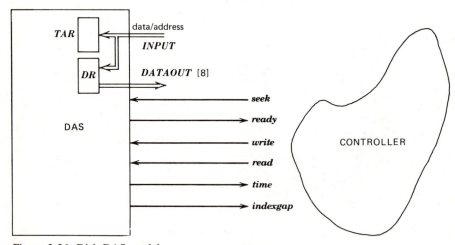

Figure 3.26. Disk DAS model.

timing signals will appear while a gap is under the read/write head. During this time, a logical-1 level can be placed on line *write* causing a new record to be written beginning at the current spot in the tract.

Note that data transfer proceeds at a fixed rate determined by the speed of the disk and independent of the clock rate of the CPU. It is thus vital that the control of the CPU be such that there is no possibility of failing to respond to a signal on line *time*.

One method of handling this problem is to provide a controller, between the DAS unit and the CPU, which will have a small *buffer* memory of its own that can temporarily store a small block of data, thus giving the CPU more time to respond. Also, disk transfer instructions may include the number of bytes to be transferred, and the controller may be used to keep track of the number of bytes transferred.

Another form of DAS is the *magnetic bubble memory*. Magnetic bubbles are minute magnetic domains that can be created or destroyed in certain magnetic materials by the application of perpendicular magnetic fields. Once set up, these bubbles are stable in the absence of a field, thus forming the basis for a nonvolatile memory. To detect the bubbles, they must be made to move. For this purpose, a loop pattern of segments of permalloy is deposited on the surface of the memory chip. Then, setting up a rotating magnetic field in a plane parallel to the surface of the chip will cause the bubbles to circulate around the permalloy loop, thus forming a magnetic shift register. The movement of the bubbles past a specific point can be detected by several methods. Note that there is a rather direct analogy to a disk, in that we again have circular movement of data, the difference being that the movement is magnetic rather than mechanical.

Figure 3.27 shows the basic organization of one of the first commercial bubble memories to appear, a 100-Kbyte unit. The memory is organized as eight loops of

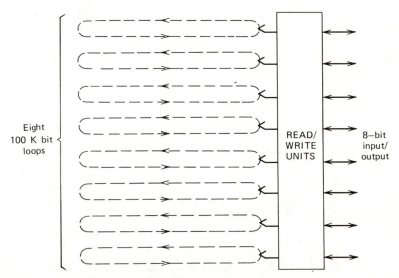

Figure 3.27. Byte-organized bubble memory system.

100 Kbits each, one loop for each of the 8 bits forming a byte. The eight loops rotate in synchronism, with the 8 bits making up each byte passing the read/write station simultaneously. It takes 1 sec to complete a full revolution of a loop, so that the data rate is 100 Kbytes/sec, with an average access time of one-half second. Bubble memories offer great advantages over disk memories in size and, potentially, cost. When bubble memories were first introduced, some enthusiasts predicted that they would someday completely replace disk memories. To date, this has not happened, primarily because disk systems have improved so dramatically in cost/performance ratio that bubble memories are not competitive. The use of bubble memories is restricted to applications where their small size and low power consumption is important.

3.7 Sequential Access Storage (SAS)

Sequential memories, of which magnetic tape is the most common type, fill the need for very large capacity at very low cost. Digital magnetic recording tape is plastic tape coated with a magnetic surface, identical except in size and quality to the tape used for home recording. The tape is wound on reels and passes from one reel to another past a read/write head (Fig. 3.28). Digital tape transports are similar in principle to home tape recorders but provide for much faster and more precise control of tape movement. The method of reading and writing is identical to that used in disk memories.

The general arrangement of data on a tape is shown in Fig. 3.29. In recently designed equipment, data is recorded in nine separate tracks on the tape. The 8 bits of a data character are written laterally across eight of the nine tracks of the tape. One of these 8 bits is typically a parity bit to establish odd or even parity over the 8-bit character. The ninth bit is used to ensure the availability of the timing signal called *sprocket* (to be discussed shortly). Establishing uniform parity for all characters assists in the detection of errors, which are primarily caused by imperfections on the tape surface.

When tape is written, consecutive characters will continue to be written at uniform

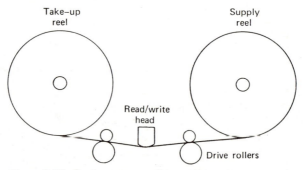

Figure 3.28. Basic structure of tape transport.

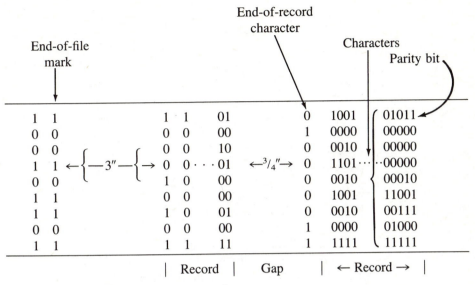

Figure 3.29. Typical data format on magnetic tape.

intervals as long as data continue to be made available. All the characters written in a single WRITE operation will constitute a *record*. When the WRITE operation ends, an *end-of-record* or *checksum* character will be generated to establish longitudinal parity over each bit position in the record, and the tape will come to a stop. When another WRITE operation is initiated, the tape will come up to speed and this process will be repeated. Because it takes time to stop and start the tape, there will be a blank interval (usually 1.9 cm) between records, known as the *interrecord gap*. In addition, many systems provide for a special one-character record known as the *end-of-file mark*, where a *file* is simply a set of records that have some logical connection. The end-of-file mark is usually placed 3 in. after the end of the last record in the file; and since it is considered a one-character record, it has its own end-of-record mark associated with it.

The general model for a sequential memory is shown in Fig. 3.30. The CPU or tape controller will initiate a write operation by a signal on line **write**. When the tape transport has reached operating speed, it will respond with a signal on line **sprocket**[3] and accept the first character from the tape write register **TWR**. New characters will be placed in **TWR** in response to each sprocket signal until **write** is returned to 0. During a write operation, the sprocket signal is generated by a clock within the SAS system. The SAS system keeps track of longitudinal parity and writes the EOR checksum character on tape at the termination of the write operation.

---

[3]The term *sprocket signal* is apparently derived from the sprocket holes in the paper tape, which actually control the mechanical movement of the tape; it has become fairly standard in referring to magnetic tape. The sprocket signals serve the same function as the signals derived from the timing track of a disk, that of marking the position of each character.

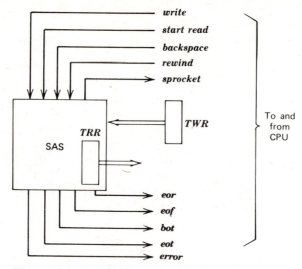

Figure 3.30. Terminal model of sequential access memory (SAS).

The SAS system will respond to a ***start read*** pulse by accelerating the tape in forward direction. The tape will have reached operating speed before the 1.9-cm gap is exhausted and the first character of the next record is encountered. Each character will be deposited in the tape read register, ***TRR,*** and its availability is indicated by a signal on line ***sprocket.*** During the read operation, the timing of the sprocket signal is determined by the characters as they read from tape. In the simplest method of recording, this signal is merely the OR combination of the bits in each character, including the timing track. When the SAS system senses the end-of-record gap, the tape is stopped and this fact is signalled on line ***eor.***

There are a number of error conditions, such as parity errors and attempts to write past the end of the tape, that can only be detected by the tape unit. Therefore, we indicate an ***error*** output on our general model, with the understanding that in any particular model there may be a number of error lines, depending on the number of error conditions defined by the designer.

Note that there is no means of addressing locations on tape. READ and WRITE operations start wherever the tape happens to be. We can move forward or backward on the tape a desired number of records. If we want to skip a record, for example, we simply issue a ***start read*** command but ignore the data being read. The ***backspace*** command will move the tape back to the immediately preceding interrecord gap, that is, one record back. We can provide for locating specific records by writing identification characters as the beginning of the record. We can then search the tape by looking for the correct identification. The ***rewind*** command rewinds the entire tape onto the supply reel. The completion of this command will be indicated by a signal on line ***bot*** (beginning of tape). Both ends of the tape should be indicated by marks on the tape that can be sensed by the system.

Reel-to-reel tape units provide the highest performance at the highest cost and are generally found only in large systems. Recording density in reel-to-reel units ranges from 800 to 6250 bytes/in., with tape speeds from 10 to 200 in./sec, providing data rates of 8 to 800 Kbytes/sec. The number of bytes on a tape will depend on the number of records or files, since the gaps take up space. A standard $10^1/_2$ in. reel of tape holds 2400 ft, providing a capacity of about 20 to 150 Mbytes per tape. The format, model, and operating sequences just described apply primarily to reel-to-reel systems.

Recently, high-speed digital tape cassettes have made an appearance. These systems must not be confused with the audio cassettes used for data storage in the early days of the microcomputer. High-speed cassettes, which are driven under reel-to-reel servo control, achieve data rates of 3 Mbytes/sec. Data can be stored at up to 40 Kbytes/in., providing a capacity of 200 Mbytes on a 4 in. × 5 in. × 1 in. cartridge.

3.8   Read-Only Memory (ROM)

The read-only memory is a device in which the stored information either is permanently fixed during fabrication or can be altered only by changes in the device structure. The basic form of the typical read-only memory is shown in Fig. 3.31. The coupling devices are usually transistors, but in some cases they may be passive circuit elements.

The address is decoded to select one word line, as was illustrated for the electronic

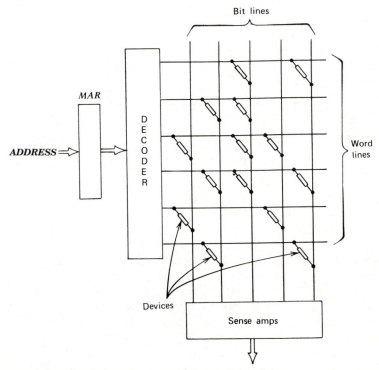

Figure 3.31. Basic structure of read-only memory.

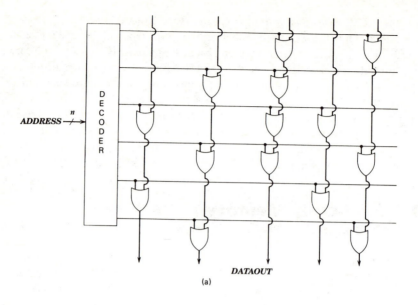

(a)

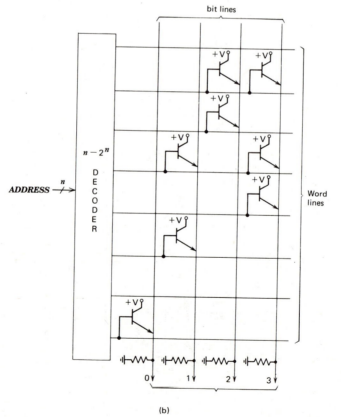

(b)

Figure 3.32. ROM models. (a) General model. (b) Transistor-coupled ROM.

memory of Fig. 3.13. A voltage is applied to the selected word line, which in turn is coupled through to a bit line wherever a coupling element is connected. Wherever a coupling device is connected, a 1 is considered to be stored; wherever there is no connection, a 0 is considered to be stored. The coupling device may be connected during fabrication, in which case the information storage is permanent. Alternately, coupling devices may be placed at each intersection with means provided for the user to destroy connections where the operator wishes 0's to be stored. Sometimes this is done by the user of the ROM passing large currents (sufficient to destroy the devices) through unwanted coupling devices.

In the static ROM, the coupling devices can be regarded simply as connections to a single ORing operation to generate the data output bits. This viewpoint is illustrated in Fig. 3.32a. This figure closely resembles the clocked RAM of Fig. 3.15 with the write line *DATAIN* and the memory elements removed. Most ROMs are transistor-coupled, as illustrated in Fig. 3.32b. In this figure, the word lines are vertical rather than horizontal, as in the previous illustrations. At each point where a 1 is to be stored a transistor is connected—the emitter to the bit line, the base to the word line. All collectors are connected to a common supply voltage. All word lines are normally held at a sufficiently negative level to cut off all the transistors so that the bit lines are at 0 volts. When a word line is selected, it is raised to a sufficiently positive level to switch the transistors on, thus raising the bit lines where a transistor is connected to a positive level. This type of ROM is commonly available in integrated circuit form. Integrated circuit ROMs are available in both bipolar and MOS types, with capacities up to several thousand words, including address decoding logic, in a single IC package. Depending on type, MOS or bipolar, access times range from about 1 μsec to less than 10 nsec. The direct compatibility, both in speed and logic levels with ordinary gates is an obvious advantage. The transistor-coupled ROM may be the only type of ROM ever encountered by many designers. Read-only memories are usually designed into systems as memories in which the user cannot change the contents, just as the name implies. Alternatively, a ROM may be viewed as a means of implementing combinational logic. Depending on the connections within the ROM, each output bit is an arbitrary Boolean function of the input variables to the decoder.

3.9 Summary and Perspective

As we stated at the beginning of the chapter, this is not intended to be an exhaustive survey. There is at least one whole category of memory that we have not treated: mass memory to handle the problems of very large stores such as census or tax records. At present, magnetic tape is the dominant medium for such applications. Its capacity is unlimited, but it has the disadvantage of requiring manual handling of the tapes. A mass memory in which the computer could have access to any part of the store without human intervention would have obvious advantages. Most research in this area has centered on optical and photographic techniques. A few systems have been developed, but this is basically an area with many difficult problems and few solutions.

Even with better access, the problems of searching very large files are formidable, and there has been much interest in the *associative,* or *content-addressable,* memory. As an example, in a hit-and-run investigation, it might be desired to search the license plate files for all owners of cars of a certain make, year, and color. But these files would be indexed under license number or owner's name, so that a complete search of the entire file would be required. In an associative memory, we would simply input the desired identifying characteristics, and all records with matching characteristics would be immediately identified, without exhaustive search. Many techniques for implementing this type of memory have been suggested, but none has even approached the low cost required for very large files. The associative memory that seems so inviting as a means of handling large files may also be used as a high-speed buffer memory. This application will be discussed in Chapter 13.

Even within the categories we have discussed, we have treated only those types that seem to have the greatest present and continuing importance. However, continued technical developments will undoubtedly produce new devices and change the relative importance of existing devices. Rather than attempt to prophesy the future (with our very cloudy crystal ball), we shall try to give you some perspective on the cost-speed relationships among the various categories of memory. These relationships are, we hope, somewhat independent of exact form of implementation and may, therefore, have some continuing validity.

In Fig. 3.33 we show a logarithmic plot of memory speed vs cost per bit. The four main types of memory—register, random access, direct access, and sequential—are represented by dark areas on the graph, since there are wide variations in speed and cost in each category. Even with these variations, however, it is notable that there are distinct intervals between the four categories, a fact that presumably accounts for the continuing importance of all four types over the past 20 to 30 years. Over this period, the graph as a whole has shifted down and to the left, that is, toward the cheaper and faster; but the relative position of the four types has changed only with

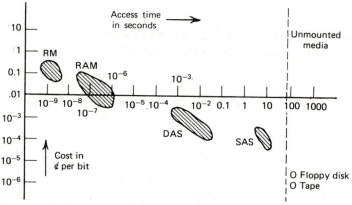

Figure 3.33. Cost/speed relationships of memory.

respect to the relative cost of complete implementations of a direct access and sequential access storage.

During the nine years between the second and third editions of this book, the cost of register memory, RAM, and DAS has decreased by a factor of approximately 100. If you compare the figure in the second edition corresponding to Fig. 3.33, you will notice the similarity in all but the cost scale factors and the position of the SAS. A significant decrease in RAM cost was predicted nine years ago; but the density increase and cost decrease of dynamic RAMs have probably exceeded almost every-ones' expectations. Even more surprising is the fact that the cost per bit of disk memories has almost kept pace.

From Fig. 3.33 it can be seen that the complete SAS system now offers little cost advantage over the DAS system. In fact, SAS is now considered by many as an I/O device rather than a memory. Tape, however, remains at this writing the favored medium for long-term off-line storage of data. Hence a data point representing the cost per bit and the access time of an unmounted tape reel has been included in Fig. 3.33. Similarly included is a data point for an independent floppy disk, which you have no doubt found convenient for the storage of smaller amounts of data.

Again, what may be expected in the future is never clear. Undoubtedly, RAM will continue to get cheaper but probably not at the rate experienced between 1975 and 1987. For smaller systems, dynamic RAMS may be organized as DAS systems, replacing the disk except for I/O purposes. Whatever the technology employed, the computer designer may always work with a hierarchy of three memory types, with SAS used for I/O purposes.

References

1. F. J. Hill and G. R. Peterson, *Introduction to Switching Theory and Logical Design*, 3rd ed., Wiley, New York, 1981.
2. A. J. Kolk, "Low-Cost Rotating Memories: Status and Future," *Computer*, Vol. 9, No. 3, Mar. 1976, pp. 30–35.
3. J. McDermott, "Semi Conductor Memories," *Electronic Design*, Vol. 24, No. 12, June 1976, pp. 78–82.
4. R. Allan, "Semi Conductor Memories," *IEEE Spectrum*, Vol. 12, No. 8, Aug. 1975, pp. 40–45.
5. E. C. Joseph, "Memory Hierarchy: Computer System Considerations," *Computer Design*, Vol. 8, No. 11, Nov. 1969, pp. 165–169.
6. L. E. Sebestyan, *Digital Magnetic Tape Recording for Computer Applications*, Chapman & Hall, London, 1973.
7. A. V. Pohm, "Electronic Replacements for Head-per-Track Drums and Disks," *Computer*, Vol. 9, No. 3, Mar. 1976, pp. 16–20.
8. G. Luecke, J. P. Mize, and W. N. Carr, *Semiconductor Memory Design and Application*, McGraw–Hill, New York, 1973.
9. D. W. Gulley, "Match DRAM Organization to Memory Requirements," *Computer Design*, Dec. 1983, pp. 73–80.
10. D. Brunner, "Is Your Dynamic RAM Refresh Scheme Killing Your Microprocessor Performance?," *Digital Design*, Feb. 1982, pp. 58–61.

11. R. Matick, *Computer Storage Systems and Technology,* Wiley Interscience, New York, 1977.

12. M. Eplick and R. Parker, "Winchester Disk Technology Spins Into New Orbits," *Computer Design,* Jan. 1983, pp. 89–102.

13. A. E. Bell, "Optical Data Storage Technology Status and Prospects," *Computer Design,* Jan. 1983, pp. 133–144.

14. *MOS Memory Data Book,* Texas Instruments, Dallas, 1984.

4 Design Conventions

4.1 Introduction

Subsequent to the publication of the first edition of this book, there has been a noticeable increase in interest in computer hardware description languages [1,2,3]. These languages have been recognized as vehicles for communications of ideas in the early stages of design. They have served as the bases of design automation processes. They have proved useful in product description, for training purposes, and in maintenance documents.

The procedure that we shall propose for digital system design will be based on one such hardware description language called AHPL. Most of this language will be presented in the next chapter. The purpose of this chapter is to interpret certain of the more basic conventions in terms of hardware. Enough of the language will be presented to permit the design of a simple vector-processing digital system. The need for a more sophisticated notation and a carefully constructed set of conventions for translating this notation into hardware will become evident in the process.

The utility of AHPL or any hardware language is based on the fact that most digital systems can be partitioned into a control section and a section containing data registers and logic, as shown in Fig. 4.1. The control section will cause register transfers to take place in the data section by sending signals on a set of control lines. In some systems, the sequencing of control will be influenced by branching information fed back from the data section. Usually, memory elements in the data section are arranged as registers. A single control level will typically cause the results of a logical computation to be transferred into all the flip-flops of one or more registers. Since the bits

75

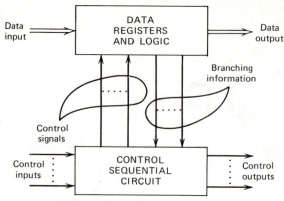

Figure 4.1. Data/control partition.

of registers are often treated uniformly, these logical computations can be conveniently expressed in a vector notation similar to APL.[1]

4.2   Register Transfers

Much of the activity of a vector-handling digital system consists of transferring vectors of information from one register to another. A computation, for example, consists of placing some Boolean function of the contents of argument registers into a destination register. It is quite possible to view a digital computer simply as a collection of registers among which data may be transferred, with logical manipulations taking place during the transfers. As we shall see, a major part of the description of a computer will consist of a schedule defining each transfer and specifying the ordering and timing in which these transfers will take place. In this section we shall describe the hardware mechanism through which a register transfer can be accomplished. The notation for expressing the simplest of these transfers as design language steps will also be presented.

Registers will be noted by strings of boldface italic capitals, such as **MA, PC,** and **AC.** Transfer of the contents of one register into another is indicated by an arrow, for example,

$$AC \leftarrow MD$$

signifies that the contents of **MD** are transferred to **AC.** The contents of the source register (**MD** in this example) are not affected by the transfer; but any previous information in **AC** is, of course, destroyed. The notation

$$AC \leftarrow 0, 0, 0, 0$$

---

[1]APL is *A Programming Language,* invented by K. E. Iverson.

will indicate that all the flip-flops in *AC* are cleared, if *AC* is a 4-bit register, whereas

$$AC \leftarrow 1, 1, 1, 1$$

will indicate that all the flip-flops in *AC* are set.

The large majority of register transfers in digital systems are clocked, that is, synchronized by a system master clock. Many flip-flops are equipped with master set and/or master clear inputs. These inputs are unclocked, but register transfers implemented through the use of these inputs are usually used only for system reset.

We assume that the control section as well as the data section of Fig. 4.1 is synchronized by the system clock. Therefore, all logic level changes on output lines from the control unit will be assumed to take place at the time of the leading or the trailing edge of a clock pulse. We shall arbitrarily choose to synchronize all state changes in both the control and data units with the trailing edge of a clock pulse. Thus trailing-edge-triggered flip-flops will be used throughout, and the system will be referred to as a *trailing-edge-triggered system*. With only slight complication one could choose leading-edge-triggered flip-flops to form a leading-edge system.

A single control level output from the control sequential circuit is illustrated in Fig. 4.2a. The assumed relationship between this control signal, which we shall label CSL, and the system clock is illustrated in Fig. 4.2b. A close correspondence exists between a control level and each clock pulse that occurs while this control level is 1. These clock pulses will be used to effect the register transfers specified by the corresponding control levels. Very often, the AND combination of a control signal and the clock will be implemented explicitly. ANDing the line CSL with the clock results in a line labelled CSP on which pulses approximately synchronized with the clock appear as shown in Fig. 4.2b.

The implementation of a clocked transfer from the 4-bit register *AR* to the 4-bit register *BR* caused by control level CSL is illustrated in Fig. 4.3, where each register is composed of flip-flops. It can be seen that the transfer is effected by the trailing edge of pulses on line CSP. *During clock periods when a pulse does not appear on this line, the contents of the register BR remain unchanged.* This is emphasized in

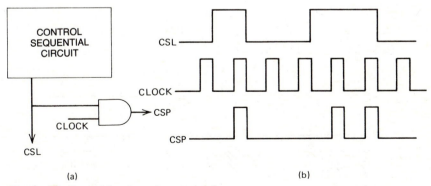

Figure 4.2. Control levels and control pulses.

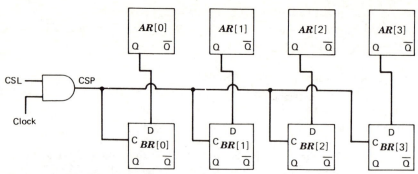

Figure 4.3. Clocked transfer.

Fig. 4.4. This simple mechanism for assuring that the contents of a register change only when a control level is present is extremely important and corresponds to the situation in software language when a variable remains unchanged until it appears on the left of an executed step. Consistent with the notation introduced in the first paragraph of this section, we represent the transfer of *AR* into *BR* by

BR ← AR

Each time the control sequential circuit is in a state corresponding to an AHPL step containing this expression, the logic level CSL will be 1, causing the transfer to take place.

The edge-triggering mechanism for bipolar circuits will serve as the synchronization model throughout the book. For MOS VLSI, an equally effective approach to synchronizing data transfers with control unit activity has been developed using the two-phase clocking scheme discussed in Section 3.5.

Very often there will be more than one vector to be transferred into the same register in a given digital system. As we shall see in Section 4.7, these transfers may take place in separate steps in a control sequence or they may be expressed in the

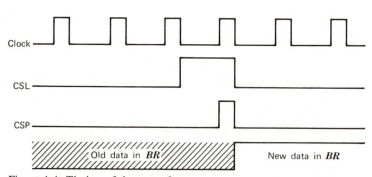

Figure 4.4. Timing of data transfers.

same step as a *conditional transfer*. That is, the vector to be transferred in a given step will be contingent to the value of one or more control inputs or feedback variables to the control circuit. In either case, there will be a separate control line from the control sequential circuit for each vector to be directly transferred into each register. Suppose, for example, that any one of three vectors can be transferred into a 4-bit register *DR*. If CSL1 = 1, *AR* will be transferred into *DR;* if CSL2 = 1, *BR* will be transferred into *DR;* and if CSL3 = 1, then *CR* will be transferred into *DR*. The implementation of these three transfers is illustrated in Fig. 4.5 for D flip-flops.

The output of the banks of AND gates will be 0 unless the corresponding control signal is 1. It will normally be assumed that no more than one control signal will be 1. Thus, if one control level, for example, CSL1, is 1, the vector *AR* will be routed to the output of the bank of OR gates. The same control level will enable a clock pulse to reach the "C" inputs of the *DR* flip-flops, thereby clocking *AR* into *DR* with timing as illustrated in Fig. 4.4.

It is often necessary to clear all the flip-flops of a register to 0 or to set them to 1. We have already presented notation for these two operations. It is unlikely that only these two operations would appear in a control sequence for a given register. Let us, therefore, consider the situation in which a 4-bit register of D flip-flops *AR* is to be set to 1 if CSL1 = 1, where *AR* is to be cleared if CSL2 = 1, and where the contents of *BR* are to be transferred into *AR* if CSL3 = 1. A Karnaugh map for the next value of flip-flop *AR,* applicable whenever a control pulse reaches the clock input of this flip-flop, is given in Fig. 4.6. We assume that no more than one of the three control signals will be 1, simultaneously giving us four of the "don't-care" entries on

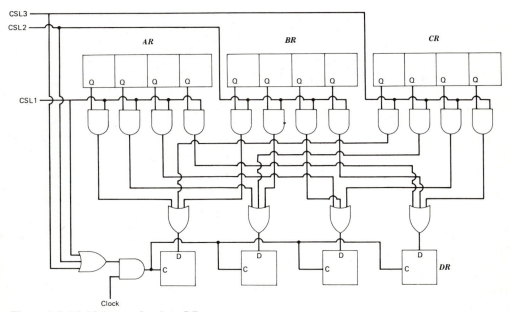

Figure 4.5. Multiple transfers into *DR*.

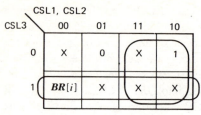

Next value of $AR[i]$ Figure 4.6. Karnaugh map for ith D flip-flop of AR.

this map. Since a clock pulse will be gated to the flip-flop clock input if and only if one of the three control signals is 1, the upper left square of the map is also a "don't-care" condition.

From the Karnaugh map, we determine expression 4.1 for the D input of flip-flop AR_i.

$$D_{AR[i]} = CSL1 \vee (BR[i] \wedge CSL3) \tag{4.1}$$

A logic block diagram of the input network of register AR is given in Fig. 4.7 as compared to the three-vector bus configuration of Fig. 4.5 are evident. Where vector constants are involved, the process of translating AHPL descriptions to network form must provide for generating configurations such as shown in Fig. 4.7.

Not all data transfers involve every flip-flop of a register. Bit numbers are used in AHPL to select individual flip-flops of a register. Consistent with Fig. 4.3 and 4.7, the leftmost flip-flop of a register is denoted by bit number 0 with bit numbers increasing to the right. Similarly, registers and flip-flops may be *catenated* using separating commas to form longer vectors. Thus expression 4.2 is a valid AHPL expression

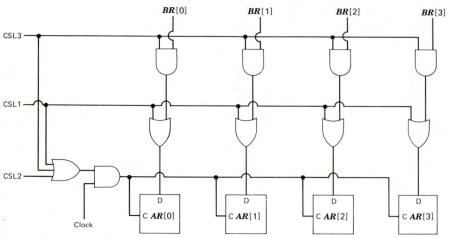

Figure 4.7. Transfer including Set and Clear.

specifying the placing of the contents of *AR*[3] in *DR*[2], the contents of *AR*[4] in *DR*[3], and the contents of *AR*[5] in *CR*[0].

$$DR[2], DR[3], CR[0] \leftarrow AR[3], AR[4], AR[5] \tag{4.2}$$

A long segment of a register may be specified by indicating the first and last bits of the segment, separated by a colon. As an example, the string *AR*[2], *AR*[3], *AR*[4], *AR*[5] could be denoted *AR*[2:5]. Expression 4.3 therefore specifies the same data transfer as does expression 4.2.

$$DR[2:3], CR[0] \leftarrow AR[3:5] \tag{4.3}$$

Critical to the design of any digital system is the ability to perform logical computations on the contents of registers and flip-flops as they are transferred into other memory elements. Expression 4.4, for example, calls for transferring the complement of the contents of a register *BR* into *AR* of the same dimension. Expression 4.5 calls for ORing the contents of *AR* and *BR* and placing the result in *CR* whereas expression 4.6 would place an AND combination of these same two registers into *CR*.

$$AR \leftarrow \overline{BR} \tag{4.4}$$

$$CR \leftarrow AR \lor BR \tag{4.5}$$

$$CR \leftarrow AR \land BR \tag{4.6}$$

A circuit realization of the latter is given in Fig. 4.8, where *AR, BR,* and *CR* are 3-bit registers. For simplicity, the AHPL transfer notation is used to identify the corresponding control line. A complete listing of the logical operations available in AHPL and the corresponding notation will be given in Chapter 5.

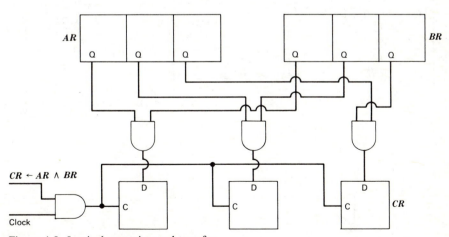

Figure 4.8. Logical operation and transfer.

4.3 Busing

In the examples of Section 4.2, we considered primarily the gating between a single pair of registers. Many times, we must provide for the gating of any one of several registers into several other registers. For example, suppose that we have two registers, *AR* and *BR,* both of which we must be able to gate to either of two other registers, *CR* or *DR*. The direct extension of the method of Fig. 4.5 to this requirement is shown in Fig. 4.9a. For each transfer desired, there must be a set of AND gates to combine the register outputs and the control levels, and there must be a set of OR gates at the input of each receiving register.

As the number of registers increases, this method gets very expensive. For example, with four registers to be gated to any one of four other registers, 16 sets of AND gates will be required; and the OR gates must all have four inputs. An alternative method that is generally less expensive is the use of an interconnection bus, as shown in Fig. 4.9b. In some cases, depending on the electrical characteristics of the AND gates, the OR gates may be replaced by direct connection on bus wires.

The notation for a bus will be the same as for a register (i.e., italic capitals), except that the name of a bus will always end in the word "*BUS.*" For example, the

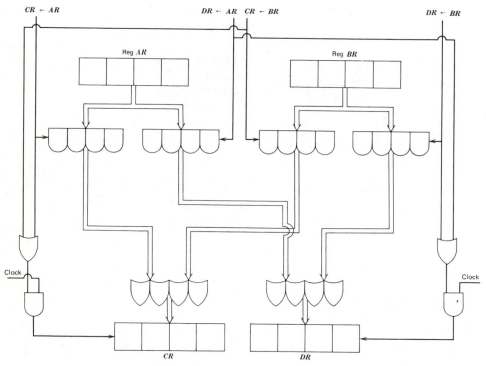

Figure 4.9a. Transfer among a group of registers.

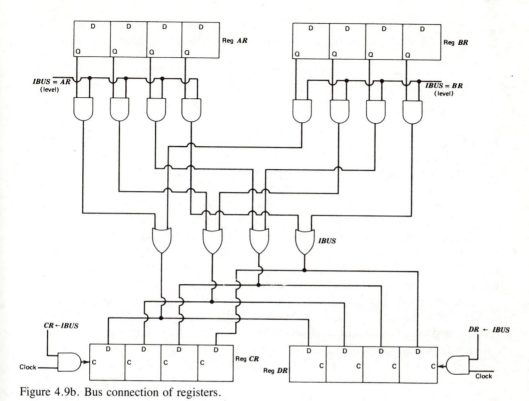

Figure 4.9b. Bus connection of registers.

bus in Fig. 4.9b will be referred to as the **IBUS.** This natural similarity will not prove inconvenient as a bus exhibits many of the characteristics of a register. The transfer of data through a bus is a two-step process. Both steps can be accomplished in one clock period. The first step uses the control level to route the data to the output of the bus. This operation differs from a transfer in that data is *not* stored by a bus. A data vector will remain at the output of a bus only *as long as the control level remains 1.* This distinction between a register and a bus must not be forgotten. The symbol " = " will be used to denote the routing of a data vector to the output of a bus. Thus the two possible connection statements routing data onto the bus in Fig. 4.9b are denoted

$$IBUS = AR \quad \text{and} \quad IBUS = BR$$

The second step of triggering the bus output into the destination register is usually accomplished by the same clock pulse that terminates the control level holding the data on the bus. This operation does not differ from that of transferring the contents of a register into a destination register. The two possible clocked transfers of the output of **IBUS** in Fig. 4.9b and the corresponding control lines will be designated

$$CR \leftarrow IBUS \quad \text{and} \quad DR \leftarrow IBUS$$

From this we conclude, for example, that the transfer of data from **AR** to **DR** through the **IBUS** can be expressed by the simple AHPL step 5 given in expression 4.7.

$$5 \; IBUS \; = \; AR;$$ (4.7)

$$DR \leftarrow IBUS.$$

The timing of this operation is illustrated in Fig. 4.10, where CSL5 is the control level corresponding to step 5.

The actual physical realization of a bus may be more complex than a simple set of gates, as implied by Fig. 4.9b. The exact form will depend on the type of input and output gates used, the number of registers connected, and a variety of other factors. The results of gating more than one register onto the bus at a time will depend on the exact form of the bus. In some cases the results may be a logical ORing of the data; in others, the result may be unpredictable. In this book we shall assume that only one register may be gated onto the bus at a time. It is permissible to pulse the data on a bus into any number of registers simultaneously.

Both methods of register interconnection, separate gating and busing, are used. To suggest the possible hardware saving achieved through the use of a bus, suppose that it is desired that a path be made available for the transfer of information *from any one of n registers to any one of m destination registers*. If busing is not used, $n \cdot m$ banks of AND gates will be required together with m banks of OR gates. If we assume b bits in each register and a unit cost for each AND gate and each OR gate, the cost of the data paths, if busing is not used, is given by Eq. 4.8.

$$\text{Cost without busing} = m \cdot b \, (n + 1)$$ (4.8)

If busing is employed, only n banks of AND gates and one bank of OR gates will be required, so that the cost of the data paths with busing is given by Eq. 4.9.

$$\text{Cost with busing} = b(n + 1)$$ (4.9)

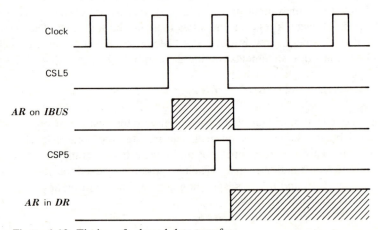

Figure 4.10. Timing of a bused data transfer.

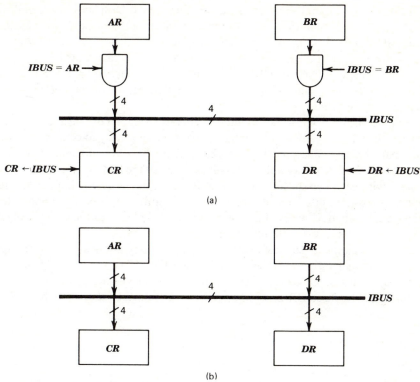

Figure 4.11. Simplified bus network notation.

Thus, when interconnections between three or more registers are required, the use of busing will permit a savings in hardware. Where not all possible paths between registers are needed, the situation is more complicated, but the analysis is similar.

Before proceeding, it will be necessary to have a simplified diagrammatic form for representing these interconnections; diagrams showing all the individual lines, as in Fig. 4.9b, are obviously impractical. Two forms of simplified notation that may be used to represent busing networks such as Fig. 4.9b are shown in Fig. 4.11. In both cases, the number of bits in each vector is indicated by the integer next to each diagonal slash. As in Fig. 4.9, each register consists of 4 bits. Control information is included in Fig. 4.11a, but is omitted in Fig. 4.11b. In both cases, the bus itself is represented by a heavy solid line.

4.4   Intersystem Busing

You may previously have heard the term *bus* used to refer to the cables used for physically interconnecting separate digital systems. Such a bus will be called a *communication bus*. Communications buses are used to make possible a savings in the number of wires interconnecting the separate equipments. Distances between devices can be as much as several hundred feet, and the buses will almost always transmit 8 or more bits. Often the cost of wire and associated installation problems will dwarf the cost of integrated circuit components used to gate vectors onto the buses. The concept of a bus as a bank of OR gates realized in any technology is inadequate if the purpose of the communications bus is assumed to be one of minimizing the cost of interconnecting cables.

   To illustrate two approaches to intersystem bus wring, let us consider four digital systems A, B, C, and D, each of which must have the capability to connect one vector to the input of a bus called the *IOBUS.* Each of the four systems must have access to the output of the *IOBUS* as well. We shall assume that the four systems are physically separated, with each system located several feet from its nearest neighbor. It will be sufficient to illustrate just 1 bit of the bus for each of the four systems along with the corresponding individual wires of the interconnecting cable. Additional bits imply only identical repetitions of the 1-bit configurations.

   Using the hardware suggested by Fig. 4.9b to satisfy this design problem results in a configuration 1 bit of which is given in Fig. 4.12a. The data lines from each of the four units must be ORed together to form the corresponding bus output bit. This is accomplished by three OR gates in systems A, B, and C as shown so that only two

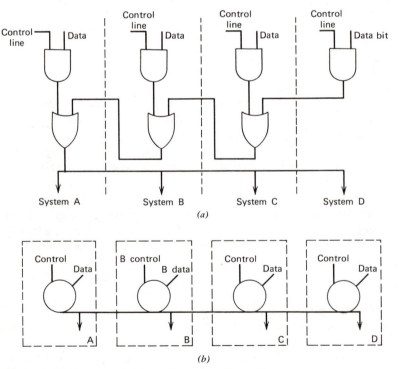

Figure 4.12. Two approaches to intersystem bus wiring.

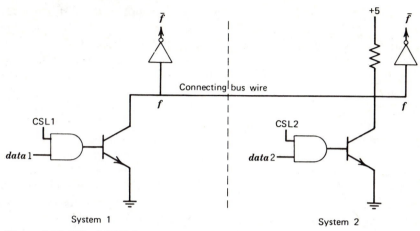

Figure 4.13. Wired NOR bus.

wires are required to connect each pair of systems within a linear arrangement. One of these routes the inputs to the OR gate whose output constitutes the bus. The other routes the bus output back to each system.

Figure 4.12b symbolizes a system with only one interconnecting wire. Such a system could function properly if each of the elements represented by circles could behave in the manner to be described for the element in system B. If the control line labelled *B control* is 1, the element must cause the interconnecting wire to assume the voltage representing the value of *B data*. If B control = 0, the device must permit the voltage on the interconnecting wire to be determined by a similar element in one of the other systems.

One commonly used physical realization that closely approximates the function described for Fig. 4.12b is the wired NOR[2] configuration of DTL logic. Figure 4.13 illustrates 1 bit of a wired NOR bus with two input and two output parts. This circuit effectively realizes expression 4.10.

$$f = \overline{(\text{CSL1} \wedge \text{data1}) \vee (\text{CSL2} \wedge \text{data2})} \tag{4.10}$$

Although the actual interconnecting bus wire is *f*, the value $\bar{f}$ represents the bus output and is available in both systems. Clearly, $f = \overline{data1}$ if CSL1 = 1, and $f = \overline{data2}$ if CSL2 = 1. If CSL1 = CSL2 = 0, then $\bar{f}$ = 0, as would be the case in Fig. 4.12a if all four control signals were 0. If CSL1 = CSL2 = 1, the value on the bus would not be meaningful in the context of intersystem communications. Clearly, some coordination scheme must be used to ascertain that no more than one system tries to use the bus at a given time. This matter will be considered in Chapters 9, 10, and 11.

---

[2]Sometimes the circuit is referred to as "wired-AND," since every source driving the bus must be at the one-level for the bus to be at the 1-level.

Another commonly used single-wire busing device is the tristate element, a considerably simplified version of which is given in Fig. 4.14. We shall refer to the two elements enclosed by rectangles and connected to +5 volts and 0 volts as controlled switches. There are a variety of physical realizations of the tristate concept depending on the logic family and the voltage and impedance levels desired on the buses. The realization most closely corresponding to Fig. 4.14a is the TTL 74125, in which the controlled switches are merely transistors with a carefully designed input network to ensure proper biasing. For our purposes, it is sufficient to say that a controlled switch is *open* if the output of the corresponding AND gate is 0 and is *closed* if the output of the corresponding AND gate is 1. The D line is the data line and the E line is the enable line. If $E = 0$, both switches are open and the gate is in the high-impedance state; that is, the data are disconnected from **ZBUS**. If $E = 1$, the upper switch is closed if $D = 1$ and the lower switch is closed if $D = 0$; that is, the output follows D. A simple NMOS implementation of the tristate bus used within a VLSI part is shown in Fig. 4.14b.

As mentioned earlier, the possibility of simultaneously connecting data to a bus from two or more separate sources is always to be avoided by the designer. As discussed in Chapter 1, a digital system is often simulated in the clock mode to verify the correctness of its design. Such simulators must respond as accurately as possible even in cases of bad design. For the wired NOR bus (including output inverters), multiple connections to the bus can be represented by simply ORing the values. For the tristate bus, the situation is more complicated. Simultaneous connection of 1 and 0 values to the same bus may result in some intermediate voltage. This voltage will depend on the technology and the number of simultaneous connections. Simulators designed for accurate representation of tristate elements must work with at least four values: "high Z" (high impedence) and the intermediate or unknown value U, in addition to 0 and 1.

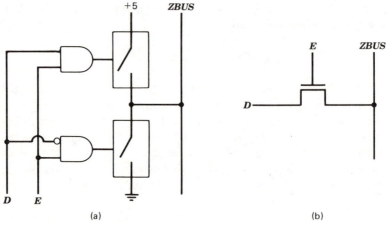

Figure 4.14. Tristate bus elements.

4.5 Sequencing of Control

We have carefully described the wiring and timing of control signals associated with the accomplishment of individual register transfers and the routing of data vectors through buses in advance of transfers. We have yet to discuss the mechanism by which a sequence of such transfers can be accomplished. It is this ability to execute and re-execute sequences of register transfers and the facility, comparable to software programming, to alter this sequencing as a function of results that makes possible the processing of algorithms via hardware. There must exist a hardware mechanism to provide for sequencing as well as notation for representing both fixed and conditional branches in sequences in our hardware description language. Sequencing notation is the subject of this section. Its realization in the form of the control sequential circuit of Fig. 4.1 will be the topic of Section 4.6. Before formally defining the branching notation of AHPL, let us illustrate the need with an example.

Example 4.1

Figure 4.15 is the system block diagram of a digital system B that provides for a selective data flow between system A and system C. A sequence of 12-bit data vectors will appear on the 12 wires forming the vector X to ultimately be accepted by system C. The function of system B is to deleted those vectors for which

$$X[0:3] \wedge X[4:7] \wedge X[8:11] = (0, 0, 0, 0) \tag{4.11}$$

The data flow is asynchronous; that is, system A places a new vector on line X after it receives a logical 1 of one-clock-period duration on line *inready*. Similarly, system C will accept a data vector from the set of 12 lines Z immediately after observing a logical 1 for one clock period on line *outready*. These control signals will appear well

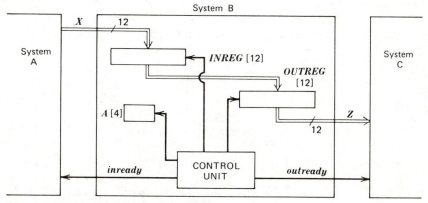

Figure 4.15. System diagram of data selector.

in advance of the need for new data on lines **X** and well before the data will be changed on lines **Z**. This will be the case, since several clock periods will be required for system B to perform its function.

The purpose of Fig. 4.15 is only to depict the general layout of the system and to serve as a list of all data registers to be used. It is not a complete wiring diagram of either the data paths or the control logic. The number of data flip-flops (28) might be considered excessive if the goal were the most economical realization of the data selector. The purpose here, however, is a straightforward sequence of transfers so that the functional sharing of registers has been disallowed.

The following is a sequence of numbered steps to be executed by the control unit of system B to implement the data selection function just described, assuming the system to operate continuously. The first step accepts a data vector and places it in a working register **INREG**. At the same time, a signal is generated to inform system A that a new data vector can now be placed on lines **X**. The realization of the signal *inready* requires only the routing of the line from the control unit representing step 1 directly to an output point and labelling the wire *inready,* as illustrated in Fig. 4.16.

1   **INREG ← X**;
       inready = 1.
2   **A ← INREG**[0:3] $\wedge$ **INREG**[4:7].
3   **A ← INREG**[8:11] $\wedge$ A.
4   s ← A[0] $\vee$ A[1] $\vee$ A[2] $\vee$ A[3].
5   GO TO (step 6 if s = 1 or step 1 if s = 0)
6   **OUTREG ← INREG**;
       outready = 1.
7   GO TO 1
END SEQUENCE
Z = OUTREG.

Step 2 ANDs together the first two 4-bit segments of **INREG** whereas the third segment is ANDed to this result at step 3. IF the resulting 4 bits are all zero, flip-flop s will be zero following step 4. Otherwise, s will be 1. Clearly, the operations of steps 2, 3, and 4 could have been condensed to one step, but it is instructive to illustrate a multistep sequence.

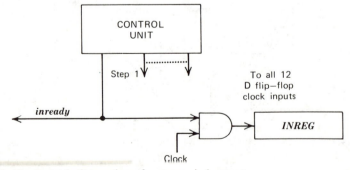

Figure 4.16. Generation of a one-period output.

Following step 4, the vector in **INREG** may be deleted from the data flow, depending on the contents of flip-flop **s**. The decision is made by the English-language branch statement included as step 5. This step causes control to be switched back to step 1, if $s = 0$, so that the next vector may be placed in **INREG**. In this event, the original contents of **INREG** are lost, and that vector is deleted from the sequence. If $s = 1$, control goes from step 5 to step 6; the data vector is placed in **OUTREG;** and system C is alerted to accept this vector by a 1 on line **outready**. Following step 6, control returns to step 1 for a new vector. This is accomplished by the unconditional branch symbolized by a FORTRAN-like GO TO in step 7. The last line is not a numbered step. The notation $Z = OUTREG$ indicates that the vector of output lines is connected to this register at all times. ∎

The sequence of steps generated in the previous example is an example of what shall be called a hardware *control sequence*. Notation is provided in all software languages to handle both fixed and conditional branches in the sequencing of transfer operations. Steps 5 and 7 of the control sequence for Example 4.1 suggest the need for expressing both concepts in our hardware description language AHPL. Including the corresponding notation in a hardware language yields a tool fundamentally as powerful as a software language.

The fixed transfer of the GO TO operation will be denoted in AHPL by

$$\rightarrow (D)$$

where D is the statement number of the next statement to be executed. Following the approach used in APL, we also allow

$$\rightarrow (F)$$

where F is a function to be determined by a logical or algebraic computation. The form of function F to be used almost exclusively throughout the book is given by expression 4.12.

$$\rightarrow (f_1(x_1, \ldots x_k), f_2(x_1, \ldots x_k), \ldots f_n(x_1, \ldots x_k))/(D_1, D_2, \ldots D_n) \qquad (4.12)$$

The $D_{i's}$ are statement numbers of the alternative statements that could be executed following completion of the branch statement. Each f_i is a Boolean function of the logic levels $x_1, x_2, \ldots x_k$, which are either control inputs or variables fed back from data unit. If the Boolean function $f_i = 1$, then D_i, the statement number in the corresponding position to the right of the "/", will be the number of the next statement to be executed. We assume for now that Eq. 4.13 will be satisfied for all i and j $(i \neq j)$

$$f_i(x_1, x_2, \ldots x_k) \wedge f_j(x_1, x_2, \ldots x_k) = 0 \qquad (4.13)$$

so that only one D_i will be selected. Expression 4.14 is a two function branch in which control continues to step 18 if the flip-flop $IR[0] = 1$ or returns to step 10 if $IR[0] = 0$.

$$17 \;\rightarrow\; (\,\overline{IR[0]},\, IR[0])/(10,\, 18). \tag{4.14}$$

For two function branches only, the function corresponding to the next step may be omitted, so expression 4.15 has the same meaning as 4.14.

$$17 \;\rightarrow\; (\,\overline{IR[0]})/(10). \tag{4.15}$$

The fixed branch in step 7 of Example 4.1 may now be expressed in AHPL as

$$\rightarrow (1) \tag{4.16}$$

The conditional of step 5 requires the notation suggested by expression 4.12 and may be written

$$5 \rightarrow (s,\, \bar{s})/(6,\, 1). \tag{4.17}$$

or as

$$5 \rightarrow (\bar{s})/(1).$$

Each AHPL statement will consist of a transfer part and a branch part. The transfer part will consist of any number (possibly zero) of transfers, output statements, or bus routes. The branch part will follow the format of expression 4.12 but will not explicitly appear if the following statement in the sequence is always to be executed next. Subject to this convention, the control sequence of Example 4.1 may be rewritten completely in AHPL, as shown in Fig. 4.17. Notice that the branch operation in the last step was combined with the preceding transfer operation to form a single step. It was not possible to combine steps 4 and 5, since the logical value on which the branch is based will not be found in *s* until after the step 4 transfer is completed. It will become clear in

> 1 *INREG* ← *X;*
>   *inready* = 1.
> 2 *A* ← *INREG*[0:3] $\wedge$ *INREG*[4:7].
> 3 *A* ← *INREG*[8.11] $\wedge$ *A.*
> 4 *s* ← *A*[0] $\vee$ *A*[1] $\vee$ *A*[2] $\vee$ *A*[3].
> 5 null
>   → (*s*, $\bar{s}$)/(6, 1).
> 6 *OUTREG* ← *INREG;*
>   *outready* = 1;
>   → (1).

Figure 4.17. AHPL control sequence for data selector.

Section 4.6 that the clock pulse that executes a transfer at a given step also effects the branch operation at the same step. In some situations, it is impossible to avoid a seemingly wasted step consisting of a branch and no transfer. In this example, we can save one clock period by eliminating flip-flop s from the design and replacing steps 4 and 5 by

4　　null
$$\rightarrow ((A[0] \vee A[1] \vee A[2] \vee A[3]), (\overline{A[0] \vee A[1] \vee A[2] \vee A[3]}))/(5,1)$$

Our goal is to generate from an English-language description of a digital system of any complexity an AHPL *control sequence* or hardware program that completely and unambiguously describes that system. A hardware realization consisting of a control section and a data section can then be derived from the AHPL sequence. The data unit will be constructed as already described. The realization of the control unit will be discussed in the next section. For now, let us consider another simple example for which the AHPL sequence has already been determined.

Example 4.2

The following AHPL sequence describes a simple system that receives a vector X and makes it available as an output after a delay, subject to the control of input signals a and b. If $a = b = 0$, the vector is not transferred. If $a = 0$ and $b = 1$, the vector is transferred without modification. If $a = 1$, the vector is first rotated, one place right if $b = 0$, two places right if $b = 1$.

1　$R \leftarrow X$;
　　$\rightarrow (\bar{a} \wedge \bar{b}, a, \bar{a} \wedge b)/(1,2,4)$.
2　$R \leftarrow R[2], R[0:1]$;
　　$\rightarrow (\bar{b})/(4)$.
3　$R \leftarrow R[2], R[0:1]$.
4　*ready* $= 1$;
　　$Z = R$;
　　$\rightarrow (1)$.

　　　Let us follow the functioning of the digital system described by this control sequence assuming the control unit to be originally in the state corresponding to step 1. The first line of step 1 indicates that the step 1 control signal causes the 3-bit vector X to be placed in a register R, which we also assume to be 3-bits in length. The second line, or branch portion, of step 1 specifies the step to be executed following the completion of step 1. If $a = b = 0$, control remains at step 1, causing a new input vector to be placed in R, while the previously received vector is discarded. If $a = 1$, step 2 is executed next. If $a = 0$ and $b = 1$, control jumps to step 4.

　　　Step 2 causes the contents of R to be rotated one position to the right, that is, $R[1] \leftarrow R[0], R[2] \leftarrow R[1]$ and $R[0] \leftarrow R[2]$. If input b is 1, control proceeds to step 3, where R is again rotated right. If b is 0, control jumps from step 2 directly to step

4. Following the execution of step 3, control always proceeds to step 4. Therefore, the branch portion of step 3 may be and is omitted. In step 4, the connection statement $Z = R$ effectively makes the contents of R available on the three lines corresponding to the output vector Z. This notation specifies that the output is available only during the one clock period while the control unit remains in the state corresponding to step 4. The same step 4 control signal causes a 1 to appear on another output line, *ready,* to indicate to any interacting digital system that a valid output vector currently appears on the lines Z. ∎

You will notice that the control sequence as given in this example is only a partial description of the system without certain information provided in the preceding paragraphs. The input and output lines, for example, were identified only in this verbal description. Also, the number of bits in R was revealed only in this same manner. This situation will not be satisfactory in the long run. *It is our intention that the AHPL description stand alone as a compete specification of a digital system.* This will be possible through the use of declaration statements, which will, among other functions, specify register length and identify input/output lines. We shall defer this subject until the complete language is presented in Chapter 5.

4.6   Electronic Realization of the Control Unit

The control unit of a digital system described in AHPL is a classical finite-state machine or clock-mode sequential circuit. Each step may be regarded as a state with the branch statement associated with the step specifying the next state as a function of the inputs. The outputs are the control signals sent to the data unit. There are many approaches to control unit realization requiring varying numbers of flip-flops and varying amounts of combinational logic. In general, there is a trade-off between memory elements and the amount of combinational logic. At one extreme would be the classical, minimal state, sequential circuit realization. In most cases, this would require extensive combinational logic with no unifying pattern. The microprogrammed control unit to be discussed in Chapter 8 is a nearly minimal state, sequential circuit. In one version of a microprogrammable control unit up to 2^n microprogram steps are available, where n is the total number of flip-flops in the control unit.

In this chapter and throughout the book, we shall use a one flip-flop per control state model as the hard-wired realization of a control unit. At the other end of the spectrum from the microprogrammable version, this model employs far from a minimal number of flip-flops with correspondingly simple combinational logic. In this model, only the flip-flop corresponding to the current control step will be in the 1 (set) state. All other flip-flops will contain 0 (reset state).

The one flip-flop per control state model is easily the most direct interpretation of an AHPL control sequence. Translating an AHPL sequence to this type of control unit will require no knowledge of formal sequential circuit synthesis. Despite the lavish use of flip-flops, we have found it difficult to improve on the overall economy of this

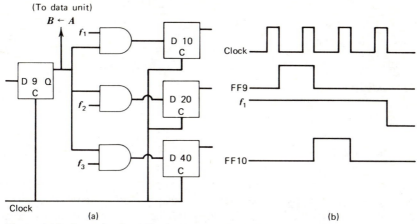

Figure 4.18. Control unit realization of a single AHPL step.

approach. It is also compatible with the concept of multiple active control states, which will become important in Chapter 9.

Let us first illustrate the translation of the following arbitrary step of an arbitrary control sequence to the corresponding portion of a control unit.

$$9 \quad B \leftarrow A;$$

$$\rightarrow (f_1, f_2, f_3)/(10, 20, 40). \tag{4.19}$$

As illustrated in Fig. 4.18a, step 9 is represented by a single flip-flop. The realization of the transfer portion of the step requires only that the output of the step 9 D flip-flop be routed to the data unit to be used as described earlier in the chapter. The branch portion translates to an array of AND gates whose outputs lead to the flip-flops corresponding to the three possible steps to be executed following step 9. Since one and only one of the three functions f_1, f_2, or f_3 will be 1, the output of one and only one of the three AND gates will be 1 while control is in step 9. If control is not in step 9, the output of all three AND gates will be 0. In Fig. 4.18b, the case in which $f_1 = 1$ and (although not shown) $f_2 = f_3 = 0$ is illustrated. Notice that the step 9 flip-flop is 1 for one clock period. The same clock pulse that executes the step 9 transfer also causes the step 10 control flip-flop to go to 1, where it remains during the following clock period. In this way, the one-period logical 1 can work its way around the control network with one and only one control flip-flop having the value 1 during any one clock period.

Example 4.2 (Continued)

Let us further illustrate the process of translating an AHPL sequence into a control unit using the control sequence determined in Example 4.2, which for convenience is repeated here.

1 $R \leftarrow X$;
   $\rightarrow (\bar{a} \wedge \bar{b}, a, \bar{a} \wedge b)/(1, 2, 4)$.
2 $R \leftarrow R[2], R[0:1]$;
   $\rightarrow (\bar{b})/(4)$.
3 $R \leftarrow R[2], R[0:1]$.
4 *ready* = 1;
   $Z = R$;
   $\rightarrow (1)$.   ■

The realization of both the control unit and the data unit is given in Fig. 4.19. Consider first the control section in the lower portion of the figure. Since both steps 1 and 2 include conditional branches, branching networks appear at the output of the two corresponding flip-flops. Notice that it is possible to go to step 4 from any of the first three steps. Consequently, an OR gate appears at the D input to step 4. If any of the three inputs to this OR gate is a 1 during a given clock period, the step 4 flip-flop will be 1 during the next clock period. The inputs to the OR gate originate in the branching networks from steps 1, 2, and 3. Similarly, an OR gate appears at the D

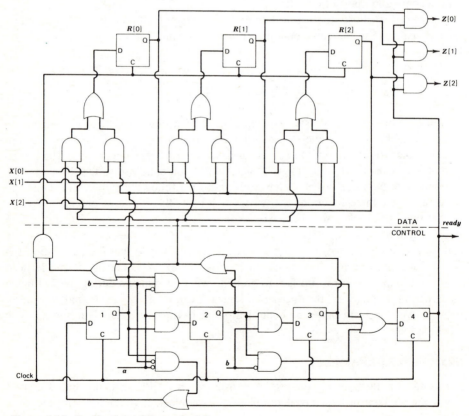

Figure 4.19. Realization of Example 4.2.

input of the step 1 flip-flop with inputs from the step 1 branching network as well as from step 4. If $a = b = 0$, when the step 1 flip-flop contains a 1, this 1 is routed back around to the D input of this same flip-flop. Therefore, this flip-flop value would remain 1. If one of the control flip-flops is initially 1 and the other three are 0, the single 1-level will propagate continuously through the network. We assume that the direct set or clear inputs can be used to establish the initial conditions.

Two control lines are routed into the data unit, one to transfer X into R, the other to rotate the contents of R to the right. The latter is the transfer specified by both steps 2 and 3. Notice that the control lines for these two steps are ORed together with only the result of this operation routed to the data unit to effect the transfer. The control line from step 4 is connected directly to the output line *ready*. It also routes the contents of R through a set of AND gates to form the output vector Z. Therefore, the output is $Z = R$, as specified when the step 4 flip-flop is 1. By implication $Z = 0$, 0, 0 at all other times.

4.7   Function-Level Simulation

Digital systems can be modeled and simulated at several distinct levels. The most accurate result may be obtained by using transistor models of the digital circuits and simulating using a simulation program such as SPICE. Simulation of large systems at the circuit level may be prohibitively expensive. Gate-level modeling and simulation will often provide sufficiently accurate results to support timing decisions related to critical path delays (see Section 7.4). Gate-level simulation divides time into finite increments, perhaps 10 to 100 increments per clock period. It is easily concluded that simulation of a network of gates and memory elements at clock-period intervals is 10 to 100 times more economical than gate-delay-level simulation.

An alternative to simulation in clock period intervals is execution of the AHPL (or other register transfer language) description itself. This approach, which resembles an interpreter of a software language converted to an intermediate form, is usually referred to as *function-level simulation*. Registers are represented by single words of the simulation host, and only those statements in an active control step are executed each clock period. Because of the precise one-to-one correspondence between the AHPL description of a clock-mode network and the network itself, as emphasized in the preceding six sections, the execution of the AHPL description can be expected to give the same results as simulation of the network. Function-level simulation uses significantly less computer time than even clock-mode event-driven[3] simulation at the network level.

A short section of output from HPSIM, one function-level simulator of AHPL, is shown in Fig. 4.20. This clock-period-by-clock-period timing trace was generated by applying a sequence of inputs on lines A, B, and X in the AHPL description of

---

[3]Event-driven simulators include mechanisms to provide that only gates whose input values change during a particular time interval are evaluated during that interval.

CLOCK #	A	B	X	R	READY	Z	STEP
1	0	0	011	000	0	000	1
2	1	0	101	011	0	000	1
3	1	0	101	101	0	000	2
4	1	0	101	110	1	110	4
5	0	0	011	110	0	000	1
6	0	1	011	011	0	000	1
7	0	1	011	011	1	011	4
8	0	0	010	011	0	000	1
9	1	1	010	010	0	000	1
10	1	1	010	010	0	000	2
11	1	1	010	001	0	000	3
12	1	1	010	100	1	100	4
13	0	0	101	100	0	000	1
14	0	0	101	101	0	000	1
15	0	0	101	101	0	000	1

Figure 4.20. HPSIM output for Example 4.2.

Example 4.2. The inputs for 15 consecutive clock periods are displayed in the first three columns of Fig. 4.20. Notice that the circut is still in step 1 during clock period 2 because inputs A and B were both 0 during the first clock period. As emphasized by the underlines, the inputs are

$$A = 1 \quad B = 0 \quad X = 101$$

during the second clock period. The clock pulse at the end of period 2 shifts these values of X into R, so that R = 101 during period 3. HPSIM evaluates the branch statement in step 1 for $A = 1$ and $B = 0$ and determines that the same clock pulse drives the circuit to step 2 for the third clock period. This control-state change is emphasized by the arrow at the right of Fig. 4.20. Further checking of the values in the figure is left to you, the reader.

Figure 4.20 displays the HPSIM output in binary form. This could be quite unwieldy where the user desires a printout of the values of a number of input, internal, and output values in a circuit of reasonable size. A hexadecimal printout option is available. You should consult Ref. 9 for further information on HPSIM.

The advantage of function-level simulation is not only its economy but also the fact that it can be used conveniently to verify the hardware expression of system concepts at the very beginning of the design process. Working the "bugs" out of an AHPL description is immeasurably easier than this same activity at the network level. Once it has been established that an AHPL description functions as intended, a more detailed simulation may be used on parts of the compiled network to verify the implementation.

4.8 The Conditional Transfer

The conditional branch offers a method of choosing between two or more transfers, which might be accomplished at a particular point in time depending on which of a set of input or feedback control values are 1. Suppose, for example, that it is desired to transfer $A \leftarrow B$ if $a = 0$ or to transfer $D \leftarrow C$ if $a = 1$. This would be accomplished using conditional branch notation as follows.

> 1
> $\quad \rightarrow (\bar{a}, a)/(2, 3)$.
> 2 $A \leftarrow B$;
> $\quad \rightarrow (4)$.
> 3 $D \leftarrow C$.
> 4

This sequence will imply the control unit hardware illustrated in Fig. 4.21a. One of the two step 2 and step 3 flip-flops in this figure may seem immediately redundant. At a given point in time, one of the two flip-flops will be 1. The output from either will cause the step 4 flip-flop to advance control to the next operation. Each flip-flop can be excited only following step 1, depending on the value of a. It would seem possible to save one control flip-flop in this case by assigning only one flip-flop, which will store a 1 during the clock period following step 1 and prior to step 4. As depicted in Fig. 4.21b, no information is stored at this step to indicate which of the two transfers $D \leftarrow C$ or $A \leftarrow B$ is to be executed. The information required to make this distinction was available as the value of a at the time of step ·1.

In most cases, the contents of flip-flop a will have remained unchanged between steps 1 and 2. If this is so, the logic level on line a can be used at step 2 to effect a choice between these two transfers. The hardware mechanism by which this is accomplished is given in Fig. 4.21c. Just as in 4.21a, a separate line is generated corresponding to each of the two transfers. A one-period logical 1 will appear on the line labeled $D \leftarrow C$ whenever this transfer is to be executed, and a similar level will appear on the line labeled $A \leftarrow B$ when that is the transfer to be executed.

The mechanism for which control is shown implemented in Fig. 4.21c will be called a *conditional transfer* and will be represented in AHPL by the notation

> 2 $A * \bar{a} \leftarrow B; D * a \leftarrow C$

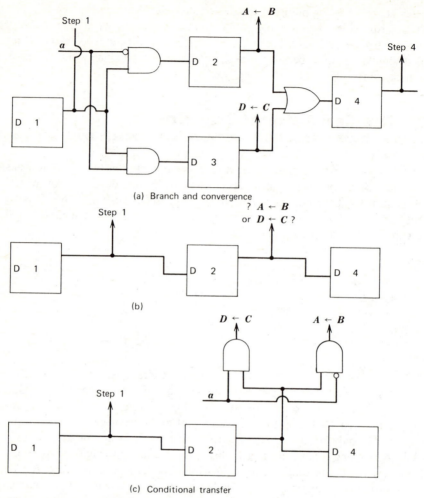

(a) Branch and convergence

(b)

(c) Conditional transfer

Figure 4.21. Equivalent control structures.

The asterisk may be translated as "if." Therefore, $A * \bar{a} \leftarrow B$ may be interpreted as "The contents of B are placed in A if and only if $a = 0$." If $a = 1$, the contents of A will be unchanged. Transfers separated by a semicolon is the notation for simultaneous transfers. In this case, one transfer will take place if $a = 1$ the other if $a = 0$. Since the two transfers are independent, it is not necessary that the two condition functions be mutually exclusive. For example, the following notation implies that both transfers take place if $y = 1$.

$$A * (y \vee f) \leftarrow B; D * (y \vee g) \leftarrow C$$

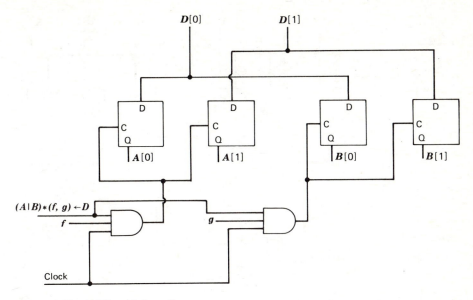

Figure 4.22. $(A!B) * (f,g) \leftarrow D$.

Sometimes only the target of a transfer will vary with the values of a set of condition variables. In this case, the notation of expression 4.20 may be used.[4]

$$(A!B!C) * (f, g, h) \leftarrow D \tag{4.20}$$

The asterisk representing "if" relates each of the registers separated by ! to the corresponding element of the vector at the right of the asterisk. If $f = 1$, then $A \leftarrow D$. If $g = 1$, then $B \leftarrow D$; and if $h = 1$, then $C \leftarrow D$. Again, no transfer takes place if $f = g = h = 0$. If more than one of the values of f, g, and h are 1, then the contents of D are simultaneously transferred to more than one register.

An asterisk or condition function on the left side of a transfer expression always indicates that a control pulse will arrive at the clock inputs to the flip-flops of a register only if the corresponding condition function is 1. This is illustrated in Fig. 4.22.

Quite often, the vector to be selected on the right side of a transfer or connection statement will be subject to the values of a set of condition variables. The notations of expressions 4.21 and 4.22 will both be assigned meaning.

$$D \leftarrow (A!B) * (f, g) \tag{4.21}$$

$$DBUS = (A!B) * (f, g) \tag{4.22}$$

---

[4]The use of this notation for a conditional transfer is actually a special application of the notation for catenating rows of a matrix, which will be introduced in Chapter 5.

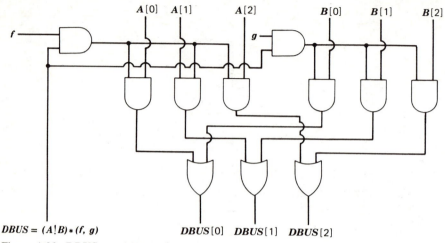

$DBUS = (A!B) * (f, g)$

Figure 4.23. $DBUS = (A!B) * (f,g)$.

The register A will be transferred into D or connected to the $DBUS$ if $f = 1$. Similarly, $D \leftarrow B$ or $DBUS = B$ if $g = 1$. When using the forms in expressions 4.21 and 4.22, it must be ascertained that no two of the condition variables are 1 simultaneously. The implementation of expression 4.22 is given in Fig. 4.23. With this realization, a vector of 0's is connected to $DBUS$ if $f = g = 0$, but a tristate bus would be floating in the high-impedance state. For this reason, it is important not to use this form for implicit realization of a vector of all 0's by connecting "nothing" to the bus. The logic network that determines the vector to be transferred into D in expression 4.21 is quite similar. The line labelled with the connection statement is connected directly to the output of a control flip-flop. In summary, the asterisk on either side of a connection or transfer statement is used to specify conditions. *Conditions on the left control the clock inputs to the registers. Conditions on the right specify busing networks for the data vectors.*

Expression 4.23 fits naturally into the language to be presented in Chapter 5 and is logically equivalent to expression 4.21.

$$D \leftarrow (A \wedge f) \vee (B \wedge g) \tag{4.23}$$

There is a difference in hardware, however, since f and g are considered data variables in expression 4.23. These variables are part of the combinational logic network and are not gated with the control signal generated for the control sequence step. This distinction will be important when the process of compiling a control sequence into a sequential network is considered formally in Chapter 7.

Suppose that the four-step control sequence given in Fig. 4.21 were specified in more detail to read

1 $a \leftarrow (X[0] \wedge X[1] \wedge X[2]) \vee B[0]$.
2
    $\rightarrow (\bar{a}, a)/(3, 4)$.
3 $A \leftarrow B$;
    $\rightarrow (5)$.
4 $D \leftarrow C$.

Notice that it is not possible to combine transfer step 1 and branch step 2, because the branch at step 2 must make use of the value of a determined by step 1. Thus three clock periods are required for the execution of steps 1, 2, 3, and 4, regardless of the value of a. The accomplishment of the same functions can be expressed as follows using conditional transfers.

1 $a \leftarrow (X[0] \wedge X[1] \wedge X[2]) \vee B[0]$.
2 $A * a \leftarrow B$; $D * a \leftarrow C$.

Clearly, only two clock periods are required for executing this sequence. The saving is possible, because a is used at the time of the actual transfer rather than one period earlier. Situations in which flip-flop value is established immediately prior to its use as the determining argument in a conditional operation are not uncommon. Conditional transfer notation will prove valuable in tightening the timing in most such cases.

4.9 Development of a Design

It is not always easy to think through a design concept while representing it only in the form of a one-dimensional language or list of branches and transfers. A two-dimensional format or a flowchart language sometimes provides a much better vehicle for guiding the thought process through the development of an algorithm. The designer should not hesitate to use the flowchart as an idea is crystallized, rendered clear, and firmly established in the designer's mind. Before a design is complete, it must be expressed in total detail in a form that can be communicated unambiguously to those involved in the later stages of the process of design construction and utilization of the system. A flowchart is less suitable as a communications tool than is a one-dimensional language description. A recommended procedure will be to use a flowchart as a starting point in the development of a complete AHPL description.

The following example is the first in which we begin with a word description of a design problem and follow through to an AHPL control sequence. A flowchart will be of considerable assistance in this process. This example will involve a simple form of communications between two separate digital systems. There are a number of special problems associated with intersystem communications that we will not allow to surface here. These will be the subject of Chapter 10.

Example 4.3

The register configuration of Fig. 4.24a illustrates the principal data paths of a special-purpose memory unit that must accept a stream of data and addresses continuously but asynchronously placed on an 8-bit vector of input lines, *X*. The communications system providing data on *X* will not be part of the design. We need only know the sequence and timing of data placed on *X* and the relationship of three control lines, ***ready, accept,*** and ***word,*** to this system. The memory consists of 2^{16} 32-bit words, an associated 32-bit data register ***DR***, and a 16-bit address register ***AR***. Each time a logical 1 is placed on line ***write,*** the word in ***DR*** is written into memory at the address currently located in ***AR***. We shall not be concerned with the internal implementation of the memory module. We shall similarly ignore the read-from memory capability, which we presume to exist using the same address and data registers.

The overall data transmission rate is sufficiently slow so that the memory interface for which an AHPL description is to be written will have ample time to deal with any 8-bit byte on *X* before a subsequent byte is placed there. Each time a byte is placed on *X*, a logical 1 will appear on line ***ready*** until the interface signals acceptance with a one-period level on line ***accept***. The data and corresponding addresses will appear in the order given in Fig. 4.24b. The 4 data bytes that are to be catenated to form a 32-bit word appear first, beginning with the most significant 8 bits. The 4 data bytes are followed by the 16-hit address in 2 consecutive bytes. Each address is followed by the first byte of the next data word, and so on. The ***ready*** signal corresponding to

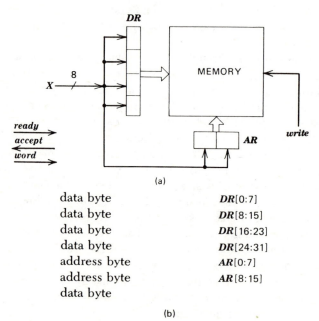

(a)

| data byte | *DR*[0:7] |
| address byte | *AR*[0:7] |

data byte   *DR*[0:7]
data byte   *DR*[8:15]
data byte   *DR*[16:23]
data byte   *DR*[24:31]
address byte   *AR*[0:7]
address byte   *AR*[8:15]
data byte

(b)

Figure 4.24. Communications memory.

each first data byte will coincide with a logical 1 on the line **word**. The latter control line provides a synchronizing capability.

Solution

Prior to transferring a data byte from **X**, it is necessary to check for a 1 on line **ready**. This check and the subsequent transfer of a data byte are represented in the flowchart of Fig. 4.25a. Also included is a mechanism for checking for the fourth data byte to alert the system that the next 2 bytes will form the address. We continue the sequence by checking for the **ready** = 1 signalling the presence of the first address byte on **X**. This is followed by a similar sequence corresponding to the second address byte. With the complete address in **AR**, we let **write** = 1 for one clock period prior to returning control to the beginning in anticipation of another data word (Fig. 4.25b).

So far, no synchronizing mechanism has been included in the flowchart to ascertain that the 6 bytes are transferred to their correct places in **AR** and **DR**. A line, **word,** has been included in Fig. 4.24 for this purpose. Let us revise the sequence so that the interface will expect the first data byte whenever a 1 is observed on line **word**. This will permit the communications system to interrupt and resynchronize the sequence at any point to begin a new data word. A check of line **word** following each observation of **ready** is added to Fig. 4.25b to form Fig. 4.26. If a 1 is detected on the line **word**, control is routed to a point to prepare for handling the first byte as shown.

It is important to realize that the flowchart of Fig. 4.26 is accurate only as a representation of the general sequence of events. It is important to distinguish this

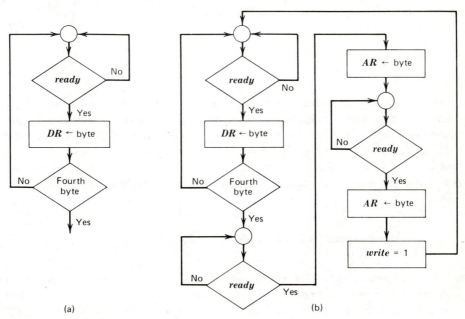

Figure 4.25. Flowchart development.

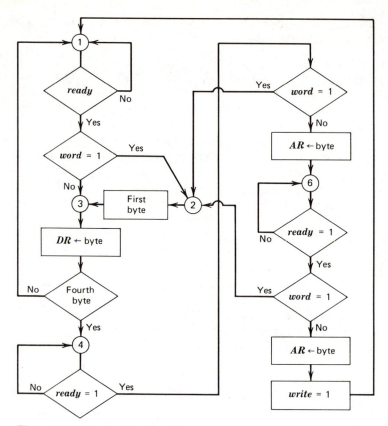

Figure 4.26. Memory interface flowchart.

form of flowchart from the more complete extended ASM chart described in Ref. [5]. There is a one-to-one correspondence between blocks of an ASM chart and the steps of the eventual AHPL description. No such direct correspondence will exist for Fig. 4.26. In fact, a number of details are yet to be incorporated in the design. These may now be filled in as the AHPL description is written. First, it is convenient to check both **ready** and **word** simultaneously, not separately as might be suggested by Fig. 4.26.

1
$\rightarrow (\overline{ready}, ready \wedge word, ready \wedge \overline{word})/(1,2,3).$
2 **CNT** $\leftarrow 0, 0.$

In step 2, a 2-bit register **CNT** is introduced. This counting register will be used to store the number of the byte to be transferred next into **DR**. If step 2 is executed prior to step 3, the latter step will cause **X** to be transferred into the leftmost 8-bits of **DR**. Step 3 also increases the number in **CNT** by 1, informs the communications system that the byte on **X** has been accepted, and effects a branch depending on the old value of **CNT**. If **CNT** contains (1,1), control proceeds to step 4 to look for the first address byte. Otherwise, control returns to step 1 in anticipation of another data byte. As before, step 4 checks both *ready* and *word*. If *ready* = 1 and *word* = 0, the first address byte is transferred into **AR** at step 5. This procedure is repeated in steps 6 and 7 for the second address byte. As indicated in the flowchart, the sequence is completed by the one period **write** = 1 in step 8.

3 (**DR**[0:7] ! **DR**[8:15] ! **DR**[16:23] ! **DR**[24:31] ∗ (($\overline{CNT[0]}$ ∧ $\overline{CNT[1]}$),
   ($\overline{CNT[0]}$ ∧ CNT[1]), (CNT[0] ∧ $\overline{CNT[1]}$), (CNT[0] ∧ CNT[1])) ← **X**;
   CNT ← (CNT[0] ⊕ CNT[1]), CNT[1]; *accept* = 1;
   → ($\overline{CNT[0] ∧ CNT[1]}$)/(1).
4 → ($\overline{ready}$, ready ∧ word, ready ∧ $\overline{word}$)/(4,2,5).
5 **AR**[0:7] ← **X**; *accept* = 1.
6 → ($\overline{ready}$, ready ∧ word, ready ∧ $\overline{word}$)/(6,2,7).
7 **AR**[8:15] ← **X**; *accept* = 1.
8 *write* = 1;
   → (1).

This is not the only control sequence that will satisfy the design problem presented. For example, the similar tasks of selecting bytes for the data register and for the address register were handled in two distinct ways. A counter was provided to count through the 4 bytes to be loaded in **DR**. Two consecutive two-step sequences were employed to load the 2 address bytes in **AR**. The latter approach adds hardware to the control unit while avoiding a register analogous to **CNT** in the data unit. The larger the number of similar activities, the greater the likelihood that using a counter will be the best approach. Choosing the overall best approach from the array of alternatives is perhaps the most difficult step in the design process. ∎

The time intervals between data bytes in the foregoing example will not necessarily be uniform. It therefore is not possible to time the information transfers with any sort of periodic signal. We term data exchanges under these circumstances as *asynchronous*. We have followed a standard technique using two control lines to communicate the availability and acceptance of data between two systems. Various forms of the control step

1   (4.24)

    → ($\overline{ready}$)/(1).

will appear throughout the book as a means of retaining control at one point in a control sequence while waiting for a control input from another system as part of an asynchronous data transmission. The realization of expression 4.24 is given in Fig. 4.27.

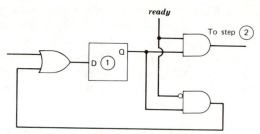

Figure 4.27. Realization of asynchronous WAIT.

4.10 Economics of Digital System Design

Most tasks that are accomplished by vector-handling digital systems are sufficiently complex that a variety of approaches are possible. The costs (both production and design) are likely to vary with the approach chosen. So will the amount of time required by the digital system to perform a given task.

In many cases, the digital system must interact with some very slow system, either physical or biological. Two examples might be desk calculators or a controller for a chemical process. For such cases, the speed of the digital system is not important. The most economical approach consistent with adequate reliability should be chosen.

Occasionally, a digital system must interact with a very fast system. In such cases, only the fastest solution may be satisfactory.

The preceding are the two extreme examples of what may be called *real-time* digital systems. In general, the speed at which a real-time digital system must operate is dictated by some other system with which it must interact. The appropriate design approach is the most economical one that will operate at the required speed.

The situation is quite different for *non-real-time* systems, of which the general purpose computer is the most common example. Such systems can operate at various *levels of performance*. In batch processing, for example, performance might be measured in terms of the dollar value of jobs executable per hour. Dollar values can be estimated when there is a past history of other digital systems performing the same type of job.

In designing a digital system, many of the choices that affect cost and speed are choices of whether to perform sets of similar operations simultaneously or sequentially. The choices range from handling bits in a word serially or in parallel to the possibility of processing more than one job at a time by the computer. Simultaneous or *parallel* operations almost always imply larger numbers of components and, therefore, greater overall cost. In addition, choices must be made between component technologies on the basis of speed and cost.

There are a finite number of essentially different combinations of choices that might be made in the design of a particular digital system. It is possible to analyze all these alternatives in sufficient detail to estimate their cost and speed. The effort one would actually devote to this would depend on the number of copies of the system to be constructed, as well as the cost of this effort in relation to the overall design cost. If such an analysis were made, the result might appear in the form of Fig. 4.28.

Each X on the figure represents a design based on some set of choices. The solid line on the figure is not a minimal mean square error fit of the data points but is rather a smooth curve approximately joining points with the lowest cost/speed ratios. The two points that are circled on the figure represent design choices, which need not be considered seriously. There are higher-speed–lower-cost alternatives available.

Notice that the dashed tangent line passes through the point on the curve that has the optimum cost/speed ratio. If cost/speed ratio were the only criterion, then the design point nearest this tangent point might be chosen. When system performance must be matched to some other system, it may be necessary to move in one direction or the other from the optimum. As mentioned, this is common in the case of real-time systems. If the designs of several subsystems of a larger system are projected to depart significantly from the economic optimum, a reconfiguration of overall system *architecture* may be in order.

Vector-handling systems that are not computers are more likely to be described by Fig. 4.28. In a complete computer, storage capacity as well as data handling speed is a factor in overall system performance. For some jobs, there is a trade-off between speed and memory capacity. The analysis of overall computer performance in terms of cost/speed characteristics and storage capacities of subsystems is an interesting but difficult problem. In many cases, it is not possible to complete as accurate an analysis as might be desired.

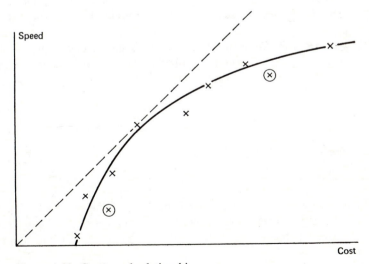

Figure 4.28. Cost/speed relationship.

Problems

4.1 Construct a logic block diagram similar to Fig. 4.3b illustrating the transfer

$$AR \leftarrow AR[1], AR[2], AR[0]$$

4.2 Construct a timing diagram for Problem 4.1 using leading-edge-triggered data flip-flops. Assume that the initial value of AR is (1, 0, 0).

4.3 Construct the logic block diagram of hardware associated with the register AR providing for the accomplishment of either of the transfers

$$AR \leftarrow \overline{AR}$$
$$AR \leftarrow BR$$

given the proper control signal. Both AR and BR are 4-bit registers.

4.4 Determine a minimal expression for D$AR[i]$ similar to Eq. 4.1, where AR must be the destination of the following four transfers:

$$AR \leftarrow 0,0,0$$
$$AR \leftarrow 1,1,1$$
$$AR \leftarrow \overline{AR}$$
$$AR \leftarrow BR$$

4.5 Suppose that the transfer $AR \leftarrow AR[2], AR[0:1]$ is to be accomplished if the control signal CSL1 is 1 and $AR \leftarrow AR[1:2], AR[0]$ is to be accomplished if CSL2 = 1. Construct a logic block diagram of the input network for the register AR that will provide for both these transfers.

4.6 Let $AR, BR, CR,$ and DR all be 8-bit registers that form part of a digital system. Included at various points in the control sequence for the system are the following transfers:

$BR \leftarrow AR$	$AR \leftarrow BR$
$CR \leftarrow AR$	$CR \leftarrow BR[1:7], BR[0]$
$DR \leftarrow AR[1:7] AR[0]$	$AR \leftarrow DR$
$BR \leftarrow \overline{AR}$	$BR \leftarrow DR$

Construct a busing diagram of the form of Fig. 4.11 showing paths for all listed transfers. Determine the total number of AND gates required to provide paths for these transfers by both methods of interconnection.

4.7 Write the AHPL control sequence from which the control unit of Fig. P4.7 was derived.

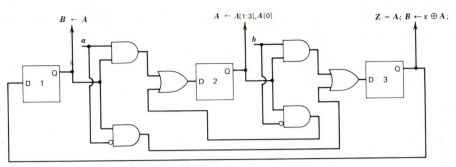

Figure P4.7.

4.8 Construct a control realization corresponding to the following AHPL sequence.

1 $Z = X \lor A$;
   $\rightarrow (a, \bar{a} \land b, \bar{a} \land \bar{b})/(2,3,4)$.
2 $A \leftarrow X$;
   $\rightarrow (1)$.
3 $A \leftarrow X[1{:}3], X[0]$;
   $\rightarrow (4)$.
4 $A \leftarrow A[1{:}3], A[0]$;
   $\rightarrow (1)$.

4.9 Construct a detailed logic block diagram of the hardware realization of both the control and data units specified by the following AHPL description, where a and b are flip-flops, x is an input, and z a single output line.

1 $a \leftarrow x \lor b$;
2 $b \leftarrow x$;
   $\rightarrow (a, \bar{a})/(1, 3)$.
3 $z = 1; b \leftarrow x \oplus b$;
   $\rightarrow (1)$.

4.10 Assume the control unit of Fig. 4.19 initially stores 1, 0, 0, 0 in the four control flip-flops from left to right. Construct a timing diagram for the contents of these four flip-flops spanning eight consecutive clock periods in which the control inputs are successively a, b = 00, 01, 11, 10, 10, 11, 01, 00.

4.11 Apply the input sequence given in Problem 4.10 to the control unit of Fig. P4.7 with the three flip-flops from left to right initially in the states of 1, 0, and 0. Obtain timing diagrams for a and b, and the output of each control flip-flop.

4.12 Construct logic block diagrams of the data unit realizations of expressions 4.20 and 4.21.

4.13 Obtain an AHPL control sequence for the sequential network of Fig. P4.13, assuming the network to be partitioned into control and data sections as shown.

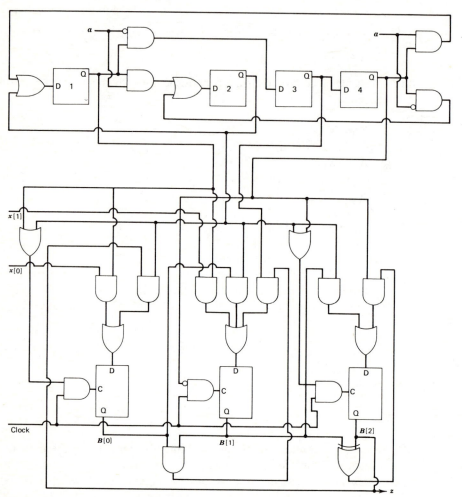

Figure P4.13.

4.14 The digital system described by the following AHPL control sequence has one output line z, an input vector X, and three single inputs a, b, and c. Operation of the system starts when a goes to 1 for one clock period. The system then carries out the transfers indicated and then raises z for one clock period as a signal that operations are complete. The external system will then establish new values of b, c, and x, and then send a 1-period level on a to start a new cycle. Reduce the sequence to an equivalent three-step sequence by employing conditional transfers. Is it possible to describe the system in fewer than three steps? Why or why not?

1 $\rightarrow (\bar{a})/(1)$.
2 $\rightarrow (\bar{b})/(4)$.
3 $B \leftarrow X \vee B$;
   $\rightarrow (\bar{c})/(5)$.
4 $D \leftarrow A \wedge B$.
5 $A \leftarrow X \oplus B$.
6 $z = 1$;
   $\rightarrow (1)$.

4.15 Construct a detailed logic network diagram of the digital circuit described by the following AHPL description. Include both the data section and control section and use the one flip-flop per control state approach.

MODULE:
INPUTS: x; a.
OUTPUTS: z.
MEMORY: r.

1 $\rightarrow (a, \bar{a})/(1, 2)$.
2 $r \leftarrow ((x \wedge r \,!\, x) * (a, \bar{a})$.
3 $z = r$; $r * a \leftarrow x$; $\rightarrow (1)$.
END.

4.16 A digital system controlling a bank of four lamps is to be driven by a very slow clock with a period equal to 0.2 sec. The lamps will be allowed to assume only one of the seven numbered patterns given in Fig. P4.16 where a zero indicates that a lamp is on, and an unlighted lamp is represented by a blank. If the only input to the system is $x = 0$, then the light patterns are to cycle as follows with a change each clock period.

Pattern	1	2	3	4	5	6	7
Lamp 1	0	0	0	0			
Lamp 2		0	0	0	0		
Lamp 3			0	0	0	0	
Lamp 4				0	0	0	0

Figure P4.16.

$$1 \rightarrow 2 \rightarrow 3 \rightarrow 4 \rightarrow 4 \rightarrow 5 \rightarrow 6 \rightarrow 7 \rightarrow 1 \rightarrow 2, \ldots$$

If $x = 1$, the sequence is

$$1 \rightarrow 7 \rightarrow 6 \rightarrow 5 \rightarrow 4 \rightarrow 4 \rightarrow 3 \rightarrow 2 \rightarrow 1 \rightarrow 7, \ldots$$

Write an AHPL sequence to describe a controller for these lamps. Let the 4-bit vector L [4] represent the outputs to the lamps. *Hint:* Consider an eight-step control sequence with no data flip-flops.

4.17 A digital system has an 8-bit vector, X, of input lines together with another input line **ready**. The system will have two output lines z and **ask**. Following each one-period level placed on line **ask**, a new vector will become available on lines X. The availability of such a vector will be signalled by a one-period level on line **ready**. Each time an input vector is exactly the same as either of the two previous input vectors, the output z should be 1 for four clock periods prior to another signal on line **ask**. The line z should be 0 at all other times. Write an AHPL sequence describing this digital system. Define the data registers as required.

4.18 (For students with background in state table minimization.) Determine a four-state (two flip-flop) realization of the control unit shown in Fig. P4.13.

References

1. Proceedings 1975 *Symposium on Computer Hardware Description Languages,* IEEE catalog no. 75CH 1010-8c, New York, Sept. 1975.
2. Y. Chu, "Why Do We Need Hardware Description Languages?" *Computer,* Dec. 1974, pp. 18–22.
3. G. J. Lipovski, "Hardware Description Languages," *Computer,* June 1977.
4. F. J. Hill and G. R. Peterson, *Introduction to Switching Theory and Logic Design,* 3rd ed., Wiley, New York, 1981.
5. F. J. Hill and G. R. Peterson, *Digital Logic and Microprocessors,* Wiley, New York, 1984.
6. R. Piloty, et al., *CONLAN Report,* Springer-Verlag, Berlin, 1983.
7. *VHDL Version 7.2 Users Manual,* Intermetrics, Bethesda, Md., 1985.
8. *VHDL Version 7.2 Language Reference Manual,* Intermetrics, Bethesda, Md., 1985.
9. Z. Navabi, *HPSIM2 User Manual,* University of Arizona Engineering Experiment Station, Sept. 1, 1984.

Introduction to a Hardware Programming Language (AHPL)

5.1 INTRODUCTION

A digital computer is a very complex device, and a complete description of a computer is going to be correspondingly complicated. We have already seen in Chapter 2 that it can take a lot of words to describe even a few of the operations of a very simple computer. Certainly, something better than the English language is going to be needed if we are to achieve efficient and concise descriptions of the design and functioning of digital computers.

There are many levels at which computers can be described: block diagrams, wiring tables, and the like. We are concerned here with a description of what the computer does in terms of the sequencing of operations and the flow of information from one point to another in the computer. Developing this description is the fundamental job of the designer. Once this description has been completed, the development of logic diagrams, schematics, wiring tables, etc., becomes largely a mechanical procedure, subject to considerable automation, as we shall discuss in later chapters.

In Chapter 4, we saw that hardware register transfers could be expressed in programming language form. We also observed that program branches could be realized as hardware. In the process, we established a few of the conventions of AHPL, the design language that will be used throughout the book. In this chapter, we shall assemble AHPL as a complete language and consider the hardware realization of those AHPL constructions not already treated in Chapter 4.

In the early stages of the development of AHPL, several languages were evaluated as to their suitability for hardware design. A suitable hardware language must permit

115

sufficient detail to describe even bit-by-bit operations and must at the same time have sufficient power to permit concise descriptions of complex operations. The language that seemed best able to meet these requirements had been developed by K.E. Iverson and was known simply as *A Programming Language* or APL [1]. Although APL is now primarily used for interactive programming, hardware description was one of the applications originally envisioned by Iverson. APL has subsequently been implemented with various modifications on several computer systems, the most widely used version being APL/370, which is available on several IBM computer systems.

Although APL lacks a number of features that are needed to represent hardware level operations, many of the standard APL conventions used with binary arguments could represent the common logic networks very well. We thus decided to adopt a notation as close to APL as possible and add other hardware related features as needed to form a new hardware description language, AHPL. Many APL operations do not suggest unique hardware realizations, so are not included in AHPL.

You, the reader, must approach the next three sections making the assumption that AHPL is critical to the overall objective of the book and must be mastered. Also it should be remembered that the emphasis in these three sections is on semantics. You will not be expected to have formed a complete picture of exactly what is permitted in AHPL until the end of Section 5.7. In this section, a complete syntax of this language is presented with as much rigor as possible given the expected background of most readers.

5.2   Operand Conventions

A function-level simulator that is available for AHPL must process an ASC-II version of the language that allows only one typeface. In print, however, it is more convenient to use different typographic conventions for different kinds of operands. The conventions to be used in AHPL are shown in Fig. 5.1.

The distinction between variables and literals is important in any computer language. In conventional programming systems, a *variable* is a name by which we refer to operands; a *literal* is an actual value for an operand. Thus, in a programming language we write

$$X = Y + 1 \tag{5.1}$$

meaning "The new value of X is to be equal to the value of Y plus one"; that is, Y is a variable and 1 is a literal. In AHPL, as in other hardware description languages, literal values are assigned to physical entities such as registers and buses. AHPL is a clock-mode language, so that a new value may be assigned to a physical entity only once each clock period. We choose to call the output of a memory element or a bus bit a *signal* rather than a variable. A value may be assigned to a signal once each clock period. The statement

$$MA \leftarrow PC$$

Type of Operand	Printed Representation
Literal value	
Numeric	Standard numerals
Function	Standard uppercase letters
Signals	
Scalar	Bold lowercase italic letters
Vector	Bold uppercase italic letters
Matrix	Bold uppercase roman letters

Figure 5.1. Typographic conventions for AHPL.

which we shall usually refer to as transfering the contents of the register, *PC,* to *MA,* can be interpreted as updating the signal outputs of register, *MA,* with the current signal value of *PC.* This update takes place at the end of each clock period in which the statement is active.

In AHPL, boldface letters or strings of letters indicate signals while numerals indicate literal values. For this reason, as in most languages, operators must not be omitted. Thus *MA* is the name of a single signal and cannot be interpreted as $M \wedge A$.

Unlike transfer statements involving signals, statements updating variables have no fixed relation to real time and do not represent actual hardware elements. We shall see later in this chapter that there is a place for variables in AHPL. These variables will appear in combinational logic unit descriptions. They will not represent physical elements in the network but will play a role in specification of the network.

A vector is simply a collection of operands arranged in a one-dimensional array. The number of elements (operands) in a vector is known as the dimension of the vector and will be denoted by ρ. Registers of more than one bit are considered to be vectors, since they consist of a number of bit positions, the contents of which are generally independent of one another. Thus, if the *PC* register has 18 bits, then $\rho\,PC = 18$; and the individual bit positions are denoted $PC[0], PC[1], PC[2], \ldots PC[17]$, with $PC[i]$ denoting the bit in the *i*th position. Note that the first position of the vector is denoted $PC[0]$, a procedure that is known as a 0-origin indexing. In some programming systems, 1-origin indexing is used. In this book, 0-origin indexing will always be assumed unless otherwise specifically stated.

A matrix is a two-dimensional array of operands, as illustrated in Fig. 5.2. The vector

$$(\mathbf{M}\langle i\rangle\,[0],\ \mathbf{M}\langle i\rangle\,[1],\ \ldots\ \mathbf{M}\langle i\rangle\,[\rho_1 - 1])$$

is known as the *i*th row of **M,** denoted as $\mathbf{M}\langle i\rangle$. Similarly, the vector

$$\begin{bmatrix} \mathbf{M}\langle 0\rangle\,[0] & \mathbf{M}\langle 0\rangle\,[1] & \mathbf{M}\langle 0\rangle\,[2] & \dots\dots\dots\dots\dots\dots\dots & \mathbf{M}\langle 0\rangle\,[\rho_1 - 1] \\ \mathbf{M}\langle 1\rangle\,[0] & \mathbf{M}\langle 1\rangle\,[1] & \dots\dots\dots\dots\dots\dots\dots\dots & & \mathbf{M}\langle 1\rangle\,[\rho_1 - 1] \\ \\ \mathbf{M}\langle \rho_2 - 1\rangle\,[0] & \dots\dots\dots\dots\dots\dots\dots\dots & & & \mathbf{M}\langle \rho_2 - 1\rangle[\rho_1 - 1] \end{bmatrix}$$

Figure 5.2. Array.

$$(\mathbf{M}\langle 0\rangle\,[j],\ \mathbf{M}\langle 1\rangle\,[j],\ \dots\ \mathbf{M}\langle \rho_2 - 1\rangle\,[j])$$

is the jth column of $\mathbf{M}$. The number of rows of $\mathbf{M}$ is ρ_1. The number of columns is ρ_2.

The most commonly encountered two-dimensional arrays in AHPL are random access memories. In this case, each row of $\mathbf{M}$ is a memory word. A stack of registers can also be treated as a two-dimensional array. As discussed in Chapter 4, $\mathbf{M}\langle i{:}k\rangle$ is a notation that can be used to form a new array consisting of rows i through k of $\mathbf{M}$. $\mathbf{M}[r{:}n]$ is an array consisting of columns r through n of $\mathbf{M}$.

5.3   AHPL Operators

In the hardware translation of AHPL, the variables or registers are capable of storing only values of one *type*, BOOLEAN (0's and 1's). Similarly, BOOLEAN is the only type of 0 and 1 are the only values processed by the most common simulator of AHPL. We shall see in Section 5.7 that a special syntax is needed for describing complex combinational logic networks. To facilitate the description of such networks for use in the process of translating them to a hardware realization, a second type, INTEGER, is necessary. It is important to realize that the use of integers and operators therein is only a descriptive mechanism. The combinational logic networks themselves process only Boolean values. The binary and unary operations of AHPL are summarized in Fig. 5.3.

Vectors and arrays of Boolean values and variables will be common in AHPL. However, the use of integers will be limited to scalar values. Binary operations on arrays and vectors using AND and OR are with one exception valid only if both operands have the same dimensions. The valid exception is the case where one of the operands is a scalar Boolean value. In this case, the operation is treated as if the scalar value is replaced with an array or vector of the same dimensions as the other operand in which every element has the same value as the scalar operand. For example,

$$x \wedge (1,\ 0,\ 1) = (x,\ x,\ x) \wedge (1,\ 0,\ 1) = (x,\ 0,\ x)$$

The following are a few more examples using the Boolean operators of Fig. 5.3. In each case $U = (1,1,0,1,0,0)$, $V = (0,1,1,1,1,0)$, $x = 1$, and $y = 0$.

Operation	Name	Value Type	Restrictions
$\bar{x}$	NOT	Boolean	Applicable to either
$x \wedge y$	AND		signals or
$x \vee y$	OR		variables
$x \oplus y$	Exclusive OR		
$x + y$	Addition	Integer	Applicable to index
$x - y$	Subtraction		variables in
$x * y$	Multiplication		combinational
x / y	Division		logic unit
$(x \; \mathcal{R} \; y)$	Relational		descriptions only
$2 \uparrow n$	Power of 2		

Figure 5.3. Binary and unary operators of AHPL.

$$U \wedge V = (0,1,0,1,0,0)$$
$$U \vee V = (1,1,1,1,1,0)$$
$$x \oplus V = (1,0,0,0,0,1)$$
$$y \oplus U = (0,0,1,0,1,1)$$

The relational operator $(x \; \mathcal{R} \; y)$ evaluates to 1 if the relation, $\mathcal{R}$, is satisfied and to 0 if the relation is not satisfied. The relation, $\mathcal{R}$, may be any of the relations that typically compare numbers, such as $=, >, \geq; <,$ or $\leq$. For example

$$(4 > 3) = 1$$

since 4 is indeed greater than 3. Similarly,

$$(4 < 3) = 0$$

Much of the special power of APL and AHPL derives from the mixed operators, which operate on various combinations of scalars, vectors, and matrices. There are a great many of these in APL, some of considerable complexity. A few of these that have been incorporated into AHPL are listed in Fig. 5.4.

The CATENATE operator simply joins vectors together to form larger vectors. Thus, if $X = (1,1,0)$ and $Y = (1,0,1)$, then

$$Z \leftarrow X, Y$$

specifies that $Z = (1,1,0,1,0,1)$. The notation $M \; ! \; N$ indicating row catenation has been added to AHPL. This operation is valid only if M and N have the same number of columns. The result is a matrix whose first $\rho_2 M$ rows are the rows of M and whose

Operator	Name	Meaning
X, Y	Catenate	$x[0] \ldots X[\rho_1 - 1], Y[0] \ldots Y[\rho_1 - 1]$
$M \, ! \, N$	Row catenate	The result is an array with the rows of **M** above the rows of **N**.
$n \, \top \, p$	Binary encode	An n element vector whose rightmost elements are the bits in a binary representation of p
$\odot / X$	Reduction	$X[0] \odot X[1] \odot X[2] \ldots \odot X[\rho_1 - 1]$
$Z = \odot / M$	Row reduction	$Z[i] = \odot / M\langle i \rangle$
$Z = \odot // M$	Column reduction	$Z[i] = M\langle 0 \rangle[i] \odot M\langle 1 \rangle[i] \ldots M\langle \rho_2 - 1 \rangle[i]$

Figure 5.4. Mixed operators in AHPL.

last ρ_2 **N** rows are the rows of **N**. One or more of the arguments of row catenation may be a vector, as illustrated by the example

$$M\langle 1:2 \rangle \, ! \, M\langle 0 \rangle = \begin{bmatrix} 0 & 1 & 1 \\ 1 & 1 & 1 \\ 0 & 0 & 1 \end{bmatrix}$$

where

$$M = \begin{bmatrix} 0 & 0 & 1 \\ 0 & 1 & 1 \\ 1 & 1 & 1 \end{bmatrix}$$

The binary encode operation of Fig. 5.4 is a special case of the standard APL encode. That is, $n \, \top \, p$ expresses the binary equivalent of the decimal number p as a n-element vector. The least significant bit of the binary number is the rightmost element of $n \, \top \, p$. This notation will provide a convenient method of expressing constants in AHPL. For example,

$$8 \, \top \, 100 = (0,1,1,0,0,1,0,0)$$

and

$$8 \, \top \, 0 = (0,0,0,0,0,0,0,0)$$

An operation that is applied to all elements of a vector or matrix to produce a simpler structure is called a *reduction*. The reduction of a vector is denoted by

$$z \leftarrow \odot/X$$

where $\odot$ may be any binary operator, and signifies that

$$z = ((\ldots ((X[0] \odot X[1]) \odot X[2]) \ldots) \odot X[p - 1])$$

Reduction is a very powerful operation that can be used in many ingenious ways. For example, if V is a logical vector,

$$z \leftarrow \vee/V$$

will be 0 if and only is every element of V is 0, and

$$z \leftarrow \wedge/V$$

will be 1 if and only if every element of V is 1.

Reduction is extended to matrices in two ways. Row reduction is denoted

$$X \leftarrow \odot/\mathbf{M}$$

and signifies that each row is reduced individually, producing a vector of dimension $\rho_2 \mathbf{M}$. Column reduction is denoted

$$X \leftarrow \odot//\mathbf{M}$$

and signifies that each column is reduced individually, resulting in a vector of dimension $\rho_1 \mathbf{M}$. For example, if

$$\mathbf{M} = \begin{bmatrix} 1 & 1 & 0 & 1 \\ 1 & 0 & 0 & 1 \\ 0 & 1 & 0 & 0 \end{bmatrix}$$

then $\vee/\mathbf{M} = (1,1,1)$, $\vee//\mathbf{M} = (1,1,0,1)$, and $\wedge/(\vee//\mathbf{M}) = 0)$.

5.4 AHPL Modules

A typical large digital system will consist of a number of interconnected subsystems or modules. Although a design problem will often be limited to a single module, it will usually be important to see clearly the relationships of that module to other modules within the system. There will be wires interconnecting modules that must have labels as outputs in one module as well as inputs in another. Certain memory elements may be capable of receiving data that might be clocked in by the control unit of more than one module. It is also important to be able to collect the transfer and connection statements associated with one subsystem so that they are immediately recognized as part of that module and no other.

We have already presented some of the AHPL conventions at the level of the individual statement. Before presenting the complete syntax, we shall consider the relationship of the individual statements to the overall system description, which may include many modules as well as combinational logic units. Not all systems are isolated with easily defined boundaries. Some may even be connected through communications links into seemingly never-ending networks. In such cases, a system boundary must be imposed by the designer. Often, bounds can be established at points of interface with equipment that is primarily nondigital. In the end, however, the designer is free to establish any system boundary that may prove convenient.

Fig. 5.5 is an informal illustration of a syntax for subdividing a bounded system with the system itself as the root. The first level of branching in the tree indicates that the procedural AHPL descriptions of the modules containing memory and control precede the FUNCTIONS consisting of combinational logic only. The outputs of a combinational logic unit may be used within any procedural module or nonrecursively within any other combinational logic units. The syntax for describing combinational logic units will be deferred until Section. 5.6.

A small set of combinational logic units are used repeatedly in a variety of digital systems. These will be introduced as needed. Perhaps the most common of these combinational logic units is the increment function

INC (*REG*)

which is an *n*-bit vector representation of a binary number determined by increasing by 1 modulo-2^n the number stored in *REG*. In hardware terms

REG ← INC(*REG*)

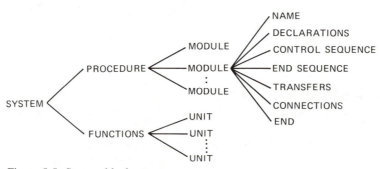

Figure 5.5. System block structure.

merely means treating **REG** as a counter and incrementing that counter. The AHPL connection description representing INC and the corresponding hardware realization will be given later.

As indicated in Fig. 5.5, the AHPL description of a module will consist of a name, a list of declarations, a control sequence, a list of individual connection statements, and a termination. The declarations include

MEMORY   (flip-flops, registers, and arrays)
INPUTS
OUTPUTS
BUSES
LABELS
COMBUSES
CLUNITS

All flip-flops, registers, and memory arrays that will appear in the control sequence of a given module must be dimensioned in a MEMORY declaration. Vectors of input and output lines as well as individual lines must be declared. The source of each input line, together with any different label in its module of origin may be given. Each BUS must be declared and dimensioned. A *communications bus,* as discussed in Chapter 4, may now be formally defined as a bus on which the contents may be determined by more than one module. A communications bus must be declared separately as a **COMBUS,** thus recording the fact that this bus must be connected to a set of input/output lines from the module. It is not necessary to also include a communications bus among the INPUT and OUTPUT declarations.

The **LABELS** declaration may be used to rename portions of larger registers. It may also be used to call for a particular hardware realization of a register such as an MSI part.

To illustrate the use of declaration statements, the initial steps of a formal AHPL description of the data selector of Example 4.1 will be given as follows.

MODULE: DATA SELECTOR
   MEMORY: *INREG* [12]; *OUTREG* [12]; A [4]; *s.*
   INPUTS: *X* [12].
   OUTPUTS: *Z* [12]; *inready; outready.*

This example illustrates the declaration of registers and individual memory elements. An *array will be dimensioned* as *M* ⟨*m*⟩ [*n*], where *m* is the number of rows and *n* is the number of columns. If *M* is a memory array, we shall assume it to have *m* words of *n* bits each.

Following the declarations is the control sequence, which will consist of a series of action statements, the syntax of which will be defined in the next section. The control sequence will be terminated by END SEQUENCE. This indicator may be followed by individual transfers and connection statements that are intended to be applicable at all times regardless of the step in the control sequence active during the current clock period. A combinational logic network generating an output as a function of the registers in a module might be included following the END SEQUENCE statement. In this case, the same output function would apply continuously regardless of the state of the control unit.

In some systems it is necessary to keep track of time in parallel with any other activities that might be in progress. This can be accomplished by incrementing a counter every clock period. Such a counting function can be specified by inserting a statement such as

$$COUNT \leftarrow \text{INC } (COUNT)$$

following the END SEQUENCE statement. All connection statements and transfers may be subject to conditional expressions consistent with the syntax to be presented in the following section. In the following partial example, a counter is incremented whenever the data flip-flop $a = 1$. The output statement is valid every clock period.

> END SEQUENCE
> $COUNT * a \leftarrow \text{INC}(COUNT)$;
> $Z = X \wedge REG.$
> END

Finally, as illustrated by this example, the overall module description must be terminated by END.

5.5   AHPL Statements

Only operations that satisfy the constraints imposed by available hardware are included in AHPL. We wish to make this point in the strongest possible way. Every AHPL step written down by the designer will represent some action on some already-specified hardware elements. The designer will always have a mental picture of the hardware involved prior to writing an AHPL step. In the remainder of this chapter, we shall develop hardware-related features for AHPL that are not in APL.

The syntax and semantics of individual statements in an AHPL control sequence will be presented in this section. The syntax will be presented in outline form, gradually working inward form the overall program sequence to the individual operations. First, however, let us look briefly at the notation on either side of the arrow in a simple transfer statement.

$$DV \leftarrow OCLV \tag{5.2}$$

The vector DV represents what we shall call the target vector. It may be a single register or a vector of one or more memory elements assembled by any of the list of already discussed *selection operators* tabulated in Fig. 5.6. The bracketed values appearing in these selection operators must be constants.

A [*j*]	The *j*th element of *A*
A [*m:n*]	Elements *m* through *n* of *A*
,	Catenation
A!*B*	Row catenation
M ⟨*j*⟩	The *j*th row of **M**
M ⟨*m:n*⟩	Row *m* through row *n* of **M**

Figure 5.6 AHPL Selection Operators

The vector ***OCLV*** on the right side of expression 5.6 represents what will be called an *origin combinational logic vector*. Each element of an ***OCLV*** is a combinational logic expression whose arguments may be elements from any of the following

1. Memory elements
2. Inputs
3. Combinational logic units
4. Buses
5. Constants

Only 0, 1, and the *n* bit encoding of a decimal number *d* ($n \top d$) will be used as constants. Particular arguments for combinational logic expressions may be selected from the foregoing elements using any of the selection operators in Fig. 5.6. These arguments may then be related by any of the logic operators listed in Fig. 5.7.

To minimize the need for parentheses in the formation of OCL expressions, the AHPL selection and logic operators will be used according to the following *precedence structure*.

1. NOT
2. All selection operators except catenate
3. $\wedge$
4. $\vee$ or $\oplus$
5. Catenate

An operation in the lower-numbered category will have the highest precedence and will be executed first. When the issue is otherwise unresolved, parentheses will be employed. In this book, parentheses may be used in some places when not absolutely required to ensure clarity.

We are now ready to examine the syntax of a control-sequence step. Any number

$\wedge$	AND
$\vee$	OR
Overbar	NOT
$\wedge$/	AND over elements of a vector
$\vee$/	OR over elements of a vector
$\oplus$	Exclusive OR

Figure 5.7. AHPL logic operators.

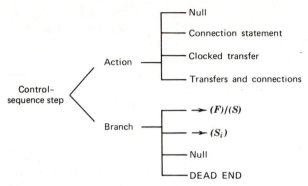

Figure 5.8. Syntax of a control-sequence step.

of such steps may be listed to form the control sequence of Fig. 5.5. Each control sequence step will consist of an action statement followed by a branch, as suggested by Fig. 5.8. This figure also indicates the four possible compositions of the action statement. In effect the action statement may consist of any number of clocked transfers and/or connection statements. The first alternative, "null," allows for steps consisting only of a branch statement.

The branch portion of a step in a control sequence may take on any of the four possible forms given in Fig. 5.8. The meanings of the first three have already been discussed. The statement DEAD END indicates that no other control state will follow the current state. This might be used to effect a HALT instruction, for example, or to terminate various paths within a set of simultaneous or parallel control sequences. The concept of parallelism will be considered in Chapter 9.

In Fig. 5.8, F represents a vector of Boolean expressions that serve as conditionals. The elements of an F vector may be generated in the same way as those of an $OCLV$, and S is a vector of statement numbers.

The three possible forms of a clocked transfer are given in Fig. 5.9, and the four forms of a connection statement are given in Fig. 5.10. The simplest clocked transfer merely transfers an origin combinational logic vector into a destination register of the same length. The remaining two forms are conditional transfers. The array $OCLM$ is merely a matrix whose rows are vectors of combinational logic expressions.

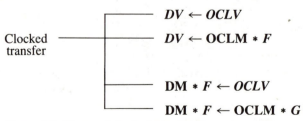

Figure 5.9. Forms of clocked transfers.

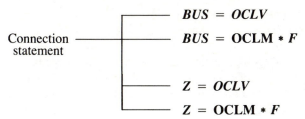

Figure 5.10. Connection statements.

If the **OCLM** is $(A \: ! \: B \: ! \: C)$, if $F = (f, g, h)$ and the **DV** is **D,** then the second transfer form represents the transfer previously given as expression 4.21.

$$D \leftarrow (A \: ! \: B \: ! \: C) * (f, g, h)$$

Similarly, if the *matrix, DM,* were to represent $(A \: ! \: B \: ! \: C)$ and the **OCLV** were **D,** the third transfer form would coincide with expression 4.20.

$$(A \: ! \: B \: ! \: C) * (f, g, h) \leftarrow D$$

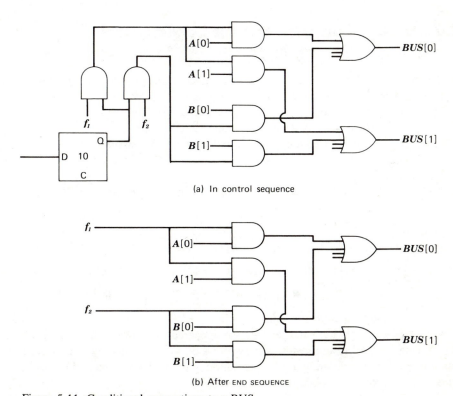

Figure 5.11. Conditional connections to a BUS.

In all cases, the expression will have meaning only if the vector of expressions selected on the right has the same number of elements as the destination vector selected on the left.

In Fig. 5.10, we distinguish the connection to a predeclared bus from a connection statement that routes an *OCLV* to a vector of module outputs when it appears in a control sequence. There is no logical difference between a connection to an output vector *Z* and connection to a bus. Where the number of anticipated inputs is very large, one would usually use a predeclared bus. Where output networks route only a few data vectors, the notation *Z* = *OCLV* may be used.

Expression 5.3 is a conditional connection to a bus of 2-bit length, the hardware realization of which is depicted in Fig. 5.11a. The same expression following END SEQUENCE would not require ANDing the condition variables f_1 and f_2 to the output of a control flip-flop resulting in the network given in Fig. 5.11b. Note the similarity to the transfer network of Fig. 4.5.

$$10 \; \boldsymbol{BUS} = (\boldsymbol{A} \; ! \; \boldsymbol{B}) * (f_1, f_2) \tag{5.3}$$

Ordinarily, only connection statements of the form *Y* = *OCLV* will appear in combinational logic unit descriptions.

5.6   Using Combinational Logic Units

In Chapter 4, we introduced the fundamental register transfer statements of AHPL and considered their hardware correspondence. We have already used sequences of such statements to describe sequential hardware activity. We have now precisely defined the accepted syntax for the type of description called an AHPL module. Let us now introduce another descriptive tool that can be employed for significantly abbreviating the expression of logic on the right side of a transfer or connection statement in a module description.

Consider the moderately complex combinational logic vector given by expression 5.4.

$$\boldsymbol{C} = (A[0]) \wedge B[0]) \oplus ((A[1] \wedge B[1]) \wedge (A[2] \wedge B[2]) \wedge (A[3] \wedge B[3])),$$
$$(A[1] \wedge B[1]) \oplus ((A[2] \wedge B[2]) \wedge (A[3] \wedge B[3])), \tag{5.4}$$
$$(A[2] \wedge B[2]) \oplus (A[3] \wedge B[3]), (A[3] \wedge B[3])$$

If this expression appeared only once within an AHPL module description, it could be written as given. If the same expression appeared more than once, added clarity and a saving in effort would result, if the expression were replaced by an abbreviation, with the description defining the abbreviation presented only once. For example, expression 5.5 could be substituted for expression 5.4.

CLUNIT: LOGIC (*A;B*)

```
┌─────────────────────────────────┐
│ Declarations                    │
│           .                     │
│           .                     │
│           .                     │
└─────────────────────────────────┘
```

BODY

```
┌─────────────────────────────────┐
│ Connections                     │
│           .                     │
│           .                     │
│           .                     │
└─────────────────────────────────┘
```

END   Figure 5.12. Combinational logic unit description.

$$C = \text{LOGIC}(A;\ B) \tag{5.5}$$

In Section 5.4 we have already introduced and used the very important combinational logic unit INC, which increments an input vector. The notations INC(*COUNTER*) or LOGIC (*A; B*) are similar to function or procedure call notation in a programming language. Here we shall refer to LOGIC(*A; B*) as a *function* or a *combinational logic unit*. This notation will be restricted to refer *only* to combinational logic networks.

The description of the network defined by LOGIC(*A; B*) will be set apart by the heading and END notation. A list of declarations will precede and be separated from a set of connections statements by the keyword BODY, as illustrated in Fig. 5.12. This is the format of a *combinational logic unit description*. The combination logic description of LOGIC (*A; B*) may consist of a single *connection statement* or a series of connection statements.

If notation for a single combinational logic unit appears more than once with the same arguments, only one network needs to be constructed with multiple connections to its output. Thus the combinational logic unit description is a vehicle for minimizing cost through the reuse of logic networks. If the notation for a given function appears more than once but with different arguments, then the network must be constructed separately for each distinct set of inputs.[1] Only one combinational logic unit description is required in any case. If the function is to be used with more than one set of arguments, dummy variables may appear in the heading of the combinational logic unit description.

Some special features will be allowed within a combinational logic unit description to simplify the expression of particularly complex networks. The writing of

---

[1] We shall see in Chapter 6 that a complex combinational network can be shared by declaring buses as its arguments.

combinational logic unit descriptions and their compilation into hardware will be considered further in Section 5.7.

In this section, we shall be content with a single example of the use of combinational logic unit notation.

Example 5.1

The digital network represented by the following AHPL module description performs a logical function on sequences of 3 bits appearing in consecutive clock periods on input line x. The "8's complement" of each sequence of 3 bits appears after a two-clock period delay on output line, z. The slicing of the bit string into 3 bit sequences is resynchronized each time control line, *go,* goes to 0. The eight's complementing function is accomplished by the combinational logic unit COMP(W), which has three output lines. The input, W, is also a 3-bit vector. Construct a logic block diagram of the data unit described by this module.

> MODULE: EIGHTS COMPLEMENTER
> INPUTS: x, go.
> MEMORY: $Y[2]$.
> OUTPUTS: z.
> CLUNITS: COMP[3] $<$: . . . .
>
> 1 $Y \leftarrow Y[1], x; z = Y[0]$;
> $\rightarrow (\overline{go})/(1)$.
> 2 $Y \leftarrow Y[1], x; z = Y[0]$;
> $\rightarrow (\overline{go})/(1)$.
> 3 $z = $ COMP[0] (Y, x) ;
> $Y \leftarrow $ COMP[1:2] (Y, x);
> $\rightarrow (1)$.
> END.

Solution

Like memory elements, inputs, and outputs, combinational logic units must be declared with the number of output lines specified. The actual syntax of the declaration will be discussed in the next section. Only two memory elements are required in the description, because the first of a sequence of outputs is generated by step 3 coincident with the third of the corresponding sequence of three inputs. The notation COMP[1:2] (Y, x) is the rightmost two out of the three output lines of the combinational logic unit, COMP, whose three bit argument is Y,x. The register Y is shared by future outputs and received inputs. In step 1, Y contains two outputs. In step 3, it contains two inputs. The resulting data unit, which can be generated from the module description without considering its function, is given in Fig. 5.13.

Descriptions of combinational logic units can be developed in any number of ways. The specification of the eight's complementing function, COMP, is most easily set forth in the multiple output Karnaugh map of Fig. 5.14a. For each input combination, the corresponding output is obtained by subtracting the binary value of the

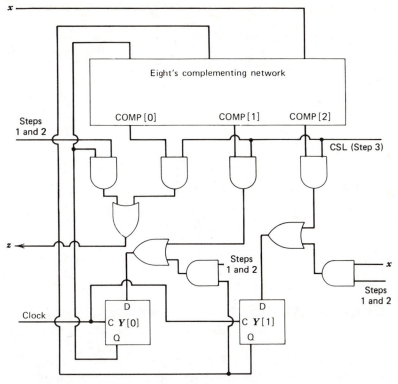

Figure 5.13. Data unit for eight's complementer.

input from eight. It is easily seen that the least significant bit of the output is the same as the input, *x*. Individual expressions for COMP[1:2] are easily obtained once the functions are copied to the individual Karnaugh maps of Fig. 5.14b and c. Expressions for the three outputs of COMP are given in Eqs. 5.6, 5.7, and 5.8.

$$\text{COMP}[0] = (x \vee Y[1]) \wedge Y[0] \ \vee \ Y[0] \wedge \overline{Y[1]} \wedge x \tag{5.6}$$

$$\text{COMP}[1] = (x \vee Y[1]) \wedge \overline{(x \wedge Y[1])} \tag{5.7}$$

$$\text{COMP}[2] = x \tag{5.8}$$

In this sample example, the functions of *x* and *Y* could have been written directly into the module description. As we have observed, this can be inconvenient for more complex functions. Notice also that the term $x \vee Y[1]$ appears in both expressions 5.6 and 5.7. If these expressions are written separately in the module description, a rather sophisticated optimizing hardware compiler would be required to avoid realizing this term twice with two separate OR gates. The syntax for describing combinational logic units, to be presented in the next section, will provide for specifying the wiring of the network COMP at the pleasure of the designer.

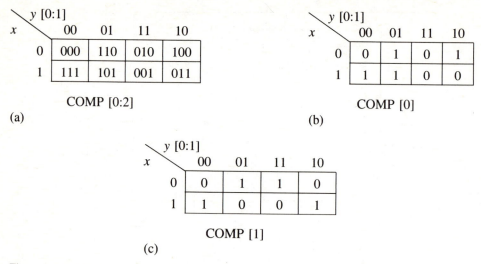

COMP [0:2]

(a)

COMP [0]

(b)

COMP [1]

(c)

Figure 5.14. Eight's complementing function.

5.7 Combinational Logic Unit Descriptions

Referring to Fig. 5.5, you will notice that the complete AHPL description of a system is broken into procedures and functions. The procedure portion consists of a set of modules that together describe the system of interest. These modules may declare and *invoke* combinational logic units that must be described in the functions portion. In the "eight's complementer of Section 5.6, we used a simple three-output combinational logic unit description. In our implementation of RIC in Chapter 6, we shall need combinational logic units to accomplish addition, to increment, to decrement, to serve as a decoder, and to facilitate the expression of reading from an array of registers. These functions will be accomplished by ADD, INC, DEC, DCD, and BUSFN, respectively.

AHPL uses a structured syntax for combinational logic unit description. (What is more structured than combinational logic?) This makes it possible for a *hardware compiler* program to process a description step by step and to generate a network wire list for the corresponding combinational logic unit. Each connection statement adds one or more gates to the network. It is the responsibility of the designer, the writer of the combinational logic unit description, to assure that the description does indeed represent an implementation of the desired logic function. In some cases, connection statements can be ordered from input to output; that is, each connection statement uses as inputs-only variables that either are inputs to the overall network or appear on the right side of prior connection statements. If this is done, verifying the network is straightforward. As with a subroutine, output values can then be computed for a set of input arguments in one pass through the list of statements.

The root syntax detailing the declaration part of a combinational logic unit

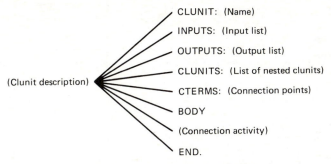

Figure 5.15. Syntax for declarations in CLUNITS.

description is given in Fig. 5.15. The syntax for declarations of inputs and outputs and nested clunits does not differ from that of modules. Internal signals that are the targets of connection statements are now also declared as CTERMS. This permits the hardware compiler program to know in advance the points that must be connected by connection statements and makes it possible to process a description in one pass.

Before presenting the complete syntax for the ⟨connection activity⟩ let us consider a simple example that requires only a series of connection statements.

Example 5.2

Develop an AHPL combinational logic unit description of a *full adder*.

Solution
The term *full adder* refers to a circuit that accomplishes the addition of two corresponding bits, one from each argument vector connected to the input of the complete adder. This process entails accepting a carry bit from the full adder stage that adds bits just lower in significance and generating a sum bit and a carry bit to the next most significant full adder. If we denote the inputs as *x, y,* and *cin,* the minimal second-order equations for the sum and carry are as follows:

$$sum = (x \wedge \bar{y} \wedge \overline{cin}) \vee (\bar{x} \wedge y \wedge \overline{cin}) \vee (\bar{x} \wedge \bar{y} \wedge cin) \vee (x \wedge y \wedge cin)$$
$$(5.9)$$

$$cout = (x \wedge y) \vee (x \wedge cin) \vee (y \wedge cin) \qquad (5.10)$$

These forms can be implemented directly as AND-OR circuits, but a simpler adder circuit can be obtained by factoring these equations into the following forms:

$$sum = x \oplus y \oplus cin$$
$$cout = ((x \oplus y) \wedge cin) \vee (x \wedge y)$$

The implementation of these forms can be described by the AHPL unit description that follows.

```
CLUNIT:      FULLADD (x; y; cin)
INPUTS:      x; y; cin
OUTPUTS:     FULLADD [2].
CTERMS:      a; b; c; sum; cout.
BODY
    a = x ⊕ y;
    b = x ∧ y;
    sum = a ⊕ cin;
    c = a ∧ cin;
    cout = b ∨ c;
    FULLADD[0] = cout;
    FULLADD[1] = sum.
END.
```

Note that the first five statements specify connections of gates, while the last two simply label the outputs. ∎

The rules for writing combinational logic unit descriptions do not require that connection statements appear in order. It is only necessary that they cause the proper network to be connected. In Chapter 14, we shall see an example, the carry look-ahead adder, in which input to output ordering cannot be achieved in an efficient description. There are many possible combinational logic units that can accomplish addition. Most are naturally ordered from input to output. The carry look-ahead adder is made more complicated by the addition of special subnetworks to reduce the propagation delay.

The combinational logic unit description just derived in Example 5.2 provides a simple illustration of the wiring process accomplished by the hardware compiler. The process is straightforward, where the wiring statements are ordered from input to output as they are in the example. To show that the result of the wiring process is the same regardless of the order of the connection statements, consider the following alternative description.

```
CLUNIT: FULLADD(x; y; cin)
    INPUTS: x; y; cin.
    OUTPUTS: FULLADD[2].
    CTERMS: a; b; c; sum; cout.
    BODY
    sum = cin ⊕ a;
    c = cin ∧ a;
    cout = b ∨ c;
    a = x ⊕ y;
    b = x ∧ y;
    FULLADD = cout, sum.
END
```

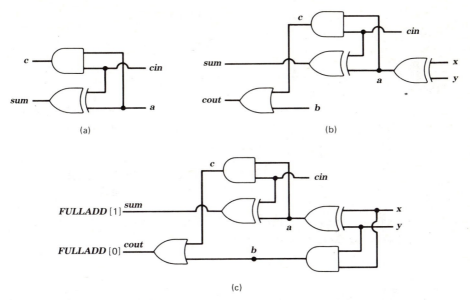

Figure 5.16. Wiring the full adder.

The wiring process is illustrated in Fig. 5.16. Fig. 5.16a is the result of wiring the first two connection statements. Adding the gates called for by the third and fourth statements results in Fig. 5.16b, and wiring the last two statements yields Fig. 5.16c. It is left to you to verify that the same network results from connecting the ordered description given in Example 5.2.

In a clock-mode simulation, the output of each combinational logic unit must be computed once each clock period. Output and internal signals of combinational logic unit descriptions can be computed by executing the wiring statements. Although the terms within a combinational logic unit description must be classified as signals, no specific time delay is associated with the evaluation a wiring statement when computing the outputs of a combinational logic unit in a clock-mode simulation. These statements are merely executed as necessary until the output of the CLUNIT is determined. One advantage of the version of FULLADD given in Example 5.2 is that it can be executed (simulated) in a single pass. This is not true for the scrambled version just given.[2]

A more detailed syntax of the body portion of a combinational logic unit description is given in Fig. 5.17. As mentioned, the syntax is structured but includes only two of the flow-control mechanisms normally found in a language such as PASCAL. Because of the natural rigidity of combinational logic, these are all that are

---

[2]Simulation of an unordered version of a combinational logic unit description may be accomplished by executing the description iteratively until the same values are obtained throughout the network for two consecutive iterations.

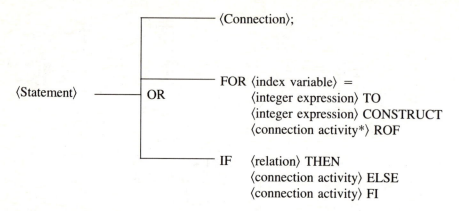

⟨Statement⟩ ——— OR

⟨Connection⟩;

FOR ⟨index variable⟩ =
      ⟨integer expression⟩ TO
      ⟨integer expression⟩ CONSTRUCT
      ⟨connection activity*⟩ ROF

IF   ⟨relation⟩ THEN
      ⟨connection activity⟩ ELSE
      ⟨connection activity⟩ FI

*A "connection activity" is a list of any number of statements.

Figure 5.17. Syntax for body of CLUNITS.

necessary. *Index variables* subject to integer operators are used to provide for replication. These index variables are just that, variables of type integer in contrast to signals. The operators allowed in expressions on index variables were tabulated in Fig. 5.3. Evaluation of these expressions is a hardware compile-time activity. The purpose of these expressions is to specify the structure of the network; index variables do not represent points in the final network. The syntax provides for nesting the IF THEN and FOR TO constructs by permitting any list of statements within these mechanisms.

Index expressions are integer arithmetic expressions of reasonable complexity consistent with Fig. 5.3. Multiplication, division, and powers of 2, expressed $2 \uparrow k$, are allowed. Similarly, the relational operators on the integer index variables are restricted to $=, <, \leq, >$, and $\geq$, as stated in Section 5.3. Index expressions are allowed in row and column selection, that is within ⟨ ⟩ and [ ], respectively. One change from the second edition is the notation for a logical minterm function of n variables. Now a minterm is simply given by the primitive function TERM(i,***BOOLVEC***), where i is an integer index specifying the minterm number, and ***BOOLVEC*** is a vector of the Boolean variables in decending binary order over which the minterm is defined. For example,

$$\text{TERM}(1;\ x,y,z) = \bar{x} \wedge \bar{y} \wedge z$$

It should be stressed that TERM is a special primitive function, which includes an integer variable among its arguments and is not itself a combinational logic unit description. Although not an efficient notation for this purpose, TERM functions may be used to form combinational logic unit descriptions of arbitrary BOOLEAN expressions in standard-sum-of-products (see [7]) form. For example,

$$x \oplus y = \bar{x} \wedge \bar{y} \ \vee \ x \wedge y$$

$$= \text{TERM}(0; \ x,y) \vee \text{TERM}(3; \ x,y)$$

Our first example of a more complex combinational logic unit description will declare and invoke copies of the combinational logic unit FULLADD just discussed. We must first introduce the syntax for declaration of CLUNITS. A new symbol, "$<$:" is used for declaring combinational logic units. The following are declarations of incrementers of two different lengths, drawing on a single description of INC with a parameter enclosed in { }.

CLUNITS: INCA[4] <: INC{4}.
CLUNITS: INCB[8] <: INC{8}.

More than one instance of both the 4-bit and the 8-bit incrementers may be created by merely invoking them in the body of the description. Invoking combinational logic units within other combinational logic units and within modules is the same. Only the number of outputs of a logic network is specified in the declaration. The arguments must be specified each time the network is invoked. In this case, the parameter enclosed by { } is merely the length of the incrementer. The number of inputs and outputs are the same and are specified by this parameter. In general, the relationship between input and output vectors and these numerical parameters is defined in the relevant combinational logic unit description. The designer must be familiar with this description before declaring a combinational logic unit.

As an example of a combinational logic unit description that exploits the syntax of Fig. 5.17, let us consider an *n*-bit *ripple-carry adder*. The FOR TO construct will prove useful in that the ripple-carry adder will consist of *n* identical full adders. In Chapter 6, we shall use a 32-bit instance of this adder in the RIC arithmetic logic unit.

Example 5.3

Write an AHPL combinational logic unit description of an *n*-bit ripple-carry adder.

Solution
Let us use a parameter, I, equal to the number of bits in each argument of the adder. Therefore, $I + 1$ outputs are required to provide a carry out. I copies of the full adder derived previously will be used, but only one declaration statement is required since the full adders are identical. The carry outputs from the full adders must be declared as CTERMS, because with one exception they are only connection points within the network. The resulting description is as given in Fig. 5.18. ■

Suppose that an 18-bit version of the ripple-carry adder described in Example 5.3 is to be used within a module description. This will require the following declaration.

CLUNIT: ADDER(XIN; YIN; cin) {I}
  INPUTS: XIN[I]; YIN[I]; cin.
  OUTPUTS: $SUMOUT$[I + 1].
  CLUNITS: FA[2] <: FULLADD.
  CTERMS: $CARRY$[I]; SUM[I].
  BODY
       $CARRY$[I − 1], SUM[I − 1] = FA(XIN[I − 1]; YIN[I − 1]; cin);
       FOR J = I − 2 TO 0 CONSTRUCT
       $CARRY$[J], SUM[J] = FA(XIN[J]; YIN[J]; $CARRY$[J + 1])
       ROF;
       $SUMOUT$ = $CARRY$[0], SUM.
  END.

Figure 5.18. Description of an n-bit adder.

ADD [19] <: ADDER{18}

Fig. 5.19 illustrates the step-by-step process executed by the hardware compiler in generating a copy of this network if ADD is invoked with actual arguments X and Y and with cin = 0. Fig. 5.19a shows the network following execution of the first statement in the body of the description of ADDER. Fig. 5.19b shows the network after one pass through the FOR loop, and Fig. 5.19c shows the network after executing the complete description.

Each invocation of the adder, whose description is given in Fig. 5.18 with a separate set of arguments, will result in the generation of a separate network. Often, however, it is useful at various points in a system description to add different vectors utilizing a single adder. This can be accomplished by declaring buses that serve as the only inputs to the adder. Various arguments can then be connected to the buses as required. Assume that the following are part of the declarations in the AHPL description of a computer.

  CLUNITS: ADD[17] <: ADDER{16}.
  BUSES: $ABUS$[16]; $BBUS$[16]; cin.

Notice that cin is a 1-bit bus, so that if necessary the source of the input carry can vary with the arguments. The same adder can now be represented at many steps in a description, provided the buses, $ABUS$, $BBUS$, and cin are always the arguments. For example,

  10 $ABUS = X; BBUS = Y; cin = 0$;
      $Z = ADD(ABUS; BBUS; cin)$.

It might be tempting not to declare cin as a bus and to invoke the adder at one point in the description as

ZA = ADD($ABUS;\ BBUS;$ 0).

and elsewhere as

ZB = ADD($ABUS;\ BBUS;$ 1).

Once again this would result in *two* separate adder networks.

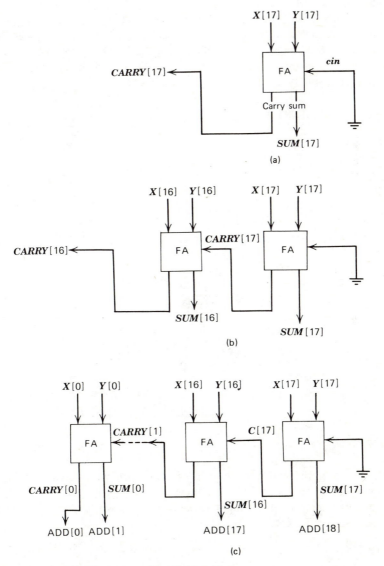

Figure 5.19. Generation of an 18-bit adder.

In Chapter 7, we will explore the role of the hardware compiler further. This program will have greater responsibility in the case of modules than it has for combinational logic unit descriptions. For the former, the compiler will be called on to accomplish a limited amount of optimization on the control unit. As illustrated, the compiler merely executes explicit instructions in generating combinational logic networks. It is worth emphasizing again that the integer index variables will not exist in the resulting hardware network. They serve only as part of a mechanism to provide for compact description. The target networks of the compiler, both combinational and sequential, process only signals of type Boolean.

To conclude this section, let us present the descriptions of two more combinational logic units that will prove constantly useful in the succeeding chapters. Generation of the first incrementer will make use of the IF THEN mechanism. Note that the name of the n-bit incrementer will be INCRMT. We shall continuously use INC in our discussion, implying a declaration of the form

INC[J] <: INCRMT{J}

Example 5.4

Write the combinational logic unit description of an I-bit incrementer.

Solution

```
CLUNIT: INCRMT(X) {I}
    INPUTS: X[I].
    OUTPUTS: TERMOUT[I].
    CTERMS: TA[I].
    BODY  FOR J = I − 1 TO  0  CONSTRUCT
            IF J = I − 1 THEN
                    TA[J] = 1
            ELSE
                    TA[J] = X[J + 1] ∧ TA[J + 1]
            FI
          ROF;
          FOR J = I − 1 TO  0  CONSTRUCT
                  TERMOUT[J] = X[J] ⊕ TA[J]
          ROF.
    END.
```

The last example will be a decoder, instances of which will be refered to as DCD. The generic version will have I inputs and $2 \uparrow$ I outputs. The outputs of a decoder are all minterms of the input variables, so we will expect its description to rest on the function TERM.

Example 5.5

Write a combinational logic unit description of an I input decoder.

Solution

        CLUNIT: DECODER(A) {I}.
            INPUTS: A[I].
            OUTPUTS: **DCDOUT**[2 $\uparrow$ I].
            BODY
                    FOR J = 0 TO (2 $\uparrow$ I) $-$ 1 CONSTRUCT
                        DCDOUT[J] = TERM(J;A)
                    ROF.
        END.   ∎

5.8 Handling of Memory Arrays in AHPL

The selection operators listed in Section 5.6 serve the function of selecting arguments from flip-flops, registers, and arrays so that they may be permanently wired into the data unit, either providing input data to a transfer or serving as the destination of a transfer. These selection operators imply permanent connections only, not logical operations or computations. This is the reason that subscripts and superscripts must be constants. Wired connections are inherently constant. Often it is necessary to select a word from a memory array as a function of the contents of a register, as in the case of a random access memory (RAM). The conditional transfer notation of Fig. 5.19 has been provided in part for this purpose. Suppose that the array M in Fig. 5.20 consists of 2^n words stored in 2^n static semiconductor registers. Let F be a vector of 2^n elements, one and only one of which will be logical 1. In this case, expression 5.11 specifies transferring the contents of the memory data register MD into one of the words of memory.

$$\mathbf{M} * \mathbf{F} \leftarrow \mathbf{MD} \tag{5.11}$$

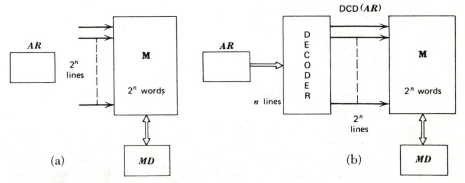

Figure 5.20. Random access memory.

By constraining the value of the elements of F such that one and only one of these values is logical 1, only one of the 2^n memory registers is clocked each time the step in expression 5.11 is executed. Usually, the location of the word in memory to be replaced will be specified by the binary number stored in an address register, labelled AR in Fig. 5.20. To complete the notation for a write-in memory operation, we must replace F in expression 5.11 by the output of a combinational logic network, which we shall call DCD. This network must be constructed in such a way that $DCD[i] = 1$ and $DCD[j] = 0$, where $j \neq i$ if the binary number stored in AR is i. The network DCD, as depicted in Fig. 5.20b, is usually referred to as an n-2^n line decoder. Clearly, DCD is an instance of the combination logic decoder defined in Example 5.5. The write-in memory operation can, therefore, be expressed in AHPL as given in expression 5.12.

$$\mathbf{M} * \text{DCD}\ (AR) \leftarrow MD \tag{5.12}$$

The logic network for reading from a static memory, as was depicted in Chapter 3, is much the same as a busing network. For a hypothetical four-word memory, the read from memory operation is given by expression 5.13.

$$MD \leftarrow (\mathbf{M}\langle 0\rangle \wedge \text{DCD}[0]\ (AR)) \vee (\mathbf{M}\langle 1\rangle \wedge \text{DCD}[1]\ (AR))$$
$$\vee (\mathbf{M}\langle 2\rangle \wedge \text{DCD}[2]\ (AR)) \vee (\mathbf{M}\langle 3\rangle \wedge \text{DCD}[3]\ (AR)) \tag{5.13}$$

A shorter form is clearly necessary to represent this operation for a memory of practical size. Again, we fall back on the combinational logic unit notation introduced in Section 5.7. Since the two-level AND-OR network implementing expression 5.13 is in effect a busing network, we use the notation BUSFN to express a generalization of expression 5.13, as follows.

$$MD \leftarrow \text{BUSFN}(\mathbf{M};\ \text{DCD}\ (AR)) \tag{5.14}$$

A formal combinational logic unit description of BUSFN is given as follows.

```
CLUNIT: BUSFN(MEM; F) {L; K}
    INPUTS: MEM⟨K⟩[L]; F[K].
    OUTPUTS: WORDOUT[L].
    CTERMS: N⟨K⟩[L].
    BODY
            FOR I = 0 TO K − 1 CONSTRUCT
            N⟨I⟩ = MEM⟨I⟩ ∧ F[I]
            ROF;
            WORDOUT = ∨//N.
    END.
```

This description is straightforward and logically complete. If F is the output of an n input decoder, the fan-in of each of the OR gates is $2 \uparrow n$. We leave it as a problem for the reader to write a logically equivalent description of BUSFN that will eliminate the prospect of prohibitively large fan-ins.

Some users of AHPL, who might not be interested in hardware realizations but will use the language to assist in describing architecture, could become impatient with the number of characters in expression 5.14 for the READ operation. A shorter alternative, such as expression 5.15, which implies the activity of BUSFN and DCD, might be more convenient for some applications. You are welcome to use this form, realizing that it will have no meaning to the AHPL hardware compiler. It may be incorporated in some future versions of the function level simulator for AHPL.

$$MD \leftarrow \text{READ}(M; AR) \tag{5.15}$$

The memory write operation may be even less satisfying after the rules for the AHPL hardware compiler are more carefully detailed in Chapter 7. The hardware compiler would treat the outputs of the decoder as control variables. Clearly, this would not be intended if **M** were a large memory. In practice, designers have had no problem avoiding this ambiguity, because large memories are usually separate modules. No suitable alternative to the write notation given by expression 5.12, which explicitly uses the transfer operator, has come to mind.

Making up the remainder of this section are three design examples. These are included to illustrate two approaches to the manipulation of small data arrays. They also provide additional illustrations of complete module descriptions and will take advantage of the complete AHPL syntax as presented in Section 5.5.

Example 5.6

A simple machine tool controller is to be designed using a read-only memory to store sequences of tool positions. Eighteen-bit numbers are used to specify the tool position in three dimensions in a way that need not concern us here.

There are four possible sequences, any of which may be requested by an operator at any time. Each sequence is 256 words long. The system hardware must include an 18-bit register, *PR*, for storing the current tool position. The tool electronics continually monitor this register through three digital-to-analog converters. Communications with the operator is provided using a start-stop flip-flop, *ss*, and a 2-bit register, *SQR*, which specifies the desired sequence. The bit combinations 00, 01, 10, and 11 in *SQR* indicate that the sequence presently being used (if any) is *A*, *B*, *C*, or *D*, respectively. *SQR* is loaded from line *SEQ*. Setting the flip-flop *ss* to 1 will cause the controller to begin reading out the sequence specified by *SQR*. If the operator causes the flip-flop *ss* to be reset to 0, the controller responds by terminating the sequence in progress and storing a vector of 18 zeros in *PR*. On completing a sequence, the controller must reset *ss* and store zeros in *PR*. A synchronizing mechanism has been provided so that the contents of *ss* and *SQR* will never change during a controller clock pulse.

Solution

The only required storage registers in addition to those just described are a 10-bit address register for the read-only memory and the read-only memory itself. These devices may be represented by the vector *AR* and the matrix **ROM,** respectively. The complete register configuration is given in Fig. 5.21. The read-only memory (*ROM*) contains 1024 eighteen-bit words in all. Sequence *A* is stored in locations 0 to 255 (decimal). In decimal, the first addresses of sequences *B, C,* and *D* are 256, 512, and 768, respectively.

The frequency of the clock source has been established to be compatible with the required data rate of the tool and is, therefore, slower than the *ROM*. Thus a word can be read from the *ROM* in one clock period. The following is a module description of the machine tool controller.

MODULE: MACHINE TOOL CONTROLLER
   MEMORY: **ROM**⟨1024⟩[18]; *PR*[18];*AR*[10]; *SQR*[2]; *ss*.
   INPUTS: *SEQ*[2]; *start; stop.*
   OUTPUTS: *OPR*[18].
   CLUNITS: BUSFN[18] <: BUSFN{18;1024};
             DCD[1024] <: DECODER{10};
             INC[10] <: INCRMT{10}.

1 *SQR* ← *SEQ*
  → ($\overline{ss}$, *ss*)/(1, 2).
2 *AR* ← *SQR*[0], *SQR*[1], 8 ⊤ 0.
3 *PR* ← BUSFN (**ROM;** DCD(*AR*)).
4 *AR* ← INC(*AR*).
  → ((∧/*AR*[2:9] ∧ *ss*), $\overline{ss}$, $\overline{(∧/AR[2:9] ∧ ss)}$)/(5, 6, 3).
5 *ss* ← 0.
6 *PR* ← 18 ⊤ 0
  → (1).
END SEQUENCE
    ss * (*start* ∨ *stop*) ← (1!0) * (*start, stop*);
    OPR = *PR.*
END.

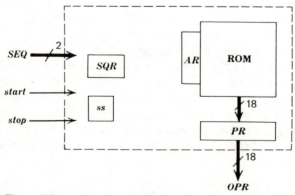

Figure 5.21. Machine tool controller, Example 5.6.

Step 1 provides a waiting loop to start operation. Notice the conditional transfer following END SEQUENCE, indicating that the *start* and *stop* lines are continuously monitored. Anytime the operator pulses the *start* line, the next clock pulse will set *ss,* and the following clock pulse will branch from step 1 to step 2 to start the sequence. Step 1 also gates the input *SEQ* into *SQR,* so that whenever the sequence starts, *SQR* will contain the number of the sequence most recently specified by the operator.

Depending on the two bits in *SQR,* the right side of step 2 will reduce to one of the four 10-bit vectors; 10 $\top$ 0, $\top$ 256, $\top$ 512, or $\top$768, which indicates whether the desired sequence is *A, B, C,* or *D.* For example,

$$10 \top 768 = 1, 1, 0, 0, 0, 0, 0, 0, 0, 0$$

Step 3 is an example of what will become a familiar read-from-memory notation. The contents of the address in **ROM** specified by *AR* are placed in *PR.*

Step 4 uses the combinational logic unit INC. This step causes 1 to be added to the binary number in *AR* so that the next word in sequence may be obtained from **ROM.** Step 4 also causes a branch to step 5 if a 256-word sequence has just been completed. Notice that although the contents of *AR* are being incremented by this same step, the branch is a function of the old value of *AR.* That is, when the last number is read from the **ROM** the last 8 bits of *AR* will all be 1's. Steps 5 and 6 clear *ss* and initialize the position information in *PR* before returning control to step 1 to await another user request. If step 4 encounters *ss* = 0 at any point, the process in progress is aborted by clearing *PR* at step 6 and control returns to step 1. ■

Example 5.6 illustrates one method of manipulating data in an array, that of treating the array as a memory and accessing individual words using an address register and an accompanying decoding network. A second commonly used approach is to treat the array as a black of shift registers and rotate the desired word to the output. A single upward rotation of the rows of a 16-row array is given by

$$\mathbf{M} \leftarrow (\mathbf{M}\langle 1:15\rangle \ ! \ \mathbf{M}\langle 0\rangle) \tag{5.16}$$

A downward rotation would be similarly expressed.

A design based on rotation of rows is closely related to a semirandom access memory and is, therefore, slower than a design based on the addressing of words in an array. Example 5.7 illustrates the use of row rotation of an array of limited size in an application in which speed is not a primary consideration.

Example 5.7

A digital module is to be designed to check for duplicate characters in a stream of 8-bit data characters. The circuit has input line data that will be 1 whenever a new data character is available on a vector of input lines *CHAR.* Transitions on these input lines are synchronized with the clock of the duplicate character checker. An output line *accept* must be provided on which a one-clock-period level will occur following acceptance of a data vector from the line **CHAR**. The only other output line is to be connected to a flip-flop *y that is to contain a 1 if and only if the most recently received character is a duplicate of any one of the 16 immediately previous characters*. The value of *y* should return to 0 when **accept** goes to 1, indicating reception of the next character. It may be assumed that the time interval between data characters will be ample to permit checking for duplicates serially.

Write a complete description of the character checker module including declarations and control sequence.

Solution

The duplicate character checker will be based on an array **SRM** of eight 16-bit shift registers. Also required are an 8-bit input data register **INR** and a 4-bit counter **CNT**. Each character received in **INR** is compared with each of the 16 characters stored in **SRM** as they are rotated to the top row. The number of rotations is monitored by **CNT**, causing the process to terminate after all 16 characters are checked. Following the last cycle of the checking operation, the character in **INR** is entered in **SRM**⟨15⟩ and the oldest word, which had previously been stored in **SRM**[0], is lost. As soon as a duplicate character is received, *y* is set to 1.

The following is an AHPL description of the duplicate character checker.

```
MODULE:   DUPLICATE CHARACTER CHECKER
          MEMORY: SRM⟨16⟩[8]; INR[8]; CNT[4]; y.
          INPUTS: CHAR[8]; data.
          OUTPUTS: accept; y.
          CLUNITS: INC[4] <: INCRMT{4}.

1   → (datā, data)/(1,2).
2 accept = 1; y ← 0;
    INR ← CHAR; CNT ← 4 ⊤ 0.
3 y * ∨/(INR ⊕ SRM⟨0⟩) ← 1;
    CNT ← INC(CNT);
    SRM ← (SRM⟨1:15⟩ ! SRM⟨0⟩);
    → (∧/CNT, ∧̄/CNT)/(4, 3).
4 SRM ← (SRM⟨1:15⟩ ! INR);
    → (1).
END SEQUENCE
END.                                          ∎
```

As a final example of memory manipulation using AHPL, let us consider a case where the memory array is external to the module being described. Fig. 3.19 showed the internal details of a 8-bit × 1 dynamic RAM. It was demonstrated how read and write operations for 1 data bit could be accomplished in response to control signals on lines **dread** and **dwrite**. It was necessary to refresh all data at least once each millisecond. This was accomplished by exciting line, **refresh,** and counting the row address lines through all possible (in that case four) address combinations. The memory

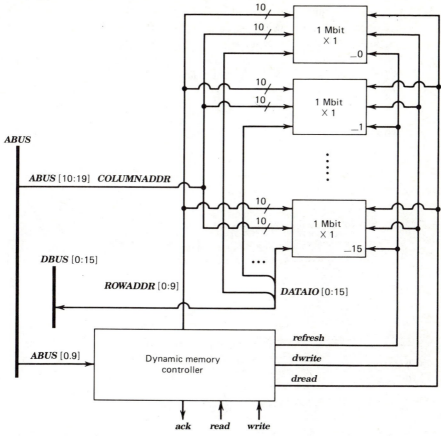

Figure 5.22. Control of dynamic RAM.

shown in Fig. 5.22 is composed of 16 much larger dynamic RAM chips that function in the same way. Now there are 10 row address lines and 10 column address lines. It remains necessary to count through all $2 \uparrow 10$ row addresses at least once each millisecond for refresh.

Example 5.8

Write the AHPL description of the controller for the 1 megabit $\times$ 16 dynamic RAM shown in Fig. 5.22. The refresh interval must not exceed 1 msec. The clock rate is 5 MHz. Note that the row address multiplexer is now part of the controller module instead of in the individual memory parts, as might have been inferred from Fig. 3.19.

Solution

In the AHPL description of the memory controller that follows, the high-order half of the address bus is routed to the row address lines of the memory chips for a read or write operation. Such an operation is precluded by step 1, when it is time to refresh.

When refresh is taking place, the output of the counter, **REFCNT,** is connected to these address lines. One clock period is used in the refreshing of each row of 1024 bits. A counter, **REFINTVL,** is provided to count continuously through the refresh interval. When this counter reaches its maximum value, a flip-flop, *startref,* which will cause refresh to begin as soon as control reaches step 1, is set. The period of this 12-bit counter is given by

$$\text{Refresh interval} = \frac{2^{12}}{5 \times 10^6} \approx 0.8\text{msec}$$

Because $2^{10}/(5 \times 10^6) = 0.2\text{msec}$ is required to refresh all rows of each chip, 25% of the available memory time is used up by refresh.

```
MODULE:     DYMEMCONTROL.
INPUTS:     read; write; ADBUS[20].
OUTPUTS:    dread; refresh; dwrite; ack; ROWADDR[10].
MEMORY:     REFRCNT[10]; REFINTVL[12]; startref.
COMBUS:     DBUS[16].
CLUNITS:    INCA[10] <: INCRMT{10};
            INCB[12] <: INCRMT{12}.
```

1 → (*read* ∧ $\overline{startref}$, *write* ∧ $\overline{startref}$, *startref*)/(2, 3, 4).
2 **ROWADDR** = **ADBUS**[0:9]; *dread* = 1;
  ack = 1;
  → (1).
3 **ROWADDR** = **ADBUS**[0:9]; *dwrite = 1; ack* = 1;
  → (1).
4 **REFCNT** ← 10 ⊤ 0.
5 *refresh = 1;* **REFCNT** ← INCA(**REFCNT**); **ROWADDR** = **REFCNT;**
  startref ← 0;
  → (∧ /**REFCNT**, ∧ /**REFCNT**)/(5, 1).
END SEQUENCE
REINTVL ← INCB(**REFINTVL**);
startref ∗ ∧/**REFINTVL** ← 1.
END.

5.9 A Timing Refinement

Often, a flowchart of a system will be developed in such a way that operations that can be accomplished at the same time or for which timing is not critical are represented by separate steps. A second pass through the AHPL sequence may reveal potential changes that could both speed up its execution and save control flip-flops. Interrelated branches can make this process more difficult than one of merely combining steps. Often, the hoped-for timing improvements can be accomplished using conditional transfers, as discussed in Section 4.7. Another approach we shall explore in this section is that of eliminating the delay associated with an individual step in the control sequence. We shall specify this in AHPL by appending the comment NO DELAY to the action portion of the step.

The one-clock-period delay associated with an AHPL step may be eliminated if neither the branch portion nor the action portion is dependent on the result of a transfer in an immediately preceding step and if such action will not destroy the proper timing relationship on input and output lines connected to other modules. In the following three-step sequence, a time delay is unnecessary at step 2, since the transfer uses only information available prior to the previous step.

1
  $\rightarrow (\bar{a})/(1).$
2 $A \leftarrow B$ NO DELAY
3 $C \leftarrow X \vee A.$

The delay associated with step 3 cannot be eliminated, since this step depends on the result of step 2. A realization of the control unit for this three-step partial sequence is illustrated in Fig. 5.23a. From the figure, it can be seen that step 2 is accomplished during the last clock period for which control remains in step 1. The following two-step sequence with a conditional transfer associated with step 1 will provide timing identical to that specified by Fig. 5.23a.

1 $A * \underline{a} \leftarrow B;$
  $\rightarrow (\bar{a})/(1).$
2 $C \leftarrow X \vee A.$

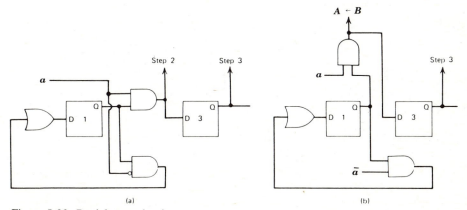

Figure 5.23. Partial control unit.

A realization of this sequence is given in Fig. 5.23b. For this simple case, the two AHPL sequences result in identical control units. This will not always be so, as the number of control gates compiled by a conditional transfer step will depend on the designer's facility with multiple-output combinational logic minimization.

The advantage of the NO DELAY notation over that of the conditional transfer lies in the ease of application. Often, it will not be worthwhile to undertake the analysis necessary to reformulate a sequence in terms of conditional transfers even though the result might be more compact. This would be particularly true in the case of complicated systems.

Example 5.9

A peripheral equipment will often be required to output signals on a number of control lines as a function of stored data. It is often convenient to interrogate this data and generate the control signals sequentially even in cases where there is no precise timing relation between the output signals. Such is the case for the following control sequence. It was subsequently discovered that none of steps 2, 3, 4, and 5 required separate clock periods for execution, so that these steps are marked NO DELAY.

<table>
<tr><td>1</td><td></td><td></td></tr>
<tr><td></td><td>$\rightarrow (\bar{a})/(1)$.</td><td></td></tr>
<tr><td>2</td><td>***out1*** $= 1$;</td><td>NO DELAY</td></tr>
<tr><td></td><td>$\rightarrow (\boldsymbol{B}[0], \boldsymbol{B}[1], \overline{\boldsymbol{B}[0] \vee \boldsymbol{B}[1]})/(3,4,5)$.</td><td></td></tr>
<tr><td>3</td><td>***out2*** $= 1$.</td><td>NO DELAY</td></tr>
<tr><td>4</td><td>***out3*** $= 1$.</td><td>NO DELAY</td></tr>
<tr><td>5</td><td>$\boldsymbol{A} \leftarrow \boldsymbol{X}$.</td><td>NO DELAY</td></tr>
<tr><td>6</td><td>$\boldsymbol{BUS} = \boldsymbol{A};$</td><td></td></tr>
<tr><td></td><td>$\boldsymbol{B} \leftarrow \boldsymbol{BUS}[4:7], \boldsymbol{BUS}[0:3]; \rightarrow (1)$.</td><td></td></tr>
</table>

A realization of the control unit corresponding to this sequence is given in Fig. 5.24. Notice that delay flip-flops are required for steps 1 and 6. The former is necessary

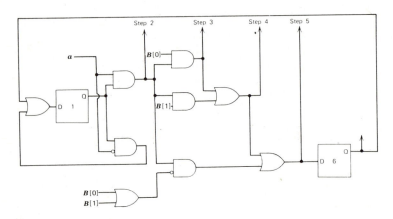

Figure 5.24. Realization of NO DELAY steps.

to hold control at one point while waiting for control input *a* to go to 1. The latter establishes a bus route whose argument is dependent on the result of step 5.

A two-step sequence equivalent to the one given here can be written using conditional transfers. We leave it as a problem for you to develop and obtain a realization of such a sequence.

5.10 Conclusions

We have now presented most of AHPL along with the corresponding hardware realization. We have provided a number of small design examples to assist you in developing a facility for the use of the design language. We are now ready to consider more complex and more important design examples. The remainder of the book will be devoted to digital computer systems and their related peripheral equipment.

Problems

Each of Problems 5.1 through 5.9 consists of two or more expressions that may or may not be valid AHPL. In each case, indicate if the expression is invalid or compute the result if it is valid AHPL. The operands used in all these expressions are given as follows.

$$U = (1,1,1,0); V = (1,0,0,1); W = (1,0,1)$$

$$N = \begin{bmatrix} 101 \\ 110 \\ 011 \\ 111 \end{bmatrix} \text{ and } x = 5; y = 2, z = -1 \text{ and } a = b = c = 1$$

5.1   (a) $U \oplus V$ (b) $U \wedge x$

5.2   (a) $U \wedge W$ (b) $N \wedge a$

5.3   (a) $(x < z)$ (b) $(z > W)$

5.4   (a) $\wedge/W$ (b) $\oplus/W$

5.5   (a) $\vee//N$ (b) $\wedge/N$ (c) U, N

5.6   (a) $(a,b,c)[1:2]$ (b) W/N (c) $N ! W$

5.7   (a) $\oplus//N$ (b) U, V (c) $U ! V$

5.8   (a) $(4 \top 5) \oplus W$ (b) $7 \top (2 \uparrow x)$

5.9   (a) $N\langle 3\rangle[0:1]$ (b) $N\langle 4\rangle[1:3]$

5.10   Add the necessary declarations and other syntax formalities to the control sequence given for the digital system developed in Example 4.3 to form a complete AHPL module description. Consider the memory to be external to the module.

5.11   Add the necessary declarations to the control sequence derived in Problem 4.16 and make other syntax modifications as required to obtain a complete module description of the network given in Fig. P4.16.

5.12   Which of the following are legitimate AHPL action statements? Register $A[2]$ has two flip-flops, $B[3]$ and $C[3]$ have three, $X[2]$ is a vector of two input lines, a and b are individual inputs, and BUS is a 3-bit bus.
(a) $b \leftarrow a$
(b) $B \leftarrow ((A, a) \,!\, (A, b)) * (C[0], \overline{C[0]})$
(c) $(A[0], B[0:1]) * a \leftarrow C$
(d) $BUS \leftarrow C$
(e) $B \leftarrow BUS \oplus C$
(f) $BUS = 0, 1, 0;$
      $C \leftarrow BUS$
(g) $C \leftarrow 4 \top 0$
(h) $B \leftarrow (B \oplus (A, a)) \oplus C$
(i) $a * B \leftarrow C$
(j) $B * a \leftarrow X, b$
(k) $\wedge/B, A \leftarrow C$
(l) $A, C[0] \leftarrow \text{INC}(B)$
(m) $\text{INC}(A \leftarrow X$
(n) $C \leftarrow (\overline{C} \,!\, B) * \text{INC}(X);$
      $(B \,!\, C) * (A[0], A[1]) \leftarrow X, a$

5.13   Construct a logic block diagram (i.e., a network wiring diagram) of all hardware specified by the following module and combinational logic unit description. Use D flip-flops.

```
MODULE:     SAMPLE.
MEMORY:     A[2].
INPUTS:     X[2]; a.
OUTPUTS:    z.
CLUNITS:    FUNC[2] <: LOGIC.
1     A ← X;
          → (a)/(1).
2     A * a ← FUNC(A; X); → (1).
```

ENDSEQUENCE
$$z = \wedge/A.$$
END.
CLUNIT: LOGIC($B; Y$).
INPUTS: $B[2]$; $Y[2]$.
OUTPUTS: $NETOUT[2]$.
CTERMS: $r; s$.
BODY
$r = B[0] \vee Y[0]$;
$s = B[1] \wedge Y[1]$;
$NETOUT[0] = r \wedge B[1]$;
$NETOUT[1] = s \vee B[0]$.
END.

5.14 A combinational logic priority network has a vector of six input wires, $X[6]$, and a vector of six output wires, $PRI[6]$. An output $PRI[j]$ is to be 1 if and only if $X[j] = 1$ and each $X[i] = 0$ for all $i < j$. Write an AHPL combinational logic unit description for this 6-bit priority network.

5.15 (a) Write a modified version of the combinational logic unit description of Problem 5.14 so that PRI can be declared for input vectors, $X[n]$, of any length n.
(b) Write the complete AHPL module description of a module that has no function other than to compute a priority vector from an input vector, $X[8]$, and to store this priority vector in a register, $R[8]$, each time a 1 appears on input line *storepri*. The outputs of R are permanently connected to a module output vector, $Z[8]$. An 8-bit instance of the priority network described in part (a) is to be declared.

5.16 Manually execute the steps of the hardware compiler to generate the logic block diagram of a 4-bit version of the incrementer described in Example 5.4.

5.17 Write a combinational logic unit description similar to that of Example 5.4 for a decrementer. When used in a module description, the decrementer will typically be declared DEC[I].

5.18 Write a combinational logic unit description for a logic function, LARGER, which will have two I-bit vector arguments, A and B. The network is to have two outputs, $LARGER[2]$, such that

$$LARGER = 0, 1 \text{ if } \perp A > \perp B$$

$$LARGER = 1, 0 \text{ if } \perp A < \perp B$$

$$LARGER = 0, 0 \text{ if } \perp A = \perp B$$

The symbol $\perp$ is borrowed from APL and is the inverse of the binary encode operation. That is, $\perp A$ yields the decimal equivalent of the binary number represented by A.

5.19 (a) Write a combinational logic unit description of the 3-bit decoder used in Fig. 3.14.
(b) Write a combinational logic unit description of the 6-bit decoder shown in Fig. 3.14 that declares the 3-bit decoder of part (a).
(c) Write a combinational logic unit description of the 12-bit decoder of Fig. 3.14 that declares the 6-bit decoder of part (b).

5.20 Write a complete AHPL module description of a simple device that will generate a periodic output on the only output line z. If the only input x is 1, the output should be repetitively five 0's followed by three 1's. If $x = 0$, the output should be repetitively six 0's followed by two 1's. Any phase relationship to an absolute time reference is immaterial, and the transient output following a change on x does not matter. Only one register, a 3-bit counter $CNT[3]$, is needed.

5.21 Write a complete AHPL module description of a hardware "last-in first-out" stack. The stack module will have control lines, **push** and **pop**, as inputs and will be connected to a 16 bit data bus called **DBUS**. Immediately following each 0 to 1 transition on line **push**, the vector currently on **DBUS** is to be pushed on the stack. A signal on line **pop** will cause the current top of the stack to be connected to the **DBUS** where it will remain until **pop** returns to 0. At the conclusion of the pop activity, the top vector is discarded and the rest of the stack is moved up. The stack is to be implemented using an array, **M**(256)[16] declared within the module and treated as a RAM, and other registers as required. **Push** and **pop** will never be 1 simultaneously.

5.22 Repeat Problem 5.21 except that the array **M** is to be wired to implement row-to-row shifts in both directions.

5.23 Rewrite the AHPL description of the dynamic memory controller of Example 5.8 so that the refresh of rows and responses to read and write operations can be alternated. Justification of this approach is that much of the refresh might be accomplished while the CPU is active internally with no need for memory reference. The need to refresh the entire memory at least once each millisecond still stands. The clock frequency remains 5 MHz.

5.24 Let N be a memory array consisting of 2^{10} eighteen-bit words. Write an AHPL sequence that will accomplish economically a search on this array similar to that described in Example 5.7. Let $A[10]$ be the 10-bit register specifying the address of a read or write operation on **N** and declare other registers as needed. If $n + 1$ is the number of words in **N** in which the first 3 bits are 1's, then these words should be stored in $N\langle 0:n \rangle$ at the conclusion of the process. Word $n + 1$ should consist of all zeros, and the contents of the remaining $2^{10} - n - 2$ words may be considered immaterial.

5.25 Modify the AHPL module description of the machine tool controller of Example 5.4 to incorporate the following improvements:
   (a) The system will stop and wait for the start of a new sequence if $\top(2^{18} - 1)$ is encountered in **PR**.
   (b) Expand the memory to 2048 words so that eight 256-word sequences can be included.

5.26 A digital communications buffer contains 32 eighteen-bit words. The buffer has its own control unit. Part of the function of the buffer is to check for longitudinal parity (i.e., parity over the 32 bits in each bit position of the word). If a parity error in one of the 18-bit positions is found, a flip-flop *pf* is to be set to 1. Write a partial control sequence in AHPL that accomplishes this parity check in an economical sequential manner. Declare memory elements as required. Consider using an array composed of eighteen 32-bit shift registers.

5.27 Let **M** be a memory consisting of 1024 eighteen-bit words with a 10-bit memory address register *AR*. Write an AHPL control sequence that will compute $\vee//\wedge/\mathbf{M}$ in an economical sequential manner.

5.28 A random sequence generator is driven by an external clock source. This generator provides a level, *z,* which is constant between clock pulses, and may or may not change, on a random basis, when triggered by a clock pulse or leading edge of a one-period level. A special-purpose computer is to be designed employing a 1-MHz clock. This computer is to provide an output clock to drive the random process at a frequency of 1 kHz. The computer must also compute the number of level changes in the random process each second. The computer must also compute and display the average number of level changes per second over the first 2^8 sec following the depression of its start button. Write in AHPL a complete module description of this special-purpose computer. Declare counters and other registers as required. Accomplish division by shifting.

5.29 Two small memory arrays, **M** and **N,** each consisting of 256 eighteen-bit words form part of a special-purpose digital system. The arrays have memory address registers *ARM* and *ARN,* respectively. At the beginning of a partial control sequence, **M** contains 256 random numbers, which are to be transferred to **N** and arranged in the order of magnitude. The largest is to be placed in $\mathbf{N}\langle 0 \rangle$. Write a partial AHPL control sequence that will accomplish this operation. Declare additional registers as required. Make use of the combinational logic unit description *LARGER* defined in Problem 5.18.

5.30   Can the comment NO DELAY be added to any of the steps in the control unit of Example 5.1? Why or why not? Is there excess delay anywhere in the control sequence for Example 5.6?

5.31   Write a two-step control sequence equivalent to the sequence of Example 5.9 by using conditional transfers to eliminate the steps designated NO DELAY. Obtain a complete logic block diagram of the corresponding control unit. Compare the number of gates with the nine gates of Fig. 5.24. Which is the most economical realization? Can the more costly circuit be minimized through Boolean manipulation to compare more favorably?

References

1. K. E. Iverson, *A Programming Language,* Wiley, New York, 1962.
2. H. Hellerman, *Digital System Principles,* 2nd ed., McGraw–Hill, New York, 1973.
3. T. D. Friedman and S. C. Yang, "Methods Used in Automatic Logic Design Generator (ALERT)," *IEEE Trans. Computers,* Sept. 1969, p. 593.
4. H. Schoor, "Computer Aided Digital System Design and Analysis Using a Register Transfer Language," *IEEE Trans. Electronic Computers,* Dec. 1964, pp. 730–737.
5. L. Gilman and A. J. Rose, APL an Interactive Approach, 2nd ed., Wiley, New York, 1975.
6. F. J. Hill, "Introducing AHPL," *Computer,* Dec. 1974, pp. 28–30.
7. F. J. Hill and G. R. Peterson, *Introduction to Switching Theory and Logical Design,* 3rd ed., Wiley, New York, 1981.
8. J. R. Duley and D. L. Dietmeyer, "A Digital System Design Language (DDL)," *IEEE Transactions on Computers,* Vol. C-17, Sept. 1968, pp. 850–861.
9. R. Piloty, "Segmentation Constructs of RTS III, A Computer Hardware Description Language Based on CDL," *Proceedings of the 1975 International Symposium on Design Languages and Their Applications,* New York, Sept. 3–5.
10. R. Piloty, et al., *CONLAN Report,* Springer-Verlag, Berlin, 1983.
11. *VHDL Version 7.2 Users Manual,* Intermetrics, Bethesda, Md., 1985.
12. *VHDL Version 7.2 Language Reference Manual,* Intermetrics, Bethesda, Md., 1985.
13. F. J. Hill, "Structure Specification with a Procedural Hardware Description Language," *IEEE Transactions on Computers,* Feb. 1981, pp. 157–161.
14. R. E. Swanson, Z. Navabi, and F. J. Hill, "An AHPL Compiler/Simulator System," *Proceedings Sixth Texas Conference on Computing Systems,* Nov. 1977.
15. D. G. Gajski, "The Structure of a Silicon Compiler," *Proceedings IEEE International Conference on Circuits and Computers,* New York, Sept. 1982, p. 272.
16. F. J. Hill, et al., "Hardware Compilation from an RTL to a Storage Logic Array Target," *IEEE Transactions on CAD,* July 1984, pp. 208–217.

Machine Organization and Hardware Programs

6.1 Introduction

In Chapter 5, we introduced a new language, AHPL, with the justification that computer hardware could be described in terms of this language. In Chapter 2, we described the architecture of a digital computer, RIC, that provides a representative example of a computer in the microcomputer/minicomputer category. In this chapter, we start the process of developing a hardware implementation of this architecture. The design will initially be set forth in the form of a hardware description in AHPL. In this chapter, we shall be working somewhere between the architecture level and the implementation level, as defined in Section 2.1. The architecture of the machine, that is, the description of the machine as seen by the programmer, was not totally completed in Chapter 2, and we shall add more detailed specifications in this chapter. At the same time, we shall stop short of the detailed description of the hardware implied by the definition of implementation in Chapter 2. Translation of the AHPL descriptions into hardware networks must wait until Chapter 7.

We shall continue to use RIC as the vehicle to illustrate what is actually a completely general procedure. Because RIC is reasonably simple, a nearly complete design can be presented without burdening you with detail. There are, however, many important features of larger computers that are not found in RIC. AHPL routines describing many of these features will be presented in later chapters. Having seen the details of a complete computer tied together in Chapters 6 and 7, you should be able to visualize the incorporation of these individual features into the overall design of larger computers.

We believe that AHPL is an excellent vehicle for teaching computer organization and is also a practical design language. The latter belief is supported by the fact that AHPL has been adopted as a design tool by a significant number of firms in the computer area since the publication of the first two editions of this book. We have already shown some correspondences between AHPL conventions and digital hardware. We shall continue this in Chapter 7, to show how a complete AHPL description of a computer can be directly translated into a description of the corresponding hardware. This process can be done automatically, and programs have been written to compile AHPL programs, that is, to translate them into hardware form. But our basic goal is to provide you with the tools required to perform the translation directly, without computer aid. Having progressed to this point, you will have a basic understanding of computer organization and design.

6.2   Basic Organization of RIC

The instruction set and the main operating registers of RIC were specified in Chapter 2. You will recall that there were four *operating registers:* the accumulator, *AC;* the index register, *IX;* the stack pointer; *SP;* and the status register, *SR.* We use the term operating register to refer to registers to which the programmer has access through instructions that specifically modify or store the contents of these registers. We also have the program counter, *PC,* which is not usually considered an operating register in the same sense as are the other registers just named. The program counter is certainly affected by branch and jump commands, but we do not have load and store commands for the program counter.

There are three additional registers that were not mentioned in Chapter 2. One is the instruction register, *IR.* Whenever a new instruction is fetched, it moves from memory to *IR,* where it is available for decoding and interpretation. Although it is used in the execution of every instruction, it is not considered an operating register since there are no instructions that specifically modify *IR.* We also need two registers in association with the memory; the memory data register, *MD,* and the memory address register, *MA.* On a memory read cycle, the address of the desired word is first loaded into *MA,* and the word stored at that location is then read into *MD,* from whence it is available to be processed in whatever manner may be desired. For a memory write operation, the address is loaded into *MA,* the word to be stored is loaded into *MD,* and then stored at the addressed location.

Given the instruction set and the register set, the next step is to specify the register interconnections and ALU capabilities necessary to realize the instruction set. Some readers may wonder how we know, "in advance," that a certain organization is required. The answer is that one usually does not. The experienced designer may be able to make a very accurate estimate of the requirements, but this is not necessary. As we shall see, it is quite practical to start with a very minimal specification, gradually expanding and refining the design as our understanding of the required sequence of operations increases.

The arithmetic-logical unit (ALU) contains the various combinational logic circuits that perform the required operations on the contents of the various registers. Given the instruction set specified in Chapter 2, we can anticipate that the ALU will include an adder, complementing logic, AND, OR, and XOR logic, and shift logic. Further development of the design may indicate the need for additional capabilities, but we need not worry about that now. Indeed, for the present we shall simply assume that the ALU will include whatever logic capabilities are needed and defer consideration of its detailed design until later.

Because the instruction set includes 32-bit arithmetic and logical operations, the ALU must have two 32-bit inputs and one 33-bit output. The execution of such instructions as AND and ADD will require that *AC* be connected to one ALU input and *MD* to the other. Assuming we wish to use the same adder for indexing, we will need to connect *IR* to one ALU input and *IX* to the other, and the branch and stack instructions will require connection of *PC* and *SP* to the ALU. We saw in Chapter 4 that the use of buses is appropriate when a number of registers need to be connected to one or more targets, or where it is desired to use one combinational logic unit with several sets of arguments. We shall use two buses, *ABUS* and *BBUS,* to provide for interconnections between the two ALU inputs and the various registers. In a similar manner, we can see that it will be necessary to route the many output vectors from the ALU to almost any register. For this purpose, we shall provide a third bus, *OBUS.* This "three-bus" structure is virtually standard in computers, as it derives naturally from the need to perform operations that combine two operands to produce a single

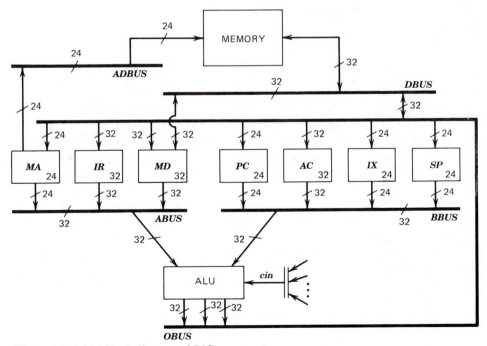

Figure 6.1. Initial block diagram of RIC.

result. Actually, one more bus is shown in Fig. 6.1, although it is not easily identifiable as such. This is the carry input to the ALU, *cin,* which is effectively a 1-bit bus supplying a third argument to the adder within the ALU. Several possible sources may be connected to *cin.*

It is also necessary to consider the connections between the CPU and the memory. The CPU must be able to send addresses and data to the memory and receive data from the memory. We noted previously that addresses will normally pass through a single register, *MA.* Even though we see no obvious need for multiple register connections to the address lines, we find it convenient to specify an additional bus, *ADBUS,* to provide the address path between the CPU module and the memory module. A bidirectional data bus, *DBUS,* is provided as the data path between RIC and memory. During a read operation the memory module will connect the desired data to the *DBUS,* which can then be clocked into the argument register, *MD,* by RIC. During a write operation, RIC can connect the output of *MD* to *DBUS.* The hardware implementation of this bidirectional *DBUS* was discussed in Section 4.4. Based on these various considerations, we shall specify an initial organization of the CPU and connections to memory as shown in Fig. 6.1. Note that *SR* is not shown in this diagram. It is not a register in the usual sense since the flags making up *SR* are quite independent, and it is not clear now just how they fit into the bus structure. Let us emphasize again, this is just a "first pass" at the internal organization. It will certainly have to be refined and expanded as we proceed with the design process, but we have to start somewhere.

6.3 Register Transfers

The execution of an instruction by a computer such as RIC consists of a series of transfers of data from register to register, with the data being processed by the ALU as required during the transfer operations. Several such register transfers will be required to accomplish a single machine language instruction such as MVT.

As discussed in Chapter 4, when registers are interconnected by buses, the execution of a single register transfer requires the generation of several control signals, to connect the various buses and registers. For the RIC organization specified earlier, signals must be generated to determine which registers are placed on the buses, and to determine which ALU output is gated into which register. For example, a basic operation is the AND transfer, in which the contents of *MD* and *AC* are ANDed and the result is placed in *AC.* The control signals and interconnections involved in this transfer are depicted in Fig. 6.2.

According to the syntax presented in Chapter 5, the AHPL step describing this AND operation is written as follows

$$ABUS = MD; BBUS = AC;$$
$$OBUS = ABUS \wedge BBUS; AC \leftarrow OBUS.$$

Given the RIC bus organization, much of the notation in the preceding register-transfer description would be repeated in every transfer statement. Because each register drives

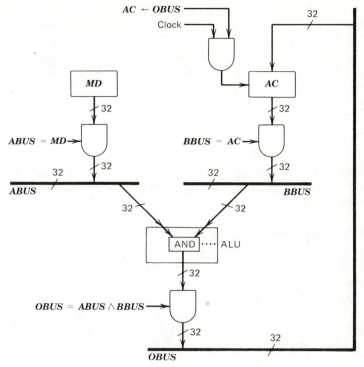

Figure 6.2. Control of AND transfer.

only one bus, the inputs to the ALU are always **ABUS** and **BBUS** and the input bus routings are known. Therefore, in discussions of RIC we shall use an abbreviated form of register transfer statement, for example,

$$AC \leftarrow MD \wedge AC$$

with the register on the **ABUS** listed first for two-operand transfers.

This form of abbreviated notation is possible in the case of single, unconditional transfers, where there generally is no ambiguity in determining the bus connections required. We choose to use abbreviated forms in this chapter so that you may more easily follow the basic function of RIC. One special precaution is that we must not specify an operation that is impossible because of the bus connections. For example,

$$AC \leftarrow AC \wedge IX$$

is impossible, because **AC** and **IX** are both on the **BBUS**. In cases in which there is any possible ambiguity, such as in conditional transfers where the bus connections might depend on the conditions, the bus routing will be fully specified.

The memory read and write operations for RIC are quite different from normal register transfers, as they involve transfers between two separate modules, the ALU and the memory. Discussion on complete notation for transfers between modules will be delayed to Chapter 9, and we shall use a simplified notation for memory read and write operations until that time. A memory read operation requires that the address be placed on the *ADBUS* and the corresponding word be read from the *DBUS*. We shall assume a synchronous memory that returns a word on the *DBUS* in the same clock period in which the address is placed on *ADBUS*, and the control line, *read*, is set to 1. Accordingly, the notation for a memory read operation will be

$$ADBUS = MA; read = 1; MD \leftarrow DBUS$$

A memory write operation will likewise be carried out in one clock period, provided that the *write* line is set to 1 at the same time that the address is placed on *ADBUS* and the word to be written is placed on *DBUS*. The notation for a memory write operation will be

$$ADBUS = MA; write = 1; DBUS = MD.$$

Note carefully that these statements do not describe the actual operations in the memory module. We cannot specify, in the description of one module, what happens in another module. These statements specify the necessary connections to the buses and lines between the two modules to achieve the desired results. A complete description of the system would also include a description of a memory module operating in a manner consistent with assumptions we have made in writing these read and write statements.

6.4 Fetch and Address Cycles

We are now ready to proceed with the first step in the design of a control unit for RIC, the writing of a control sequence. This will be an AHPL program consisting of routines to execute the RIC instructions. The complete sequence of operations required to carry out a single instruction will be referred to as an *instruction cycle*. Each instruction cycle will consist of at least two parts, a *fetch cycle* and an *execute cycle*. If the instruction includes an address, there will be one or more *address cycles*. In the fetch cycle, a new instruction is fetched from memory. The address, if any, will be processed in the address cycles, as required by the address mode. The operations required by that instruction are then carried out in the execute cycle.

During the fetch cycle, the contents of the program counter, *PC*, are first shifted to the memory address register, *MA*, and *PC* is incremented in preparation for the next instruction fetch. The memory executes a read operation, leaving the addressed word in *MD*. The instruction is then transferred from *MD* to *IR*. These steps of the fetch cycle, which are common to all instructions, are shown here.

1    $MA \leftarrow PC.$
2    $ADBUS = MA; MD \leftarrow DBUS; read = 1; PC \leftarrow INC(PC).$
3    $IR \leftarrow MD.$

Notice that there are two separate operations in step 2. This is possible because the read from memory operation does not use the internal bus structure. The **PC** can be routed to the **BBUS** and the incremented **BBUS** returned to **PC** through the **OBUS** at the same time the contents of the external **DBUS** are clocked into **MD**.

The instruction is now in **IR**. But what kind of an instruction is it, 32-bit or two 16-bit? To answer this question, we use a branch condition at step 4 to test bit 4, which according to Fig. 2.2 indicates whether or not the instruction is 32-bit.

4   → ($\overline{IR[4]}$)/(16-bit instruction sequence).

If **IR**[4] = 0, control branches to an as yet unnumbered step that will start the sequence for 16-bit instructions.

If control reaches step 5, the instruction is identified as a 32-bit instruction, but there are two basic types of 32-bit instructions. For branch instructions, we have a 16-bit opcode and a 16-bit displacement. For all other 32-bit instructions, we have an 8-bit op code (including address mode bits) and a 24-bit address. Fig. 2.9 tells us that IR[0:3] = 0111 specifies a branch instruction. Step 5 tests these bits to branch to a sequence to implement branch instructions.

5   NO DELAY
       → ($\overline{IR[0]} \wedge IR[1] \wedge IR[2] \wedge IR[3]$)/(Branch sequence).

Note that this is a NO DELAY step. This is possible since **IR** was loaded at step 3 and the delay at step 4 allows for propagation of the new values of **IR** through all the branch logic, so that all subsequent branches on **IR** can be NO DELAY steps. Indeed, step 4 and subsequent branches on **IR** could be combined into a single complex branch statement. We have chosen to separate them to clarify the logic involved.

If control reaches step 6, we know we have a 32-bit instruction with address and we are ready to start the address cycles. Unless, of course, the "address" is not an address at all but an immediate address, that is, an operand. Consistent with Fig. 2.4 step 6 tests **IR**[5] to identify this case. Step 7 accomplishes the sign extension of the 24 bits of immediate data available in **MD** to 32 bits and branches to step 22, where actual execution is accomplished for all instructions for which immediate addressing is valid.

6   NO DELAY
       → ($\overline{IR[5]}$)/(8).
7    $MD[0:7] \leftarrow \overline{(8 \top 0)} \wedge MD[8]$;
       → (22).

The sequencing through the address cycles will depend on the address mode. Step 8 tests for indirect addressing.

8   NO DELAY
       → ($\overline{IR[7]}$)/(11).

If *IR*[7] = 1, we enter the indirect address cycle at step 9, which moves the address portion of the instruction from *MD* to *MA*. The address could just as well have been taken from *IR,* but we have used *MD* for consistency with later steps. Step 10 then reads the indirect address to *MD*.

> 9   *MA* ← *MD*[8:31].
> 10   *ADBUS* = *MA; MD* ← *DBUS; read* = 1.

Step 11 delivers the *effective address,* that is, the actual address that will be used to access the operand, to *MA*. This could be broken up into several steps, but we have used a conditional transfer to shorten the sequence. If *IR*[6] = 0, the address is moved directly from *MD* to *MA*. If *IR*[6] = 1, the address is indexed before being moved to *MA*.

> 11   *MA* ← (*MD*[8:31] ! ADD[1:24](*MD*[8:31]; *IX*)) * ($\overline{IR[6]}$, *IR*[6]).
> 12   Start of execute cycle . . .

Example 6.1

It was indicated in Section 6.3 that AHPL steps would be abbreviated and that specific bus connections would not be given, if only one possible set of connections could be implied by the abbreviated step. This assertion is true for step 11, but using the 32-bit busing structure forces some changes in the expression. Rewrite step 11 making the bus connections explicit.

Solution

A step 11 that will not cause the hardware compiler to generate unnecessary implicit buses is given as follows. Consistent with Fig. 6.1, *MD* and *IX* are routed to the adder through the *ABUS* and *BBUS,* respectively. There is no carry input, so the 1-bit carry bus, *cin,* must be connected to 0.

> 11   *ABUS* = *MD; BBUS* = 8 ⊤ 0,*IX; cin* = 0;
>   *OBUS* = (*ABUS* ! ADD[1:32](*ABUS; BBUS; cin*)) * ($\overline{IR[6]}$, *IR*[6]);
>   *MA* ← *OBUS*[8:31].

6.5   Execute Cycles for Addressed Instructions

If the opcode of the instruction is such that we have reached step 12, we know that we have one of 15 addressed instructions to execute, with the effective address to be used in the instruction in *MA*. At this point, we could include a 15-way branch to separate sequences for each of the instructions, but the more common approach is to divide the instructions into categories based on various common features. To implement the various branches, we first need to know the specific opcodes for the various instructions. These are listed for the first time in Fig. 6.3.

Operation	Opcode ($IR[0:3]$)
SBC	0 0 0 0
SUB	0 0 0 1
ADC	0 1 0 0
ADD	0 1 0 1
ORA	1 0 0 0
AND	1 0 0 1
XOR	1 0 1 0
MVT	0 0 1 0
MVF	0 1 1 0
CMP	0 0 1 1
BIT	1 0 1 1
INC	1 1 0 0
DEC	1 1 0 1
JSR	1 1 1 0
JMP	1 1 1 1

Figure 6.3. Opcodes for addressed instructions.

First, from the other instructions we separate JMP and JSR, for which the address is not used to access memory but is transferred to *PC* as the address of the next instruction. Recalling that step 5 separated opcode 0111 for the branch sequence, we see that $IR[1:3] = 111$ is enough to identify the JMP command. This is shown in Fig. 6.4a, where we show the various opcodes on a Karnaugh map. Note that the Boolean function in step 12 isolates BRA and JMP, but BRA is effectively a "don't care," since it has already been separated.

12   NO DELAY
        $\rightarrow (\wedge/IR[1:3])/(14)$.
13      $PC \leftarrow MA$;
        $\rightarrow (1)$.

If the instruction is not a JMP, control branches to step 14. Step 13 executes JMP by transferring the effective address to *PC* and branching back to step 1 to fetch the new instruction. At step 14, control separates for execution of the JSR instruction. The final subroutine address (after possible indexing or indirect addressing) was stored by step 9 in *MA*. Before control is transferred to step 32 for execution of JSR, step 15 moves this address to $IR[8:31]$ so that *MA* is free for addressing the stack in the process of saving the current contents of *PC*.

14   NO DELAY
        $\rightarrow (\wedge/IR[0:2])/(16)$.
15      $IR[8:31] \leftarrow MA$;   "to JSR"
        $\rightarrow (32)$.

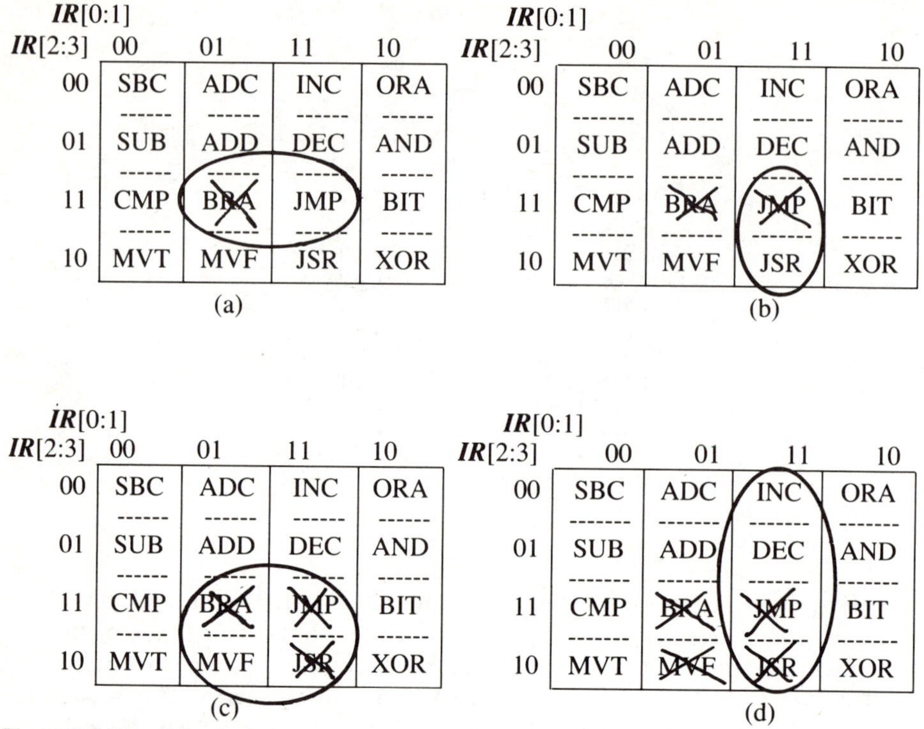

Figure 6.4 Branching logic in decoding OPCODES.

The logic implementing this last branch decision takes advantage of the fact that the values of *IR*[0:3] specifying JMP are now "don't cares" as are those for BRA, as shown in Fig. 6.4b. Since the JSR instruction involves the stack, we shall defer further discussion of this instruction until later, when we discuss the stack operations.

Once control reaches step 16, it is known that the address formed in *MA* will be used to access memory. All instructions, except MVF, start by reading memory, so a branch is specified at this step to separate MVF (Fig. 6.4c).

16   NO DELAY
        $\rightarrow$ (*IR*[1] $\wedge$ *IR*[2])/(19).
17   *MD* ← *AC*.
18   *write* = 1; *ADBUS* = *MA*; *DBUS* = *MD*;
        $\rightarrow$ (1).

Step 16 branches to step 19 if the command is not MVF. Steps 17 and 18 execute MVF by moving the contents of *AC* to *MD* and then writing them to memory. For

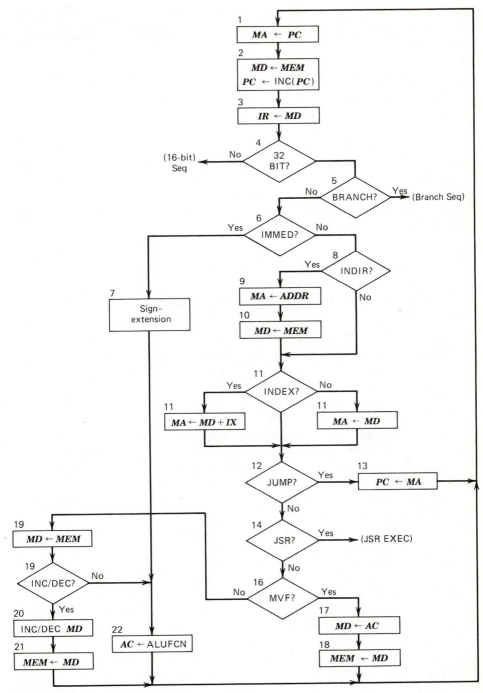

Figure 6.5. Initial flowchart of RIC.

the instructions that read an operand from memory, step 19 brings the operand to **MD.**. The flowchart of Fig. 6.5 will clarify the operations of the fetch and execute cycles to this point.

$\quad$ 19 $\quad$ **ADBUS = MA; MD ← DBUS; read = 1;**
$\qquad$ → ($\overline{IR[0] \wedge IR[1]}$)/(22).

At step 19, the hardware control process is ready to execute any of the 13 instructions involving an operand from memory, of which 11 involve the accumulator. Separated for execution by step 20 are the two instructions that do not use the accumulator, INC and DEC. The implementation of the step 19 branch takes advantage of the fact that the values of **IR**[0:3] specifying JMP and JSR are "don't cares" at this point, as shown in Fig. 6.4d.

$\quad$ 20 $\quad$ **MD ← (INC(MD) ! DEC(MD)) * ($\overline{IR[3]}$, IR[3]);**
$\qquad$ **zff ← ⋁/OBUS;nff ← OBUS[0].**
$\quad$ 21 $\quad$ **write = 1; ADBUS = MA; DBUS = MD;**
$\qquad$ → (1).

Step 20 increments or decrements the operand brought from memory and sets the Z and N flags in accordance with the results; step 21 writes the modified operand back into memory.

Once step 22 is reached, we are ready to execute an instruction that calls for the contents of **AC** and **MD** to be applied to the ALU with a result determined by the opcode placed on **OBUS** and then, except for CMP and BIT, routed to **AC**. Note that the path from step 7, the branch for immediate addressing, rejoins the main sequence at this point. The operand is now in **MD,** although it was obtained in a unique way for each of the addressing modes.

The ALU consists of a set of logic units to perform the operations ADD, AND, OR, and XOR. The **ABUS** and **BBUS** are permanently connected to the inputs of all these units. The connections to these buses and the connection of the appropriate ALU output to the **OBUS** are determined by the operation to be executed. The required connections are shown in Fig. 6.6a, including carry-in connections to the adder for operations that use the adder. The logical expressions controlling these connections must be developed using Karnaugh maps similar to those used in Fig. 6.4 to determine branch expressions. Now the combinations of values of **IR**[0:3] corresponding to INC, DEC, JMP, JSR, BRA, and MVF are all "don't cares." The AHPL statements reflecting these connections form step 22 of the sequence. Most of this must be left as a problem for the reader, but the connection control expressions for the **ABUS** and **OBUS** are developed in Fig. 6.6b and c, respectively. Where subtraction is involved (instructions SBC, SUB, and CMP), **MD** is connected to the **ABUS**. For all other cases, **MD** is connected to the **ABUS.** The Karnaugh map of the appropriate control expression is given in Fig. 6.6b. Possible connections to the **OBUS** are the adder output, the AND of **ABUS** and **BBUS,** the OR of these buses, the EXOR of these buses, and the **ABUS** directly. The Karnaugh maps of the corresponding five disjoint control expressions are given in Fig. 6.6c.

	ABUS	BBUS	OBUS	cin
ADD	*MD*	*AC*	ADD	0
ADC	*MD*	*AC*	ADD	*cff*
SUB	$\overline{MD}$	*AC*	ADD	1
SBC	$\overline{MD}$	*AC*	ADD	*cff*
MVT	*MD*	✕	*ABUS*	✕
.ORA	*MD*	*AC*	*ABUS* $\vee$ *BBUS*	✕
AND	*MD*	*AC*	*ABUS* $\wedge$ *BBUS*	✕
XOR	*MD*	*AC*	*ABUS* $\oplus$ *BBUS*	✕
BIT	*MD*	*AC*	*ABUS* $\wedge$ *BBUS*	✕
CMP	$\overline{MD}$	*AC*	ADD	1

Note: ADD = ADD(*ABUS; BBUS; cin*)

(a)

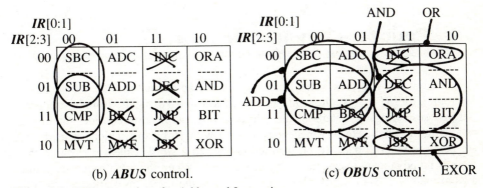

(b) **ABUS** control. (c) **OBUS** control.   EXOR

Figure 6.6. ALU connections for Addressed Instructions.

22     $ABUS = (MD \; ! \; \overline{MD}) * ((\overline{IR[0]} \wedge \overline{IR[1]} \wedge (\overline{IR[2]} \vee IR[3])),$
$(\overline{IR[0]} \wedge \overline{IR[1]} \wedge (\overline{IR[2]} \vee IR[3])));$
$BBUS = AC; \; cin = (cff \wedge \overline{IR[3]}) \vee (\overline{IR[1]} \wedge IR[3]);$
$OBUS = (ADD[1{:}32](ABUS; \; BBUS; \; cin) \; ! \; ABUS \wedge BBUS$
$! \; ABUS \vee BBUS \; ! \; ABUS \oplus BBUS \; ! \; ABUS)$
$* \; ((\overline{IR[0]} \wedge IR[2]) \vee (\overline{IR[0]} \wedge IR[3]),$
$IR[0] \wedge IR[3], \; IR[0] \wedge \overline{IR[2]} \wedge \overline{IR[3]},$
$\overline{IR[0]} \wedge IR[2] \wedge \overline{IR[3]}, \overline{IR[0] \wedge IR[2] \wedge IR[3]});$
$AC * (\overline{IR[2] \wedge IR[3]}) \leftarrow OBUS;$
$cff * (\overline{IR[0]} \wedge (\overline{IR[2]} \vee IR[3])) \leftarrow ADD[0](ABUS; \; BBUS; \; cin);$
$zff \leftarrow \overline{\bigvee/OBUS}; \; nff \leftarrow OBUS[0];$
$vff * (\overline{IR[0]} \wedge (\overline{IR[2]} \vee IR[3])) \leftarrow$
$(\overline{ABUS[0]} \wedge \overline{BBUS[0]} \wedge \overline{ADD[1](ABUS; \; BBUS; \; cin)}) \vee$
$(\overline{ABUS[0]} \wedge \overline{BBUS[0]} \wedge ADD[1](ABUS; \; BBUS; \; cin));$
$\rightarrow (1).$

The ninth line of step 22 specifies the clocking of the result into *AC* except for CMP and BIT. The remaining lines specify the setting of the four flags. The setting of the carry, zero, and negative flags should be self-explanatory. The overflow flag is set if the signs of the two operands applied to the adder are the same but the apparent sign of the result is different. In considering this equation, keep in mind that the two buses are 32-bit, while the output of the adder is 33 bits.

We have now completed the fetch and address cycles and the execute cycle for the addressed 32-bit instructions. You should be aware that we have used many more steps than needed, in the interests of clarity. For example, the decisions at steps 4, 5, 6, and 7 could be combined into a single multiway decision, but we have used separate steps to clarify the logic used in designing the sequence. Approaches to speeding up the sequence will be considered in Chapter 7.

6.6 Register-Only Instructions

We are now ready to look at the processing of the 16-bit instructions. As we saw in Sec. 6.4, if bit $IR[4] = 0$, the sequence branches at step 4 to handle 16-bit instructions. Before considering the details of these instructions, we need to consider the modifications in the fetch sequence necessary to deal with 16-bit instructions. Clearly, we are going to wish to pack 16-bit instructions two to a word. Unless we can do that, there is no advantage to having 16-bit instructions. When the fetch sequence obtains a word with two 16-bit instructions, it will process the upper instruction in much the same way discussed in the last section, except that only the upper 16 bits will be used. When this has been done, instead of going back to memory to get another instruction, the machine will next process the instruction in the lower half of the instruction word. This process is illustrated in the flowchart of Fig. 6.7.

To control the processing of 16-bit instructions, we add the second half flag, *shf*. When a new instruction word is fetched at step 1, *shf* is set to 0. If bit 4 of the instruction is 0, the sequence branches at step 4 to step 50 to process 16-bit instructions. Following processing of the instruction in the upper half of the instruction word, step 100 checks *shf*. If it is 0, indicating that the instruction just processed was in the upper half of the instruction word, step 101 shifts the lower instruction to the upper half of *IR*, and sets *shf* to 1. Control then returns to step 50 and the second instruction in the word is executed. When control returns to step 100, *shf* now equals 1, and control branches to step 1 to fetch a new instruction word.

Why shift the lower instruction to the upper half? Could not the instruction be executed where it is? It could, but this would make the design more expensive. We have already set up decoding logic to interpret the codes in the upper half of *IR*, and duplicating this logic for the lower half would be expensive. For example, all the control sequence steps interpreting the opcode assume that it is located in *IR*[0:3]. If we did not move the lower 16-bit instruction, its opcode would be in *IR*[16:19], requiring that we either duplicate the opcode logic or reconnect it. Moving the lower instruction to the upper half does exact a time penalty, but this is generally the preferred

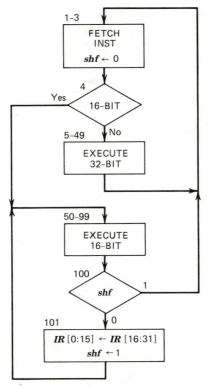

Figure 6.7. Fetch sequence for 16-bit instructions.

Operation	OpCode
ADD	0 1 0 1
ADC	0 1 0 0
SUB	0 0 0 1
SBC	0 0 0 0
AND	1 0 0 1
ORA	1 0 0 0
XOR	1 0 1 0
CMP	0 0 1 1
BIT	1 0 1 1
MVT	0 0 1 0
Shift/rotate	0 1 1 0

Figure 6.8. Register-only instructions.

procedure. We should also note that this procedure assumes that there will be a 16-bit instruction in the lower half of the word. We cannot start a 32-bit instruction in the lower half of one word and continue it in the next. If the program is such that a 16-bit instruction in the upper half of an instruction word should be followed by a 32-bit instruction, a NOP (no operation) instruction must be placed in the lower half. These sorts of constraints may seem awkward, but they must be regarded as a penalty we pay for the flexibility of having instructions of more than one length.

Having put a 16-bit instruction in position for execution, we first separate register-only instructions from other 16-bit instructions. Register-only instructions include all the operations listed in Fig. 6.3 that involve *AC,* except MVF, plus the shift/rotate instructions. The instructions are listed in Fig. 6.8 along with the opcodes. For convenience, we also repeat the format for 16-bit two-address instructions in Fig. 6.9. You will note that the opcodes are the same as for the *AC* and memory instructions, except that the shift/rotate instruction has replaced MVF.

Let RFN(*AD1*) and RFN(*AD2*) represent the registers specified by *AD1* and *AD2,* respectively. Then two-operand instructions such as ADD and AND will have the meaning

$$\text{RFN}(\textbf{AD1}) \leftarrow \text{RFN}(\textbf{AD1}) \odot \text{RFN}(\textbf{AD2})$$

where $\odot$ stands for the arithmetic or logical operation specified by the opcode. For MVT the operation will be

$$\text{RFN}(\textbf{AD1}) \leftarrow \text{RFN}(\textbf{AD2})$$

Since *AD1* and *AD2* can both specify any register, there is no need for the MVF command, and we have used its opcode for shift/rotate.

We noted earlier that the bus structure of Fig. 6.1 will not permit direct execution of an operation such as

$$AC \leftarrow AC \vee IX$$

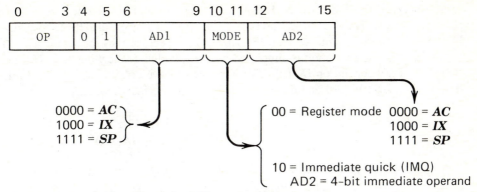

Figure 6.9. Two-address format for RIC.

because *AC* and *IX* are both on the *BBUS*. However, the desired result can be obtained by first routing the contents of the register specified by RFN(*AD2*) to *MD*, which is on *ABUS* and is not needed for memory access for register-only instructions. We also note that *AD2,* which is the operand for immediate quick, is in *IR,* which is also on *ABUS*. Thus, for two-operand instructions, *AD1* will specify the operand on *BBUS* and *AD2* will specify the operand on *ABUS*.

Understanding of the branches in the control sequence will be facilitated by a map of the register-only opcodes, as shown in Fig. 6.10. We note that opcodes with *IR*[0:1] = 11 are unused. These will be reserved for other types of 16-bit instructions. On this basis, the first branch of the 16-bit sequence will be

50       $\rightarrow$ (*IR*[0] $\wedge$ *IR*[1])/(other 16-bit).

The entries for *IR*[0:1] = 11 may now be treated as "don't cares," as shown in Fig. 6.10. Assuming opcode 0111 will not be used and is also a "don't care," step 51 to branch to the shift/rotate sequence may be written as follows.

51   NO DELAY
         $\rightarrow$ (*IR*[1] $\wedge$ *IR*[2])/(Shift/Rotate).

Step 52 begins execution of the two-address instructions by moving the operand specified by *AD2* to *MD*. Note that it is unnecessary to move the immediate operand

	IR[0:1]			
IR[2:3]	00	01	11	10
00	SBC	ADC	✕	ORA
01	SUB	ADD	✕	AND
11	CMP	✕	✕	BIT
10	MVT	SH/ROT	✕	XOR

Figure 6.10. Opcodes for Register-only Instructions.

to **MD** because **IR** is on **ABUS**. However, doing so simplifies the next step, since one operand will always be in **MD** no matter what the mode. Note also the two separate high-order 8-bit vectors moved with **IR** to **MD,** made necessary by the sign-extension. Notice that the step 52 logic is simplified by the fact that connections to **ABUS** and **BBUS** need not depend on **IR**[10]. This is so because we do not care what is on the **ABUS** when **IR**[10] = 0 and do not care what is on the **BBUS** when **IR**[10] = 1.

52     $BBUS[8:31] = (AC[8:31] \ ! \ IX \ ! \ SP) * (\overline{IR[12]},$
                       $IR[12] \wedge \overline{IR[13]}, IR[12] \wedge IR[13]);$
      $BBUS[0:7] = (8 \top 0 \ ! \ AC[0:7]) * (IR[12], \overline{IR[12]});$
      $ABUS[0:27] = (28 \top 0 \ ! \ 28 \top 0) * (\overline{IR[12]}, IR[12]));$
      $ABUS[28:31] = IR[12:15];$
      $OBUS = (ABUS \ ! \ BBUS) * (IR[10], \overline{IR[10]});$
      $MD \leftarrow OBUS.$

You will note the one-to-one correspondence between the squares of Fig. 6.10 and the squares in Figs. 6.6b and c, including the six "don't cares." We are, therefore, in a position to express execution of the instructions left in Fig. 6.10 in much the same form as in step 22. That is, steps 22 and 53 will be nearly identical. The exceptions are that three possible vectors are conditionally connected to the **BBUS** and there are three alternative target registers. Also shown are steps 100 and 101, which provide for execution of two 16-bit instructions in each instruction word, as shown in Fig. 6.7. In order that steps 100 and 101 function correctly, it is necessary to add to step 1 a statement that will clear **shf.** This is included in the RIC control sequence given in the Appendix.

53     $ABUS = (MD \ ! \ \overline{MD}) * (((\overline{\overline{IR[0]} \wedge \overline{IR[1]} \wedge (\overline{IR[2]} \vee IR[3])}),$
                 $(\overline{IR[0]} \wedge \overline{IR[1]} \wedge (\overline{IR[2]} \vee IR[3]))));$
      $BBUS = (AC \ ! \ 8 \top 0, IX \ ! \ 8 \top 0, \underline{SP}) * (\overline{IR[6]},$
                 $IR[6] \wedge \overline{IR[7]}, IR[6] \wedge IR[7]);$
      $cin = (cff \wedge \overline{IR[3]}) \vee (\overline{IR[1]} \wedge IR[3]);$
      $OBUS = (ADD[1:32](ABUS; BBUS; cin) \ ! \ ABUS \wedge BBUS$
                $! \ ABUS \vee BBUS \ ! \ ABUS \oplus BBUS \ ! \ ABUS) *$
                $((\overline{IR[0]} \wedge \overline{IR[2]}) \vee (\overline{IR[0]} \wedge \overline{IR[3]}),$
              $IR[0] \wedge \overline{IR[3]}, IR[0] \wedge IR[2] \wedge \overline{IR[3]},$
         $\overline{IR[0] \wedge IR[2]} \wedge IR[3], IR[0] \wedge IR[2] \wedge IR[3]);$
      $AC * \overline{IR[6] \wedge (IR[2] \wedge IR[3])} \leftarrow OBUS;$
      $(SP \ ! \ IX) * (IR[2] \wedge IR[3]) \wedge IR[6] \wedge (\overline{IR[7]}, IR[7])$
                                   $\leftarrow OBUS[8:31];$
      $cff * (\overline{IR[0]} \wedge (\overline{IR[2]} \vee IR[3])) \leftarrow ADD[0](ABUS; BBUS; cin);$
      $zff \leftarrow \vee/OBUS; nff \leftarrow OBUS[0];$
      $vff * (\overline{IR[0]} \wedge (\overline{IR[2]} \vee IR[3])) \leftarrow$
             $(\overline{ABUS[0]} \wedge \overline{BBUS[0]} \wedge \overline{ADD[1](ABUS; BBUS; cin)}) \vee$
             $(ABUS[0] \wedge BBUS[0] \wedge \overline{ADD[1]} (ABUS; BBUS; cin));$
      $\rightarrow (100).$

100   NO DELAY
        $\rightarrow (shf)/(1)$.

101     $IR[0:15] \leftarrow IR[16:31];\ shf \leftarrow 1;$
        $\rightarrow (50)$.

The shift/rotate instruction is a register-only instruction, but the instruction format differs from those considered previously because no address is needed, shifting and rotating being available only on **AC**. The format for this instruction is repeated in Fig. 6.11. Bits 0–4 establish that this is the 16-bit shift/rotate instruction, shift if bit 5 = 0, rotate if bit 5 = 1. Bit 10 indicates the direction of shift or rotate, and bits 11 through 15 specify the shift/rotate distance as a 5-bit number. Bit 6 indicates whether or not the carry is included in rotates, or whether shifts are arithmetic or logical.

As given in Fig. 2.15, there are seven distinct shift operations, LSR, ASR, SHL, ROR, RRC, ROL, and RLC. The basic logic for shifting was shown in Chapter 4, and simply calls for gates to route each output bit to the input position to the left or right. The implementation of these seven operations requires similar logic, except that the leftmost and rightmost bits require special treatment as does the carry flag. These seven AHPL statements can be combined into a single conditional transfer based on the controlling bits in the instruction. However, this provides only for a shift or rotate of 1 bit, whereas the instruction format permits us to specify shifts of up to 31 bits. There are two approaches to providing shifts of more than 1 bit. One is to provide special logic for multiple shifts. This approach will be investigated later. A simpler approach is to employ looping in the control sequence. If we were programming a computer that had only single-bit shifts and we needed a shift of several bits, we would simply use several successive shift instructions. We can accomplish the same purpose in the control sequence by introducing a shift counter, **SHC,** that will be initialized with the desired shift count from **IR**[11:15]. We shall then set up a loop, shifting and decrementing the shift counter until it reaches 0. The net result is the same as accomplished by multiple shift commands, except that we need only fetch one shift instruction.

Step 51 branched to the shift/rotate sequence, which we shall start at step 60 by transferring the shift count from **IR**[11:15] to the 5-bit shift counter **SHC.** Note that we decrement the count as we transfer it, so that the final shift will be made while the count is 0.

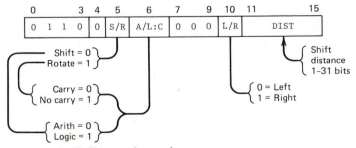

Figure 6.11. Shift/rotate instruction.

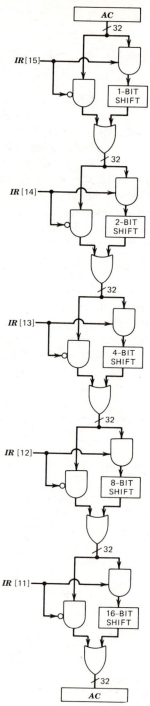

Figure 6.12. Combinational logic for multiple shifting (carry flag omitted for simplicity).

60      $SHC \leftarrow \text{DEC}(IR[11:15])$.

Step 61 accomplishes a 1-bit shift or rotate, decrements the shift counter, and tests the counter to determine if the shift should be repeated. It should be noted that the rather complex step 61 is written without explicitly incorporating the RIC bus structure. This form does not disguise the actual shift/rotate mechanism. The nontrivial problem of translating step 61 to a form expressing explicit bus connections will be left as a problem for the reader.

61      $AC[0] \leftarrow (AC[0] \mathbin{!} AC[1] \mathbin{!} AC[31] \mathbin{!} \overline{cff} \mathbin{!} 0) *$
$$(\overline{IR[5] \wedge IR[6] \wedge IR[10]}, \overline{IR[10]},$$
$$IR[5] \wedge IR[6] \wedge IR[10], IR[5] \wedge \overline{IR[6]} \wedge IR[10],$$
$$IR[5] \wedge IR[6] \wedge \overline{IR[10]});$$
$AC[1:30] \leftarrow (AC[0:29] \mathbin{!} AC[2:31]) * (IR[10], \overline{IR[10]});$
$AC[31] \leftarrow (AC[30] \mathbin{!} AC[0] \mathbin{!} cff \mathbin{!} 0) * (IR[10],$
$$\overline{IR[5] \wedge IR[6] \wedge IR[10]},$$
$$IR[5] \wedge \overline{IR[6]} \wedge IR[10], IR[5] \wedge \overline{IR[10]});$$
$cff * (IR[5] \wedge \overline{IR[6]}) \leftarrow (AC[31] \mathbin{!} AC[0]) * (IR[10], \overline{IR[10]});$
$SHC \leftarrow \text{DEC}(SHC);$
$\rightarrow (\bigvee/SHC, \overline{\bigvee/SHC})/(61, 100).$

Although step 61 certainly looks very complicated, the corresponding logic is not all that complex, but this approach is relatively slow for multiple shifts. An alternative approach is to provide sufficient logic to carry out any desired shift in one step. It would be impractically expensive to provide separate logic for each possible shift length, from 1 to 31, but an intermediate approach is more realistic. We note that each bit of the shift distance specification calls for a shift by a power of two. If bit 15 = 1, a shift of 1 bit is required; if bit 14 = 1, a shift of 2 bits is required; if bit 13 = 1, a shift of 4 bits is required, and so forth. Shifts of any number of bits can be accomplished by providing shift logic for 1, 2, 4, 8, or 16 bits, together with logic to route the word through any combination of these shift networks as may be required. Figure 6.12 suggests the organization of this shift logic required. We leave it to you to develop an AHPL description of this shift network.

6.7 Branch Commands

Assembly language branch commands, in their simplest form, test one of the four flags for a specified condition. If the condition is met, a branch is made to an instruction at a specified distance relative to the current instruction; if not, the next sequential instruction is executed. The eight branch commands, one for each possible value of the four flags as tabulated in Fig. 2.10, can, when used in combination, accomplish any desired branch as a function of the flag bits. That figure also indicates two other types of branches, Branch Always (BRA), and Branch to Subroutine (BSR). Branch Always, like JMP, is unconditional, but uses relative addressing like other branch commands. Branch to Subroutine functions like other branches, except that it pushes the address of the next instruction on the stack, thus saving it as the return address after completion of the subroutine. Branch to Subroutine offers the same advantages relative to JSR as do regular branches relative to JMP. If we use JSR to transfer control to a subroutine, the subroutine must be in a fixed location, independent of the location of the main routine. With BSR, the entire program, including subroutines, can be located anywhere in memory as long as the relative locations remain constant. The use of BSR also makes it possible to make a branch to a subroutine conditional. For example, we might want to call a divide routine only if the denominator is not 0.

While branches on the values of individual flags are the most obviously useful, it is sometimes necessary to be able to branch on certain combinations of the flags. For example, a branch on "greater than 0" will require a check of both the N and Z flags. One very common requirement in programming is a check of the relative magnitude of two numbers. To make such a check, we use the CMP command, which sets the flags on the basis of the operation

$$AC - M\langle \perp MA \rangle^1$$

without changing the contents of *AC*. For unsigned numbers, a check of the C and Z flags will suffice to determine the relative values. If $Z = 1$, then $AC = M\langle \perp MA \rangle$. If $Z = 0$, then $C = 1$ indicates $AC < M\langle \perp MA \rangle$; and $C = 0$ indicates $AC < M\langle \perp MA \rangle$. For signed numbers, the situation is more complex. Figure 6.13 summarizes the conditions of the flags for various situations after execution of the CMP command on signed numbers. There are two possible conditions of the flags for oppositely signed numbers, depending on whether the subtraction produces overflow.

The relations between *AC* and $M\langle \perp MA \rangle$ for each combination of values of flag

Relative Values	Signs		Resulting Flags		
$AC = M \perp MA$			$Z = 1$	$N = 0$	$V = 0$
$AC > M\langle \perp MA \rangle$	Both positive		$Z = 0$	$N = 0$	$V = 0$
	Both negative		$Z = 0$	$N = 0$	$V = 0$
	AC pos, **M** neg		$Z = 0$	$N = 1$	$V = 1$
	AC pos, **M** neg	or	$Z = 0$	$N = 0$	$V = 0$
$AC < M\langle \perp MA \rangle$	Both positive		$Z = 0$	$N = 1$	$V = 0$
	Both negative		$Z = 0$	$N = 1$	$V = 0$
	AC neg, **M** pos	or	$Z = 0$	$N = 0$	$V = 1$
			$Z = 0$	$N = 1$	$V = 0$

Figure 6.13. Values of Flags After CMP.

---

[1] $\perp$ is an APL operator that encodes the binary number in *MA* to form a decimal integer. Although not in AHPL, $\perp$ is the inverse of the AHPL operator $\top$.

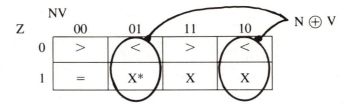

*It might appear that this combination of flags could result from a compare of 10000... and 1000..., but the signs used in overflow determination would be based on the first argument and the 1's complement of the second argument (01111...). Therefore, V = 0.

Figure 6.14. Map of Relative Magnitudes indicated by Flags.

bits may be summarized in a Karnaugh map, as shown in Fig. 6.14. The three combinations of values marked "don't care" will indeed never occur. From this map, we can now determine the logical functions of the flags representing each of the arithmetic relations between the two arguments of the compare command. These functions are listed in Fig. 6.15. The Boolean expression, $N \oplus V$, which is required in four of these functions, is depicted on the Karnaugh map.

All these functions are provided for by the branch instruction format shown in Fig. 6.16. Implementing the branch function will only require ORing various combinations of flags specified by bits 7 through 15. Bit 4 = 1 of Fig. 6.16 indicates that this is a 32-bit instruction, and the opcode 0111 indicates a branch. Bit 5 indicates regular branch or branch to subroutine, and bit 6 indicates whether a branch is to be executed if the specified function or its complement is 1. Bits 16 through 31 specify the 16-bit displacement to be added to *PC* if the branch is taken. Bits 7 through 14 allow the machine language programmer to specify the true or complemented values of each of the four flags. Bit 15 is used to specify inclusion of the expression $N \oplus V$ in the branch function. In each pair of bits, a 1 in the first bit calls for a branch if the flag = 1, and 1 in the second bit causes a branch if the flag = 0. Setting both bits to 1 for any flag will provide Branch Always.

If branches are set for more than one flag, the combinations will be ORed and bit 6 will specify a branch on the resultant function equal to 0 or 1. For example, *IR*[5:15] = 0 00 01 00 00 01 will cause a branch on

Relative Values	Logical Function	Branch Mnemonic
$AC = M\langle \perp MA \rangle$	Z	BEQ
$AC < M\langle \perp MA \rangle$	$N \oplus V$	BLT
$AC \leq M\langle \perp MA \rangle$	$Z \vee (N \oplus V)$	BLE
$AC \geq M\langle \perp MA \rangle$	$\overline{N \oplus V}$	BGE
$AC > M\langle \perp MA \rangle$	$\overline{Z \vee (N \oplus V)}$	BGT

Figure 6.15. Boolean expressions for branch functions.

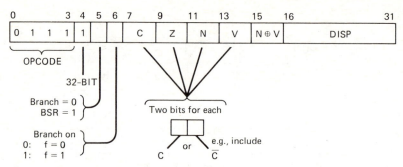

Figure 6.16. Format for branch instructions.

$$\overline{Z} \lor (N \oplus V) \qquad\qquad (BGT)$$

The design of this instruction format provides an interesting example of the interaction of hardware and software requirements in computer architecture. It was first discovered that tests of the four flags N, Z, V, and C were insufficient. Therefore, the function $N \oplus C$ was added; and the *microcoded* format of Fig. 6.16, allowing ORing and complementing of the flags and flag functions, was developed. The result is a complex instruction format, very powerful but not easy to use. It is likely that few programmers will have the patience to master it fully, and the burden of finding ways to exploit its power will primarily fall on the designer of the assembly language for the computer. The typical programmer will use only the branch mnemonics provided in the assembly language.

We are now in a position to write the branch sequence that will start at step 30, with the actual branch function.

30    $\rightarrow ((\lor/(\textbf{\textit{IR}}[7{:}15] \land (C,\overline{C},\ Z,\overline{Z},\ N,\overline{N},\ V,\overline{V},\ N \oplus V))) \oplus \textbf{\textit{IR}}[6])/(1).$

If the branch condition is not met, control returns to step 1 to fetch the next instruction in sequence. Step 31 determines whether or not the command is branch to subroutine. If so, steps 32 through 34 push the current contents of **PC** on the stack. These steps are required by the instruction JSR as well, so control for JSR and BSR merge at step 32 (see the branch at step 15). This is the first encounter with the implementation of an instruction involving the stack. PSH, POP, and RTS will be considered in the next section. Recall that the stack pointer in RIC points at the data word at the top of the stack, so that **SP** must be decremented at step 32 before a word can be placed on the stack.

31   NO DELAY
       $\rightarrow (\overline{\textbf{\textit{IR}}[5]})/(35).$
32    $\textbf{\textit{MA}} \leftarrow DEC(\textbf{\textit{SP}}); \textbf{\textit{SP}} \leftarrow DEC(\textbf{\textit{SP}}).$

33      $MD \leftarrow 8 \top 0, PC$
34      $ADBUS = MA; DBUS = MD; \underline{write} = 1.$
35      $ABUS = (16 \top 0, IR[16:31] ! 16 \top 0, IR[16:31] ! 8 \top 0, IR[8:31])$
$$* ((IR[16], IR[16]) \wedge IR[0], IR[0]);$$
$BBUS = 8 \top 0, PC; cin = 0;$ "accommodate JSR"
$OBUS = (ABUS ! ADD[1:32](ABUS; BBUS; cin)) * (IR[0], \overline{IR}[0]);$
$PC \leftarrow OBUS[8:31];$
$\rightarrow (1).$

Finally, step 35 causes the new program address to be placed in **PC**. For BSR, it adds the displacement from **IR**[16:31] to the contents of **PC**. Note the conditional connection to **ABUS** to provide the required sign extension for the displacement, which is considered to be a signed number. For JSR, the new program address has been stored in **IR**[8:31] by step 15 and must be moved to **PC** by step 35. There are 2 bits that distinguish the JSR opcode from that of the branch instructions. In this case, we use bit **IR**[0], which is 1 for JSR.

Notice that we are reusing rather than repeating two short sequences of AHPL code. In writing software, this would be a serious breach of the structured programming philosophy. In hardware, shortening of the control sequence results in a reduced chip area requirement for the control unit implementation. Even in the world of VLSI, such savings cannot be dismissed.

6.8   Special-Purpose Instructions

A few instructions discussed in Chapter 2 have not yet been implemented. For lack of a better name, we shall refer to those instructions, which do not fit neatly into any of the categories considered so far, as *special-purpose* instructions. The remaining instructions specified in Chapter 2, PSH, POP, SEC, CLC, NOP, HLT, and RTS, are all 16-bit instructions, since none of them require an address. You will recall, from Section 6.6, that we did not use opcodes with **IR**[0:1] = 11 for 16-bit instructions, so all these opcodes are available for these miscellaneous instructions. Since there are so few of these instructions, it is likely that we could handle all of them with an 8-bit format, but the complications involved in handling a third instruction length are just not worth the trouble. We shall, therefore, use 16-bits for these instructions, even though we will not need all the bits. The 16-bit instructions with **IR**[0:1] = 11 will be divided into four categories, as shown in Fig. 6.17.

System instructions (SYS) will include instructions that affect the general operating state of the system without manipulating data or modifying registers. The IOT category will include all instructions specifically involving input/output operations and the interrupt system of the computer. The *supervisory group* (SUPV) of instructions

$IR[0:1]$

$IR[2:3]$ 00   01   11   10

$IR[2:3]$	00	01	11	10
00	╳	╳	SYS	╳
01	╳	╳	IOT	╳
11	╳	╳	SUPV	╳
10	╳	╳	MISC	╳

Figure 6.17. Categories of 16-bit special purpose instructions.

include instructions specifically intended for use only by the machine operators or system programmers, not usually available to ordinary users. Finally, the *miscellaneous group* (MISC) will include any instructions that do not fit in any other category. For the remaining instructions defined in Chapter 2, HLT and NOP will be in the SYS group and PSH, POP, SEC, CLC, and RTS will be in the MISC group.

As noted earlier, we need only a few more bits for the special-purpose instructions so far defined, but we shall specify four more bits of opcode, $IR[6:9]$, for these instructions, which will allow for 16 instructions in each category. This should be ample for any likely future expansion. The opcodes for the presently defined instructions are listed in Fig. 6.18.

We start at Step 50 with a branch to this group of instructions, which will start at step 70

50   NO DELAY
      $\rightarrow (IR[0] \wedge IR[1])/(70)$.

At step 70, we make a four-way branch to the four categories of instructions specified in Fig. 6.17. Since we are implementing only two of the categories at present, we could simplify this branch. Making the full four-way branch now will provide for adding the other categories later.

$IR\ [0:9]$	Instruction
1100 01 0000	NOP
1100 01 0001	HLT
1110 01 0000	CLC
1110 01 0001	SEC
1110 01 0100	PSH
1110 01 0101	POP
1110 01 0111	RTS

Figure 6.18. Opcodes for special-purpose instructions.

70   NO DELAY
      $\rightarrow$ (DCD(IR[2:3]))/(71, 110, 130, 170).

The system group starts at Step 71. For NOP, the sequence simply goes to the second 16-bit instructions or returns via step 100 to step 1. Otherwise (for now), the instruction must be HLT, which calls for a DEAD END, that is, the clock is turned off, and the state of the machine is "frozen" until restarted.

71   NO DELAY
      $\rightarrow$ ($\vee$/ IR[6:9])/(100).
72   DEAD END.

The MISC group starts at step 130, again with a four-way branch to simplify future expansion.

130    $\rightarrow$ (DCD(IR[6:7]))/(131, 140, 150, 160).

Step 131 implements CLC and SEC.

131    $cff \leftarrow IR$[9];
       $\rightarrow$ (100).

Execution of PSH, POP, and RTS starts at step 140, with PSH carried out in steps 141 through 143.

140    $\rightarrow$ (IR[9])/(144).
141    $SP \leftarrow$ DEC(SP); $MA \leftarrow$ DEC(SP).
142    $MD \leftarrow AC$.
143    $ADBUS = MA; DBUS = MD; write = 1$;
       $\rightarrow$ (100).

POP and RTS are very similar, since both pull a word off the stack. For POP, the word goes to AC; for RTS, the word goes to PC.

144    $MA \leftarrow SP$.
145    $ADBUS = MA; MD \leftarrow DBUS; read = 1; SP \leftarrow$ INC(SP).
146    $AC * IR$[8] $\leftarrow MD$;
       $PC * IR$[8] $\leftarrow MD$[8:31];
       $\rightarrow$ (100).

The AHPL sequence is now complete for all instructions defined to this point. In the next chapter, we shall consider some of the hardware implications of this sequence.

6.9 *Options in Computer Structures*

In the preceding sections, we have studied the design of the RIC computer in considerable detail. We have done so because we believe that it is pedagogically advantageous to follow through the design of at least one specific machine in a consistent and comprehensive manner. The concentration on this particular machine is not intended to imply that this is in any sense the only reasonable design or even a preferable design. Although RIC has many features in common with various real computers, the number of possible variations and options in organization is virtually unlimited. Now that you have the essential features of one specific design well in hand, it is appropriate to look briefly at some possible options.

Any attempt to classify options would be most difficult without some bounds on the nature of the system under discussion. As noted in Chapter 1, the basic characteristics and structure of digital computers were first set forth in a systematic manner by the mathematician John von Neumann, in 1945. Since that time, computers conforming generally to the organization he set forth have been classified as *von Neumann machines,* and it is a measure of the significance of his contributions that the vast majority of computers built over the years have been von Neumann machines. In this section, we shall restrict our discussion to features consistent with the general notion of a von Neumann organization. Elsewhere in the book, we shall consider other possibilities.

Von Neumann's analysis dealt with very general concepts, and it is difficult to arrive at a precise definition of what is or is not a von Neumann machine. The characteristic most commonly cited as distinguishing the von Neumann organization is the storage of data and instructions in the same form, in the same random access memory. This characteristic in turn implies other structural features, including separation of registers and logic from memory, a program counter and an instruction register, and input/output facilities. Figure 6.19a illustrates the essential features of a von Neumann structure. This structure also implies the division of the instruction cycle into three basic parts, as shown in Fig. 6.19b. Clearly, RIC includes all these features.

Available options with the von Neumann organization can be classified in terms of options in structuring the three blocks of Fig. 6.19b. The number of options available in the instruction execution block is essentially unlimited. Some possible categories of instructions were discussed earlier. One particularly important group of instructions, the arithmetic instructions, will be discussed in detail in Chapters 15, 16, and 17. Options in the accessing of arguments will be the subject of the next section.

The sequence of instructions actually fetched and executed is often called the *instruction stream.* The function of block 1 in Fig. 6.19b is to fetch each instruction in turn from the instruction stream and make it ready for execution. Within the instruction fetch cycle, there are essentially two types of options available. The first concerns the manner in which the address of the next instruction is obtained. One method is to include the address of the next instruction in each instruction. Then the instruction fetch requires moving the next instruction address from the instruction

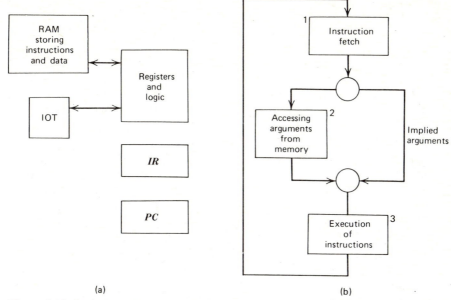

(a)   (b)

Figure 6.19. Basic Von Neumann organization.

register to the memory address register and reading the new instruction into the instruction register. This option was employed in a few early computers, but the standard technique used today is that used in RIC. The program is assumed to be stored in sequential locations in memory, and a program counter is used to keep track of the next instruction address. Branch instructions can change the next instruction address, but they do so by modifying the program counter so that the fetch cycle uniformly refers to the program counter for the instruction address.

The second option in the fetch cycle is in the number of words per instruction. Machines with longer words may pack two or more instructions in a word, whereas machines with shorter word lengths, especially microprocessors, may require several words per instruction. The basic structure of the fetch cycle for a machine with more than one instruction per word is shown in Fig. 6.20a. If an instruction has m-bits, the usual technique is to execute the instruction in the most significant m-bits of the instruction register. After the fetch of an instruction word, each individual instruction must in turn be shifted into the correct position. Also note that n is not necessarily a constant for a given machine; that is, some instructions may occupy a full word, others only part of a word. In such cases the opcode will contain information to set the appropriate value of n as was done in RIC.

The basic fetch cycle for the case in which more than one word may be required per instruction is shown in Fig. 6.20b. This time, n indicates the number of words per instruction and, again, it is not necessarily constant for a given machine. If this is the case, the number of words in the instruction will usually be specified in the first instruction word. As shown in Fig. 6.20b, if additional words are required, they are

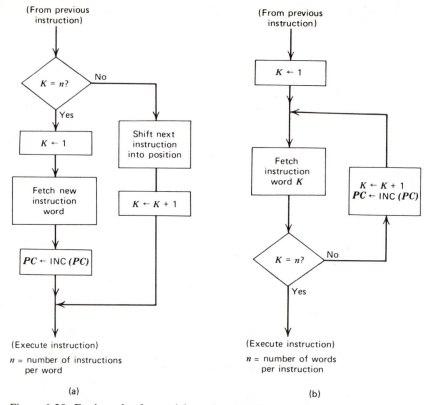

Figure 6.20. Fetch cycles for partial-word and multiple-word instructions.

fetched from successive memory locations until *n* words have been assembled into the instruction register.

Example 6.2

Write in AHPL the steps of the control sequence that specify the instruction fetch for a computer that employs a 12-bit 2^{18}-word RAM. Instructions that require an operand from memory must consist of 24 bits (i.e., two computer words). Instructions that do not require an argument from memory are 12-bit instructions. Bit $IR[0] = 0$ for one-word instructions, and $IR[0] = 1$ for two-word instructions. For compactness memory references may be expressed using BUSFN.

Solution

Since the following is only a partial control sequence, declarations are omitted, and the memory is assumed to be in the same module as the CPU. As implied, *PC* and *MA* are 18-bit registers whereas *IR* is 24 bits and *MD* is 12 bits. The first instruction word is always placed in $IR[0:11]$

1   $MA \leftarrow PC$.
2   $MD \leftarrow$ BUSFN (**M;** DCD (**MA**)).
3   $IR[0:11] \leftarrow MD$.
4   $\rightarrow$ (**IR**[0])/(execution of one-word instructions).
5   $PC \leftarrow$ INC(**PC**); $MA \leftarrow$ INC (**PC**).
6   $MD \leftarrow$ BUSFN (**M;** DCD(**MA**)).
7   $IR[12:23] \leftarrow MD$.
8   Accessing of argument

This control sequence is clearly an example of Fig. 6.20b, where n is restricted to the values 1 and 2.

If a memory word is 32 bits, for example, an instruction might consist of more than one word but not necessarily an integral number of words. This implies an instruction fetch approach combining the notions of both Fig. 6.20a and Fig. 6.20b. An interesting architectural interpretation of this situation is to view the instruction stream of 8-bit bytes (or 16-bit halfwords), leaving the identification of desired bytes within larger words to the implementation level. We shall see an example of this in the next section.

6.10   Addressing Options

Let us now turn our attention to the options available in the accessing of arguments in block 2 of Fig 6.19b. The term *argument* is used in a very broad sense here, to include operands to be processed, results to be stored, and addresses for branch operations. Thus every instruction requires access to at least one argument. In the interest of simplicity, we have shown the access to arguments only once in Fig. 6.19b, although the storing results will usually occur after the execute phase.

Arguments may be broadly grouped into two classifications, *addressed* and *implied*. Implied arguments are the contents of registers whose use is specified by the opcode itself. For instance, ADD and AND imply the accumulator as the source of one operand and the destination of the result. This mode of access is indicated by a straight-through line in block 2 of Fig. 6.19b because no steps are required to move the arguments into position for execution. The processing of the registers implied by the opcode automatically accesses these arguments.

Addressed arguments are those that require access to memory. There is complication here in that registers are memory devices, and in many modern computer systems the memory may include a whole hierarchy of devices rather than just one main memory. Here we use the term *memory* in the basic von Neumann sense: to denote a separate section of the computer system consisting of 2^n information storage locations, identified by n-bit addresses. An addressed argument requires the generation of an n-bit address, which is in some way specified by the instruction. This address generation and memory access is indicated as block 2 in Fig. 6.19b. The options available in this block are the subject of the remainder of this section.

The design decisions that must be made in setting up an addressing scheme have been separated into the four degrees of freedom listed in Fig. 6.21. The tree in this figure is provided as a means of graphically depicting the great variety of combinations of approaches to address determination that are available. Each terminal node of the tree corresponds to one combination. The ordering of the four degrees of freedom was selected solely for the convenience of illustration.

The first option is how many arguments are to be accessed in memory. As discussed in Chapter 1, the single-address format, in which one argument is addressed and the others are implied, is the most common. However, some machines do use two- or three-address formats. Multiple-address instructions are often stored in several words, as discussed in the last section. The options of single or multiple arguments are depicted as separate branches from the root node of the tree depicted in Fig. 6.21. Although a continuation is shown only for the single-address branch, a complete tree would have branches corresponding to the next degree of freedom from each nonterminal node. Thus terminal nodes would exist corresponding to all combinations of choices for the four addressing parameters.

The next choice (the second level of branching) is the number of words per argument. The amount of information obtained from each location in the memory is assumed to be one word. Most machines use one word per operand, but in some machines operands may be spread over several consecutive locations. In such machines, the instruction usually specifies the location of the first word in the operand; accessing then continues through successive locations until the entire operand has been processed.

The next choice (third degree of freedom) is how many accesses to the memory must be made to obtain each operand (or each word of an operand). The leftmost branch on the decision tree represents *immediate addressing,* in which the argument

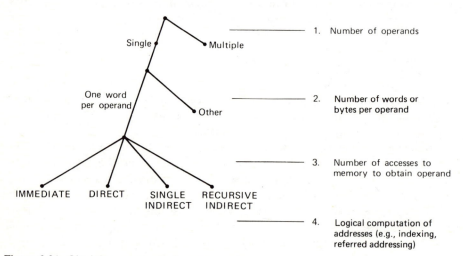

Figure 6.21. Obtaining arguments from memory.

is a part of the instruction so that no additional accesses to memory are required. This form of addressing may seem out of place on the decision tree, since no address is generated nor is a memory access made. A reasonable argument could be made that this is a form of implied addressing, except that the use of an immediate argument is not usually implied by the opcode, but is rather specified by an address mode. This is simply a special case that does not fit neatly in either of the two categories, addressed and nonaddressed instructions.

Direct addressing and single-level indirect addressing, which are used in RIC, require one and two additional memory accesses, respectively. *Recursive indirect addressing,* which is not provided in RIC, will allow any number of successive memory accesses before the operand is finally obtained. This is accomplished by replacing the indirect addressing specification bit as well as the address in *IR* after each successive memory access. The operand is not read from memory until a 0 in this bit position is encountered (see Problem 6.1).

The fourth and final degree of freedom is less convenient to depict in the tree structure because of the large number of possibilities. Indexing is allowed in RIC, which calls for an address to be formed by adding the contents of an index register to a vector from *IR*. In general, addresses can be generated *as combinational logic functions of any registers or combinations of registers.* Another example of this fourth degree of freedom is the use of the opcode to specify a register within the CPU that contains the address. We shall call this *referred addressing* or *register indirect addressing.*

The third and fourth degrees of freedom are logically independent in that the third provides for the determination of addresses by successive operations in time whereas the fourth involves a single, one-time determination of the address in terms of combinational logic. The examples in this section and Section 6.11 will illustrate various combinations of these two types of options.

In some computers, an address of sufficient length to specify any word in the memory space may never appear in the instruction stream. However, a complete address might be formed by exercising some of the options in levels 3 and 4 of Fig. 6.21, such as indirect addressing or referred addressing. For example, when an indirect address cycle is executed in RIC, a full 32-bit word is fetched but only 24 bits are used. If RIC were to be modified to use the full 32 bits, its address capacity would be increased to 2^{32} = 4096M words. To accomplish this, we must increase the size of *MA* and *PC* to full word length.

This modification does not fully solve the problem because an address is still needed in the instruction, even with indirect addressing. The usual procedure is as follows. During the fetch cycle, a full-length address (32 bits in RIC) is transferred from *PC* to *MA* and an instruction fetched. During execution of an addressed instruction, a partial address (24 bits in RIC) is transferred to the corresponding position of *MA* and catenated to the most significant position (8 bits in RIC) left in *MA* by the instruction fetch.

When such a scheme is used, it is common to consider the memory as being divided into *pages.* The most significant portion of an address, which is not changed by direct addressing, is known as the *page number;* the least significant portion, normally taken from the instruction, is known as the *page address* or *page offset*. The complete full-length address is known as the *absolute address*. As an example, consider a machine with 24-bit words, in which the standard single-address instruction consists of an 8-bit opcode and a 16-bit address. In such a case, the upper 8 bits of an absolute address would be the page number and the lower 16 bits would be the page address, dividing the 16M word address space into 256 pages of 64K words each. For example, if the upper 8 bits are 00 (hex) we are on page 0 with addresses running from 000000 to 00FFFF. For the first 8 bits = 01 (hex), we are on page 1, with addresses running from 010000 to 01FFFF, and so forth.

The page number designated by the leading bits of **PC** is known as the *current page*. As long as direct addressing is used, the program will be executed on the current page. Indirect addressing need not used unless it is necessary to move off the current page. For machines with large pages, such as the 64K pages just discussed, many programs could be executed without leaving the current page. When necessary, however, indirect addressing on memory reference instructions can refer to data locations on any page. Indirect jumps will reset the program counter, providing a new current page number as required.

The preceding paragraphs describe the basic principles by which indirect addressing can be used to increase the addressing capacity of computers. In machines using this technique, additional refinements are often incorporated to provide for simpler programming. Let us now consider as an example a machine that has a word length of only 12 bits, making the problem of address capacity particularly severe.

Example 6.3

Figure 6.22 shows the basic organization of a 12-bit, 4K computer.

Devise an instruction format for addressed instructions and a page-addressing scheme. Also devise a convenient means to use memory locations to serve the function of index registers. Use only one word per instruction.

Solution

Three bits is about the minimum possible for opcodes if the machine is to do anything at all, and 1 bit will be required to designate indirect addressing. Thus we have a maximum of 8 bits available for page addresses, which would allow for 16 pages of 256 words each. However, as a matter of programming convenience, we shall instead divide the memory into 32 pages of 128 words each, with bit 4 used to choose between the current page or page 0, as shown in Fig. 6.23. Thus, if Z/C = 0, the page address is taken on page 0; if Z/C = 1, the page address is taken on the current page.

This zero-current page choice does not increase address capacity. With an 8-bit page address, the direct addressing range would be 256 words. With this method, the range is still 256 words, 128 on page 0 and 128 on the current page. But there is a programming advantage. Many locations on page 0 will be used as *pointers,* containing the addresses of standard subroutines or tables of constants. For example, we might have standard subroutines for multiplication and division. These could be stored at convenient places in memory, and their starting addresses could be stored on page 0.

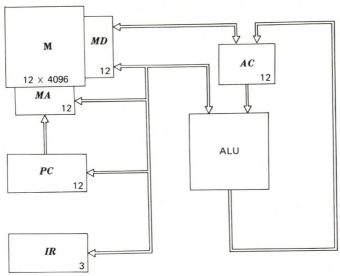

Figure 6.22. Organization of a simple 12-bit computer.

Then programs located anywhere in memory could refer to these routines by an indirect reference through page 0.

The page 0 feature also makes it convenient to provide an indexing feature using standard memory locations. The first eight locations on page 0 (absolute addresses 000 to 007 hex) will be used as *autoindex* registers. When an indirect reference is made to these locations, the contents will be incremented by one and rewritten in the same location, and the incremented number will be used as the effective address. For example, if the contents of location 004 were 163 hex and the command were

MVT I Z 4 (Z indicates page 0)

then 163 would be read from location 4 and incremented to 164, 164 would be rewritten in location 4, and the contents of location 164 would be loaded into the accumulator. It can be seen that this feature would provide a very convenient means of stepping through an array of data. The basic flowchart for the fetch cycle of this machine is shown in Fig. 6.24. We shall leave the task of writing an actual control sequence as an exercise for the reader. ■

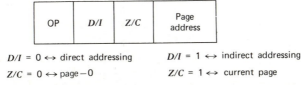

D/I = 0 ↔ direct addressing   D/I = 1 ↔ indirect addressing

Z/C = 0 ↔ page−0   Z/C = 1 ↔ current page

Figure 6.23. Instruction format for 12-bit computer, Example 6.3.

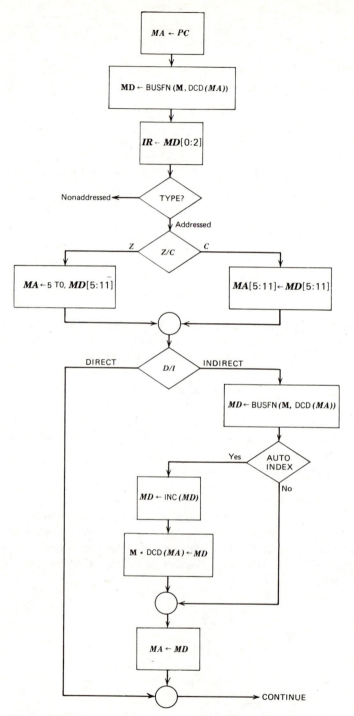

Figure 6.24. Fetch cycle for 12-bit computer, Example 6.3.

It should not be inferred from the preceding discussion that paging is a concept restricted to machines functioning in this particular manner. Many 8-bit microprocessors use 16-bit addresses, providing a 64K address space, fetched in 2 bytes from memory. It is common to consider the first byte as a page number and the second byte as a page address, thus dividing the address space into 256 pages of 256 words each. However, there is no use of indirect addressing to obtain addresses longer than can be obtained in an instruction, and no concept of current page.

Another technique for address modification, found primarily in larger machines, is *base addressing*. In this scheme, at least one *base address register* is provided

Whenever an argument is accessed in memory, a page address from *IR* is added to or catenated with a base address register to form the absolute address. Such an operation will usually be transparent to the user although an instruction for loading each base address register must be provided.

In addition to increasing addressing capacity, base addressing also facilitates *relocatability,* a characteristic important in large machines operated in either a batch or a multiprogramming mode by executive or monitor software. The executive or monitor is responsible for allocating memory in the most efficient manner, so as to accommodate as many programs as possible. A compiler does not anticipate the best arrangement in memory for a program and associated data files. Usually, it assumes each program to begin at address 0. The executive or monitor then loads a starting address in a base address register assigned to the program at load time to locate the program where it fits best in terms of the current state of memory.

Example 6.4

Relocatability through base addressing may be included in RIC by adding a 24-bit register, *BASE,* and making a few modifications in the control sequence given in Sections 6.4 through 6.8. The *BASE* register may be cleared, saved, or loaded by adding this one additional register to the operand lists for the 16-bit two-operand instructions. This will be left as a problem for the reader. The approach to implementing relocatability will assume that *PC* will at all times contain the actual address of the instruction to be executed. The base address must be added to every address used in the execution of an instruction, that is, either a data address or the address of a next instruction for JMP or JSR.

Identify and modify those parts of the RIC code given in Sections 6.4 through 6.8 to provide for adding *BASE* to any addresses used in the execution of an instruction.

Solution

Step 1, $MA \leftarrow PC,$ need not be changed since *PC* will always contain the absolute address of the next instruction to be executed. Step 9, used in indirect addressing, must be modified to appear as follows.

> 9 $MA \leftarrow ADD(MD[8:31]; \textbf{BASE}).$

The final effective address for all instructions, including JMP and JMS, is computed by step 11, which already involves the addition of the index register. To accomplish base addressing, step 11 must be replaced by two steps as follows. Each addition now has two arguments and can be accomplished through the RIC bus structure. We assume that *BASE* will be connected to the *BBUS*.

> 11 $MA \leftarrow$ ADD $(MD,[8:31]; BASE)$;
> $\rightarrow (IR[6])/(12)$.
> 11A $MA \leftarrow$ ADD$(MA; IX)$.
> 12   . . .

The stack pointer, *SP,* is another register that must continuously contain an address in the area of the process in execution. Unlike *PC,* the stack pointer is accessible to and can be loaded by the user. It cannot, therefore, be assumed to contain a relocated address. Each time the contents of *SP* is placed in *MA, BASE* register must be added. This will require that step 32 in the implementation of JSR be modified as follows.

> 32 $MA \leftarrow$ DEC(SP); $SP \leftarrow$ DEC(SP).
> 32A $MA \leftarrow$ ADD$(MA; BASE)$.

The registers *SP* and *BASE* cannot be added directly since they are connected to the same bus. An identical modification must be made in step 141 in the implementation of PSH. For POP and RTS, it is again necessary to replace the single step 144 by

> 144 $MA \leftarrow SP$
> 144A $MA \leftarrow$ ADD$(MA; BASE)$

The preceding is simple enough in principle, and there will be no problems as long as a single program is being executed. However, relocation through the use of a base register will usually be used only in a multiprogramming environment, in which monitor or executive software is controlling the program stream assigning programs to different areas of memory, and controlling the switching from one program to another. All programs will be compiled or assembled using a standard starting address, START. When the monitor loads a program for execution, it will choose an appropriate location based on the current operating situation. The displacement of the program location from START will be saved by the monitor in a location NEWPROG. The monitor itself will have a fixed location in memory, starting at location MONITOR.

Assume we have a program running. *PC* will contain the actual location of the current instruction being executed, and *BASE* will contain the displacement of the current program from START, so that every address generated by the program will be displaced into the region for this program. To switch contexts, we need to jump to the region of a new program, but we have to be careful, since the JMP address will also be displaced by the contents of *BASE*. The first step is to return to the monitor by executing the following two instructions, which will have to be placed at the end of every program.

```
MVT BASE #0
JMP MONITOR
```

The first instruction clears the **BASE** register so that the second will jump to the absolute address of the monitor. When the monitor is ready to start the new program, it will execute the following instructions.

```
MVT  NEWPROG
MVT  BASE AC
JMP  START
```

The first two steps move the displacement of the new program to **AC** and then to **BASE.** The JMP instruction then loads START + **BASE,** that is, START + contents(NEW-PROG), the absolute address of the new program, into **PC** to start execution of the new program.

6.11 Argument Access in a Multiregister Organization

As we have noted, memory speed is one of the main limiting factors in the speed of computers. Even with developing memory technology, it is likely that there will always be a gap between the speed of large capacity memory and the speed of registers and logic. One consequence of this fact is that instructions involving only register transfers will always be faster than those requiring memory access. If programs could be arranged to do many register-to-register instructions for each memory reference, overall execution time would be significantly reduced. The more registers that are available, the more that can be done between memory references.

As the number of high-speed registers increases, it becomes convenient to organize them as a small but fast static memory. Arguments can then be specified by short addresses, eliminating the need for separate opcodes for similar operations on different registers. Since the number of registers is small, they can be addressed with a small number of bits, making two-address and even three-address instruction formats practical. This notion has already been illustrated with the 16-bit two-argument instructions found in RIC.

As a final example of the operand fetch options depicted in Fig. 6.21, let us consider a 32-bit architecture using an array of 16 32-bit general purpose registers. For many of the instructions, no distinction needs to be made between registers containing addresses, such as index registers and stack pointers, and registers containing data. There will inevitably be exceptions to this philosophy of uniformity of registers, (for example, if the program counter and stack pointer are part of the array, particular registers must be permanently designated to serve these purposes), but we shall not dwell on these exceptions in this section. Like RIC, this machine will address to the level of 32-bit words and will have an address length of 24 bits. This architecture will be a superset of the RIC architecture, and one design goal will be to make the writing of an assembler to translate RIC programs to object code for this register array computer as straightforward as possible. Given this compatibility at the assembly language level, we shall take the liberty of referring to the register array computer as RIC II. Clearly, RIC II will not be compatible with RIC at the machine code level.

The data path structure of RIC II is given in Fig. 6.25. Only two operand instructions will be considered here, and 32-bit registers **AR** and **BR** will hold these operands following the operand fetch process. The ALU will be used in the computation of the operand address as well as in the execution phase. The uniform high-speed register array is declared **R**⟨16⟩[32].

RIC II will also serve as an example of an instruction stream divided into intervals of 8-bit bytes. The first byte of an instruction will always contain 8 bits of opcode that will specify the particular instruction and indicate the number of operands required by the instruction. Following the opcode byte will be an operand specifier for each operand, consisting of 1 to 4 bytes. Figure 6.26a shows a segment of the instruction stream for a two-operand instruction. The first byte of each operand specifier indicates a register in **R**⟨16⟩[32] and specifies the addressing mode for that particular operand. How the register is used will depend on the addressing mode. If index addressing is specified, then three additional instruction stream bytes are included in the operand specifier to form a 24-bit displacement address to which the low-order 24 bits of the designated register in the array, **R**, can be added as an index. If indexing is not specified, then the operand specifier will consist of only 1 byte.

Figure 6.26b depicts an opcode byte for a two-operand instruction, as indicated by the fact that bits 4 and 5 are both 0. Other combinations of these 2 bits will specify other instruction formats, none of which will be discussed here. The first 4 bits will

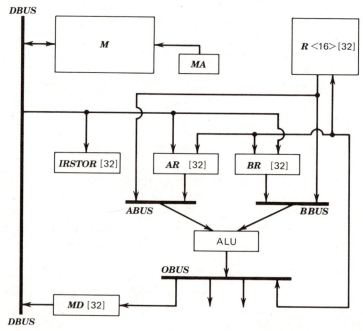

Figure 6.25. Register array computer.

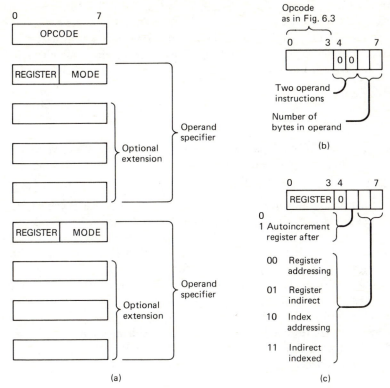

Figure 6.26. Two-operand instructions in byte interval instruction stream.

specify opcodes consistent with those tabulated for RIC in Fig. 6.3. Actually, only those instructions remaining in Fig. 6.4d are consistent with the two-operand format. The other bit combinations considered here as "don't cares" are available for future expansion. We shall assume that the second operand address will also serve as the address of the destination of the result. The last 2 bits of the opcode byte specify whether the operand will consist of 8, 16, 32, or 64 bits. Operand lengths other than the 32-bit operands that will be specified by 10 in these 2 bits will be left for the problem set.

The interpretation of the first byte of an operand specifier is illustrated in Fig. 6.26c. The first four bits are the register number in **R.** Bit 4 will be 0 for the addressing modes to be discussed. This bit could be made 1 for additional addressing modes such as immediate. If bit 5 is 1, the designated register will be incremented following determination of the operand. Bits 6 and 7 will specify four possible addressing modes as tabulated. *Register addressing* means that the designated register contains the operand. *Register indirect* means that the register contains the address of the operand. Index addressing requires the 3-byte displacement from the instruction stream, to which the last 24 bits of the designated index register are added, to form the effective address of the operand. In indirect indexed addressing, the displacement address is treated as the address of a word in memory that is added to the designated index register to obtain the effective address of the operand (low-order 24 bits in each case).

Here we are only illustrating what can be done, so, not all useful addressing modes have been included. The architecture described herein is somewhat suggestive of that of the Digital Equipment Corp. VAX in which many of the ideas were first implemented.

Example 6.5

Determine the string of bytes that will implement the RIC MVT and MVF instructions with direct or absolute addressing. Let $R\langle 8 \rangle$ be treated as the accumulator.

Solution

The MVT instruction in which the first operand specifier is that of the source and the second is the target is given in Fig. 6.27a. The first 4 bits of the opcode correspond to MVT from Fig. 6.3. The addressing mode for the source is indexed with $R\langle 1 \rangle$ as the designated index register. Clearly, this register must contain 0. The address in the instruction stream is represented by A's. Refer to Problem 6.31 for another approach to absolute addressing. The second operand specifier is register addressing, so no displacement bytes are required.

The opcode for MVF as given in Fig. 6.27b is the same as for MVT. Only the operand specifiers are reversed. Thus, no separate implementation of MVF is required in RIC II. The opcode in RIC for MVF could be a NOP in RIC II. A NOP in the set of 8-bit opcodes is necessary, given that all branching must be to word boundaries.

∎

So far, we have partially discussed the architecture of a register array based RIC II. Consistent with the advice of Section 2.2, the definition of the architecture has been in terms of natural language and whatever tools of illustration that could be brought to bear. So far, nothing has been said of implementation and no AHPL descriptions have been provided. Implementation of the byte interval instruction will necessarily be awkward in a machine with a basic memory data bus of 32-bits. The problem is worsened somewhat for RIC, which is addressable only to the 32-bit word as compared to the byte addressable VAX, for example. We illustrate the implementation of the address computation for two operand RIC II instructions in the following example.

00100010	Opcode (MVT)	00100010	Opcode (MVT)
00010010	Register/mode	10000000	Register/mode
AAAAAAAA		00010010	Register/mode
AAAAAAAA		AAAAAAAA	
AAAAAAAA		AAAAAAAA	
10000000	Register/mode	AAAAAAAA	

          (a)   (b)

Figure 6.27. Instruction Stream for (a) MVT and (b) MVF.

Example 6.6

Write an AHPL description of the implementation of the fetch of the first operand for two-operand instructions in the byte interval instruction stream of RIC II. Declaration of data paths and data registers may be assumed consistent with Fig. 6.25 and need not be shown. Include the declarations of the necessary control registers. The number of memory references to the instruction stream is to be minimized. Assume that the processor clock period is shorter than the memory access time, dictating asynchronous memory read operations. Register transfers may be used in the description without specification of the precise bus connections.

Solution

To minimize the number of memory references to the instruction stream, each set of 4 instruction bytes obtained from a 32-bit memory location must be stored in a register, **IRSTOR,** and shifted left byte-by-byte as the bytes are processed. A 2-bit register, **BYTPT,** is to count the bytes used. An 8-bit register, **IR**, is included from which the opcode will be decoded, and another 8-bit register, **REGMD**, is included for interpreting the register number and addressing mode.

MEMORY: **IRSTOR**[32]; **BYTPT**[2]; **IR**[8]; **REGMD**[8]   "control only"

Step 100 is the beginning point for execution of any instruction. Here the opcode is shifted into **IR**. As in RIC, all jump operations will be to word boundaries. This constraint is insufficient to synchronize the byte stream with word boundaries, since the number of bytes in each instruction will depend on the addressing mode. Thus, it is necessary to allow for a possible fetch of 4 instruction bytes following the processing of each byte. Whether a fetch is carried out will depend on the value of **BYTPT**, but no time will be consumed by the check when there is no fetch. For example, steps 101 and 102, which fetch a new instruction word, are skipped unless **BYTPT** is 11, indicating that the last byte has been shifted from **IRSTOR**. Because the access time of the external RAM is longer than one clock period, the memory read operation is modeled as asynchronous. Thus control waits at step 102 until **dataready** indicates that the instruction word is available.

100   **IR, IRSTOR**[0:23] ← **IRSTOR; BYTPT** ← INC(**BYTPT**);
       → ($\overline{\wedge/BYTPT}$)/(103).
101   **MA** ← **PC; PC** ← INC(**PC**).
102   **read** = 1; **IRSTOR** * **dataready** ← **DBUS**;
       → ($\overline{dataready}$)/(102).
103   → (**IR**[4] $\vee$ **IR**[5])/("other than 2-operand instructions").

Control continues at step 104 only for the two-operand instructions. For these, the next step is to place the byte, which specifies the register associated with the first operand and the addressing mode, into **REGMD** for interpretation. This is accomplished by step 104. Again, steps 105 and 106 are executed only if it is necessary to access memory for another 4 instruction bytes. Step 108 is executed only if the addressing mode is either register or register indirect. For register mode, the actual operand is transferred to *AR*, and for register indirect, the address of the operand is placed in *MA*.

104   *REGMD, IRSTOR*[0:23] ← *IRSTOR; BYTPT* ← INC(*BYTPT*);
        → ($\overline{\wedge BYTPT}$)/(107).
105   *MA* ← *PC; PC* ← INC(*PC*).
106   *read* = 1; *IRSTOR* * *dataready* ← *DBUS;*
        → ($\overline{dataready}$)/(106).
107   NO DELAY   → (*REGMD*[6])/(109).
108   *AR* * $\overline{REGMD}$[7] ← BUSFN(**R;** DCD(*REGMD*[0:3]));   "register"
        MA * *REGMD*[7] ← BUSFN[8:31](**R;** DCD(*REGMD*[0:3]));
        → (*REGMD*[7], $\overline{REGMD[7]}$)/(122, 123).   "register indirect"

The indexed and indirect indexed addressing modes both require that a 3-byte address be obtained from the instruction stream. This is accomplished by steps 109 through 117. If a memory reference is unnecessary, only three clock periods will be required.

109   *AR*[8:15], *IRSTOR*[0:23] ← *IRSTOR; BYTPT* ← INC(*BYTPT*);
        → ($\overline{\wedge BYTPT}$)/(112).
110   *MA* ← *PC; PC* ← INC(*PC*).
111   *read* = 1; *IRSTOR* * *dataready* ← *DBUS;*
        → ($\overline{dataready}$)/(111).
112   *AR*[16:23], *IRSTOR*[0:23] ← *IRSTOR; BYTPT* ← INC(*BYTPT*);
        → ($\overline{\wedge BYTPT}$)/(115).
113   *MA* ← *PC; PC* ← INC(*PC*).
114   *read* = 1; *IRSTOR* * *dataready* ← *DBUS;*
        → ($\overline{dataready}$)/(114).
115   *AR*[24:31], *IRSTOR*[0:23] ← *IRSTOR; BYTPT* ← INC(*BYTPT*);
        → ($\overline{\wedge BYTPT}$)/(118).
116   *MA* ← *PC; PC* ← INC(*PC*).
117   *read* = 1; *IRSTOR* * *dataready* ← *DBUS;*
        → ($\overline{dataready}$)/(117).

Only for indirect indexed addressing is it necessary to go to memory to obtain an address. This is done by steps 119 and 120 after the indexed addressing case has been branched to step 121 where the indexing operation takes place. All the addressing modes, except register mode, converge at step 122 where the operand is accessed from memory and placed in *AR*. All four modes have converged at step 123 where the designated register is incremented, if the autoincrement bit, *REGMD*[5] = 1.

118   NO DELAY   → ($\overline{REGMD[7]}$)/(121).
119   *MA* ← *AR*[8:31].   "indirect"
120   *read* = 1; *AR* * *dataready* ← *DBUS;*
        → ($\overline{dataready}$)/(120).

121   *MA* ← ADD[9:32](*AR;* BUSFN(**R;** DCD(*REGMD*[0:3]))). "indexed"
122   *read* = 1; *AR* * *dataready* ← *DBUS*.
       → ($\overline{dataready}$)/(122).
123   **R** * (DCD(*REGMD*[0:3]) ∧ *REGMD*[5] ←
                                    INC(BUSFN(**R;** DCD(*REGMD*[0:3])))).
124   "Continue with fetch of second operand"

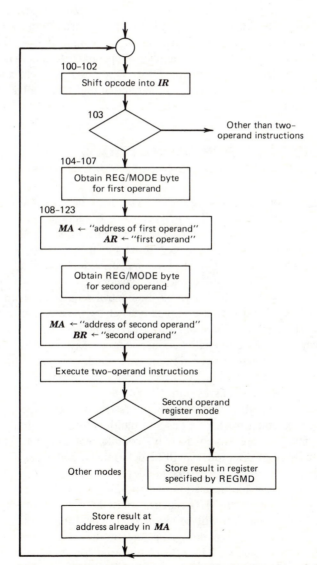

Figure 6.28. Execution of two-operand instructions in register array machine.

The fetch of the second operand of a two-operand instruction would be a repetition of steps 104 through 123 of Example 6.6, except that the result would be left in **BR**. At the conclusion of the execution of a two-operand instruction, the address determined for the second operand will still be in **MA**. This address can then be used directly for storing the result. Thus a separate sequence of steps to determine a third address is not needed. This is depicted in Fig. 6.28, which also shows the handling of the exception, that is, register mode addressing. In this case, the identity of the target register remains in **REGMD**, enabling the immediate storage of the result in the array, **R**.

In closing this section, we should note that RIC II exhibits most of the options identified in the previous two sections. The byte interval instruction stream combines the instruction fetch options of Figs. 6.20a and b. Looking at Fig. 6.26, we see that a RIC II instruction can process varying number of operands. Although not illustrated, a variety of operand lengths are provided for. Direct and indirect addressing are included, and considerable computation on the internal registers can take place during address determination.

6.12   Multiple-Cycle Instructions

Now that the instruction fetch and argument access have been treated in some detail, let us now turn our attention briefly to the third or execution phase. The memory reference instructions considered so far were executed by a single transfer of information from one register to another register. In later chapters, as we consider instructions useful in computers with particular problem distributions, we shall find that some instructions require many consecutive register transfers.

In general, the approach to designing the control sequencing hardware will be the same, regardless of instruction complexity. Let us illustrate, using fixed-point multiplication as an example. There are various possible approaches to the multiplication of numbers that may be negative. Since storage may be in the form of one's complements, two's complements, or sign and magnitude, various schemes are used to effect multiplication of all these formats. To preserve continuity, let us defer a discussion of the various alternatives until Chapter 15.

The simplest, although not necessarily the fastest or least expensive, approach to multiplication is keeping track of signs and multiplying the magnitudes. Here let us assume that numbers are stored as two's-complement integers. Thus, prior to multiplication, the sign of the product will be determined, and all two's-complement negative numbers will be replaced by magnitudes.

Since the fixed-point multiplication of two 32-bit numbers may result in a 64-bit product, another register, the **MQ** register, must be added to store the 32 least significant bits of the product. It will be necessary to count the number of bits of the multiplier that have been treated at any given stage in the process; so a 5-bit counter, designated **SHC**, will be added. The **cff** will be used for storage of the sign. The described hardware configuration may be found in Fig. 6.29.

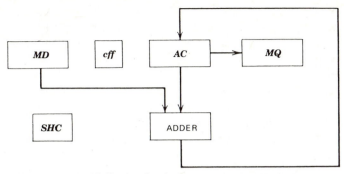

Figure 6.29. Multiplication hardware.

Only the basic data paths involved in multiplication are shown in Fig. 6.29. In practice, busing would almost certainly be used. As we have seen, however, we need not concern ourselves with the bus arrangement in writing the control sequence. We shall assume that the bus configuration is such that all transfers required in the following sequence can be implemented.

The multiplication instruction is not included in RIC. Similarly, several of the registers in Fig. 6.29 are not available in RIC. Therefore, let us visualize multiplication as part of another computer, encompassing all the features of RIC but with an extended arithmetic capability, including multiplication.

Let us pick up the operation at a point in the control sequence following the fetch cycle and the identification of the instruction. The multiplier is in the *AC* from the previous instruction. The multiplicand has just been read from storage and placed in *MD*. Control has diverged to the point of the actual beginning of the instruction. The operation begins with the clearing of *cff* to prepare for sign determination. The first three steps convert the multiplier to sign and magnitude form, leaving the magnitude in *MQ* and the sign in *cff*. The next three steps place the magnitude of the multiplicand in *MD* and leave the sign of the final product in *cff*. Two's complements, where necessary, are obtained by complementing individual bits and adding one to the least significant bit. Notice that *cff*, which has initially reset to 0, is complemented once if the multiplier is negative and once if the multiplicand is negative. Thus it ends up 0 if and only if the signs are the same.

1    $cff \leftarrow 0$;
       $\rightarrow (\overline{AC[0]})/(3)$.
2    $AC \leftarrow \text{ADD}[1:32](32 \top 0; \overline{AC}; 1); cff \leftarrow \overline{cff}$.
3    $MQ \leftarrow AC; AC \leftarrow MD$.
4    $\rightarrow (\overline{AC[0]})/(6)$.
5    $AC \leftarrow \text{ADD}[1:32](32 \top 0; \overline{AC}; 1); cff \leftarrow \overline{cff}$.
6    $MD \leftarrow AC$.

Before proceeding, let us consider the basic multiplication process in some detail. Since the basic arithmetic process of a computer is addition, multiplication is generally

carried out by successive addition. In this technique, the decimal multiplication of
203×576 would be carried out as shown inn Fig. 6.30a. For the binary case, the
process is even simpler, since the only multiplier bits are 0 or 1. Thus, for each
multiplier bit, the multiplicand is either added once or not added at all. A typical
binary multiplication is shown in Fig. 6.30b.

From this, it is seen that the basic binary multiplicative process involves in-
specting each multiplier bit in turn, adding and shifting for a 1, and shifting without
adding for a 0. As shown in Fig. 6.30, the partial products are successively shifted
left before addition, finally resulting in a product having twice as many bits as the
initial operands. This process would be impractical in a computer, since it would
require a double-length adder, for example, a 64-bit adder for a machine with 32-bit
operands.

To avoid this difficulty, addition, if required, is performed as each bit of the
multiplier is inspected; and the resultant sum is then shifted right, providing a relative
left shift of the next partial product. To provide for the double-length product, the *AC*
and *MQ* registers are catenated for right-shifting. The multiplier is initially loaded into
MQ, the multiplicand into *MD*, with *AC* initially cleared. As the product is shifted
into *MQ*, the multiplier is shifted out so that the multiplier bit to be inspected is always
in the low-order position of *MQ*. This process of multiplication is illustrated in Fig.
6.31 for the same multiplications as Fig. 6.30b. The dotted line in *MQ* indicates the
boundary between the developing partial product and the remainder of the multiplier.

The first step in the implementation of this process stores a string of zeros in
AC and sets the multiplication counter *SHC*, to zero. This is followed by a loop that
adds a product vector to *AC* and shifts the result right. This loop will be executed 32
times. When $\perp(31) = SHC$, the process will terminate. Thus, at the conclusion of
32 cycles, the product will be found with the least significant bits in *MQ* and the
remaining bits in *AC*. The *AC* will not overflow at any step, since the magnitude of
the multiplicand is less than or equal to $2^{31} - 1$.

7	$SHC \leftarrow 5 \top 0; AC \leftarrow 32 \top 0.$	
8	$\rightarrow (MQ[31])/(10).$	
9	$AC, MQ \leftarrow 0, AC, MQ[0:30];$	
	$\rightarrow (11).$	
10	$AC, MQ \leftarrow \mathrm{ADD}[1:31](AC; MD), MQ[0:30].$	
11	$SHC \leftarrow \mathrm{INC}(SHC);$	
	$\rightarrow (\overline{\wedge /SHC})/(8).$	

Notice that a separation of control is specified, depending on whether a given
bit of the multiplier is 1 or 0. The reason for this is a physical one; the shift operation
will require less time than the add followed by a shift (perhaps 5:1). Thus, if half the
multiplier bits are zero, this approach will reduce the overall multiplication time by a
factor of almost 2. Since the multiplicand is in positive form, the leading bit (the sign
bit) is 0 so that there can be no overflow. Hence the leading bit of the sum will always
be 0, as desired for shifting into *AC*[0].

After consideration of all 32 bits, the contents of both *MQ* and *AC* are complemented if the *cff* is 1. The process of complementing a double-length result is rather
cumbersome. This alone might suggest looking for another approach to multiplication.

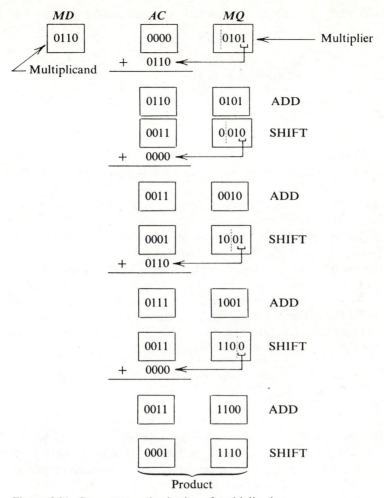

Figure 6.31. Computer mechanization of multiplication.

$$
\begin{array}{r}
576 \\
\times\ 203 \\
\hline
576 \\
576 \\
576 \\
000 \\
576 \\
576 \\
\hline
\text{(a)}\quad 116{,}828
\end{array}
\qquad
\begin{array}{r}
0110 \\
0101 \\
\hline
0110 \\
0000 \\
0110 \\
0000 \\
\hline
\text{(b)}\quad 0011110
\end{array}
$$

Figure 6.30. Multiplication by successive addition.

For completeness, the following sequence, although awkward, does complete the process.

12	→ $(\overline{cff})/(15)$.
13	*cff, MQ* ← ADD(32 T 0; $\overline{MQ}$; 1).
14	*cff, AC* ← ADD(32 T 0; $\overline{AC}$; *cff*).
15	Exit to next instruction

6.13 Summary

In this chapter, we have presented a language with which the engineer can approach the design of a computer or a computer subsystem. It is not an algorithmic design procedure. The designer is not relieved of the responsibility of optimizing this AHPL description of the control unit for a particular application.

It is hoped, however, that this chapter and Chapter 7 will provide the engineer with a place to start. We have developed the complete control sequence (except for IOT) for a typical single-address machine. We have also introduced some more complex systems of addressing and a basic multiple register organization. We have hardly scratched the surface in terms of possible computer organizations, and many other possibilities will be discussed in succeeding chapters.

Problems

6.1 Multiple indirect addressing is possible. Such a scheme would allow an address obtained by indirect addressing to be the address of another address, which might be the data address or the address of another address. RIC can be made to function in this manner by replacing bits 5:7 in the instruction register, as well as the address bits, with each indirect access.

   (a) Modify steps 4 through 10 of the RIC control sequence to implement this modification. It may be necessary to add steps, which may be called 10A and 10B.

   (b) Alternatively, only bit 7 of **IR** could be replaced with each indirect access. Discuss the advantages and disadvantages of this latter approach.

   (c) Given multiple indirect addressing, would it be possible to specify the addressing mode with only 2 bits rather than with 3?

6.2 Suppose that the only addressing modes allowed for jump operations in a modified version of RIC are direct and indirect. Suppose that no branch relative operations are included but are replaced by a conditional jump absolute operation, JPC, which uses instruction bits 5 and 6 to specify the jump conditions (bit 7 specifies direct or indirect addressing). Modify steps 1 through 15 of the RIC control sequence accordingly and include sufficient steps to implement JMP, JPC, and JSR. The JPC conditions are tabulated here.

IR [5:6]	jump if
0 0	Z = 1
0 1	N = 1
1 0	C = 1
1 1	V = 1

6.3   Some computers, particularly microprogrammed (see Chapter 8) computers, branch at one point for separate execution of all 32-bit instructions rather than share steps as is done in RIC. Modify the RIC control sequence so that control branches at step 13 to 15 separate control sequences to implement each of the operations tabulated in Fig. 6.3. Compare the number of AHPL steps required by the two approaches.

6.4   Consider a simplified RIC with no 16-bit instructions, so that only an 8-bit instruction register is required. Modify steps 1 through 11 of the RIC control sequence accordingly.

6.5   Suppose an addressing mode, specified by $IR[5:7] = 111$, and calling for indexing before indirect addressing is added to RIC. Modify steps 1 through 11 of the RIC control sequence accordingly.

6.6   Modify steps 1 through 11 of the RIC control sequence as described in Problem 6.5, but also allow multiple indirect addressing as discussed in Problem 6.1. If $IR[7] = 1$, indirect addressing continues. The significance of bits $IR[5:6]$ after all indirect addressing is complete is given here.

IR [5:6]	
0 0	Direct (address is now available)
0 1	Used only before indirect addressing
1 0	Immediate (24-bit data word available)
1 1	Available address must be indexed

6.7   Repeat Problem 6.6, but allow indexing ($IR[5:6] = 11$) after the indirect addressing at any level.

6.8   Rewrite step 20 of the RIC control sequence showing explicitly all bus connections. Be certain that the step is consistent with the bus configuration shown in Fig. 6.1.

6.9   Repeat Problem 6.8 for step 32 of the RIC control sequence.

6.10   A certain computer has only 8-bit instruction and data words. If the first
3 bits of an instruction are all 1's, the instruction is to be executed in
two event times. Bits 3, 4, and 5 control the first event time and bits 6
and 7 the second. If bit 3 is a 0, the first event time is a NOP. If bit 3
is a 1, bits 4 and 5 specify rotate or shift (enter a 0 in the vacated bit
position) operations as follows.

	Bit	4	5	
		0	0	Rotate *AC* left
		0	1	Rotate *AC* right
		1	0	Shift *AC* left
		1	1	Shift *AC* right

The action of the second event time is specified as follows.

	Bit	6	7	
		0	0	No operation
		0	1	Set *AC*
		1	0	Clear *AC*
		1	1	Complement *AC*

Write an AHPL sequence to implement these instructions.

6.11   In some computers, the index registers can be automatically incremented
or decremented each time they are used. This makes it possible to avoid
the inclusion of instructions for incrementing the index register in assembly language loops. Modify RIC by adding two addressing modes that
provide for incrementing the index register after it is used. Modify RIC
steps 1 through 11 to incorporate the addressing modes tabulated here.

IR [5:7]	Addressing mode
1 1 0	Indexed with autoincrementing of *IX*
1 1 1	Indirect indexed with autoincrementing of *IX*

6.12   Suppose a machine with exactly the same instruction set as RIC is to be
designed and named RIC16. RIC16 will differ in that the memory data
bus will consist of only 16-bits and the 24-bit address will address individual 16-bit words. Operands will usually consist of two consecutive
words in memory. Jumps and branches to any 16-bit word are allowed
in RIC16.

(a) Rewrite the first 22 steps of the RIC control sequence transforming it into a sequence for RIC16.

(b) Why would RIC16 not be considered assembly language compatible with RIC?

(c) Suppose it is now desired to design a processor called RIC32, which will be assembly language compatible with RIC16. RIC32 will merely be faster than RIC16 in that an operand can be obtained with one memory reference rather than two. In what way will the instruction and data fetch implementations in RIC32 be more complicated than in the original RIC?

6.13 A microprocessor is to be designed with 16 address output lines and an 8-bit data bus so that it is capable of addressing $2\uparrow16$ 8-bit words. An instruction may consist of one or more consecutive bytes in memory. We will be concerned with the instruction fetch and the execution of certain 2- or 3-byte instructions. Assume the microprocessor to have, among other registers, a 16-bit *PC*, one 8-bit *AC*, two 16-bit index registers *IA* and *IB*, an 8-bit instruction register, and a 16-bit memory address register. This memory address register may be assumed to be connected to the 16-address output lines. The data bus is a COMBUS that may be connected to the output of any 8 bits of a register. Two control outputs, *read* and *write*, are to be included. The addressed data will appear on the data bus during the same clock period in which *read* = 1. A one-period level on line *write* will also cause the execution of a write operation.

The first byte of an instruction may be interpreted as given in Fig. P6.13. Notice that there are only two addressing modes, immediate and indexed. Immediate addressing means that the data byte or bytes im-

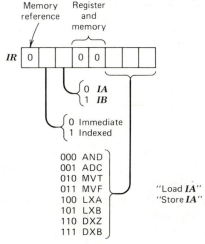

Figure P6.13.

mediately follow the 8-bit instruction byte in memory. In the indexed addressing mode, a 16-bit address is formed by adding the 8-bit byte following the instruction byte to the contents of a 16-bit index register.

Write a partial, but formal, AHPL description of the microprocessor module. Include the control sequence for the instruction fetch, the address formation for all memory reference instructions ($IR[0] = 0$), and the execution of all eight register and memory instructions ($IR[3:4] = 00$). Include declarations, simply omitting declarations of any hardware not used in your partial control sequence. LXA and DXA mean load and deposit, respectively, the index register. The index registers are 16-bit registers, so two consecutive data bytes in memory must be used in these instructions. It is not necessary to predefine an internal bus structure prior to writing the control sequence.

6.14 Consider a digital computer with a 32-bit word length and the same registers and bus organization as in RIC (PC, AC, IX, and SP on the $BBUS$). The set of 32-bit addressed instructions are slightly different. After control has branched away for execution of some addressed instructions (listed in the figure as "don't cares"), the instructions depicted in Fig. P6.14 that use AC are to be executed in a single step. The meaning of each mnemonic is the same as in RIC except for MATCH, which is the same as XOR except that it has no effect on AC.

$IR[0:1]$

$IR[2:3]$	00	01	11	10
00	SBC	ADC	X	AND
01	SUB	ADD	X	BIT
10	CMP	X	X	XOR
11	X	MVT	X	MATCH

Figure P6.14

(a) Write the AHPL expression for connections to the $ABUS$ in the step that executes the instructions in Fig. P6.14.

(b) Write an AHPL expression for cin (carry-in to the adder) for this execution step.

(c) Write an AHPL expression for connections to the $OBUS$ for this execution step.

(d) Write an AHPL expression for the transfer statement into zff (zero flag) in this execution step.

(e) Write an AHPL expression for the transfer statement into vff (overflow flag) in this execution step.

6.15 A hardware saving can be achieved in the RIC ALU by sharing logic between the ADD and the EXOR operations. Write a combinational logic unit description for a unit that will accomplish both ADD and EXOR. There will be two separate output vectors, a 32-bit XOR output and a 33-bit ADD. The input arguments will be the same as those of the adder. The adder will be ripple carry as discussed in Chapter 5. Use as few logic gates as possible. What, if any, modifications in RIC step 22 would be required by the use of this unit?

6.16 Consider a computer with an 18-bit word length and an instruction word as given in Fig. P6.16. The machine has 18-bit registers *IR*, *MD*, and *AC*; and 13-bit registers *PC*, *IA*, *IB*, and *MA*. The last two opcodes indicate instructions that do not use the 13-bit address. Write in AHPL the control sequence of the computer beginning with the instruction fetch up through the execution of the instructions given by the first 6 opcodes.

0		2 3	4 5		17
OPCODE			ADDRESS		

3 4	
0 0	Direct
0 1	Indirect
1 0	Index *IA*
1 1	Index *IB*

OPCODE			Mnemonic	
0	0	0	OR	
0	0	1	ADC	
0	1	0	JPA	Jump if $AC > 0$
0	1	1	JMP	
1	0	0	JSR	
1	0	1	DCA	Store and clear *AC*
1	1	0	IOT	
1	1	1	Nonaddressed	

Figure P6.16.

6.17 Suppose one more 24-bit register called *BASE* and one more 32-bit register, *MQ*, have been added to RIC. Rewrite the appropriate portions of steps 52 and 53 so that these two registers can be processed by the 16-bit two operand instructions in just the same way as *AC*, *IX*, and *SP*.

6.18 Let a modified RIC consist of eight general purpose 32-bit registers **REG**⟨8⟩ [32] in place of *AC*, *IX*, and *SP*. Consider only the two-address register-only instructions of Section 6.6. Let the AD1 and AD2 codes for the eight registers be 0000 through 0111, respectively. Modify RIC steps 52 and 53 to implement all the two-address operations in Fig. 6.8 for this new configuration.

6.19   Modify step 61 of RIC explicitly including all bus connections. The step must be made consistent with Fig. 6.1.

6.20   Modify RIC step 61 to accomplish multiple bit shifting in one clock period as suggested by Fig. 6.12. Assume that the shift distance as specified by instruction bits 11 through 15 will never exceed 7 bits in either direction.

6.21   Using the format of Fig. 6.16, code the 32-bit branch instruction that would be generated by the assembler for each of the following. Each number proceeded by $ is a relative address in hexadecimal.
(a) BLE $9 (b) BGE $00FF (c) BGT $2 (d) BRA $FFFF "branch always"

6.22   Suppose the format of the branch instructions in Fig. 6.16 were changed so that bit 6 would not cause the overall branch function to be complemented but would correspond to $(\overline{N \oplus V})$. Rewrite step 30 of the RIC control sequence accordingly. Which of the branch operations listed in Fig. 6.15 could no longer be realized?

6.23   Suppose the code $IR[0:9] = 1110\ 01\ 0010$ corresponding to CMC (complement cff) is to be added to the table in Fig. 6.17. Modify, as necessary, RIC steps 130 through 146 to provide for implementation of this operation.

6.24   Modify steps 130 through 146 of the RIC control sequence so that the stack will point at the first vacant location at the top of the stack rather than at the last data word already pushed on the stack.

6.25   As suggested by Example 6.3, indirect addressing may be used to increase the address space of a computer. Modify the register configuration and the first 22 steps of RIC to allow 32-bit addresses.

6.26   Write in AHPL the control sequence for the computer of Example 6.3.

6.27   The base addressing scheme of Example 6.4 may cause problems in connection with RTS. Carefully discuss the nature of these difficulties and how they can be avoided either by programming or by further modifications in the hardware.

6.28   Code sufficient bytes of the RIC II byte stream to accomplish each of the following.

		1st operand	2nd operand	
(a)	ADC	$R\langle 4 \rangle$;	$M\langle 00FF \text{ hex} \rangle$	
(b)	SUB	$(M\langle 00FFFF \rangle)$	$R\langle 4 \rangle$	"indirect"

6.29   Fill out the RIC II control sequence as follows.

(a)   Photocopy and mark steps 104 through 123 to form steps 124 through 143, which fetch the second operand.
(b)   Write the steps that store the RIC II result after execution.

6.30   (a) Modify step 108 of the RIC II control sequence to explicitly reflect all connections in the RIC II bus structure.
(b) Repeat for step 121.

6.31   Suppose the program counter is included as $R\langle 0 \rangle$ in the 16-register array discussed in Section 6.11. In this case, how might immediate addressing be accomplished using the register indirect mode, if RIC II were modified to provide addressing of individual bytes? What, if any, modifications would be required in the control sequence of that section? Describe why the JMP instruction might now be eliminated from the opcode list of Fig. 6.3?

6.32   A computer, RIC IIa, which could be more economical than RIC II to realize as a VLSI chip (it may also execute faster because of less delay in the instruction decode logic), will have the same register array and bus structure as RIC II. A word instruction stream rather than a byte stream will be employed. An instruction will consist of one, two, or three words. The first word will consist of the opcode (8-bit for purposes of the problem but expandable to 16-bits) and reg/mode bytes for both operands. A second word will contain the operand extension for the first operand, if required. A third word could contain the extension for the second operand. Write in AHPL the equivalent of RIC II steps 100 through 123 for this new configuration.

6.33   This problem is concerned with writing the AHPL description of a two-address machine. That is, two arguments may be obtained from the random access memory or one argument can be read from memory and a result deposited in memory by a single instruction. For simplicity, we assume that the random access memory contains only $2 \uparrow 10$ 24-bit words. Unless bits $IR[0:2] = 111$, the instruction word will take the following form.

It will be observed that indirect addressing is allowed while indexing is omitted for convenience. Arbitrarily, we shall assume that, when indirect addressing is specified, it refers to ADDRESS 1 only. Of the seven possible memory reference instructions, two are of particular interest. These are

010   AND   AND the contents of the memory location specified by AD-DRESS 1 with *AC* and deposit the result at the location specified by ADDRESS 2. *AC* is left unchanged.

011   JMP   JMP to ADDRESS 2 if and only if the content of the location specified by ADDRESS 1 is 0.

The machine has a 24-bit instruction register, *IR*; a single 10-bit memory address register, *MA* (only one memory access can be performed at a time); a 24-bit memory data register, *MD*; a 24-bit accumulator, *AC*; an extra 24-bit working register, *WK*; and a 10-bit program counter, *PC*. Write an AHPL sequence representing a hard-wired control unit for this machine. Include the fetch cycle and allow for indirect addressing. Carry the execute cycle through for only the two instructions AND and JMP. Indicate the point where control diverges for the instructions represented by opcode 111, and indicate the point where control for the instructions AND and JMP diverges from that of the other memory reference instructions.

References

1. Y. Chu, *Computer Organization and Microprogramming,* Prentice–Hall, Englewood Cliffs, N.J., 1972.
2. R. M. Kline, *Digital Computer Design,* Prentice–Hall, Englewood Cliffs, N.J., 1977.
3. G. A. Blaauw, *Digital System Implementation,* Prentice–Hall, Englewood Cliffs, N.J., 1976.
4. F. J. Mowle, *A Systematic Approach to Digital Logic Design,* Addison–Wesley, Reading, Mass., 1976.
5. M. M. Mano, *Computer System Architecture,* Prentice–Hall, Englewood Cliffs, N.J., 1976.
6. H. Hellerman, *Digital Computer System Principles,* 2nd ed., McGraw–Hill, New York, 1973.
7. T. Bartee, *Digital Computer Fundamentals,* 4th ed., McGraw–Hill, New York, 1977.
8. A. S. Tannenbaum, *Structured Computer Organization,* 2nd ed., Prentice–Hall, Englewood Cliffs, N.J., 1984.
9. F. J. Hill, and G. R. Peterson, *Introduction to Switching Theory and Logical Design,* 3rd ed., Wiley, New York, 1981.
10. D. P. Siewiorek, C. G. Bell, and A. Newell, *Computer Structures: Principles and Examples,* McGraw–Hill, New York, 1982.
11. *MC68000 16-Bit Microcessor User Manual,* 3rd ed., Prentice–Hall, Englewood Cliffs, N.J., 1982.

12. J. K. Iliffe, *Advanced Computer Design,* Prentice–Hall, Englewood Cliffs, N.J., 1982.
13. *VAX Architecture Handbook,* Digital Equipment Corp., Maynard Mass., 1981.
14. F. J. Hill, and G. R. Peterson, *Digital Logic and Microprocessors,* Wiley, New York, 1984.
15. R. Piloty, et al., *CONLAN Report,* Springer-Verlag, Berlin, 1983.

7 Hardware Realizations

7.1 Introduction

In the last chapter, we showed how the functioning of a digital system can be described in terms of an AHPL control sequence. The next step in the design process is to translate this description into hardware. Some of this has already been done. In Chapter 6, we developed the basic data structure of the system, that is, the internal organization of registers, buses, and processing logic, in parallel with the writing of the control sequence. Another major part of the design process is the development of the control unit. In Section 4.6, a particular form of hard-wired control unit was introduced. For readers whose primary objective is to gain an understanding of computer functioning from the user's point of view, the material on hardware in preceding chapters will be adequate for most purposes. Such readers may prefer to skim over the materal on hardware in Sections 7.2 and 7.3. Sections 7.4 and 7.5 are directed primarily to readers who expect to design digital systems and who have the objective of filling in some of the fine points of hardware realizations that are not evident from previous chapters.

Section 7.2 deals with the problems of starting and stopping complex digital systems. Although not essential to the developments in succeeding chapters, this material is important if real systems are to be built. Section 7.3 deals with the problems of controlling devices that cannot respond in a single clock period. This material is very important to the designer. Section 7.4 provides a detailed analysis of propagation delays in the data paths and the control unit. This material is critical, since it is these delays that set the basic limit on the speed of any digital system.

Section 7.5 is concerned with hardware compilers. The use of computers to mechanize parts of the design process is virtually a necessity in the design of computers or other systems of comparable complexity. It is easy to write a statement such as

20   *cff, AC* ← ADD(*AC; MD; cin*)

and it is clear what is to occur. But the actual implementation will require the wiring of hundreds of connections, every one of which must be individually specified. The manner in which computers take over such detail work is discussed in Section 7.5. This material is not essential to later chapters but is very helpful in providing a clearer picture of the manner in which the necessary hardware can be determined from the control sequence.

As a final note, most of the material in this chapter is based on the use of a *hard-wired* control unit. This type of control unit offers maximum speed and is usually preferable for special-purpose realizations and computers with limited instruction sets. Another type of control unit is the *microprogrammed* control unit. These are usually slower than hard-wired units but will often lead to quicker chip design for VLSI realization of computers with complex instruction sets. Microprogramming will be treated in Chapter 8.

7.2   Starting, Stopping, and Resetting

One of the more subtle problems associated with the design of a control unit is how to get it started. With the control unit design we have so far assumed, once a single-clock-period level has been established at the input to any single D flip-flop, the desired sequence of levels will propagate through the sequence of control flip-flops. Thus, to start operations at step 1, flip-flop 1 of the control unit must be set and all others must be reset. To accomplish this, we use the direct SET and RESET inputs of the D flip-flops making up the control unit. A line labelled *reset* will be connected to the SET input of flip-flop 1 and to the RESET input of all the other flip-flops in the control unit. The line *reset* will be held active as long as the reset button is pushed. When the button is released, the next clock pulse will advance control from step 1 to step 2, and the sequence will proceed from there.

With this method, the system will automatically start through its sequence after being reset. That is probably acceptable for a computer, but it might be desirable in some cases for the system to remain in a reset state while preparations for the new operating cycle are carried out. This can be accomplished very simply by making step 1 a wait state for a *start* signal, as shown in Fig. 7.1.

Figure 7.2 shows the realization of the first few steps of a typical control sequence with both *start* and *reset* lines; it also shows the timing of a typical reset-start sequence in which we have assumed that the system happened to be at step 3 of the sequence at the time of the reset.

When the *reset* line goes low (on most flip-flops the direct inputs are activated by the signal going low) flip-flop 1 is set and all other flip-flops in the control unit

1 → (*start*)/(1)
2 Start of main sequence

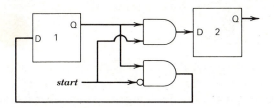

Figure 7.1. Implementation of RIC step 1a.

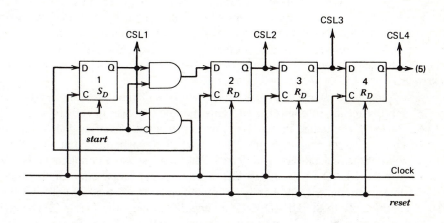

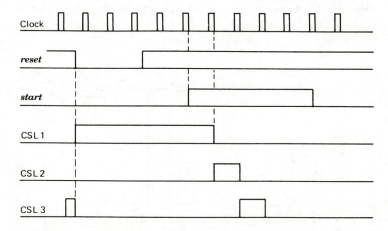

Figure 7.2. Reset-start sequence.

are reset. When the *reset* line goes high, step 1 is enabled and the *start* signal is tested. As long as *start* is low, control will remain at step 1. When *start* goes high, control moves to step 2 to start the normal sequence. This reset action will be indicated by the statement

    CONTROLRESET (1)

appearing after the END SEQUENCE statement, with the number in parenthesis indicating the control step to which the system returns when reset.

    The reset button provides for resetting the system when it is already in operation, but means must also be provided to reset the system when it is first turned on. It might seem that the solution is simple, turn the system on and then reset it by pushing the button. However, unless precautions are taken, a digital system will come on in a completely random state when power is first applied and might do something undesirable or even dangerous before it could be reset. To prevent this, most systems provide electronic means whereby the *reset* line is automatically driven active as soon as power is applied and held there for a short time, long enough for the power supplies to reach steady state and the clock oscillator to stabilize. The *reset* line then goes inactive automatically and the system proceeds with its normal sequence, or waits for *start* signal.

    The foregoing system of start and reset will be suitable if control step 1 can be entered only by means of control reset. This may be the case in some systems, but not necessarily in computers in which the implementation of various halt commands must be considered. In chapter 6, the HLT instruction was indicated at step 72, but consideration of the realization was deferred. The simplest way to implement the HLT command is the DEAD END at step 72, indicating that propagation of the control level is simply terminated. The hardware implementation of steps 70 and 71 which, branch conditionally to the DEAD END at step 78, is shown in Fig. 7.3. The AND gate leading to step 78 obviously serves no purpose but is included for clarity. Since nothing is connected to the output of this gate, the HLT instruction simply causes the active control level to disappear, leaving all flip-flops in the control unit in the reset state. The syntax DEAD END represents no hardware but indicates that nothing is connected to the output of corresponding control step.

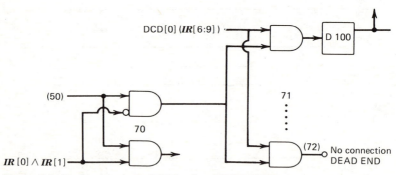

Figure 7.3. Implementation of HLT using DEAD END.

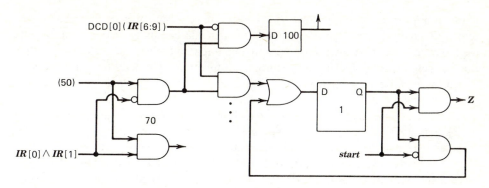

Figure 7.4. Implementation of HLT by return to step 1.

Because DEAD END, as described here, will leave all control flip-flops reset, the computer cannot be started again without a control reset to enable step 1. If a reset operation affected nothing but the control unit, this would be satisfactory; but a computer reset is often used to shut everything down and start over when something goes wrong. In addition to resetting the control unit, it may also reset the I/O devices, the interrupt system, the status indicators, and even the data registers. HLT is often used to stop a program to give the operator a chance to intervene, without otherwise affecting the status of the program, so that a computer reset would be undesirable. We shall, therefore, implement HALT by returning control to step 1, to wait for a *start* signal without otherwise affecting the status of the computer. This is done at step 71, as shown in Fig. 7.4, and step 72 is eliminated.

With this implementation of HLT, the timing of the *start* signal must be considered more carefully. A modern computer executes an instruction in a few microseconds or less and can execute a complete program in a small fraction of a second. If a *start* signal is derived directly from a manual push button, the computer might complete the program, execute a HALT, and return to step 1 before the button has been released, in which event it would start again. Such false restarts can be prevented by the use of a *single-level generator*.

The single-level generator can be described by three statements included following END SEQUENCE. This requires declaration of two memory elements, *stff* and *slf*, and a CTERM, *slstart*, to provide a control connection to the implementation of the control sequence. (In some versions of the AHPL simulator, it will be necessary to declare *slstart* as an output even though it will not really be connected outside of the RIC module.)

    END SEQUENCE
        CONTROLRESET (1);
        stff ← start;
        slf ← stff;
        slstart = stff ∧$\overline{slf}$.
    END.

It might appear that the flip-flop *stff* would be unnecessary if *start* were connected directly to the input of *slf*. We should note that the computer start button may be depressed at random at any point in time without regard to the system clock. The flip-flop *stff* actually accomplishes a synchronizing function. (We defer further discussion of synchronization to Chapter 9. At that point, we shall see that this elementary synchronizing mechanism may in some cases be insufficient.) The implementation of the partial hardware description just given is shown in Fig. 7.5a, with the corresponding timing diagram given in Fig. 7.5b. We note that *slstart* is 1 for only one clock period. It remains 0 until *stff* goes to 1 and returns to 0 as soon as *slf* goes to 1.

The hardware techniques just described will be adequate for most digital systems other than computers, but there are also software aspects to be considered in starting and resetting computers. A computer control unit can basically do just one thing, read an instruction and execute it, so that a computer cannot be started in any useful sense unless it has a program to start executing. To provide this software component of the start/reset process, most CPUs include a ROM containing a start-up program that will, at the very minimum, allow the user to enter commands through a keyboard. On power up or reset, the *reset* line, in addition to resetting the control unit to the start of the fetch sequence, will reset the program counter to the address of the first instruction of the start-up program. The start-up program will usually establish appropriate starting conditions in the system and then turn control over to the operating system software. It is important to note that this start-up program is a part of the CPU itself, is normally transparent to the user, and is located in a separate address space accessible only during start-up or reset. Because the computer has its initialization steps built in, there is rarely any need for a separate start button, a single reset button being sufficient to start the computer over and bring it to a condition where it is ready to start accepting commands from the user.

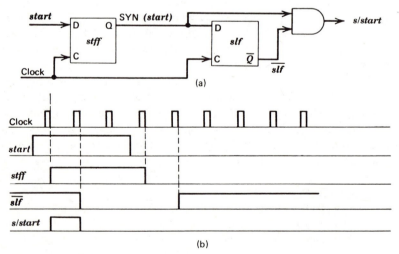

Figure 7.5. Single-start-level generation.

7.3   Multiperiod Operations

In writing the RIC control sequence in Chapter 6, we assumed that all transfer operations could be completed in one clock period. However, there are many cases in which transfers or logic operations may require more than one clock period. Memory access is one such situation. Because of cost, main random access memory is often realized in technology that is slower than register memory. Since the majority of transfers involve registers, the clock rate is set accordingly, and any slower transfers will require multiple clock periods.

As discussed in Chapter 3, many different technologies may be considered for implementing random access memories. These many types of memories differ greatly in signal and timing requirements. In terms of the control sequence steps required to control them, the majority of memory systems can be grouped into three categories, which we shall refer to as *clocked, slow synchronous,* and *asynchronous.* The clocked memory is the simplest to handle, being logically equivalent to an array of clocked registers. Such as memory is fully compatible in speed with the control unit. The general model for a clocked memory is shown in Fig. 3.13. There are address lines, separate input and output lines for data, and a single control line, **write enable,** which is equivalent to the clock line for a register.

Clocked memories are usually small arrays of registers that will be located on the same VLSI chip as the CPU. For these memories, the notations discussed in Chapter 5, for example

$$MD \leftarrow \text{BUSFN}(\mathbf{M}; \text{DCD}(MA))$$

for read and

$$\mathbf{M} * \text{DCD}(MA) \leftarrow MD$$

for write, accurately characterize the hardware that implements these one-clock-period operations.

Larger memories, which are typically found in separate IC packages are best represented as separate modules. Where the memory access time is more than one clock period, the slow synchronous or asynchronous memory models are appropriate. The dynamic MOS memory discussed in Chapter 3 is the most natural member of the slow synchronous memory family. An AHPL description of the internal functioning of a memory package is not required for modeling the device as a slow synchronous memory. It is only necessary to interpret the input-output specifications of the package in terms of the timing and AHPL description of the CPU. The simplest solution, and the one adopted in many 8-bit microprocessors, is merely to make the CPU clock rate compatible with that of available memory packages and to still accomplish read and write operations in one clock period. Let us consider a more interesting case in which

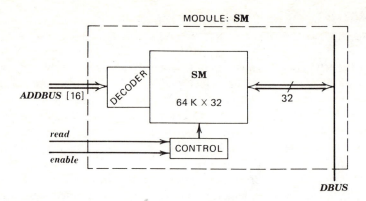

Figure 7.6. Model of a slow synchronous memory.

the CPU has a clock frequency approximately three times the speed of the available memory.

Figure 7.6 shows a typical slow synchronous memory model organized as 64K 32-bit words. The memory module might actually consist of several IC packages. Addresses are provided on a 16-bit *ADBUS* and data are transferred along a 32-bit bidirectional *DBUS*. The line, *read,* will be 1 for a memory read operation and 0 for a write. The *ADBUS* and *read* lines will typically be required to be stable for a period of time before *enable* goes to 1 initiating the memory operation.

Example 7.1

A memory module similar to Fig. 7.6 has a nominal speed of 2 MHz. This memory is to be used with an implementation of RIC with a clock rate that will be assumed to be 5 MHz. A closer look at the memory specifications indicates that the address and read lines must be stable 0.1 μsec ahead before *enable* goes to 1. In the worst case, the output data in a read operation will not be available until 0.35 μsec after the onset of *enable.* Write typical control sequences that will accomplish properly timed read and write operations within this version of RIC.

Solution

The timing requirements for the memory are shown in Fig. 7.7 superimposed on three RIC clock periods. If *MA* is loaded by the leftmost clock pulse and *read* = 1 during the first clock period, the *ADBUS* and *read* signals will stabilize at least 0.1 μsec prior to an *enable* signal that might be turned on during the second clock period. If *enable* does go to 1 during the second clock period, the data will be available to be triggered into a RIC register by the clock pulse at the end of the third period. Even though we have no AHPL description of the memory module, we can describe in AHPL the RIC steps necessary to interface with these memory specifications.

Because of the bus and separate control lines, the memory must be declared as

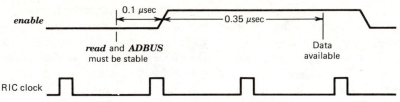

Figure 7.7. Timing of slow synchronous memory example.

a separate module and the communication lines must be added to the declarations for RIC.

OUTPUTS: *ADBUS*[16]; *read; enable*
COMBUSES: *DBUS*[32]

These lines could similarly be declared as INPUTS and COMBUSES in the description of the memory module. We shall assume that *ADBUS* will be driven by the low-order 16 bits of *MA,* as specified by the statement

ADBUS = *MA*[8:23]

after END SEQUENCE.
    With this and connections as indicated, a typical read sequence would appear as follows.

2   *MA* ← *PC*.
3   *read* = 1.
4   *enable* = 1; *read* = 1.
5   *enable* = 1; *read* = 1; *MD* ← *DBUS*.

The clock pulse at the end of step 2 establishes the address in *MA* and thus on *ADBUS*. At the beginning of step 3, *read* is set to 1. At the start of step 4 and after a delay of one period, *enable* is set to 1 and *read* continues at 1. This condition is held through step 5, until the data word is transferred into *MD* from *DBUS* by the clock pulse at the end of step 5, two clock periods after *enable* was set to 1.
    A typical write sequence would appear as follows, assuming the address to be already available in *MA*.

8   *MD* ← *AC*.
9   *DBUS* = *MD; read* = 0.
10   *DBUS* = *MD; enable* = 1; *read* = 0.
11   *DBUS* = *MD; enable* = 1; *read* = 0.   ■

Sometimes a memory will be so slow with respect to the clock rate of the CPU that it may be tempting to model it as an asynchronous memory. The distinction between this and the slow synchronous model is that an asynchronous model implies the existence of a control line on which the memory will inform the CPU that data are available. This control line will usually not be synchronized to the CPU clock, so some sort of synchronizing mechanism will be necessary. When we discuss the issue of synchronization in Chapter 9, we shall find that this is a serious drawback. An important advantage of the slow synchronous approach, as discussed in the previous example, is that no external control input is required. In effect, the CPU anticipates the "*worst case*" response of the memory to a request for data and times the data transfer accordingly.

An example of an asynchronous memory module that can be interfaced to a CPU with a 16-bit word length is shown in Fig. 7.8. The memory module includes the memory itself (8192 × 16), address and data registers (*MAR* and *MDR*), address and data I/O lines (*MEMADBUS* and *DBUS*), control input lines (*read* and *write*), and a control output line, *ack*. The control lines are at the 0-level when the memory is not in use. To initiate a memory operation, the CPU will gate appropriate information onto the address and data lines and drive *read* or *write* to logical 1. The memory will respond by gating *MEMADBUS* into *MAR* and, for a write operation, *DBUS* into *MDR*. When a write operation is complete or when data have been placed on the *DBUS* in response to a *read*, the memory will raise *ack* to the 1-level. At this point, the CPU may lower *read* or *write* and clear the address and data lines. It is important to note that the CPU "sees" the memory only in terms of the communication lines. The registers *MAR* and *MDR* are part of the asynchronous memory model and will not be reflected in the CPU sequence in any way. The dynamic memory and controller of Example 5.8 were modeled as an asynchronous memory.

Included in the declarations section of the mating CPU module are the following INPUT and OUTPUT declarations.

INPUTS: *ack.*
OUTPUTS: *read; write.*
COMBUSES: *MEMADBUS*[13]; *DBUS*[16].

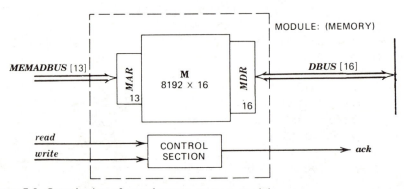

Figure 7.8. Organization of asynchronous memory module.

A memory address register, **MA,** is not necessarily required in the CPU. In a simpler organization than RIC, the memory address register might never be used as the argument of an operation within the CPU. Often, it is only an intermediate storage of addresses that are transferred from the **IR** or **PC.** Alternatively, the outputs of these registers could be connected directly to **MEMADBUS.** It is desirable to retain **MD,** since this register can often be used to store an argument after a memory cycle is complete, or even an argument not obtained from memory.

The following is a typical control sequence for fetching an instruction from the asynchronous memory.

2   **MEMADBUS = PC; read = 1;**
        $\rightarrow (\overline{ack})/(2)$.
3   **IR ← DBUS.**
4   "continue"

Because we no longer have an **MA** register, the new step 2 connects the output of **PC** to **MEMADBUS.** Step 2 also sets **read** to 1 and waits for **ack** to go up, acknowledging satisfaction of the read request. Step 3 then transfers the word from **DBUS** to **IR.** Note that there is no need to pass the instruction word through **MD.**

The control unit and timing diagram for these new steps are shown in Fig. 7.9. The logical 1 on **read** is provided by connecting CSL2 to the **read** line through an

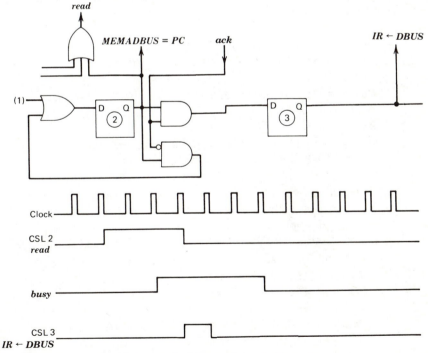

Figure 7.9. Instruction fetch control with asynchronous memory.

OR gate. The other inputs to the OR gate will be the control levels from other read steps in the sequence. Control holds at step 2 until **ack** goes up. It is important that another memory reference does not begin until **ack** has returned to zero. Adding a step to check for this would result in what is called a *completely responsive handshake*. This concept will be developed in Chapter 9.

Sometimes, multiperiod delays can be encountered in combinational logic units within the CPU itself. In such cases, a timing sequence very similar to that used in conjunction with a read or write from or to a slow synchronous memory may be used to allow for the extra delay before the output of the combinational logic unit is transferred into a register. The delay in adders is usually reduced using some form of look-ahead (see Chapter 14) to be comparable to the period of the system clock. In the following example, we assume that this is not the case.

Example 7.2

Consider a 32-bit computer with a clock rate of 5 MHz but with an adder with a worst-case propagation delay of 0.5 μsec. Write a partial control sequence for execution of addition that will allow for the adder delay but will not slow down other memory reference operations, in particular AND and MVT.

Solution

It is necessary to separate the step executing the addition from the execution of other instructions. This is accomplished by the following partial control sequence, which explicitly shows AND and MVT as well as ADD.

> 17 $\rightarrow$ (DCD(**IR**[0:3]))/(18,19,20, "other operations").
> 18   **ABUS = MD; OBUS = ABUS; AC $\leftarrow$ OBUS;**
> $\rightarrow$ (24).
> 19   **BBUS = AC; ABUS = MD; OBUS = ABUS $\wedge$ BBUS;**
>   **AC $\leftarrow$ OBUS;** $\rightarrow$ (24).
> 20   **BBUS = AC; ABUS = MD;**
>   **OBUS** = ADD[1:32] (**ABUS; BBUS; cin**); **AC $\leftarrow$ OBUS;**
>   **cff** $\leftarrow$ ADD[0] (**ABUS; BBUS; cin**); $\rightarrow$ (24).

To complete the solution, we must replace step 20 by a sequence of three steps that will implement a 0.6 μsec delay before the result of addition is clocked into the accumulator and carry flip-flop. The AND and MVT operations are still accomplished in one clock period. Notice that the flags other than **cff** are omitted for clarity.

> 20-1   **BBUS = AC; ABUS = MD.**
> 20-2   **BBUS = AC; ABUS = MD.**
> 20-3   **BBUS = AC; ABUS = MD.**
>   **OBUS** = ADD[1:32] (**ABUS; BBUS; cin**); **AC $\leftarrow$ OBUS;**
>   **cff** $\leftarrow$ ADD[0] (**ABUS; BBUS; cin**); $\rightarrow$ (24).   ■

Where propagation through combinational logic requires more than two or three clock periods, it may be useful to declare a counter to count the waiting clock periods. In the following steps, 32 clock periods are allowed for completion of a slow operation.

20     $CNT \leftarrow 5 \top 0$.
21     $ABUS = MD; BBUS = AC;$
      $OBUS = \text{SLOWOP}(ABUS; BBUS);$
      $AC * (\wedge/CNT) \leftarrow OBUS; CNT \leftarrow \text{INC}(CNT);$
      $\rightarrow (\overline{\wedge/CNT})/(21)$.
22   "continue"

7.4   Propagation Delays and Clock Rate

We have noted in previous sections that one purpose of the delay provided by control flip-flops is to allow the results of previous transfers to propagate. Let us now look at this problem more closely, to determine what kind of delays may be encountered and what other factors may be involved. As an example, consider the following two steps, which might be encountered in the multiplication sequence of an 16-bit computer employing a bus organization similar to that of RIC. These two steps begin the conversion of a two's complement argument to sign-magnitude form. At step 6, the argument is transferred to AC. If the number is positive, AC is transferred into the multiplier-quotient register, MQ, in step 7. If not, the bit-by-bit complement of AC is transferred to MQ.

6     $BBUS = MD; OBUS = BBUS; AC \leftarrow OBUS.$
7     $ABUS = AC; OBUS = (ABUS \,!\, \overline{ABUS}) * (\overline{AC[0]}, AC[0]);$
      $MQ \leftarrow OBUS.$

Figure 7.10 shows the control and data circuitry involved in these transfers, and a partial timing diagram. In this figure, t will denote the time of the trailing edge of the clock pulse controlling the transfers in step n, and Pn will denote the corresponding pulse applied to the clock input of the destination register.

As discussed in Chapter 3, all logic elements introduce delays. For trailing-edge-triggered flip-flops, which are assumed here, the delay is from the trailing edge of the clock pulse until the resultant change appears at the output. For gates, the delay is from the time of any input change until any resultant change at the output. Although there will always be a difference in delays between specific logic elements, within certain logic families (such as TTL) these delays are approximately uniform. For MOS VLSI, the situation is more complicated. The delay of a gate will be very much dependent on layout, in particular on the length of fan-out leads from the gate output. A thorough treatment of this issue requires circuit analysis and, therefore, lies outside the scope of this book. To introduce the relation between path delay and clock rate,

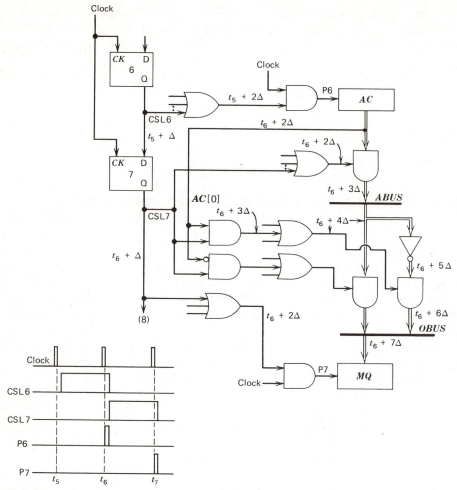

Figure 7.10. Propagation delays in a transfer.

we assume the hypothetical situation in which there exists a uniform delay, Δ, for all logic elements.

The clock pulse at t_5 turns on control flip-flop 6, so that CSL6 goes up at $t_5 + \Delta$, passes through an OR gate that combines signals from all steps loading the AC register, and arrives at the AND gate that controls the clocking of AC at $t_5 + 2\Delta$. If it is assumed that the logic inputs to AC are stable, the next clock could arrive at any time after this. The clock pulse at t_6 turns off CSL6 and turns on CSL7 at $t_6 + \Delta$. This same clock pulse also passes through the AND gate and clocks AC at $t_6 + \Delta$ so that the new value of AC is available at $t_6 + 2\Delta$. Then CSL7 passes through an OR gate and reaches the bank of AND gates between AC and $ABUS$, also at $t_6 + 2\Delta$ so that the new value of AC is available at the input to the $ABUS$ at $t_6 + 3\Delta$.

Next, we must note that buses are logic elements, generally banks of AND/OR gates, and also introduce delays. Therefore, the output of the **ABUS** does not reach its new value until $t_6 + 4\Delta$. There are two paths to the **OBUS**, for direct and inverted transfer. For inverted transfer the output of the inverter bank is available at $t_6 + 5\Delta$, at which time it can be gated through to the **OBUS**, provided that the control signal is available. Also, CSL7 is applied to the AND gates controlling the conditional transfer at $t_6 + \Delta$, but the **AC**[0] signal is not available until $t_6 + 2\Delta$, so that the outputs of the AND gates are available at $t_6 + 3\Delta$ and pass through the OR gates to the AND gate banks, controlling the **OBUS** inputs at $t_6 + 4\Delta$. For the inverted transfer, the data arrive after the control level and are available at the input to the **OBUS** at $t_6 + 6\Delta$. Finally, the **OBUS** introduces its own delay so that the new data are not available at the logic inputs to **MQ** until $t_6 + 7\Delta$. The level controlling the clock has been available since $t_6 + 2\Delta$, but the clock interval must be at least 7Δ for proper operation.

In the preceding example, the minimum interval between clock pulses was seven times the delay of a single logic element. Of this time, only two delay times were needed for the actual loading of the register; the remaining times were associated with the delays in the control and data paths involved in the succeeding transfer. This raises a question as to how cumulative propagation delays are affected by NO DELAY steps. The following six-step example arose as part of left and right rotate operations through the busing structure of SIC, an 18-bit computer treated in detail in the previous edition of this book. Because steps 5, 26, and 27 involve a branch to step 30, and the latter three steps are NO DELAY, step 30 is accomplished during the nominal step 5 clock period. Therefore, all the steps shown must be considered in conjunction with the transfer in step 30.

4    $BBUS = MD; OBUS = 0, BBUS; IR \leftarrow OBUS[1{:}18].$

5    $\rightarrow (IR[0] \wedge IR[1] \wedge IR[2])/(25).$

25   NO DELAY
      $\rightarrow (\overline{IR[3]}, IR[3])/(26, \text{I/O Seq.}).$

26   NO DELAY
      $\rightarrow (IR[5])/(30).$

30   NO DELAY
      $ABUS = AC;$
      $OBUS = ((ABUS, lf) \,!\, (ABUS[17], lf, ABUS[0{:}16])) * (\overline{IR[4]}, IR[4]);$
      $lf, AC \leftarrow OBUS; \rightarrow (33).$

33    $\rightarrow (IR[10]/(40).$

Step 4 loads the instructions into **IR**; step 5 is the branch for addressed or nonaddressed instructions; step 25 is the branch for operate or I/O instructions; step 26 is the branch for rotate or nonrotate instructions in event time 1; step 30 is the rotate transfer; and step 33 is the initial branch in event time 2. Figure 7.11 shows the control circuitry and data paths for these steps. The clock pulse at t_4 loads **IR** and also turns on CSL5. However, the ANDing of the first 3 bits of **IR** is not available

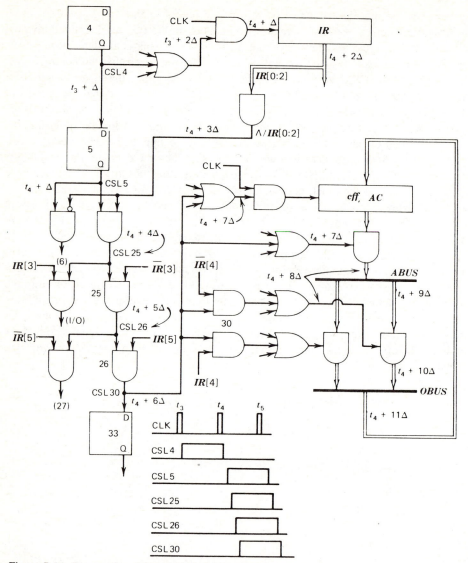

Figure 7.11. Propagation delays in NO DELAY steps.

until $t_4 + 3\Delta$, so that the output of the step 5 branch logic is not available until $t_4 + 4\Delta$. This signal must then propagate through the logic for steps 25 and 26 so that CSL30, which controls the rotate transfer, is not available until $t_4 + 6\Delta$. To this delay must be added the propagation delay through the data paths so that the *OBUS* output is not available for loading into *lf, AC* until $t_4 + 11\Delta$, four delay times later than in the simpler transfer of Fig. 7.10.

A first reaction to this might be that this is just one special case in the control sequence and would not slow down the machine that much in a typical mix of instructions. But if we are to have a uniform clock rate, allowing the same time for all steps, we have to allow for the worst case. Thus, even if this were the only situation requiring 11Δ, and all other steps could be completed in the 7Δ determined in the previous example, we would be required to slow the system clock to allow for this case.

It may be that such a slowing of the clock, in this case by about 40%, cannot be tolerated. If so, what are the alternatives? One approach is to consider this as a special case requiring the insertion of extra delay. In this case, the simplest solution would probably be to make step 30 a delay step, that is, insert a control flip-flop at step 30. This would not speed up this particular sequence of operations but would spread it over two clock periods, one associated with step 5, the other with step 30.

Alternately, we may note that step 30 is carried out in the same clock period as step 5. Even though CSL30 is delayed relative to CSL5, the step 30 transfer is completed by the same clock pulse, at t_5, that would have completed any transfers at step 5 had there been any. Thus we see that NO DELAY transfers and branches are essentially extensions of the branch logic of the preceding delay step. There is no theoretical reason why we could not consider all the logic associated with steps 25, 26, and 30 as a part of the step 5 logic, described by a complex conditional transfer and multiway branch at step 5 (see Problem 7.7). Recognizing that this is the case, we then see that the number of levels of logic could be reduced by combining terms, with a resultant decrease in the propagation delays. In Chapter 6, we noted that we made several decisions sequentially that could have been combined in a single multiway branch, in the interests of clarifying the structure of the sequence. We see now that such sequential decisions exact a time penalty even though NO DELAY steps may be used. The designer must decide in each case whether the extra time is justified.

Once the designer decides that the control sequence is complete, he or she will then develop the circuit for the corresponding control unit, either manually or with the aid of a hardware compiler program. The designer will then check critical path delays just as we did earlier, to look for potential improvements. When he makes changes, he will correct the control sequence accordingly. If he is using a hardware compiler, he will probably recompile the circuit and then check to see that it came out the way he intended. Depending on the skill of the designer, he may go around this loop several times before he is satisfied that the design is a simple as he can get it. The design of a digital system is a very complex task; you should not expect to get it right the first time.

7.5   Hardware Compilers

In the last section and elsewhere, we have mentioned hardware compilers, without any indication of just what they are or do, beyond a general implication that they somehow mechanize the design process. Because the design and manufacture of a computer is such a complex process, a great deal of effort has been directed toward developing ways to use computers themselves in the design process, primarily because the speed and accuracy of a computer is essential for handling the thousands, even millions, of small details involved in the process of designing and building a computer. Each computer or chip manufacturer has his own approach, and nomenclature in this field is not at all standardized. We use the term *hardware compiler* to signify a program that accepts as an input an AHPL control sequence and certain sequence-independent information and that produces a complete network description of the system. A network description may take a variety of forms but will probably include block diagrams and wiring lists. Block diagrams, as we have seen, show the relationships between various elements in pictorial form, in varying degrees of detail. Wiring lists are lists of the connections between every input and every output of every element (gates, registers, flip-flops, etc.) in the system.

The basic input to the compiler is the AHPL sequence. The declaration section of the AHPL description directly specifies the registers and buses, and the inputs and outputs. However, the logic elements required to implement the control unit and the interconnections required in the data unit are only indirectly specified by the sequence itself. In preceding chapters, we discussed a type of control unit in which there is a very direct relationship between each step in a control sequence and the corresponding hardware in the control unit. We also discussed the gating in the data unit and the manner in which the control signals control the data flow. Clearly, the hardware compiler must include a set of rules for translation of the control sequence into a corresponding hardware configuration. This set of rules will be based on the designer's choice of the form of hardware realization to be used so that the design of the compiler itself is a basic component of the computer design. The hardware compiler does no logic minimization on the Boolean expressions provided by the designer. It does eliminate duplicate connections to declared and undeclared buses and optimize logic within the control unit.

The task of compiling an AHPL module description to hardware can be divided into the following three phases.

    I. Control state assignment and compilation of the control unit.
    II. Generation of data unit wire list from transfer and connection statements.
    III. Insertion of interconnections between the control and data units.

Any assignment of control steps to combinations of control-state-variable values that uniquely identifies each step can be used. Of most interest are the two limiting cases: (1) One flip-flop per control state; (2) A minimal number of control state variables. For the latter cases, the compilation process consists of using the branch statements to develop a state table or transition table of the control unit and obtaining a PLA (programmed logic array) realization using a PLA-generation program. For the first alternative, the branch statements can be replaced by equivalent transfer statements and the control unit can be treated as a special case by the process that compiles the data unit. This approach will be illustrated following our consideration of the data unit.

The second or data unit compilation phase is the most interesting and will receive the majority of our attention. A flowchart representation of this phase is given in Fig. 7.12. To illustrate the hardware compilation process, we have chosen the module MULTISHIFT, which was deliberately contrived to illustrate most of the activities depicted in Fig. 7.12. You should not be concerned with the function of this module.

MODULE: MULTISHIFT.
MEMORY: $A[18]$; $CNT[3]$.
INPUTS: a; b; $X[6]$.
OUTPUTS: z; *look*; $A[0:5]$.

1    $A \leftarrow 0, A[0:16]$;
     $\rightarrow (a)/(3)$.

2    $A \leftarrow 0, A[0:16]$;
     $\rightarrow (1)$.

3    $CNT \leftarrow a, b, 0$;
     $A[0:11] \leftarrow X, A[0:5]$;
     $\rightarrow (b)/(1)$.

4    $A \leftarrow 1, A[0:16]$;
     $CNT \leftarrow INC(CNT)$;
     $\rightarrow (\wedge/CNT)/(4)$.

5    $A[0:5] \leftarrow ((A[6:11] \wedge A[12:17])!(A[6:11])) * (\bar{b}, b)$;
     $A[6:17] * b \leftarrow X, A[0:5]$; *look* = 1;
     $\rightarrow (1)$.

END SEQUENCE
     CONTROLRESET (1);
     $z = A[17]$.
END.

The data network compiler is not concerned with branch statements or the order of execution of transfers and connection. Step 1 of Fig. 7.12 causes a table of all transfers to be formed without regard to order but with a list of source conditions and clock conditions. The transfer table for the foregoing control sequence is given in Fig. 7.13. Notice that transfers that may occur at the same step with the same target are listed separately. For example, $A[0:5]$ is always clocked at step 5. However, two separate transfers are listed with the target, one with source condition $5 \wedge \bar{b}$, the other with $5 \wedge b$. The latter notation indicates that $A[6:11]$ is connected to the data inputs of $A[0:5]$ if and only if control is in step 5 and $b = 1$. Notice that the same transfer appears in both steps 1 and 2. This transfer is listed only once with source and clock condition $1 \vee 2$.

The second step of the compiling process is to partition the target vectors so that only flip-flops with potentially identical input networks are allowed to remain in the same target segment. This involves inspection of the targets in the transfer table

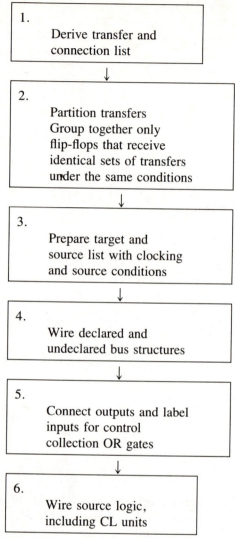

Figure 7.12. Compiling of data network.

to identify blocks of flip-flops that are common targets of various transfers. For example, the flip-flops of $A[12:17]$ are all targets of transfers in entries 1, 4, and 7 of Fig. 7.13 and of no other transfers. Thus $A[12:17]$ remains a segment. The right sides of transfers must also be examined to identify parts of transfers that are actually identical. The last 17 bits of transfers 1 and 4 in Fig. 7.13 are identical, but the first bits are not. Therefore, the target flip-flop $A[0]$ will have a different input network than flip-flops $A[1:17]$ and must be treated separately. Continuing this process gives the following list of target segments.

$A[0]$ $A[1:5]$ *CNT* $A[6:11]$ $A[12;17]$ *look* z

	Target Source	Source Conditions	Clock Conditions
1	$A \leftarrow 0, A[0:16]$	$1 \vee 2$	$1 \vee 2$
2	$CNT \leftarrow a, b, 0$	3	3
3	$A[0:11] \leftarrow X, A[0:5]$	3	3
4	$A \leftarrow 1, A[0:16]$	4	4
5	$CNT \leftarrow INC(CNT)$	4	4
6	$A[0:5] \leftarrow A[6:11] \wedge A[12:17]$	$5 \wedge \bar{b}$	5
7	$A[6:17] \leftarrow X, A[0:5]$	5	$5 \wedge b$
8	$look = 1$	5	N/A
9	$A[0:5] \leftarrow A[6:11]$	$5 \wedge b$	5
10	$z = A[17]$	ALL	N/A

Figure 7.13. Transfer and connection list.

Once partitioning has been accomplished, step 3 of Fig. 7.12 calls for the tabulation of each segment of target flip-flops with a list of all conditions for which this segment of flip-flops is clocked. For each segment, a list of all source vectors and corresponding source conditions is also tabulated. The table for this example is given in Fig. 7.14.

There are two target entries in Fig. 7.14 for which clocking conditions do not apply: the output connections z and **look**. The same would be true for declared buses

Target Segment	Source	Source Condition	Clock Condition
$A[0]$	0 $X[0]$ 1 $A[6] \wedge A[12]$ $A[6]$	$1 \vee 2$ 3 4 $5 \wedge \bar{b}$ $5 \wedge b$	$1 \vee 2 \vee 3 \vee 4 \vee 5$
$A[1:5]$	$A[0:4]$ $X[1:5]$ $A[7:11] \wedge A[13:17]$ $A[7:11]$	$2 \vee 4 \vee 1$ 3 $5 \wedge \bar{b}$ $5 \wedge b$	$1 \vee 2 \vee 3 \vee 4 \vee 5$
CNT	$a, b, 0$ $INC(CNT)$	3 4	$3 \vee 4$
$A[12:17]$	$A[11:16]$ $A[0:5]$	$1 \vee 2 \vee 4$ 5	$1 \vee 2 \vee 4 \vee (5 \wedge b)$
$A[6:11]$	$A[5:10]$ $A[0:5]$ X	$1 \vee 2 \vee 4$ 3 5	$1 \vee 2 \vee 3 \vee 4 \vee (5 \wedge b)$
$look$	1	5	N/A
z	$A[17]$	ALL	N/A

Figure 7.14. Target-segment source list.

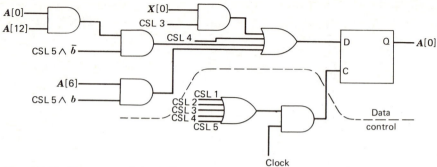

Figure 7.15. Data network for $A[0]$.

with outputs that fan out to various target flip-flops. All declared outputs, memory elements, and buses should appear as target entries in the table.

For each segment of target flip-flops, the source list forms to inputs to an undeclared busing network. Step 4 of the compiling process generates the busing networks from the target and source list of Fig. 7.14. As an illustration, the input network for the single-target flip-flop $A[0]$ is given in Fig. 7.15. Only three AND gates are required to accommodate data $X[0]$, $A[6]$, and $A[6] \wedge A[12]$. The step 4 control signal CSL4 is connected directly to the OR gate to cause a 1 to be loaded into $A[0]$. The flip-flop will be clocked for steps 1 and 2 while all inputs to the data OR gate are 0, causing 0 to be loaded into the flip-flop. Enclosed by dashed lines in Fig. 7.15 is the only source logic generated by step 6 of the hardware compiler. The OR gate with inputs that are the five clocking conditions is generated by step 5. Since the only other source with more than one source condition is logical 0, no other control collection OR gate is required.

Let us now turn our attention to the control unit realization phase of the compilation process. As mentioned previously, we might code the control steps using a minimum number of state variables and turn the resulting control state transition table over to a PLA generation program. Alternatively, we can represent each step by a separate control flip-flop and translate the branch statements of each step to transfer statements. To do this for the example MULTISHIFT, the hardware compiler will create a vector of control flip-flops $C[1:5]$ to correspond to the numbered steps. Once this is accomplished, the branch statement at each step may be translated to a set of transfer statements into the appropriate control flip-flops. No information is lost during this translation process. The result for MULTISHIFT is shown following. The original data unit transfers that have already been compiled are omitted.

1    $C[2] \leftarrow \overline{a}; C[3] \leftarrow a.$
2    $C[1] \leftarrow 1.$
3    $C[1] \leftarrow b; C[4] \leftarrow \overline{b}.$
4    $C[4] \leftarrow \wedge/CNT; C[5] \leftarrow \wedge/CNT.$
5    $C[1] \leftarrow 1.$

Target	Source	Source Condition
$C[2] \leftarrow \bar{a}$		$C[1]$
$C[3] \leftarrow a$		$C[1]$
$C[1] \leftarrow 1$		$C[2] \vee C[5]$
$C[1] \leftarrow \underline{b}$		$C[3]$
$C[4] \leftarrow \underline{b}$		$C[3]$
$C[4] \leftarrow \wedge CNT$		$C[4]$
$C[5] \leftarrow \wedge CNT$		$C[4]$

Figure 7.16. Control unit transfer connection list.

This control unit description can now be processed by the procedure given in Fig. 7.12. The application of step 1 leads to the transfer connection table of Fig. 7.16. Because all control flip-flops are clocked every clock period, no clock conditions are applicable (imposing no clock conditions is actually a slight variation of the compiling process for the data unit) and this column is omitted from the table. Because the targets are already single flip-flops, no further partitioning happens in step 2 of the compiling process. Step 3 of the compiling procedure assembles the various sources of each control flip-flop to form the target/source list of Fig. 7.17.

From Fig. 7.17, the control unit can be wired as was done for the partial data unit of Fig. 7.15. One distinction will be that the system clock will be connected directly to the clock input of each control flip-flop. The resulting control unit is given in Fig. 7.18. It is left to you to verify that the same network would result if the individual branch statements were implemented at the output of the respective control flip-flops, as was done in Chapter 5. Only the position of the gates on the diagram is different.

The control unit of MULTISHIFT module included no NO DELAY steps. Example 7.3 will demonstrate that such steps cause no special problems. A no-delay step will require a 1-bit bus rather than a flip-flop as a control target.

Target	Source	Source Condition
$C[1]$	1 b	$C[2] \vee C[5]$ $C[3]$
$C[2]$	$\bar{a}$	$C[1]$
$C[3]$	a	$C[1]$
$C[4]$	$\bar{b}$ $\wedge / CNT$	$C[3]$ $C[4]$
$C[5]$	$\wedge / CNT$	$C[4]$

Figure 7.17. Control unit target source list.

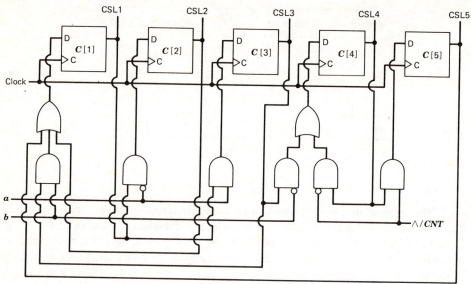

Figure 7.18. Multishift control unit.

Example 7.3

Tabulate the transfer connection list for the control unit resulting from the following AHPL control sequence.

1    $A \leftarrow INC(A)$.

2    $\rightarrow (A[0] \wedge A[1] \wedge A[2])/(1)$.

3   NO DELAY
     $\rightarrow (A[3] \vee A[4])/(6)$.

4   NO DELAY
     $B \leftarrow \overline{A}$.

5    $B \leftarrow (INC(B) \mathbin{!} 8 \top 0) * (x, \overline{x})$;
     $\rightarrow (B[0])/(5)$.

6    $B \leftarrow \overline{B}$;
     $\rightarrow (1)$.

Solution

Corresponding to the six control steps, we use control flip-flops and bus bits, $C[1{:}2]$, $CBUS[3{:}4]$, and $C[5{:}6]$. Stripping away the data unit statement and replacing branches by transfers and connections yields

Target Source	Source Condition
$C[2] \leftarrow 1$	$C[1]$
$C[1] \leftarrow \wedge /A[0:2]$	$C[2]$
$CBUS[3] = \overline{\wedge/A[0:2]}$	$C[2]$
$C[6] \leftarrow A[3] \vee A[4]$	$CBUS[3]$
$CBUS[4] = \overline{A[3] \vee A[4]}$	$CBUS[3]$
$C[5] \leftarrow 1$	$CBUS[4]$
$C[5] \leftarrow B[0]$	$C[5]$
$C[6] \leftarrow \overline{B[0]}$	$C[5]$
$C[1] \leftarrow 1$	$C[6]$

Figure 7.19. Realizing control unit with NO DELAY steps.

1   $C[2] \leftarrow 1$.
2   $C[1] \leftarrow \wedge/A[0:2]; \; CBUS[3] = \overline{\wedge/A[0:2]}$.
3   $C[6] \leftarrow A[3] \vee A[4]; \; CBUS[4] = \overline{A[3] \wedge A[4]}$.
4   $C[5] \leftarrow 1$.
5   $C[5] \leftarrow B[0]; \; C[6] \leftarrow \overline{B[0]}$.
6   $C[1] \leftarrow 1$

Application of step 1 of Fig. 7.12 yields the transfer connection table of Fig. 7.19. We leave it as a problem for the reader to determine the target-segment/source list. ∎

A complete hardware compilation of RIC would be much to voluminous to include in this section. One hardware type, the bus, was missing from the MULTI-SHIFT example just considered. Buses are treated as targets by the compiler just as are registers. The only distinction is that with buses there are no clock conditions. A similar situation was encountered for the output *look* in MULTISHIFT. As an illustration of the application of the hardware compiler to a bus with a large number of inputs, let us consider only the *ABUS* in RIC.

Before proceeding with the compilation, we must recall that a notational shortcut was permitted in the generation of the control sequence in Chapter 6. The bus connections, that is, the path through the busing structure, were expressed explicitly only where they were not a "direct" implication of Fig. 6.1. A version of the control sequence with only explicit bus connections must be available before the transfer and connection table of Fig. 7.20 can be derived. Most of this task will be left for you, but let us consider one or two steps, where the word "direct" may have been interpreted liberally. Two such steps are listed here. Step 20 will involve the *ABUS*, because *MD* is connected to that bus. Step 32 requires the *ABUS* because the two's complement of 1 must be added to *SP*, which is connected to the *BBUS*.

20   $MD \leftarrow (INC(MD) \; ! \; DEC(MD)) * \overline{(IR[3], IR[3])};$
       $zff \leftarrow \vee/OBUS; \; nff \leftarrow OBUS[0]$.
32   $MA \leftarrow DEC(SP); \; SP \leftarrow DEC(SP)$.

Target	Source	Source Condition
ABUS	MD	$\overline{3, 9, 11, 20, 146}$ $22 \wedge (\overline{IR[0]} \wedge \overline{IR[1]} \wedge (\overline{IR[2]} \vee IR[3]))$ $53 \wedge (\overline{IR[0]} \wedge \overline{IR[1]} \wedge (\overline{IR[2]} \vee IR[3]))$
	$\overline{MD}$	$22 \wedge (\overline{IR[0]} \wedge \overline{IR[1]} \wedge (\overline{IR[2]} \vee IR[3]))$ $53 \wedge (\overline{IR[0]} \wedge \overline{IR[1]} \wedge (\overline{IR[2]} \vee IR[3]))$
	$\overline{16 \top 0}, IR[16:31]$	$35 \wedge IR[16] \wedge IR[0]$
	$16 \top 0, IR[16:31]$	$35 \wedge \overline{IR[16]} \wedge IR[0]$
	$8 \top 0, IR[8:31]$	$35 \wedge IR[0]$
	$\overline{32 \top 0}$	32, 141
	IR	60, 101
ABUS[0:7]	$\overline{(8 \top 0)} \wedge MD[8]$	7
ABUS[8:31]	MA	13, 15
ABUS [0:27]	$\overline{28 \top 0}$	$52 \wedge IR[12]$
	$28 \top 0$	$52 \wedge \overline{IR[12]}$
ABUS[28:31]	IR[12:15]	52

Figure 7.20. Transfer connection list for RIC **ABUS**.

The relevant part of step 20 may be rewritten as follows. We note that the **BBUS** may be left unconnected (effectively $32 \top 0$) for incrementing, which is accomplished by connecting 1 to **cin**. For this same reason, no entry need be made in the source list for **ABUS** where something on the **BBUS** is incremented. Step 20 requires only the entry of 20 in the list of source conditions for **MD** in Fig. 7.20.

> 20   **ABUS** = **MD**; **BBUS** = $\overline{(32 \top 0)}$ * **IR**[3];
>   **cin** = **IR**[3]; **OBUS** = ADD[1:32] (**ABUS; BBUS; cin**);
>   **MD** ← **OBUS**.

A revision of step 32 shows $\overline{32 \top 0}$ connected to the **ABUS**. It also illustrates the legal simultaneous clocking of **OBUS** into two targets. This step results in the entry of 32 in the source condition list for the source $32\top0$ in Fig. 7.20.

> 32   **ABUS** = $\overline{32 \top 0}$; **BBUS** = **SP**;
>   **cin** = 0; **OBUS** = ADD[1:32](**ABUS; BBUS; cin**);
>   **MA** ← **OBUS; SP** ← **OBUS**.

The table in Fig. 7.20 is completed by identifying and including an entry for each use of the **ABUS** throughout the RIC control sequence. You may wish to verify some of the entries using the complete, but condensed, RIC sequence given in Appendix A.

The partitioning of **ABUS** according to step 2 in Fig. 7.12 results in only four target segments that have distinct sets of source vectors. Once this partition is accomplished, each source entry in Fig. 7.20 is sliced into the same size segments as the relevant target segments. These source slices are then entered in the target-segment/source table for the corresponding segment (unless an identical slice is already listed) with the corresponding source conditions added to the list for that source slice. For **ABUS** targets only, the result is Fig. 7.21.

The compilation process described in this section should not be taken as an exact description of any specific compiler. We have overlooked many details and simplified many steps in the interest of clarity. Our intent has been to illustrate the basic character of the compilation process and to show that a control sequence can be converted to a hardware design by a completely algorithmic procedure, not dependent in any way on human insight or intuition. This algorithmic character is necessary in a computer program, but it is a serious limitation on the flexibility of the designer. It is not possible to provide rules to deal in an optimum fashion with every possible design problem that may arise. The application of a limited number of standard procedures by the compiler will result in designs that will be accurate but often less than optimum. To allow for optimization, the designer can be provided with opportunities to intercede and modify the designs produced by the computer.

By procedures such as that just described, the compiler will develop an initial design. The designer will then review the design, making modifications if they are necessary. At this point, assuming a good compiler, we shall have a design that will accurately implement the sequence written by the designer, but this is no guarantee that the system will meet all the initial specifications. Therefore, the next step may be a simulation to verify correct operation. There are many kinds of simulations; one possibility would be to perform a logic simulation at the individual instruction level. Inputs corresponding to each instruction would be fed to a computer model of the system logic, and the logic flow for the entire sequence would be simulated to verify that the system did what it was supposed to do. If the simulation reveals errors, the designer will correct the design and repeat the process until no further errors are found.

The next steps in the process will depend on the electronic and mechanical realizations chosen by the designer. Once simulation of the abstract net list produced by the hardware compiler has yielded satisfactory results, the next step might be to let the compiler generate a VLSI layout of the system. When the layout is complete, the designer will be provided another opportunity to intervene and make corrections. Another simulation may then be run to check on the effect of circuit delays. This phase of the design is likely to be very interactive, with the designer intervening frequently to edit the layout.

From the preceding description, we can see clearly that the hardware compiler must have available a large amount of information beyond that provided by the control sequence itself. The sequence identifies the major components of the system and

Target	Source	Source Conditions
ABUS[0:7]	MD[0:7]	3, 9, 11, 20, 146 $22 \wedge ((\overline{\overline{IR[0]} \wedge \overline{IR[1]} \wedge (\overline{IR[2]} \vee IR[3])}))$ $53 \wedge ((\overline{IR[0]} \wedge \overline{IR[1]} \wedge (\overline{IR[2]} \vee IR[3])))$
	$\overline{MD[0:7]}$	$22 \wedge ((\overline{\overline{IR[0]} \wedge \overline{IR[1]} \wedge (\overline{IR[2]} \vee IR[3])}))$ $53 \wedge ((\overline{\overline{IR[0]} \wedge \overline{IR[1]} \wedge (\overline{IR[2]} \vee IR[3])}))$
	8 ⊤ 0	$52 \wedge IR[12],$ $35 \wedge (\overline{IR[0]} \vee IR[0] \wedge IR[16])$
	$\overline{8 \top 0}$	$32, 141, 52 \wedge IR[12]$ $35 \wedge (IR[0] \wedge IR[16])$
	$IR[0:7]$	60, 101
	$(8 \top 0) \wedge MD[8]$	7
ABUS[8:15]	MA[0:7]	13, 15
	MD[8:15]	3, 9, 11, 20, 146 $22 \wedge ((\overline{\overline{IR[0]} \wedge \overline{IR[1]} \wedge (\overline{IR[2]} \vee IR[3])}))$ $53 \wedge ((\overline{IR[0]} \wedge \overline{IR[1]} \wedge (\overline{IR[2]} \vee IR[3])))$
	$\overline{MD[8:15]}$	$22 \wedge ((\overline{IR[0]} \wedge \overline{IR[1]} \wedge (\overline{IR[2]} \vee IR[3])))$ $53 \wedge ((\overline{IR[0]} \wedge \overline{IR[1]} \wedge (\overline{IR[2]} \vee IR[3])))$
	8 ⊤ 0	$52 \wedge \overline{IR[12]}$ $35 \wedge IR[0] \wedge \overline{IR[16]}$
	$\overline{8 \top 0}$	$32, 141, 52 \wedge IR[12]$ $35 \wedge IR[0] \wedge IR\overline{[16]}$
	IR[8:15]	$60, 101, 35 \wedge \overline{IR[0]}$
ABUS[16:27]	MD[16:27]	3, 9, 11, 20, 146 $22 \wedge ((\overline{\overline{IR[0]} \wedge \overline{IR[1]} \wedge (\overline{IR[2]} \vee IR[3])}))$ $53 \wedge ((\overline{IR[0]} \wedge \overline{IR[1]} \wedge (\overline{IR[2]} \vee IR[3])))$
	$\overline{MD[16:27]}$	$22 \wedge ((\overline{IR[0]} \wedge \overline{IR[1]} \wedge (\overline{IR[2]} \vee IR[3])))$ $53 \wedge ((\overline{IR[0]} \wedge \overline{IR[1]} \wedge (\overline{IR[2]} \vee IR[3])))$
	IR[16:27]	35, 60, 101
	12 ⊤ 0	$52 \wedge \overline{IR[12]}$
	$\overline{12 \top 0}$	$32, 141, 52 \wedge IR[12]$
	MA[8:19]	13, 15

Target	Source	Source Conditions
ABUS[28:31]	*MD*[28:31]	$3, 9, 11, 20, 146$ $22 \wedge ((\overline{IR[0]} \wedge \overline{IR[1]} \wedge (\overline{IR[2]} \vee IR[3])))$ $53 \wedge ((\overline{IR[0]} \wedge \overline{IR[1]} \wedge (\overline{IR[2]} \vee IR[3])))$
	$\overline{MD[28:31]}$	$22 \wedge ((\overline{IR[0]} \wedge \overline{IR[1]} \wedge (\overline{IR[2]} \vee IR[3])))$ $53 \wedge ((\overline{IR[0]} \wedge \overline{IR[1]} \wedge (\overline{IR[2]} \vee IR[3])))$
	IR[28:31]	$35, 60, 101$
	IR[12:15]	52
	$\overline{4 \top 0}$	$32, 141$
	MA[20:23]	$13, 15$

Figure 7.21. Target-segment and source list.

specifies what the system is to do. But this description could correspond to a variety of physical realizations. As we noted earlier, the compiler structure includes the rules of correspondence between various types of control sequence steps and a specific hardware realization. Thus, when the designer designs the compiler he or she is specifying the hardware details. In writing the compiler, he will have in mind the type of sequences to be realized, just as he will have some sort of hardware in mind when he writes the sequence. The compiler can be used to realize a variety of sequences, and a given sequence can be realized in a variety of ways. Thus the two phases of the design are carried out separately, but they are not independent of each other.

One question that the designer of a compiler must resolve is what information should be built into the structure of the compiler, and what information should be provided as input data. Consider the matter of specifying the actual logic elements to be used. Should this be built into the compiler or should one of the inputs be a list of library circuits elements to be used in a given system? If an input list is to be used, should the designer be able to specify elements from any family of logic, or should he be restricted to a single family or logic, or even to a subset of elements within a single family? Allowing the widest possible range of elements increases the versatility of the compiler but makes it more complicated, since it has to have rules for dealing with a variety of situations. Restricting the compiler to a limited number of elements will make it simpler but will limit its applicability.

All these factors pose difficult problems for the designers of compilers and other software used in computer design and manufacture. The design of such software is a very big job and represents a sizable investment. To get the maximum return on the investment, the design should be as flexible and versatile as possible. But the more flexible and versatile it is, the more it costs in the first place. Further, no matter how versatile it may be, many new developments cannot be anticipated. Inevitably, technological innovations will come along that offer significant improvements in cost or performance but cannot be incorporated into existing software. Then the designers must decide if the projected improvements warrant the cost of developing new software. Despite all these problems, it is safe to predict that computer aids to computer design are here to stay, simply because the job cannot be done without them.

7.6   Optimizing the Control Sequence

In Section 7.4, we considered the impact of delay in combinational logic units. In some cases, we found it necessary to add steps to the control sequence, and therefore extra clock periods, to allow sufficient time for propagation through long combinational logic paths. On the other side of the coin, might there be cases where more clock periods are specified than are actually needed? A brief consideration of this possibility is the topic of this section.

Fig. 7.22 is a control graph showing steps 4 through 50 of the RIC control sequence. Branch-only steps are represented by circles and transfer steps by rectangles. The notation "ND" adjacent to a step indicates that the step is NO DELAY. We notice first that the branch step 4 is not a NO DELAY step, because the branch condition is a function of the instruction register that is loaded at step 3. With the exception of step 30, all branch steps connected by a reverse path through only branch steps to step 4 are already designated NO DELAY. These branch steps are all executed during the same clock period as step 4. Whatever data registers might be involved in the branch conditions of these branch steps, those data registers were last clocked prior to step 4. Because branch steps 12, 14, 16, and 31 are only functions of $IR[0:7]$, which was last clocked at step 3, these steps may also be labelled NO DELAY. A NO DELAY step 30 may result in a long combinational logic path. Evaluation of this possibility will be left as a problem for you.

So far, no transfer steps have been designated NO DELAY, but consider transfer steps 7 and 9, which are also connected through NO DELAY steps to branch step 4. There is nothing to prevent the execution of these two steps during the same clock period as step 4, because the branch step does not use the bus structure. Every other transfer step depicted in Fig. 7.22 is directly preceded by another transfer or is connected back through a path of NO DELAY branch steps to another transfer. All transfers except read and write to memory require the bus structure. Therefore, no two transfers can be accomplished simultaneously unless one uses the bus structure and the other is an unrelated read or write with no conflicting transfers into **MD**. No pair of consecutive transfers in Fig. 7.22 meet this criteria, so no other steps may be marked NO DELAY.

Steps 4 through 10, with steps 7 and 9 marked NO DELAY, as suggested, are repeated as follows.

4      $\rightarrow (\overline{IR[4]})/50)$.   "16-bit instructions"

5   NO DELAY   "branch instructions"
        $\rightarrow (\overline{IR[0] \wedge IR[1] \wedge IR[2] \wedge IR[3]})/(30)$.

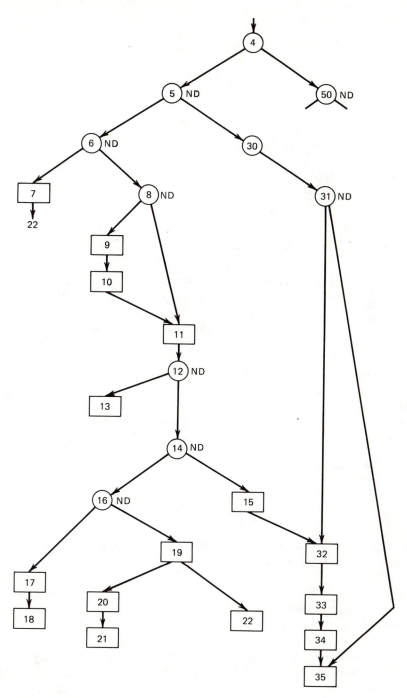

Figure 7.22. Partial RIC control graph.

6   NO DELAY
    $\rightarrow (\overline{IR[5]})/(8)$.

7   NO DELAY
    $MD[0:7] \leftarrow \overline{8\top0} \wedge MD[8]$;
    $\rightarrow (22)$.

8   NO DELAY
    $\rightarrow (\overline{IR[7]})/(11)$.

9   NO DELAY
    $MA \leftarrow MD[8:31]$.

10   $ADBUS = MA; MD \leftarrow DBUS; read = 1$.

Example 7.4

Suppose that a not-quite program-compatible computer that is similar to RIC but is addressable to 16-bit halfwords is to be designed to function with a 16-bit data bus. Illustrate how the bus structure can be used simultaneously with a read operation to permit a 32-bit instruction to be obtained from RAM in two consecutive clock periods.

Solution

In the solution that follows, we are ready to begin execution of a 32-bit instruction after four clock periods. Notice that the incremented *PC* is clocked from the *OBUS* into two targets coincident with the read of the high-order half of the instruction from memory, and this half of the instruction is decoded to control branching while the low-order half is read from memory.

1   $MA \leftarrow PC$.

2   $ADBUS = MA; read = 1; IR[0:15] \leftarrow DBUS$;
    $MA \leftarrow INC(PC); PC \leftarrow INC(PC)$.

3   $ADBUS = MA; read = 1; IR[16:31] \leftarrow DBUS$;
    $\rightarrow (\overline{IR[4]})/(\text{16-bit instruction execution})$.

4   NO DELAY   "branch instructions"
    $\rightarrow (\overline{IR[0]} \wedge IR[1] \wedge IR[2] \wedge IR[3])/(30)$.
"*PC* must be incremented coincident with next memory reference"

If the designer is also willing to underwrite the chip area necessary to provide for connections of *PC* directly to the *ADBUS,* as well as the path from *DBUS* to *IR*[0:15], the number of clock periods used by the instruction fetch can be reduced to two, as shown following. Now it is possible to increment *PC* through the bus structure coincident with both memory reads. Leaving the low-order 16 address bits in *MD* at the beginning of the final address determination is not an inconvenience.

1     $ADBUS = PC; read = 1; IR[0:15] \leftarrow DBUS;$
      $PC \leftarrow \text{INC}(PC).$

2     $ADBUS = PC; read = 1; MD \leftarrow DBUS; PC \leftarrow \text{INC}(PC);$
      $\rightarrow (\overline{IR[4]})/(\text{16-bit instruction execution}).$

3   NO DELAY   "branch instructions"
      $\rightarrow (\overline{IR[0]} \wedge \overline{IR[1]} \wedge \overline{IR[2]} \wedge \overline{IR[3]})/(30).$
      "Low-order 16 address bits are in MD."

It might be noted that this same technique, connecting PC and IR directly to the memory buses, would permit combining steps 1, 2, and 3 of the original RIC sequence into a single step.   ■

Many microprocessors further reduce the number of clock periods required for instruction execution by overlapping the instruction fetch with the final steps of execution. This feature is more critical for the 16-bit version of RIC or for 8-bit microprocessors where two or three memory references are sometimes required to obtain a single instruction. This is actually a form of parallel control and is most easily discussed with the benefit of some fundamental concepts to be introduced in Chapter 9.

Another approach to speeding up operations is to assume that a memory operation is going to be needed and go ahead with it in parallel with some operation that does not need memory. For example, step 4 of the RIC sequence does nothing except wait for the opcode to stabilize in IR so it can be tested. Since many instructions will read memory, either for indirect addressing or to obtain an operand, some time can be saved by doing a memory read during step 4.

4     $ADBUS = MD[8:31]; read = 1; MD \leftarrow DBUS;$
      $\rightarrow (\overline{IR[4]})/(50).$

If the instruction calls for indirect addressing or a direct read, the memory access has already been done. If not, no harm has been done, the word read into MD will just be discarded. This works only if the memory is fully synchronous and exacts an additional cost in the form of additional connections, from MD to $ADBUS$. Nevertheless, this approach can save a lot of time in a typical program and is well worth considering.

Problems

7.1   The first two steps of the modified RIC control sequence given at the beginning of Section 7.2 are still inadequate for a microprocessor enclosed in a package with a limited number of I/O pins.

(a)   For this case, modify the initial steps of the control sequence to provide a mechanism for loading the fixed address, FFFFFF(hex), into *PC* when the start button is depressed. Indicate the step to which control will return following the completion of each instruction.

(b) Repeat part (a) except now let the starting address be located at FFFFFF(hex).

7.2 Modify the description of the single-start-level generator given in Section 7.2 so that the start button and reset button may be combined. Let the signal reset be the line that resets the computer to its initial state as specified by CONTROL RESET. Provide for the one-period level, *slstart,* to occur at least one full clock period after the onset of the signal on line, *reset.* Assume that the *reset* signal is asynchronous to the system clock, but neglect any instability problems related to possible coincidence of the rising edge of reset with the triggering edge of the clock.

7.3 Modify steps 1 to 23 of the RIC control sequence to incorporate the slow synchronous memory model (Fig. 7.6) for the computer main random access memory. Wherever possible, accomplish internal CPU activities while waiting for data to become available from memory.

7.4 Repeat Problem 7.3 using the asynchronous memory model of Fig. 7.8.

7.5 Repeat Problem 7.4, but now assume that the asynchronous memory has a *dataready* signal and that it is desired to transfer words into *MD* as soon as *dataready* appears rather than waiting for *ack* to go down. Assume that *dataready* will go up as soon as the word is available and down at the same time as *ack.* It may be assumed that data rewrite in dynamic memory takes place during the interval, never greater than six clock periods, between the onset of *dataready* and the fall of *ack.*

7.6 Let Δ be the delay of each gate in the implementation of RIC and let the time necessary to clock data into a memory element be 2Δ. Assume that step 19 is executed immediately before step 22.

(a) Determine the total worst case number of gate delays associated with the execution of step 22. Assume that a ripple-carry adder for which a combinational logic unit description was given in Chapter 5 is used. If $\Delta = 5$ nsec, what constraint is imposed on the RIC clock frequency by this path?

(b) Suppose that the clock frequency must be twice the maximum value determined in step 3. Modify the control sequence in the vicinity of step 22 to make this possible. Add additional steps, if necessary.

(c) Further modify the control sequence determined in part (b) so that instructions not requiring the adder will require no more clock periods than necessary for execution.

7.7 Assume that step 61 of RIC has been modified as suggested in Problem 6.17 to accomplish multiple-bit shifting in one clock period. Let Δ be the delay of each gate in the implementation of RIC and let the time necessary to clock data into a memory element be 2Δ. How many gate delays must be allowed for in the worst case logic path in the implementation of step 61? If $\Delta = 5$ nsec, what constraint is imposed on the RIC clock frequency by this path?

7.8 Determine the following for the machine tool control module developed in Chapter 5 functioning manually as a hardware compiler.

(a) A transfer and connection table of the form given in Fig. 7.13.
(b) A target-segment and source list of the form given in Fig. 7.14.
(c) From the table found in part (b), construct the data and clock networks of the form given in Fig. 7.15 for $AR[0]$.

7.9 Repeat Problem 7.8 for the duplicate character checker module developed in Chapter 5. Construct the network for $SRM\langle 15\rangle[0]$.

7.10 Determine the control unit target source list (Fig. 7.17) for the machine tool controller module.

7.11 Repeat Problem 7.10 for the duplicate character checker.

7.12 Repeat Problem 7.10 for the machine tool controller, this time making a minimal memory element state assignment of the control flip-flops. Assign the values of three control flip-flops as follows: step 1; 000, step 2; 001,. . . . .

7.13 Determine the control unit target source list (Fig. 7.17) for the first 22 steps of RIC.

7.14 Determine a connection and transfer table similar to Fig. 7.20 for the RIC *BBUS*. Partition the *BBUS* into homogeneous target segments. Determine the target-segment and source list similar to Fig. 7.21 for the RIC *BBUS*.

7.15 Construct a control graph for steps 50 through 146 of RIC. Using this graph, indicate any additional steps that can be designated NO DELAY.

7.16 Note in the modified RIC control sequence of Section 7.6 that step 9 is executed during the same clock period as step 4. Let Δ be the delay of each gate in the implementation of RIC and let the time necessary to clock data into a memory element be 2Δ. How many gate delays must be allowed for in the path leading to the execution of step 9? If $\Delta = 5$ nsec, what constraint is imposed on the RIC clock frequency by this path?

7.17 Combine steps 5, 25, 26, and 30 as given in Section 7.4 into an equivalent single step with conditional transfers and connections and a multiway conditional branch. Assume that step 6, the I/O sequence, step 50, and step 27 are separate. The purpose of this change would be to reduce the delay associated with the branching logic leading to step 30. What is now the worst case delay associated with this step?

7.18 Modify the control sequence of RIC as suggested at the end of Section 7.6, adding direct connections to *ADBUS* and *DBUS* to combine steps 1 through 3 into a single step and doing a memory read in step 4. Make any other modifications necessitated by these changes.

7.19 Modify the RIC control sequence to overlap the fetch of the next instruction with the final steps in the execute phase. Indicate clearly any hardware modifications necessary to accomplish this.

References

1. T. S. Hedges, et al., "The Siclops Silicon Compiler," *Proceedings IEEE International Conference on Circuits and Computers*, New York, Sept. 1982, p. 277.
2. F. J. Hill, "Introducing AHPL," *Computer*, Dec. 1974, p. 28.
3. R. E. Swanson, Z. Navabi, and F. J. Hill, "An AHPL Compiler/Simulator System," *Proceedings Sixth Texas Conference on Computing Systems*, Nov. 1977.
4. D. G. Gajski, "The Structure of a Silicon Compiler," *Proceedings IEEE International Conference on Circuits and Computers*, New York, Sept. 1982, p. 272.
5. F. J. Hill, and G. R. Peterson, *Digital Logic and Microprocessors*, Wiley, New York, 1984.
6. R. Piloty, et al., *CONLAN Report*, Springer-Verlag, Berlin, 1983.
7. *VHDL Version 7.2 Users Manual*, Intermetrics, Bethesda, Md., 1985.
8. *VHDL Version 7.2 Language Reference Manual*, Intermetrics, Bethesda, Md., 1985.
9. F. J. Hill, "Structure Specification With a Procedural Hardware Description Language," *IEEE Transactions on Computers*, Feb. 1981, pp. 157–161.
10. F. J. Hill, et al., "Hardware Compilation from an RTL to a Storage Logic Array Target," *IEEE Transactions on CAD*, July 1984, pp. 208–217.
11. *MC68000 16-Bit Microprocessor User Manual*, 3rd ed, Prentice–Hall, Englewood Cliffs, N.J., 1982.
12. F. J. Hill, and G. R. Peterson, *Introduction to Switching Theory and Logical Design*, 3rd ed., Wiley, New York, 1981.
13. M. A. Breuer, *Design Automation of Digital Systems*, Prentice–Hall, Englewood Cliffs, N.J., 1972.

8

Microprogramming

8.1   Introduction

The concept of a microprogram was first presented by M. V. Wilkes of Cambridge University Mathematical Laboratory in 1951 [1,2,3,4]. This may seem particularly remarkable if one recalls that the vacuum tube and the relay were the only switching devices available at that time. This was only eight years after the introduction of the first electrical computing machine, which incidently used the relay as the principal component. The concept was used infrequently until the introduction of the IBM system 360 in 1964. All but the fastest and most sophisticated model in the 360 series relied on microprogramming in the control unit design. A primary reason for this approach was to permit reasonably efficient *emulation* of earlier IBM computers on the system 360. The assurance that existing customer programs could be used directly on the new computer was no doubt a valuable marketing technique for IBM.

In Chapter 6, we learned to express the control function for a digital system as a sequence of AHPL steps very much like a program. Why not store this program in some type of memory and read the AHPL steps out in program sequence? Each time such an AHPL step is read, it could cause a branch (within the AHPL program) or a register transfer within the computer. This is microprogramming. In effect, the control unit of a microprogrammable computer consists principally of a memory rather than a large network of flip-flops and logic. Most often, this memory will be a read-only memory (ROM). The instructions stored in the ROM are called *microinstructions*. Each microinstruction corresponds to an AHPL step. Usually, a ROM will be cheaper than a read-write memory with the same access time.

254 Microprogramming

In addition to possible economy, other advantages of a microprogram include the possibility of modifying the instruction code and the apparent architecture of the machine. Also, a ROM may make possible cheaper storage and faster execution of frequently used subroutines such as multiplication, division, and, in the case of scientific applications, trigonometric functions. In the early stages of the design process, the designer must carefully weigh these factors against certain drawbacks, to be pointed out in succeeding sections, in the context of the intended application for the proposed computer. The designer will then decide to what extent, if any, microprogramming will be used in the design of the control unit.

8.2   Controlling the Microprogram

It is easy to say "Store the AHPL program in read-only memory," but how is this done? We must consider two basic problems. First, some correspondence must be established between the vectors of 1's and 0's that can be stored in memory and the AHPL program steps. Second, we must control the reading of program steps from memory and their execution. Clearly, it is impossible to avoid including a certain amount of hard-wired control circuitry.

In Fig. 8.1a we see a simplified diagram of the essential items of RIC hardware. The items of hardware that would be found in a microprogrammable version of RIC are shown in Fig. 8.1b. The most important observation to make from Fig. 8.1 is that the two versions of RIC are identical except for the control units. Even the terminal characteristics of the control unit are the same. That is, precisely the same sequence of transfer pulses appears on the same control lines in both versions. Only the means by which these control signals are generated is different.

The performance similarity of microprogrammed machines and nonmicroprogrammed machines should not be pushed too far. The control sequences for the two machines of Fig. 8.1 must necessarily be identical because both machines were defined to be RIC. This is not to say that the type of control unit, microprogrammed or hard-wired, will not influence the layout of the other parts of a digital system. As we shall see in subsequent sections, the choice of a microprogrammable control unit of realistic cost will impose certain constraints on the form of a control sequence that can be implemented. These constraints are not imposed by a hard-wired control sequencer.

The control sequencer of Fib. 8.1a is replaced by a ROM, two registers *MAR* and *MIR*, a *microsequencer,* and a network of decoding logic. Much of this chapter is devoted to demonstrating how these components might function as a control unit. The microsequencer is a small, hard-wired control sequencer. This is necessary to facilitate the transfer of vectors between the ROM, *MIR*, and *MAR* within the control unit. Only instructions are stored in the read-only memory.[1] Therefore, a word may be read from the ROM directly into the *microinstruction register, MIR.* No special

---

[1]For some machines, this constraint is modified to permit the reading of constants from the ROM.

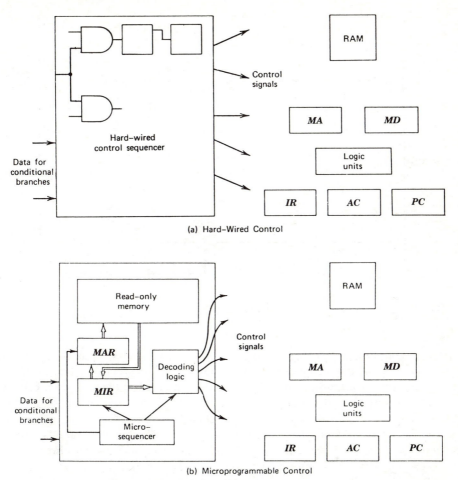

Figure 8.1. Two types of control units (a) Hard-wired control (b) Microprogrammable control

memory data register for the read-only memory is required. The **MIR** stores the microinstruction currently being executed. This microinstruction either will cause a transfer pulse to be issued from the control unit or will cause a branch within the control sequence. The *microaddress register, MAR,* functions as both a program counter and an address register for the read-only memory. Again, this is possible because every address is the address of an instruction. You may observe that a microprogrammable control unit is almost a computer within a computer.

Under certain circumstances, the microinstruction register **MIR** will not be required. If the control memory output-word is continuously available as a function of **MAR,** the output lines from this memory can themselves be used to effect the proper transfer and branch operations within first transferring the information into **MIR.** In

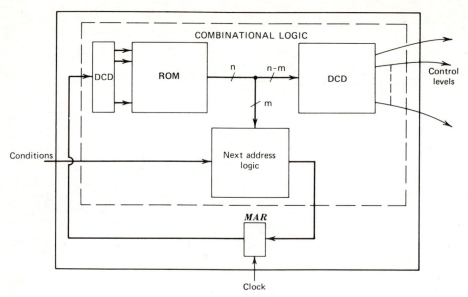

Figure 8.2. ROM-based control sequential circuit.

this case, the microprogrammable control unit can be represented as shown in Fig. 8.2. This configuration assumes that each microinstruction specifies a branch, if necessary, as well as a transfer, and is deliberately arranged in the form of a classical Moore model sequential circuit. The register *MAR* stores the current state of the machine. The sequential circuit has only one state per word in the ROM or potentially one state per step in the control sequence. If, as is usually the case, no other microprogram would result in the same sequence of output control levels, the circuit of Fig. 8.2 is the minimal state control sequential circuit. This is, a 2^n state control sequence is realized by a control circuit consisting of n flip-flops rather than up to 2^n flip-flops as could be the case in a hard-wired control sequencer. As mentioned previously, the minimal state realization of a control circuit is not necessarily the best, or even the overall most economical, realization.

There are inputs to the control unit that serve to control conditional branches within the *microprogram*. Very often these lines, which are shown in Fig. 8.1b, come from the instruction register, *IR*.

It is the decoding logic of Fig. 8.1b, in conjunction with the microsequencer, that makes it possible to interpret the vector in *MIR* as an AHPL step. Our approach here will be gradually to uncover the structure of these units and the reasons why they are so structured. We shall not start by showing all the details of the coding of a microinstruction but rather shall specify these details only as they arise naturally in the discussion. When an *MIR* is employed, the execution of a microinstruction is a two-step process.

1. Place a word from the ROM in *MIR*
2. Issue a control level and/or update *MAR*

If no asynchronous transfers are specified, two clock periods are required per microinstruction. By contrast, in a machine with a hard-wired control sequencer or in the circuit of Fig. 8.2, each step in the control sequence will be executed in one clock period.

You might conclude that the use of an **MIR** would decrease the speed of a microprogrammable computer by a factor of two. This would not necessarily be the case, since the clock rate to be established for the configuration of Fig. 8.2 will depend on the propagation delay through the ROM and the decoding logic in series with any combinational logic in the data unit. The inclusion of **MIR** will break this logic into two parts, each with a maximum delay shorter than the original maximum delay. Thus the clock frequency could be increased, although not doubled, if **MIR** is used. We shall see that it is possible to extend the complexity of the microsequencer beyond the simple two-step procedure described here. In this case, the faster clock rate would be advantageous. We have chosen to use **MIR** throughout the discussion of a microprogrammable RIC primarily to simplify notation. Most of the subsequent discussion is equally applicable to a model similar to Fig. 8.2 with each instance of **MIR** translated as the output of the ROM.

The delay associated with the ROM will probably always make the microprogrammable approach slower than the fastest hard-wired control sequencer. We shall find that the number of microinstructions necessary to accomplish a task will usually exceed the number of steps in a control sequence for a hard-wired implementation of the same task. Various sophistications can be added to lessen the time penalty inherent in microprogramming. Still, it is safe to say that a machine with a hard-wired control sequencer can always be made to operate faster than an apparently identical machine that relies on microprogramming. Most of the commonly available 16- and 32-bit microprocessor chips have been realized through microprogramming, but the primary reason has probably been the easier organization of the design process and greater predictability of control-unit chip area.

Consideration of our primary microprogamming design example, RIC, will begin in the next section. In preparation, let us consider the description of the simplest possible microsequencer given use of the microinstruction register, **MIR,** and separation of branch and transfer microinstructions. The latter is often done to reduce the length of a microinstruction word. This will, of course, increase the total number of microinstructions; but, because branches are associated with a minority of steps in a control sequence, the total number of bits in the *control memory* will be reduced. Although the control memory is not always a read-only-memory, it will be referred to as ROM in the following microsequencer description as a simple method of distinguishing it from the main random access memory of the computer.

1    $MIR \leftarrow$ BUSFN(**ROM**; DCD(MAR)).
2    $\rightarrow (MIR[0])/(4)$.
3    $MAR \leftarrow$ (INC(MAR) ! $MIR[16:31]$) $* (\bar{g}, g)$;
     NO DELAY $\rightarrow (1)$.
4   "execute connections and transfers as functions of MIR";
     $MAR \leftarrow$ INC(MAR);
     NO DELAY $\rightarrow (1)$.

This microsequencer is not completely general, but it is consistent with the microprogrammable version of RIC to be discussed in the next section. We have assumed that the most significant bit in each microinstruction will be used to distinguish between branch and transfer microinstructions. If $MIR[0] = 1$, a branch is executed at step 3. If $MIR[0] = 0$, step 4 sends control signals to the data unit to activate connections and transfers. We note that both steps 3 and 4 are NO DELAY steps, so that every microinstruction is executed in two clock periods. The branch at step 2 requires a separate clock period because it must await the placing of a microinstruction in MIR. It is also assumed that the ROM address space is 64K words, that only two-way branches are allowed, and that the address of a successful branch is found in the last 16 bits of the microinstruction. The branch is conditioned on g, a complex function of microinstruction bits and condition lines from the data unit. If $g = 0$, the next microinstruction in order will be the next to be executed. Two-way branching in the microprogram will be sufficient for the description of RIC in the next section. Some microprogrammable computers have employed more complex multiway branching, a topic that will be deferred until Section 8.9.

8.3 A Microprogrammable RIC

We pointed out in Chapter 6 that the bus structure of a computer is usually laid out before the writing of a control sequence begins. This significantly constrained what could eventually be written into the description. In the case of a microprogrammable computer, the bus structure must necessarily be specified at the outset, but this is only a part of the constraints that will be placed on the microprogram description of the machine. In addition, all branch functions, and possible bus connections and transfers, must be listed in advance. As suggested in the last section, the microsequencer must be designed and the meaning of all bits of the branch or transfer microinstruction formats must be assigned meanings at the start.

So far, each of the activities discussed is a function performed by the designer of the microprogrammable computer. In order that these functions not be confused with microprogramming, the three phases of implementation and utilization for a microprogrammable machine are summarized in Fig. 8.3. So far, we have considered only the hardware phase. This phase will have been completed once the unit leaves the manufacturer's installation. The task of supplying the microprogram may be accomplished by the manufacturer, may fall to the user, or may be done by the manufacturer according to the user's specification. At one time, a selling point of a microprogrammable minicomputer was the potential to modify the control unit by supplying a revised microprogram. It is important to recognize that *supplying a microprogram is the limit of the user's ability to restructure the machine*. There is no provision for user modification of the microsequencer. For example, the list of branch functions is fixed. An exercise or example may call for augmenting the list of branch functions prior to writing a specific microprogram. In practice, all such branches must be anticipated during the design process and included in the branch list. As a pedagogical

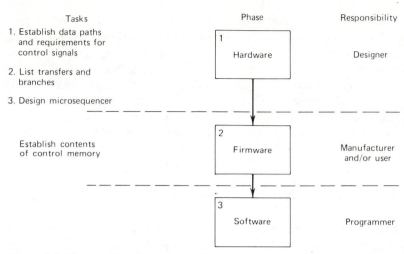

Figure 8.3. Phases of implementation.

tool, we have chosen to introduce branch functions as needed rather than supply an exhaustive list in advance.

In Fig. 8.4, we repeat the RIC bus structure given earlier in Fig. 6.1. Connections to the memory data and address buses are omitted, because all connections and transfers associated with memory read and write operations will be controlled by two "read" and "write" bits in the microinstruction. Included are transfers into the flag bits and the carry-in line to the CPU that will require some special attention in the formulation of the transfer microinstruction format. Also added to the bus structure is the 5-bit

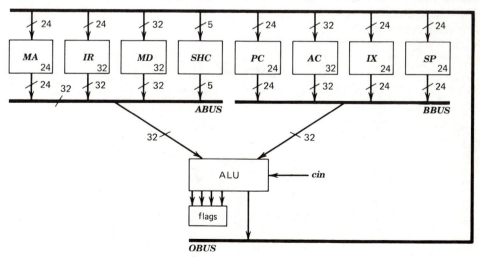

Figure 8.4. Microprogrammable RIC.

counter, **SHC,** which transparent to the user, can serve a variety of microprogram functions. Connecting this register to the bus structure, rather than supplying a separate incrementing capability, will increase the number of microprogram steps and slow down the instruction execution. To control separate incrementing of this register, and to provide for other parallel activities would lengthen the microinstruction. The advantages and disadvantages of this approach will be considered in Section 8.4.

Although the diagram of Fig. 8.4 served our needs in Chapter 6 by identifying the pairs of registers that could serve as arguments of the ALU, it does not actually show all the vectors that can be connected to the three buses. Various combinations and rotations of the bits of the registers shown are connectable to the **ABUS** and **BBUS,** and there are several outputs from the ALU connectable to the **OBUS.** To actually determine the list of vectors connectable to each bus, a preliminary control sequence must be available.

Each microinstruction will control the activity that takes place during one time step (actually two clock periods) of execution of a RIC instruction. It will control all bus connections and transfers that will take place during and at the end of that time step. The format of a transfer microinstruction for the microprogrammable RIC is given in Fig. 8.5a. Consistent with the microsequencer presented in the previous section, bit 0 of the transfer microinstruction is 0. Bits 1 through 3 are, for now, unused. The next four 5-bit fields are used to specify the connections to **ABUS, BBUS, OBUS,** and the target of the transfer. The last eight bits (24–31) will be assigned special functions. Provision has been made for up to 32 connections to each bus and 32 targets. Quite likely, this is more than will actually be required. To avoid unnecessary congestion at this point, we have listed in Fig. 8.6, with one exception, only those connections and transfers required in the realization of the RIC control sequence

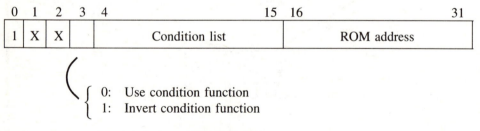

0	1	2	3	4 8	9 13	14 18	19 23	24 31
0	X	X	X	*ABUS*	*BBUS*	*OBUS*	Target	Special bits

(a) Transfer

0	1	2	3	4 15	16 31
1	X	X		Condition list	ROM address

$$\left\{ \begin{array}{l} 0: \quad \text{Use condition function} \\ 1: \quad \text{Invert condition function} \end{array} \right.$$

(b) Branch

Figure 8.5. Branch and transfer microinstructions.

MIR[4:8]	Connections to ABUS	MIR[9:13]	Connections to BBUS
0 0 0 0 0	32 ⊤ 1	0 0 0 0 0	8 ⊤ 0, *PC*
0 0 0 0 1	*MD*	0 0 0 0 1	8 ⊤ 0, *IX*
0 0 0 1 0	8 ⊤ 0, *MA*	0 0 0 1 0	*AC*
0 0 0 1 1	*MD*	0 0 0 1 1	32 ⊤ 1
0 0 1 0 0	28 ⊤ 0, *IR*[12:15]	0 0 1 0 0	8 ⊤ 0, *AC*[8:31]
0 0 1 0 1	$\overline{(28 \top 0)}$, *IR*[12:15]	0 0 1 0 1	8 ⊤ 0, *SP*
0 0 1 1 0	27 ⊤ 0, *SHC*	0 0 1 1 0	Specified by
0 0 1 1 1	$\overline{32 \top 0}$		*IR*[6:9]*
0 1 0 0 0	16 ⊤ 0, *IR*[16:31]	0 0 1 1 1	by *IR*[12:15]
0 1 0 0 1	$\overline{16 \top 0}$, *IR*[16:31]	0 1 0 0 0	32 ⊤ 0
0 1 0 1 0	32 ⊤ 0	0 1 0 0 1	*MQ*
.	.	0 1 0 1 0	32 ⊤ 0
.	.	.	.
.	.	.	.

MIR[14:18]	Connections to OBUS	MIR[19:23]	Target
0 0 0 0 0	*ABUS*	0 0 0 0 0	*MA*
0 0 0 0 1	*BBUS*	0 0 0 0 1	*IR*
0 0 0 1 0	*ABUS* ⊕ *BBUS*	0 0 0 1 0	*PC*
0 0 0 1 1	ADD[1:32] (*ABUS;BBUS;cin*)	0 0 0 1 1	*MD*
0 0 1 0 0	*ABUS* ∧ *BBUS*	0 0 1 0 0	*IX*
0 0 1 0 1	*ABUS* ∨ *BBUS*	0 0 1 0 1	*SP*
0 0 1 1 0	*cin*, *BBUS*[0:30]	0 0 1 1 0	*AC*
0 0 1 1 1	*BBUS*[1:31], *cin*	0 0 1 1 1	Specified by
0 1 0 0 0	*ABUS*[16:31], 16 ⊤ 0		*IR*[6:9]*
0 1 0 0 1	*ABUS* ∧ *MD*[8]	0 1 0 0 0	*SHC*
0 1 0 1 0	*BBUS*	0 1 0 0 1	*IR*[8:31]
0 1 0 1 1	*BBUS*[1:31], *BBUS*[0]	0 1 0 1 0	*MD*[0:7]
.	.	0 1 0 1 1	*MQ*
.	.	0 1 1 0 0	"no target"
.	.	0 1 1 0 1	*shf*
		.	.
		.	.

*See Fig. 2.8.

Figure 8.6. Partial list of bus connections and targets.

given in Chapter 6. Not all targets listed consist of 32 bits. It is assumed that these targets will always receive the appropriate number of rightmost bits from the *OBUS*.

Also shown in Fig. 8.5b is the format for branch microinstructions. We have chosen to use 32-bit microinstructions and, therefore, a 32-bit ROM word length. That this is the same as the word length of main RAM is a coincidence. In general, there is no relation between word lengths of the main memory and the control memory.

Entries seven and eight in the list of *BBUS* connections, and entry eight in the list of targets, provide for connections and transfers conditioned on fields in the instruction register. These are the fields that select the arguments and result registers for the two-address instructions as described in Fig. 2.8. Implementation, for example, of row 00111 in the target list will merely require using the control line DCD[7] from the decoder of **MIR**[19:23] to enable a second decoder of **IR**[6:9] whose 16 outputs would select the actual target register.

Each of the four 5-bit fields in the transfer microinstruction will serve as the input of a separate 5 to 32 decoder. The outputs of the decoders will be control lines that actually effect the connections to the buses and gate the transfer pulses to the registers. A logic block diagram that tried to depict these connections for RIC would be prohibitively complex. Instead, we illustrate in Example 8.1 the ideas involved by decoding a 3-bit field of the microinstruction of an arbitrary computer and by using the outputs to control connections to a 6-bit bus.

Example 8.1

Figure 8.7 lists the vectors that must be connected to the 6-bit **QBUS,** one of the buses of a small microprogrammable computer. The vector to be connected to **QBUS** by a particular microinstruction is specified by 3 bits of the microinstruction register, **MIR**[2:4]. For example, if **MIR**[2:4] $= 0,0,1$, then zeros are to be connected to the first 3 bits of the **QBUS,** and **RA**[3:5] to the last 3 bits. Construct a detailed logic block diagram of the **QBUS,** including the decoder in the control unit that generates control levels to effect connections to the **QBUS.**

Solution

A single step in the AHPL description of the microsequencer will call for placing the appropriate vector from Fig. 8.7 on the **QBUS.** The array of bus inputs on the right side of the AHPL step given as expression 8.1 is abbreviated **QM** in Fig. 8.8.

$$QBUS = (RA \ ! \ 3 \top 0, RA[3:5] \ ! \ RA[0:2], RB[3.5] \ ! \ RB \ !$$
$$6 \top 0 \ ! \ 6 \top 1 \ ! \ 6 \top 8 \ ! \ 6 \top 10) * DCD(MIR[2:4]) \qquad (8.1)$$
$$= QM * DCD(MIR[2:4])$$

Vector to Be Placed on *QBUS*	*MIR*[2:4]
RA	0, 0, 0
3 ⊤ 0, *RA*[3:5]	0, 0, 1
RA[0:2], *RB*[3:5]	0, 1, 0
RB	0, 1, 1
6 ⊤ 0	1, 0, 0
6 ⊤ 1	1, 0, 1
6 ⊤ 8	1, 1, 0
6 ⊤ 10	1, 1, 1

Figure 8.7. Inputs to **QBUS.**

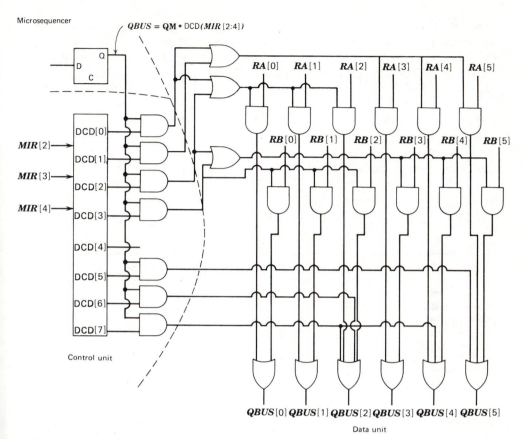

Figure 8.8. Implementation of **QBUS** and **QBUS** control.

Only one step of the microsequence is shown in Fig. 8.8 along with the portion of the control unit that decodes **MIR**[2:4] and the realization of the **QBUS** in the data unit.

Notice that none of the OR gates making up **QBUS** has more than four inputs (three of the OR gates have only two inputs) even though eight vectors are listed in Fig. 8.7. By appropriate ORing of the control levels, the various combinations of bits from **RA** and **RB** result in only two connections to each **QBUS** OR gate. For example, only **RA**[0:2] and **RB**[0:2] need be routed to the first 3 bits of **QBUS**, because 3 T 0 is the **QBUS**[0:2] output if all input lines are 0. The routing of the constants listed as the last four entries in Fig. 8.7 is accomplished by connecting the respective control levels directly to the **QBUS** OR gates, much the same as in the implementation of a ROM. Notice that no connection to DCD is required to cause 6 T 0 to be placed on the **QBUS**.   ■

Just as with connections and transfers, the branch functions that will be needed in microprograms must be anticipated in advance and assigned to combinations of values in a field of the branch microinstruction. Fig. 8.5b is consistent with the microsequencer of the previous section, which allows only two way branches. Bits 1 and 2 will be left unused, given this simple microsequencer. Bit $MIR[3]$ will indicate whether the selected branch function should be 1 or 0 to effect a branch. A list of as many as 2^{12} branch functions together with the complement of each function is possible. Certainly fewer functions will be used, but the number is still smaller when compared with $2^{2^{16}}$ possible functions of the first 16 bits of the instruction register. Indeed, the available bits in Fig. 8.5b might be used to provide some form of multiway branch capability. We shall, however, leave this topic for Section 8.9. If a microinstruction branch condition is satisfied, $MIR[16:31]$ will be the next value of MAR.

A list of branch functions sufficient for implementation of all the RIC control sequence found in Chapter 6 is given in Fig. 8.9. We note that all the first 16 bits of the instruction register are included individually in the list. These 16 individual bit

$MIR[4:15]$	Branch function
000000 000000	$IR[0]$
000000 000001	$IR[1]$
000000 000010	$IR[2]$
000000 000011	$IR[3]$
000000 000100	$IR[4]$
000000 000101	$IR[5]$
000000 000110	$IR[6]$
000000 000111	$IR[7]$
000000 001000	$IR[8]$
000000 001001	$IR[9]$
000000 001010	$IR[10]$
000000 001011	$IR[11]$
000000 001100	$IR[12]$
000000 001101	$IR[13]$
000000 001110	$IR[14]$
000000 001111	$IR[15]$
000000 010000	$IR[0] \wedge IR[1] \wedge IR[2] \wedge IR[3]$
000000 010001	$\wedge /IR[1:3]$
000000 010010	$\wedge /IR[0:2]$
000000 010011	$IR[1] \wedge IR[2]$
000000 010100	$IR[0] \wedge \overline{IR[1]}$
000000 010101	$(\vee/(IR[7:15] \wedge (C,\overline{C},Z,\overline{Z},N,\overline{N},V,\overline{V}, N \oplus V))) \oplus IR[6]$
000000 010110	$\vee/SHC$
000000 010111	$\vee/IR[6:9]$
000000 011000	shf
000000 011001	(Unconditional)
000000 011010	$MQ[31]$
000000 011011	$AC[0]$
000000 011011	cff
. . .	. . .

Figure 8.9. List of RIC branch functions.

functions and their complements could, if necessary, be used in a series of branch steps to effect any one of the branch functions in the control sequence of Chapter 6. The more complex functions identified in a step-by-step review of the control sequence are included to save steps.

Recall that an overall branch function, g, was included in the microsequencer description given in Section 8.2. The table in Fig. 8.9 defines this function. Notice in the table, the function corresponding to $MIR[4:15] = 000000\,010101$. This function of IR and several flags is 1, and causes a branch, if a selected flag-bit is 1. The controlling flag-bit is selected by the instruction register. The same approach may be used to generate the composite branch function, g. To ease the writing of the expression for g, let us use $F[0:12]$ to represent the last 13 branch functions in Fig. 8.9, beginning with $\overline{IR[0]}\wedge IR[1]\wedge IR[2]\wedge IR[3]$. Now we may simply decode the condition list field of MIR and AND the result bit by bit with the branch functions to form Eq. 8.2. Recall that bit $MIR[3]$ specifies whether control should be transferred, if the listed function is 1 or if it is 0.

$$g = \bigvee/(DCD[0:28](MIR[4:15]) \wedge (IR[0:15], F[0:12)) \oplus MIR[3] \qquad (8.2)$$

8.4   Flags and Special Bits

In Fig. 8.10, we repeat the RIC transfer microinstruction format, emphasizing the eight special bits $MIR[24:31]$. If bit $MIR[24]$ is a 1, the N, V, and Z flags will be clocked. The logic functions connected to the D inputs of these flip-flops will be generated in the ALU and will always be the same. Determination of these expressions

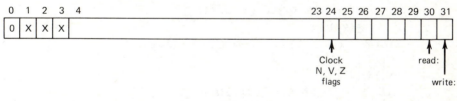

(a)

MIR[25:27]	cff activity	MIR[28:29]	Connection to cin
0 0 0	cff not clocked	0 0	cin = 0
0 0 1	cff ← ADD[0]	0 1	cin = 1
0 1 0	cff ← BBUS[0]	1 0	cin = cff
0 1 1	cff ← BBUS[31]	1 1	cin = AC[31]
1 0 0	cff ← c̄f̄f̄		
1 0 1	cff ← 0		
1 1 0	cff ← 1		

(b)

Figure 8.10. Special bits in transfer microinstruction.

will be left as a problem for you. Bits *MIR*[30] and *MIR*[31] will cause read and write operations from and to the external memory to take place. An active control line from *MIR*[30], for example, will cause **read** = 1 and the memory data bus to be clocked into *MD*. The address bus is always connected to *MA*. Read and write operations may take place at the same time as transfers through the bus structure. The only restriction is that a read does not take place at the same time that *MD* is a target of a transfer from the *OBUS*.

The interpretation of bits *MIR*[25:29], which control the carry input to the ALU and the carry flip-flop activity are given in Fig. 8.10b. When any of bits *MIR*[25] through *MIR*[27] is 1, the carry flip-flop, *cff*, will be clocked. Six separate bits can be connected to the D input of this flip-flop depending, for example, on whether the microinstruction uses the adder or implements a rotate. Four possible bits can be connected to *cin*, the carry input to the ALU, depending on the values of *MIR*[28:29]. The usefulness of complementing *cff* and connecting *AC*[31] to *cin* will be apparent as we discuss a multiplication microprogram in the next section.

In the last section, we developed the function, *g*, to complete step 3 (implementing branching) of the microsequencer given in Section 8.2. Now with the tables in Figures 8.6 and 8.10, we are able to complete step 4 of the microsequencer. Each of the *ABUS* connection entries in Fig. 8.6 can be considered as a row of a connection matrix **OCLMA**. Similarly, let the *BBUS* vectors be the rows of **OCLMB**, the *OBUS* vectors be the rows of **OCLMO**, and the target vectors the rows of **TM**. A notational problem exists for targets of length less than 32 bits. Imagine segments of a dummy placeholder register catenated at the left of the actual target to fill out the 32 bits. This register will never be actually implemented. Now we can rewrite the description of the microsequencer in terms of the matrices just defined with the flag transfers and connections to *cin* made explicit.

1　　*MIR* ← BUSFN(**ROM**; DCD(*MAR*)).
2　　　→ ($\overline{MIR[0]}$/(4).
3　　*MAR* ← (INC(*MAR*) ! *MIR*[16:31]) * ($\overline{g}$, *g*);
　　　NO DELAY　　　→ (1).
4　　NO DELAY
　　　ABUS = **OCLMA** * DCD(*MIR*[4:8]);
　　　BBUS = **OCLMB** * DCD(*MIR*[9:13]);
　　　OBUS = **OCLMO** * DCD(*MIR*[14:18]);
　　　TM * $\overline{\text{DCD}[12](MIR[19:23])}$ ∧ DCD(*MIR*[19:23]) ← *OBUS*;
　　　cin = (0 ! 1 ! *cff* ! *AC*[31]) * DCD(*MIR*[28:29]);
　　　cff * (∨/*MIR*[25:27]) ← (ADD[0] ! *BBUS*[0] ! *BBUS*[31] !
　　　　　　　　　　　　　　　　　　　　　　$\overline{cff}$! 0 ! 1) * DCD[1:6](*MIR*[25:27]);
　　　nff * *MIR*[24] ← *OBUS*[0];
　　　zff * *MIR*[24] ← $\overline{\vee/OBUS}$;
　　　vff * *MIR*[24] → " Chapter 6, step 23 "
　　　read = *MIR*[30]; **write** = *MIR*[31];
　　　DBUS = *MD* * *MIR*[31]; *MD* * *MIR*[30] ← *DBUS*;
　　　MAR ← INC(*MAR*);
　　　→ (1).

It should be pointed out that the preceding is more than a description of the microsequencer. It is now a complete description of the microprogrammable computer, including the data unit. Note that *MD* is included in **TM** and is separately the target of a transfer from *DBUS*. The further refinement of step 4, required to accurately represent in AHPL the implied or declared bus at the input of *MD* will be left as a problem for the reader.

8.5 Microcoding

Just as coding software directly in machine language is a tedious process, so is coding a microprogram directly in the instruction formats discussed in the past two sections. Our purpose in this section is to encode a microprogram segment corresponding to a few steps in the RIC control sequence to illustrate the interpretation of the various bits in the transfer and branch microinstruction formats. In the process, we shall notice why the number of microinstructions will almost always exceed the number of steps in a hard-wired control sequence implementing the same process. At the end, we shall conclude that, although easy to understand, the microprogramming template described in Sections 8.3 and 8.4 is not optimal with respect to execution time or the number of microprogram steps or chip area given VLSI implementation. Performance optimization usually comes through specialized modification of the microsequencer once the scope of the control sequence is well established.

An interesting illustration will result from microcoding RIC steps 51, 52 and 53 given in Section 6.6 to implement two-address instructions. Because step numbers will not correspond to address locations, we start with the premise that the branch corresponding to step 1 will be located at address 100 (hex). For ease of reading in the coding in Fig. 8.11, addresses are represented in hexadecimal with the remaining coding in binary. Spaces are used to separate the appropriate fields of both types of microinstructions. Don't-care bits will be represented by X's.

We see from this code that the single step 52 in the hard-wired control sequence is replaced by seven microprogram steps, two or four of which must be executed for a given two-address instruction. The problem lies in the limited conditional transfer

Step	ROM address	Microinstruction		
51	100	1XX0 000000 010011		
52	101	1XX1 000000 001010	107	
52	102	1XX0 000000 001100	105	
52	103	0XXX 00100 00111 00000 00011 0000XX00		
52	104	1XX0 000000 011001	108	"unconditional"
52	105	0XXX 00101 00111 00000 00011 0000XX00		
52	106	1XX0 000000 011001	108	
52	107	0XXX 00100 00111 00001 00011 0000XX00		
53	108			

Figure 8.11. Microcoding RIC steps 51 and 52.

capability provided in the microinstruction format. We note that the values 00111 in the **BBUS** field provided for the same conditional connection of **AC, IX,** or **SP** to the **BBUS** in all four of the transfer microinstructions listed. However, no connection to the **ABUS** conditioned on **IR**[12] or connection to the **OBUS** conditioned on **IR**[10] are listed. It was, therefore, necessary to branch to three (the connection to the **ABUS** selected by **IR**[12] does not matter, if **IR**[10] = 0, because the **ABUS** is not used in that case) separate transfer steps on the basis of these two bits. Including more conditional connections in the lists, particularly those that are used frequently, would have the effect of shortening microprograms and reducing the instruction execution times. There are, of course, innumerable possible combinations of register lists and condition functions. Including more of these in the connection target list of Fig. 8.6 serves to constrain the microprogram.

Two unconditional transfers are found in the code. These could be eliminated by adding 16 bits to provide for an unconditional transfer in every transfer microinstruction. Such an approach would reduce execution time but would result in an overall increase in the number of bits in the ROM.

In step 53, it is again possible to connect **AC, IX** or **SP** conditionally to the **BBUS** (conditioned on **IR**[6:9]) by inserting 00110 in the **BBUS** field. The target of the **OBUS** may be similarly conditional on **IR**[6:9]. However, connections to the **OBUS** and the special bits, **MIR**[24:31], are dependent on the particular instruction being executed. It is, therefore, necessary to separate control for the 10 instructions depicted in Fig. 8.12a. The transfer microinstructions implementing ADC and ADD are, because of the don't cares in Fig. 8.12a, easily isolated by the branches conditioned on first **IR**[1] and then **IR**[3]. Impementation of these two operations is coded in Fig. 8.12b. Branches on all bits **IR**[0:3] are necessary to isolate the remaining eight operations; the coding of these is left to the reader.

Notice that the ADD and ADC operations differ only in the special bit fields selecting the carry input to the adder, as enclosed in Fig. 8.12b. In both cases, 00001 connects **MD** to the **ABUS,** 00110 makes the **BBUS** connection conditional, 00011 connects the output of the adder to the **OBUS,** and 00111 makes the **OBUS** target conditional on **IR**[6:9]. The first special bit causes the N, V, and Z flags to be clocked. The next two cause the carry-out from the adder to be transferred into the carry flip-flop. It is assumed in Fig. 8.12b that RIC step 100 is coded at location 200 (hex) in the ROM.

Figures 8.12a and 8.12b demonstrate the inconvenience resulting from the absence of a multiway branch capability. Section 8.9 will explore, in general, approaches to adding limited multiway branches. The most important application of multiway microprogram branching is for one-time decoding of the opcode, and branching at once to a set of separate locations in the control ROM for the implementation of each possible instruction. The relatively little further branching, which will be required in the execution of most of the instructions, can easily be accomodated using two-way branch instructions. This technique is employed in many microprogrammed microprocessors. Although use of the control ROM may be even less efficient, the more important consequence of this arrangement is that fewer microinstructions and, therefore, less time is required in the execution of each machine instruction. We illustrate this technique in the following example.

IR [2:3]	IR [0:1] 00	IR[1] 01	11	10
00	SBC	ADC	✕	ORA
01	SUB	ADD	✕	AND
11	CMP	✕	✕	BIT
10	MVT	✕	✕	XOR

} IR [3]

(a.)

step	ROM address		microinstruction	
53	10B	1XX1	000000 000001 111	
53	10C	1XX0	000000 000011 10F	
53	10D	0XXX	00001 00110 00011 00111 10011000 "ADC"	
53	10E	1XX0	000000 011001 200 "unconditional"	
53	10F	0XXX	00001 00110 00011 00111 10010000 "ADD"	
53	110	1XX0	000000 011001 200 "step 100 at 200hex "	
53	111	1XX0	000000 000000 "con'd to form 8-way branch"	
•	•	•	•	
•	•	•	•	

(b.)

Figure 8.12. Microcoding RIC step 53.

Example 8.2

Consider a computer that, like RIC, has 16-bit and 32-bit instructions. Like RIC (Fig. 2.2), the first 8 bits of each 32-bit instruction include the opcode and addressing modes. In contrast to RIC, the opcode and mode bits are also grouped in $IR[0:7]$ for 16-bit instructions. The format for two-address instructions is given in Fig. 8.13a. For shift and rotate instructions, the critical bits are also grouped in $IR[0:7]$, leaving only the shift distance and unused bits in $IR[8:15]$. The small number of miscellaneous instructions needed in this computer can also be represented by unused bit combinations in $IR[0:7]$. Describe, using AHPL, an approach to separating the opcode mode combinations for execution in 256 separate memory areas.

Solution

The branch shown in Figure 8.13b divides the control memory into 256 equal pages (256 words) on the basis of $IR[0:7]$. Implementing this branch requires only a simple modification of step 3 of the microsequencer given in the previous section. We add a single entry to the branch list of Fig. 8.9 that will represent the multiway branch. We choose the last possible entry in the table for which $\bigwedge/MIR[4:15] = 1$. For this case, the 16 address bits in the microinstruction are disregarded. Step 3 may now be rewritten as follows.

$$3 \quad MAR \leftarrow (INC(MAR) \; ! \; MIR[16:31] \; ! \; IR[0:7],8 \top 0)$$
$$* \; (\overline{\bigwedge/MIR[4:15]} \wedge (\bar{g}, g), \bigwedge/MIR[4:15])$$

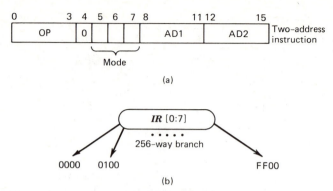

Figure 8.13. Multiway branch on opcode.

Some instructions will require considerably less than 256 words of ROM. The unused words need not actually be implemented; but this would require random pruning of lines from the ROM decoder, something that could cause problems in the VLSI realization. The step 3 just presented can be further modified to allow the multiway branch to 256 arbitrary locations in ROM by adding another small ROM containing these 256 addresses. The opcode bits would serve as an index into this ROM. This technique is similar to what has been called *nanoprogramming* in references 10 and 12 (we would prefer to reserve this term for realizing the microsequencer through microprogramming, something unlikely ever to be used), so we label this ROM, **NANOROM.** This approach is realized by rewriting step 3 as given here.

3     $MAR \leftarrow (INC(MAR) \ ! \ MIR[16:31] \ !$
      $BUSFN(\textbf{NANOROM}; DCD(IR[0:7]))$
                              $* \ (\overline{\wedge/MIR[4:15]} \wedge (\bar{g}, g), \wedge/MIR[4:15])$

A microsequencer including step 3 as presented here could allow the section of ROM corresponding to each instruction to contain the exact number of words used to implement that instruction. At the end of the design process, the size of the ROM and perhaps the number of microaddress bits can be reduced. ∎

8.6 An Assembly Language for Microprograms

The first commercially available computers were programmed in machine code, but the tedium of this process soon triggered the development of assembly language and then higher-level languages. The short examples found in the previous section have probably convinced you that microcoding is no less tedious. What form should an assembly language for microprograms take? First, we observe that microcode describes clock-mode hardware at the same level as AHPL. Equally important is the fact that while AHPL is completely general and can be used to describe any clock-mode hardware, the hardware functions describable in microcode are firmly constrained by the design of the corresponding microsequencer. This would suggest that the general form of register transfer syntax used in AHPL could be adapted to form a microassembly language, but this language would be much simplified, thereby reflecting the constraints imposed by the microsequencer.

In this section, we shall define an assembly language, called MICRAL, for microprograms for the machine just discussed (*MICRoAssembly Language*). Each step of MICRAL will correspond to one microinstruction. The MICRAL representation of a transfer step must specify a connection to each bus and a transfer from the *OBUS* to a target register. A bus connection statement in MICRAL will have an abbreviation *A, B,* or *OB* for *ABUS, BBUS,* or *OBUS,* respectively, on the left side of the " = " with one of the vectors in Fig. 8.6 on the right. The abbreviated bus notation will also be used in the expressions to the right of the " = " sign. Since no ambiguity will result, leading zeros may be omitted in MICRAL. Since the arguments of CLUNTS in the ALU are always the same, these will be omitted, too. Where the rightmost bits of the *OBUS* are used in a transfer, the number of bits is fixed by the target and will not otherwise be specified in MICRAL. The two operations, read and write, to the RAM will simply be written in MICRAL as *READ* and *WRITE.* Sixteen bit control memory addresses will be given in hexadecimal form.

The string, NVZ, will be included as a statement in any microinstruction in which these flags are to be clocked. If *cff* is clocked or *cin* is relevant, corresponding transfer and connection statements will be included as constrained by Fig. 8.10b. None of the information omitted from MICRAL in the foregoing discussion will be required by a microassembler program that will generate microcode from a MICRAL statement. The information provided in each statement will be sufficient to permit identification of the corresponding entries from Figures 8.6, 8.9, and 8.10. As in AHPL and unlike in most assembly languages, steps will be numbered and symbolic addresses will *not* be used. Processing MICRAL will be much simpler than processing AHPL because for each bus the parser need only distinguish a source form those listed in the appropriate table in Fig. 8.6. Similarly, once the *OBUS* is determined to be the source, the target need only be distinguished from among the targets listed in the final table in Fig 8.6.

All these features will simplify the writing of the microassembler, which will be discarded after the final microcode has been generated, while leaving the assembly code no less readable. Unlike for AHPL, our interest in MICRAL is transient. Our goal is to show that a simple but useful microassembly language can be written, once the microsequencer of a microprogrammable computer has been completely specified. We are, therefore, content to leave a few details of MICRAL syntax to be elaborated during the discussion of an example.

As an example, let us write a RIC microprogram to accomplish multiplication as discussed in Section 6.12. Each numbered step will represent a microinstruction. The MICRAL step numbers representing ROM locations begin arbitrarily at 1000 (hex). To the extent possible, the corresponding steps from the original AHPL sequence are listed within quotation marks at the right. As expected, there are more microinstructions than steps in the original sequence. Microinstructions 1000 to 1009 accomplish sign determination and conversion to sign and magnitude form. The first step of the original sequence must be separated into a transfer followed by a branch microinstruction. The simplified AHPL branch notation given in step 1001 will be universal in MICRAL. Step 1003 illustrates the expression of connecting the output of a combinational logic unit without its arguments. In this case of the microprogrammable RIC, the arguments of the adder are always the *ABUS, BBUS,* and *cin.*

1000	$cff \leftarrow 0.$	"1"
1001	$\rightarrow (\overline{AC[0]})/(1004).$	
1002	$cff \leftarrow \overline{cff}; B = AC; OB = \overline{B}; AC \leftarrow OB.$	"2"
1003	$A = 32 \top 0; B = AC; cin = 1; OB = \text{ADD}; AC \leftarrow OB.$	
1004	$B = AC; OB = B; MQ \leftarrow OB.$	"3"
1005	$A = MD; OB = A; AC \leftarrow OB.$	"4"
1006	$\rightarrow (\overline{AC[0]})/(1009).$	
1007	$cff \leftarrow \overline{cff}; B = AC; OB = \overline{B}; AC \leftarrow OB.$	"5"
1008	$A = 32 \top 0; B = AC; cin = 1; OB = \text{ADD}; AC \leftarrow OB.$	
1009	$B = AC; OB = B; MD \leftarrow OB.$	"6"

Step 7 in the original sequence loads two registers simultaneously with the same vector. This cannot be accomplished in the microprogrammable version. Only one target can be selected in a transfer microinstruction. This is of less interest, because a different counting mechanisms will be used in the microprogram. At step 100A, *SHC* is initially loaded with all 1's, and the successively decremented values are compared with zero, just as would be done in the implementation of the rotate instruction. The check is accomplished at step 1010. The addition conditioned on *MQ*[31], and the shift right into *MQ* that implements the actual multiplication, is implemented by steps 100C through 100F.

100A	$B = \overline{32 \top 0}; OB = B; SHC \leftarrow OB.$	"7"
100B	$A = 32 \top 0; OB = AC A; \leftarrow OB.$	
100C	$\rightarrow (\overline{MQ[31]})/(1014).$	"8–10"
100D	$A = MD; B = AC; cin = 0; OB = \text{ADD}; AC \leftarrow OB.$	
100E	$B = MQ; cin = AC[31]; OB = cin,B[0:30]; MQ \leftarrow OB.$	
100F	$B = AC; cin = 0; OB = cin, B[0:30]; AC \leftarrow OB.$	
1010	$\rightarrow (\sqrt{/SHC})/(1013).$	"11"
1011	$A = 27 \top 0,SHC; B = \overline{32 \top 0}; cin = 0;$	
	$OB = \text{ADD}; SHC \leftarrow OB.$	
1012	$\rightarrow (100C).$	

As in the original routine, steps 1013 through 101A convert the result back to 2's complement form, if the result is negative.

1013	$\rightarrow (\overline{cff})/(101A).$	"12"
1014	$B = AC; OB = \overline{B}; MD \leftarrow OB.$	"13"
1015	$\overline{B} = MQ; OB = \overline{B}; AC \leftarrow OB; cff \leftarrow 0.$	

1016	$A = 32 \top 0$; $B = AC$; $cin = 1$; $OB = $ ADD;	
	$cff \leftarrow$ ADD[0]; $AC \leftarrow OB$.	
1017	$B = AC$; $OB = B$; $MQ \leftarrow OB$.	
1018	$A = MD$; $OB = A$; $AC \leftarrow OB$.	"14"
1019	$A = 32 \top 0$; $B = AC$; $cin = cff$; $OB = $ ADD;	
	$AC \leftarrow OB$; $cff \leftarrow$ ADD[0].	
101A	$\rightarrow$ "next routine"	"15"

To include a multiplication instruction in this version of RIC, an opcode must be found. Ideally, multiplication would be a memory reference instruction. One could perhaps replace SUB in the list in Fig. 6.3 with MUL (multiplication). The equivalent of SUB could be accomplished by setting *cff* prior to SBC. The resulting computer would not be *upward compatible* with the hard-wired RIC of Chapter 6, because a RIC program involving SUB would not execute on the new machine. Another approach would be to implement a 16-bit two-address instruction which would move *AC* to *MQ*. After the other argument is loaded into *AC,* a special 16-bit multiplication instruction could begin by transferring the first argument from *MQ* to *MD*. Further consideration of this choice will be left as a problem for the reader.

The use of MICRAL has certainly made the discussion of the multiplication microprogram easier to follow. Such documentation advantages might not be sufficient to dictate the writing of a microassembler for a particular computer design project. The microassembler is dependent on the existence of final versions of tables such as given in Figures 8.6, 8.9, and 8.10, which are realized in the form of the microsequencer. It is not inconceivable that such tables will continue to evolve throughout the entire design process. It is difficult to anticipate every bus connection in advance. Perhaps the appropriate compromise is the use of a less than all-inclusive language like MICRAL, together with a combination of hand assembly and computer cross assembly.

8.7 Extending the RIC Microsequencer

Repeated in Fig. 8.14a is the format for a RIC transfer microinstruction. Notice that bits *MIR*[1:3] are unused. It is only necessary that the transfer format in Fig. 8.14a be applicable for one combination of values of these bits. For other sets of values, bits *MIR*[4:31] can be used to specify some other type of transfer activity. Some options of interest are tabulated in Fig. 8.14b. Input/output operations may require *responsive signalling*. That is, the duration of certain control outputs may depend on other control inputs. For convenience, we have allowed a separate category of microinstructions for this possibility. To specify the format of this type of microinstructions and to detail its processing by the microsequencer will require the background of Chapter 10. Similarly, input/output may require certain synchronous operations that cannot be accomplished through the busing structure. Again, we allow for this eventuality but provide no details.

0	1	2	3	4	8	9	13	14	18	19	23	24	31
0	X	X	X	*ABUS*		*BBUS*		*OBUS*		Target		Special bits	

(a) Synchronous bused transfer.

MIR[0:3]	Operation
0 0 0 0	Bused transfer
0 0 0 1	Other synchronous operations
0 0 1 0	Asynchronous operations
0 0 1 1	"Unused"
0 1 0 X	$OBUS = ROM(\langle MIR[3:18]\rangle)$;
	$TM * DCD(MIR[19:23]) \leftarrow OBUS$
0 1 1 X	"As above with indexing"
1 X X X	Branch

(b)

Figure 8.14. Categories of RIC microinstructions.

Of more interest is the fifth entry in Fig. 8.14b, which causes a constant to be read from anywhere within the control memory, ROM, as specified by *MIR*[3:18]. This operation will require a separate address path, as illustrated in Fig. 8.15. The three-input address bus, *MADDRBUS,* is entirely combinational, with three 16-bit banks of AND gates and a bank of OR gates as shown. The transfer of the constant from the *OBUS* to the desired register in **TM** is specified by *MIR*[14:23], exactly as listed in Fig. 8.6 for an ordinary bused transfer. For the transfer of the constant from the *OBUS* to the target, the only additional hardware will be one gate for ORing two control lines at the output of the microsequencer.

Obtaining a single constant from a location in the control ROM known in advance can be accomplished by using a microinstruction for which *MIR*[0:2] = 0, 1, 0. This approach is insufficient if it is desired to step through or index into an array of constants in the control ROM. For this type of activity, it is necessary to access the ROM via some type of microprogram programmer-transparent data register. For this purpose, we introduce the data microaddress register, *DMAR,* also shown in Fig. 8.15. Each time this register is used, its contents will be obtained as the sum of a micro index register, *IMIC,* and *MIR*[3:18]. *DMAR* is required, because formation of the sum will require the *OBUS*. This bus cannot, of course, be used for two purposes during the same clock period. The microsequencer, as extended to implement Fig. 8.14b, follows. One possible addition to what is shown would be to permit the use of the special bits *MIR*[24:31] in a "fetch constant" microinstruction in the same way as in a bused transfer.

1   *MADDRBUS* = *MAR;*
     MIR $\leftarrow$ BUSFN(**ROM;** DCD(*MADDRBUS*)).
2    $\rightarrow$ (*MIR*[0], $\overline{MIR[0]}$ $\wedge$ (DCD[0:2] (*MIR*[1:3]), DCD[2:3] (*MIR*[1:2])))
     /(3, 4, "other synchronous", "asynchronous", 5, 6).

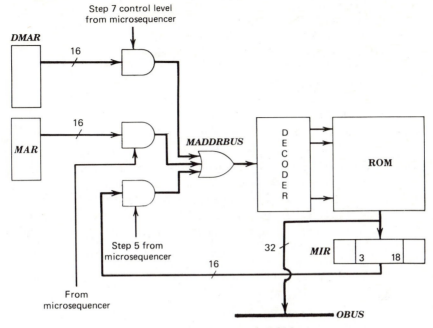

Figure 8.15. Reading a constant from the control, ROM.

3   **MAR**   ← (INC(**MAR**) ! **MIR**[16:31]) * ($\bar{g}$, g);
       NO DELAY   → (1).

4   NO DELAY
       ABUS = **OCLMA** * DCD(**MIR**[4:8]);
       BBUS = **OCLMB** * DCD(**MIR**[9:13]);
       OBUS = **OCLMO** * DCD(**MIR**[14:18]);
       TM * $\overline{\text{DCD}[12](\textbf{MIR}[19:23])}$ $\wedge$ DCD(**MIR**[19:23]) ← **OBUS**;
       cin = (0 ! 1 ! *cff* ! **AC**[31]) * DCD(**MIR**[28:29]);
       cff * ($\vee$/**MIR**[25:27]) ← (ADD[0] ! **BBUS**[0] ! **BBUS**[31] !
                                       $\overline{cff}$! 0 ! 1) * DCD[1:6](**MIR**[25:27]);
       nff * **MIR**[24] ← **OBUS**[0];
       zff * **MIR**[24] ← $\overline{\vee/\textbf{OBUS}}$;
       vff * **MIR**[24] ← "see Chapter 6, step 23"
       read = **MIR**[30]; **write** = **MIR**[31];
       MD * **MIR**[30] ← **DBUS**; **DBUS** = **MD** * **MIR**[31];
       MAR ← INC(**MAR**);   → (1).

5   NO DELAY
       MADDRBUS = **MIR**[3:18];
       OBUS = BUSFN(**ROM**; DCD(**MADDRBUS**));
       TM * DCD(**MIR**[19:23]) ← **OBUS**;
       MAR ← INC(**MAR**); → (1).

6   NO DELAY
        ABUS = 16 ⊤ 0, *MIR*[3:18];
        BBUS = 16 ⊤ 0, *IMIC; cin* = 0;
        OBUS = ADD[1:32] (*ABUS; BBUS; cin*);
        DMAR ← *OBUS*[16:31].

7   *MADDRBUS* = *DMAR;*
        OBUS = BUSFN(**ROM;** DCD(*MADDRBUS*));
        TM * DCD(*MIR*[19:23]) ← *OBUS;*
        MAR ← INC(*MAR*);   → (1).

Step 5 accomplishes the reading of an individual constant from the control ROM into the specified register in **TM.** This, like most other microinstructions, requires two clock periods. Where indexing is employed, *IMIC* is added to *MIR*[3:18] at step 6, and the constant is actually read from the ROM at step 7, which cannot be a NO DELAY step. Therefore, microinstructions denoted by *MIR*[0:2] = 011 require three clock periods for execution.

In referring to the reading of constants from ROM in MICRAL, it will be sufficient to use the following notation, where the constant may be expressed in hexadecimal.

"target" ← "constant"

for example,

MD ← 0000000F

Assigning the constant to a memory location can be a function accomplished by the assembler for MICRAL. If *IMIC* is involved, the notation may be simply

"target" ← **ROM** ⟨"address"; *IMIC*⟩

where "address" is a four-hex digit constant that will be placed in bits 3 through 18 of the microinstruction.

It must be possible to load values into *IMIC,* and to increment and decrement this register, if it is to serve as an index register as just described. To provide for this, it is only necessary to add *IMIC* to the list of *OBUS* targets and the list of specifiable connections to the *BBUS* given in Fig. 8.6. Thus the new data path implications of adding microindexing are as depicted in Fig. 8.16.

With the addition of the just-described features to RIC microprogramming, one would expect to implement more complex operations at the microprogramming level than just the basic RIC instructions. Each operation so implemented would necessarily be represented in the RIC II instruction set. We shall not worry about the specific opcodes.

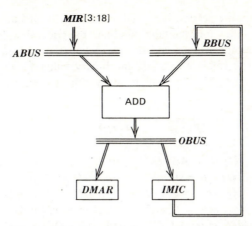

Figure 8.16. Data path for control memory indexing.

Example 8.3

Write in MICRAL a microprogram that will convert a four-digit BCD (binary coded decimal) number to binary. Assume that at the beginning of the operation these four digits are stored in the low-order half of the accumulator. The least significant digit is in $AC[28:31]$.

Solution

Our approach to this problem will be *table lookup*. Each digit will have 10 possible binary values. For the least significant digit, the bit representations for the BCD and binary values are the same. For each of the other digits, a separate table of the corresponding binary values will be placed in the control ROM. The table for the second digit, containing 10 values—0, 1010, 10100 through 1011010 (90 decimal)—will be stored in ROM beginning at location 0800 (hex). The table for the third digit, containing 10 values 0, 32⊤100, through 32⊤900 will begin at 0810 (hex). The table for the most significant digit, containing values 0 through 32⊤9000, will begin at 0820 (hex). Steps 200 through 202 leave the least significant digit in AC. Next, steps 203 through 206 rotate the next BCD digit to the right end of MQ.

200	$B = AC; OB = B; MQ \leftarrow OB.$	
201	$MA \leftarrow 0000000F$	(1st 8 bits don't reach target)
202	$A = 8 \top 0, MA; B = AC; OB = $ AND; $AC \leftarrow OB.$	
203	$B = MQ; cin = 0; OB = cin,BBUS[0:30]; MQ \leftarrow OB.$	
204	$B = MQ; cin = 0; OB = cin,BBUS[0:30]; MQ \leftarrow OB.$	
205	$B = MQ; cin = 0; OB = cin,BBUS[0:30]; MQ \leftarrow OB.$	
206	$B = MQ; cin = 0; OB = cin,BBUS[0:30]; MQ \leftarrow OB.$	

Step 207 masks the second digit and places this 4-bit number in **IMIC**. From here it is used as an index into the table to obtain the equivalent binary number times 10 (decimal). This number is then added to the accumulating result in **AC**. Steps 20A through 210 repeat the rotation and add the binary value for the third digit to **AC**. Following steps 211 through 217, which process the last digit, the resultant binary number is left in **AC**.

207	$A = 8 \uparrow 0, MA; B = MQ; OB = $ AND; $IMIC \leftarrow OB$.
208	$MD \leftarrow$ **ROM** $\langle 0800; IMIC \rangle$.
209	$A = MD; B = AC; OB = $ ADD; $AC \leftarrow OB$.
20A	$B = MQ; cin = 0; OB = cin,BBUS[0:30]; MQ \leftarrow OB$.
20B	$B = MQ; cin = 0; OB = cin,BBUS[0:30]; MQ \leftarrow OB$.
20C	$B = MQ; cin = 0; OB = cin,BBUS[0:30]; MQ \leftarrow OB$.
20D	$B = MQ; cin = 0; OB = cin,BBUS[0:30]; MQ \leftarrow OB$.
20E	$A = 8 \uparrow 0, MA; B = MQ; OB = $ AND; $IMIC \leftarrow OB$.
20F	$MD \leftarrow$ **ROM** $\langle 0810; IMIC \rangle$.
210	$A = MD; B = AC; OB = $ ADD; $AC \leftarrow OB$.
211	$B = MQ; cin = 0; OB = cin,BBUS[0:30]; MQ \leftarrow OB$.
212	$B = MQ; cin = 0; OB = cin,BBUS[0:30]; MQ \leftarrow OB$.
213	$B = MQ; cin = 0; OB = cin,BBUS[0:30]; MQ \leftarrow OB$.
214	$B = MQ; cin = 0; OB = cin,BBUS[0:30]; MQ \leftarrow OB$.
215	$A = 8 \uparrow 0, MA; B = MQ; OB = $ AND; $IMIC \leftarrow OB$.
216	$MD \leftarrow$ **ROM** $\langle 0820; IMIC \rangle$.
217	$A = MD; B = AC; OB = $ ADD; $AC \leftarrow OB$. ■

One potential improvement in the microprogram of Example 8.3 is apparent. Replacing each of the three sets of four 1-bit right shifts by a single 4-bit right shift would eliminate nine of the 24 microinstructions, thereby reducing execution time by 37%. Of less importance is a similar saving in ROM space. A 4-bit shift could be provided by adding

$$0,0,0,0,BBUS[0:27]$$

to the list of connections to the **OBUS** in Fig. 8.6. There is certainly room for this vector in the list and the 4-bit shift is generally useful, so that in an actual design environment the decision would probably be made to add it to the list.

One more deficiency remains in the facility for reading constants from the control ROM. It might be desirable to use the constant in an operation without first loading it in a register. Only registers transparent to the programmer, for example **SHC,** can be used in this way. An improvement might be to route the constant to the **ABUS** or **BBUS** rather than to the **OBUS** so that it could immediately become an argument of the ALU. Using **MIR** bits to specify the operation and target would leave insufficient bits of **MIR** to specify an address in ROM. For this purpose, a few important constants could be added to the **ABUS** and **BBUS** connection lists of Fig. 8.6.

8.8 **Further Flexibility**

So far, we have established a basic reference model in relationship to which other microprogrammable machines might be discussed. The use of this model as a standard for comparison is justified primarily by the simplicity of the microsequencer and the fact that no more than two clock periods are required for execution of a microinstruction. No attempt shall be made to consider any specific real-world microprogrammable machines. There are, however, features that have not been included in the extended RIC that might be valuable in a microprogrammable machine. We shall consider some of these features briefly in this section. Three possible categories of features are tabulated in Fig. 8.17. In general, the incorporation of any of these features will increase the complexity of the microsequencer.

The features listed in categories I and II are clearly intended to enhance the overall capability of the machine in question. The basic clock rate at which the microsequencer can operate is a function of technology. If microinstructions can be executed in one clock period, there is clearly no further improvement to be made in the rate of execution of microinstructions. Thus the capability of a microprogrammable machine can be further enhanced only by providing an organization that can accomplish more in each individual microinstruction and will, therefore, require fewer microinstructions to accomplish a given higher-level function. In some sense, this is the purpose of each of the features in categories I and II.

As has been mentioned, the incorporation of item Ia in the organization of a microprogrammable machine will increase (perhaps double) the number of bits in each microinstruction. Usually, this will result in an increase in the total number of bits of ROM. However, since the total number of microinstructions would be reduced, the speed at which the task would be accomplished would increase correspondingly. Items

---

I.
    a.   Simultaneous branches and transfers
    b.   Parallel data paths
    c.   Transfer and control functions in common microinstruction
    d.   Multiple functions in data path
    e.   Increased branching capability

II.
    a.   Indexing within microprograms
    b.   Microprogram subroutines

III.
    a.   Economical approach to small special purpose jobs
    b.   Convenience of user microprogramming

Figure 8.17. Desirable features for microprogramming.

b, c, d, and e will generally have the same effect of increasing performance by shortening the microprograms for specific tasks at the price of increasing the number of bits in a microinstruction. The term *horizontal microprogramming* has been used to describe machines designed in accordance with this philosophy. An example of Ib might be two parallel busing structures so that any two data transfers could take place simultaneously. More commonly, there might be separate input/output data paths that could be used in parallel with a transfer through the busing network. In the extended RIC, we have provided for distributing control levels to peripheral equipments via microinstructions for which *MIR*[0:3] = 0, 0, 0, 1. With a longer instruction word, this could be accomplished simultaneously with data transfers, as suggested by Item Ic. Item Id will be illustrated by the following example, while Item Ie is the subject of the next section.

Example 8.4

Suppose the extended RIC is to be redesigned somewhat so that every vector input to the **BBUS** may be shifted right either 0, 1, 2, or 16 bits before using it as an argument of any of the networks leading to the **OBUS**. This shifting must be accomplished without increasing the number of clock periods required to execute a microinstruction. Rewrite the appropriate portion of the AHPL description of the extended RIC microsequencer to provide for this operation.

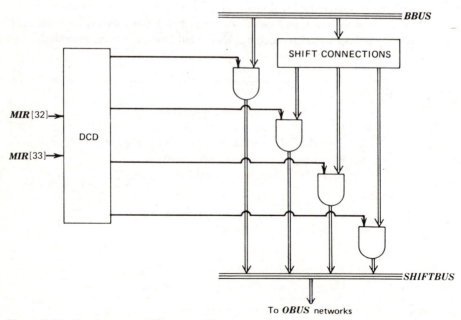

Figure 8.18. Simultaneous shifting capability.

Solution

The cited shifting capability is made possible by adding a four-input 32-bit bus called the **SHIFTBUS** that receives the shifted data from the **BBUS,** as shown in Fig. 8.18. The **SHIFTBUS** will thus replace the **BBUS** as an argument in all networks leading to the **OBUS**. It is also necessary to add 2 bits to each microinstruction. The two additional bits of the microinstruction register **MIR**[32:33] are decoded as shown in Fig. 8.18 to gate the desired data vector onto **SHIFTBUS**.

The matrix **OCLMSH,** listing the inputs to **SHIFTBUS,** is given by Eq. 8.3.

$$\textbf{OCLMSH} = (\textbf{BBUS} \,!\, \textbf{BBUS}[31],\textbf{BBUS}[0:30] \,!\, \textbf{BBUS}[30:31],\textbf{BBUS}[0:29]$$
$$!\, \textbf{BBUS}[16:31],\textbf{BBUS}[0:15]) \qquad (8.3)$$

Only step 4 of the extended RIC microsequencer, which implements bused transfers, needs to be modified. The new form of this step is given as follows.

4 NO DELAY
   ABUS = **OCLMA** * DCD(**MIR**[4:8]);
   BBUS = **OCLMB** * DCD(**MIR**[9:13]);
   SHIFTBUS = **OCLMSH** * DCD(**MIR**[32:33])
   OBUS = **OCLMO** * DCD(**MIR**[14:18]);
                                  "**SHIFTBUS** replaces **BBUS** in **OCLMO**"
   TM * $\overline{\text{DCD}[12](\textbf{MIR}[19:23])} \wedge \text{DCD}(\textbf{MIR}[19:23]) \leftarrow \textbf{OBUS;}$
   cin = (0 ! 1 ! **cff** ! **AC**[31]) * DCD(**MIR**[28:29]);
   cff * ($\vee$/**MIR**[25:27]) ← (ADD[0] ! **SHIFTBUS**[0] !
                    SHIFTBUS[31] ! $\overline{\textit{cff}}$! 0 ! 1) * DCD[1:6](**MIR**[25:27]);
"no changes in the remaining statements".

The only delay added by incorporating the shifting operations is the two levels of gating making up the **SHIFTBUS**. This may be short compared to the delay of the most complicated logic network leading to the **OBUS** and may not, therefore, necessitate lengthening the clock period. ■

In Example 8.4, a new resource, in this case a shifting network, that could be controlled by separate bits of a microinstruction was added. In general, the greater the number of such independently controlled resources, the more *horizontal* is the microprogramming approach [10].

One application of microprogramming is the design of special-purpose processors that will be permanently dedicated to one specific function, such as a communications terminal or a process control computer. Often, the variety of operations specified for these machines is small, although these few operations may be quite complex, so that software can be kept to a minimum. Often, the speed of execution specified for these instructions will be moderate as well.

Consider now a microprogrammable machine that might be designed to satisfy the range of applications discussed in the preceding paragraph. Usually, such a machine would be individually microprogrammed by the manufacturer or the user to accomplish a set of operations suitable to the individual application. In such a machine, the features listed in category III of Fig. 8.17, namely, economy and ease of microprogramming, become most important. When low cost is a design criterion, it is desirable to reduce the overhead associated with the control memory. This can be accomplished to some extent by reducing the word length and designing a microinstruction format in which all bits of *MIR* are meaningful in every microinstruction. Typically, a machine with a minimum word length will require a larger number of microinstructions to accomplish a given task than will a horizontal microprogrammable machine with longer word length. Thus the memory configuration of the former suggests the term *vertical microprogramming,* as illustrated in Fig. 8.19a.

To compensate in part for the inability to accomplish multiple tasks in parallel, designers of vertical machines have succumbed to the temptation of allowing individual microinstructions to specify the multiple operations to be executed sequentially. Since microinstruction bits are not available to specify these sequential operations independently, the vertical microinstructions become inflexible, much like assembly language instructions. This inflexibility tends to make microprogramming easier (i.e., feature IIIb).

Sequential operations within microinstructions imply a more complicated multiclock-period microsequencer. One might argue that vertical microprogramming is not microprogramming at all. Less drastically, we might visualize a spectrum of microsequencers from the reference model of Fig. 8.2 to a complete control unit. We leave it to you to draw the line between microprogramming and programming in a primitive assembly language.

The category II features, indexing (already included in RIC) and subroutines within microprograms, are sufficiently useful to warrant inclusion in many vertical as well as horizontal microprogrammable machines. That these features can be realized while only slightly complicating the microsequencer will be illustrated by the following example.

Some provision for subroutines within the microprogram must be made in any machine where complex manipulations of blocks of data are to be accomplished by microprograms. In Chapter 6, we introduced a "stack" as a means of storage of return addresses for subroutines in ROM. A simpler, single-register approach is illustrated in the following example.

Example 8.5

Add to the control unit hardware and modify the microsequencer so as to include subroutine capability within the microprogram in the extended RIC.

(a)   (b)

Figure 8.19. Origin of terms in microprogramming (*a*) Vertical (*b*) Horizontal

MIR[0]	MIR[1]	MIR[2]	
0	X	X	Transfer
1	0	X	Branch
1	1	0	Branch to subroutine
1	1	1	Return from subroutine

Figure 8.20. Microcode for subroutine branch.

Solution

Since the control memory is a ROM, some other provision must be made for storage of the address in ROM to which the microprogram must return following completion of the subroutine. The 16-bit register, **SUBR**, will be used for this purpose. Because only one such address can be stored, only one level of subroutine is possible. That is, a subroutine cannot be called from within a subroutine.

There must be a microinstruction calling for return from a subroutine as well as a microinstruction for entering a subroutine. The corresponding microcodes are given in Fig. 8.20. Bit **MIR**[1] is now used to distinguish a branch from a subroutine call. Bits **MIR**[3:15] have no meaning in a "branch to subroutine" microinstruction, since only **MIR**[16:31] is required to specify the address of the subroutine. Only the first 3 bits of the "return from subroutine" microinstructions are meaningful.

The RIC microsequencer can be modified to conform to Fig. 8.20 by merely writing a more complex step 3. Now one of three addresses, INC(**MAR**), **MIR**[3:18], or **SUBR** is placed in **MAR**, depending on bits **MIR**[1:2] and the branch conditions. If the microinstruction is a branch to a subroutine, the incremented value of **MAR** is placed in **SUBR**.

2      $\rightarrow$ (MIR[0], $\overline{MIR[0]} \wedge$ (DCD[0:2](MIR[1:3]), DCD[2:3](MIR[1:2])))
       /(3, 4, "other synchronous", "asynchronous", 5, 6).
3   **MAR** $\leftarrow$ (INC(**MAR**) ! **MIR**[16:31] ! **SUBR**) * ($\overline{MIR[1]} \wedge \bar{g}$,
          ($\overline{MIR[1]} \wedge g$) $\vee$ (MIR[1] $\wedge \overline{MIR[2]}$), MIR[1] $\wedge$ MIR[2]);
       SUBR * (MIR[1] $\wedge \overline{MIR[2]}$) $\leftarrow$ INC(**MAR**);
       NO DELAY $\rightarrow$ (1).

A limited subroutine-nesting capability could be easily added by using a four-word or possibly eight-word hardware stack in place of **SUBR**. See Problem 8.34.

8.9 Branching Improvements

In Section 8.5, we had no difficulty in providing for the coding of any register transfer that appeared to be useful. It was necessary in Section 8.6 to simplify the control sequence to conform to the lack of conditional transfers and the constrained branching format of the microprogrammable extended RIC. In general, it is branching and conditional transfers that are most severely restricted by a microprogramming approach.

The RIC control sequence of Chapter 6 liberally used instruction bits and data bits to branch at various points within the sequence. The wired approach makes it possible to connect directly to any bit or combination of bits of any registers in the machine to control a branch operation. For large machines with several high-speed data registers, the amount of information embodied in a particular branch condition is overwhelming. Consider, for example, a machine with 16 registers of 32 bits each. Let f_i be the Boolean function that gates a pulse through a particular path of a particular branch operation. The number of possible ways to specify this function is given in Eq. 8.4.

$$N(f_i) = 2^{2^{16(32)}} = 2^{2^{512}} \tag{8.4}$$

Thus, in the most general case, 2^{512} bits would be required to specify the function. Another $\rho(MAR)$ bits would be required to provide the address of the next microinstruction in the event the branch condition is satisfied. Compared to assembly language, a much larger number of branch functions is required in microprogramming.

In a microprogramming approach, the branch function and the branch address must be specified by the bits in a microinstruction. Clearly, not all functions enumerated in Eq. 8.4 would be of interest. However, if the designer of a large machine enjoyed the freedom of the hard-wired control approach, he would likely specify more branches than could be coded in a microinstruction if a large block of bits were set aside for the branch address.

We have not even discussed multiple branches as yet. Often, it is desirable to provide a conditional branch to more than two points in the microprogram. When you consider the possibility of providing bits to specify more than one address in a microinstruction, the need for some other approach becomes obvious. There are many ways to add to the flexibility of branch commands. Two such schemes will be presented in this section. Both achieve this greater branching capability at the price of considerably more complex logic between the **ROM** and **MAR** and wasted space in the **ROM.** Before providing you with details of examples of these two schemes, let us examine the general structure of address logic within the microprogrammable control unit.

In Fig. 8.21, we illustrate the logic structure associated with the two-way branching approach used so far. The OR gates that route the two alternative addresses to the input of **MAR** are represented as a bus. In Figs. 8.22a and 8.22b, we see the logic structure for the two more-complex branching schemes mentioned. In both cases, we have increased the number of alternative addresses that can be routed to the input of **MAR.** In both cases, the addresses are completely generated by combinational logic so that the address is formed and placed in **MAR** in one clock period. The distinction between these two networks is primarily the handling of data that specify branch conditions.

In Fig. 8.22a, the branch conditions are still selected by bits of **MIR,** just as in the two-way branch scheme. The bits used to select branch conditions may vary, the multiway branches are possible, since more than two addresses are formed from bits in **MIR** and **MAR.**

In Fig. 8.22b, there is no selection or condition function. Instead, the vector

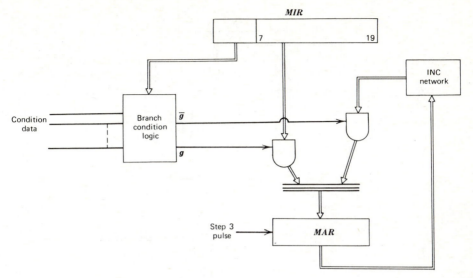

Figure 8.21. Two-way branch logic structure.

MIR[1:3] is simply decoded to select one of, in this case, eight alternative addresses. The vector MAR, is incremented only in the event of a transfer. Inputs from the machines data registers are used in the formation of alternative addresses.

Further discussion of the two approaches will consist of supplying the details of one example of each scheme.

Scheme I. Branch microinstructions in a particular system, employing an 18-bit, 2^{15}-word ROM, may take one of four forms depending on MIR[1] and MIR[2]. These formats are illustrated in Fig. 8.23.

The first format specifies an unconditional branch to any address in the ROM. The second format is a two-option branch, with one option being the next instruction in sequence. Eight bits are provided to specify a branch function from a fairly long list of 2^8 such functions. If the branch condition is satisfied, the new 15-bit address is formed as given by expression 8.5,

$$MAR \leftarrow MAR[0:7], MIR[11:17] \qquad (8.5)$$

Notice that the most significant 8 bits of MAR are not changed. The first two formats together provide an improvement over the approach of the previous sections. The longer list of branch functions is achieved at the price of only an occasional extra microinstruction.

Example 8.6

Suppose that the current address of a microprogram employing the branching scheme of this section is 357D hex. From here it is desired to branch to 8000 if a branch

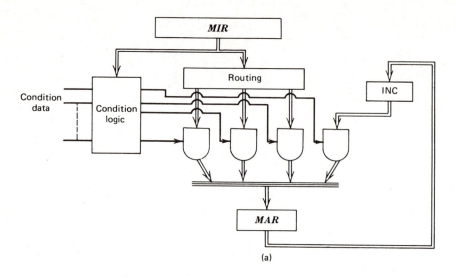

(a)

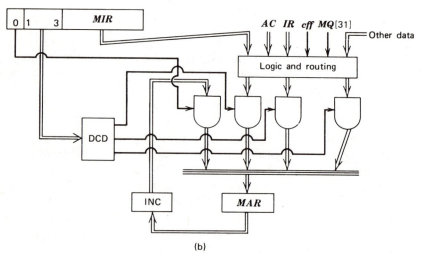

(b)

Figure 8.22. Alternative branching structure (a) Scheme I (b) Scheme II.

condition, $f = 1$, is satisfied, and to continue in sequence otherwise. The two-step operation may be expressed in MICRAL as follows:

Hex address
357D → $(f = 1)/357F$
357E → (8000)

The format 3 branch instruction provides for 32 possible three-way branches. Depending on functional values, the next microinstruction is taken from the next

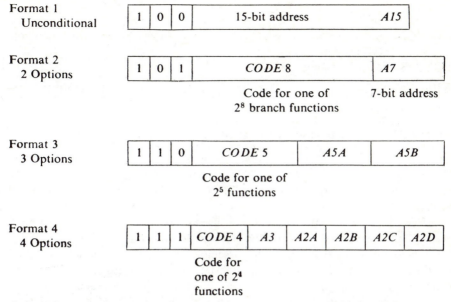

Figure 8.23. Branch instruction formats.

address in sequence or from an address formed from *A5A* or *A5B*. Either of these 5-bit vectors can be used as the least significant 5 bits of an address, as was done for format 2.

Format 4 provides for a four-way branch, as specified by one of 16 branch functions. The most significant 3 bits of the new address will always be *A3;* the next 2 bits will be *A2A* or *A2B* or *A2C* or *A2D;* and the last 10 bits will always be zeros.

Most any three- or four-way branch can be accomplished using a format 3 or 4 branch microinstruction together with one or more unconditional branches. The principle disadvantage of the scheme just discussed is the long lists of branch functions. These lists would be difficult to remember. In addition, the associated decoding logic would be very costly.

Scheme II. The preceding limitations can be overcome by not storing the complete address of either alternative next instruction as bits of the branch microinstruction in the ROM. Instead, this address can be assembled from bits in various registers. Thus the branch is a function of these data bits, and multiple branches are possible.

We shall describe one possible approach to assembling a branch address. With this introduction, you should be able to develop any number of similar schemes. Our approach is not optimized for any particular computer or for any prospective set of microprograms. In fact, it may not be particularly good in any application. It is convenient to explain, however, and it illustrates most types of options available to the designer. In this example, a ROM address will consist of 12 bits. We shall assemble this address by selecting three 4-bit blocks from a set of five such blocks and ordering them in a manner prescribed by the bits of the microinstruction. These blocks of 4

BLOC1	$MIR[4:7]$,
BLOC2	Assembled from zeros and the value of one of eight functions of various data bits
BLOC3	A special 4-bit register
BLOC4	$cff, \overline{cff},$ 0, or 1 $MQ[31], \overline{MQ}[31], 0,$ or 1 $AC[0], \overline{AC[0]}, 0,$ or 1
BLOC5	$IR[0:3]$

Figure 8.24. Available blocks of microaddress bits.

bits are taken from a variety of sources. The five available blocks of bits are listed in Fig. 8.24.

The 18-bit branch microinstruction is used to specify and assemble these blocks into a 12-bit address. The bits of **MIR** are used as shown in Fig. 8.25.

There are 3 bits that specify the assembly of blocks into an address. One bit combination specifies an unconditional transfer, so only seven permutations of three of the five blocks are allowed. These are given in Fig. 8.26, along with the bit combination that specifies each. For example, if bits $MIR[1]$, $MIR[2]$, and $MIR[3]$ are all zero, then the address of the next microinstruction becomes

BLOC3(4 bits), $MIR[4]$, $MIR[5]$, $MIR[6]$, $MIR[7]$, BLOC4(4 bits)

Depending on how the bits of block 4 are assigned, this instruction would cause a branch to one of 16 adjacent addresses. If $MIR[1]$, $MIR[2]$ and $\mathbf{MIR}[3]$ are all 1, $MIR[16:17]$ is taken as the address of an unconditional transfer.

The last 7 bits of **MIR** are used in a way that permits a great deal of flexibility in the composition of BLOC4. The bits of BLOC4 are assigned as shown in Fig. 8.27. Only 3 bits are available to control the composition of BLOC2. We therefore use the bits to choose one of eight functions of the data vectors. These functional values are inserted in BLOC2, as shown in Fig. 8.28. A particular f_i might be any useful function of the bits in the data register. For example, $\sqrt{}/AC$ would very likely be included.

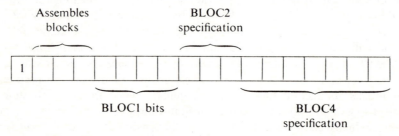

Figure 8.25. Branch microinstruction.

MIR[1]	MIR[2]	MIR[3]	First 4 Address Bits	2nd 4 Bits	3rd 4 Bits
0	0	0	Block 3,	Block 1,	Block 4
0	0	1	3,	1,	2
0	1	0	1,	3,	2
0	1	1	3,	4,	1
1	0	0	3,	4,	5
1	0	1	1,	5,	4
1	1	0	1,	3,	4
1	1	1	Unconditional Transfer		

Figure 8.26. Assembly of a microaddress.

You will immediately see ways to improve the scheme described herein. Our purpose has been to suggest a general approach and certain specific techniques that a designer may find useful in a particular design situation. One possibility, which we have not considered, would be the inclusion of blocks of bits from the present contents of *MAR* in an extended version of Fig. 8.26. No doubt, the final choice of a branching scheme for a proposed computer would be the result of interaction between individuals or groups working on different aspects of the system design. One would expect modifications as the overall design of the computer progressed.

Consider, as an example, the branch microinstruction of Fig. 8.29a. Bits 1, 2, and 3 are 101; so the next address is given by blocks 1, 5, and 4. BLOC1 is specified by the branch microinstruction as 1001. Since the last 7 bits of *MIR* are zero, BLOC4 is composed of all zeros. The 4 bits forming the center of the next address are taken as the first 4 bits of the instruction register, *IR*. Presumably, these bits are the opcode of the instruction under execution. Thus the 16-way branch provides a method of simultaneously separating control into separate sequences for 16 instruction types. The addresses of the next microinstructions are the first words of 16 consecutive 16-bit blocks. The addresses of the first words in each block range from 900 to 9F0 hex.

It is assumed that the 16 separate instruction sequences will require no more than 16 operations before reconvergence or further branching. Certain of the alternative

MIR[11]	0	1		
BLOC4$_0$	0	1		
MIR[12], MIR[13]	00	01	10	11
BLOC4$_1$	0	1	$\overline{cff}$	$\overline{cff}$
MIR[14], MIR[15],	00	01	10	11
BLOC4$_2$	0	1	$MQ[31]$	$\overline{MQ[31]}$
MIR[16], MIR[17]	00	01	10	11
BLOC4$_3$	0	1	$AC[0]$	$\overline{AC[0]}$

Figure 8.27. Assignment of bits in BLOC4.

MIR[8],	MIR[9],	MIR[10]	$BLOC2_0$,	$BLOC2_1$,	$BLOC2_2$,	$BLOC2_3$
0	0	0	0	0	0	f_1
0	0	1	0	0	0	f_2
0	1	0	0	0	0	f_3
0	1	1	0	0	0	f_4
1	0	0	0	0	f_5	0
1	0	1	0	0	f_6	0
1	1	0	0	0	f_7	0
1	1	1	0	0	f_8	0

Figure 8.28. Composition of BLOC2.

instruction sequences will likely require fewer than 16 operations. Thus unused ROM locations may remain in the various blocks. One of the unpleasant implications of any branch scheme of the type discussed in this section is that the use of these randomly distributed ROM locations elsewhere in the microprogram is very awkward.

Consider as a second example the microinstruction stored at F18 in the ROM, as shown in Fig. 8.30. Bits 1, 2, and 3 of *MIR* are 011 so that the address of the next microinstruction is composed of blocks 3, 4, and 1, respectively. The BLOC3 register contains 1111, as shown in the figure. Similarly, the block 1 bits from *MIR* are placed in *MAR* as shown. The last 7 bits of *MIR* specify block 4 as *cff*, as indicated in the box in Fig. 8.30. These bits are also placed in *MAR* as indicated. Notice that if *cff* is zero, the 12 bits inserted in *MAR* differ from the original bits only in bit *MAR*[11]. Thus if *cff* = 0, the next instruction in sequence is executed. If **cff** = 1, control branches to location F59 of the ROM.

Thus it is possible to accomplish the simple, single-condition branch used exclusively in previous sections. Clearly, such branches cannot be specified with complete flexibility. You will agree that the expression of the branch microinstructions for this approach in MICRAL, or any other assembly language, will be awkward; the writing of the necessary assembler will also be much more difficult.

Assembles four blocks BLOC2 Specification

1 1 0 1 1 0 0 1 0 0 0 0 0 0 0 0

BLOC1   BLOC4
(a)

1,0,0,1,*IR*[0],*IR*[1],*IR*[2],*IR*[3],0,0,0,0
(b)

Figure 8.29. Sixteen-way branch.

$$\text{F18: } 1\ 0\ 1\ 1\ 1\ 0\ 0\ 1\ 0\ 0\ 0\ 0\ 1\ 0\ 0\ 0\ 0\ 1$$

| 0 *cff* 0 1 |

$$\text{BLOC3} = 1111 \qquad \overbrace{1\ 1\ 1\ 1 \quad 0\ \textit{cff}\ 0\ 1 \quad 1\ 0\ 0\ 1}$$

Note F18 hex = 1111 0001 1000

Figure 8.30. Single-condition branch.

8.10 Timing Optimization

As mentioned in Section 8.2, the fastest possible microprogrammable control unit would probably be described in a single AHPL step with only one register in the microinstruction loop. Each microinstruction would include bits to specify both a branch and a transfer. The configuration shown in Fig. 8.31a employs a 64-bit mi-

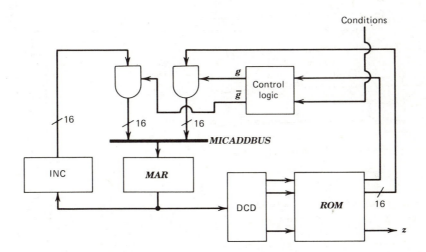

```
MODULE:MICROCONTROL.
MEMORY: MAR[16]; ROM ⟨2 ↑ 16⟩ [64].
INPUTS: c.
OUTPUTS: Z [32].
ENDSEQUENCE
MAR ← (INC(MAR)!BUSFN[16:31](ROM; DCD (MAR))) * (g̅, g);
Z = BUSFN[32:63] (ROM; DCD (MAR)).
END.
```

(b.)

Figure 8.31. Microprogrammable control unit without *MIR*.

croinstruction and functions without the register, *MIR,* as discussed in Section 8.2. To simplify the discussion, the microprogrammable control unit is treated as a separate module in the partial AHPL description of Fig. 8.31b. The microinstruction bits used to effect the transfers and connections are regarded as outputs of the module.

The simple configuration of Fig. 8.31 is attractive, because it maps directly onto the classic Mealy model of a finite-state machine. The minimal state assignment takes the form of the *MAR* with the output and next state logic realized by the ROM, incrementer, and the condition logic. The disadvantage is the long worst-case delay path. It might be the path from the clocking point of *MAR* through the decoder, the ROM, the condition logic, and the implicit next microaddress bus back to the input of *MAR.* The clock period must, of course, be sufficiently long to allow for propagation around this loop. More likely, the worst-case delay is the path from the clocking point of *MAR* through the ROM, through the conditional connection of some data bus at the input of the ALU, through the worst-case logic unit within the ALU, and through the ALU output bus to the input of a target register.

An interesting alternative to Fig. 8.31 is another single-clock-period micropro-

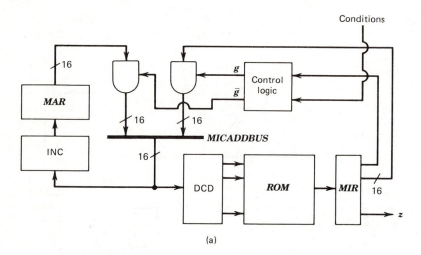

(a)

MODULE: MICROCONTROL.
MEMORY: *MAR*[16]; *MIR*[64]; **ROM**⟨2 ↑ 16⟩ [64].
INPUTS: *g*.
OUTPUTS: Z[32].
ENDSEQUENCE
MICADDBUS = (*MAR* ! *MIR*[48:63]) * ($\bar{g}$, *g*);
Z = *MIR*[0:31];
MAR ← INC (*MICADDBUS*);
MIR ← BUSFN (**ROM**; DCD (*MICADDBUS*)).
END.

(b)

Figure 8.32. Removing *MAR* from the microinstruction loop.

grammable control unit depicted in Fig. 8.32. Both *MAR* and *MIR* are included, but *MAR* is removed from the microinstruction loop. The microinstruction currently being executed is stored in *MIR* while the declared microaddress bus, *MICADDBUS,* points at the next microinstruction. Depending on the familiar conditions function, *g,* either *MAR* or a field in *MIR* is connected to this bus. Each clock pulse loads the incremented *MICADDBUS* into *MAR* at the same time that the addressed microinstruction is transferred into *MIR.* As before, there is only one register, this time *MIR,* in the next microinstruction loop. Now, however, the decoder and ROM are not in the probable worst-case delay path into the data unit. Consequently, one would expect the configuration in Fig. 8.32 to support a higher clock frequency than that of Fig. 8.31. Some literature, such as that describing the AMD 2909 and 2911 bit-slice controllers, has called the structure of Fig. 8.32 a *microinstruction pipeline;* but application of this term is probably not justified.

8.11   Microprogram Controllable Bit-Slice Data Unit

Up to now, we have looked on a computer, both control and data sections, as an integrated unit, perhaps realized on a single IC chip. When no standard microprocessor chip is satifactory for a particular application, it is often possible to assemble a set of IC chips to form a data unit. Similarly, special-purpose chips are available that, when used together with a user-programmable ROM, can form a microprogrammable control unit. Using these two chip sets, a computer with a unique instruction set can be developed in a few months with relatively little design cost. This approach is suggested in Fig. 8.33.

The earliest chip-family designed for control unit realization featured the AM2909 or AM2911 [14]. Simply adding a four-word stack to the list of connectables to *MICADDBUS* in Fig. 8.32 will result in a configuration essentially the same as the AM2911. Adding a ROM and some decoding logic on the output of the microinstruction yields the essentials of box A of Fig. 8.33. All that has been said about microprogrammable control units in the previous sections is applicable to Fig. 8.33. In this section, we shall focus briefly on the relationship between the control outputs of box A and the data chips in box B.

After considering this section, the instructor is in an excellent position to treat, in more detail, particular families of data-unit chips using the manufacturer's data manuals. Space is not available in this volume to treat even one such family completely. Furthermore, many new chip sets will be introduced during the lifetime of this book. Bit-slice and RISC (reduced instruction set computers, see Section 17.4) chip sets are some examples.

Historically, bipolar integrated circuits have been faster than MOD ICs but have been realizable only with lower device densities. The speed advantage made the bipolar technology attractive for the realization of the data-unit chips of box B. When the first

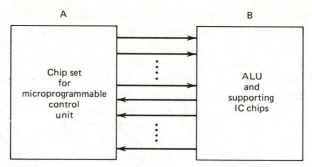

Figure 8.33. Multichip microprogrammable computer realization.

such chip sets were designed, a sufficient density to permit realization of a complete data unit on a single chip could not be attained. The result was the *bit-slice* concept. Each bit-slice package contained a 4-bit slice of the ALU together with similar slices of the data registers and *A, B,* and *O* buses. An 8-bit computer could be formed from two such slices, a 16-bit computer from four slices, and so forth. The control inputs of each slice were connected identically to the control outputs from box A. The carry-

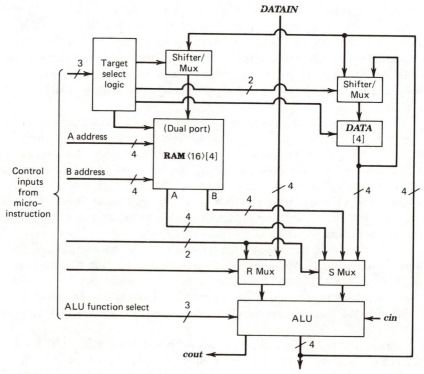

Figure 8.34. Bit-slice ALU chip.

out bit from the 4-bit ALU on a chip was connected to the carry-in of the slice to its left.

The earliest bit-slice ALU chip was the AM2901 [14]. The 4-bit ALU of Fig. 8.34 is very similar in concept, but is not identical in every detail to the AM2901. Of particular interest is the 16-word dual-port RAM, which makes it possible to realize a register array architecture as discussed in Section 6.11. The RAM has two separate address input fields so that any two words can be read out simultaneously. If so desired, the two outputs from the RAM can furnish both arguments of the ALU. If a result is to be written back into RAM, it will be written in the word identified by address B. All 17 control bits shown entering at the left of the ALU slice originate at the microinstruction output from box A of Fig. 8.33. In addition to the two address fields, there is a 3-bit field that selects the ALU arguments, a 3-bit field that selects one of eight possible ALU functions, and a 3-bit field that accomplishes shifts of the ALU output and selects the target. Note that the R and S multiplexers, together with the target select multiplexer, accomplish the functions of *ABUS, BBUS,* and *OBUS,* respectively, in RIC. Rather than provide more detailed specifications of Fig. 8.34, we leave it to you to obtain these specifications for the actual devices from the appropriate manuals.

8.12   Observations

Microprogramming is a widely used method of controlling the execution of machine language instructions. It can be applied at a variety of levels with hard-wired control sequencers of greater or lesser complexity for controlling microprogram execution. The simplest application of microprogramming would limit the use of branching within the microprogram to separating all instructions at the beginning of the execution sequences. Assembly language branches could be accomplished by merely making a transfer to the program counter, *PC,* dependent on a data bit. We saw in Section 8.7 that a more elaborate microprogramming approach could be justified only by storing routines, which would otherwise be part of system software, in a large ROM.

When a ROM is used in the control unit, the overall machine speed is limited by the access time of the ROM. Thus, wherever the cost per computation is a governing factor, the access time of the ROM must be of the same order of magnitude as the time required for a data transfer between high-speed registers. The clock rate would probably be specified according to this access time of the ROM. If the resulting clock period is significantly longer than the delay of the register transfers, the system will not be operating at maximum efficiency.

To improve machine speed, it is often desirable to fetch a succeeding microinstruction from the ROM while one microinstruction is being executed. This overlap is similar to the more general notion of *instruction look-ahead,* which will be discussed in Chapter 17. As is the case for look-ahead, a branch microinstruction may cause a succeeding microinstruction already read from the ROM to go unused.

Microprograms will usually include a large number of branch operations. This can be verified by noticing the frequency of branches on the AHPL sequence of Chapter 6. In the hard-wired control unit, a branch instruction does not require a clock period. If every other operation were a branch, a 50% saving in execution time could be achieved if special references to the ROM memory for branch operations could be eliminated from the microprogramming approach. Thus branch and transfer operations are often combined in a single microinstruction, even though a register performing the function of *MIR* is included. The original Wilkes model followed this approach.

Whether or not branch and transfer operations should be combined depends on the frequency of branch operations and the cost of lengthening the ROM word to accommodate both operations. A way to express the cost added to the ROM might be in the cost of storing zeros. A combined transfer and increment *MAR* microinstruction will contain mostly zeros in the branch section (in fact, mostly zeros altogether). In a semiconductor ROM, an active device must be provided for each bit. This device is open-circuited in the last stage of the manufacturing process if the bit is 0.

Problems

   8.1   Realize the control sequence of Example 4.2 as a microprogrammable control unit of the form suggested in Fig. 8.2. Your solution should consist of a complete bit pattern for the ROM as well as a gate-by-gate logic block diagram of the "Next Address Logic." A decoder for the output control levels will not be required.

Note: **Let each microinstruction consist of 12 bits, 2 bits for each of four possible next addresses and 1 bit for each of the output control levels.**

   8.2   An alternative realization of a microprogrammable control sequential circuit is illustrated in Fig. P8.2 (a Moore model sequential circuit with all combinational logic realized by the ROM). Realize the control sequential circuit of Example 4.2 according to this format. Your solution should define the layout of a microinstruction and include a complete bit pattern of the ROM.

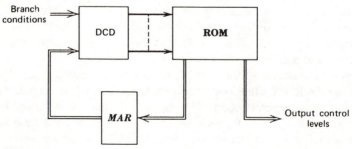

Figure P8.2.

8.3 Assume that the clock period of a microprogrammable computer is sufficiently long to permit the propagation of the value of *MAR* through the decoder, the **ROM,** and then the execution decoding logic, and execution logic in time to permit updating *MAR* and clocking the data into the appropriate target register, all in a single clock period. Under these circumstances, a one-step microsequencer may be used. Eliminate *MIR,* and rewrite the four-step microsequencer of Section 8.2 as a set of connections and transfers after the END SEQUENCE. For clarity, express the connections and transfers of step 4 as given in Section 8.4.

Note: **BUSFN(ROM; DCD(*MAR*)) may replace *MIR* as it is used in steps 2, 3, and 4. It may be necessary to add additional transfer conditions.**

8.4 Using the simplified busing notation of Fig. 4.11 and other notational simplifications as necessary, construct a logic diagram of the data unit of the microsequencer (including the ROM) obtained in Problem 8.3. This is not the data unit of the computer itself. Treat the control signals that implement transfers and connections involving **OCLMA, OCLMB, OCLMO,** and **TM** as outputs from the microsequencer. Treat the logic implementing the function *g,* as a black box.

8.5 Discuss why a microprogrammable control unit cannot itself be called a computer.

8.6 Suppose it is desired to make every microinstruction in the microprogrammable RIC both a transfer and a branch. Assume that all the bits in the transfer portion of the microinstruction as given in Fig. 8.5a, except bit 0, are still necessary, but that bits 0 through 2 of the branch microinstruction of Fig. 8.5b are not needed. Format a combined branch/transfer microinstruction given a control ROM made up of 64K 56-bit words. What is the maximum allowed number of two-way branch functions.

8.7 Consistent with the assumptions made in Problem 8.3, write an AHPL description of a single-step microsequencer, given the ROM and microinstruction format formulated in Problem 8.6.

8.8 In Fig. 8.6, we noticed that *IR*[6:9] controls the connections to the *BBUS* if *MIR*[9:13] = 00110. Use the information in Fig. 2.8 to construct a partial logic diagram of connections to the *BBUS*. Use the notation illustrated in Fig. 4.11a, and include only those connections corresponding to *MIR*[9:13] = 00110 and *MIR*[9:13] = 00111. Include all the relevant control lines.

8.9 Part of Eq. 8.2 for *g* is the 29-bit vector AND operation

$$DCD[0:28](MIR[4:15]) \wedge (IR[0:15], F[0:12])$$

Write the actual Boolean expressions for the last five elements in this vector.

8.10   The AHPL description of the RIC microsequencer given in Section 8.4 is not quite accurate with respect to implementation of transfers into **MD**. Note that **MD** is an entry in the target matrix, **TM,** and is also a target of a transfer from the **DBUS.** For this reason, a two-input vector busing network is required at the input to **MD.** Rewrite all statements in step 4 of the microsequencer relevant to transfers in **MD.**

Note: **Simply delete one row from the transfer statement involving *TM*, and write the appropriate single transfer statement for target *MD*.**

8.11   Suppose that 3 bits of **MIR** were available for specifying connections to *cin* (see Fig. 8.10b). If *AC*[0] could be included in this list of connections for *cin,* what entry could be deleted from the list of **OBUS** connections without impairing the ability to write a microprogram implementing the shift and rotate instructions?

8.12   Complete the microcoding of step 53 of the RIC control sequence as begun in Section 8.5. Now express this microprogram in MICRAL.

8.13   Write a microprogram to implement step 61 of the RIC control sequence as given in Chapter 6.

(a)   Express this microprogram in MICRAL.
(b)   Now manually assemble the MICRAL program derived in part (a) to RIC microcode.

8.14   Express in MICRAL the instruction fetch and operand address portion of RIC as given by steps 1 through 11 of the RIC control sequence.

8.15   Suppose the opcode for multiplication is to replace that for SUB in the table of RIC memory reference instructions. Suppose step 19 of the RIC control sequence is to begin at location 0500 in the control ROM. Beginning at this location, write in MICRAL a microprogram that will assume that the operand address is in **MA** and will prepare for the multiplication microprogram that begins at ROM location 1000 (see Section 8.6). This microprogram should separate from the other memory reference instructions at the most appropriate point.

8.16   Construct a set of tables similar to those given in Fig. 8.6 to support the register bank RIC II as given in Section 6.11. Include in the tables only sufficient vectors to provide for the microcoding of those activities that are fully defined in Section 6.11.

(a) Use the transfer microinstruction format given in Fig. 8.5a.

(b) Assume a 36-bit microinstruction with the addition of a 4-bit field to identify a register in the array, **R.**

8.17 Assume an equal delay Δ for each logic gate and each transfer into a memory element. Compute the worst-case delay for step 5 of the RIC microsequencer of Section 8.7. Include all the delay from the trailing edge of the clock pulse, which excites step 5 and loads *MIR,* until the vector is available at the output of the *OBUS* for transfer into **TM.** Assume that the combinational logic units DCD and BUSFN used in the control memory each constitute a delay of 4 Δ.

8.18 If a constant less than 32 bits or fewer significant bits with sign-extension is satisfactory, such a constant could be incorporated within a microinstruction itself. This is very similar to immediate addressing. Revise the extended RIC microsequencer of Section 8.7 to implement this approach for *MIR*[0:2] $=$ 010.

(a) How can a 24-bit constant together with the target register field be fit into the transfer microinstruction format?

(b) Rewrite step 5 of the RIC microsequencer to cause a 24-bit constant from *MIR* with sign-extension to be clocked into the target register.

(c) Suggest a more convenient overall transfer microinstruction format. What impact might this change have on the allowed clock frequency?

8.19 Write in MICRAL a RIC microprogram that will convert a 16-bit binary number, found in *AC,* to BCD format. At the end of the microprogram, the appropriate number of BCD digits will be found at the rightmost end of *AC.* Assume that an additional combinational logic unit BCDADD(*ABUS; BBUS; cin*) is available for connection to the *OBUS.* This unit is an 8-digit BCD adder.

Note: **Treat the number as four hexadecimal digits with four tables in ROM containing the possible digits multiplied by the appropriate power of 16.**

8.20 (a) Write a combinational logic unit description for the BCDADD used in Problem 8.19.

Note: **Make use of the already available full adders employed in the combinational logic unit, ADD(*ABUS; BBUS; cin*) and correct, as appropriate, each set of 4-sum bits and every fourth carry.**

(b) Now write ADD and BCDADD as a single combinational logic unit so that the hardware compiler would generate only one set of full adders.

8.21   Using the same tabular approach as in the microprogram of Section 8.6, write a RIC assembly language (software) subroutine to convert a four-digit BCD number, stored in $AC[16{:}31]$, to binary. Assume that ADC (absolute) requires six clock periods and that the 4-bit shift requires nine clock periods in the hard-wired RIC. For simplicity, assume all other instructions used in the routine also require six clock periods each, and determine the total number of clock periods required by the program. What is the ratio of assembly language time to microprogram time for accomplishing this function?

8.22   Repeat the analysis of Problem 8.21 for multiplication. Write a RIC assembly language multiplication program to accomplish multiplication and compare time consumption with the microprogram of Section 8.6. Make the same execution cycle assumptions as in Problem 8.21.

8.23   Using statements after END SEQUENCE, rewrite the seven-step RIC microsequencer of Section 8.7 so that the connections to the *ABUS* and *BBUS* are functions of *MIR* bits only, and not of the microsequencer step. Determine the number of gates and gate inputs saved by this modification. Can a similar modification be made with respect to the *OBUS?* Why or why not?

8.24   A RIC microprogram is to be written as part of a special version of this machine for information-retrieval applications. A special instruction that will search a list of words in the RAM beginning with the address specified by *IX* is to be included. If one of these words is the same as the contents of *AC,* the instruction will terminate by leaving the corresponding address in *IX.* If no match is found, $32 \top 0$ will be left in *IX.* The number of words in the list will have previously been placed in *SHC.* Write in MICRAL a microprogram for execution of this single instruction.

8.25   Write in MICRAL a *RIC* control microprogram that will divide (discarding the remainder) a 31-bit positive integer in AC by $2^{\perp \mathbf{SHC}}$. A number between 0 and 15 has been placed in *SHC* by a previous sequence. The answer will be left in *AC.* Microcode two instructions only: the first transfer microinstruction appearing in your sequence and the first branch microinstruction appearing in your sequence.

8.26   Consider the microprogrammable extended RIC with the ability to retrieve constants from the ROM, as listed in Fig. 8.14, included. Suppose the rightmost 8 bits of the *AC* are a coded character that is the same as one of 20 eight-bit characters stored at consecutive locations in the ROM. Write in MICRAL a sequence of microinstructions that will compare *AC* with the list of characters until the identical character is found. A number between 1 and 20, which identifies this character, is to be left in *IX.*

8.27 A proposed computer is to have 2^{13} 16-bit words of random access memory. Certain memory reference instructions are to be two-address instructions. For example, an instruction might call for adding the contents of two locations in the random access memory and leaving the result in a high-speed register. The machine will have eight high-speed registers, one of which must serve as a program counter and two of which must serve as an instruction register. The remaining five may serve as data registers (the output of the random access memory could be connected to a bus), accumulators, index registers, or whatever. A carry flag is associated with only one register. The last 26 bits of the instruction registers contain the 13-bit addresses of the two arguments. The leftmost 6 bits may be used to specify the opcode, indexing, and indirect addressing. The 26 address bits of the instruction register double as the memory address registers. Thus a fetch cycle would call for placing the contents of *PC* in the first 13 address bits and $\top(\bot PC + 1)$ in the other 13-bit address register.

Set up a system of buses to handle data in the machine under microprogram control. Devise a system of microprogram control branches and transfer operations to allow as much flexibility as possible. Use a 24-bit ROM. Make your specifications sufficiently complete to allow unambiguous coding of microinstructions.

8.28 Devise a suitable instruction list for the machine discussed in Problem 8.27. Include an instruction that will add two arguments from the random access memory and place the result in a high-speed register. Also include an instruction that will take the two's complement of a 16-bit word from a random access memory location and place the result in another location of the random access memory. Write microprograms for these instructions in an appropriate AHPL-like microassembly language.

8.29 Suppose that the extended RIC microinstruction has been lengthened to 40 bits to provide greater horizontal microprogramming capability. Rewrite the AHPL description of the microsequencer so that the additional 10 bits can be used to specify one-period levels on any or all 10 control output lines to peripheral equipments.

8.30 Supply a detailed schematic diagram of the block labelled Routing in Fig. 8.22a to realize the precise branching format specified in Fig. 8.23. Show the 20 *MIR* flip-flops and the inputs to each AND gate leading to the address bus. Avoid any unnecessary gates.

8.31 Use one of the formats of Fig. 8.23 to specify the bit pattern of a microinstruction that will effect a four-way branch to one of the following four hexidecimal addresses.

3C00   3000   3800   3400

Assume the branch function code to be 1110.

8.32 Write the bit pattern of a scheme II microinstruction that will branch to 8D2 if $MQ[31] = 0$ and 8D0 if $MQ[31] = 1$.

8.33 Assume that a control unit is to be constructed using a ROM that will cost 1 cent per bit regardless of the length of a word. Suppose one step in the control sequence out of four is a branch. Twenty bits will be required to microcode a transfer operation, and 20 bits will be required to microcode a branch. Compute the costs of the ROM for separate branch and transfer operations, and for branches and transfers combined in the same microinstruction. Assume a total of 4000 branch and transfer steps in the control sequence. Assume that the cost of storing zeros is also 1 cent per bit. Neglect the decoder. What will be the percentage decrease execution time achieved by combining branches and transfers. If the cost of the ROM is 10% of the cost of the overall machine, compare the cost performance ratios for the two approaches.

8.34 Consider the microprogrammable control unit of Fig. 8.32. Modify the corresponding AHPL description by adding a four-word circular stack to accommodate ROM addresses. The stack will be used in a manner similar to the register **SUBR** of Section 8.8. A 2-bit stack pointer will also be needed. Also add another external input vector connectable to **MICADD-BUS**. This vector could be some function of the contents of an instruction register to permit a multiway branch as a function of an instruction decode. Let the vector connected to **MICADDBUS** be controlled by an input, $S[2]$, rather than by the function **g**. (If literature on the AMD 2909, 2910, or 2911 is available, compare the resulting description with these parts.)

References

1. S. S. Husson, *Microprogramming Principles and Practice,* Prentice–Hall, Englewood Cliffs, N.J., 1970.
2. M. V. Wilkes, "The Best Way to Design an Automatic Calculating Machine," *Report of Manchester University Computer Inaugural Conference,* July 1951, pp. 16–18.
3. M. V. Wilkes and J. B. Stringer, "Microprogramming and the Design of the Control Circuits in Electronic Digital Computers," *Proc. Camb. Phil. Soc.,* Vol. 49, Part 2, 1953, pp. 230–238.
4. M. V. Wilkes, W. Redwick, and D. Wheeler, "The Design of a Control Unit of an Electronic Digital Computer," *Proc. IRE,* Vol. 105, 1958, p. 21.
5. G. B. Gerace, "Microprogram Control for Computing Systems," *IRE Trans. Elec. Computer,* Vol. EC-12, 1963.
6. *MOS Memory Data Book,* Texas Instruments, Dallas, 1984.

7. H. Katzan, Jr., *Microprogramming Primer*, McGraw–Hill, New York, 1977.

8. G. H. Bush, "Microprogramming," *IBM Technical Report*, No. 00–158L, SDD Division, Poughkeepsie, N.Y., March 7, 1967.

9. J. K. Iliffe, *Advanced Computer Design*, Prentice–Hall, Englewood Cliffs, N.J., 1982.

10. G. F. Casaglia and I. C. Olivetti, *"Nanoprogramming vs. Microprogramming,"* *Computer*, Jan. 1976, pp. 54–58.

11. A. K. Agrawala and T. G. Rausher, "Microprogramming Perspective and Status," *IEEE Transactions on Computers*, Vol. C-23, Aug. 1974, pp. 817–837.

12. E. Stritter and N. Tredennick, "Microprogrammed Implementation of a Single Chip Microprocessor," *SigMicro Newsletter*, Vol. 9, No. 4, Dec. 1978.

13. E. Stritter and T. Gunter, "A Microprocessor Architecture for a Changing World," *Computer*, Feb. 1979.

14. *AM2900 Bipolar Microprocessor Family Data Book*, Advanced Micro Devices, Sunnyvale, Calif.

9 Intersystem Communications

9.1 Introduction

All large data processing facilities constitute a network of interacting, vector-handling digital systems. Each of these systems includes at least an elementary control unit. These systems with their control units might be regarded as a set of separate intelligences organized to cooperate in accomplishing a computational task. One might observe a tenuous analogy with an industrial organization or committee of people, united to work on a particular problem.

Fortunately, the coordination of digital systems is less difficult, and their individual capacities are used more efficiently, than is the case with most committees of people. The intelligence of certain digital systems (such as tape transports) is so rudimentary that they can function only in close communication with another system. In a computation facility, there is nearly always a very strong committee chairman, usually but not always the central processor, which closely coordinates the activity of the individual digital systems.

Prior to our first major encounter with system interaction in the discussion of input/output in Chapter 10, it will be desirable to develop a means of describing intersystem communications. The problem of interconnecting two systems and providing for their communication is called *interfacing*. Problems arise in interfacing at the circuit design level, the sequential circuits level, and at the systems level. Although very real to the person who must design an interface, circuit problems, such as level conversion and impedance matching, can be conveniently divorced from a systems treatment. The sequential circuit problem involved in interfacing is *synchronization*. The discussion of this problem in Section 9.4 will be applicable throughout the book.

The remainder of the chapter will be devoted to an analysis of communications at the systems level. Some representation of the communications activity must be integrated in AHPL. Data lines and control lines that interconnect systems will be declared in both systems. This is, of course, consistent with the usual practice of constructing digital systems separately and connecting them as a final step.[1] The timing of communications between systems is part of the control function. We must, therefore, provide notation for sending and receiving signals in AHPL.

Closely related to multiple control is the notation of *parallel processing*. Parallel operations can be specified at several levels. Parallel operations can be handled with the notation already available. In its most sophisticated form, parallel processing clearly involves multiple control. It is an intermediate form, *parallel sequences* of operations, that will be considered in the next section. As parallel sequences become longer and more complex, the distinction between this format and multiple control becomes less clear.

9.2 Parallel Operations

No one can avoid the observation that performing a set of computing operations simultaneously or in parallel will require a shorter time than performing the same operations in sequence. In every context, the degree of parallelism is limited by operations whose arguments are dependent on the results of other operations. In some cases, this dependence is unavoidable. In others, it is a function of a particular analysis or approach to a problem. It is often difficult to ascertain which is the case.

There are many ways in which parallelism can be built into a computer. The simplest, perhaps, is the processing of bits of data words simultaneously in arithmetic or logical operations, rather than serially. This form of parallelism is almost universal. Only in special-purpose computers, which are locked into situations in which continuous availability is required but computation speed is unimportant, can the small savings in cost permitted by serial-by-bit operations be justified.

Other commonly employed parallelisms include simultaneous I/O and execution of different programs in a batch-processing environment. Sometimes, two or more complete central processors share the same peripherals and memory and operate in parallel. When look-ahead is employed, it is possible to have more than one machine instruction in various stages of execution at one time. The overall time saving achieved by this technique is heavily dependent on having an object program with a minimum of interdependence between consecutive operations. Another technique, which is even more problem dependent, involves the use of a single control unit to control the

---

[1]Individually controlled systems are not always mounted in physically separate units. Certain system pairs must be mounted in very close (centimeters) proximity to maximize communications speed.

functioning of an array of processors that perform almost identical computations. The notion of several processors concurrently active on the same problem is receiving considerable attention at present. The availability of inexpensive microcomputers makes the concept of obtaining large-scale computing power by interconnecting many small computers very attractive.

The benefit to be obtained by executing machine instructions in parallel is largely determined by factors beyond the control of the computer designer. This is not the case for the sequence of register transfers making up the execution of an individual instruction. Parallel execution of register transfers within a control sequence should be maximized. This is especially important when fast synchronous memories are used, making possible a memory reference each clock period.

In Chapters 6 and 7, we saw many examples of the simplest form of parallelism, the carrying out of several register transfers in a single machine cycle. No special notation is required, and the only precaution to be observed is that the simultaneous transfers must not conflict in any way. For example, the following step, which includes two transfer statements, would be invalid because *MA* is simultaneously the target of both transfers.

1 $MA \leftarrow PC; MA \leftarrow INC(PC).$

Sometimes, transfers that appear to be logically independent may conflict because of common data paths. For example, the transfers

$MA \leftarrow PC$ and $AC \leftarrow MD$

appear to be logically independent, but they cannot be carried out simultaneously through the bus structure of Fig. 6.1 because of conflicts on the *OBUS*.

When asynchronous operations are involved, it may not be possible to express parallel activity by simply merging independent statements into one sequence of steps. It may not be known in advance how many clock periods will be required for each operation. In this case, it is necessary to permit multiple control levels to propagate simultaneously through independent paths in the control unit. Consider the situation in which the contents of an index register are to be added asynchronously to *AC* at the same time that an asynchronous reference to memory is being made. Description of these kinds of concurrent activity requires that control be channelled into two separate paths. The existing AHPL branching notation can be used to specify branching to two separate steps simultaneously if we allow more than one branch function to be 1.

$8 \rightarrow (\bar{a}, a, a)/(9, 10, 20).$ (9.1)

Expression 9.1, for example, would cause control to branch to steps 10 and 20 simultaneously if $a = 1$. An unconditional divergence to steps 10 and 20 could be written as

$\rightarrow (1,1)/(10, 20).$ (9.2)

For convenience, we shall define expression 9.3 to have the same meaning as expression 9.2.

$$\rightarrow (10, 20). \tag{9.3}$$

Let us return now to the asynchronous memory reference and asynchronous addition, which must be executed in parallel. We assume the former to be preceded by a synchronous transfer and the latter to be followed by a synchronous transfer.

  1 *IA ← X*;
       → (A2, B2).
  A2 *startadd* = 1.
  A3 → ($\overline{sumready}$)/(A3).
  A4 *AC ← ADD(AC; IA).*   NO DELAY
  A5 *AC ← AC*[17], *AC*[0:16];
       DEAD END.
  B2 *MA ← PC.*   NO DELAY
  B3 *read* = 1.
  B4 *MD * dataready ← DATAIN*;
       → ($\overline{dataready}$)/(B4).
   5 (Sequences continue)

In this sequence it was assumed that the asynchronous addition would require less time for completion than would the memory reference. When it is known that one or the other of the parallel sequences will always terminate first, there need be no hardware provision for convergence of the paths, as illustrated in Fig. 9.1.

In many cases, the relative completion times of two or more parallel sequences may be unknown. In this case, a special convergence circuit must be provided. The symbol and application of such a circuit are illustrated very simply in Fig. 9.2. The output of the step 5 convergence circuit will be a one-period level coincident with the second of the one-period levels that arrive on each of the two input lines. It is assumed that the inputs will always be connected to the outputs of control flip-flops whose values will remain 1 for only one clock period.

We introduce the term CONVERGE to specify the convergence hardware suggested in Fig. 9.2. This notation is illustrated as follows, now assuming the relative time delays of the addition and memory references of Fig. 9.1 to be unknown.

  B4   → ($\overline{dataready}$)/(B4).
   5   CONVERGE (A5, B4).
   6   etc.

A logic block diagram for one simple realization of the convergence circuit is given in Fig. 9.3 together with the corresponding state diagram. The control input

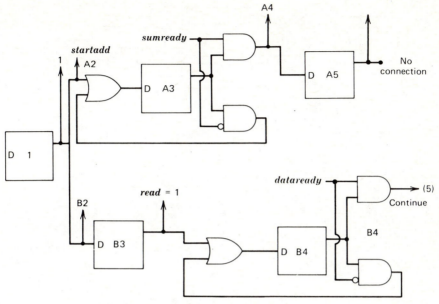

Figure 9.1. Parallel sequences without convergence.

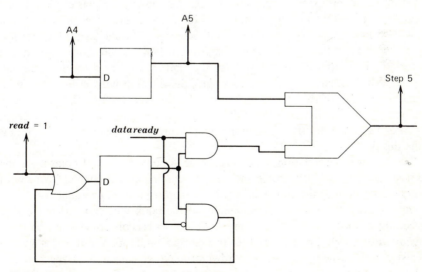

Figure 9.2. Convergence of parallel sequences.

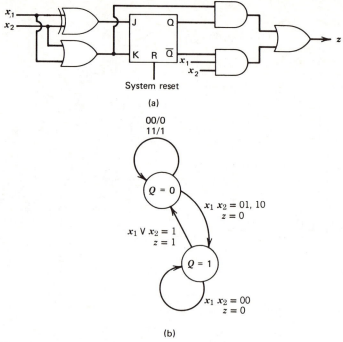

(a)

(b)

Figure 9.3. Convergence circuit.

lines, x_1 and x_2, are one-period levels from control flip-flops in the same module and are, therefore, synchronized to the same clock. As shown, the master clear input of the flip-flop in Fig. 9.3 must be connected to the system reset line in order to assure that it will be in the $Q = 0$ state prior to the occurrence of a 1-level on either input. As long as both x_1 and x_2 are 0, nothing happens. If both x_1 and x_2 arrive in the same clock period, the output z will go to 1 for the same period as a result of the lower AND gate. When either x_1 or x_2 arrives singly, the flip-flop will set but there will be no output as a result of the assumed clock mode timing, which ensures that the flip-flop output will not change until after the input signal is gone. When the other input arrives, the OR gate will drive the z output to 1 through the upper AND gate and will reset the flip-flop.

We shall use the notation for divergence and convergence of control, as introduced here, as part of AHPL in the succeeding sections of this chapter. We shall not give further attention to the particular hardware approach to convergence.

Our attention throughout the remainder of the book will be restricted to developing control sequences. It will be convenient not to be concerned with the relative time required by parallel paths. Thus we use the same notation for all cases and leave the decision as to whether or not a hardware convergence circuit is needed to the "translation to hardware" step.

Example 9.1

A digital process controller is to be designed. The principal difference between this controller and the machine tool controller of Example 5.6 is that this controller must operate at the maximum possible data transfer rate. The register configuration for the controller is shown in Fig. 9.4. With each control level appearing on input line *request* a word is read from the random access memory *M*. Each word is multiplied by a constant that is stored in register *KK*, and is then placed in *CR*. The use of data vectors in *CR* by the external process is controlled by the exchange of signals of lines *ready* and *request*. The digital controller supplies a one-period *ready* level as soon as a new data vector is placed in *CR*. To indicate that the data has been accepted and that it is ready for another vector, the external process places a level on line *request*. The registers *KK* and *MA* can be loaded through control panel switches. The memory may be regarded as a separate module that holds a data word on the vector of output lines *DATA* until a subsequent *read* signal arrives.

Solution

We shall examine two possible designs for the control unit of the process controller. The control sequences are given in Fig. 9.5. The sequence of Fig. 9.5a is straight-forward. First, a word is read from memory; then it is multiplied by the constant in *KK*, and then it is placed in the register *CR*. The notation of step 19 indicates that a *ready* level is supplied to the external system, and control waits at step 20 for a *request* level indicating that the external process is ready for a new word. Following a *request* level, control returns to step 1 to cause the next word to be read from memory.

The disadvantage of the sequence of Fig. 9.5a is that three time-consuming operations, read from memory, multiplication, and the asynchronous transfer, are done sequentially. In the sequence of Fig. 9.5b, these three operations are done in parallel for three different data words. This approach assumes that, when *dataready* appears, the word read from memory will remain stable on the *DATA* lines until a new *read* request is issued. Each word from memory must pass through each of the three steps

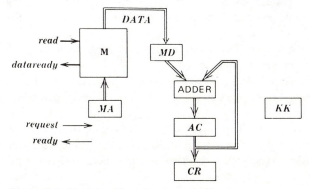

Figure 9.4. Registers for process controller.

1	*read* = 1;	1	→ (A2, B2, C2).	
2	→ ($\overline{datareaddy}$)/(2).	A2	*ready* = 1.	
3	*MD* ← *DATA*;		DEAD END	
	MA ← INC(*MA*).	B2	*read* = 1.	
4	First step of multiplication	B3	→ (*dataready*, $\overline{dataready}$)/(16, B3).	
		C2	First step of multiplication	

17	Last step of multiplication	C15	Last step of multiplication	
18	*CR* ← *AC*.	16	CONVERGE (B3, C15)	
19	*ready* = 1.	17	→ ($\overline{request}$)/(17).	
20	→ (*request*, $\overline{request}$)/(1, 20)	18	*CR* ← *AC; MD* ← *DATA*;	
			MA ← INC(*MA*);	
			→ (1).	

(a)   (b)

Figure 9.5. Control sequences for process controller.

sequentially. However, while one data word is being read from *CR*, a second word is being readied for output through multiplication by *KK,* and a third data word is being read from memory. With each pass through the control sequence, each of three words advances one step in the process.[2] After convergence, step 18 moves the data ahead and increments *MA*. Since the *request* level remains 1 until the next *ready* level, convergence can be accomplished in two steps, avoiding the necessity of a more complicated three-input convergence circuit. We have been careful to ascertain that no register is involved in more than one of the three asynchronous operations. It is for this reason that the three parallel sequences must converge before data are moved synchronously from memory to the registers used in multiplication and between *AC,* which stores the product, and *CR*. ∎

When two parallel control sequences specify transfers involving the same set of registers, care must be taken to assure that the following two rules are always satisfied.

Rule 9.1: A single register (bus) can be the target of no more than one transfer (connection) in the same clock period.

Rule 9.2: A register must not be read at a time when the correctness of its contents is contingent on the completion of an ongoing asynchronous activity.

As pointed out in Chapter 4, the result of trying to transfer two vectors into a register simultaneously is unpredictable. Rule 9.2 applies to a register that may be the target of a transfer asynchronous to other activities involving that register. Satisfaction

---

[2]This process is a simple example of *pipelining,* a technique that will be discussed in some detail in later chapters.

of both rules was ensured in Example 9.1 by carefully enforcing the convergence of the three asynchronous sequences before data were passed between registers involved in the separate asynchronous activities.

9.3   Asynchronous or Unsynchronized?

At this point, it is useful to consider carefully the meaning of the term *asynchronous*. The official IEEE definition of a *synchronous computer* is as follows:

> A computer in which each event, or the performance of each operation, starts as a result of a signal generated by a clock.

Thus, *synchronous* simply means "clocked." However, asynchronous does not mean unclocked. The IEEE definition for an *asynchronous computer* is as follows:

> A computer in which each event or the performance of each operation starts as a result of a signal generated by the completion of the previous event or the operation.

Note that this definition says nothing about a clock signal. The completion signal may or may not be synchronized to a clock. Let us consider some examples. In a ripple-carry adder, the time for carry propagation will depend on the numbers being added. In the worst case, a carry may propagate from the least significant bit position to the most significant bit position. For a fully synchronous operation, sufficient time must be allowed for this worst-case propagation. However, this worst-case propagation from one end to the other rarely occurs because there are usually bit positions in which both operands are 0, and the carry will not propagate further. On the average, carrys will propagate fully in about one-fifth the worst-case time. The *carry-completion adder* includes extra logic that will issue a signal when all carrys have fully propagated. The timing of this signal is a function of delays through the logic and the numbers being added and is totally independent of the clock.

Next, let us consider multiplication, which is usually done by multiple addition and shifting. In the simplest form of multipliers, the number of add/shift cycles will be equal to the number of bits in the multiplier, so that the number of cycles is fixed for fixed-length multipliers, and the operation is synchronous. More complex multipliers sometimes include logic to make multiple shifts in a single cycle when strings of zeros are detected in the multiplier. Such a multiplier is synchronous in the sense of being fully clocked, but the number of cycles required for completion will depend on the numbers being multiplied, so the circuit will need to generate a completion signal and is, in that sense, asynchronous.

There are comparable examples in the area of memory. We might have a large, relatively slow RAM operating on a clock different from the CPU clock, and returning a *ready* signal at a time totally independent of the the CPU clock. In another case, we might have a shift register-memory synchronized to the CPU clock, but with the number of cycles for access determined by where the addressed location is in the memory. In this case, both devices could be considered asynchronous and both are clocked, but the slow RAM would not be considered synchronous with the CPU.

In an attempt to sort all this out, we shall specify the following restrictions and definitions.

1. *All* operations within a single module must be *synchronous,* that is, timed by a common clock. Operations within a module will be considered *asynchronous* when there are parallel sequences within a module and the relative timing between steps in these sequences is not fixed.
2. Interconnected modules will be considered *synchronized* if they operate on a *common clock,* but will usually be *asynchronous* in the sense that there need be no fixed relationship between specific steps in the sequences of different modules.
3. Interconnected modules will be considered *unsynchronized* if they do *not* operate on a common clock.

All this may seem to you like splitting hairs, but the distinctions are very important because the techniques for dealing with unsynchronized systems and asynchronous systems are very different. The techniques for handling asynchronous operations and modules primarily involve organizing the sequences in appropriate ways. Dealing with unsynchronized modules primarily requires synchronization of signals between modules by electronic techniques. These problems will be discussed in Section 9.5.

9.4 Interacting Processes and Interacting Modules

The user looking from the outside of a large digital system sees many input and output ports that seem to be simultaneously receiving and sending information. The users' manuals describe many internal activities that are said to take place simultaneously. What is controlling all these activities? How is it that these activities seem to cooperate rather than compete? Are these parallel operations controlled by a single intelligence or several?

That parallel control sequences and separate control sequences might not be totally different can be argued in terms of the figurative model shown in Fig. 9.6. A portion of a control sequencer featuring three parallel sequences is represented by Fig. 9.6a. Only the paths of propagation of the control level within the control unit are shown. The transfers that take place are left to your imagination.

Figure 9.6b differs from Figure 9.6a only in that the individual parallel branches have become more complicated. A control level can circulate in a path containing a loop for a long time. When such is the case for two or more paths, one might argue that the convergence circuit serves to provide occasional communications between the separate control sequences in these paths. The controller example of the last section

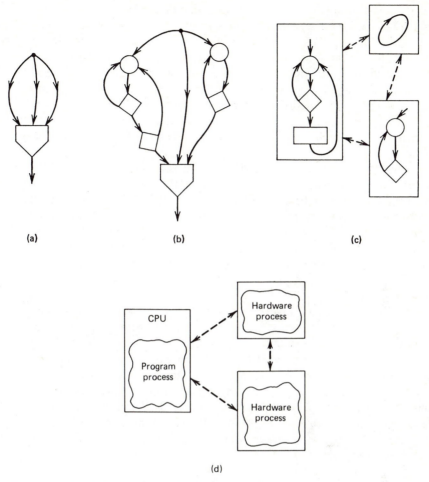

Figure 9.6. Parallel sequences and multiple control.

would have a form similar to Fig. 9.6b, since the multiplier sequence would certainly contain loops.

In Fig. 9.6c, the individual control loops have been formally separated to form distinct control units. Two-way communications between these separate units is indicated by dashed arrows. We shall not further develop parallel control of the type suggested by Fig. 9.6a and 9.6b. Where used, parallel control within a module will be a fairly obvious extension of the techniques already developed. Where greater complexity is required, it is usually better to use the approach of separate modules, which will be the topic of the remainder of this chapter.

The digital world has assigned the word *process* to represent an active or inactive locus of control. A consistent use of the word "process" in software circles is as "an independent routine belonging either to the system or a user." Separate hardware processes exist in Figs. 9.6 b and c. More than one process may be active within a module; but each module will be controlled by at least one process, even if it be a single step. Chapter 6 discussed in great detail the particular hardware process responsible for executing routines within CPU. When this particular process is active in the execution of a routine, it is no longer credited with an identity separate from that of the executing software process. It is, if you will, the embodiment of the executing software program. This notion is emphasized graphically in Fig. 9.6d. In this figure, only one process is shown within the CPU module. In general, there may be other simultaneously executing processes within the CPU module in addition to the program process.

When the control section is divided into separate units, the data section must be similarly divided. A basic requirement of the AHPL method of system description is that all components must be assigned to a specific module. Thus, if the control section is to be divided into separate units, the entire system must be divided into distinct modules, with the various components of the data sections being declared in separate modules. This may seem a fairly obvious idea in principle, but there are some problems. As long as all data transfers take place within a single module, there is nothing different from the situation in systems made up of only one module. However, when data must be transferred from one module to another, the situation becomes more complex. Since two separate sequences are involved, Rules 9.1 and 9.2 of the previous section must be satisfied. Satisfaction of these rules will require the exchange of certain information between the interacting modules.

Figure 9.7 illustrates a typical situation, in which data developed by a process in Module I is to be transferred to a register in Module II. Rule 9.1 requires that only one transfer into *CRII* occur during any one clock period. This is most simply accomplished by letting the control unit of Module II control the transfers into *CRII*. At some point in the sequence for Module II, we will have the statement

$$CRII \leftarrow DATAI$$

with no other transfer into *CRII* in the same step. To satisfy Rule 9.2, this transfer must take place only if Module I has completed the process that develops *DATAI*. When this condition is satisfied, Module I will send a signal, *dataready*, to Module II and this signal will be used to control the loading of *CRII*, as shown in Fig. 9.8a.

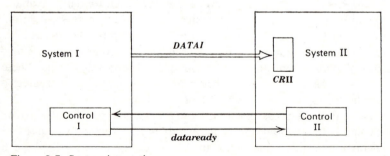

Figure 9.7. System interaction.

MODULE I   MODULE II

          ·   ·

          ·   ·

          ·   ·

    process to   ·
    develop
    DATAI

          ·   ·

          ·   8   ***CRII * dataready ← DATAI:***
10   *dataready* = 1 ⟶⟶⟶⟶⟶⟶⟶   → (*$\overline{dataready}$*)/(8).

          ·   ·

          ·   ·

(a)

MODULE I   MODULE II

          ·   ·

          ·   ·

          ·   ·

    process to   ·
    develop
    DATAI

          ·   ·

9   → *$\overline{ready}$*)/(9) ⟵⟵⟵⟵⟵   7   ***readyf*** = 1.
                                          8   ***CRII * dataready ← DATAI:***
10   *dataready* = 1 ⟶⟶⟶   → (*$\overline{dataready}$*)/(8).

          ·   9   ***readyf*** = 0.

          ·   ·

                                       ENDSEQUENCE
                                          ready = readyf.

(b)

MODULE I   MODULE II

          ·   ·

          ·   ·

          ·   ·

    process to   ·
    develop
    DATAI

          ·   ·

          ·   8   ***CRII * dataready ← DATAI.***
10   *dataready* = 1 ⟶⟶⟶   → (*$\overline{dataready}$*)/(8).
    → (*$\overline{accept}$*)/(10) ⟵⟵⟵   9   ***accept*** = 1.

(c)

Figure 9.8. Intermodule signalling.

At first glance, it might seem that this would work, but the problem is not that simple. Note that step 10 in Module I holds *dataready* at 1 for only one clock period. Unless module II happens to be at step 8 at that time waiting for *dataready*, this approach will not work. One solution is to let Module II tell Module I when it is ready to receive data, as shown in Fig. 9.8b. Here we define a flip-flop, *readyf* in Module II that drives a line *ready*. When Module I has completed the process that develops a value for *DATAI,* it checks *ready* to see if Module II is ready for data, holding at step 9 until that condition exists. At that point, it is sufficient to raise *dataready* to 1 for only one clock period, since Module II is waiting for it. Following the completion of the transfer, Module II turns off *ready* in preparation for the next transfer.

Another method to accomplish the same purpose is shown in Fig. 9.8c. In this case, Module I holds *dataready* at 1 until Module II returns an *accept* signal after clocking the data into *CRII*.

There are many other variations on these signalling patterns. The lines may have different names, and the order of signalling may vary. Sometimes the receiving device will signal first, sometimes the sending device will signal first. Some signals will have a fixed duration, some will hold active until some sort of acknowledgment is received. Whatever the details, the basic process corresponds to the definition of asynchronous operation given earlier; that is, a new process starts on receipt of a signal that some other process has been completed. The *ready* signal indicates that Module II has completed the process of preparing to receive data. The *dataready* signal indicates that Module I has completed the process of developing the *DATAI* signal. The *accept* signal indicates that Module II has completed the process of receiving that data. The principle is completely general; interacting systems coordinate their activities by exchanging completion signals, indicating when one process has been completed so that any other process dependent on the completion of that first process can be started.

The example used in the previous section to illustrate parallel sequences may also be reworked in terms of interacting modules. This is done in Example 9.2, which illustrates the communication between modules using the approach of Fig. 9.8b.

Example 9.2

Redesign the process controller in such a way that each of the three parallel sequences of Fig. 9.5b is accomplished by a separate module.

Solution
The process controller is laid out as three separate modules in Fig. 9.9. The memory had previously been treated as a separate module. The multiplication is now accomplished in a separate module, leaving the third module to keep track of the memory address and to interact with the controlled process. Since the memory will be integrated into the system as an off-the-shelf item, a detailed AHPL description of only the multiplier and process controller are given as follows.

    MODULE: MULTIPLIER.
      INPUTS MEMORY: *DATA* [12].
      INPUTS SWITCHES: *CONSTANT* [6]; *refill.*

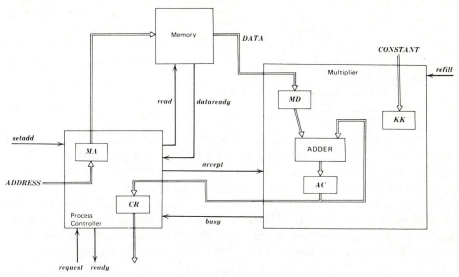

Figure 9.9. Multimodule process controller.

INPUTS PROCESS CONTROLLER: *accept.*
MEMORY: *AC* [18]; *KK* [6]; *busy; MD* [12].
OUTPUTS: *AC*; *busy.*

1 → ($\overline{accept}$)/(1).
2 *busy* ← 1; *MD* ← *DATA*. NO DELAY
3 First step of multiplication

.
.
.

16 Last step of multiplication
17 *busy* ← 0;
→ (1).
END SEQUENCE
KK ∗ *refill* ← *CONSTANT*.
END.

MODULE: PROCESS CONTROLLER
INPUTS MULTIPLIER: *AC* [18]; *busy*.
INPUTS MEMORY: *dataready.*
INPUTS PROCESS: *ADDRESS* [12]; *request; setadd.*
MEMORY: *MA* [12]; *CR* [18].
OUTPUTS: *CR; ready; read; MA*; *accept.*
1 *ready* = 1; *read* = 1.
2 → ($\overline{dataready}$)/(2).

$$3 \quad \rightarrow (\overline{busy})/(3).$$
$$4 \quad \rightarrow (\overline{request})/(4).$$
$$5 \quad CR \leftarrow AC; \; MA \leftarrow \text{INC}(MA); \; accept = 1;$$
$$\rightarrow (1).$$

END SEQUENCE

$$MA * setadd \leftarrow ADDRESS.$$

END.

These AHPL sequences are complete even to the point of providing for the external control signals, *setadd* and *refill,* by which the user can insert a new address in *MA* or a new constant in *KK.* It is assumed that such action will take place only when activity is held up by the withholding of a *request* signal. In this way, Rule 9.1 is satisfied even though the AHPL specification of these loading operations is written following "END SEQUENCE." Once a new address signal has been placed in *MA,* the corresponding number will appear in *CR* only after three *request* signals.

In this example, the need to wait for completion of three separate functions (1. read from memory, 2. multiplication, and 3, use of data) has not been eliminated by separating the control unit into modules. In fact, this is the primary function of the process-controller module. No hardware convergence circuit is required, since now the *busy* level from the multiplier remains 0 and the *request* level remain 1 until responded to by the process controller. One possible timing sequence is illustrated in Fig. 9.10. Following receipt of the one-period *dataready* level, at least two more clock periods are required to check for *busy* = 0, indicating completion of multiplication and for *request* = 1. In Fig. 9.10, these lines have already assumed these respective values prior to the *dataready* signal and will retain the values until the check is made. Once all three signals have been received, a one-period *accept* level is issued to the multiplier, which causes it to accept a new vector from lines *DATA,* begin multipli-

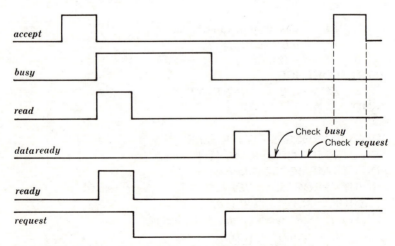

Figure 9.10. Timing of control signals.

cation, and set *busy* to 1. Signals on lines *read* and *ready* are also issued by the process controller, and the chain of events is repeated.

It should be noted that the control signal *busy* from the multiplier proved very convenient for the process controller, since it would remain zero indefinitely or until receipt of a subsequent one-period *accept*. This is contrasted with the line *dataready,* which must be watched constantly for the occurrence of a one-period level. This form of the signal *busy* is made possible by defining *busy* as a data flip-flop external to the control unit.

So far, no mention has been made of Rule 9.2. The process controller assures that this rule is satisfied by executing the transfers

$$CR \leftarrow AC \text{ and } MA \leftarrow \text{INC}(MA)$$

and causing the transfer

$$MD \leftarrow DATA$$

to be executed by the multiplier during the two clock periods in which it knows that none of the three asynchronous operations are in progress.

9.5   Unsynchronized Subsystems

Design in the clock mode (subject to the clock-mode assumption) is by far the easiest and most convenient approach to the design of sequential circuits. The large majority of existing digital systems have been designed this way. A digital system represented by an AHPL description is assumed to be a clock-mode system.

The clock-mode assumption may be restated as follows.

In a circuit operating in the clock mode, all input transitions and all state variable transitions must be synchronized by a clock pulse, and all the variables must be stable before the next clock pulse. Usually these transitions are in synchronism with either a rising or a falling edge of the clock.

Within many systems there are subsystems for which this assumption is not satisfied. A few logic levels may change values at random without regard for the system clock. Distance between modules of a single system may make it impossible to synchronize them with the same clock. This problem is most likely to occur at high frequencies, where the clock period may be of the same order of magnitude as the propagation delay in typical wire connections. An unsynchronized subsystem is depicted in Fig. 9.11a. The design can be expressed in AHPL by separating and by identifying it as a separate module, as illustrated in Fig. 9.11b. As illustrated, a *synchronizer* is placed on each control line from module A to the primary module B.

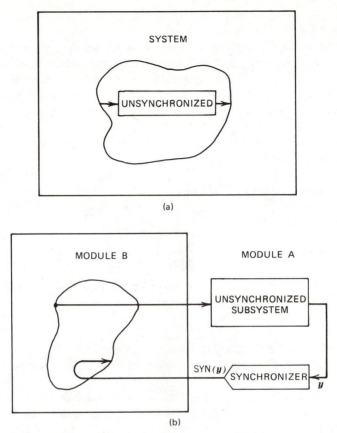

Figure 9.11. Asynchronous subsystems in AHPL.

We assume that module A is unsynchronized with respect to the module B clock. It is necessary that signals on line *y* be synchronized to the module B clock before they can be used in that system.

There are many reasons why an input from module A might not be synchronized with the internal clock of module B: (1) module A might be driven by an internal clock not synchronized within the clock of module B; (2) module A might not be a clock-mode system; (3) there might be a significant transmission line delay between modules A and B, so that the inputs would be delayed, and therefore unsynchronized, even if it were possible to drive the two modules with the same clock. Even with these reasons in mind, the designer of module B should probably not concede the use of a synchronizer without a fight. If steps can be taken to adjust specifications or physical location so that the two modules can be driven by the same clock, the designer of module B is well advised to make the attempt. The engineering time saved and the greater confidence in the reliability of the final product are well worth some time spent on intersystem design.

Try as one might, a system designer may finally have no choice but to deal with some unsynchronized inputs. In Fig. 9.12, we see module B with examples of two possible kinds of inputs. The vector *DATA* is an input to the data section or a data input, whereas *x* is a control input. If these signals arrive at module B unsynchronized with the clock, then some steps must be taken to synchronize them so that module B can operate in the clock mode. As is typically the case, the function of the control input, *x,* is to indicate when the data input lines, *DATA,* are stable and are to be accepted by module B. If module B monitors the line *x* to determine when *DATA* is stable before clocking it into the register, *CR,* there is no need to provide for synchronizing the lines, *DATA,* within module B. A similar argument with respect to other input data vectors reduces the problem of input synchronization to synchronizing the control inputs.

To make our example more specific, let us assume that the only appearance of *DATA* within the AHPL description is in step 10 as follows.

10     $CR * x \leftarrow DATA;$
        $\rightarrow (\bar{x}, x) / (10,11).$

Since the transfer of *DATA* into *CR* is conditional on *x,* we need not worry about synchronizing the data lines, but let us examine the problems that result if we fail to synchronize the control input *x.* Fig. 9.13 is a realization of step 10 using falling-edge-triggered D flip-flops. Suppose that *x* is an unsynchronized control input that goes to 1 immediately ahead of the falling edge of a clock pulse. A 1 signal appears at point *a* one gate delay after the transition on line *x.* The level at point *a* is used to gate a clock pulse that will cause the transfer $CR \leftarrow DATA$ to take place. The resultant control pulse may be a narrow spike as shown, which may or may not be sufficient to effect the desired transfer. Even in a case in which the step 10 transfer did not occur, the signal at point *a* may have appeared at the input of control flip-flop 11 in time for the trailing edge of the clock to set this flip-flip to 1. This situation is depicted in Fig. 9.13 by the shaded area on the step 11 waveform, which indicates that the

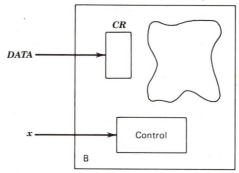

Figure 9.12. Clock-mode module B with unsynchronized inputs.

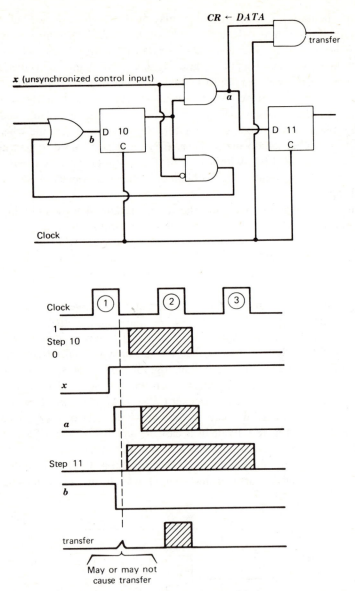

Figure 9.13. Effect of unsynchronized control input.

value is uncertain. It is also possible that gate delays will be such that point **b** will still be 1 at the time of the trailing edge of clock pulse 1 even though **a** reached the value 1 prior to this edge. This could result in 1's appearing simultaneously in control flip-flops 10 and 11. These two 1's could then propagate independently within the control unit, causing a sequence of erroneous transfers. On the other hand, a different combination of gate delays could cause 0's to appear at the input of both flip-flops 10 and 11 coincident with the trailing edge of the clock pulse. In this case, the control level signal would be lost. Again, these various possibilities are represented by the shaded areas for steps 10 and 11.

Now that we have observed the potential danger associated with an unsynchronized control input, let us consider what might be done to synchronize that input. First, let us transfer x into a "synchronizing" flip-flop, r, in a statement following the END SEQUENCE and modify step 10 as follows:

10    $CR * r \leftarrow DATA;$
     $\rightarrow (\bar{r}, r) / (10, 11).$

.
.
.

END SEQUENCE
     $r \leftarrow x.$
END.

Now the branch and transfer in step 10 are controlled by r rather than by x. This means that r must be set to 1 by x one clock period before the transfer in step 10 is accomplished, and the control can continue to step 11. The argument that this measure will solve the synchronization problem is the following.

Argument for a Synchronizing Flip-Flop: It is assumed that whenever x goes to 1, it will remain at 1 for several clock periods. If a transition in x from 0 to 1 occurs very near a clocking transition, this transition may or may not set r to 1. No matter! If r is set, the transfer in step 10 and the branch to step 11 will be accomplished during the next clock period. If not, r will be set one period later, and step 10 will be executed two periods later. Either behavior is acceptable.

If you are tempted to breathe more easily at this point, don't! Unfortunately, the flip-flop r may not behave precisely as assumed in the foregoing argument. A number of researchers have verified empirically and argued theoretically that simultaneous transitions on the clock and data inputs of a flip-flop can leave the output gates of the device in the linear region. (See, for example, Ref. 11.) The result is that the output may oscillate for an entire clock period without settling to either the old or a new logical value.

For an illustration of this behavior, consider Fig. 9.14, which shows the pair of cross-coupled gates connected to the flip-flop output. Every type of bipolar flip-flop will have this pair of gates at the output. The rest of the flip-flop, which will vary with the type, is represented by the box. A similar argument can be made for the MOS flip-flops within LSI parts. Suppose the flip-flop output is initially 0. Point a in the circuit will be normally 1 but must be driven to 0 for a period of time to cause the output, z, to go to 1. The third waveform of Fig. 9.14 shows, without verification, what can happen when the **D** input goes to 1, too close to the triggering clock transition. This tiny zero-going pulse may not have sufficient energy to drive z to +5 volts or even past the threshold of about 2.5 volts for logical 1. In this case, the output of both gates in the cross-coupled pair will be between 1 and 2.5 volts when the pulse

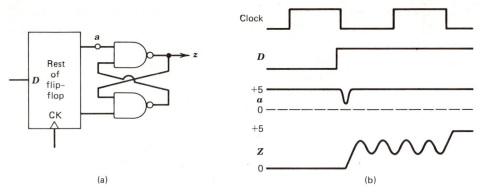

Figure 9.14. Oscillations in a synchronizer flip-flop.

on *a* has disappeared. The result is the oscillation of *z* shown in the last waveform, which can persist until the next triggering clock edge.

We have not shown that the synchronization is hopeless. What has been demonstrated by the research in this area is that there will always be finite probability of failure in the synchronization process. It is up to the designer to reduce this probability of failure to a point that it is no more significant than the probability of other failures such as shorts and opens within the system. This is done by reducing the minimal interval between a data transition and the clock transition within which trouble will result. Even without synchronization, the interval might, for example, be only 1 nsec out of a 500-nsec clock period for a failure probability of 0.2%. Computation of this probability is beyond the scope of this book (see Ref. 2), but it is improved by merely adding the fallible synchronizing circuit just described. The probability of oscillations is less than the probability of one of the forms of erroneous behavior of Fig. 9.13 given an unsynchronized *x*. Also, the oscillation may die out in one clock period, depending on the magnitude of the pulse at point *a*. Other steps that might be taken to reduce further the risk of synchronization failures are

1. Modify the circuit design of the synchronizing flip-flop, usually by increasing gain, so that oscillations will die out more quickly.
2. Connect the input of a second synchronizing flip-flop, *s*, between the input of the unsynchronized input, *x*, and the D input of the flip-flop, *r*.
3. Extend the length of time allowed for the oscillations to die out before the synchronized input is used.

We can apply points 2 and 3 to reduce the risk of synchronization problems in the system of Fig. 9.12 by modifying the statements after the END SEQUENCE as follows.

END SEQUENCE
    r * (∧/*CNT*) ← *s*; *s* * (∧/*CNT*) ← *x*;
    CNT ← INC(*CNT*).
END.

Now *r* and *s* are updated less frequently. If the counter, *CNT,* is modulo 8, for example, then *s* and *r* are triggered only once every eight clock periods. Whenever *s* goes into oscillation, these oscillations have eight clock periods to die out before *r* is affected. The disadvantage is, of course, a possible eight-clock-period delay in the acceptance of *DATA* after this vector is available. If this response time is too slow for a particular application, the only choice is circuit enhancement or toleration of a larger probability of failure.

If you are uncomfortable with the complexity of synchronization, heed our earlier advice and make every effort to arrange to drive all systems with the same clock. Alternatively, as discussed in Chapter 7, let the synchronous master module anticipate responses from the other unsynchronized portions of the system. In most cases, this simply means to allow enough time for data supplied by an unsynchronized module to become available and stable without expecting a control signal from the unsynchronized module to tell us this.

Occasionally, two or more systems will operate synchronously even though "multiple clock" signals may be active. This can be the case if the clock periods of all active clocks are multiples of the period of a single master clock. This can be achieved by simply counting down the master clock to generate lower frequency clocks in peripheral modules. The overall system can be made to function reliably if the timing of control signals issued by the faster systems are carefully related to control signals received from the slower systems.

9.6 Completely Responsive Signalling

In Section 9.4, we illustrated interactive control signalling between modules. We saw three examples of activity in one module waiting only for signalled completion of activity in another module. Under certain circumstances, it may be necessary to sense both the beginning and end of an activity to assure satisfactory communications between two modules. Let us begin our discussion with the consideration of another example.

Example 9.3

A simple printing device has eight input lines designated as the vector *CHAR* and two control inputs labelled *print* and *feed.* Its only output is a single line labelled *wait.* Each time a one-period level is placed on line *print,* the character represented on lines *CHAR* in ASCII code will be printed. Each time a one-period level is placed on line *feed,* a combination of carriage return and line feed is executed. Following either one-period level, the line *wait* will go to 1 until the operation is complete.

Three control lines and the 16-bit *IOBUS* connect the printer interface to a CPU. The control line *ready* from the printer interface must be recognized as 1 by the CPU before a data vector is placed on the *IOBUS*. This will prevent another request when a printer operation is in progress. When a data word has been placed on the *IOBUS,* the CPU will so indicate with a 1-level on a line *datavalid.* When the interface has accepted this data word, it must respond with a one-period level on the line *accept.* Each data word will contain two ASCII characters packed as vectors *IOBUS* [8:15] and *IOBUS* [0:7]. Design an interface to satisfy these requirements.

Solution

The interface will use a 16-bit data register, *DR,* so it can release the *IOBUS,* together with an 8-bit register, *CR,* the outputs of which are permanently connected to the printer input lines, *CHAR.* A flip-flop, *first,* will be used to indicate which of the two characters in a word is being printed.

```
    MODULE: PRINTER INTERFACE.
        MEMORY: DR[16]; CR[8]; first.
        OUTPUTS: CHAR[8]; ready; accept; print; feed.
        INPUTS: datavalid; wait.
        COMBUSES: IOBUS[16].
    1   ready = 1;
        → (datavalid̄)/1.
    2   DR ← IOBUS; accept = 1; first ← 1.
    3   CR ← (DR[8:15]! DR[0:7]) * (first, first̄).
    4   feed = RETURN(CR); print = RETURN (CR).
    5   Null.
    6   → (wait)/(6).
    7   first ← 0;
        → (first, first̄)/(3, 1).
    END SEQUENCE
        CONTROLRESET(1);
        CHAR = CR.
    END.
```

RETURN is a combinational logic function that is 1 if *CR* contains a carriage-return character. Step 6 causes control to wait for the completion of the printing of the character. Step 5 is included to allow the printer an extra clock period to react by setting *wait.* After the completion of a printing operation, step 7 either returns control to step 3 to print the second character, or to step 1 to wait for another data word. ■

Two basic types of signalling are used in intersystem communications, *nonresponsive* and *responsive.* In *nonresponsive* signalling, the sending device simply places a signal on the communications lines for some fixed period of time and then proceeds, assuming that the receiving device has taken whatever action may be required. In *responsive* signalling, the sending device places a signal on the communications line and holds it there until the receiving device acknowledges receipt of the signal. Nonresponsive signalling is usually simpler but is reliable only when the sending and receiving devices are carefully synchronized, preferably on the same clock. Responsive signalling is more reliable in most cases, since it requires verification at each step in the communication process, but it requires more hardware and is usually slower than nonresponsive signalling.

Many systems employ a mixture of these two approaches to signalling, as does the printer interface of the last example. The interface holds the signal *ready* at 1 until the CPU responds with the signal *datavalid,* indicating that data are on the bus. The CPU then holds the data on the bus until the interface responds with the signal *accept.* This partially responsive *three-line handshake* is quite satisfactory for the printer interface of Example 9.3, in which the transmitter and receiver are driven by the same clock and several clock periods are required to handle the data after an *accept* is issued. Consider, however, a system in which (1) the receiver requires only one clock period to handle a data character after an *accept* is issued, and (2) the transmitter and receiver are physically separated so that a propagation delay of one or more clock periods exists on the control lines between the devices. In this case, the partially responsive handshake would not be reliable, since *ready* could be returned to 1 after a character is received and processed and *the system could be looking for a new datavalid signal before the datavalid signal corresponding to the character, just received, has returned to 0.*

Figure 9.15 depicts the potential problem with the partially responsive handshake like that used in Example 9.3. Notice that the onset of the second *ready* = 1 is contingent only on the processing of data within the printer. In this case, the data are handled very quickly by the receiving device and *ready* goes back to 1 before the lowering of *datavalid* (in response to the *accept* reaching the transmitting device) has been observed at the receiver. The result is that the same data is accepted twice by the receiver.

The completely responsive handshake given in Fig. 9.16 eliminates the problem just described by simply not allowing *ready* to return to 1 until *datavalid* has been observed to return to 0. Now each transition on the line *ready* occurs only after an indication from the transmitter; and each transition on line *datavalid* occurs only after

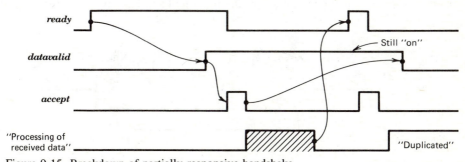

Figure 9.15. Breakdown of partially responsive handshake.

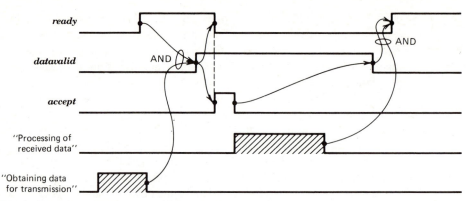

Figure 9.16. Completely responsive handshake as observed at the receiver.

an indication from the receiver. This is the definition of *completely responsive* signalling. We have observed the elimination of the potential problem of receiving the same data twice at the receiver. Requiring that ***datavalid*** go to 1 only after ***ready*** is observed, and that ***datavalid*** return to 0 only following the ***accept*** similarly eliminates the possibility of sending two data vectors for one ***ready*** = 1 level, given a long transmission delay.

It might be observed that the onset of the ***accept*** signal in Fig. 9.16 coincides with the return to 0 of line ***ready***. Therefore, what information is provided by line ***accept*** that cannot be obtained by watching for the fall of line ***ready***? The answer is "None," of course. The signalling depicted in Fig. 9.17 is completely responsive, with each transition contingent on the prior observation of a particular transition on the other line. Now the positive transition on line ***ready*** indicates just that "ready," whereas the negative transition signals acceptance of data.

The three-line version of the completely responsive handshake is sometimes used for convenience. The IEEE 488 bus is an example. Under the IEEE 488 bus protocol, data may be simultaneously broadcast to more than one instrument. Separate ***ready*** and ***accept*** lines allow for ANDing control signals from multiple devices. Where pin-limited integrated circuits are involved, the two-line handshake is often used.

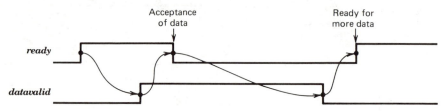

Figure 9.17. Two-line fully responsive signalling.

9.7   Interconnection of Systems

It is often necessary to provide for the transfer of data among several independent modules. As suggested in Section 4.4, the most efficient method of implementing such a transfer network is through the use of a data bus. If one or more of the modules is a computer or a CPU, the most common arrangement for data transmission is the I/O bus, which from a logical point of view simply consists of a set of n lines providing bidirectional transfer of n-bit words between **MD** in the CPU and the data registers of the I/O devices, as shown in Fig. 9.18. If there are no direct transfers between I/O devices, the principal saving achieved by the use of an I/O bus is in cabling. As shown in Fig. 9.18, the bus is routed serially from device to device rather than routing two cables between each device and the central processor. In addition, the switching located at the input to the central processor is simpler (although the switching at each I/O device is more complicated).

Since the registers connected to the bus are located in separate devices, each module must generate the control levels required to place data on the **IOBUS** and to trigger data from the **IOBUS** into local registers. To accomplish the transfer of a data vector from device A to device B requires to device A to first generate a 1 on the control line routing a data register to the **IOBUS**. This level must then remain 1 until system B clocks the vector from the **IOBUS** into its data register.

Clearly, some procedure must be provided through which a sending module will know when the **IOBUS** is not in use by another module and through which a receiving register will know when data are available on the bus. This coordinating procedure usually becomes the responsibility of one designated module. If one of the modules is a CPU, this unit will usually retain control of the **IOBUS**. Thus, in addition to the I/O bus, there must be paths provided for transmission of control information between the CPU and the I/O devices.

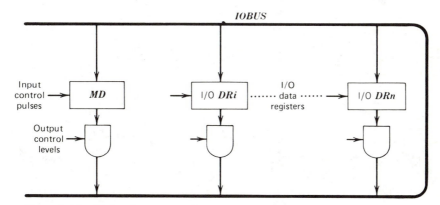

Figure 9.18. I/O bus interconnections.

Some control information can be passed back and forth between peripherals and the CPU in vector units in much the same manner as data. Historically, a special bus called the *command/status bus* has been implemented for this purpose, as depicted in Fig. 9.19a. (We shall see in the next chapter that memory mapped input/output has made the command/status bus redundant in more recent computers.) Other control information, for example, the handshake signals discussed in Section 9.4, must be exchanged on individual lines. Some of these will take the form of 1-bit buses conforming to the topology of, but logically separate from, the command/status bus. A few control lines, such as interrupt lines, which will be discussed in the next chapter, must be connected uniquely between the CPU and each peripheral, as shown in Fig. 9.19b.

Let us focus now on the control of input/output without using unique control lines to the individual I/O devices. In addition to the command/status bus itself, there may be three 1-bit control buses, *ready, datavalid,* and *accept,* that are connected to the CPU and all peripheral devices. Given this configuration, all activity must be initiated by the CPU. This will be accomplished by broadcasting a command on the command/status bus. There must be one additional CPU control output connected to all I/O devices to alert them to the presence of such a command on the command/status bus. Here, we shall call this line *csready.* A few bits of each command must serve

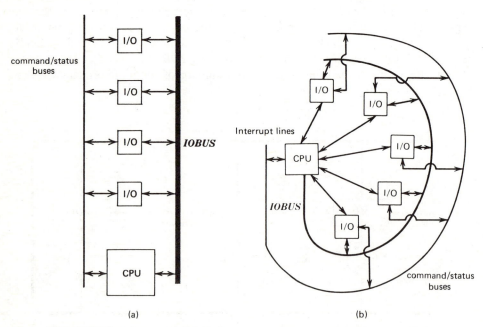

Figure 9.19. *IOBUS* and command/status bus.

as a short address vector to identify the device for which the command is intended. The remaining bits may be coded in any desired way to make up the actual command.

Every peripheral device will include a number of flip-flops that store the current status of that device. The status information of interest will vary with the device but will always include the state of progress in executing an active command. From time to time, a device will be instructed by the CPU to send its status to the CPU on the command/status bus. Such a request for status may be made while the peripheral device is already engaged in the transfer of data or a block of data. The ability to respond to a request for status at any time implies some form of parallel loci of control within the device.

Further illustration of communications through the command/status bus requires a specific example, as partially detailed in Fig. 9.20. In addition to the 16-bit *IOBUS,* which is not shown in Fig. 9.20, there is a 12-bit *CSBUS* on which commands are transmitted from the master module to the peripheral modules, and on which status information is transmitted from the peripheral modules to the master module. A 1 will appear on a line *csrdy* from the master module whenever a command is placed on the *CSBUS.* A subset of these command bits will be used as an address, to indicate which of the peripheral modules is to receive the command. When a *csrdy* signal appears, each module will check these bits to determine if a response on its part is in order.

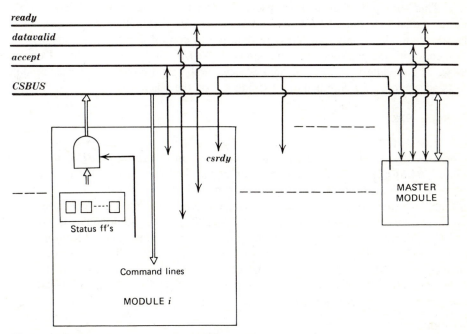

Figure 9.20. *CSBUS* control of communications.

A set of flip-flops storing various internal status information must be included in each module. A module will respond to a request-for-status command by connecting its register of status flip-flops to the *CSBUS*. Not every module will use all the possible status flip-flops. Similarly, some of the command lines will be of no interest to particular modules.

The lines *ready, datavalid,* and *accept* will each be treated as a 1-bit bus. As shown in Fig. 9.20, any module will be able to place a one-level on any of these three buses, and the bus level may be observed by any module. The only distinction between these buses and other communications buses discussed so far rests in the fact that each is only a *1-bit* bus. For convenience, the word *bus* does not appear in the names of these three control lines. Nevertheless, *ready, datavalid,* and *accept* are *communications buses* in every sense and must be declared as such. The hardware of each of these buses will be similar to the hardware for a single bit of any other communications bus.

At any given time, only one module can be allowed to transmit data. We shall usually assume only one receiving device. If the control were not buses, it would be possible to have multiple receivers by using an ANDing of *ready* and *accept* signals from all receivers to control the handshake process. A peripheral module will be notified when it is to assume either of these roles by a command from the master module. The control of data transfers through the *IOBUS* will be partially responsive as in Example 9.3.

This same procedure will be observed when a status vector is transferred to the master module via the *CSBUS*. Since commands are transmitted at the pleasure of the master module, only two lines are required to control a command transmission. As mentioned, the presence of a command on *CSBUS* will be signalled by a 1 on line *csrdy*. The module with the indicated device number will advise the master module of its acceptance of a command by placing a 1 on the bus *accept*.

Example 9.4

The same printing device considered in Example 9.3 is to be interfaced to the I/O system of Fig. 9.20. When a command is placed on the 12-bit *CSBUS*, the first 3 bits, *CSBUS*[0:2] will specify the number of the device for which the command is intended. The printer will be device 010. Although there are 9 bits, *CSBUS*[3:11], available for specifying commands, the printer will be subject to only two commands, which will be specified by *CSBUS*[3]. If *CSBUS*[3] $= 0$, the printer is to accept a word for printing. If *CSBUS*[3] $= 1$, the printer interface is to send status information to the CPU over the *CSBUS*. Either operation is to be controlled by the three-line interactive handshake. The printer interface will have only one status bit, a flip-flop *busy,* the contents of which may be transmitted over *CSBUS*[0]. The interface indicates that it cannot accept another data word by setting *busy* to 1.

Solution
The declarations are similar to those for Example 9.3 except that all the lines between the interface and the CPU, except *csrdy,* are now communications buses and must be

declared after COMBUS. The following sequence is more complicated, primarily because of the need to be ready to respond to a request for status at any time.

MODULE: PRINTER INTERFACE.
    MEMORY: DR[16]; CR[8]; *busy; first.*
    OUTPUTS: $CHAR$[8]; *print; feed.*
    INPUTS: *wait; csrdy.*
    COMBUSES: $IOBUS$[16]; $CSBUS$[12]; *ready; datavalid; accept.*

1    $\rightarrow$ *(csrdy* $\wedge$ $CSBUS$[0] $\wedge$ $CSBUS$[1] $\wedge$ $\overline{CSBUS[2]}$)/(1).
2   *accept* = 1;
       $\rightarrow$ ($\overline{CSBUS}$[3], $\overline{CSBUS}$[3], $CSBUS$[3])/(1, 1A, 3.)
3    $\rightarrow$($\overline{ready}$)/(3).
4    $CSBUS$[0] = *busy; datavalid* = 1;
       $\rightarrow$ ($\overline{accept}$, *accept*)/(4,1).
1A   *ready* = 1;
       $\rightarrow$($\overline{datavalid}$)/(1A).
2A $DR \leftarrow IOBUS$; *busy* $\leftarrow$ 1; *accept* = 1; *first* $\leftarrow$ 1.
3A-6A   Same as 3-6 in Example 9.3
7A   *first* $\leftarrow$ 0; *busy* * $\overline{first}$ $\leftarrow$ 0;
       $\rightarrow$ (*first*, $\overline{first}$)/(3A, 8A).
8A   DEAD END.
END.

Step 1 waits for a *csrdy* signal occurring while device 2 is specified. Step 2 indicates that the command has been received with *accept* = 1 and determines if the command is an output data command or a request for status. If $CSBUS$[3] = 0, control branches to two parallel sequences. Steps 1A to 8A accept a data vector and print two characters as was done in Example 9.3. At the same time, control returns to step 1 so that the interface is ready to respond to a request for status while the device is still busy with a printing operation. The CPU will not issue a subsequent output data command while *busy* = 1; there will be no second attempt to branch to 1A until the original control level has exited this sequence at the step 8A DEAD END.

If $CBUS$[3] = 1 at step 2, control branches to step 3 to wait for a *ready,* which will indicate that the $CSBUS$ is free. Step 4 holds *datavalid* at 1, which indicates that the requested status bit *busy* has been placed on the $CSBUS$ and holds *busy* on the bus until another *accept* is received telling the device to return to step 1. The interface may be asked to respond to a request for status many times during an ongoing print operation. Clearly, the interface control unit would be much simpler if the *busy* line could be routed directly to the CPU, eliminating the need for parallel sequences.

The sequence of Example 9.3 is a shorter sequence because it does not provide for control of the printer by the CPU. The sequence in that example is started by the printer, indicating that it is ready to receive data. The sequence of Example 9.4 is a complete sequence, putting the CPU in control and allowing it to check the status of the printer.   ■

9.8   PMS Descriptions

We have seen many occasions where a logic block diagram has been helpful in the study and understanding of an AHPL description. We have used a semiformal notation in diagrams such as Fig. 9.20 to describe connections on a wire-by-wire level. This notation would be tedious indeed, if one were to try to use it to describe an entire multiuser computer system. Often, one wishes to communicate graphically information relating the pieces of larger systems without resorting to the level of detail found in an AHPL description or in a logic block diagram like Fig. 9.20. In planning a system, one is not ready to talk about clock period by clock period timing or detailed logical operations on data. Rather, the designer is more likely to be interested in the compatibility of major components of the system with respect to their capacity to process, store, and communicate quantities of information.

The analysis and the clock stimulation of digital systems based on their AHPL descriptions is a *time-domain* activity. Those readers with experience in design and analysis of linear systems are aware that both *frequency-domain* and time-domain tools are useful in that regard. Time-domain analysis and simulation is most useful when the precise response of a system to one particular stimulus is of interest. The frequency domain is used when the focus is on average responses to classes of stimuli within particular frequency ranges. Measures of the overall information-handling capacity of a system are available in the frequency domain. The *Fourier transform* formally relates time-domain descriptions of linear systems to frequency-domain descriptions. In many cases, this transform can actually be computed to obtain a frequency-domain description from the differential equations in the time domain.

Are frequency-domain representations of digital systems of interest? Yes, as in linear systems, this is the way average information-handling characteristics of a system must be expressed. One approach to frequency-domain description of digital systems, the PMS language, is the topic of this section. Unfortunately, the digital computer is the ultimate nonlinear system, and no mathematical relationship, such as the Fourier transform, can be expected to exist from a time-domain language like AHPL to PMS. Obtaining frequency-domain information from an AHPL description must be an *ad hoc* process.

The graphical language called PMS (Processor, Memory, Switch) was invented at Carnegie–Mellon University [7] and has been used at Digital Equipment Corporation as an aid to system planning. We will find a variation of this language helpful in communicating the ideas of the next three chapters. In fairness to the inventors of PMS, we shall use this term when referring to the language, recognizing that it has been adapted to our pedagogical needs. Unlike for AHPL, we shall make no claim that this graphical language is completely precise or machine processable. Still, we shall consider our version of PMS to be sufficiently consistent to serve as a useful tool for use in working the exercises at the end of the chapter.

Figure 9.21 shows a simple computer system that includes examples of each of the primitive elements of a PMS representation of a computer system. The first three numbered boxes suggest the name of the language: P for processor, M for memory,

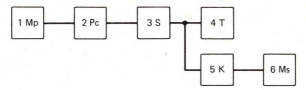

Figure 9.21. PMS diagram of an early computer system.

and S for Switch. A typical switch might be a bus that interconnects a set of several sources or destinations of information. Unlike previous notation for buses, the box labelled S represents, together as appropriate, control wires, status wires, address vectors, as well as data lines. The lowercase "p" in box 1 is optional, indicating primary storage such as random access memory. The lowercase c in box 2 optionally indicates that the processor is the CPU. The element in box 4 is a T for transducer, a device that transforms binary encoded information to or from another form, often human supplied (a keyboard) or human readable (a printer). A *modem* or a digital communications equipment (DCE) would be another example of a transducer. The K in box 5 is a controller or an interface unit. Box 6, Ms, represents secondary storage (DAS or SAS). The connecting lines will be called *links*, L. The lines representing links do not explicitly show a direction of information flow. Links are often, but not always, bidirectional. We now see that the elements of PMS are actually P, M, S, K, T, and L.

Figure 9.21, as it stands, is a perfectly good PMS diagram, although the information it contains is limited to structural interconnections. The diagrams become more useful when indication of information processing, storage, and communications capacities are indicated. Numerical values for storage capacity can be accurate. It is expected that values for communications rates and particular processing speeds will be approximate. Throughput of a processor is, of course, very much application and data-dependent. For purposes of this book, we shall introduce the following three notational forms to indicate these capacities.

$<n$: = The element's maximum transmission or processing capacity is n bytes/sec.

$@n$: = The element requires n bytes/sec.

$\$\$m$: = The element can store m bytes.

An application of the $@n$ notation might be a refresh driver for a CRT display (T). $<n$ could be included in a P or S box or written adjacent to a link. Any of the forms $<n$, $@n$, or $\$\$m$ might be included in a secondary storage box, Ms, depending on the context of the discussion. Concise English-language clarification of a PMS element may be included beside or within an enlarged box.

PMS may be employed at more than one level of detail. As planning of a system becomes more specific, it is often convenient to replace a single PMS element by a more detailed PMS description of that element. A nesting of more than one level of

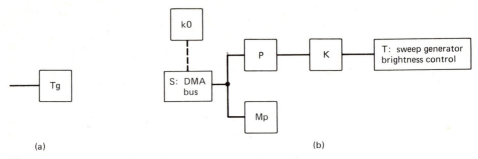

(a)   (b)

Figure 9.22. CRT graphics terminal.

this PMS substitution is possible, but at some point PMS must give way to AHPL description (or some other hardware description language), logic block diagrams, analog models, and/or software programs to provide increased detail. No precise rules for substitution of another description medium within PMS have been formulated.

Example 9.5

As an example of PMS substitution, consider the transducer, Tg, in Fig. 9.22a, which represents a graphics terminal. As required, the more detailed description of Fig. 9.22b may be substituted for Tg. This description shows a microprocessor supplying, through an interface unit, refresh data to the sweep generator brightness control transducer. The processor shares primary storage through a DMA (direct memory access: a subject to be discussed in the next chapter) switch an RS-232 (see section 12.4) interface unit K0. The optional dashed line indicates a control connection. Thus K0 also arbitrates the DMA activity.   ■

It is generally agreed that, given the foregoing discussion, the first PMS description prior to any substitution should be called the highest level of description. AHPL is the lowest level of description treated herein. Lower-level descriptions would be those useful for the gate level and circuit simulations.

Problems

9.1   The following is an AHPL description of a counter module. Following control reset, will $Z[1]$ ever be 1? Will $Z[0]$? List for 12 consecutive clock periods following control reset all active control states for each clock period. Assume that $x = 0$.

MODULE: DUAL COUNTER.
INPUTS: x.
MEMORY: A [3]; B [3].
OUTPUTS: Z [2].

1    $B \leftarrow 3 \top 0; A \leftarrow 3 \top 0;$
     $\rightarrow (x, \bar{x}, \bar{x})/(1, 2, 3).$
2    $A * B[2] \leftarrow 3 \top 0; Z[0] = \wedge/A;$
     $\rightarrow (x, \bar{x} \wedge A[2], \bar{x})/(1, 3, 5).$
3    $B \leftarrow \text{INC}(B).$
4   DEAD END
5    $A \leftarrow \text{INC}(A); Z[1] = \wedge/B;$
     $\rightarrow (x, \bar{x})/(1, 2).$
END SEQUENCE
  CONTROL RESET (1).
END.

9.2   For the module described in Problem 9.1,

(a)   Construct a one flip-flop per control state realization of the control unit.
(b)   (For students with background in sequential circuits) Generate a state diagram for this control sequential circuit and construct a realization using a minimal number of flip-flops.

Hint Note: **Consider a state for each of the 16 combinations of active and inactive control steps.**

9.3   The following is an AHPL description of a module designed to facilitate the transfer of data between two memories. Rewrite the module description using parallel control sequences to improve the overall transfer rate. Both the READ and WRITE operations take several clock periods to accomplish. Add a mechanism to ensure that the word read from the first address will be written in the first address and so forth.

(a)   Assume that the read operation will always require less time than the write operation.
(b)   Assume that the time required by both operations is variable and that is not known which will take longer.

MODULE: TRANSFER CONTROL
        INPUTS: *XA*[12]; *XB*[12]; *DATAIN* [8]; *go; ready; done.*
        OUTPUTS: *READADD*[12]; *WRITEADD*[12]; *read; write;*
            DATAOUT[8].
        MEMORY: *DATA* [8]; *READADD* [12]; *WRITEADD* [12].
1    $WRITEADD \leftarrow XA; READADD \leftarrow XB;$
     $\rightarrow (\overline{go})/(1).$
2    $WRITEADD \leftarrow \text{INC}(WRITEADD);$
     $READADD \leftarrow \text{INC}(READADD).$
3    $read = 1;$
     $\rightarrow (ready)/(3).$

4        $DATA \leftarrow DATAIN$.
5        $write\ =\ 1$;
         $\rightarrow$ (**done, done**)/(5, 2).
END SEQUENCE
         CONTROLRESET(1).
         $DATAOUT = DATA$.
END.

9.4   The multimode process controller depicted in Fig. 9.9 (the version in
          Example 9.1 has the same problem) works fine if two consecutive mean-
          ingless output vectors can be tolerated while the process gets underway.
          Rewrite the MULTIPLIER and PROCESS CONTROLLER modules to
          provide a start signal to resynchronize the process after a new address is
          loaded in MA. Also ensure that control output **ready** will not go to 1
          until the word read from the initial address multiplied by KK is available
          in CR.

9.5   Discuss the possibility of parallel control sequences in a microprogrammed
          machine. Can parallel sequences exist within the microprogrammed con-
          trol unit? How? Can parallel sequences be used outside the micropro-
          grammed control unit? Can separate units be employed in a micropro-
          grammed machine? How?

9.6   What possible source of trouble exists in the module described by the
          following AHPL sequence?

1        $CNT \leftarrow$ INC (CNT);
         $\rightarrow$ ($\wedge/CNT$)/(1).
2        $Z = 1$.
END SEQUENCE
   $CNT * x \leftarrow 8 \top 0$.
END.

9.7   Rewrite the AHPL description of the following module so that the two
          asynchronous memory references and the shifting can all be accomplished
          in parallel, thereby speeding up the overall data transfer rate. Assume
          that $DATAIN$ is the output of one memory module and $DATABUS$ is the
          input of another. Let $ADDBUS$ be the address lines for both memories.
          Add registers, if necessary. For convenience, let the data in the destination
          register be offset two memory locations from that in the original memory.

MODULE: SHIFTINGTRANSFER.
INPUTS: SW[4]; $DATAIN$[16]; $busy1$; $busy2$; go.
OUTPUTS: $read$; $write$.
COMBUSES: $ADDBUS$[12]; $DATABUS$[16].
MEMORY: MA[12]; CNT[4]; DR[16].

1    $MA \leftarrow 12 \top 0; \rightarrow (\overline{go})/(1)$.
2    $CNT \leftarrow SW$.
3    $read = 1; \rightarrow (\overline{busy1})/(3)$.
4    $\rightarrow (busy1)/(4)$.
5    $DR \leftarrow DATAIN$.
6    $DR \leftarrow DR[1:15], DR[0]; CNT \leftarrow INC(CNT)$;
     $\rightarrow (\bigvee/CNT)/(6)$.
7    $write = 1; \rightarrow (\overline{busy2})/(7)$.
8    $MA * \overline{busy2} \leftarrow INC(MA); \rightarrow (busy2)/(8)$.
9    $\rightarrow (go, \overline{go})/(2,1)$.
ENDSEQUENCE
  CONTROLRESET(1);
  DATABUS = DR; ADDBUS = MA.
END.

9.8   Consider a 16-bit *DBUS* version of RIC as described in Example 7.4. Let the first three steps of this example replace the first five steps of RIC, but use RIC steps 6 through 35 as given in Appendix A. Assume that a separate incrementing capability independent of the bus structure is available. Make modifications, where appropriate, in only steps 6 through 35 to provide for the overlap of the execution of the instruction fetch with the final step or steps of execution of the previous instruction. Express the overlap in AHPL by simultaneously branching to an execution step while also branching back to step 1. Make use of the DEAD END notation. Each step, including a "→ (1)" and preceding steps as appropriate, should be considered. In some cases, two steps of overlap are possible, in some cases one, in some cases none. Assure that Rule 9.1 is always satisfied.

9.9   A digital computer is being designed using a technology for which oscillations at the output of a memory element that has been driven into the metastable region will always die out in less than 3.5 μsec. A reliable synchronization mechanism is required for a control input, *x,* to the computer. Write in AHPL, after the END SEQUENCE, the statements describing hardware that will provide this synchronization. Write a declaration statement for any memory elements used. Assume that the computer clock period is 1 μsec.

9.10   Rewrite the AHPL description of the printer interface of Example 9.3 to incorporate completely responsive signalling.

(a)   Three line,
(b)   Two line as suggested by Fig. 9.17.

9.11   Rewrite the AHPL description for the communications memory module of Example 4.3. The single-line *ready* is to be replaced by lines *ready* and *datavalid*. Lines *accept* and *word* retain their former significance. Control communications should now conform to the completely responsive three-line handshake of Fig. 9.16. It should no longer be necessary to assume that the communications memory is in a position to accept data whenever data are available.

9.12 Repeat Problem 9.11 for the duplicate character checker of Example 5.5. In this case, the single line *data* should be replaced by lines *ready* and *datavalid*.

9.13 Suppose that the duplicate character checker of Example 5.5 is connected to the busing structure suggested by Fig. 9.19a. Let the three control lines be *ready, datavalid,* and *accept*. Data are to be accepted from an 8-bit *IOBUS*. Rewrite the AHPL description of this module accordingly.

9.14 Construct a PMS diagram of a 16-bit minicomputer with 64K of primary memory and with a separate *IOBUS.* Included on the bus will be a tape transport, a graphics terminal, an alphanumeric CRT terminal, a 30 character per second printer (parallel interface), and two 300 baud modem ports. The tape transport specifications are 1600 bits/in. and 100 in./sec. The graphics terminal has internal display memory. Assume all I/O on the bus is buffered with a maximum of 100,000 16-bit transfers to or from memory each second. Indicate using standard symbols as many data rates and data specifications as possible on the PMS diagram. Include as much detail as permitted by PMS.

9.15 A data communications terminal (DTE) includes its own control unit. The portion of the control unit that will cause received data to be stored in the memory of a minicomputer is to be designed. Data will pass in only one direction. Receiving data is a high-priority operation for the minicomputer. When a full buffer of data is available, the computer suspends all other activity while storing this data in memory. Connections

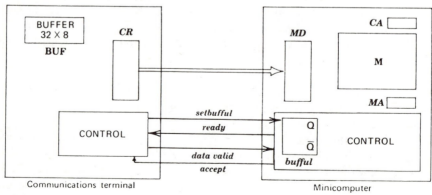

Figure P9.15

between the terminal and the computer are shown in Fig. P9.15. The semiconductor buffer in the terminal contains (when full) 32 eight-bit characters. Pairs of consecutive characters are combined to be stored as 16-bit words in the minicomputer memory. These words can be transferred directly from *CR* in the terminal to *MD* in the minicomputer. The first portion of the terminal control sequence is concerned with communications on a telephone line so that the 32 eight-bit characters are properly placed in the buffer. After the buffer has been filled, a level from the terminal will cause a flip-flop, *bufful,* in the computer to be set to 1. This flip-flop functions in much the same way as the interrupt flip-flops to be discussed in Chapter 10.

(a) Write the last portion of the control sequence for the terminal beginning with the step that generates the *setbufful* signal. This sequence will interact with the computer to cause the 32 characters to be stored in memory. Once the computer has processed the interrupt, it will respond with a signal on line *ready*. The three-line handshake then continues to completion.

(b) At step 1 in the control sequence, prior to the fetch operation, the computer pauses to examine the contents of *bufful*. If *bufful* = 0, the instruction fetch is carried out. If *bufful* = 1, control branches to step 100 to provide communications with the terminal. Write step 1. Write the sequence, beginning at step 100, that writes the data in memory. The next address at which data is to be stored in memory is available in *CA*. This address is kept current by software when a transfer sequence is not in progress.

References

1. *IEEE Standard 488-1975*, Institute of Electrical and Electronic Engineers, New York, 1975.
2. *IEEE Standard 796-1983*, Institute of Electrical and Electronic Engineers, New York, 1975.
3. J. C. Cluley, *Compute Interfacing and Online Operation*, Crane Russak, New York, 1975.
4. J. E. McNamara, *Technical Aspects of Data Communications*, Digital Equipment Corp., Maynard, Mass., 1977.
5. F. J. Hill and G. R. Peterson, *Digital Logic and Microprocessors*, Wiley, New York, 1984.
6. F. J. Hill, "Structure Specification With a Procedural Hardware Description Language," *IEEE Trans. on Computers*, Feb. 1981, pp. 157–161.
7. D. P. Siewiorek, C. G. Bell, and A. Newell, *Computer Structures: Principles and Examples*, McGraw–Hill, New York, 1982.
8. *MC68000 16-Bit Microprocessor User Manual*, 3rd ed., Prentice–Hall, Englewood Cliffs, N. J., 1982.

9. T. J. Chaney, and C. E. Molnar, "Anomalous Behavior of Synchronizer and Arbiter Circuits," *IEEE Trans. on Computers,* C-22, April 1973, pp. 421–422.

10. B. Liu and N. C. Gallagher, "On the 'Metastable Region' of Flip-Flop Circuits," *Proc. of the IEEE,* April 1977, pp. 581–583.

11. G. R. Couranz and D. F. Wann, "Theoretical and Experimental Behavior of Synchronizers Operating in the Metastable Region," *IEEE Trans. on Computers,* C-24, June 1975, 1975, pp. 604–616.

12. L. R. Marino, "General Theory of Metastable Operation," *IEEE Trans. on Computers,* C-30, No. 2, February 1981, pp. 107–115.

10 Interrupt and Memory-Mapped I/O

10.1 Introduction

In the last chapter, we investigated the basic procedures whereby reliable communications can be provided between independent digital modules or systems. These techniques are very general and are certainly not restricted to situations involving computers. However, the most common example of digital communications is found in the communications between computers and their input/output devices. In this chapter, we are concerned with the application of the techniques introduced in the last chapter to computer input/output systems. The importance of input/output in a computer system can scarcely be overstated, since this is the means by which the computer communicates with the "outside world." The computer is normally in control of the input/output process, but, as noted in the last chapter, there are situations in which a peripheral device must be able to initiate communications. Interrupt is a part of the communications problem because it is the means by which peripherals can request the "attention" of the computer when it is busy with other activities. Input/output operations are not the only reasons for interrupt, but they are probably the most common. Also, the special machine instructions dealing with interrupt are usually grouped with I/O instructions; therefore, it seems logical to consider interrupt and I/O together.

Among the most common I/O transducers are modems, printers, CRTs, keyboards, and floppy disk drives. These are all electromechanical devices of great complexity, but details of how they are constructed will not be considered here. We are concerned only with how the computer communicates with these devices. With regard to communications with the computer, all these devices have three special character-

345

istics that account for the special nature of the I/O problem. First, their operation is completely asynchronous with respect to the central processor. Second, their speed of operation is often orders of magnitude slower than that of the central processor. For example, the data rate of a typical printer would be 300 chars/sec, compared with a typical CPU rate of a million operations/sec. Third, their data format is usually quite different from that of the central processor.

From the standpoint of communication with the CPU, magnetic tape and disk are generally considered to be I/O devices because they share these same three special characteristics. We have previously considered these types of devices as memory, but this is simply a matter of point of view. These devices are memory in the sense that the CPU can store information in them and later retrieve it without human intervention; but they are I/O in the sense of requiring special techniques to deal with their characteristics of slow, asynchronous operation and special data formats.

There is probably more variation from computer to computer in the areas of interrupt and I/O design than in any other area of computer design. This being the case, we cannot hope to cover all possible techniques. In line with our belief that learning best proceeds from the specific to the general, we shall develop specific "typical" interrupt and I/O systems, and then comment on the variations and options open to the designer.

10.2   Memory-Mapped Input-Output

In the first two editions of this book, the emphasis was on *classical input-output* using the separate ***IOBUS*** and command/status bus as discussed in the last chapter. More recently, an alternative approach called *memory-mapped I/O* has become increasingly popular. The memory-mapped approach eliminates the need for the ***IOBUS*** and command/status bus as separate from the address and memory data buses in small computer systems. This is particularly attractive where the CPU is an integrated circuit package (i.e., a microprocessor).

Fig. 10.1 uses PMS to contrast the topology of the classical and memory-mapped I/O approaches. In Fig. 10.1a, the switch Sp represents the address and data buses while S represents the ***IOBUS*** and command/status bus or ***CSBUS***. The switch S' in the memory-mapped I/O organization of Fig. 10.1b must represent the function of all four of these buses. There are four obvious activities that must take place over the switch S (IOBUS and CSBUS) in Fig. 10.1a. These include the output of data, the input of data, the input of a status vector from a peripheral to the CPU, and the output of a command. The command includes the device ID as well as the actual command bits. The second column of Table 10.1 indicates the bus that accommodates each of these activities in the classical I/O organization.

The last column in Table 10.1 suggests how each of these five communications activities might be accommodated using only the buses making up switch Sp. Commands and data may be transmitted to peripherals using the data bus in much the same way data are written in RAM. Similarly, the input of status and data from a peripheral

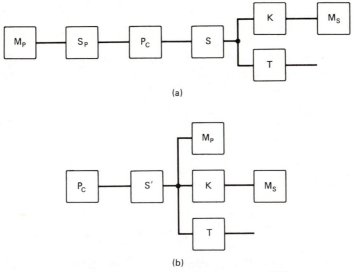

Figure 10.1. (a) Classical I/O vs (b) memory-mapped I/O.

will resemble a READ operation. You are probably familiar with microprocessor-based systems that function in just this way. In some fashion it was necessary to adjust the timing of either the read and write or the input-output to make them compatible. It is often preferable to accomplish read and write to RAM in a synchronous fashion with one clock period for each operation. Input-output to peripheral devices requires an asynchronous handshake, as discussed in Chapter 9. In some memory-mapped systems (e.g., the 8-bit 6502) all I/O is accomplished in synchronous fashion. In others (e.g., the Motorola 68000), an asynchronous handshake is provided for all read and write operations.

TABLE 10.1   Media for Classical and Memory-Mapped I/O

Activity	Classical I/O	Memory-mapped I/O
Output of command		
Device ID	*CSBUS*	Address bus
Command	*CSBUS*	Data bus
Input of status	*CSBUS*	Data bus
Output of data	*IOBUS*	Data bus
Input of data	*IOBUS*	Data bus
Read		
Address	Address bus	Address bus
Data	Data bus	Data bus
Write		
Address	Address bus	Address bus
Data	Data bus	Data bus

Of special interest is the handling of the device ID. In the classical approach introduced in Chapter 9, this ID will probably consist of 3 to 5 bits to identify one of a small number of devices. Broadcasting the device number on the address bus means that many more bits are available to specify the address of a device, 24 bits in the case of RIC. Of course, the addresses assigned to peripheral devices cannot conflict with those assigned to active random access memory. Still, the number of addresses required for I/O devices will be negligible compared to the total address space. For this reason, several addresses may be assigned to each I/O device to accommodate data registers and multiple command and status registers as required in individual cases.

It is also important to note that while Table 10.1 specifies that the address and data buses will support input-output, so that $S' = Sp$, it also implies that these buses must be time-shared. All activities require the data bus, so only one operation, read, write, or I/O, can take place at a time. On the positive side, special input-output instructions are required in classical I/O. For memory-mapped I/O, input of data or status is accomplished by the normal read instruction. Whether data or status is read is determined by whether a data register or a status register is addressed. Output of a command or data is accomplished by write.

Example 10.1

Design a special interface for connecting the simple printer of Examples 9.3 and 9.4 to the address and data buses of RIC to facilitate memory-mapped I/O. Provide for flexibility in the assignment of the device in the RIC address space. Assume that only the low-order 16 bits of the RIC data bus will be used to be consistent with these two examples. Assume that all read and write operations are synchronous, requiring a single clock period.

Solution

In Example 9.4, the interface was required to accept a command as part of the input status and output data operations. This was necessary because the mechanism for device identification is classically included in the command. Now, there will be no commands to the interface, only a write operation for output data and a read operation for input status. The printer interface will be assumed to contain two registers—a data register and a status register. The output of data will be accomplished by a write to the data register. The only means that will be provided for the computer to assess the progress of a print operation will be to read the status register from the interface. In this case, the status register will consist of only one flip-flop, **busy,** which will be connected to *DBUS*[0].

It seems natural to assign the data and status registers to consecutive addresses in the RIC address space. The high-order 23 address bits will be the same for the two registers, for *DR* the bit *ADBUS*[23] $= 0$, and for the status register *ADBUS*[23] $= 1$. Connections of the printer interface to the RIC buses are illustrated in Fig. 10.2. When the values that correctly address the printer interface appear on *ADBUS*[0:22], enable will be 1. The box labelled "Address logic" must necessarily be outside of the printer

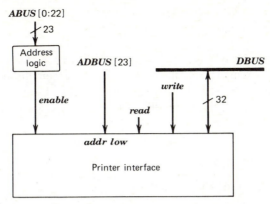

Figure 10.2. RIC connections to printer interface.

interface module if its two consecutive addresses are to be left unassigned. The following is the AHPL description of the modified printer interface.

MODULE: RIC/PRINTER INTERFACE
MEMORY: *DR*[16]; *CR*[8]; *busy; first*
INPUTS: *enable; addrlow; read; write; wait*
OUTPUTS: *CHAR*[8]; *print; feed.*
COMBUS: *DBUS*[32].

1   *DR* * (*write* $\wedge$ *enable* $\wedge$ $\overline{addrlow}$) $\leftarrow$ *DBUS*[16:31];
          $\rightarrow$($\overline{write \wedge enable \wedge \overline{addrlow}}$)/(1).
2   *first* $\leftarrow$ 1; *busy* $\leftarrow$ 1.
3   *CR* $\leftarrow$ (*DR*[8:15] ! *DR*[0:7]) * ($\overline{first, first}$).
4   *feed* = RETURN(*CR*); *print* = $\overline{\text{RETURN}(CR)}$.
5   null.
6     $\rightarrow$ (*wait*)/(6).
7   *first* $\leftarrow$ 0; *busy* $\leftarrow$ *first*;
          $\rightarrow$ ($\overline{first, first}$)/(3,1).
END SEQUENCE
          CONTROLRESET (1); *CHAR* = *CR*;
          DBUS[0] = *busy* * (*enable* $\wedge$ *read* $\wedge$ *addrlow*).
END.

Parallel control must still be present so that status may be read while a print operation is in progress, but the one-clock-period synchronous read feature makes it easy to implement. The required connection for "read status" is simply written after ENDSEQUENCE. The bit **addrlow** could have been omitted from the description here and in step 1, since in this simple example it will always be a 0 for a write and 1 for a read. It has been included for the sake of generality. The fact that only 16 data bits are used by the printer interface must be known by the systems programmer. Other peripherals may use all 32 bits.   ■

Since the ***busy*** *bit will end up in **AC**[0]* following a status read, a program-controlled output of 2 data bytes to the printer could be accomplished by the following very simple sequence of assembly language instructions. The symbolic addresses of the printer data and status registers are PRNTDATA and PRNTSTATUS, respectively.

CHK	MVT	PRNTSTATUS
	BMI	CHK
	MVT	DATA
	MVF	PRNTDATA

Providing for easy checking of bits of more complete status registers will require some special input-output instructions. This will be the topic of a subsequent section.

10.3   Interrupt System for RIC

Many possible situations can call for interrupt of the main program. Internal interrupts usually result from some sort of error condition, such as a memory parity error, a jump out of range, or a divide by zero. External interrupts most frequently result from requests for service from external devices. The very term *interrupt* is often misleading, as it implies an anomalous, unexpected situation that takes the CPU away from what it is "normally" doing. When the interrupt is caused by an error condition, this is the case. But errors are, we hope, rare events. The vast majority of interrupts come about in the course of input/output operations. You will even see the phrase "interrupt-driven system," referring to a system that spends most of its time waiting for some external device to request attention. A phrase such as *request for service* would be more descriptive, but *interrupt* is the accepted term.

Interrupt systems vary widely in detail, but certain basic features are common to virtually all computers. First, there must be one or more interrupt request lines that, when driven active, will interrupt the computer when it reaches an appropriate point in its operating sequence. In some systems, driving an interrupt request line active will set a flag that will remain set until the CPU responds. In other systems, the line must be held active until the CPU responds. The difference is primarily an electronic detail; the end result is the same. Second, steps must be built into the control sequence whereby the CPU can check the status of the interrupt lines or flags at appropriate intervals. This part of the process, the requesting of interrupts and checking for interrupt requests, is usually a hardware feature that proceeds automatically with little or no intervention by the programmer.

The next part of the interrupt process involves checking to determine where the interrupt request came from and allowing the programmer to decide whether or not the CPU should respond. This part of the process usually involves a combination of hardware and software. Finally, if a response to the interrupt is appropriate, the CPU must jump to an interrupt program or subroutine. The means for jumping to the interrupt program is usually a hardware feature. The program itself, which determines the response to the interrupt, that is, what is to be "done about it" is left entirely to the discretion of the programmer.

Let us now illustrate some of these concepts by designing an interrupt system for RIC. We shall start by designing a very simple system, of the type that will be found in small microprocessors, and shall then investigate some more complex alternatives. The RIC CPU will be provided with an active-high interrupt request line (*irq*). As long as this line is low, it will have no effect on the operations of the processor. This line will be connected to any devices in the system that are to be allowed to interrupt the CPU, and any of these can cause *irq* to be 1 (active). Each time RIC enters the fetch cycle, it will check *irq*. If *irq* = 0, the next instruction will be fetched in the normal manner. If *irq* = 1, the CPU will enter an interrupt cycle, provided that interrupts have not been disabled. When a computer system is initially installed, it will be determined, by the connections to the *irq* line, which devices will have the capability of interrupting. However, it is clearly important that the programmer be able to determine whether or not interrupts will be permitted at any particular time. For this reason, we will include an interrupt enable flag, (*ief*). This flag, like the carry flag, can be set or cleared by instructions provided for that purpose. When this flag is cleared, interrupts are disabled and *irq* cannot affect the processor. When *ief* = 1, the processor will be interrupted at the start of the fetch cycle if *irq* = 1.

To implement the interrupt cycle, we start by inserting a step 1A at the start of the fetch cycle.

1A $\rightarrow ((\overline{irq \wedge ief}), (irq \wedge ief))/(1,200)$.

1   *MA* ← *PC*.

         (Continue with normal fetch cycle)

If *irq* is low or interrupts are disabled, the sequence continues with the normal fetch cycle. If *irq* is active and interrupts are enabled, the sequence branches to step 200, which is the start of the interrupt sequence.

200   *ief* ← 0.
201   *SP* ← DEC(*SP*).
202   *MA* ← *SP; MD* ← 8 ⊤ 0, *PC*.
203   *ADBUS = MA; DBUS = MD; write* = 1.
204   *ADBUS* = 24 ⊤ 0; *MD* ← *DBUS; read* = 1.
205   *PC* ← *MD*[8:31];
         → (1A).

The interrupt cycle is basically a hardware jump to a subroutine. Step 200 clears *ief* to prevent any further interrupts until the interrupt routine has responded appropriately to the current interrupt. Steps 201 through 203 push the contents of the program counter, the address of the next instruction in the main program that has been interrupted, on the stack in preparation for return to the main program after completion of the interrupt routine. The second part of any jump to a subroutine is to load the address of the subroutine into *PC*. In the case of JSR, the address is a part of the instruction. For a jump to an interrupt subroutine, step 204 of the sequence obtains the contents of location 000000 in memory, which has been reserved for the address of the interrupt routine. This address, which must have been loaded into location 000000 by the programmer, will be transferred to *PC;* and a jump to step 1 will result in a fetch of the first instruction of the interrupt subroutine.

You should note carefully that this process does not "do anything about" the interrupt. The hardware process only preserves the address at which the the main program was interrupted and forces a jump to a routine to "do something about" the interrupt. It is the responsibility of the user of the machine to provide a routine to deal with interrupts and to load the address of this routine into the reserved location at 000000. The writing of interrupt routines is largely beyond the scope of this book. However, because we are concerned with designing the hardware interrupt systems so as to facilitate efficient processing of interrupts, a brief discussion of the main features of interrupt programs is in order.

The first part of the interrupt program will often involve inquiries to determine what occurrence or device generated the interrupt. As noted previously, several devices may be connected to the *irq* line and thus have the capability to generate an input. If that is the case, the interrupt program will usually start by issuing inquiries to the various devices to determine which one generated the interrupt. Having determined which device interrupted, the CPU will then send a signal to that device acknowledging the interrupt, at which point the device will remove the active signal from *irq*. The CPU will then take whatever action is appropriate to deal with the interrupt condition. If this action will require the use of any of the general-purpose registers, their contents will have to be pushed onto the stack to preserve the status of the interrupted program.

One important consideration in interrupt programs is the question of whether interrupts of the interrupt program should be allowed. Consider a situation where a computer is controlling an industrial process. Some interrupts may be generated by measurements indicating that emergency conditions exist that require immediate corrective action. Another interrupt may indicate that a printer is requesting that another line of text be sent. When an interrupt occurs, the interrupt system immediately prevents further interrupts by clearing *ief,* so that the interrupt program can determine the source of the interrupt. If it is determined that the interrupt was caused by one of the emergency conditions, no further interrupts should be allowed until appropriate corrective action has been taken. In this event, *ief* will be left cleared. If the interrupt comes from the printer, it is likely that the interrupt system will be re-enabled by setting *ief,* because no harm will be done if the printer is momentarily delayed in receiving the next line of text.

When the actions required to deal with the interrupt have been completed, control must be returned to the interrupted program. The first step in the return portion of the interrupt program will be clear *ief* if it was set to enable interrupts of the interrupt program. Next, if the contents of any registers have been pushed on the stack, they must be pulled off the stack and restored. The final instruction in the interrupt program will be RTI (ReTurn from Interrupt), which is implemented by steps 210 through 213. Because RTI is a separate instruction, step 210 will be reached, like the first step implementing any other instruction, following the instruction fetch and branching on the decoding of the instruction.

210   *ief* ← 1.
211   *MA* ← *SP; SP* ← INC(*SP*).
212   *ADBUS* = *MA; MD* ← *DBUS; read* = 1.
213   *PC* ← *MD*[8:31];
        → (1A).

This sequence is essentially the same as RTS, pulling the return address off the stack and returning to fetch the next instruction of the interrupted program. The only difference is that step 210 sets *ief*. This is necessary to restore the status of the interrupted program fully, because *ief* must have been set in that program for the interrupt to have occurred in the first place.

Reduced to essentials, the interrupt process described herein is simple enough. Prior to fetching each new instruction, the CPU checks for an interrupt request. If one is present and interrupts have been enabled, the address of the next instruction to be executed in the interrupted program is pushed on the stack and the address of a subroutine to deal with the interrupt routine is fetched from a reserved location in memory. When the interrupt routine is complete, the RTI instruction retrieves the address of the interrupted program from the stack and proceeds with that program from the point of interrupt. A critical "fine point" in this process is the timing of the disabling and enabling of the interrupt system as the computer switches from one program or subroutine to another.

The process of switching from one program to another is often referred to as *context switching*. When interrupting one program to execute another, it is essential that all information necessary to resume execution of the original program be preserved before the execution of the new program starts. This collection of information needed to continue execution of the interrupted program defines the *status* or *context* of the program. If the contexts of the two programs are mixed, disaster is sure to occur.

As an example, suppose we omit step 200 of the interrupt sequence and leave it to the programmer to disable the interrupt system as a part of the interrupt subroutine. The interrupt sequence moves the address of the interrupt routine to *PC* and returns to step 1A to fetch the first instruction of that routine. When that occurs, the CPU will find *irq* still active, since the original interrupt has never been acknowledged. The CPU will thus be interrupted again, and the CPU will enter an endless loop, responding to the same interrupt over and over. A possible remedy is to let step 205 return to step 1 instead of 1A, so that *irq* will have no effect on the fetch of the first instruction of the interrupt subroutine. If that first instruction clears *ief,* the process can then proceed smoothly. But, suppose the programmer forgets to clear *ief* on the first instruction of the interrupt routine. (And you may absolutely rely on programmers to forget to do things they should do). Then the CPU will be interrupted on the fetch of the second instruction of the interrupt routine. The interrupt sequence will now push the second address of the interrupt routine on the stack, while the various registers will reflect the status of the interrupted main program. The result is mixed context and, no matter what happens from this point on, any attempt to return to the original program is doomed to failure.

Similar observations apply to the re-enabling of the interrupt system on RTI (see Problem, 10.4). These problems emphasize the importance of complete understanding of the interrupt process by the computer architect. If the hardware parts of the interrupt sequence are not properly designed, no amount of ingenuity on the part of programmers can keep things from going wrong. On the other hand, no amount of ingenuity on the part of the designer can produce a system that is immune to programmer errors. All computer systems are an inseparable mix of hardware and software, and both designers and programmers must be aware of the ways in which the hardware and software interact.

One area where interrupt systems differ is in the amount of information automatically saved when an interrupt occurs. In the system as described earlier, we have provided for saving the absolute minimum amount of information needed to preserve the context of the interrupted program. By contrast, some computers will automatically save the contents of all the operating registers. The rationale for doing this is that it is much faster do it automatically with a hardware sequence than to do it with software in the interrupt program. On the other hand, if any of the registers are not needed by the interrupt program, the time spent saving their contents is wasted. In the case of RIC, there are two registers other than *PC* that will almost certainly be used in even the simplest interrupt programs, the accumulator and the status register. On that basis, we shall modify the preceding sequences to provide for automatic saving and restoring of *AC* and *SR*.

200	*ief* ← 0.
201	*SP* ← DEC(*SP*).
202	*MA* ← *SP; MD* ← 8 ⊤ 0, *PC; SP* ← DEC(*SP*)
203	*ADBUS* = *MA; DBUS* = *MD; write* = 1;
	MA ← *SP; MD* ← 24 ⊤ 0, *SR; SP* ← DEC(*SP*).
204	*ADBUS* = *MA; DBUS* = *MD; write* = 1;
	MA ← *SP; MD* ← *AC*.
205	*ADBUS* = *MA; DBUS* = *MD; write* = 1.
206	*ADBUS* = 24 ⊤ 0; *MD* ← *DBUS; read* = 1.
207	*PC* ← *MD*[8:31];
	→ (1A).

You will note that we have taken full advantage of the transfer timing that permits changing a register at the same time its previous contents are being used. for example, in Step 202 we decrement *SP* in preparation for the write of *SR* at the same time we transmit the address for storing **PC** to **MA.** In Step 203, we transmit the address for **SR** to **MA** and the contents of **SR** to **MD** at the same time we write the contents of **PC** to the stack. In this manner, we accomplish the saving of **SR** and **PC** at the expense of only two additional steps. By contrast, pushing these two registers on the stack by programming would require the execution of three instructions, involving about 20 steps.

The RTI sequence must be similarly modified to retrieve **AC** and **SR** from the stack.

210	*ief* ← 1.
211	**MA** ← **SP; SP** ← INC(**SP**).
212	**ADBUS** = **MA; MD** ← **DBUS; read** = 1; **MA** ← **SP; SP** ← INC(**SP**).
213	**ADBUS** = **MA; MD** ← **DBUS; read** = 1; **AC** ← **MD; MA** ← **SP; SP** ← INC(**SP**).
214	**ADBUS** = **MA; MD** ← **DBUS; read** = 1; **SR** ← **MD**[24:31].
215	**PC** ← **MD**[8:31]; →(1A).

Again, because of the use of overlapping steps, this modification requires only two additional steps.

The interrupt system just described, with only one interrupt line, is known as a *non-vectored* interrupt system. There are usually a number of possible interrupt sources connected to this line, so that the interrupt program must include a software *polling* routine to identify which device generated the interrupt. We saw that using a hardware sequence to save the registers can save considerable time compared to a software routine to accomplish the same purpose. Let us consider the possiblity of using hardware to identify the interrupt source. For this purpose, each possible interrupt source will have a separate interrupt line, for example, *int1* to *int15* for a system with 15 possible interrupt sources. These lines will be ORed together to drive the *irq* line of the computer and will also *vector* (i.e., point) the computer to a location containing the address of a subroutine to deal with a specific interrupt source. Such a system is known as a *vectored interrupt system*. There are many possible ways to construct a vectored interrupt system. Fig. 10.3 illustrates one possible approach.

As noted in the preceding paragraph, the separate interrupt lines are OR'ed to drive the *irq* line to the computer. They also provide the inputs to a 15 × 4 ROM that generates a 4-bit binary output indicating the number of the interrupt line, that is, 0001 to 1111. The 24 bits of **ADBUS** are fed to a NOR gate, which produces a 1 only if the address is all 0's, that is, hex 000000. The low-order 4 bits of the address are fed to a quad 2-to-1 multiplexer controlled by the NOR gate along with the 4-bit code generated by the ROM. If the address is anything but 000000, the signal to the G1 input of the multiplexer will be 0, and the low-order 4 bits of the address will pass on through without modification. If the address issued by the computer is 000000, the signal to G1 will be 1 and the 4-bit vector from the ROM will become the low-

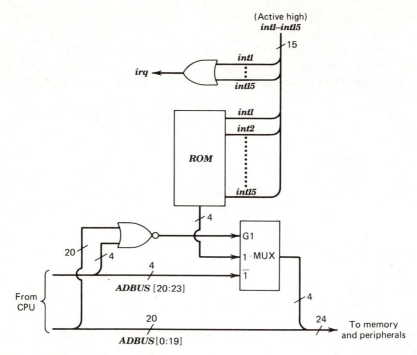

Figure 10.3. Interrupt vectoring system.

order 4 bits of address. The computer is thus vectored to a location in the range 000001 to 00000F, corresponding to the number of the interrupt source. These locations will have been previously loaded with the addresses of the routines for the various interrupt conditions. It should be noted that, with this scheme, the address 000000 cannot be included in the address space at all. Because any reference to this address generates a signal that an interrupt is being processed, it cannot be read or written to. It cannot even be used to store the address of an interrupt routine, because there is no possible way to write that address into location 000000.

In the interrupt system described earlier, the programmer can block interrupts entirely through the use of the *ief* flag. Individual interrupts can then be blocked by control of the polling routine. With multiple interrupts, a hardware procedure for controlling individual interrupts is usually included. The use of the mask register (*MR*) will permit the programmer to enable or disable individual interrupt sources selectively. The necessary hardware is shown in Fig. 10.4. *MR* is a 16-bit register with bit-0 unused, the other 15 bits corresponding to the 15 interrupt lines. The programmer can load *MR* with 0's and 1's as desired, with a 1 indicating that the corresponding interrupt line is enabled, a 0 indicating that it is disabled.

It will probably have occurred to you that the system shown in Fig. 10.3 will work only if there is only one interrupt present at any given time. If more than one enabled interrupt line goes high at the same time, the ROM will be accessed on more

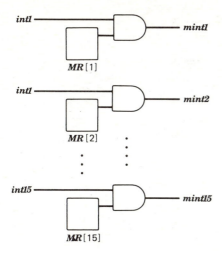

intl — minth

intl — mint2

intl5 — mintl5

Figure 10.4. Masking of interrupt signals.

than one address line and the output vector will be meaningless. In any vectored system there must be some method of deciding which interrupt will take priority when two or more occur at the same time. One method is to use a *priority network* such as shown in Fig. 10.5. Here is is assumed that priority is in numerical order, that is, **intl** has the highest priority and **int15** has the lowest priority. In this network, only one output line will be active at a time, corresponding to the currently active interrupt line with the highest priority. The active address line going to the ROM will be the highest priority active interrupt line that has been enabled by the programmer.

A priority network with n inputs may be described by the following combinational logic unit description.

```
CLUNIT: PRI(X){n}.
    INPUTS: X[n].
    OUTPUTS: OUT[n].
    CTERMS: Y[n].
BODY
    OUT[0] = X[0];
    Y[0] = X[0];
    FOR I = 1 TO n − 1 CONSTRUCT
        OUT[I] = X[I] ∧ Y[I − 1];
        Y[I] = Y[I − 1] ∨ X[I]
    ROF.
END.
```

Invoking this description for $n = 15$ will result in the network given in Fig. 10.5, with **minti** = $X[i]$ and **PRIi** = $OUT[i]$.

A limitation of this method is the fact that the priority is fixed once the interrupt

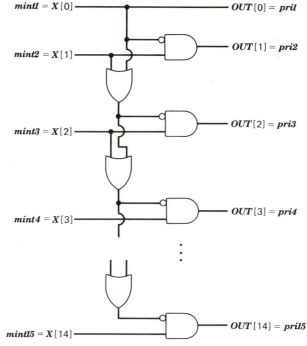

Figure 10.5. Interrupt priority network.

sources have been connected to specific inputs to the network. A programmer has limited control of priority through the mask register. For example, a programmer can give *int2* a higher priority than *int1* by turning off *int1,* but the priority cannot be reversed with both enabled. The complete vectored interrupt system combining all these features is shown in Fig. 10.6.

A complete interrupt control unit such as shown in Fig. 10.6 can easily be implemented on a single VLSI chip, which can be connected between the CPU and the various peripherals. This approach is widely applied in microcomputer systems. In such as system, *MR* will occupy a location in the address space and the programmer will establish the desired masking by writing to this location. In mainframe computers, comparable hardware may be included as a part of the CPU, in which case *MR* may be added to the register set, rather than being in the address space. Programming details will differ, but the basic operation will be the same.

More complex systems will allow the programmer to change the priorities of various interrupt sources. This feature is particularly likely to be found in systems intended for interrupt-driven environments. In such systems, there may be no "main program" in the usual sense. Instead, the system may be continually switching between different processes associated with different interrupt sources. Typically, each process will be assigned a priority by the programmer, which can be changed at any time. Each interrupt source may have a register in its control unit that can be loaded with

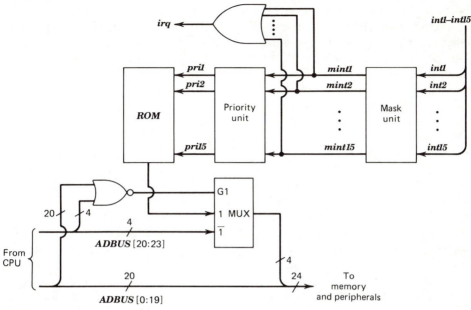

Figure 10.6. Vectored interrupt control unit.

the assigned priority. When a device signals an interrupt, it also signals its priority. This priority is automatically compared with the priority of the process currently being executed. If the process requesting interrupt has a higher priority, it will interrupt the current process. If not, it will go into a queue with other processes waiting to interrupt, positioned in the queue according to its relative priority. When the current process is complete, the highest-priority process in the interrupt queue will commence execution. Such systems allow dynamic control of system priorities to adjust to changing conditions. For example, the importance of servicing a given unit may depend on how long it has been since it was last serviced. In this case, the priority could be increased at regular intervals.

10.4 Options in the Control of Input-Output Transfers

In Section 10.2, we saw a simple example of a *program controlled output* transfer. This simplest approach has the drawback of being the most wasteful of CPU time. The amount of lost CPU time will, of course, depend on how soon before the printer is ready the loop

```
CHK    MVT    PRNTSTATUS
       BMI    CHK
```

is actually entered. Improvement can be achieved by either (1) entering the loop after an interrupt is received from the printer indicating that data is ready or (2) including other activity in the same loop so that PRINTSTATUS is checked only periodically interspersed with other operations. As we learned in the previous section, more over-head is associated with each interrupt than can be justified by the output of just one word. The second option still uses many cycles of the CPU for mere status checking and is often inconvenient to implement.

Further improvement would seem to require taking routine input-output com-pletely out of the hands of the hardware process that controls instruction execution. In this section, we shall explore ways in which this can be accomplished by first establishing blocks of data in consecutive memory addresses and then providing to another process the parameters necessary to control the actual series of I/O transfers. Areas of memory reserved for storing blocks of data for I/O will be referred to as *buffers*. Input or output of single words, often control parameters, will be left under program control. Usually, this type of information will be read or written from or to a continuously accessible register in a single memory cycle without a status check.

The most clear-cut and now the most common approach to taking input-output out of the hands of the executing program is called *direct memory access* (DMA), as symbolized by Fig. 10.7b. In Figs. 10.7a and b we see two possible routes for a data transfer between primary and secondary storage. In Fig. 10.7a, the route is by way of a CPU data register (*AC* in RIC I). This is the path for a program-controlled transfer. In the case of Fig. 10.7b, the data word does not pass through the CPU. To make possible the use of this path, it is necessary to temporarily deprive the CPU of the right to use the bus S' and award the right to the secondary storage controller. A special hardware process is required to serve as an *arbitrator* of the control of the bus S'. This is the function of controller K' in Fig. 10.7b, an AHPL description of which will be given in Section 10.6.

Various types of input/output systems may be categorized in terms of the possible combinations of true or false for the three statements A, B, and C that follow. We

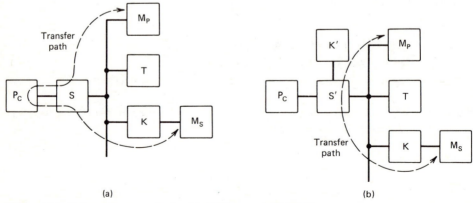

(a)   (b)

Figure 10.7. Information transfer by (a) CPU control (b) DMA.

have already observed that for DMA at least statements A and C must be true. It must be possible for a process other than program execution and a process in a device outside of the CPU to gain control of S'. This discussion presumes memory mapped I/O, although a similar analysis is possible given use of the IOBUS.

A. A process other than program execution can gain control of the data and address buses (S').
B. Control of the bus (S') is arbitrated and granted on a cycle-by-cycle basis.
C. A process in a device outside of the CPU may be granted the right to place an address on bus S'.

The map of Fig. 10.8 lists the form of I/O transfer corresponding to each meaningful combination of the truth values of statements A, B, and C. The chart shows that true DMA requires that the bus arbitrator K' accept requests for bus control and separately grant use of the bus every clock period (or every memory cycle if the memory is asynchronous or if the memory cycle is a multiple of the CPU clock period). This provision maximizes the frequency of activity on S' by allowing external devices to use memory cycles available while the program process executes steps not requiring memory access. Another approach to DMA would require the program process to possibly relinquish control of the bus only between instructions. This approach, labelled *Simple DMA* in Fig. 10.8, is easier to implement but less effective.

Where only statement A is true, a process other than the program execution process, but only one within the CPU, can gain control of S'. The implementation of this alternative has been called *buffered I/O* and was very commonly used in classical computer organizations. In the days of expensive logic, buffered I/O was more economical to implement than was DMA because most of the implementation was centered in the CPU. The controllers in the peripheral equipment remained rather simple. The disadvantage of buffered I/O is that sets of control lines similar to the interrupt lines of Fig. 9.15b must fan in from each peripheral equipment to the CPU. Given the current state of affairs of inexpensive logic within pin-limited IC chips, the balance has tipped in favor of DMA. No example of buffered I/O implementation will be given herein. The interested reader is referred to Chapter 10 of the second edition.

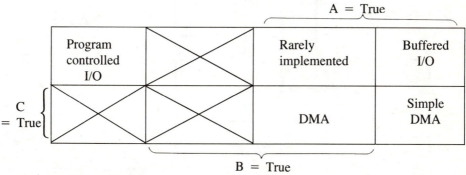

Figure 10.8. I/O transfer options.

If all the preceding statements are false, the only option is program-controlled I/O. Of course, program-controlled I/O will always be an available option for handling exceptional cases.

10.5   A Device Controller for RIC DMA

In general, several peripherals may be connected to the primary memory bus S′ of RIC. The RIC primary memory bus is a synchronous bus with transactions to and from memory taking place in one clock period. In Section 10.9, we shall argue the advantages of placing a second bus, in this case asynchronous, between peripherals and the primary memory bus. In this section, however, we shall illustrate the mechanism through which DMA could be accomplished by a peripheral directly across this primary memory bus. Fig. 10.9 focuses on the organization of a single peripheral. We shall develop the mechanism necessary to transfer a block data between a buffer area within RIC memory and a buffer in the peripheral. Processing the data within a peripheral will be left for Chapter 11, where a number of devices will be considered.

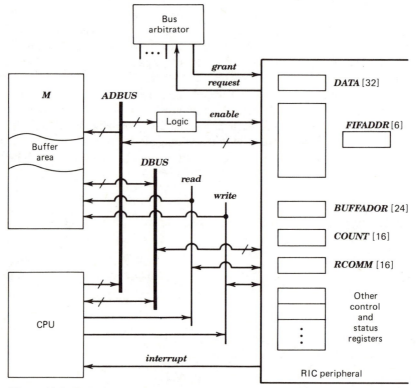

Figure 10.9. DMA across the RIC primary memory bus.

An address space consisting of 16 spaces will be allocated to each peripheral. The low-order address XXXXX0 will be assigned to the 32-bit data register, **DATA**. The next three addresses will be assigned to control registers, **BUFFADDR**[24], **COUNT**[16], and **RCOMM**[16], respectively. The fact that these registers are less than 32 bits means only that some high-order bits of the **DBUS** will not be involved in a read or write operation. The remaining 12 addresses will be assigned to a bank of 12 additional control and status registers that will control the handling of the data by a particular device but will not be discussed here. The buffer in the peripheral will be a small static RAM, **FIFO**⟨64⟩[16], organized to function in a first-in first-out fashion. An address register, **FIFADDR**[6], is provided for the **FIFO** so that data can be entered by address from the low end of the **FIFO**, eventually to be read out in the same order.

The bits in the transfer control/status register, **RCOMM**, are assigned as follows. (Note that *input* and *output* are relative to memory.) *Full* and *Empty* indicate the status of the buffer stack.

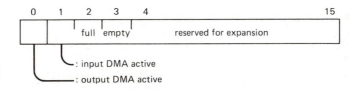

The CPU may read the status of **RCOMM** at any time. Completion of a DMA activity or filling or emptying the **FIFO** may cause the peripheral to generate an interrupt that will cause RIC to check status. The CPU will initiate a DMA activity by initializing **BUFFADDR** and **COUNT** by write operations and then writing a 1 to the appropriate bit **RCOMM**[0] or **RCOMM**[1]. (We assume that bits 2 and 3 are read-only from **DBUS**.) During the DMA process, the peripheral must signal the arbitrator with a 1 on line *request* each time it desires use of the bus. The request may remain on until a one-period reply is received on line *grant*. The read or write operation must take place during the clock period immediately following the period in which *grant* is 1. The potential for intolerably long logic path delay in the request-grant path will be considered in the next section.

A partial AHPL description of the I/O device follows. Those registers involved in program control read or write or DMA implementation are declared; only the steps implementing DMA output from RIC memory are given.

MODULE: RICPERIPHERAL
  MEMORY: **FIFO**⟨64⟩ [16]; **DATA**[32]; **COUNT**[16]; **RCOMM**[16];
                 BUFFADDR[24]; **OTHERREG**⟨12⟩ [16]; **FIFADDR**[6].
  INPUTS: *enable*; *grant*.
  OUTPUTS: *request*; *interrupt*.
  COMBUSES: **ADBUS**[24]; **DBUS**[32]; *read*; *write*.

1    $FIFADDR \leftarrow 6 \top 0$;
     $\rightarrow (RCOMM[0], RCOMM[1], \overline{RCOMM[0]}\wedge\overline{RCOMM[1]})/(2, ?, 1)$.
2    $request = 1$;
     $\rightarrow (grant)/(2)$.
3    $ADBUS = BUFFADDR$; $read = 1$; $DATA \leftarrow DBUS$.
4    $FIFO * DCD(FIFADDR) \leftarrow DATA[16:31]$;
     $RCOMM[3] \leftarrow 0$;
     $FIFADDR \leftarrow INC(FIFADDR)$.
5    $FIFO * DCD(FIFADDR) \leftarrow DATA[0:15]$;
     $FIFADDR \leftarrow INC(FIFADDR)$;
     $BUFFADDR \leftarrow INC(BUFFADDR)$;
     $COUNT \leftarrow DEC(COUNT)$.
6    $\rightarrow ((\vee/COUNT) \wedge (\vee/FIFADDR))/(2)$.
7    $interrupt = 1$; $RCOMM[0] * (\overline{\vee/COUNT}) \leftarrow 0$;
     $RCOMM[2] * (\overline{\vee/FIFADDR}) \leftarrow 1$.

·
·
·

ENDSEQUENCE
CONTROLRESET(1);
$DBUS = DATA * (read \wedge enable \wedge DCD[0] (ADBUS[20:23]))$;
$DBUS[16:31] = (RCOMM!OTHERREG) * (read \wedge enable$
                                    $\wedge DCD[3:15](ADBUS[20:23]))$;
$DATA * (write \wedge enable \wedge DCD[0](ADBUS[20:23])) \leftarrow DBUS$;
$BUFFADDR * (write \wedge enable \wedge DCD[1](ADBUS[20:23])) \leftarrow$
                                                        $DBUS[8:31]$;
$COUNT * (write \wedge enable \wedge DCD[2](ADBUS[20:23])) \leftarrow DBUS[16:31]$;
$RCOMM[0:1] * (write \wedge enable \wedge DCD[3] (ADBUS[20:23])) \leftarrow$
                                                        $DBUS[16:17]$;
$OTHERREG * (write \wedge enable \wedge DCD[4:15](ADBUS[20:23])) \leftarrow$
                                                        $DBUS[16:31]$.
END.

We note that the read and write operations are implemented as single clock-period operations after ENDSEQUENCE. It is assumed that control waits at step 1 when no DMA block transfer is in progress. By writing a 1 to $RCOMM[1]$, the CPU causes DMA input to memory to begin. Similarly, a 1 written to $RCOMM[0]$ will cause control to go to step 2 to begin DMA output from memory. For each transfer, a bus request is issued to the arbitrator at step 2. If a grant appears, the desired reference to RAM is accomplished by step 3 during the very next clock period. Steps 4 and 5 break the data word into two halfwords for storage in the **FIFO.** The **FIFO** address is incremented during each of these steps. Only step 5 increments $BUFFADDR$ to the address of the next 32-bit word in the buffer area of RAM. As part of the initialization by the CPU, the register $COUNT$ was set to the number of words in the

RAM buffer area. The counter is decremented each time control reaches step 5; and when **COUNT** reaches 0, the DMA activity is complete. We also check for the possibility that the **FIFO** has been filled at step 6. If either the **FIFO** is full or the transfer is complete, an interrupt is generated and DMA activity stops.

For a specific peripheral device, additional steps will be included to move the information on to secondary storage or to a transducer. These steps might begin after DMA is complete, another process could be simultaneously active with the DMA. Interaction between these two processes would be delicate, since both would be accessing the **FIFO**. A third and more likely alternative would be for control to switch back and forth between DMA mode and local storage or send mode on a word-by-word basis. This approach will require some modification in the preceding steps.

10.6 Design of an Arbitrator for a Fast Synchronous Bus

In this section, we shall design an arbitrator that will control access to the primary memory bus of RIC and allow direct memory access as discussed in the previous section. Fig. 10.10a depicts a particular configuration including a CPU and three controllers for I/O devices whose requests for direct memory access must be arbitrated

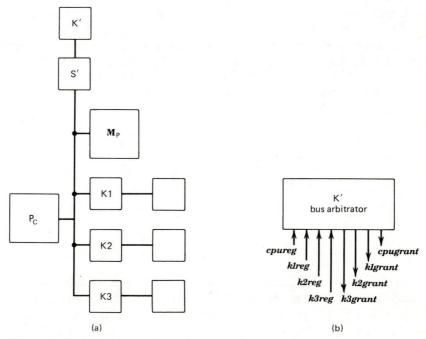

(a)

(b)

Figure 10.10. Arbitration of RIC primary memory bus.

by the bus controller K′. You will note the modified placement of the S′ and K′ boxes in Fig. 10.10a from the usual PMS notation. The notation of Fig. 10.10a will be used when the bus is arbitrated by an external controller rather than a CPU. We assume that each controller and the CPU are connected directly to the arbitrator by a line labelled *request*, and a line labelled *grant*, as shown in Fig. 10.10b.

Various computer systems have used other approaches to arbitration that do not require the convergence of all request lines at a central point. An example is a chain topology used in the Digital Equipment Corporation Unibus. The amount of combinational logic required by the scheme of Fig. 10.10b will be shown to increase faster than linearly as the number of request and grant lines increases. This factor and IC pin limitations are disadvantages of this approach. However, convergence of the request lines always offers the potential for the most rapid response. Our approach shall be to rely on the parallel arbitration of Fig. 10.10b and to look for a hierarchy of buses and controllers as the means of accommodating large numbers of peripherals.

The simplest criteria for resolving simultaneous DMA requests is a fixed ordering of priority among the various devices. To explore this alternative, let us assign the highest priority to the CPU, second highest to K1, and so on. As with the example in the previous section, the three peripheral controllers will be designed so as not to request the bus for two separate transactions during two consecutive clock periods. No such restriction need be placed on the CPU, since it is the highest priority device and will receive a grant during each period it makes a request. Consistent with the RICPERIPHERAL module of the previous section, *the use of the bus will always take place during the clock period immediately following the bus grant signal.* Fig. 10.11 characterizes the behavior expected from the arbitrator. To avoid unnecessary detail, use of the bus is represented in the figure only for the case of the CPU.

The bus arbitrator may be expressed in AHPL as follows. It can be seen that the arbitrator consists essentially of the combinational logic unit DMAPRI. Given the order of priorities and restrictions on the request signals discussed earlier, this network can be a four-input version of the network PRI introduced in Section 10.3 to establish interrupt priority.

> MODULE: ARBITRATOR
> INPUTS: *cpureq*; *k1req*; *k2req*; *k3req.*
> OUTPUTS: *cpugrant*; *k1grant*; *k2grant*; *k3grant.*
> LABELS: *REQUEST* = *cpureq, k1req, k2req, k3req*;
>   *GRANT* = *cpugrant, k1grant, k2grant, k3grant.*
> ENDSEQUENCE
>   *GRANT* = DMAPRI(*REQUEST*).
> END.

So far, we have considered only a fixed-priority assignment with the CPU having the highest priority. There are drawbacks both to fixed priority and to assigning highest priority to the CPU. If the number of control steps are reduced to a minimum and timing optimized, the CPU may attempt to access memory every other cycle. For an 8-bit microprocessor where several memory accesses are required to obtain an instruc-

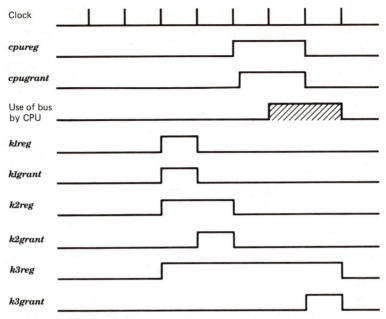

Figure 10.11. Expected response of DMA arbitrator.

tion, the percentage of CPU accesses is even higher. As will be illustrated in the following example, CPU domination of memory may make it impossible for a peripheral controller to move data to RAM at the rate it is read from secondary storage.

Example 10.2

Devise a priority scheme for the arbitrator that guarantees that the DMA bus will accommodate the data rates of all peripherals shown in the PMS diagram of Fig. 10.12.

Solution

We note the bus specification to be 8 Mbytes/sec. Since the word length on the bus is 32 bits, the clock rate is 2 MHz. When the secondary storage device controlled by K1 is active at its maximum data rate, it will require 25% of the bus capacity. The controller K3 could require 10%. If the CPU used no more than 50% of the bus capacity, the system could function. There can, however, be no guarantee of this if the CPU has highest priority and can retain control of the bus for successive memory cycles. One simple approach that has been used is to simply assign the CPU the lowest priority. Alternatively, highest priority could be rotated from device to device, so that all have equal access to service. Some order of priority must be in effect at any given time so that one of a set of simultaneous requests can be selected. ∎

Any decision such as suggested by the previous example to limit the access to memory on the part of RIC would force significant modifications in the RIC control

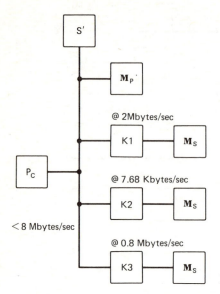

Figure 10.12. Priority determination.

sequence. If RIC were able to expect the arbitrator response illustrated by Fig. 10.11, it would not actually check the incoming grant signal, and the control sequence would be modified only to the extent of adding a *cpureq* $= 1$ one step in advance of every read or write operation. If *cpugrant* is not automatically forthcoming, it must be checked each time a request is issued. Steps 1 and 2 from Section 6.4 are shown here for the case where the grant is automatic.

1   *MA* $\leftarrow$ *PC*; *PC* $\leftarrow$ INC(*PC*); *cpureq* $= 1$.
2   *ADBUS* $=$ *MA*; *read* $= 1$; *MD* $\leftarrow$ *DBUS*.

If *cpugrant* is not automatic, the value of *cpureq* must be held at 1 until *cpugrant* is received. Clearly, the program counter cannot be allowed to increment repeatedly while control waits at step 1. In this case, the incrementing operation is moved to step 2 with the following result.

1   *MA* $\leftarrow$ *PC*; *cpureq* $= 1$;
       $\rightarrow$ (*cpugrant*)/(1).
2   *ADBUS* $=$ *MA*; *read* $= 1$; *MD* $\leftarrow$ *DBUS*;
       PC $\leftarrow$ INC(*PC*).

Other pairs of steps involving memory operations will require similar modifications on a case-by-case basis.

Example 10.3

Modify the AHPL description of the arbitrator just presented to implement the scheme of rotating the order of priority as discussed in Example 10.2. Include the modified combinational logic unit description, DMAPRI.

Solution

In addition to providing a more complicated combinational logic unit, it is necessary
to add a shift register, *RPRI*, which will be rotated left each clock period and will
continuously store a 1 only in the flip-flop corresponding to the highest priority request
line.

> MODULE: ARBITRATOR
>   INPUTS: *cpureq*; *k1req*; *k2req*; *k3req*; *reset*.
>   OUTPUTS: *cpugrant*; *k1grant*; *k2grant*; *k3grant*.
>   MEMORY: *RPRI*[4].
>   LABELS: *REQUEST* = *cpureq, k1req, k2req, k3req*;
>   *GRANT* = *cpugrant, k1grant, k2grant, k3grant*.
> ENDSEQUENCE
>   *RPRI* ← (*RPRI*[1:3],*RPRI*[0] ! 1,0,0,0) * ($\overline{reset,reset}$);
>   *GRANT* = DMAPRI(*REQUEST*; *RPRI*).
> END.

The modification given here may seem simple, but the resulting combinational
logic unit is quite complex. Separate expressions are shown for each of the four grant
lines. It would be possible to condense the description into a single line within a FOR
statement using another combinational logic unit, RIGHT, where RIGHT(Y) =
Y[3],Y[0:2]; but this would add nothing to the clarity. For a larger number of request
lines, this option would be helpful, although logic complexity would suggest the use
of DMAPRI only for a small number of lines. This more compact description will be
left as a problem for you.

> CLUNIT: DMAPRI(X;RP).
>   INPUTS: X[4]; RP[4].
>   OUTPUTS: *OUT*[4].
> BODY
>   *OUT*[0] = X[0] $\land$ (RP[0] $\land$ $\overline{RP[3]}$ $\land$ $\overline{X[3]}$ $\lor$ RP[2] $\land$ $\overline{X[2]}$ $\land$ $\overline{X[3]}$
> $\lor$ RP[1] $\land$ $\overline{X[1]}$ $\land$ $\overline{X[2]}$ $\land$ $\overline{X[3]}$);
>   *OUT*[1] = X[1] $\land$ (RP[1] $\lor$ RP[0] $\land$ $\overline{X[0]}$ $\lor$ RP[3] $\land$ $\overline{X[3]}$ $\land$ $\overline{X[0]}$
> $\lor$ RP[2] $\land$ $\overline{X[2]}$ $\land$ $\overline{X[3]}$ $\land$ $\overline{X[0]}$);
>   *OUT*[2] = X[2] $\land$ (RP[2] $\lor$ RP[1] $\land$ $\overline{X[1]}$ $\lor$ RP[0] $\land$ $\overline{X[0]}$ $\land$ $\overline{X[1]}$
> $\lor$ RP[3] $\land$ $\overline{X[3]}$ $\land$ $\overline{X[0]}$ $\land$ $\overline{X[1]}$);
>   *OUT*[3] = X[3] $\land$ (RP[3] $\lor$ RP[2] $\land$ $\overline{X[2]}$ $\lor$ RP[1] $\land$ $\overline{X[1]}$ $\land$ $\overline{X[2]}$
> $\lor$ RP[0] $\land$ $\overline{X[0]}$ $\land$ $\overline{X[1]}$ $\land$ $\overline{X[2]}$).
> END.   ∎

10.7 External Address Determination

We saw in Section 6.10 that there are many addressing modes (e.g., indirect or referred)
in which the actual address of the data is not included directly in the instruction stream

but is a function of registers in the CPU. If an address determined according to any of these addressing modes falls into the address space of a peripheral device, it may be further modified as a function of registers in that device. This technique can be used to extend the effective address space assigned to a peripheral device.

In the "classic" form of indirect addressing (see Fig. 2.4), the effective address of the data is stored in a location in memory. In the execution of an indirect address cycle, the address of the location containing the effective address is sent out on *ADBUS* and the contents of this location are sent back to the CPU on *DBUS*. The CPU then sends this effective address out on *ADBUS* to indicate the location of the actual data. The entire process is controlled entirely by the CPU. As seen by the memory, the process simply consists of two complete memory cycles in no way different from any other memory cycles.

The role of the addressed device is more active if the contents of an addressed register are used as the indirect address for a secondary address space local to the device. For example, suppose a peripheral device includes one special register, *IN-DIR*[8], and a local array **LOCARRAY**$\langle 256 \rangle)[32]$ that is assigned only one address, conveniently FFFFFF in RIC address space. A write to FFFFFF may be redirected to any location in the array, as specified by *INDIR*, by including statement 10.1 in the AHPL description of the device.

$$\textbf{LOCARRAY} * (\textit{write} \wedge (\wedge/ADBUS) \wedge \text{DCD}(\textit{INDIR})) \leftarrow \textit{DBUS} \qquad (10.1)$$

The register *INDIR* contains the indirect address to a local address space. This register may be manipulated locally or written into by RIC, if one more location in RIC address space is assigned to this peripheral module.

There are many programming applications of indirect addressing, including parameter passing following subroutine calls, and at least one special attraction to the hardware designer. That is, referred addressing can provide for addresses longer than the number of address bits in an instruction or instruction stream. In RIC, the main address length is 24 bits. When an indirect reference is performed, the CPU gets back 32 bits. If all were used, as a 32-bit address, we would have access to an address space of 4 billion locations, instead of 16 million. External indirect addressing, as discussed in the previous paragraph, similarly increases the total number of addressable locations.

External indirect addressing through locations in peripherals is useful if those peripherals include the ability, within their own loci of control, to update, maintain, and generally manipulate these addresses so that actual loading of addresses by the CPU will be a relatively infrequent occurrence. Consider the DMA peripheral discussed in Section 10.5. A pointer to **FIFO** is initialized in register *FIFADDR*; and the CPU loads *COUNT* and *BUFFADDR*. The peripheral then takes over control of these registers as an array of words are transferred to RIC memory. Indeed, *FIFADDR* could be considered to contain an external indirect address except that it is controlled by the peripheral, not by the CPU. If RICPERIPHERAL were designed for program controlled transfers rather than DMA, triggering read statement 10.2 would result in the transfer of a word from **FIFO** to the RIC accumulator. The function, *enable* = 1, indicates that the single location of **FIFO** in RIC address space has been addressed.

$$DBUS[16:31] = \textbf{FIFO} * (\textbf{\textit{enable}} \wedge \textbf{\textit{read}} \wedge \text{DCD}(\textbf{\textit{FIFADDR}})) \qquad (10.2)$$

Program control of the transfer of the **FIFO** array would involve a status check to ascertain that **FIFADDR** had been incremented before each read operation. The buffer address in primary memory would be under control of the CPU.

It may seem pointless to attempt to expand a 24-bit or 32-bit address space by mapping individual addresses into small arrays. The reason for so doing is usually organizational convenience. The designer of the overall memory map of a system may be reluctant to assign to peripheral devices a larger section of the memory space than might ever be used. As peripherals are replaced with updated devices, it is important to localize any required changes in the operating system. This can imply that the allocated memory space not be increased, which is possible through the use of external indirect addressing. As a device increases in capability and sophistication, the number of control registers may be expected to increase. An indirect array of control registers is illustrated in Example 10.4.

Example 10.4

Write a partial AHPL description of a device to be connected to the RIC primary memory bus that allows for an array of 256 32-bit control and status registers. Include the statements after ENDSEQUENCE needed to provide for reading or writing to the array. Only two RIC addresses 00FFFE and 00FFFF are allocated for this purpose. Write the short sequence of RIC assembly language instructions necessary to write a command into the fifteenth word of the array.

Solution

The layout described herein is depicted in Fig. 10.13. As in statement 10.1, **INDIR** is declared as an 8-bit register, whereas the array of control registers is declared as **CMDSTAT**⟨256⟩[32]. The necessary statements to implement reading or writing to this array are given as follows.

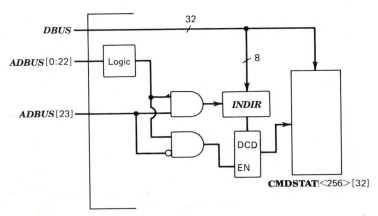

Figure 10.13. Indirect control registers.

ENDSEQUENCE
INDIR * (*write* $\wedge$ ($\wedge$($\overline{ADBUS}$[0:7], *ADBUS*[8:23]))) $\leftarrow$ *DBUS*[24:31];
CMDSTAT * (*write* $\wedge$ ($\wedge$($\overline{ADBUS}$[0:7], *ADBUS*[8:22], $\overline{ADBUS}$[23]))
$\wedge$ DCD(*INDIR*)) $\leftarrow$ *DBUS*;
DBUS = **CMDSTAT** * (*read*$\wedge$($\wedge$($\overline{ADBUS}$[0:7], *ADBUS*[8:22],
$\overline{ADBUS}$[23]))$\wedge$ DCD(*INDIR*)).
END.

Writing a command to row 0F of CMDSTAT is accomplished as follows. The assembly language symbol # indicates immediate addressing, and $ indicates a hexadecimal constant.

MVT	# $0F
MVF	$00FFFF
MVT	"address of command"
MVF	$00FFFE

10.8 Slow Direct Addressing

In the next section, we shall add to the RIC computer system an *asynchronous bus*, that is, a bus under control of a two-line, completely responsive handshake. This bus, to be called RICBUS, will not replace the synchronous primary memory bus but will be interfaced to it. If RIC is to have program control of any transactions on RICBUS, it must be subject to the handshake. The facility to respond to such a handshake must be added to the RIC control sequence. There is no room in the opcode to add an asynchronous memory reference instruction. However, there are as yet three unused combinations of addressing mode bits.

Our approach will be to add one more addressing mode, called *slow direct*. This mode will be applicable for all memory reference (not including branch, JMP, and JSR) instructions, but in practice it is likely to be used only in conjunction with MVT and MVF. Use of this mode will be very infrequent. Only specific devices containing hardware to generate compatible handshake signals will respond. The primary memory,

IR[5:7]	Addressing Mode	Mnemonic
000	Direct	MVT ADDR
001	Indirect	MVT (ADDR)
010	Indexed	MVT ADDR, X
011	Indirect indexed	MVT (ADDR), X
100	Immediate	MVT #ADDR
110	Slow direct	MVTSL ADDR

Figure 10.14. RIC addressing modes with slow direct.

for example, will not respond to the slow direct addressing mode. Figure 10.14 repeats the addressing mode tabulation of Fig. 2.4 with the slow direct mode added.

Inclusion of slow direct addressing requires further modification of the RIC control sequence. The first five steps—including step 5, which separates the nonmemory reference branch instructions—remain the same. Step 6 must be modified to use bit *IR*[6] to distinguish slow direct from immediate addressing. For slow direct addressing, step 7A is added to place the address in *MA* and continue to step 16 where execution begins for memory reference instructions.

5   NO DELAY
       $\rightarrow (\overline{IR[0]} \wedge IR[1] \wedge IR[2] \wedge IR[3])/(30).$ (Branch instructions)

6   NO DELAY
       $\rightarrow (\overline{IR[5]}, IR[5] \wedge \overline{IR[6]}, IR[5] \wedge IR[6])/(8,7,7A).$

7     $MD[0:7] \leftarrow \overline{8 \top 0} \wedge MD[8];$
       $\rightarrow (22).$

7A $MA \leftarrow MD[8:31];$
       $\rightarrow (16).$

The next step that must be modified is step 18, which must implement the write handshake for the MVF instruction. In step 18, we wait for an acknowledge signal to be returned on line *ack* if the addressing mode is slow direct. For this mode, an additional step 18A that waits for *ack* to go low completing the completely responsive handshake is also necessary.

16   NO DELAY
       $\rightarrow (\overline{IR[1] \wedge IR[2]})/(19).$

17    $MD \leftarrow AC.$

18    $write = 1; ADBUS = MA; DBUS = MD;$
       $\rightarrow (\overline{IR[5]}, IR[5] \wedge ack, IR[5] \wedge \overline{ack})/(1, 18A, 18).$

18A $\rightarrow (ack, \overline{ack})/(18A, 1).$

A similar handshake is necessary for a read from memory. This handshake is provided by modifying step 19 in the same way as step 18 and adding step 19a. A NO DELAY step 19B is included for convenience to separate the INC and DEC instructions. Step 21 must be modified to provide for asynchronously rewriting the results of these two instructions, but this task will be left as a problem for you.

19    $ADBUS = MA; MD \leftarrow DBUS; \underline{read} = 1;$
       $\rightarrow (\overline{IR[5]}, IR[5] \wedge ack, IR[5] \wedge \overline{ack})/(19B, 19A, 19).$

19A $\rightarrow (ack)/(19A).$

19B   NO DELAY
       $\rightarrow (\overline{IR[0] \wedge IR[1]})/(22).$

You will notice that a single input control line, *ack*, was used in both the read and write handshakes. For the write operation, *ack* will function in place of both *ready* and *accept* used in the three-line handshake. For reading, the *ack* signal replaces *datavalid*. The significance of each transition in the read and write handshakes is indicated in Fig. 10.15.

In the case of the write handshake, the correspondence between the timing diagram and the active steps in RIC as well as the active steps of the slave in which the data are written are shown. The control sequence of a slave that sees the signals from RIC during the same clock period in which they are issued and requires no extra clock periods for handling the received data follows. The line *addressenable* will be 1 if the address placed on *ADBUS* by RIC corresponds to an address in the address space allocated to the slave.

10   *DATAREG* ∗ (*write*/*addressenable*) ← *DBUS*;
        → ($\overline{write/\backslash addressenable}$)/(10).
11   *ack* = 1;
        → (*write*)/(11).

The resulting handshake in Fig. 10.15a requires four clock periods. For purposes of timing computations in this chapter and Chapter 11, this will be regarded as the fastest possible handshake on any asynchronous bus. A two-period handshake is possible, if the sum of propagation delays in both directions between RIC and the slave

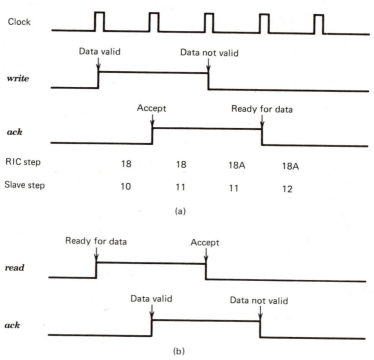

Figure 10.15. Timing of four-period read and write handshakes.

can be accommodated in a single clock period. Pursuit of this unlikely alternative will be left as a problem for you.

10.9   A Generalized Asynchronous Bus

Until now, we have used the term *bus* to refer to a vector of homogeneous lines to which values may be connected by more than one source. At this point, let us acknowledge, as was done when PMS notation was introduced, that the term bus has also come to be used in reference to a collection of lines including an address bus, a data bus, and all associated control lines. The protocol describing the timing relationship between control lines also falls within the definition of a particular bus, under this interpretation of the word *bus*.

There is no single standard bus, but there are a variety of bus standards that are widely used. The IEEE 488 standard bus is widely used in the field of instrumentation. A few of the other configurations that satisfy the term bus as characterized by the first paragraph are the UNIBUS, the S-100 bus, and the MULTIBUS.

There is little commonality among the bus configurations just listed and other generalized buses. There is space in this book to deal with only one such bus, which we shall call RICBUS. It shares various features with many of the real-world buses, but it is identical to none of them. RICBUS bears as much resemblance to most of these configurations as they do to one another. Our goal has been to keep RICBUS as simple as possible, consistent with using it as a vehicle to introduce the important concepts associated with using a bus that is not the primary memory bus.

The relation between RICBUS and RIC is characterized in PMS-like notation in Fig. 10.16. Both the RICBUS and the primary memory bus with DMA have an independent controller. This is suggested by the location of the S (switch) block at the end of the bus rather than between a processor and the bus, as was the case when that processor had permanent control of the bus. RICBUS is a 16-data-bit bus that

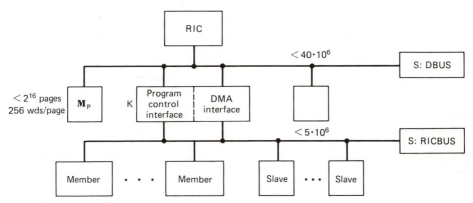

Figure 10.16. Two-level RIC bus structure.

includes 16 address bits, providing an address space of $2 \uparrow 16$ 16-bit words. The bus lines are tabulated in Fig. 10.17. Because the RICBUS has half the word length of the primary memory bus and requires a handshake, its bandwidth (in bytes/sec) can be no better than one-eighth the bandwidth of the primary memory bus. Based on a 10-MHz clock, this bandwidth is 5×10^6 bytes/sec, as given in Fig. 10.16. We assume that the bus handshake will require no fewer than four clock periods, as shown in Fig. 10.15.

There are many reasons why a two-level bus structure might be employed. To maximize the clock rate, it is desirable that the primary memory bus be confined to the smallest possible physical area. The asynchronous RICBUS might be extended a few feet to reach the location of physically adjacent peripheral devices. Likewise, connecting an uncertain number of additional devices to the primary memory bus would slow the clock rate and make its actual specifications more difficult. Supporting microcomputers, with the need to communicate to other RICBUS devices, might also be attached to RICBUS. Peripherals designed to communicate with the 16-bit micro-computers via RICBUS could also be linked to RIC through the same bus. Finally, the RICBUS under some other name might have been available prior to the design of RIC.

The interface between RICBUS and the primary memory bus will actually consist of two independent modules. One will route slow direct read and write requests from RIC to and from any registers in any devices in the address space of RICBUS. The second, and easily the more complicated, interface provides a path through which a device on RICBUS can accomplish a DMA transfer of a page of data to or from primary memory. For the purpose of bulk input/output, we regard the address space of the primary memory bus as consisting of 2^{16} pages of 256 words each. As suggested by the memory map of Fig. 10.18, the 16 most significant (four hexadecimal) digits of **ADBUS** specify a page number. The remaining 8 bits (page address) identify the word within a page. Many DMA block transfers to and from the primary memory will be in page units. Because DMA transfers must be made to areas of physically realized RIC memory, two separate regions of 256 consecutive pages are set aside for program

RICBUS lines	Function
RBDATA [16]	16-bit data word (RIC halfword)
dma	0: **RBADDR** specifies RICBUS address
	1: **RBADDR** specifies **ADBUS** [8:23]
high	0: DMA to low-order halfword
	1: DMA to high-order halfword
RBADDR [16]	Address
BUSREQ [8]	Control
BUSGRANT [8]	Control
busread	Control
buswrite	Control
busack	Control

Figure 10.17. Tabulation of RICBUS lines.

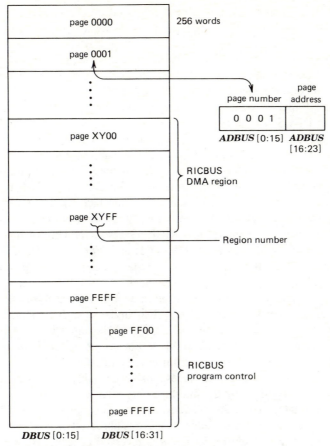

Figure 10.18. RIC memory address space.

control I/O and DMA. The location of the 256-page region for DMA transfers is subject to control by the RIC operating system, which can write a most significant address byte, XY, to a control register in the DMA interface. When a RIC peripheral gains control of RICBUS and places an address on the **RBADDR**, it must be clear whether this is the address within another device on RICBUS or within the DMA region of the primary memory. A line **dma** is provided for this purpose. For an address on RICBUS **dma** = 0, and for DMA activity **dma** = 1. Either the DMA interface may be considered outside the RICBUS address space or **dma** may be considered as an additional address bit.

Both the data and address lengths differ between RICBUS and the primary memory bus. The program control interface must perform some type of translation as well as interfacing control lines to permit RIC to access registers in devices on the RICBUS in the slow direct addressing mode. The program control interface will always function as a bus master on RICBUS, never as a slave, and will be the highest priority device on RICBUS. Typically, control and status information will be transferred to peripheral device registers in the program control mode. These registers will be relatively few in number and will be 16-bit, consistent with RICBUS. The approach will be to disregard the high-order 16 bits of **DBUS**, reading or writing only **DBUS**[16:31]. To facilitate address translation, the RICBUS address space is assigned as the last 256 pages of the RIC address space. As shown in Fig. 10.18, it is only meaningful to write to the last 16 bits of words in these pages. When reading these pages, the high-order 16 bits on DBUS will be 0's.

Figure 10.19 shows the address space looking back from a RICBUS peripheral that has become bus master. If **dma** = 1, it will be addressing RIC primary memory through the DMA interface in the region specified by the 8-bit region number currently stored in the interface. If **dma** = 0, some other RICBUS slave will be addressed. RIC words will be passed to or from the DMA interface by the busmaster in two consecutive halfwords, always the high-order halfword first. For clarity and increased reliability in the event of an interrupted RICBUS grant, the control line, **high**, will be 0 when a low-order halfword is on **RBDATA**; and **high** = 1 will indicate a high-order halfword. Should RICBUS be used as a stand-alone bus independent of RIC, the lines **dma** and **high** would not be implemented.

To the primary memory bus, the program control interface will always appear as a slave. When the interface is activated by RIC in the slow direct addressing mode, it will always seek to become master of RICBUS. The input and output lines that connect the program control interface to the two buses are assembled in Fig. 10.20.

An AHPL description of the program control interface follows. The interface provides the same form of completely responsive handshake on both buses. Each control transition is passed on by the interface only after a similar transition has been received. The first statement issues a request to become busmaster of RICBUS whenever a read or write to the RICBUS address space is observed on the primary memory bus. Control waits in step 1 until a **busgrant** is received. The RICBUS request stays

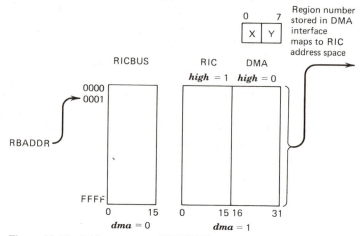

Figure 10.19. Address space of RICBUS master.

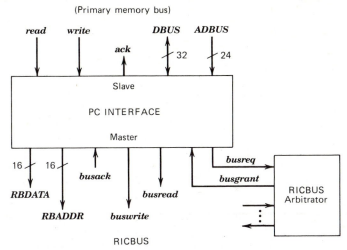

Figure 10.20. PCINTERFACE.

active, retaining control of that bus until the transfer is complete. Step 2 passes the read or write activity on to the RICBUS. When a *busack* signal is received from the target slave on RICBUS, control goes to step 3 to pass the acknowledge back to RIC on line *ack*. If the operation was a read, the data from **RBDATA** is connected through to the **DBUS.** In the case of a read operation, *busread* is held 1 in step 3 so that the slave will hold the data on RICBUS. Step 4 releases the bus and holds *ack* = 1 until *busack* has gone to 0. This action concludes the completely responsive handshake.

MODULE:	PCINTERFACE
INPUTS:	*read*; *write*; *ADBUS*[24]; *busgrant*; *busack*.
OUTPUTS:	*ack*; *busreq*.
MEMORY:	*busreqff*.
COMBUSES:	*DBUS*[32]; *RBDATA*[16]; *RBADDR*[16]; *busread*; *buswrite*.

1   *busreqff* ← (*read* $\vee$ *write*) $\wedge$ ($\wedge$/*ADBUS*[0:7])
      → ($\overline{busreqff}$ $\wedge$ *busgrant* $\wedge$ $\overline{busack}$)/(1).

2   *RBDATA* = *DBUS*[16:31] $*$ *write*; *RBADDR* = *ADBUS*[8:23];
     busread = *read*; *buswrite* = *write*;
      → ($\overline{busack}$)/(2).

3   *ack* = 1; *busread* = *read*; *buswrite* = *write*;
     DBUS[16:31] = *RBDATA* $*$ *read*; *RBADDR* = *ADBUS*[8:23];
        → ((*read* $\vee$ *write*) $\wedge$ ($\wedge$/*ADBUS*[0:7]))/(3).

4   *ack* = 1; *busreqff* ← 0;
      → (*busack*, $\overline{busack}$)/(4,1).

ENDSEQUENCE
     CONTROLRESET(1); *busreq* = *busreqff*.
END.

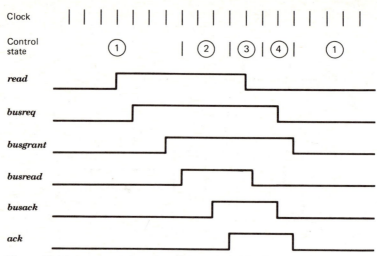

Figure 10.21. Read activity relayed through RICBUS.

A timing trace for a typical read operation relayed through RICBUS is shown in Fig. 10.21. From the AHPL description, it can be seen that the data are held on the primary memory bus until **read** has returned to 0. The responsive signalling relationship among the signals in Fig. 10.21 is evident from the description of PCIN-TERFACE. The numbers of clock periods of delay are consistent with the design of the RICBUS arbitrator and a typical slave to be given in Sections 11.2 and 11.3.

So far, nothing has been said about interrupts from RICBUS members. For the purpose of these discussions, all interrupt lines will be routed directly from the individual devices to RIC. We will not consider any possible consolidation of interrupts at the RICBUS interface level, although such consolidation may be advantageous when the time comes to write the RIC operating system.

It may be useful to connect more than one RICBUS to the primary memory bus. This is not precluded, although one of the arguments in favor of RICBUS was to minimize the number of physical connections to the primary memory bus. A second RICBUS will require a separate set of 256 RIC memory pages to represent its address space.

Problems

10.1   Consider the communications memory of Example 4.3. Assume that the data word is to be placed somewhere in the address space F00000 to F0FFFF in the RIC primary memory rather than in a special RAM. Assume the 16-bit address along with the data is to be passed on to RIC via memory map read operations and that RIC will write the data at the proper location in memory using indirect addressing. Add to the 16-bit register, *AR,* a high-order 16 bits, which will include status bits to provide separate indications of whether a new data word and/or address word are available. Write a revised AHPL description of this device properly interfaced to RIC. Let the data and address registers occupy address FFFF00 and FFFF01 in the RIC address space.

10.2   A 256-word by 32-bit hardware stack is to be placed in the RIC address space at location FFFF02. The internal stack pointer will also be accessible from RIC at address location FFFF03. A push operation could be accomplished by a write to location FFFF02 and a pop by a read from the same location. Write an AHPL description of this device properly interfaced to the RIC primary memory bus. What modification would be required in RIC to allow this stack to be used to restore the return addresses of subroutines?

10.3   Suppose that any device that might have caused an interrupt of a RIC program will have a 1 in bit-0 of a status register. Write a RIC assembly language program that will identify the interrupting device. Assume that the status registers of the 16 possible devices occupy addresses 000F00 through 000FF0 and that this is the priority order of the devices. Let the starting addresses of the interrupt routines be 0FF000, 0FF100, through 0FFF00, respectively. Execution of the routine should conclude with a jump to the proper interrupt program. Will it matter in what order the devices are polled? Why or why not?

10.4   Is it possible for a RIC program to be interrupted by two devices in succession without any instructions of the main program being executed between the two interrupts? Justify your answer.

10.5   Suppose the interrupt vectoring network of Fig. 10.6 is to be considered a separate module. Write a AHPL description of that module. Suppose the mask register is located at FFFFFF in the RIC address space.

10.6   Suppose it is desired to give RIC the power to establish any arbitrary priority order among the interrupt lines shown in Fig. 10.6. What is the minimum number of register bits that would need to be added to the module to provide for this? Suppose, instead, an array **PRIORID**⟨16⟩ [4] is used with the first row identifying the highest priority line, and so forth. Subject to this assumption, write a combinational logic unit description of a new priority network, ARBPRI, which will generate the 16 input lines to the ROM.

10.7   Rewrite the AHPL module description of problem 10.5 to include a circulating shift register in which only 1 bit would be 1. The flip-flop containing a 1 would indicate the current highest priority interrupt. The next line to the right would be second highest priority, etc. The priority-indicating register should rotate each time an interrupt occurs. It will be necessary to rewrite the combinational logic unit description of the priority network.

10.8   Consider the restricted form of DMA represented by square A $\overline{B}$ C in Fig. 10.8 in which a peripheral can gain control of the bus only between the execution of RIC instructions. If this approach is employed together with the architecture implied by the PMS chart of Fig. 10.7a, a separate bus control module would not be employed. Assume only three external equipments with DMA privilege whose requests for memory access would be routed directly to RIC. Modify the first few steps of RIC to allow it to yield to the highest priority device desiring memory access rather than begin execution of an instruction. Add steps to the control sequence as necessary.

10.9   Consider a 16-bit minicomputer similar to that of Problem 9.14 except with memory-mapped I/0. All peripheral devices are the same. Construct a PMS chart with as much detail as possible for this new computer system.

10.10   Suppose the CPU in FIG. 10.9 is not RIC but is instead a processor with a 24-bit address space and a 16-bit data bus. The register configuration, with the exception of the register **DATA** of the RIC peripheral, is unchanged, and all bus control lines function in exactly the same manner.

      (a)   Modify the partial AHPL description of the output DMA activity in RICPERIPHERAL so that it will function with the new bus configuration.

      (b)   Add the necessary steps to the description of part (a) to provide for DMA input.

10.11   Modify step 21 of the RIC control sequence and add additional steps as necessary, so that RIC instructions INC and DEC can be used with the slow direct addressing mode.

10.12   Suppose that the register **DATA** in the RIC peripheral of Fig. 10.9 need not be accessible via program control. The 16 registers, **BUFFADDR**, **COUNT**, **RCOMM**, **OTHERREG**⟨13⟩, and an indirect address register **INDIR**[4] must be accessible in this manner. However, only two addresses, 00FFFF (for **INDIR**) and 00FFFE (for the other registers), are assigned to the device. Modify the statements after ENDSEQUENCE in the description of RICPERIPHERAL to provide program control access to these registers using external indirect addressing.

10.13 Modify steps 18 and 18A of the RIC control sequence, as given in Section 10.8, and steps 10 and 11 of the slave so that the write handshake requires only two clock periods. The *write* signal must reach the slave and the *ack* signal must propagate back in the same clock period. Avoid any strictly combinational logic loops.

10.14 Suppose the *COUNT* register in the RIC peripheral of Fig. 10.9 is set to three before output DMA is activated. If the **FIFO** store is initially empty, construct a clock-period-by-clock-period timing diagram showing all control lines that change at any time during the DMA activity. Values should be shown from when the control leaves step 1 until this DMA activity is complete. Assume that the CPU executes one memory read following transfer of the first word to the peripheral but that no other memory requests will occur.

10.15 Suppose the 16-bit minicomputer of Problem 10.9 provides for a 16-bit address. Let the entire configuration of devices associated with this computer be connected to RICBUS. Construct a PMS diagram of the resulting system, including RIC. Assume that the minicomputer has been modified so that it can function as a bus member.

  (a) Will the modifications just made be sufficient to permit communications between the minicomputer and its peripherals in the program control mode? Why or why not? Assume that the *busread*, *buswrite*, and *busack* control lines on RICBUS are compatible with the control lines of the individual devices.
  (b) Describe in one or two sentences what further modifications must be made to permit the tape transport to function in DMA mode with the minicomputer RAM.
  (c) Will the modifications made for part (b) be sufficient to permit DMA access by the tape transport to the RIC primary memory? Why or why not?

10.16 The hardware stack memory of Problem 10.2 is to be redesigned to function as a RICBUS slave. Two successive write operations will constitute a push, and two successive reads will be required for a pop. If only one write operation is followed by a read, the push will be aborted. An incomplete pop will be similarly aborted. Write a complete AHPL description of this device.

10.17 A synchronous bus called EQUIBUS consists of a 16-bit address bus, *EQUIADDR*, and a 8-bit data bus, *EQUIDATA*. Only three of the devices that will be connected to EQUIBUS are to be able to request control of the bus. All other devices are to be slaves only. All three potential masters of EQUIBUS enjoy equal status; and once a device is granted access to EQUIBUS, it will remain bus master until it no longer requests the bus. The three bus request inputs are to be declared as *BUSREQ*[3]. The corresponding three busgrant outputs are to be declared as *BUSGRANT*[3]. A three-output combinational logic unit COUNTPRI(*CNT*; *BUSREQ*) is available. The outputs of COUNTPRI are 0 unless one of the *BUSREQ* lines is 1. In that case, the output line corresponding to the current highest-priority active input line will be 1. The priorities are ordered by the contents of the 2-bit counter, *CNT*, which must be incremented every clock period.

(a)   Write a complete AHPL module description of the arbitrator.
(b)   Write a combinational logic unit description of COUNTPRI.

References

1. R. Matick, *Computer Storage Systems and Technology*, Wiley Interscience, New York, 1977.
2. D. P. Siewiorek, C. G. Bell, and A. Newell, *Computer Structures: Principles and Examples*, McGraw–Hill, New York, 1982.
3. G. A. Blaauw, *Digital System Implementation*, Prentice-Hall, Englewood Cliffs, N.J., 1976.
4. M. M. Mano, *Computer System Architecture*, Prentice-Hall, Englewood Cliffs, N.J., 1976.
5. R. M. Kline, *Digital Computer Design*, Prentice-Hall, Englewood Cliffs, N.J., 1977.
6. H. Hellerman, *Digital Computer System Principles*, 2nd ed. McGraw-Hill, New York, 1973.
7. J. B. Peatman, *The Design of Digital Systems*, McGraw-Hill, New York, 1972.
8. F. J. Hill and G. R. Peterson, *Digital Logic and Microprocessors*, Wiley, New York, 1984.
9. *MC68000 16-Bit Microprocessor User Manual*, 3rd ed., Prentice-Hall, Englewood Cliffs, N.J., 1982.
10. J. K. Iliffe, *Advanced Computer Design*, Prentice-Hall, Englewood Clilffs, N.J., 1982.
11. *VAX Architecture Handbook*, Digital Equipment Corp., Maynard, Mass., 1981.
12. *IEEE Standard 488-1975*, Institute of Electrical and Electronic Engineers, New York, 1975.
13. J. E. McNamara, *Technical Aspects of Data Communications*, Digital Equipment Corp., Maynard, Mass., 1977.
14. A. L. Scherr, "A Perspective on Communications and Computing," *IBM Systems Journal*, Vol. 22, Nos. 1 and 2, 1983, p. 5–9.
15. *Data Communications Network Interfacing and Protocols*, Institute of Electrical and Electronic Engineers, New York, 1981.
16. I. Flores, *Peripheral Devices*, Prentice-Hall, Englewood Cliffs, N.J., 1973.

11 Peripherals and Interfacing

11.1   Introduction

Thus far, we have looked at the computer primarily from the point of view of the CPU. In the last chapter, we looked out at RICBUS from RIC. Now we shall turn our attention to the characteristics of peripheral devices that might be connected to RICBUS. For most of these devices, we shall be concerned with designing a controller so that they can communicate with RIC across the 16-bit RICBUS. Often, a digital storage or input/output unit will be manufactured in a "stripped-down" form so that, with the addition of a small amount of hardware, it can be made compatible with any one of several distinct digital systems. Designing and adding this hardware is termed *interfacing*. The added hardware may be called the *interface*. Within the framework of AHPL, the interface may be a separate module or treated as a part of the devices module.

Consideration of a representative subset of peripheral devices will expose most of the problems to be encountered in the interface design. In the next few sections, we interface such a set of peripherals to RICBUS. Investigating the data-handling properties of representative peripherals will be a secondary objective to be accomplished simultaneously. We shall find the PMS chart to be of help in this regard. A graphics terminal, a tape transport, and a disk drive are the topics of the last three sections of this chapter. Interfacing serial communication devices to RICBUS is left for Chapter 12.

Before we can knowledgeably interface to RICBUS, we must complete the definition of that bus begun in the last chapter. This is done with the specification of the RICBUS controller in Section 11.2. Much of the interface to RICBUS will be the same for any device. Once the controller has been designed, we are able to specify a *template* that must be satisfied by any RICBUS member.

The 16-bit RICBUS need not necessarily be connected to the 32-bit RIC through the dual interface discussed in Chapter 10. The illustration of the design of a RICBUS slave in Section 11.3 considers RICBUS in its more natural state as the primary memory bus of a 16-bit computer.

11.2 The Multimaster RICBUS

All data transactions discussed for *DBUS,* the RIC primary memory bus, involve either the CPU or the primary random access memory. Some bus organizations permit a more democratic allocation of the bus resources. As the name implies, a *multimaster* bus organization permits a number of (but not necessarily all) devices on the bus to become the *bus master*. Once a device becomes a bus master, it is permitted to place an address on the address bus. This address will be in the address space of another device connected to the bus. This addressed device then becomes the *bus slave*. While placing the address on the address bus, the bus master will activate either *read* or *write,* which will themselves be 1-bit buses. If *write* $= 1$, data will be written by the master to the slave. If *read* $= 1$, data are read from the slave. While one device is the bus master, no other device is permitted to drive the address bus, data bus, or bus control lines.

To facilitate the multimaster bus organization, there must exist a controller with the responsibility of determining which device will be the bus master. Again, this controller will be called the "bus arbitrator." It will not be unusual for more than one device to desire to become the bus master at the same time. In that event, the arbitrator must implement some criteria for deciding which device will be allowed to become the bus master. One priority scheme used on the original Digital Equipment Corporation UNIBUS and elsewhere is based on the relative placement of devices along the bus. That is, the closer of any two devices to the bus arbitrator will have the higher priority. A second possibility is to route bus request lines in parallel from each device capable of being a bus master to the arbitrator, as was discussed in Section 10.6. Priority among the devices can then be enforced by a priority network within the arbitrator similar to that used to establish interrupt priority in Section 10.3. We shall adopt the latter approach for RICBUS.

In Section 10.9, it was indicated that the two-level bus structure of Fig. 10.16 offered a variety of advantages. It was also established in Section 10.9 that the second-level bus for RIC would include 16 address bits and 16 data bits. For program control access to RICBUS, a parameter established by switches on the RICBUS-*DBUS* interface will locate the 16-bit address space of RICBUS within the 24-bit RIC address space. In Fig. 10.18 this was the last 256 pages in the RIC address space.

DMA transfers are accomplished to addresses in the RIC address space. The first 8 bits of this address (the *region number*) are specified by a register in the DMA interface module. The contents of this register may be modified at any time by the RIC operating system. The low-order 16 bits of the address are placed on ***RBADDR*** by the bus master engaged in the DMA transfer. Clearly, this protocol for the DMA interface will not support a situation in which two bus members are simultaneously activated for DMA to different 256-page regions of RIC address space. It would be necessary to halt all other DMA activity temporarily, if a file is to be transferred directly from disk to a user area of memory.

The DMA portion of the interface must also provide for storing two consecutive 16-bit words received from RICBUS to form a 32-bit RIC data word. Similarly, it must store a 32-bit word obtained via DMA from the RIC memory and pass it on to the current RICBUS master in two successive RICBUS read cycles. The portion of the RICBUS interface that permits program-controlled access by RIC to any device on RICBUS was detailed in Section 10.9. In this section, we shall concentrate on developing an AHPL description of a RICBUS controller that will make possible the design of a reliable DMA section of the RICBUS-***DBUS*** interface. The architecture of the DMA interface itself is somewhat specialized; this design will be left as a problem for the reader.

The RICBUS controller will be separate from any data-handling device connected to RICBUS. Devices connected to RICBUS fall into two classes, *members* and *slaves*. Only a member may become the bus master. To reduce the complexity of the controller, the number of members is limited to eight, but the only limit to the number of slaves is the RICBUS address space. A member may, of course, be treated as a slave by another bus master. The program-controlled interface to the ***DBUS*** must be a member while the DMA interface is a slave.

It is important that RICBUS be designed so that *deadlock* can be avoided. Just as at the software level, a hardware deadlock can occur if two processes each need the same two resources to accomplish an activity. Suppose that neither process will release an acquired resource until its activity is complete. If each process simultaneously acquires one of the two resources, neither can complete its activity; and the resources are never released. This is deadlock. Figure 11.1 illustrates how deadlock might occur on the RIC bus structure, if RICBUS is carelessly defined. As shown by the heavy line, RIC has acquired the ***DBUS*** to execute a write to a target on RICBUS in the slow direct addressing mode. Simultaneously, another RICBUS member has become the RICBUS master in order to execute a DMA transfer to the primary memory. Suppose that the RICBUS control has been designed so that a member retains control of the bus until its activity is complete. The DMA activity cannot be completed because the DMA interface cannot gain control of ***DBUS***. The slow direct handshake cannot be completed because the program control interface cannot gain access to RICBUS. This is a deadlock that can be, and must be, precluded at the hardware level.

Although other approaches are possible, we take the following two steps to eliminate the possibility of deadlock in the RIC bus structure.

1. Make the program control interface a "privileged member" on RICBUS with a constant highest priority with the assumption that any other bus master will be "kicked off" if this privileged member issues a bus request.

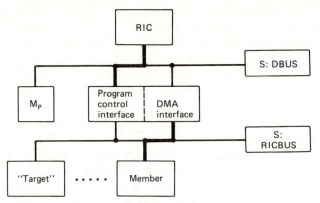

Figure 11.1. Equal priority deadlock.

2. Design all other RICBUS members so that a data transfer activity will be repeated if unexpectedly interrupted.

These measures will allow the infrequent slow direct memory references by RIC to be carried out to completion; and because RIC is the only process that will acquire the **DBUS** first, they will be sufficient to prevent deadlock.

Both the AHPL description and the logic block diagram for the critical step 2 of the RICBUS controller are given in Fig. 11.2. The requests to acquire the bus appear on eight lines, **BUSREQ**. The privileged member corresponds to **BUSREQ**[0]. During any clock period, no more than one of the bits of the register **GRANT** will be 1 to indicate the current bus master. The shift register, **RING,** contains a bit for each bus member, except the privileged member. This register is initialized with a 1 in one flip-flop and 0's in others. The **RING** is rotated to the right each time the bus is relinquished by a master, as indicated by the satisfaction of equation 11.1.

$$\vee/(\textbf{\textit{BUSREQ}} \wedge \textbf{\textit{GRANT}}) = 0 \qquad\qquad (11.1)$$

The **GRANT** register is updated each time equation 11.1 is satisfied or a bus request is received from the privileged member. If **BUSREQ**[0] = 0, the bus master is determined by the combinational logic unit, ROTPRI(**RING; BUSREQ**[1:7]). This network is similar to the priority network described in Chapter 9, except that the 1 in the register **RING** indicates the request line that currently has the highest priority. If the privileged member initiates a request on **BUSREQ**[0], the controller goes to step 3, where it remains as long as that request was active. When the slow direct read or write operation is complete, the original value of **GRANT** is restored, and control returns to step 2, so that the DMA activity in progress can be carried out to the conclusion.

Throughout the next two chapters, a number of peripherals will be described with interfaces designed for connection to RICBUS. Most of these will be designed as bus members. A member will probably have two simultaneously active control states. One will monitor the address bus, ready to respond as a slave to any read or

MODULE: RICBUSCONTROL.
INPUTS: *BUSREQ*[8].
OUTPUTS: *BUSGRANT*[8].
MEMORY: *GRANT*[8]; *RING*[7]; *GRANTSAVE*[8].
1   *RING* ← 7 ⊤ 1.
2   *GRANT* * $\overline{\vee/(BUSREQ \wedge GRANT)}$ ← 0,
                                               ROTPRI(*RING;BUSREQ*[1:7]);
               RING * ($\overline{\vee/(BUSREQ \wedge GRANT)}$)) ← *RING*[6], *RING*[0:5];
               GRANTSAVE * *BUSREQ*[0] ← *GRANT;*
               → ($\overline{BUSREQ[0]}$)/(2)
3   *GRANT* ← (1,0,0,0,0,0,0,0! *GRANTSAVE*)
                                       * (*BUSREQ*[0], $\overline{BUSREQ[0]}$);
               → (*BUSREQ*[0], $\overline{BUSREQ[0]}$)/(3,2).
ENDSEQUENCE
               CONTROLRESET(1); *BUSGRANT* = *GRANT*.
END.

(a.)

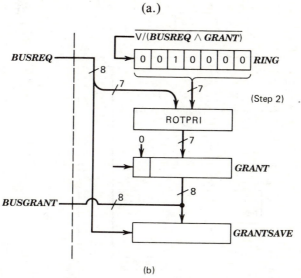

(b)

Figure 11.2. RICBUS controller.

write operation within the address space of that device. Simultaneously, a second
process will manage the data storage or transmission activity unique to that device
and will interact with the RICBUS controller and the RICBUS DMA interface to
transfer blocks of data to and from the primary memory as required. When this latter
process is ready to transfer data, it will issue a bus request signal. The data transfer
will begin when a busgrant is received from the controller. As stated earlier, the
member may be forced to relinquish control of RICBUS at any time. The member
must be able to recover smoothly and continue the DMA activity when it regains
control of the bus.

In Fig. 11.3, we show a flowchart that can serve as a template to which any RICBUS member must be consistent. We shall follow the template in the design of RIC peripherals in the next several sections. The block marked with an asterisk is specific to the particular device and may be more complex than the implementation of all the remainder of the chart. If the DMA interface is the slave, the wordstream to be sent to the RIC memory is treated as a series of 16-bit halfwords on RICBUS with each low-order halfword following the corresponding high-order halfword. Once

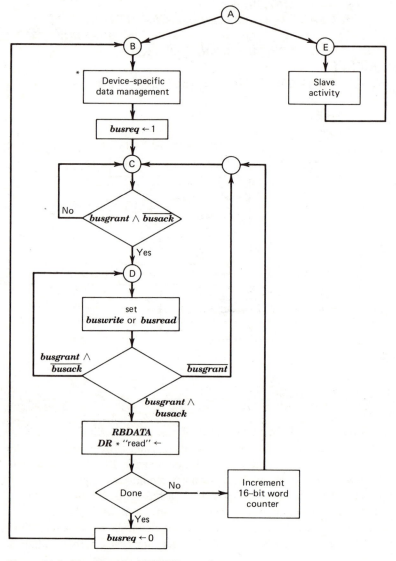

Figure 11.3. Template for RICBUS member.

a block of words is ready, often stored in a small RAM buffer, the *busreq* line is set to 1. Transmission of the pairs of 16-bit words begins when a *busgrant* is received from the controller.

The completely responsive handshake that we have adopted for RICBUS takes place between either *busread* or *buswrite* and the line *busack* activated by the slave. If any time during a transfer *busgrant* disappears, the same transfer will begin again, when the *busgrant* reappears. Therefore, the interface must be sensitive to situations where *dma* goes off and then back on again with the old values of **RBADDR**. The DMA interface must also be able to return to its state at the beginning of the unfinished transfer. The same step (point C) that checks for *busgrant* begins the handshake by verifying that *busack* = 0. This will prevent misinterpretation of an acknowledge that might be left active for one or two clock periods by the slave of the previous bus transaction.

Other approaches to a protocol for RICBUS members and the DMA interface are possible. Indeed, more than one protocol might be allowed. We shall restrict our attention to the approach just presented, which will serve to illustrate most of the issues associated with a multilayer bus structure and avoid unnecessary complications in the design of RICBUS members. Simplification of the DMA interface would probably slow the transaction or require more address bits on RICBUS.

11.3   Design of a RICBUS Slave

So far, we have discussed RICBUS as if it would be used only when interfaced to the RIC primary memory bus. Like other standard buses, it can be used independently. Indeed, it can accommodate a 16-bit microprocessor to the extent of implementing 64K of its memory space. For some applications, this is sufficient. In this section, we shall consider the design of a slave device in what would almost certainly be a stand-alone application of RICBUS. At the end of the section, it might be observed that the control programs attributed to a 16-bit microprocessor could equally well be implemented in RIC. It will be equally easy to draw the conclusion that dedication of a RIC to such a task would be uneconomical.

The layout of Fig. 11.4 suggests that RICBUS is stretched over a considerable distance. The bus interconnects a basketball scoreboard with its controller, which might be separated by as much as 200 ft. This version of RICBUS could only be implemented using special line drivers and receivers on all the data and control lines. Given the line delays of duration equal to or greater than a clock period, synchronization of the control lines will be required. A competitive, and perhaps more economical, approach would use asynchronous serial communications between the controller and the scoreboard. This approach will be left as a problem for Chapter 12.

We shall limit our attention to the design of the slave module that will interface the actual scoreboard with RICBUS. It is possible that this module, SCRBOARD, will only be addressed by the processor under program control. Whether the control panel will access the scoreboard directly as a bus member will be an open question,

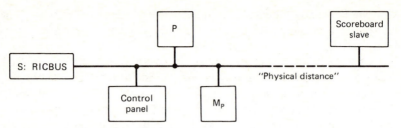

Figure 11.4. Stand alone RICBUS.

if RICBUS will allow this possibility. In addition to the team scores, most existing scoreboards provide additional information such as team fouls and the total personal fouls of the last player to commit a foul. Much more information, such as team rebounds and individual scoring, would be of interest to the truly dedicated fan. From the point of view of the interface module, the selection and identification of the information items to be provided are irrelevant. For this purpose, we assume an array of 256 16-bit indirect registers, **DISPLAY,** whose contents will be under control of the processor via RICBUS. The RICBUS address of the 8-bit indirect pointer to this array will be FFF1(hex). The row of **DISPLAY** selected by **POINTER** will be reached through address FFF0. Individual items will be defined by the control program and connections from the array to the scoreboard, neither of which shall be considered here. Provision for the animation observed on some scoreboards would require a somewhat larger display array.

Of special interest is the scoreboard timing display. Accurate timing is most easily provided by a mechanism independent of the CPU. In this case, it will be physically located in the scoreboard. A separate module with a periodic output whose period is exactly 1 sec will be assumed. The synchronized form of this signal will be labelled **synsec.** A reliable synchronizing mechanism for this signal and the bus control lines will be assumed; but not explicitly included in the module description.

Following is a module description of the scoreboard interface. The "A" sequence represents the simple activity of the scoreboard itself. The "B" sequence represents the interface of the scoreboard slave to RICBUS. The latter set of steps will be similar for any RICBUS slave.

The registers connected to display the numbers of minutes and seconds remaining are **MINUTES** and **SECONDS,** respectively. The processor must have the capability of modifying these values, holding them constant, or allowing them to increase under the control of **synsec.** For this purpose, we provide the 8-bit command register **CMD.** The check for positive and negative transitions on line **synsec** assures that step 4A will be active just once each second. If $CMD[0] = CMD[1] = 0$, the time will be decremented each period on line **synsec.** If $CMD[0] = 1$, the time will not be decremented. If $CMD[1] = 1$, the values of **MINUTES, SECONDS** will be replaced by the value of **NEWTIME,** a 16-bit register in the RICBUS address space. The address of **NEWTIME** is FFF2, of the displayed time is FFF3, and of **CMD** is FFF4. Addresses FFF5 through FFFF are unimplemented.

MODULE: SCRBOARD.
INPUTS: *synsec; buswrite; busread; RBADDR*[16].
MEMORY: **DISPLAY**⟨256⟩[16]; **MINUTES**[8]; **SECONDS**[8];
               NEWTIME[16]; **POINTER**[8]; **CMD**[8].
COMBUSES: **RBDATA**[16]; *busack; dma.*

1   → (2A, 2B).
2A   → ($\overline{\textit{synsec}}$)/(2A).
3A   → ($\overline{\textit{synsec}}$)/(3A).
4A   (**MINUTES,SECONDS**) * ($\overline{\textit{CMD}[0]}$ $\bigvee$ *CMD*[1]) ← (**NEWTIME** !
        TIMEDEC(**MINUTES, SECONDS**)) * (*CMD*[1], $\overline{\textit{CMD}[1]}$);
        → (2A).
2B   → $\overline{((\textit{busread} \bigvee \textit{buswrite}) \bigwedge (\bigwedge \textit{RBADDR}[0:11]) \bigwedge \textit{dma})}$/(2B).
3B   **NEWTIME** * (*buswrite* $\bigwedge$ DCD[2](**RBADDR**[12:15])) ← **RBDATA;**
        POINTER * (*buswrite* $\bigwedge$ DCD[1](**RBADDR**[12:15])) ←
                                                              RBDATA[8:15];
        CMD * (*buswrite* $\bigwedge$ DCD[4](**RBADDR**[12:15])) ←
                                                              RBDATA[8:15];
        DISPLAY * (*buswrite* $\bigwedge$ DCD[0](**RBADDR**[12:15])) $\bigwedge$
                                        DCD(**POINTER**)) ← **RBDATA**.
4B   *busack* = 1;
        RBDATA = ((**MINUTES,SECONDS**) * (*busread* $\bigwedge$
                                        DCD[3](**RBADDR**[12:15]));
        RBDATA = **DISPLAY** * (*busread* $\bigwedge$
                        DCD[0](**RBADDR**[12:15]) $\bigwedge$ DCD (**POINTER**));
        → (*busread* $\bigvee$ *buswrite*, $\overline{(\textit{busread} \bigvee \textit{buswrite})}$)/(4B, 2B).
END SEQUENCE
        CONTROLRESET(1).
END.

The module consists of two simultaneously active loops that are asynchronous to each other. One communicates with RICBUS, while the other updates the displayed time. These two loops operate on the same set of registers. The satisfaction of Rule 9.2 results from the uniformly decreasing values of **MINUTES, SECONDS.** System users are not aware of whether these values are sampled or reset just before or after they are decremented. For simplicity, the time-decrementing function is lumped into a single combinational logic unit description, TIMEDEC, which incorporates the relation between seconds and minutes.

11.4 Competition for BUS Capacity

We have suggested the PMS chart as a means for relating the capacity of a bus to the data requirements of the various bus members. It might be inferred that one merely adds the data rates of all devices connected to the bus and compares this number with the bus capacity. This approach would be overly conservative because not all members will be active at any particular time. At the other extreme, the operating system might enforce a protocol in which only one member is allowed to request the bus at one time. Under this approach for RICBUS, the complex bus arbitrator described in the last section would have been included for nothing.

Under certain ideal conditions, the sum of the data rates of active members might be allowed to approach the bus capacity. This would require that all devices request the bus periodically for the transfer of *packets of data* of uniform size. It would also require that each device include sufficient internal data buffering to allow it to wait a full data period for its turn on the bus. Situations that do not conform to this ideal are difficult to analyze.

Let us consider a case where a conflict can arise with only two active members whose total average data rate can be significantly less than the bus capacity. Suppose one member, P, transfers data through a bus in packets of n bytes at the constant data rate r. The other member requests the bus at irregular intervals but may transfer a packet of as many as H bytes, once it gains control of the bus. For a typically inconsiderate member $n \ll H$. This situation is depicted in the PMS chart of Fig. 11.5a. We ignore the overhead of the **busreq − busgrant** handshakes associated with exchanging control of the bus.

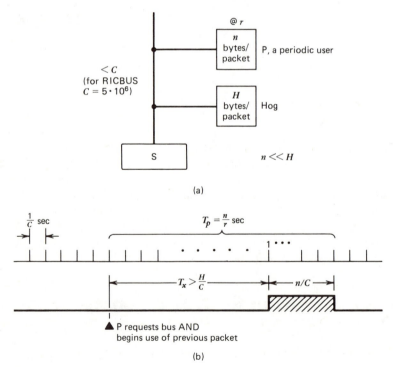

(a)

(b)

Figure 11.5. Bus competition.

For device P, the period T_p between the ends of two consecutive data packets is given by equation 11.2.

$$T_p = \frac{n}{r} \qquad (11.2)$$

If the bandwidth in bytes/sec of the bus is C, the time interval used up by a single byte (no matter if more than 1 byte are placed on the bus once) is $1/C$. Therefore, a data packet from member P consumes n/C sec, and the bus hog can retain control of the bus for as much as H/C sec. We assume that member P has sufficient buffering capability, that it can request the bus for the next packet as soon as processing of the previous packet begins. In the worst case given in Fig. 11.5b, the hog will gain control of the bus just one clock period before P can make a request. Now H/C periods will elapse before P finally gets the bus. Therefore,

$$\frac{n}{C} + \frac{H}{C} < \frac{n}{r} \qquad (11.3)$$

if data are to be always transferred successfully. The maximum packet size, H, is given by equation 11.4.

$$H(\text{max}) = \left(\frac{n}{r} - \frac{n}{C}\right) \cdot C = n \cdot \left(\frac{C}{r} - 1\right) \qquad (11.4)$$

Application of equation 11.4 will provide information on which to judge particular bus configurations in succeeding sections.

11.5 Graphics and Alphanumeric Display Terminals

Over the years, several approaches have been developed for the display of data in graphic and alphanumeric forms on the familiar CRT. Some systems permit the beam to be moved about arbitrarily with user-supplied data, controlling at will the vertical and horizontal position of the beam. This approach results in crisp, striking line drawings on the screen. In some cases, special phosphors are used that allow the image to persist on the screen for periods of time in the order of seconds to permit more complex data manipulations between refreshes of the screen. Of late, the most common approach to graphics display has been to sweep the beam (or beams) repetitively across the screen to cover it with horizontal scan lines, similar to the approach used in television. Among the advantages of this approach is the ease of combining graphic and alphanumeric displays and easier coordination of multiple beams in color applications.

The subject of this and the next section is not graphics display processing. Our interest is restricted to the problems arising from the storage and movement of the data required to refresh and modify the images on these terminals. For color terminals, much more data is needed, because it is necessary to control the intensity of three beams at each distinct point or pixel of the display. User-determined color values (up to 24 bits) are usually stored in a separate fast memory that is addressed using indices stored in the display buffer. This feature can be readily incorporated in the general approach we shall use to illustrate a monochrome graphics display.

Let us consider a display terminal with 512 scan lines and 512 × 512 *pixels*. Storing "on" or "off" values to provide for continuous refresh of each pixel will require 2^{18} bits or 32K bytes of information. Let us assume that each byte stored will control the value of the beam at eight consecutive pixels on a horizontal scan line. This is not the most convenient approach for incorporation of alphanumeric information, but with the aid of some special ROMs, character streams could be converted into this format. This task will not be considered here. Various approaches can reduce the data storage requirements for purely alphanumeric terminals to approximately the number of characters displayable on the screen. If the refresh buffer is considered to be the low-order half of 64K separately addressed bytes of RAM, Fig. 11.6 shows the hex addresses of bytes in the RAM as they correspond to positions on the scan line. Each row requires 64 bytes to store 512 pixels.

Testing and experience have revealed that a CRT screen must be refreshed at a rate of about 30 Hz to avoid flicker perceptible by the user. This implies that data must be accessed and supplied to the terminal at a rate given by equation 11.5.

$$\text{Refresh rate} = 32{,}768 \times 30 \text{ Hz} = 0.98 \text{ MHz} \qquad (11.5)$$

Figure 11.7 uses PMS-like notation to illustrate the alternatives that have been considered over the years as graphics display terminals have been incorporated into computer systems. Three possible locations of the display terminal are shown. These are (1) on the RIC primary memory bus, (2) on RICBUS, and (3) remotely located at the end of a serial communications channel. Also at issue is the location of the display refresh memory.

The first alternative for the terminal with the display memory as shown would make sense if only a single terminal were used and the computer were a personal computer rather than the somewhat more capable 32-bit RIC. In the past, when graphics terminals were a novelty, this approach was used for larger computers (there may have

```
0000 0001 0002  . . . . . . . . . . . . . . . . . . . . . . . 003F
0040 0041                                        007F
0080                                               .
   .                                               .
   .                                               .

7FC0 7FC1  . . . . . . . . . . . . . . . . . . . . . . . . . . 7FFF
```
Figure 11.6. Screen mapping of the display buffer.

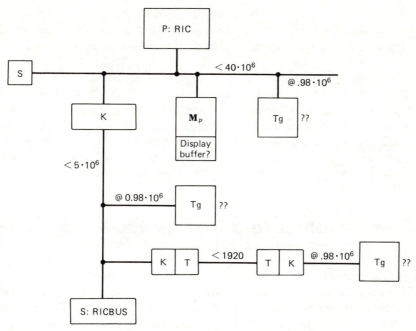

Figure 11.7. Location of graphics terminals and display buffer.

been an I/O bus). A more suitable alternative is the connection of the terminal directly to RICBUS. RICBUS could accommodate the movement of data from the primary memory to refresh one or two terminals, if all data were passed across the bus in packets no larger than those sent to the graphics terminals.

Example 11.1

Imagine that during the continuous refresh of an unbuffered graphics terminal on RICBUS as in Fig. 11.7, display data are sent from the primary memory to the graphics terminal in 4-byte packets. If only one other device is interested in RICBUS, what is the maximum number of bytes that this device can transfer, while remaining busmaster, without interfering with refresh of the terminal?

Solution
This is an immediate application of equation 11.4 derived in the previous section. For RICBUS, we established that $C = 5$ MHz in Section 10.9. The number of bytes per packet is $n = 4$, and from equation 11.5, $r = 0.98$ MHz. Therefore, for the other device on RICBUS we compute the data packet size, H, from equation 11.4.

$$H = 4 \cdot (5/(0.98) - 1)$$

$$= 16.4 \text{ bytes}$$

In addition to consuming about 20% of the bus capacity, the graphics terminal would force a complicated internal buffering on another RICBUS member, such as a disk drive, that would more naturally work with data in units of about 512 bytes. ■

Clearly, the operation of the entire system is severely constrained if the graphics terminal is separated from its refresh data base by RICBUS. As is clear from Fig. 11.7, separating the terminal from its refresh base by a serial communications channel is impossible. As we shall show in Chapter 12, the depicted data rate of 1920 bytes/sec is the maximum that would normally be attempted using the RS-232 convention for serial transmission. All this suggests that *a graphics terminal intended for general applications can be expected to have its refresh memory local to or internal to the terminal*.

11.6   A Graphics Terminal for the RIC System

We saw in Section 11.4 that it was not feasible to design a graphics terminal for RIC that did not contain sufficient internal memory to store the data required to refresh the screen completely. Instead, let us provide for RIC a graphics terminal that will be self-contained, needing to communicate with the rest of the RIC system only when it is necessary to save a screen image on disk for future use or to place an image from disk on the screen. Moving images between the disk and the screen will be accomplished using DMA, with the transfer rate dictated by the transmission medium. Any transfer rate will be tolerated by the graphics terminal, but potential user-dissatisfaction will establish some lower bound. Transfer directly from terminal to disk is an attractive proposition; but to simplify our analysis, here we shall treat the transfer as a two-step process. To transfer the contents of the screen to the disk, RIC will first initiate a DMA transfer between the graphics terminal and the primary memory and will then cause the disk memory to read the block from the primary memory via DMA. We shall focus on the former.

The mapping of memory locations onto the scan lines will be as suggested in Section 11.5. Each scan line will require 64 bytes of memory, a total of 32K bytes for the 512 scan lines. Two possible positions for a graphics terminal with internal memory within a RIC-based computer system are shown in Fig. 11.8. As suggested by that PMS diagram, the 32K screen memory can be loaded through the RICBUS in less than a second.

Example 11.2

Also illustrated in Fig. 11.8 is an alternate version of the graphics terminal that would not need to be located in the immediate vicinity of the RIC system, but could be located elsewhere and connected to the RICBUS through a serial communications medium. Select an appropriate minimum data transmission rate R to recommend for a channel, connecting this device to the RICBUS assuming it is necessary to communicate complete screen images to and from RIC.

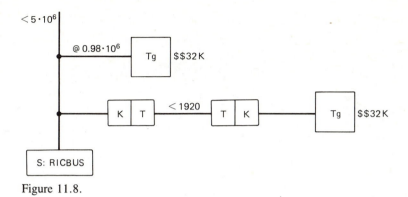

Figure 11.8.

Solution

A lower bound on the time required to transmit a complete screen image from RIC to the terminal is given by equation 11.6, where R is in bytes/sec.

$$\text{Load time} = \frac{32,768}{R} \text{ sec} \tag{11.6}$$

As we shall see in Chapter 12, the least expensive and the most commonly used data transmission equipment for use on the switched telephone system offers data rates of up to 120 char/sec. If $R = 120$, a total of 273 sec or 4.55 min would be required before the complete image would appear on the screen. Few users would tolerate such a slow response. Other standard voice channel data rates available, depending on equipment and the transmission medium, are given by 30×2^n up to a maximum of 960 or 1920 char/sec. For $R = 1920$, the screen load time would be 17 sec., probably an acceptable figure. ∎

In the foregoing example, it was assumed that complete screen images would be transmitted between RIC and the graphics terminal. This might well be the preferred method for a complicated image generated by a graphics tablet. It is to be expected that RIC could also create an image on the terminal screen by executing a program that would send a series of commands to the terminal. These commands would cause the terminal to take actions such as "draw a line" or "fill a space." To accept and react to such commands requires a level of intelligence in the terminal most easily achieved by including an internal computer that takes the form of the 8-bit microprocessor found Fig. 11.9.

A contemporary graphics terminal is also likely to accept input from both a keyboard and an electromechanical drawing tablet. Figure 11.9 is a more detailed PMS chart that may be substituted for the graphics terminal box connected directly to the RICBUS in Fig. 11.8. Consistent with PMS notation, the random access memory used to store the screen image is labelled Mp in Fig. 11.9. The tasks that must be accomplished by the graphics terminal may be listed as follows.

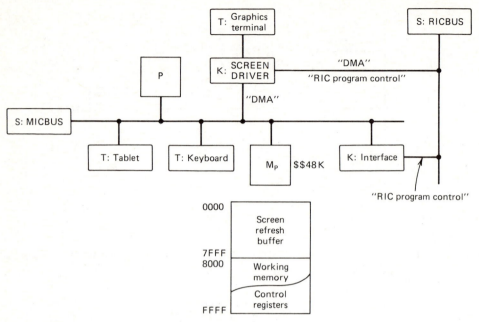

Figure 11.9. Layout of RICBUS graphics terminal.

1. Refresh the CRT screen at a rate of 30 Hz.
2. Perform computations and adjust the contents of the screen memory in response to user inputs through the graphics tablet.
3. Respond to RIC commands as observed on the RICBUS.
4. Control the DMA transfer of data between RIC and Mp.

The box P is a microprocessor that will be assigned tasks 2 and 3. Entering a diagonal line through the graphics tablet and keyboard will require modifications of the contents of several bytes of the screen driver memory, and therefore considerable computation on the part of the microprocessor. To provide for this computation, Mp will consist of somewhat more than 48K bytes out of the 64K bytes in the 16-bit Mp address space. The low-order 32K bytes will store the screen image. Registers in the tablet, keyboard, and RICBUS interface controller will share the high-order half of the microprocessor address space with the working memory. Tablet and keyboard entries will be at the pace of a human user; hence the relatively low required data rate of 10 bytes/sec. Specifics of the processing inputs from the tablet and keyboard is a software topic that will not be considered further here.

As discussed in Section 11.5, refreshing the entire screen 30 times per second will require the transfer of data form memory at a rate of 980,000 bytes/sec. If we assume a basic clock rate throughout the graphics terminal of 10 MHz, this data rate would be impractical for programmed control transfer and would be best achieved through direct memory access. For this purpose, we provide the controller module.

SCREENDRIVER, which will have direct access to the memory bus for accomplishing tasks 1 and 4. A third module, designated as a controller, will accept commands for the microprocessor and provide a variety of status information to RIC. This module will communicate under program control with RIC. SCREENDRIVER will transfer screen images to and from RIC via DMA on the RICBUS and will accept data from the microprocessor memory via DMA. Status and command registers in SCREEN-DRIVER will be accessed by RIC under program control.

We see in Fig. 11.10 an illustration of the data flow in SCREENDRIVER during the process of refreshing the screen. The 15-bit register **ADDRCNT** plays the central role. This register contains the address of the next memory byte needed by the refresh process. The most significant 9 bits of this register also specify the current scan line. Just after the first byte of a line is fetched via DMA, bits **ADDRCNT**[0:8] are loaded into a register that drives a D/A converter, whose output in turn controls the vertical position of the beam. The control section of SCREENDRIVER must generate a signal to start the sweep of the beam after ample time has been provided for the beam to return to its initial position at the left of the tube. Once triggered, the horizontal sweep is driven by a linearly increasing voltage whose timing is independently adjusted. The data byte is shifted left in **SCRNREG** each clock period in which the scan is active. The most significant bit of this register turns on the beam.

A total of 2^{18} bits must circulate through **SCRNREG** 30 times per second, so a lower bound on the clock frequency is given by equation 11.7.

$$\text{Rbit} = 2^{18} \times 30 \text{ Hz} = \left(\frac{30}{4}\right) \times 2^{20} \approx 7.5 \text{ MHz} \tag{11.7}$$

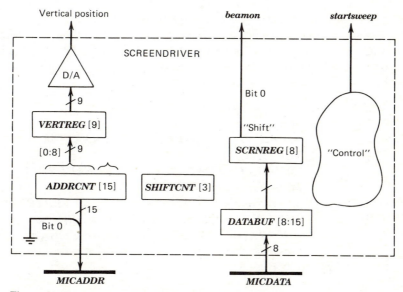

Figure 11.10. Dataflow in SCREENDRIVER module.

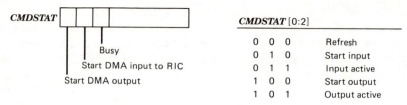

Figure 11.11. Command and status for SCREENDRIVER.

Connecting SCREENDRIVER to the 10-MHz RIC clock and shifting **SCRNREG** each clock period will allow time for reverse traversals of the beam while accomplishing a refresh at approximately 30 Hz. During at least seven out of eight clock periods, when no new data byte is loaded into **SCRNREG,** the microprocessor will have access to the bus. We assume that the DMA controller for MICBUS functions like the equal priority controller of Example 10.3.

    Although the algorithms for priority determination differ between the bus arbitrators of MICBUS and RICBUS, the set of input and output signals are the same. (The exceptions are the signals *dma* and *high* which are only on RICBUS.) In the declarations that follow, we have used names differing only in the prefix that identifies the bus for all corresponding lines on the two buses. Steps 1 to 3 initialize in preparation for refresh of the first scan line. After generation of each scan line, control converges at step 4 where a check is made of the command-status register. Control will branch out of the refresh process if RIC desires that a new image be transferred to the screen or if the current image is to be stored. The meaning of the only three implemented bits of the register **CMDSTAT** is given in Fig. 11.11. Step 5 makes secondary application of the counter **SHIFTCOUNT** to allow reverse traversal by the beam while the vertical position moves down one line. The registers **CMDSTAT** and **BUFFADDR,** in which RIC will load the low-order 16 bits of the address of the first 4 image bytes, occupy consecutive locations in the last 256 pages of RIC address space.

MODULE:	SCREENDRIVER.
INPUTS:	*busgrant; micbusgrant.*
MEMORY:	*ADDRCNT*[15]; *SHIFTCNT*[3]; *SCRNREG*[8]; *VERTREG*[9]; *CMDSTAT*[8]; *DATABUF*[16]; *BUFFADDR*[16]; *halfwdbit; busreqff.*
OUTPUTS:	*busreq; micbusreq; beamon; startsweep; VERTREG*[9].
COMBUSES:	*MICADDR*[16]; *MICDATA*[8]; *RBADDR*[16]; *RBDATA*[16]; *micbusread; micbuswrite; busread; buswrite; dma; high; busack.*

   1   *CMDSTAT*[0:2] ← 3 ⊤ 0;
       → (2, 50).

2     $ADDRCNT \leftarrow 15 \top 0$; $SHIFTCNT \leftarrow 3 \top 0$;
      $micbusreq = 1$;
      $\rightarrow (\overline{micbusgrant})/(2)$.

3     $micbusread = 1$; $MICADDR = 0, ADDRCNT$; $SCRNREG \leftarrow$
                                                      $MICDATA$;

4     $\rightarrow (\overline{CMDSTAT}[0] \wedge \overline{CMDSTAT}[1], CMDSTAT[0], CMDSTAT[1])$
      $/(5, 22, 13)$.

5     $SHIFTCNT \leftarrow INC(SHIFTCNT)$; $VERTREG \leftarrow ADDRCNT[0:8]$;
      $\rightarrow (\overline{\bigwedge/SHIFTCNT})/(5)$.

6     $startsweep = 1$.   (Begin a scan line)

7   NO DELAY
      $SHIFTCNT \leftarrow 3 \top 0$;
      $\rightarrow (8A, 8B)$.

8A $SHIFTCNT \leftarrow INC(SHIFTCNT)$; $SCRNREG \leftarrow SCRNREG[1:7],0$;
      $beamon = SCRNREG[0]$;
      $\rightarrow (\overline{\bigwedge/SHIFTCNT[0:1]}, \bigwedge/SHIFTCNT[0:1])/(8A, DEADEND)$.

8B $ADDRCNT \leftarrow INC(ADDRCNT)$.

9B $micbusreq = 1$;
      $\rightarrow (\overline{micbusgrant})/(9B)$.

10B $micbusread = 1$; $MICADDR = 0, ADDRCNT$;
      $DATABUF[8:15] \leftarrow MICDATA$.

11B $SCRNREG * (\bigwedge/SHIFTCNT) \leftarrow DATABUF[8:15]$;
      $beamon = SCRNREG[0]$;
      $\rightarrow (\overline{\bigwedge/SHIFTCNT})/(11b)$.

12B   NO DELAY
      $\rightarrow (\overline{\bigvee/ADDRCNT[9:14]}, \bigvee/ADDRCNT[9:14])/(4, 7)$.

The kernel of the refresh process is the closely coordinated parallel sequences 8A and 8B through 12B. Step 8A shifts the current byte of screen data through **SCRNREG** while steps 8B through 10B fetch the next byte via DMA. No more than the seven clock periods in which step 8A is active are available for the fetch of the data byte. This will be sufficient given the equal priority arbitration between SCREEN-DRIVER and the microprocessor. The last pixel of a byte is placed on the screen by step 11B while the new byte is transferred into **SCRNREG.** Unless the end of a scan line has been reached, steps 8A and 8B are reexcited following step 11 without additional delay.

Transfer of a screen image to or from RIC primary memory and the refresh memory is a two-step process. Checking equation 11.6 again suggests that this could probably be accomplished in less than a second even under program control. This approach would imply both a RIC program and a microprocessor program and a fairly complicated bus interface module. Equally well, both steps could employ DMA. A major goal of this chapter is to illustrate DMA on RICBUS, so we choose this approach. Because the hardware for DMA on MICBUS is already included in SCREENDRIVER, we shall let this module manage the image transfer as well.

13    $ADDRCNT \leftarrow 15 \top 0$; *halfwdbit* $\leftarrow 0$; *CMDSTAT*[2] $\leftarrow 1$.

14   *micbusreq* $= 1$;   "MICBUS"
      $\rightarrow (\overline{micbusgrant})/(14)$.

15   *micbusread* $= 1$; *MICADDR* $= 0$, *ADDRCNT*;
      DATABUF[0:7] $\leftarrow$ *MICDATA*; *ADDRCNT* $\leftarrow$ INC(*ADDRCNT*).

16   *micbusreq* $= 1$;
      $\rightarrow (\overline{micbusgrant})/(16)$.

17   *micbusread* $= 1$; *MICADDR* $= 0$, *ADDRCNT*;
      DATABUF[8:15] $\leftarrow$ *MICDATA*; *ADDRCNT* $\leftarrow$ INC(*ADDRCNT*).

18   *busreqff* $\leftarrow 1$;   "RICBUS"

19    $\rightarrow (\overline{busgrant \wedge \overline{busack}})/(19)$.

20   *RBDATA* $=$ *DATABUF*; *dma* $= 1$;
      RBADDR $=$ *BUFFADDR*; *buswrite* $= 1$; *high* $= \overline{halfwdbit}$;
      $\rightarrow (\overline{busgrant \wedge \overline{busack}}, busgrant \wedge \overline{busack}, busack)/(19, 20, 21)$.

21   *BUFFADDR*,*halfwdbit* $\leftarrow$ INC(*BUFFADDR*,*halfwdbit*);
      busreqff $* \overline{\vee/ADDRCNT} \leftarrow 0$;
      CMDSTAT[0:2] $* \overline{\vee/ADDRCNT} \leftarrow 3 \top 0$;
      $\rightarrow (\overline{\vee/ADDRCNT}, \vee/ADDRCNT)/(2, 14)$.

Steps 14 through 17 obtain two consecutive bytes from the refresh memory, and steps 18 through 20 pass the combined halfword across RICBUS to the DMA interface. The completely responsive handshake specified by the template of Fig. 11.3 is implemented. The DMA interface will combine two such halfwords to form a single RIC word before completing the second step of the transfer (across the primary memory bus). **BUFFADDR** is the address of a 32-bit RIC word, so it must be incremented only once every other pass through step 20. We provide for this by adding a least significant bit, **halfwdbit**, to the incrementing process for **BUFFADDR**. Conveniently, the line **high**, which is used to route the first of two halfwords to the high-order half of the addressed RIC word, may be connected to the complement of **halfwdbit**. The output transfer of an image beginning at step 22 is the inverse of steps 13 through 21.

22    $ADDRCNT \leftarrow 15 \top 0$; *halfwdbit* $\leftarrow 0$; *CMDSTAT*[2] $\leftarrow 1$.

23   *busreqff* $\leftarrow 1$;   "RICBUS"
      $\rightarrow (\overline{busgrant \wedge \overline{busack}})/(23)$.

24   *RBADDR* $=$ *BUFFADDR*; *busread* $= 1$; *dma* $= 1$;
      high $= \overline{halfwdbit}$; *DATABUF* $*$ *busack* $\leftarrow$ *RBDATA*;
      $\rightarrow (\overline{busgrant \wedge \overline{busack}}, \overline{busgrant} \wedge \overline{busack}, busack)$
      $/(24, 23, 25)$.

25   *micbusreq* $= 1$;   "MICBUS"
      $\rightarrow (\overline{micbusgrant})/(25)$.

26   *MICDATA* $=$ *DATABUS*[0:7]; *MICADDR* $= 0$, *ADDRCNT*;
      micbuswrite $= 1$; *ADDRCNT* $\leftarrow$ INC(*ADDRCNT*).

27   *micbusreq* $= 1$;   "MICBUS"
      $\rightarrow (\overline{micbusgrant})/(27)$.

28    $MICDATA = DATABUF[8:15]; MICADDR = 0, ADDRCNT;$
      $micbuswrite = 1; ADDRCNT \leftarrow INC(ADDRCNT).$

29    $BUFFADDR, halfwdbit \leftarrow INC(BUFFADDR, halfwdbit);$
      $busreqff * \overline{\bigvee/ADDRCNT} \leftarrow 0;$
      $CMDSTAT[0:2] * \overline{\bigvee/ADDRCNT} \leftarrow 3 \top 0;$
      $\rightarrow (\overline{\bigvee/ADDRCNT}, \bigvee/ADDRCNT)/(2, 23).$

At the beginning of the description, step 50 is activated in parallel with step 2 to provide for simultaneous slave activity that must respond to the RICBUS asynchronous protocol. Steps 50 through 52 make possible the reading and writing to the command/status register and the writing of a primary memory buffer area address in **BUFFADDR.** You will notice the strong resemblance to steps 2B through 4B of the scoreboard slave.

50    $\rightarrow \overline{(ENABLE(RBADDR) \wedge (busread \vee buswrite)dma)}/(50).$

51    $CMDSTAT[0:1] * (buswrite \wedge \overline{RBADDR}[15]) \leftarrow RBDATA[8:9];$
      $BUFFADDR * (buswrite \wedge RBADDR[15]) \leftarrow RBDATA.$

52    $RBDATA[8:15] = CMDSTAT * busread; busack = 1;$
      $\rightarrow (\overline{ENABLE(RBADDR) \wedge (busread \vee buswrite)},$
                          $ENABLE(RBADDR) \wedge (busread \vee buswrite))/(50, 52).$

END SEQUENCE
      CONTROLRESET(1);
      $busreq = busreqff.$
END.

11.7   A Magnetic Tape Transport Controller

Magnetic tape transports are among the most complex of standard computer peripherals. A tape transport is capable of a variety of activities, requiring a large number of commands and a considerable amount of status information. Data is commonly written in blocks of several thousand characters, which are written or read as units, making DMA operation a virtual necessity. Tape data is read or written 1 byte at a time, requiring assembly or disassembly of words, except in computers with 8-bit memory words. As a result of all these complications, tape transports are invariably equipped with their own peripheral controllers, to relieve the CPU of the burden of all these details. Commercial tape transports will normally be equipped with their own custom controllers, so it may be that many readers will never have the need to design a tape transport controller. Nevertheless, consideration of the design of such controllers will illustrate many basic techniques of I/O interfacing and will provide an example of DMA transfer via the RICBUS.

We will assume a 9-track tape unit, with data recorded in 8K-byte blocks at the standard density of 1600 bpi, which is the same as 1600 bytes per inch in the 9-track format. With this density a block will occupy 5 in., with 3/4-in. interblock gaps, providing a capacity of 5000 blocks (40 MB) on a 2400-ft tape. Data must be written or read one block at a time; once you start on a block, you cannot stop in the middle. DMA can easily be set up on a page-by-page basis, with each page consisting of 256 32-bit words, that is, 1K bytes. Thus a block transfer to or from the tape will require a DMA transfer of 8 pages. We could design a peripheral controller capable of direct DMA operations on the primary memory bus, similar to the controller of Section 10.5. However, large computer systems usually have a number of tape units and the number of connections available on the primary memory bus must be very limited. Instead, we will put the transport controller on RICBUS, interfacing to the main buses through a single RICBUS DMA interface. Each controller will occupy only a few locations in the RICBUS address space, permitting any desired number of tape units to be connected to RICBUS.

The RICBUS DMA interface has been described briefly in the previous sections, but the timing of operations in a tape transport is sufficiently critical that it is helpful to further consider the timing of RICBUS DMA operations. DMA operations through RICBUS were considered in the design of the graphics controller, but the timing of DMA operations was not a real problem. The graphics interface could adjust its transfer rate as required to match the capabilities of the DMA system. By contrast, a tape transport must transfer data at a fixed rate. Once a tape comes up to speed, it cannot adjust the data transfer rate to accommodate the DMA system. *Overrun*, a situation in which the tape transport provides or requests data at a rate beyond the capabilities of the DMA system, is a very real possibility. The timing of the tape transport and the DMA system must be closely coordinated to provide the maximum possible data transfer rate. We will not carry out a design of the RICBUS DMA interface but will describe its operation in just enough detail to proceed with the design of the tape transport controller. As seen by the RIC main buses, the RICBUS DMA interface will function in exactly the same manner as the DMA peripheral of Section 10.5, capable of requesting control of the primary memory bus from the bus arbitrator and then carrying out direct transfers to or from memory. In all other respects, the RICBUS DMA interface will function as a slave on RICBUS, accessible to RIC only via a RICBUS master, such as a tape transport controller. RIC will send the necessary commands to set up a DMA operation to the tape controller via the program control interface on RICBUS, and the controller will then set up the operations of the RICBUS DMA interface as may be required.

From an architectural view, the RICBUS DMA interface will consist of three registers, connected to the primary memory bus and RICBUS as shown in Fig. 11.12. The **DMASTAT** register will be permanently assigned address FFFE in the RICBUS address space and will be used for reporting status information, such as overrun, with regard to DMA operations. The upper 8 bits of **DMADDR** will be assigned address FFFF and will be loaded with the upper half of the page number identifying the DMA area in main memory. The lower 16 bits of **DMADDR** and the data register **DMADATA** do not have addresses in the RICBUS space but are "transparent" registers used for connecting the address and data buses of RICBUS with the primary memory bus.

Figure 11.13 is a flowchart of the RICBUS DMA interface. Before carrying out

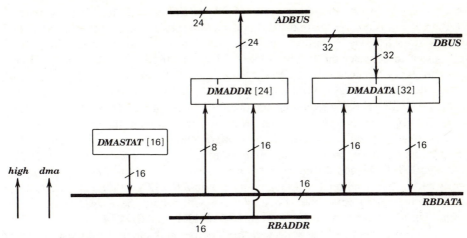

Figure 11.12. Register connections—RICBUS DMA interface.

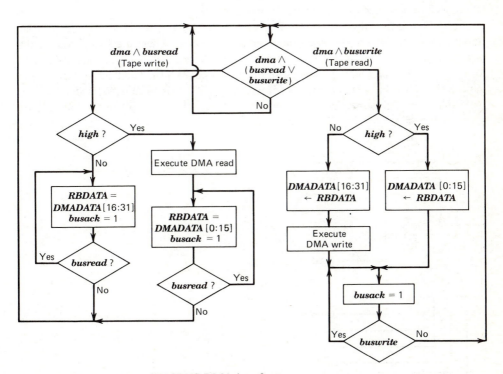

Figure 11.13. Flowchart of RICBUS DMA interface.

actual DMA transfers, the upper 8 bits of **DMADDR** must be loaded by a write to location FFFF. As suggested in the earlier discussion, these 8 bits could also be loaded directly from RIC via the primary memory bus, but it is convenient for purposes of this design to consider the RICBUS DMA interface strictly as a slave on RICBUS, accessible only to masters on RICBUS. For purposes of controlling DMA operations, we use the two RICBUS control lines *dma* and *high*. Activating *dma* will signal that a DMA operation is being requested and that the address of **RBADDR** is not an address in the RICBUS space but is the lower 16 bits of an address in the main memory.

Activating *dma* and *busread*, with *high* active, will cause a DMA read to **DMADATA** from the main memory address formed by the catenation of the 16 bits sent over **RBADDR** and the upper 8 bits previously loaded into **DMADDR**[0:7]. The upper half of the word read will then be placed on **RBDATA**. If *dma* and *busread* go active with *high* inactive, the DMA interface will ignore the **RBADDR** lines and simply put the lower half of the word in **DMADATA** on **RBDATA**.

Activating *dma* and *buswrite* with *high* active will simply load the word from **RBDATA** into the upper half of **DMADATA**. If *high* is inactive, driving *dma* and *buswrite* active will load the word from **RBDATA** into the lower half of **DMADATA** and then initiate a DMA write, at the address specified by the catenation of the 16 bits on **RBADDR** and the 8 bits previously loaded into **DMADDR**[0:7]. Note that the lower 16 bits of **DMADDR** may not physically exist, but may be realized simply in a connection of **RBADDR** to the lower 16 bits of **ADBUS**. However, this is a detail of realization that need not concern us here.

The basic model of the tape transport is indicated in Fig. 11.14. There are four input control signals: *write*, *read*, *forward*, and *reverse*. There are five output status signals: *sprocket*, *lpc*, *gap*, *bot*, and *eot*. Finally, there are the bidirectional 8-bit data lines, **TDATA**. The reading and writing of the *sprocket* bit is handled entirely by the tape deck; only 8-bit ASCII characters appear on the **TDATA** lines. A WRITE operation is initiated by activating line *write*, which will start the tape. When the tape comes

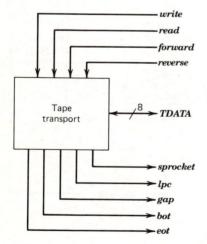

Figure 11.14. Basic model of tape transport.

up to speed, an internal oscillator in the tape deck will generate the *sprocket* signal at the appropriate intervals for recording at the density of 1600 bpi. Data to be recorded should then be placed on the *TDATA* and held until the *sprocket* line goes inactive. As the data are recorded, the controller will compute the longitudinal parity check character (LPC) to be recorded at the end of the block. When 8K characters have been recorded, three blank characters will be recorded, followed by the LPC character, after which *write* will be turned off to end the operation.

A READ operation will start when the *read* signal goes active. When the tape comes up to speed, the *sprocket* signal will go active each time a character is read, indicating that a character read from the tape will be stable on the *TDATA* lines for the duration of the *sprocket* signal. The LPC character will be found by the tape drive electronics by detecting the three blank characters, and the presence of the active *lpc* signal during *sprocket* will indicate the reading of the LPC character, at which time *read* should be turned off to terminate the read operation.

In addition to READ and WRITE, the tape transport will respond to three other commands, SPACE, BACKSPACE, and REWIND. SPACE will move the tape at high speed to the next interblock gap, BACKSPACE will move backward to the previous interblock gap, and REWIND will move back to the beginning of the tape. The signal *gap* will go active when the tape moves into the interblock gap, as detected by the absence of any recorded characters. It will go inactive when a character is detected after the tape starts moving. The beginning and end of the tape are marked by reflective markers on the tape that are sensed by *photoelectric detectors*. When either is sensed, the tape will be automatically stopped and the appropriate signal, *bot* (beginning of tape) or *eot* (end of tape) will go active. A SPACE operation will be carried out by driving the signal *forward* active and holding it active until the *gap* signal is detected, and a BACKSPACE will be carried out by driving the *reverse* signal active until *gap* is detected. A REWIND will be accomplished by setting *reverse* active until *bot* is detected.

The register model for the tape controller is shown in Fig. 11.15. Register *TDR*[16] provides for assembly or disassembly of 16-bit words to provide communications between *TDR* and *RBDATA*. *TADDR* will receive the lower 16-bits of the starting address for the DMA transfer from RIC via the program control interface. The register *TSTAT* will consist of status flags such as *busyf*, *dmactf*, *pef* (parity error), *eotf*, *botf*, *lpef* (longitudinal parity error), and *gapf*. Although these flags will be specific bits in *TSTAT*, in the interest of clarity they will be referred to by the individual names, as was the case with the flags in RIC. The register *TINT* will be used to enable interrupts due to various status conditions. The setting of a given status bit will cause an interrupt if the corresponding bit of *TINT* is set, except for *busyf* and *damactf*, where the flag going inactive, indicating completion, will cause an interrupt. This arrangement will allow the programmer to monitor the tape transport system through programmed status checking or interrupts, as appropriate in a particular situation. Register *TCOM* will be used to send commands, such as DMA read or write, backspace, and space, to the interface.

The controller will be located in the RICBUS address space by external addressing logic driven by the upper 14 bits of *RBADDR* bus. The registers within the controller

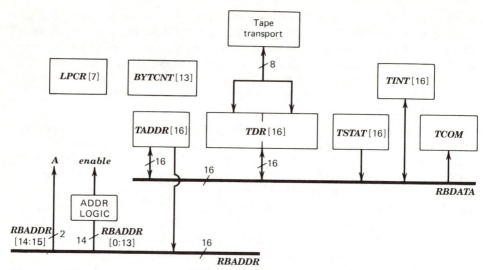

Figure 11.15. Register connections in tape transport controller.

are selected by the addressing bits *A*[2], connected to the low-order 2-bits of ***RBADDR***. Register ***TSTAT*** will be selected by *A* = 00, ***TADDR*** by 01, ***TINT*** by 10, and ***TCOM*** by 11. There is also a 13-bit counter ***BYTCNT*** to count the 8K bytes as they are written to tape, and a 7-bit ***LPCR***, used for longitudinal parity checking. The assignment of control bits in ***TCOM*** is summarized in Fig. 11.16.

MODULE:	TAPE CONTROLLER.
MEMORY:	***TDR***[16]; ***TADDR***[16]; ***TSTAT***[16]; ***TCOM***[16];
	TINT[16]; ***BYTCNT***[13]; ***LPCR***[7]; *first*; *writef*;
	readf; *busreqf*; *reversef*; *forward*.
INPUTS:	*A*[2]; *enable*; *sprocket*; *lpc*; *gap*; *bot*; *eot*.
OUTPUTS:	*write*; *read*; *forward*; *reverse*.
COMBUSES:	***RBDATA***[16]; ***RDADDR***[16]; *busreq*; *busgrant*; *busread*;
	busack; *high*; *buswrite*; *dma*; ***TDATA***[8].

1   → (2,5).
2   → ($\overline{enable}$, *enable* ∧ *buswrite*, *enable* ∧ *busread*)/(2, 3, 4).
3   (***TADDR*** ! ***TINT*** ! ***TCOM*** * (DCD[1:3](*A*)) ← ***RBDATA***.
4   ***RBDATA*** = ***TSTAT*** * (*busread* ∧ DCD[0] (*A*)); *busack* = 1;
      → ($\overline{enable}$, *enable*)/(2, 4).
5   → ($\overline{enable \wedge buswrite \wedge \text{DCD}[3]\ (A)}$)/(5).
6   → (√/***TCOM***, ***TCOM***[0:4])/(5, 10, 35, 60, 70, 80).

Following the declarations, the sequence starts by diverging to two parallel loops. One loop, steps 2 to 4, monitors RICBUS for reads or writes to the controller registers and executes the RICBUS protocol to carry out the transfers. This is the slave activity of the template in Fig. 11.3. The main sequence starts at step 5, waiting for new commands to be loaded to ***TCOM***, and step 6 checks to see what the command is. If

Control Bit	Meaning
TCOM[0]	Activate DMA write to tape
TCOM[1]	Activate DMA read from tape
TCOM[2]	SPACE
TCOM[3]	BACKSPACE
TCOM[4]	REWIND

Figure 11.16. Control bit assignments.

no bits are set, control returns to 5, otherwise the sequence branches to execute one of the five possible commands. Note that this branch assumes that only one command bit will be set.

Before proceeding to the actual sequence for a DMA read operation, let us consider the timing involved in writing data on tape. (It should be noted that a DMA read involves a read of main memory, which requires a write to tape. This is a frequent source of confusion, the fact that a read of one device requires a write to another, and the designer must be sure to keep clear which is which.) Fig. 11.17 shows the timing

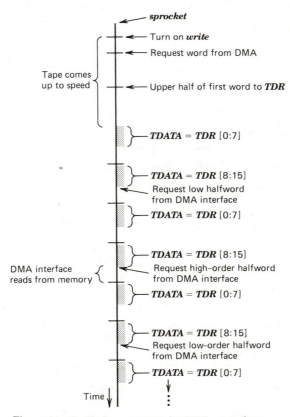

Figure 11.17. Timing of TAPE WRITE operation.

of a DMA write to tape. Note that time progresses vertically downward on this diagram. After activating write to turn on the transport, the controller will request a DMA read with **high** active, which will initiate a DMA read from main memory. When the word has been read into **DMADATA**, the upper half will be placed on **RBDATA** and clocked into **TDR**. The two bytes of the halfword are then individually connected to **TDATA** for the duration of the next two **sprocket** signals. When the second of these **sprocket** signals goes down, another DMA read request will be issued, with **high** inactive, resulting in the lower half of the word in **DMADATA** being sent to **TDR** and connected to **TDATA** as two separate bytes. When **sprocket** for the second byte goes down, another DMA read request will result in a DMA read from memory, and the whole process will be repeated. It is important that the DMA request be issued as soon as **sprocket** goes inactive to provide the maximum possible time for a DMA cycle.

The active DMA read sequence starts at step 10 by clearing the command bit, setting the DMA active flag, clearing the error flags, and clearing **LPCR** and **BYTCNT**. It then requests the bus by activating **busreq**, which will remain active until the DMA operation is complete. The sequence then activates the tape transport by raising the **write** line and setting the *first* flip-flop, which will control which half of **DMADATA** is transferred on each RICBUS cycle. In this design, **busreq** will remain 1 throughout the transfer of an 8KB block, thereby precluding sharing RICBUS with a simultaneous DMA activity of another peripheral. The possibility of interleaving transfers from two active bus members will be discussed at the end of the section.

10 *dmactf* ← 1; **TCOM**[0] ← 0;
    lpef ← 0; *pef* ← 0; *lpcf* ← 0;
    LPCR ← 7 ⊤ 0; **BYTCNT** ← 13 ⊤ 0.

11 *busreqf* ← 1;
    → ($\overline{busgrant}$)/(11).

12 *writef* ← 1; *first* ← 1.

13 → ($busgrant \wedge \overline{busack}$, $busgrant \wedge \overline{busack}$)/(13, 14).

14 **RBADDR** = **TADDR**; *high* = *first*; *busread* = 1;
    TDR * *busack* ← **RBDATA**; *dma* = 1;
    → ($\overline{busgrant}$, *busack*, $busgrant \wedge \overline{busack}$)/(13, 15, 14).

15 **LPCR** * *sprocket* ← **LPCR** ⊕ **TDR**[0:6];
    BYTCNT * *sprocket* ← INC(**BYTCNT**);
    → ($sprocket$)/(15).

16 **TDATA** = **TDR**[0:6],ODDPAR(**TDR**[0:6]);
    → ($\overline{sprocket}$)/(16).

17 **LPCR** * $\overline{sprocket}$ ← **LPCR** ⊕ **TDR**[8:14];
    BYTCNT * $\overline{sprocket}$ ← INC(**BYTCNT**);
    → ($\overline{sprocket}$)/(17).

18 **TDATA** = **TDR**[8:14],ODDPAR(**TDR**[8:14]);
    first * $\overline{sprocket}$ ← $\overline{first}$;
    TADDR * ($\overline{sprocket} \wedge \overline{first}$) ← INC(**TADDR**);
    → ($sprocket$, $\overline{sprocket} \wedge eot$, $\overline{sprocket} \wedge \overline{eot}$)/(18, 23, 19).

19 NO DELAY
    → ($\vee$/**BYTCNT**)/(13).

20      $\overline{(sprocket)}/(20)$.

21      $TDATA = (8 \top 0 \; ! \; LPCR, \text{ODDPAR}(LPCR)) *$
                                         $(\overline{\bigvee BYTCNT}[11{:}12], \bigvee BYTCNT[11{:}12])$;

        $BYTCNT * \overline{sprocket} \leftarrow \text{INC}(BYTCNT)$;

        $\rightarrow (sprocket)/(21)$.

22      $\rightarrow (BYTCNT[11] \bigvee BYTCNT[12])/(20)$.

23      $writef \leftarrow 0$; $dmactf \leftarrow 0$; $busreqf \leftarrow 0$; $wlef \leftarrow eot$;

        $\rightarrow (5)$.

Step 13 is the first step in a RICBUS transfer, checking to see that the bus is clear, but with an important difference. Because *busreq* is held active, *busgrant* should stay active. If it does not, it means that RIC has claimed RICBUS briefly to check status. Handling of this possibility is consistent with the template of Fig. 11.3. Step 14 requests a 16-bit word from the DMA interface, with **high** active or inactive, depending on the value of *first*, and transfers the requested word to *TDR*. Step 15 waits for *sprocket* to go active and increments the byte count and updates the longitudinal parity check character when this happens. Step 16 holds that data and lateral parity bit on *TDATA* while *sprocket* is active. Steps 17 and 18 repeat this operation for the lower byte in *TDR*.

The branch in step 18 differs from that in step 16 in that it checks for end of tape when *sprocket* goes down. When the writing of a block is started, there is no assurance that there is enough room left on the tape for a complete block. Following the writing of each pair of bytes, step 18 will check to see if the end of tape has been reached, branching to step 23 in that event. Step 18 also complements *first* , so that step 14 will alternate between reading the upper and lower halves of *DMADATA* in the RICBUS DMA interface. This step also increments *TADDR* to the next address in the DMA space if all 4 bytes of a word have been written to tape. Assuming end of tape has not been reached, step 19 checks to see if all 8K bytes have been written. If not, control branches back to step 13 to obtain the next 2 bytes from the DMA interface. If all 8K bytes have been written, steps 20 through 22 write three all-0 bytes and the lpc character. Step 23 deactivates the DMA operation. If the end-of-tape was reached before all 8K bytes have been transferred, step 23 sets the length error flag, *wlef*, indicating that the DMA read operation has been interrupted before completion. This flip-flop is a part of the status register, *TSTAT*.

The sequence for a DMA read operation, starting at step 35, will be left as an exercise for the reader. The other three operations are relatively simple by comparison. The backspace operation will be shown as an example.

70      $reversef \leftarrow 1$; $busyf \leftarrow 1$;

        $\rightarrow (gap)/(70)$.

71      $\rightarrow \overline{(gap)}/(71)$.

72      $reversef \leftarrow 0$; $busyf \leftarrow 0$;

        $\rightarrow (5)$.

Step 70 turns on the **reverse** signal and sets the **busyf** flag and then waits for **gap** to go down, indicating that the tape has moved out of the gap between blocks.

Step 71 then waits for the next *gap* back and then terminates the operation. You may have noted several flags used to drive output lines that have to be held active for extended periods. The steps after END SEQUENCE will specify the connections of these flags to the output lines.

        END SEQUENCE
                CONTROLREST(1);
                write = writef; read = readf; busreq = busreqf;
                reverse = reversef; forward = forwardf.
        END.

In the foregoing design, the tape transport has been allowed to maintain control of RICBUS throughout the transfer of a block of data. An upper limit on the data transfer rate that might be expected from a tape transport would be about 1 MB/sec. This limit is only 20% of the capacity established for RICBUS. In general, more than one peripheral could be actively engaged in a DMA activity at the same time. To avoid confusing the DMA interface, data must be transferred in units of 32-bit words, so the tape transport controller, just described, must retain control of RICBUS while four bytes are read from tape. Fig. 11.15 provides only a 2-byte data buffer. So RICBUS could be relinquished during the read of a block only for 2-byte intervals while this register is filled. Under these constraints, not even two tape transports could share RICBUS.

Example 11.3

Suppose that a RICBUS tape transfer controller for a tape unit, which reads data at a rate of 500 KB/sec, is provided with a 4-byte data buffer in addition to the hardware depicted in Fig. 11.15. If two such transports are simultaneously engaged in input DMA to RIC, compute the RICBUS bandwidth available to other activities. Use the 10-MHz RIC clock and neglect any time that might be used by the RIC program control interface to access command registers.

Solution

The 4-byte data buffer is filled by the tape transport in 8 μsec. Two clock periods are required by the handshake that regains control of RICBUS for each 4-byte transfer. From Section 10.9, we recall that four periods are used up by the transfer of each halfword on RICBUS. The register TDR may be connected to RICBUS while the buffer register accepts data from the transport. Thus each 4-byte transfer ties up RICBUS for 1 μsec within the 8-μsec fill interval. Together the two transports would tie RICBUS 2 out of each 8 μsec., so 75% of the RICBUS bandwidth would be available for other activity.   ∎

In this example, the time required to request RICBUS and receive a grant was not insignificant because data were transferred across RICBUS in one-word units. Such overhead factors are less important where larger data buffers can be provided in the peripherals.

11.8   Summary

In this chapter we have faced all the major considerations associated with connecting peripherals to an independent bus such as RICBUS, with direct memory access to the central processor. We considered one case, the graphics terminal, where data were to be transferred infrequently in very large 32K-byte blocks, but not at a rigid data rate. The final example was an unbuffered tape transport where blocks of data were transferred at a fixed data rate dictated by the mechanical motion of the tape transport.

No peripherals in the DAS (direct access storage) category were considered. In itself a treatment of disk storage would be of interest to many readers. However, the interface of a disk drive controller to RICBUS will present no problems not considered in conjunction with the tape transport. As discussed in Chapter 3, a file can be located much more quickly in DAS than in SAS (sequential access storage). Once a file is located, the data transfer rates are similar. The upper limit for disk transfer rate is only greater than the upper limit for tape transports by a factor of three or four. When active, a high-speed fixed disk is less likely to share a bus with another peripheral. CPU communication with memory must, of course, not stop when a disk or tape is engaged in DMA.

A simple error control mechanism applicable to tape transports was implemented in the description in Section 11.7. Because data are arranged serially on each track of a disk, these devices more closely resemble serial communications systems. The error control implementations to be discussed in Section 12.8 for communications systems may be applied to disk drives as well.

Problems

11.1   On RICBUS there are members and slaves. Can the same distinction be made for devices on the RIC primary memory bus, given the implementation of DMA on that bus? Assume that RICBUS is interfaced to this bus. What modules must necessarily be slaves on the primary memory bus? Is it likely that there will be additional slaves on that bus? What modules must necessarily be primary memory bus members?

11.2   Suppose that during the early stages of design formulation for the RIC computer system it was agreed that the RIC operating system program would absolutely assure that no more than one RICBUS member would be activated to perform DMA at a given time. In addition, no transactions would be allowed on RICBUS other than those involving the primary memory bus. It is still necessary to avoid deadlock with the program control interface, but the RICBUS arbitrator can be considerably simplified. Let the request lines of the seven RICBUS members (excluding the program control interface) be ORed together and a single grant line be fanned out to all seven devices.

(a)   Consistent with this description, modify and simplify as much as possible the AHPL description of RICBUSCONTROL.

(b)   Write a combinational logic unit description of the new grant priority network.

11.3   Given the DMA interface as discussed in Chapters 10 and 11, is it possible, simultaneously and successfully, to activate two RICBUS members for DMA to two separate 256-page regions of primary memory? Why or why not? If two members are never simultaneously activated for DMA, is it possible that two RICBUS members, not including the program control interface, would simultaneously request a busgrant? Why or why not?

11.4   Envision a new arbitration scheme for RICBUS in which bus members including the program control interface have equal priority. A "timeout" counter is provided such that the **GRANT** register will be updated at least once every 16 clock periods whether or not the request associated with the current grant has disappeared. Also, the now 8-bit **RING** register is to be rotated at least once every 16 clock periods.

(a)   Modify the AHPL description of RICBUSCONTROL accordingly.

(b)   Does a permanent deadlock occur under this arbitration scheme? If not, can bus time be wasted by a temporary deadlock situation?

(c)   If your answer to the last question is yes, what is the absolute worst case upperbound on the number of clock periods that could be consumed by unproductive deadlock?

(d)   How would this arbitration scheme complicate the design of the DMA interface and RICBUS members?

11.5   Write an AHPL description of the DMA interface for RICBUS. Assume that the address of all control registers are in the last few words of RIC page FFFF.

11.6   A nuisance associated with the interface between RIC and RICBUS as discussed in Chapters 10 and 11 is the necessity of two separate write operations, one to the RICBUS member and one to the DMA interface to establish the initial address of a DMA block transfer to or from the primary memory. Are there ways in which this function can be reduced to a single write? Suggest an approach, and discuss what modifications this would imply in RICBUS or the bus interface.

11.7   A simple display panel displays a row of 16 alphanumeric characters that are driven by the contents of the registers in array **DISPLAY**$\langle 16\rangle[8]$. Also on the panel is a row of eight binary switches. An interface is to be designed that will connect the display panel as a slave to RICBUS. The switches may be declared as the input vector *switch*[8] to the interface module. Write a complete AHPL module description of the interface that will allow any master of RICBUS to read the switch vector and change the contents of the display on the panel.

11.8 A periodic generator of random bytes on lines $X[8]$ is to be interfaced to RICBUS. The frequency, R, at which these bytes are relentlessly generated is subject to control only by a switch on the device. These bytes are purely random, but consecutive bytes may be correlated (controlled by physical switches on the device) in ways important to programs using blocks of bytes from the process. Therefore, individual bytes must not be missed. The generator does not handshake but supplies a *strobe* signal, characterized by Fig. P11.8. Each byte is to be written in the low-order portion of a RIC word. A register **BUFFADDR**[16] will be loaded with the low-order 16 bits of primary memory space where the bytes are to be placed via DMA. A register, **COUNT**[16], will be loaded with the number of bytes desired for the block. RIC will sense completion of a block transfer by reading back **COUNT** and checking it for 0. Blocks of bytes must necessarily be independent, and there is no way to control the starting point of a block. Only one 16-bit data register, **DATAREG**, to store a single halfword is allowed.

(a) Write an AHPL description of the RICBUS interface "controller" for the random process. *Hint*: The RICBUS DMA interface must be supplied with a zero halfword preceding each data halfword.

(b) Suppose that RIC is to execute in a program control loop that checks for completion of a block transfer $R/4$ times per second. Considering only RICBUS traffic, what is the maximum frequency, R, at which the generator can operate without losing a byte, if no other RICBUS members are active?

(c) Given the data rate obtained in part (b), what portion of available time on the primary memory bus will be consumed by the DMA activity?

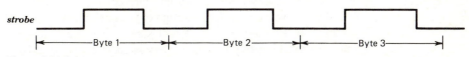

strobe

|←——————Byte 1——————→|←——————Byte 2——————→|←——————Byte 3——————→|

Figure P11.8.

11.9 Modify the AHPL description obtained in Problem 11.8 to include an interrupt at completion of the process or in the event a byte is missed. The register **COUNT** is to be set to FFFF (hex) as soon as a byte is missed.

11.10 What data rate would be required to refresh a strictly alphanumeric terminal consisting of 24 lines of 80 characters each, sufficiently fast to avoid flicker? Assume eight scan lines per line of characters.

(a) Suppose such a terminal has, unrealistically, only 1 byte of internal storage. At what data rate would it be necessary to supply characters to the terminal?

(b) Use the development of Section 11.4 to compute the number of bytes that might be transferred by another bus member across a shared bus, between bytes to the terminal. Assume an asynchronous (four-period handshake) 8-bit bus and a clock rate of 10 MHz.

(c) Repeat parts (a) and (b) after an 80-character buffer is added to the terminal, so that characters can be passed across the bus in 80-bit packets.

11.11 Assume that the terminal of Fig. 11.10 is modified to include 80 bytes of internal storage and is connected to RICBUS. Compute the data transmission rate to the terminal required to support refresh at 30 Hz. If 80 character packets are sent to the terminal over RICBUS, what is the maximum number of bytes another RICBUS member can transmit, while remaining the bus master, without interfering with the screen refresh process?

11.12 Suppose the alphanumeric terminal of Problem 11.10 includes a keyboard and a RAM connected to a MICBUS arrangement, similar to Fig. 11.10. There is no need to transmit screen images to and from RIC, and the transmission of individual characters will be controlled by the microprocessor through the program control interface. Write an AHPL description of a module similar to SCREENDRIVER that will refresh the screen from the first 24 × 80 bytes of RAM. Assume 480 pixels per scan line. Also assume availability of a ROM whose six outputs will yield the six pixels of each scan line allocated to each character. There are 10 address input lines for the 7-bit ASCII code and 3 bits to code the eight scan lines for each character.

11.13 (a) Write an AHPL description of an interface between MICBUS and RICBUS that will complete the design of the alphanumeric terminal discussed in Problem 11.12. It will supply characters, one at a time, to a fixed location in RIC primary memory through the DMA interface. It will receive characters, one at a time, from RIC under program control. *STATUS*[0] = 1, when the interface is storing a new character just received from RIC; *STATUS*[1] = 1, when a character has been placed in the interface data register to be sent to RIC; and *CMD*[0] = 1 indicates that RIC is ready to accept the character.

(b) RIC must separately write to *CMD*[0] for each character it will receive. Which will require more RICBUS time? DMA as implemented, or allowing RIC to read the character by program control? Which will require the most RIC time?

11.14 The refresh by SCREENDRIVER in the graphics terminal of Fig. 11.9 is actually accomplished at a rate somewhat greater than 30 Hz. Assuming that all else on MICBUS is totally inactive, compute as closely as possible the actual refresh rate by tracing the timing from the AHPL description of the module.

11.15 Modify the AHPL description of the tape transport controller given in Section 11.7 to include the one 32-bit buffer register discussed in Example 11.3. The revised controller must function in a manner consistent with that example.

11.16 Rework Example 11.3 assuming a tape transport transfer rate of 200 KB/sec.

11.17 Suppose the two tape transports of Example 11.3 are reading data from distinct 256-page regions of RIC memory. Under these conditions, compute the portion of RICBUS bandwidth available for other activity.

11.18 A special magnetic tape cassette unit includes sufficient internal hardware so that it appears to the user as an ideal tape on which individual characters on either side of the read/write head can be read or overwritten without disturbing other characters on the tape. Each time the cassette receives a one-period level on an input line labelled *read*, it reads one 8-bit character from tape and makes it available on seven-level output lines designated by the vector Z. Similarly, a one-period level on line *write* will cause the cassette unit to enter the values present on seven input lines designated by the vector X as an 8-bit character on tape. The maximum frequency of reading or writing is 500 character/sec. Therefore, a period of 2 msec must be allowed between successive *read* or *write* levels. An output line labelled *cassetteready* from the cassette unit is provided to prevent too-frequent requests. If the unit is presently engaged in a read, write or rewind operation, *cassetteready* = 0. Once such an operation has been completed, *cassetteready* will be 1 until another *read* or *write* pulse is received.

If the characters on tape are visualized as a numbered string, the unit, when *cassetteready* = 1, may be considered as resting between character $i - 1$ and character i. Either of these characters can be read or overwritten by the next *read* or *write* pulse. An input line to the cassette unit labelled *reverse* is provided to distinguish between these two cases. If *reverse* = 1 when a pulse arrives, character $i - 1$ is read or overwritten and the unit ends up between characters $i - 2$ and $i - 1$. If *reverse* = 0, character i is read or overwritten and the unit advances one character. The remaining input line to the cassette is labelled *rewind*. A pulse on this line will cause the tape to be rewound. After *cassetteready* returns to 1, the unit will be resting before the first character on tape.

When in this state, the unit will not respond to a reverse read or write. A line, *error*, from the cassette unit will be set whenever an attempt is made to read or write past either end of the tape. It will be reset by the next *read* or *write* in the opposite direction.

A controller for this device is to be designed to provide an interface to RICBUS. All data transfer will be done under program control. A 16-bit data register, *DR*, will be assigned address FFF0 in the RICBUS address space. RIC will only ask the cassette unit to read or write in the forward direction. Therefore, only 6 bits of a command/status register *CMDSTAT*[16] are used. The meanings of these bits are tabulated as follows.

CMDSTAT[0] = 1	Beginning of tape
CMDSTAT[1] = 1	Indicates that a rewind operation must begin
CMDSTAT[2] = 1	If RIC desires two characters from the unit
CMDSTAT[3] = 1	If a halfword is waiting in *DR* to be read
CMDSTAT[4] = 1	If a halfword is in *DR* to be written on tape
CMDSTAT[5] = 1	End of tape

Write an AHPL module description of this interface controller.

11.19 The control and data connections to a simplified 360 rpm magnetic disk recording system are shown in Fig. P11.16a. The data are formated internally so that 8-bit bytes may be received at the data input and will appear at the data output. The system consists of 4 disks with 64 tracks/disk. When a pulse of at least 0.1 μsec (one-period level) appears on line *seek*, the disk system will select a disk and orient the corresponding read/write head on a track as specified by an 8-bit address. This address will be assumed to be present on the eight data input lines at the time of the *seek* pulse. Each track is formatted so that each actual data record is preceded by several bytes of record identifying information. Thus the search for a particular record within a track may be accomplished by software. Data bytes and identifier bytes are all accepted and supplied indiscriminantly by the disk system. A pulse on line *restore* will reorient each read/write head to a position at the center of the corresponding disk. The seek and restore operations will require between 10 and 320 msec, depending on the track in question.

When *read* = 1, 4 μsec timing pulses will appear on line *time* at 36 μsec intervals, as shown in Fig. P11.19b. A valid data byte is available as *DATOUT* for a 10 μsec period around each 4 μsec *time* pulse. If write = 1, a byte from vector *IN* will be accepted for recording on disk while *time* = 1. Once during each revolution of the disks, the line *index* will be logical 1 for 40 μsec. This marks the beginning of a track, and no pulse will appear on *time* during (and in the case of read for 40 μsec after) this interval.

Design a RICBUS interface controller for this disk memory. Assume

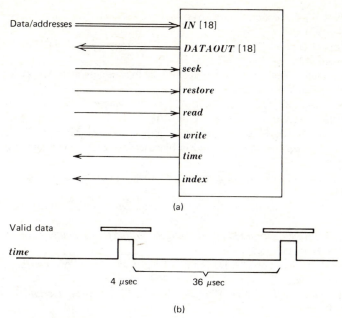

Figure P11.19.

that data from the disk will be packed into 32-bit words in RIC memory. The controller must include an 8-bit register, **TRACK**, in which RIC can write the number of a track to or from which data are to be transferred. Transfers will be via DMA and will always begin at the start of a track. The number of bytes to be written on a track will be placed in **COUNT**[16] in advance, but a mechanism must be provided through which RIC can terminate an input transfer as its option. (A few extra bytes won't hurt.) Include separate 16-bit command and status registers with as many bits as necessary defined in such a way as to place disk operation under the control of RIC. The restore function should be automatic once the system is idled. Write a complete AHPL module description of the controller.

11.20 Approximately how many bits, including identifier bytes, may be recorded on each track of the disk system of Problem 11.19? If the system were left unchanged, except that the speed were increased to 3600 rpm, would program controlled data transfer be adequate? Under what conditions?

References

1. F. J. Hill, and G. R. Peterson, *Digital Logic and Microprocessors*, Wiley, New York, 1984.

2. R. Matick, *Computer Storage Systems and Technology*, Wiley Interscience, New York, 1977.

3. M. Eplick and R. Parker, "Winchester Disk Technology Spins Into New Orbits," *Computer Design*, Jan. 1983, pp. 89–102.

4. A. E. Bell, "Optical Data Storage Technology Status and Prospects," *Computer Design*, Jan. 1983, pp. 133–144.

5. D. P. Siewiorek, C. G. Bell, and A. Newell, *Computer Structures: Principals and Examples*, McGraw–Hill, New York, 1982.

6. *VAX Architecture Handbook*, Digital Equipment Corp., Maynard, Mass., 1981.

7. *IEEE Standard 488-1975*, Institute of Electrical and Electronic Engineers, New York, 1975.

8. *IEEE Standard 796-1983*, Institute of Electrical and Electronic Engineers, New York, 1975.

9. J. C. Cluley, *Computer Interfacing and Online Operation*, Crane Russak, New York, 1975.

10. L. L. Sebestyen, *Digital Magnetic Tape Recording for Computer Applications*, Chapman & Hall, London, 1973.

11. R. W. Watson, et al., "A Design of a Display Processor," *Proceedings AFIPS Fall Joint Computer Conference*, 1969, p. 209.

12. D. H. Straayer, "Hoisting The Color Standard," *Computer Design*, July 1982, pp. 123–136.

13. *Floppy Disk Formatter/Controller, TMS279X*, Data sheet, Texas Instruments, Houston, 1984.

14. F. Hopgood, et al., *Introduction to the Graphical Kernel Systems*, Academic Press, New York, 1983.

15. F. E. Langhorst, "Working Toward Standards in Graphics," *Computer Design*, July 1982, pp. 177–182.

Serial Communications and Error Control Implementation

12.1 Justification

Since publication of the previous edition of this book, interest in data communications has grown enormously. Much of this interest has been sparked by the general availability of the microcomputer. So far, we have discussed communication through a data bus between modules in close proximity. As we shall verify in Section 12.3, handshake control is not convenient for the transfer of data over longer distances. Typically, data are transmitted between digital systems serially by individual bits. The interconnections between systems that provide these communications are usually called a computer network. Some basic terms needed in a discussion of computer networks will be defined in the next section.

Over the years, standards have been proposed and, to a lesser extent, adopted for control of serial communications. The earliest standard was EIA (Electronics Industry Association) standard RS-232, which was appropriate if the network was the voice telecommunications network. This simple standard for the communication of alphanumeric characters over the telephone network came into being well before the computer became the focal point of information interchange. As the need arose to transmit information between digital systems, this standard was conveniently available. In 1977, EIA published a successor to the RS-232 standard, called RS-449. The new RS-449 is an expanded version of, and is logically consistent with, the earlier standard. Because of this consistency and a reluctance to introduce still more control lines, the discussion of the physical level of data communications in Section 12.4 will be limited to RS-232. Other standards and protocols will be the subject of subsequent sections.

Early on, RS-232 proved quite satisfactory where modulation of data for transmission over a communications system, such as the telephone network, was involved. Unfortunately, this standard has been informally adopted as a control mechanism for passing data between minicomputers and microcomputers and adjacent peripheral equipment. This is an application for which this standard was never intended [8].

With the ever-increasing interconnections of computer systems, it has become important to communicate data over computer networks in units of messages or complete files with reliable error control mechanisms. Proposed as a potential IEEE standard, 802 [11] is a set of conventions, or protocols, that addresses file transmission from the physical level (e.g., RS-232) through the network level to the user level. Because this is a book on hardware, we shall address those lower layers of protocol most likely to be implemented by hardware in the last sections of this chapter. The protocol responsible for error control falls just above the physical level.

As discussed in Chapter 3, random access memory is becoming increasingly affordable with more and more bits on each IC chip. Because individual bit failures within a chip are now more likely, it has become important to make memory boards or systems tolerant of such failures. Error control mechanisms for random access memories can resemble those of communications systems, sequential memories, and SRAMs. Therefore, the final section on RAM ERROR control takes advantage of the background just developed.

12.2   Network Topologies and Classifications

Sending information between widely separated digital systems is quite different from passing vectors across a bus within an integrated circuit chip. Although justifying arguments will be left to the next section, data transfers between remote systems do in fact take the form of serial streams of bits. Transmission occurs in the form of finite sequences of bits called *messages* or *packets*. Handshaking control signals are not transmitted. Often there are large numbers of potential sources and destinations of data, called *nodes,* which are interconnected by a network of transmission facilities. The network topologies of interest are depicted in Fig. 12.1. A circuit interconnecting two nodes is called a *link*.

Digital communications can take place over networks intended for analog voice communications as well as over networks designed especially for data transmission. In the basic star network of Fig. 12.1a, all transmission must take place through two links interconnected by the central node or switch. Transmission over voice circuits through a campus switchboard is an example of the star network. Transmission between two computers on campuses in separate states must necessarily involve a network more complicated than the star, very likely the unconstrained graph of Fig. 12.1b. A transmission between two nodes, A and B, in the unconstrained graph can take place over many possible paths, one of which is shown by double lines in Fig. 12.1b. A path that is not the shortest may be used, if all circuits in some link of the shortest path are otherwise engaged.

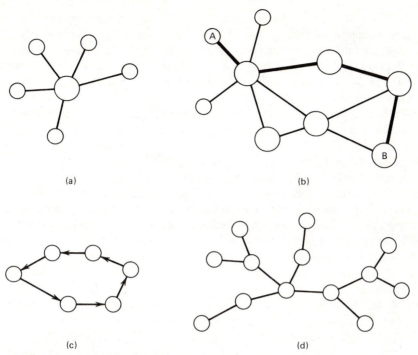

Figure 12.1. Topologies of data communications networks. (a) Star. (b) Unconstrained graph. (c) Ring. (d) Unrooted tree.

A two-way voice conversation requires that a path be established in the communication network and maintained throughout the duration of the call. This method of message control may be employed in data communications as well. A network controlled in this manner is called a *switched* network. Because links in long-distance networks are a costly resource, it is desirable to maximize the amount of traffic that can be handled by a network consisting of links with a particular bandwidth. It has been demonstrated that more traffic can be handled by a given network if messages can be passed through the network one link at a time. If a path forward from a node is unavailable, a message may simply be stored at that node until a link becomes available. A network that is controlled in this manner may be called a *store and forward network*. This type of network is well suited to the communication of data files. The cost of message storage at a node is decreasing more rapidly than is the cost of bandwidth on transmission media, so the store-and-forward network becomes increasingly more attractive. The ARPA network and several commercial data communication networks function in this manner.

Much attention has been devoted to the problem of control of the transfer of information by one application level user on a computer to another user on a remote computer. As we shall see in more detail in Section 12.8, several levels (six or seven) of control activity or *protocols* are required. Where the number of nodes in a network is limited and all nodes are in close proximity (less than 1 mile), the message control problem is simplified. Such a network is called a *local area network* (LAN). Nodes in a local area network are unlikely to be connected as the unconstrained graph of Fig. 12.1b. Figs. 12.1 a, c, and d are all possibilities, with the latter two of particular interest. The unrooted tree of Fig. 12.1d is constrained in that no more than one path is permitted between any two nodes. Control of an unrooted tree network is usually distributed with all nodes having equal access. One and only one node can transmit information at a given time. A node desiring to transmit gains control of the network via a *contention protocol*. In a contention network, each node desiring to transmit must be able to monitor the network to determine if it is idle. Should two nodes find the network idle and begin to transmit at once, both must detect this collision and back off to begin transmission sometime later. Some form of distributed priority mechanism might decide which of the nodes would be the first to try again to transmit. In contrast to the bus arbitrator, any arbitration mechanism mechanism for the network must be implemented within the individual nodes. The ETHERNET [15] is perhaps the most familiar example of a contention type local area network.

The *ring* network of Fig. 12.1c offers an alternative mechanism for control of transmission in a local area network. In this topology, messages are circulated in a stream around the loop. The stream is divided into a set of message slots with a token indicating the beginning of the stream. A node desiring to transmit waits for a vacant message slot to arrive and then inserts a message including an address of the destination node in the slot. The destination node, like all nodes, continuously monitors the message stream. When it observes its own address at the appropriate point in the message, the message is accepted. For both the ring and the contention networks, the upper limit for the average transmission rate by a given node is equal to f/n, where f is the bandwidth of an individual link and n is the number of nodes. The actual data rates obtained will depend on the implementation of the respective protocols.

12.3   Non-responsive Serial Communications

Up to this point, we have limited our discussion to communication between digital devices in close physical proximity and linked together by a common busing configuration. Let us now increase the distance between two devices until they are certainly not housed in the same building and are quite possibly separated by a considerable distance. Now the problem of communications between the devices is governed by a new set of constraints. As the distance increases, the use of eight or more data lines in parallel often becomes economically unattractive. The three-line handshake approach may also appear less attractive simply because it requires three separate control lines.

The handshake or responsive approach to data transmission will also impose an increasingly significant time delay on the communications process as distance increases. As pointed out in Chapter 9, a completely responsive handshake should be used if the propagation delay between receiver and transmitter exceeds one or two clock periods.

1 **ready** = 1
  → ($\overline{datavalid}$)/(1)
2 **accept** = 1
  → (**datavalid**)/(2)
3 "Begin storage"

.

.

.

$n-1$ "End storage"
  → (1)

(a)

1 **ready** = 1
  → ($\overline{datavalid}$, **datavalid**, **datavalid**)/(1,2,3)
2 **accept** = 1
  → (**datavalid**, $\overline{datavalid}$)/(2,n)
3 "Begin storage"

.

.

$n-1$ "End storage"
n CONVERGE ($n-1$,2)
  → (1)

(b)

Figure 12.2. Receiver sequences.

This avoids the possibility of the receiver's issuing a new **ready** before the previous **accept** has been observed by the transmitter. The completely responsive control sequence for the receiver shown in Fig. 12.2a does not begin to store a received data character until **accept** has been returned to 0.

Figure 12.3 depicts the timing of a moderate distance data transmission controlled by the completely responsive three-line handshake of Fig. 12.2a. The delay associated with the propagation of a control signal between devices is T. For open-wire transmission, the delay is 3.2 μsec/km, but for a coaxial cable it may typically be 6 μsec/km. Beginning at a point where the transmitter has a character ready and has just been made aware that the receiver is also ready, the transmitter establishes **datavalid** = 1, which is observed by the receiver after a delay T. The receiver then issues an **accept** = 1, which is observed by the transmitter again after delay T. The transmitter drops **datavalid** on receiving **accept**. After another delay of T, the receiver sees that **datavalid** = 0. It then drops **accept** and begins to store the data just received. After these data are stored, receiver control returns to step 1 to issue a new **ready** = 1, puts a new data character on line, and sets **datavalid** to 1. This completes the cycle associated with the transmission of one character. It can be seen from Fig. 12.3 that the total transmission time for a character is $S + 4T$. For N-bit characters, the data transmission rate in bits/sec is thus given by Eq. 12.1, where S is the time required for storage of a character.

$$R = \frac{N}{S + 4T} \tag{12.1}$$

It is possible for the receiver to begin storage of a character while still holding **accept** at 1. This is implemented by the partially parallel control sequence of Fig. 12.2b. In this case, the data transmission rate is given by Eq. 12.2 if $S > 2T$.

$$R = \frac{N}{S + 2T} \tag{12.2}$$

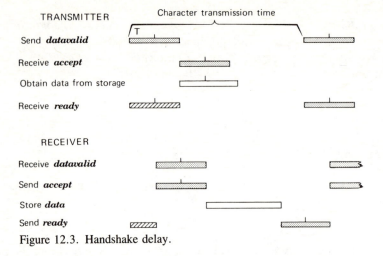

Figure 12.3. Handshake delay.

The corresponding data rate for $S \leqslant 2T$ is given by Eq. 12.3.

$$R = \frac{N}{4T} \tag{12.3}$$

Example 12.1

Assuming completely responsive signaling, compute the maximum data transmission rate, R, for eight data lines (one character) in parallel and for only one data line. Assume that the slower of the receiving and transmitting devices has a storage time, S, of 20 μsec. The distance between the devices is 30 miles; the propagation delay is 10 μsec/mile. Could either of the communicating devices be a tape transport that reads at a rate of 50,000 characters/sec?

Solution
The propagation time delay is given by

$$T = 30 \text{ miles} \times 10 \text{ μsec/mile} = 300 \text{ μsec}$$

For serial transmission, the data rate may be computed using equation 12.3.

$$R_{\text{serial}} = \frac{10^6}{4 \times 300} = 833 \text{ bits/sec}$$

If 8 bits are transmitted in parallel on eight wires, the data rate is then

$$R_{\text{parallel}} = \frac{8 \times 10^6}{4 \times 300} = 6667 \text{ bits/sec} \qquad \blacksquare$$

Even the data rate for 8-bit parallel transmission is insufficient to permit the continuous flow of data from the magnetic tape transport into the communications channel. The alternatives would be to consider a random access data buffer with intermittent reading from the tape transport or, as we shall see, broadband nonre-sponsive transmission.

Often the requirement to extend data communications networks over greater distances coincides with the need to include a larger variety of devices within the network. Typical networks will include equipment from more than one manufacturer. Sometimes, CPUs from different manufacturers will be interconnected. These machines will have a variety of word lengths, and communications on an I/O bus equal in length to the word length of one of the machines in the network is usually not practical. Instead, a standard specifying communications in the form of series of 8-bit characters has been agreed on. Sequences of characters are arranged in messages, with specific characters used to identify the beginning and end of messages. It then becomes a job of the receiving device to identify messages and to translate the information contained in these messages to a form locally usable. This task will usually be accomplished by a combination of hardware and software. This approach is *nonresponsive* transmission. Data rates for nonresponsive transmission will not depend directly on the distance between communicating terminals.

The message format is usually severely constrained when communications are confined to a computer and a set of remote time-sharing terminals. In this case, message identification may be handled entirely by hardware. The only message translation at the terminal involves recoding of individual characters to a form representable on a CRT. This is also a hardware function.

By far the most common approach to the transmission of 8-bit bytes is in a serial-by-bit fashion. This mode, in which only one communication line or channel is required, serves as a standard for communications between equipment supplied by various manufacturers [4]. Serial-by-bit communications may be either synchronous or asynchronous at the byte level, and individual bits may be either clocked or un-clocked. These two distinct concepts will now be discussed.

One asynchronous serial communications mode is the 11-bit/character, 10-char-acter/sec teletype format. In this mode, the line is normally at the logical 1 level between characters, as shown in Fig. 12.4. The transmission of a character is signaled by a logical-0 start bit at the beginning of a character. The start bit is of 9.09 msec duration, as are each of the remaining 10 bits in the character. The start bit is followed by 8 information bits and then two logical 1 stop bits. The line must be at logical 1

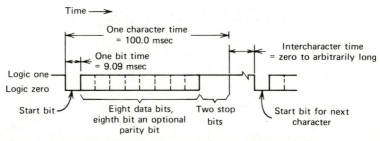

Figure 12.4. Asynchronous 10-character/sec serial transmission.

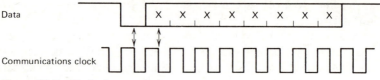

Figure 12.5. Clocked transmission.

for at least 2 × 9.09 msec following the last information bit before another start bit can appear. The actual time at which the line remains logical 1 before another start bit occurs may, of course, be much longer.

The 11-bit/character mode provides for communication without additional clocking or synchronization regardless of the characteristics of the communications channel. Asynchronous unclocked serial transmission at 30 characters/sec (300 bit/sec) is now more common. For this mode, the second stop bit is eliminated, resulting in 10-bit characters.

For transmission rates greater than 1200 bits/sec, the data are usually clocked. If the data transmission is accomplished by a direct wire link between the transmitter and receiver, a second connecting wire can be used by the transmitter to provide timing information. The Electronics Industry Association Standard RS-232 specifies clocking as illustrated in Fig. 12.5. Notice that there is one clock cycle/data bit, with the 1-to-0 transition on the clock line occurring at the midpoint of each bit. The receiver can depend on this transition to indicate times when the data line can can be reliably sampled. You should not confuse the low-frequency communications clock with the much faster logic clock, which synchronizes all register transfers and control state transitions.

Clocked data transmission may be either asynchronous or synchronous by character. Synchronous transmission requires that successive 8-bit characters be packed together so that the first bit of each succeeding character will follow immediately after the last bit of the preceding character. Some method of synchronization must be employed at the beginning of a message so that the receiving system will be able to

Character format

Bit timing	ASYNCHRONOUS	SYNCHRONOUS
Unclocked	110–1200 bits/sec Character-oriented	Seldom used
Clocked	1200–2400 bits/sec Character-oriented	2400–9600 bits/sec Message-oriented

Figure 12.6. Serial nonresponsive data transmission modes.

identify the first bit of each character. Synchronization procedures are discussed in Refs. 1 and 2.

Various combinations of clocked and unclocked, synchronous and asynchronous communications modes are employed over voice-grade telephone channels, which will be discussed in the next section. Typical applications of each mode are listed in Fig. 12.6.

12.4 Voice-Grade Data Communications Channels

One natural advantage of nonresponsive serial-by-bit data transmission is that it can readily be carried out using the voice-grade telephone network. A standard voice channel has a bandwidth of 3200 Hz. Thus, some means of modulating the baseband (sequence of logic levels) data signal is required, so that it may be represented by frequencies within this range. This fact makes necessary another piece of equipment between a data terminal, or serial interface to a computer or other digital device, and the communications channel. This piece of equipment may be referred to as a MODEM (modulator-demodulator) or as a data communications equipment (DCE). The place of the MODEM in a data communications link is illustrated in Fig. 12.7.

A few remarks on the communications channel and typical MODEMs are in order. Our primary goal, however, is a mastery of the design of an interface between a MODEM and a data terminal. This topic is independent of your background in communications.

A typical MODEM designed to transmit and receive data at the lowest data rates of 110 and 300 bits/sec will use the simplest possible means of modulation, FSK, or frequency-shift keying. This simply means that the channel will be driven by a sinusoidal signal of one frequency, perhaps 270 Hz, during each interval when the MODEM input is logical 1 (mark) and by a different frequency, perhaps 1070 Hz, when the MODEM input is logical 0 (space). The logic levels can then be recovered in the receiving MODEM by a simple filtering scheme. Two other frequencies will support simultaneous transmission in the opposite direction.

MODEMs designed for use at higher data rates will use other types of modulation schemes. A theoretical upper limit for the data rate for any channel with bandwidth W was derived by Shannon [5]. In Eq. 12.4, C is the upper limit of the data rate and S/N is the ratio of the magnitude of the transmitted signal to the magnitude of spurious noise signals caused by imperfections in the network.

Figure 12.7. Data communications link.

$$C = W \log_2 (1 + S/N) \tag{12.4}$$

A value of $S/N = 1000$ is considered very satisfactory. For this signal-to-noise ratio, the upper limit of the data rate that can be transmitted on a voice-grade telephone channel would be given by Eq. 12.5.

$$C = 3200 \log_2 (1000) = 32,000 \text{ bits/sec} \tag{12.5}$$

Because of limitations in all existing modulation schemes and to imperfections within the switched telephone network, data rates that can be handled by available MODEMs all fall considerably short of the limit just obtained. A list of MODEMs available from AT&T, with their respective characteristics is given in Table 12.1.

The term *full duplex* listed under the MODEM 103 indicates that this device is capable of transmitting data and receiving data simultaneously from the communications channel. The term *half duplex* indicates that transmission may be accomplished in either direction but in only one direction at a time. A period of time is required to reverse the direction of transmission in a half-duplex system. Depending on the nature of the telephone circuit established, this time can vary from several milliseconds to as much as 10 sec. It is interesting to note that simultaneous bidirectional transmission is available on a two-wire pair only at the slowest data rate.

The reader may be aware that most long distance telephone transmissions is accomplished via microwave links. Using three levels of frequency multiplexing, as many as 1800 voice channels are superimposed on a single microwave radio beam. The bandwidth of this carrier channel must be 4 kHz × 1800 = 7.2 MHz. It is possible to transmit data at higher rates by entering the multiplexing process above the voice channel level. For example, the bandwidth of 60 voice channels or 240 kHz

TABLE 12.1   AT&T MODEM Specifications.

	MODEM Type			
	103	**212**	**201**	**203**
Data rate on switched telephone network	≤ 300 bits/sec	≤ 1200	2000	3600, 4800
Private line data rate	≤ 300 bits/sec	≤ 1800	2400	4800, 7200, 9600; 10,800
Type of modulation	FSK	QDPSK	Phase modulation	Amplitude modulation
Synchronous/ asynchronous	Asynchronous	Asynchronous	Synchronous	Synchronous
Clocking	Clocked or unclocked	Clocked or unclocked	Clocked	Clocked
Directional; capability	Full duplex or half duplex	Full duplex	Half duplex	Half duplex

could be used as a single data transmission channel. This approach requires special equipment for local transmission from the user's site to a telephone central office. Few readers will be involved in larger bandwidth/higher data rate transmission at the hardware level; for this reason, it will not be treated further. The interested reader is referred to Ref. 1.

We are now ready to turn our attention to the design of a data terminal to function in conjunction with an asynchronous MODEM such as the Western Electric 212 and to the interfacing of other digital devices to a MODEM. The EIA Standard RS-232 specifies all lines interconnecting a data terminal equipment (DTE) and a MODEM or DCE for serial data transmission. This specification also describes in detail the function of each line. There are a total of 21 standard lines that can interconnect the two devices. Not every line will be used in every interface. The subset of these lines with which we shall concern ourselves is shown in Fig. 12.8. Each line is named and is assigned a two-letter symbol for use in AHPL. The letters bear no relation to the names but are consistent with the RS-232 identifiers. The first letter of the identifiers for the two data lines is *b;* the first letter of each control line identifier is *c;* and each clock line identifier begins with *d.*

The same lines in Fig. 12.8 are used whether the DTE and DCE are to be used full duplex or half duplex. The function of a line may differ slightly for the two cases, however.

Lines *ba* and *bb* must be held at logical 1 (mark) when inactive. If the operation is full duplex, both lines may be active simultaneously. Otherwise, only one may be active. When the DTE wishes to transmit data, a 1 level is placed on line *ca*. The DCE will respond with a 1 on "clear to send" if the channel is available. Line *ca*

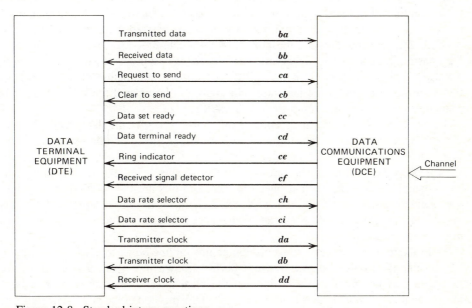

Figure 12.8. Standard interconnections.

should never be raised if line **cb** is already high, indicating that a previous transmission is not yet complete. Lines **cc** and **cd** continually indicate whether the DTE and DCE are turned on and functioning. Whenever the DCE is receiving a signal from the channel, a 1 level is placed on line **cf** to alert the DTE to monitor the "received data" line.

If two MODEMs are to be connected through the switched telephone network, a channel must be established using a dialing procedure. Dialing may be a feature of the MODEM or may be accomplished by an auxiliary telephone. During the dialing process, the MODEM appears not ready to the initiating terminal. Whenever a ring frequency is detected by the receiving MODEM, this fact is passed on to its DTE by a 1 on line **ce**. If the receiving DTE is not ready (**cd** = 0), its MODEM will appear as busy. If the DTE is ready to respond, it will issue a "request to send" and transmit a mark for a period of time followed by a message of greeting.

A logical 1 on line **cf** indicates that the MODEM is currently receiving information from the communications channel. Some MODEMs are designed to function at more than one data rate. Lines **ch** and **ci** are provided so that a single switch can be designed into either the DTE or DCE to select one of two data rates. If information transmission is to be carried out in the clocked mode, the clock signal is always generated at the transmitting end. As indicated by the presence of two lines **da** and **db**, the transmitter clock may be located in either the DTE or DCE. The synchronizing signal is transmitted on the communications channel and detected at the receiving end by various methods that will not be discussed here [1, 7]. The received clock signal is passed on to the DTE on line **dd**.

The flowchart of Fig. 12.9 describes that portion of an asynchronous serial DTE that interacts with a full-duplex modem. As has been the practice throughout the book, the signal lines listed and used in the chart are assumed "active high," that is, having the value 1 when active. The point most strongly emphasized in the flowchart is that, once the DTE is turned on and initialized, two separate processes must be active, one for transmitting and one for receiving. Usually these two processes will interact with a third process, which might be the CPU, the transducer function of a terminal, or the controller for a bus. The last case will apply in particular if the DTE function is implemented on a separate chip such as a UART.

The top of the flowchart is entered on "power on." As the data-terminal-ready line, **cd**, is turned on, the transmitted data line, **ba**, is set to the idle mark condition. If the DCE is also found to be ready, **cc** = 1, control passes to both the transmit and receive processes. In the receive process, control waits at point A until a start bit is encountered on the receive-data line, **bb**. The data bits are then shifted serially into the receive register. If the previously received character has not been taken from this register and placed in a buffer register, a character is lost and an error condition called *overrun error* is activated.

In the transmit process, transmission begins on line **ba** as soon as a character to be transmitted is observed in a transmit buffer. Shown in Fig. 12.9 is a handshake mode, that allows for the possibility that the clear-to-send line, **cb**, may still be 1 indicating that the modem is still completing the transmission of the previous character. As soon as **cb** = 0, request-to-send line **ca** is activated, and the DTE begins to send

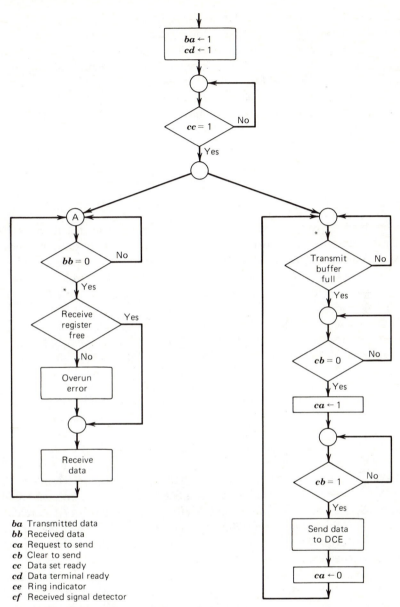

ba Transmitted data
bb Received data
ca Request to send
cb Clear to send
cc Data set ready
cd Data terminal ready
ce Ring indicator
cf Received signal detector

*Must interact with a third process that places data in the
 transmit buffer and accepts data from the receive register.

Figure 12.9. Flowchart for asynchronous DTE.

the data bit serially to the DCE after *cb* has gone to 1. Alternately, RS 232 allows the DCE to assume responsibility for allowing the modem time to transmit the last stop bit. In this case, the handshake is not used and the transfer of data can begin anytime *cb* is observed to be 1. This DTE will actually function successfully with a half-duplex modem that would deny the DTE the right to transmit, while a character was being received, by holding clear-to-send inactive.

Figure 12.9 is only a template that must be satisfied by a DTE. Implementation of the serial receive and transmit data boxes and inclusion of supplementary control functions will vary with the individual DTE. The following is perhaps the simplest possible example.

Example 12.2

Design an interface for the simple printer of Example 9.3 so that it will serve as a receiving terminal for a 10-character/sec, asynchronous unclocked communications channel. It will be recalled that the printer has a vector of 8 input data lines *CHAR* [8]. It has only two control inputs, *print* and *feed*. The only control output is labelled *wait*. Following a *print* level, *wait* will be 1 for 0.09 sec; following a *feed* level, *wait* will be 1 for 0.18 sec.

It may be assumed that each line of received characters will be followed by a carriage-return character and then a line-feed character. This is standard practice where the output terminals are teletypewriters. Assume a 1 MHz system clock.

Solution

The printer will be a receiving terminal only and will have no opportunity to communicate the signal on line *wait* back along the communications channel. The interface must, therefore, provide for receiving a continuous stream of characters at a rate of 10 characters/sec while ignoring line *wait*. Since the printing of a character requires 0.09 sec, some provision must be made for a one-character buffer register, that is, for receiving the next character while the preceding character is printed. For this purpose, we use the registers *DATA* [8] and *CHAR* [8]. The bits from *bb* are initially shifted into *DATA* and then transferred to *CHAR,* after which *DATA* is reloaded.

Notice that the carriage-return/line-feed operation initiated by a one-period level on the line *feed* requires almost 0.2 sec. This operation, which will be initiated by a carriage-return character in *CHAR*, will not be completed in time to allow the following character to be printed. Fortunately, this following character will always be a line feed that may be safely ignored, since a line feed has already been initiated. A special flip-flop *pass* will be included, which can be set to 1 to cause the next character following a carriage return to be ignored.

Because the printer will receive data only, the transmit half of the prototype in Fig. 12.9 may be ignored. The fact that printing a character takes a shorter time than receiving the character together with *pass* mechanism eliminates the possibility of overrun error, so no check will be made. Two counters must be provided, *BITCOUNT* [3] to count the number of bits received and *COUNT* [14] to count the 1 MHz system clock down to 110 bits/sec. The period is 9090 μsec or approximately 2400 hex. Examination of the potential timing error is left to Problem 12.1. The AHPL description of the printer control module follows.

Control waits at step 2 for a start bit. Once a start bit is detected, the counter after ENDSEQUENCE is reset. It is allowed to count through half a 9090-μsec clock period to mark the center of the period. The counter is reset again at step 5 and allowed to count through an entire period to mark the point at which the first data bit is sampled. This bit and successive bits are shifted into the *DATA* register at step 7. Once the character is received, it is printed or a signal on line *feed* is generated, as discussed previously.

MODULE: PRINTER TERMINAL
INPUTS: *bb*; *cc*.
MEMORY: *CHAR*[8]; *DATA*[8]; *BITCOUNT*[3]; *COUNT*[14]; *cd*; *pass*.
OUTPUTS: *CHAR*[8]; *feed*; *print*; *cd*.
CTERMS: *a*.

1   *cd* ← 1; *pass* ← 0;
      → ($\overline{cc}$)/(1).

2   *BITCOUNT* ← 3 ⊤ 0;
      → (*bb*)/(2).

3   *a* = 1.

4   → ($\overline{COUNT[1] \land COUNT[4]}$)/(4).

5   *a* = 1.

6   → ($\overline{COUNT[0] \land COUNT[3]}$)/(6).

7   *BITCOUNT* ← INC(*BITCOUNT*);
      DATA ← *DATA*[1:7], *bb*;
      → ($\overline{\land/BITCOUNT}$)/(5).

8   *CHAR* ← *DATA*;
      → ($\overline{\lor/((8 \top 13) \oplus DATA)}$)/(10).   (Check carriage return)

9   *print* = $\overline{pass}$; *pass* ← 0;
      → (11).

10   *feed* = 1; *pass* ← 1.

11   *a* = 1.

12   → ($\overline{COUNT[0] \land COUNT[3]}$, *COUNT*[0] $\land$ *COUNT*[3])/(12,2).

ENDSEQUENCE
    CONTROLRESET(1);
    COUNT ← (14 ⊤ 0 ! INC(*COUNT*)) ∗ (*a*, $\overline{a}$).
END.

In Section 12.7, we shall look into the general topic of computer network protocols. We shall learn that the RS-232 convention just discussed is an example of a physical level protocol. More recent alternative protocols to RS-232 are its successor RS-449, which includes still more control lines, and CCITT recommendation X21, which includes a minimum number of control lines.

12.5   An Asynchronous Receiver-Transmitter

LSI circuit packages capable of receiving and transmitting serial data in accordance with RS-232 at user-selected baud rates have been on the market for several years. Part of the function of these chips is parallel-to-serial and serial-to-parallel data conversion. They may be incorporated into complete DTEs in various ways. In this section, we shall express in AHPL a simplified version of a generalized serial asynchronous receiver-transmitter. In the next section, we shall incorporate several such devices into a multiport DTE to be interfaced to RICBUS.

Although available chips will accept as many as eight different baud rates, our device, to be called SERIALRT, will function at 300 baud, 1200 baud, or 9600 baud. No external communications clock of the form shown in Fig. 12.5 will be employed, which may preclude operation with a modem at 9600 baud. Consistent with Fig. 12.9, transmit and receive will be two separate activities. The module, SERIALRT, will be driven by a 10-Mhz clock. The duration of a data bit at 9600 baud is 104.2 μsec. A 10-bit counter driven by the 10-Mhz clock will count from 0 to its maximum value in a period of 102.4 μsec. The error per bit period will be 1.7 μsec and the cumulative error over 10 periods is 17 μsec. With no error, data will be sampled by the receiver at the center of each clock period. Because the cumulative error is significantly less than half a bit period, data will be sampled reliably if the receiver is resynchronized by the start bit of each character.

For 1200 baud, 3 bits are added to the counter and 2 more bits are added to form a 15-bit counter for 300 baud. Because the baud rates are related by powers of 2, the relative error remains the same in all three cases. One counter, $RCNT$[15], is actually used to provide receiver timing while a separate counter, $TCNT$[15], controls the independent transmit process, allowing for full duplex operation. For baud rates of 1200 and 9600, two and five bits, respectively are left out of the branch expression that checks the count. An input vector $BAUD$[2] specifies the baud rate as follows.

$BAUD$[0:1]		Baud rate
0	0	300
0	1	1200
1	1	9600

The receive process begins with the wait for the start bit at step 4R. We ignore the fact that bb is an unsynchronized input. Determination of whether a separate synchronizing mechanism is required will be left as a problem for the reader. Step 6R is a wait for the counter to count through half a bit period. Notice that satisfaction of the branch function depends on a different counter bit for each baud rate. Steps 6R and 7R provide the one-period interval between the center of the start bit and the center of the first data bit. Again, the number of bits of $RCNT$ actually checked depends on the values of **BAUD.** Each data bit is sampled as control passes through step 9R eight times.

MODULE: SERIALRT
INPUTS: *bb*; *cc*; *cb*; *TDATA*[8]; *accept*; *datastrobe*; *SRTCNTRL*[4].
OUTPUTS: *ba*; *ca*; *cd*; *rfull*; *tempty*; *RECDATA*[8]; *ERROR*[3].
MEMORY: *RSHIFT*[8]; *TSHIFT*[8]; *RCNT*[15]; *TCNT*[15];
           RBITCNT[3]; *TBITCNT*[3]; *cdff*; *caff*; *baff*; *ERROR*[3];
           RDR[8]; *TDR*[8]; *tfull*; *tempty*.
LABELS: *parityenable*, *echoenable*, *BAUD* = *SRTCNTRL*.

1   *cdff* ← 1; *baff* ← 1; *ERROR* ← 3 ⊤ 0.

2   → ($\overline{cc}$)/(2).

3   → (4R, 4T).

4R   *RBITCNT* ← 3 ⊤ 0;
      → (*bb*)/(4R).

5R   *RCNT* ← 15 ⊤ 0.

6R   *RCNT* ← INC(*RCNT*);
      → $\overline{(RCNT[5] \wedge BAUD[0] \wedge BAUD[1] \vee RCNT[2] \wedge BAUD[1]}$
                                $\overline{\vee RCNT[0]})$/(6R).

7R   *RCNT* ← 15 ⊤ 0.

8R   *RCNT* ← INC(*RCNT*);
      → $((\overline{(/\wedge RCNT[0:1]} \vee BAUD[1]) \wedge (\overline{/\wedge RCNT[2:4]} \vee BAUD[0])$
                             $\wedge (\overline{/\wedge RCNT[5:14]}))$/(8R).

9R   *RBITCNT* ← INC(*RBITCNT*);
      RSHIFT ← *RSHIFT*[1:7], bb;
      → ($\overline{/\wedge RBITCNT}$)/(7R).

10R *RCNT* ← 15 ⊤ 0.

11R *RCNT* ← INC(*RCNT*);
      → $((\overline{(/\wedge RCNT[0:1]} \vee BAUD[1]) \wedge (\overline{/\wedge RCNT[2:4]} \vee BAUD[0])$
                           $\wedge (\overline{/\wedge RCNT[5:14]}))$/(11R).

12R *ERROR*[0] ← $\overline{bb}$;   "framing error if no stop bit"

13R *ERROR*[2] * *parityenable* ← ODDPARITY(*RSHIFT*);
      RDR ← *RSHIFT*; *rfull* ← 1;
      ERROR[1] * *rfull* ← 1;   "overrun error"
      TDR * *echoenable* ← *RSHIFT*;
      tempty * *echoenable* ← 0.
      → (4R).

Following acceptance of the data, a check is made for the stop bit. If a 0 is found on line *bb*, a framing error condition exists. The statement expressing acceptance of the received data by another module is found after ENDSEQUENCE. If, after the receive process has reached step 13R, *RDR* still contains the last received data byte, as indicated by *rfull* = 1, an overrun error has occurred. Like the baud rate indicator, the parity and echo enable signals are provided by some type of external controller. If *echoenable* = 1, the received character is passed over to the transmit sequence for return transmission and display. Used in conjunction with the instincts of a human data source, echo provides a primitive mechanism for correcting transmission errors. Clearly, the echo process will not function properly if a conflicting data stream is being transmitted.

The transmit process begins with a handshake with the clear-to-send line after a character has been placed in register *TSHIFT*. For the sake of clarity, we have omitted the mechanism for disabling the handshake in the event that the clear-to-send line is not used. The start bit and 8 data bits are placed on line *ba* by the loop including steps 7T through 12T. Steps 13T and 14T generate the stop bit.

4T $TSHIFT * \overline{tempty} \leftarrow TDR$;
     $TBITCNT \leftarrow 3 \top 0$;
     $\rightarrow (tempty)/(4T)$.

5T $tempty \leftarrow 1$;
     $TSHIFT[0] * parityenable \leftarrow \mathrm{ODDPARITY}(TSHIFT[1:7])$;
     $\rightarrow (cb)/(5T)$.

6T $caff \leftarrow 1$;   "Request to send"
     $\rightarrow (\overline{cb})/(6T)$.   "Wait for clear to send"

7T $TCNT \leftarrow 15\top 0; baff \leftarrow 0$.   "Start bit"

8T $TCNT \leftarrow \mathrm{INC}(TCNT)$;
     $\rightarrow \overline{((\wedge TCNT[0:1] \vee BAUD[1]) \wedge (\wedge TCNT[2:4] \vee BAUD[0])}$
     $\overline{\wedge (\wedge TCNT[5:14]))}/(8T)$.

9T $baff, TSHIFT[0:6] \leftarrow TSHIFT$.

10T $TCNT \leftarrow 15\top 0$;

11T $TCNT \leftarrow \mathrm{INC}(TCNT)$;
     $\rightarrow \overline{((\wedge TCNT[0:1] \vee BAUD[1]) \wedge (\wedge TCNT[2:4] \vee BAUD[0])}$
     $\overline{\wedge (\wedge TCNT[5:14]))}/(11T)$.

12T $TBITCNT \leftarrow \mathrm{INC}(TBITCNT)$;
     $\rightarrow (\overline{\wedge TBITCNT})/(9T)$.

13T $TCNT \leftarrow 15\top 0; baff \leftarrow 1$.   "stop bit"

14T $TCNT \leftarrow \mathrm{INC}(TCNT)$;
     $\rightarrow \overline{((\wedge TCNT[0:1] \vee BAUD[1]) \wedge (\wedge TCNT[2:4] \vee BAUD[0])}$
     $\overline{\wedge (\wedge TCNT[5:14]))}/(14T)$.

15T $caff \leftarrow 0$;
     $\rightarrow (4T)$.

ENDSEQUENCE
   CONTROLRESET (1) ; $ba = baff; ca = caff; cd = cdff$;
   $RECDATA = RDR; rfull * accept \leftarrow 0$;
   $TDR * datastrobe \leftarrow TDATA; ERROR * accept \leftarrow 3TO$;
   $tempty * datastrobe \leftarrow 0$.
END.

Found after ENDSEQUENCE are the mechanisms for accepting data for transmission from a local module and for passing received data on to that module. No handshake is required.

12.6 Interfacing Serial Ports to RICBUS

In the last section, we designed a single asynchronous serial transmitter-receiver that will appear to a modem as a DTE. Like similar commercially available parts, the SERIALRT may be incorporated into terminal at the opposite end of a communications medium from the CPU; or they may be interfaced to the CPU bus structure. Ports can be interfaced individually to RICBUS. If RIC is to communicate with many remote devices, a more efficient approach is to let one controller service several terminals, as depicted in Fig. 12.10.

There are many ways to organize a concentrator. One such layout is shown in Fig. 12.11. By allowing one controller to service several ports, data can be concentrated in larger blocks for more efficient DMA. This is particularly important if many of the devices at the other end of the communications link are user CRT terminals. Input from these terminals often comes at the rate of 0 to 5 characters/sec. No matter what the input character rate, RIC must initiate a DMA transfer a few times each second so that it can respond to user input on a timely basis. By collecting the data from eight ports, as in Figs. 12.10 and 12.11, into a single buffer, called **DATAINBUF,** the expected size of a data block will be larger when a DMA transfer is initiated.

Notice that, in contrast to the single-input buffer, eight output buffers, labelled **DOB,** are used. Output from RIC, even to a CRT terminal, will usually be in units of several lines, enough to fill an individual buffer. In addition, the scan of input by the operating system is most efficiently accomplished with a single buffer in primary memory. Output is written to known addresses, so the number of output buffers in primary memory is immaterial.

Also shown in Fig. 12.11 are some command and status registers, addressable in RICBUS address space. The composite status of the concentrator is reflected in **STATCOMP.** The low-order 8 bits is a count of the number of bytes waiting in **DATAINBUF.** This vector also provides an address for access to **DATAINBUF.** Each of the high-order 8 bits of **STATCOMP** indicates the status of an individual output

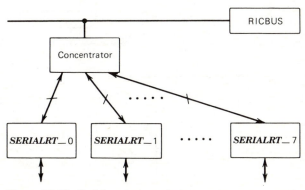

Figure 12.10. Serial port concentrator.

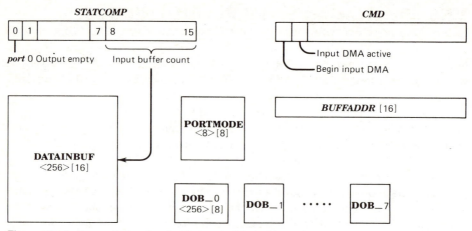

Figure 12.11. Concentrator data buffers and addressable registers.

buffer. For example, *STATCOMP*[0] = 1 if **DOB__**0 is empty and SERIALRT__0 is ready for a data byte. Only the first 2 bits of the command register, *CMD,* which control input DMA, will concern us here. The array **PORTMODE** consists of eight registers; each of which controls the mode of the corresponding SERIALRT. The meaning of these bits is given in Fig. 12.12. **DATINBUF** is a first-in first-out (FIFO) array of 16-bit words. The low-order half of a word is the data byte. The high-order half of the word provides information about the byte, including the port it came from and any errors that might have occurred during its reception. The first 2 bits may be used to mark the end of a block after its transmission to primary memory.

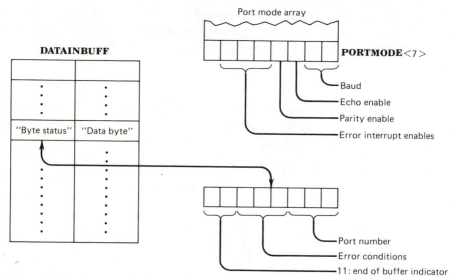

Figure 12.12. Command and status interpretations.

Clearly, there are several simultaneous activities that must take place within the concentrator module, including response to program control transfers from RIC, DMA output to the eight output buffers, interface of the output buffers to the serial transmitters, and management of the input buffer. Response to RIC program control will not differ from that activity in any other RICBUS member. Once the approach to input management has been made clear, you should be able to fill in similar details for the output case. We shall, therefore, restrict our attention to input management that will include both interface to the serial receivers and input DMA. In the following module description, only signals and memory relevant to input are declared. The reader can fill out the declarations as he adds the description of output activity.

In Chapter 13, an extension of AHPL will be provided that will formalize the interconnection of multiple copies of identical modules. Here we do it informally be letting the eight rows of **RECDATA**$\langle 8 \rangle$[8] and **ERROR** $\langle 8 \rangle$[3] represent the eight similarly named pairs of output vectors from the serial receiver-transmitters. Similarly, the rows of **SRTCNTRL**$\langle 8 \rangle$[4] represent control inputs to eight identical modules. Each bit of *RFULL* represents an input line from and each bit of *ACCEPT* represents an output line to a corresponding SERIALRT.

To avoid simultaneous writes to *STATCOMP* or words in **DATAINBUF,** we shall approach input management with a single locus of control that will address its subtasks sequentially. Step 1 separates this control locus from the other activities that are left for you. The concentrator must be prepared to accept characters from the character buffer in each of the serial receivers at the rate of 960 characters/sec. Thus, it must check and possibly accept a character from each unit at least once each millisecond. It must continuously check these modules while waiting for a busgrant and must limit the time required by a DMA to somewhat less than a millisecond. RICBUS accepts 3.33×10^6 16-bit words each second. Therefore, the entire 256 words of **DATAINBUF** can easily be transmitted within that time. Once the concentrator has received a busgrant, only RIC can interfere. One would not expect RIC slow direct addressing to take a significant part of any 1-msec time slice. If it happened, the result would be overrun errors recorded with some of the data bytes.

Step 1 initializes registers as required and branches to the separate simultaneous activities. If RIC has set up a DMA write activity, a bus request is activated at step 2 and control checks at step 3 for a busgrant. If the CONCENTRATOR has not been granted the bus, control continues to step 5, which is active for eight clock periods while a word is entered in **DATAINBUF** for each receiver with *rfull* active.

If a RICBUS grant is received, control passes to step 6 to begin DMA. In step 6, the process begins by entering a marker at the end of the block of words in **DATAINBUF.** Steps 7 through 13 send, beginning with row 0, the rows of **DATAINBUF** to RIC memory until the marker is encountered. The control sequence beginning with step 7 is written to conform completely to the template of Fig. 11.3 beginning at point C. If a bus grant is lost, we assume that it will be regained in time to complete the DMA transfer before time runs out for servicing the receiver transmitters. Once the marker has been encountered to indicate that **DATAINBUF** has been emptied, step 14 terminates the DMA, reinitializes *STATCOMP*[8:15], and returns control to step 2 for another check of the receiver modules.

MODULE: CONCENTRATOR.
INPUTS: **RECDATA**⟨8⟩[8]; **RFULL**[8]; **ERROR**⟨8⟩[3]; *busack; busgrant.*
OUTPUTS: *ACCEPT*[8]; **SRTCNTRL**⟨8⟩[4]; *busreq.*
MEMORY: **DATAINBUF**⟨256⟩[16]; **PORTCNT**[3]; **STATCOMP**[16]; **DR**[16]; **PORTMODE**⟨8⟩[8]; **CMD**[16]; **BUFFADDR**[16]; *busreqff.*
COMBUSES: *RBDATA*[16]; *RBADDR*[16]; *busread; buswrite; dma; high.*

1   *STATCOMP*[8:15] ← 8⊤0;
     → (2, "output", "program control response").

2   *busreqff* ∗ *CMD*[0] ← 1; *CMD*[1] ∗ *CMD*[0] ← 1.

3   → ($\overline{busgrant}$, *busgrant*)/(4,6).

4   *PORTCNT* ← 3⊤0.

5   **DATAINBUF** ∗ (DCD(*STATCOMP*[8:15])∧(∨/(*RFULL*∧
           DCD(*PORTCNT*))))
       ← 0,0, BUSFN(**ERROR**; DCD (*PORTCNT*)),
         PORTCNT, BUSFN(**RECDATA**; DCD(*PORTCNT*));
   ACCEPT = *RFULL*∧DCD(*PORTCNT*);
   PORTCNT ← INC(*PORTCNT*);
       STATCOMP[8:15] ∗ ∨/(*RFULL*∧DCD(*PORTCNT*))
              ← INC(*STATCOMP*[8:15]);
   → (∧/*PORTCNT*, $\overline{\wedge/PORTCNT}$)/(5,2).

6   **DATAINBUF** ∗ DCD(*STATCOMP*[8:15]) ← $\overline{16⊤0}$;
   STATCOMP[8:15] ← 8⊤0.

7   *DR* ← $\overline{16⊤0}$.

8   → (*busgrant*∧$\overline{busack}$)/(8).   "see template"

9   *RBADDR* = *BUFFADDR*; *RBDATA* = *DR*;   "write handshake"
   buswrite = 1; *dma* = 1; *high* = 1;
   → ($\overline{busack}$∧*busgrant*, *busack*, $\overline{busack}$∧$\overline{busgrant}$)/(9,10,8).

10   *DR* ← BUSFN(**DATAINBUF**; DCD(*STATCOMP*[8:15])).

11   → (*busgrant*∧$\overline{busack}$)/(11).

12   *RBADDR* = *BUFFADDR*; *RBDATA* = *DR*;   "write handshake"
   buswrite = 1; *dma* = 1; *high* = 0;
   → ($\overline{busack}$∧*busgrant*, *busack*, $\overline{busack}$∧$\overline{busgrant}$)/(12,13,11).

13   *BUFFADDR* ← INC(*BUFFADDR*);
   STATCOMP [8:15] ← INC(*STATCOMP*[8:15]);
   → (∧/*DR*)/(7).

14   *CMD*[0:1] ← 0,0; *busreqff* ← 0;
   STATCOMP[8:15] ← 8⊤0;
   → (2).

ENDSEQUENCE
CONTROLRESET(1);
SRTCNTRL = **PORTMODE**[4:7];
busreq = *busreqff.*
END.

12.7 Computer Network Protocols

Whole books [9] have been written on the subject of protocols for computer networks. We can hardly expect to do justice to the topic in a single section. Our purpose here is to provide a general background to support further reading and to facilitate our discussion of those levels of protocols that can be implemented directly in hardware.

Suppose a user of a mainframe computer system desires to send a file over a data network to a user of another large computer system in another state. A goal in the design of the network was to make this operation as painless as possible for the user. Therefore, the process with which he will interact will hide from him a series of other processes, each of which will accomplish some activity necessary for the transmission of the file. Some of these processes, beginning with the one visible to the user, are listed here.

5. File and Destination Identification.
4. Mapping of the agreed-on service on the transmission facilities available (*Transport Level*)
3. Subdivision of files into packets, routing packets over available links, and ordering of received packets. (*Network Level*)
2. Error-free transmission of packets over individual data links. (*Data Link Level*)
1. Physical transmission of serial data.

The rules implemented at each end of the transmission or segment of the transmission for accomplishment of any one of these or similar activities is called a *protocol*. Each protocol is expressed in such a way as to hide all lower-level activities. With perhaps the exception of levels 1 and 2, the breakout of data transmission activities given in this list is not written on stone. More levels of protocol are possible. Figure 12.13 illustrates the relationship between an arbitrary number of levels of activity. The RS-232 standard discussed in Section 12.4, RS-449 standard, and CCITT recommendation X21 are examples of level 1 protocols.

In Fig. 12.13, level n provides a service to its user, level $n + 1$. To accomplish this, it uses the functions made available by level $n - 1$. The internal structure of the levels above or below n are not known by level n. Each level consists of a process at each end of the transmission that implements the activites necessary to offer an enhanced service to the level above. The protocol for level n is the set of rules implemented by the two processes at that level. Control information and data are exchanged across the interface between levels n and $n + 1$. This can be either control for level n at either end of the transmission or data destined for level $n + 1$ at the other end. A process, therefore, has three interfaces, one with each level above and below and one with the corresponding process at the other end of transmission.

Whatever is placed in message by one level of protocol is treated as data by, and is transparent to, lower levels of protocol. The structure of a message as it is processed by protocol level $n - 1$ is depicted in Fig. 12.14. At the transmitting end, level $n - 1$ adds header and trailer characters to the message that will provide control

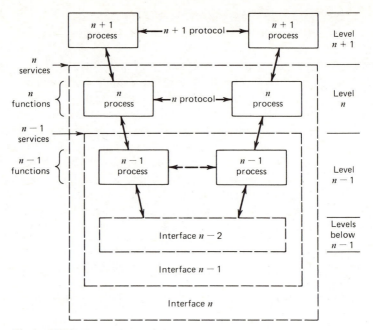

Figure 12.13. Protocol structure.

information needed by the level $n - 1$ receiving process to implement the level $n - 1$ protocol. Similar header and trailer characters may have been added to the message by level n. To level $n - 1$ these head and trailer characters are treated just as if they were part of the original message. If there exists a level $n - 2$, still another header and trailer may be added to the message as it is passed down to this level at the transmitting end.

You might be more comfortable to see a single standard set of network protocols. There is no single set of protocols used in all networks. Some may use more than the five levels listed here, some fewer. The functions of the various levels will vary from network to network. This must necessarily be so, as network characteristics vary. A token ring local area network must be approached differently from a switched public data network. This is not to say that standards are not of interest. The closer two networks are able to adhere to a single "recommendation," the easier it is to establish

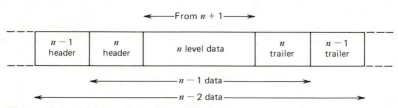

Figure 12.14. Message formation.

compatability and data exchange between the two networks. Several organizations are interested in such standards, including CCITT (International Consultative Committee for Telephones and Telegraphs), ISO (International Standards Organization), IEEE, and EIA. Some agreement exists at the two lowest levels that must be found in some form in any network. Perhaps the strongest authority is a series of X (X1, X25, etc.) recommendations [9, 11] issued by CCITT that address issues at various levels of protocols. Space will not permit addressing the recommendations in detail.

In contention networks as depicted in Fig. 12.1c and in switched networks following the topology of Fig. 12.1d in which a fixed path is established from trans-mitter to receiver for the duration of the message, the protocol processes are invoked only at the original transmitter and the ultimate receiver. In token ring topologies such as Fig. 12.1c and in store and forward version of the general network of Fig. 12.1d, protocol processes must be invoked at intermediate nodes. This notion is illustrated by Example 12.3.

Example 12.3

Suppose that the level-3 protocol is responsible for identification of the destination of a message packet in a store and forward communications network. Construct a diagram showing the extent to which the message must be interpreted at an intermediate node in order to provide for forwarding it over an available link in the direction of the destination.

Solution

First receiving and then in-reverse-order transmission processes for protocol levels 1, 2, and 3 must be invoked, as shown in Fig. 12.15. Here it is necessary to process the level-3 header or trailer to determine the packet destination so that routing can take place. The message as originally passed to level 3 at the source node is left undisturbed.

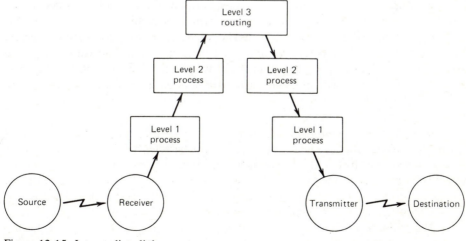

Figure 12.15. Intermediate link.

CCITT recommendation X21 for the physical level includes only six signal lines in addition to grounds. In contrast, RS-449 and CCITT recommendation V24 include seven more signal lines than does RS-232. It is difficult to resolve the issue of simplicity and economy vs flexibility even at the physical level. We shall see in the next section that there is also more than one protocol at the data link level.

12.8   Data-Link Protocols

In asynchronous communications, the unit of information in a transmitted message is 1 byte. The receiver is alerted to the beginning and end of a message by the start and stop bits, respectively. In synchronous communications, messages consist of long sequences of information bits with no start or stop bits included, thereby effecting 20% savings in transmission time per message. Usually, messages are subdivided into frames to ease buffering requirements at the receiving node and to reduce lost time, if errors occur and retransmission is required.

As indicated in Section 12.5, echo provides a convenient means of error control for the most common application of asycrhonous communications—interaction between a computer and a data entry device such as a CRT terminal. When a data file is returned to the terminal for display or hard-copy printout, an occasional error is not fatal. Similar errors cannot be tolerated when files (for example programs) are communicated from system to system for storage and execution. With echo obviously not applicable, the parity bit is the only convenient error control mechanism available for asyncrhonous character-by-character communications. For this reason, synchronous file transmission is the preferred method. Each of the synchronous communication protocols to be discussed in this section adds at least one 16-bit string of bits to each message for purposes of error control. These bits are usually called the *cyclic redundancy check* or CRC.

In addition to error control, the second function of the data-link protocol is to limit the flow of message frames to a rate with which the receiver can keep pace. This can be accomplished by requiring the sending node to wait for an acknowledgment frame from the receiver before sending another frame. If transmission delays are significant, a sliding window algorithm [16], which allows more than one frame to be in the transmission path simultaneously, can be used to increase channel use. An acknowledgment mechanism must be included in the message format, as we shall illustrate for the HDLC protocol.

In asynchronous communications, each character may be considered as an independent message frame. The beginning of a one-character frame on the transmission medium is indicated by a start bit. It remains necessary in synchronous communications to alert the receiver to the beginning of a message frame. This is accomplished by including, at the beginning of each message, a special sequence of bits called a *flag*, or by a sequence of one or more special synchronization characters.

The majority of messages when passed to the data link level by the level-3 protocol will be a sequence of bytes or 8-bit characters. The header and trailer information added by the data link protocol may also be conveniently regarded as sequences of bytes. There is nothing, however, to prevent the data links treating these catenated bytes that must eventually be serialized as an arbitrary string of bits. Fig. 12.16 depicts three data-link protocols. Two of these, BISYNC and DDCMP used by IBM and DEC, respectively, pass messages to the physical level still organized in characters. The third, HDLC (high-level data-link control), which continues to gain in popularity, produces a message that must be regarded as a string of bits.

The character-oriented protocols may be used in *hybrid* as well as in purely synchronous communications networks. An example of what might be referred to as hybrid would be a program for transferring files between a personal computer and a mainframe over the public telephone network using economical asynchronous 1200 baud MODEMS. The physical level must transmit and receive asynchronously by character while features of higher-level (usually synchronous) protocols such as error control must be included. KERMIT is one such program.

Some mechanism must be added at the data-link level to provide for identifying the end of a message or frame. Although the approaches differ, the weaknesses of both BISYNC and DDCMP lie in this feature. As shown in Fig. 12.17b, DDCMP provides in the header a count of the number of characters in the message. This method is particularly sensitive to undetected transmission errors that might affect the count field. Lost characters can cause problems with frame synchronization [16].

BISYNC places an end of transmission (ETX) character following the text. The problem lies in the possibility that an ETX might be found somewhere in the text of a message. This possibility is addressed by a technique called *character stuffing*. That is, an escape (ESC) character is placed by the data-link protocol in front of each such ETX character, so that it will be ignored. What about an ESC in the text? This character may simply be preceded by another ESC. Ambiguity is thus removed at the price that this data-link protocol can accept only messages in a character code compatible with its own.

Most *long-haul* networks use bit-oriented protocols in which the information

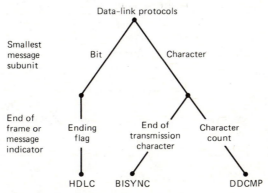

Figure 12.16. Distinguishing characteristics of data-link protocols.

portion of a frame is merely a string of bits. The standard message or frame format for one such bit-oriented protocol, called HDLC (high-level data-link control), is shown in Fig. 12.18a. It can be seen that both the beginning and ending flags for an HDLC frame are 01111110. Once again, six consecutive 1's in the text of a frame could be misinterpreted as the "end of frame" flag. In this case, the remedy is bit-stuffing. The HDLC protocol scans the message and inserts a 0 following every string of five consecutive 1's. This function and the equally easy removal of the added 0's at the receiving end can be most efficiently accomplished by hardware. Inserted and removed 0's are not included in the error-check process. For this approach to work, the transmitter must be constantly in control of what is sent to the receiver between messages. This might not be possible during start-up periods, and spurious frames received at start-up must be eliminated by the error-control mechanism, in this case the 16 frame-check bits.

In addition to text and flags, the HDLC frame includes a 16-bit framecheck, a control byte, and an address byte. The address byte must clearly be supplied and interpreted by the network level protocol. Three types of command bytes are shown in Fig. 12.18b. A supervisory control byte would typically be sent alone in an informationless frame. Within an information frame, the sequence field of the control byte indicates the number of the frame. Because only 3 bits are available in the sequence field, frames must be numbered modulo-8. As indicated in Fig. 12.18c, there are three supervisory messages which might be returned by the node receiving information. In each case, the field "Next" will indicate the number of the next message expected. For example, a REJ message will indicate that errors were found in frame "Next" and transmission should resume with that frame. If all is well, sending an acknowledgment in an information frame headed in the other direction will save channel capacity. It is only necessary to place the number of the next frame in order in the "Next" field.

No message numbers are included in the third type of control field, called

SYN	SYN	SOH	HEADER	STX	TEXT	ETX OR ETB	BCC

← Direction of serial data flow

(a)   BISYNC message format

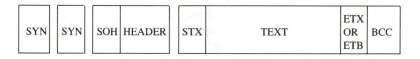

SYN	SYN	C L A S S	COUNT 14 BITS	FLAG 2 BITS	RESPONSE 8 BITS	SEQUENCE 8 BITS	ADDRESS 8 BITS	CRC 1 16 BITS	INFORMATION UP TO 16,363 8-BIT CHARACTERS	CRC 2 16 BITS

(b)   DDCMP message format

Figure 12.17. Character Oriented Message Formats.

nonsequenced in Fig. 12.18. The five unspecified bits can specify up to 32 additional control messages, which vary among HDLC-like protocols. The P/F bit can be used in various ways, one of which is to indicate the last frame in a transmission.

If at the transmitting node the control byte, like the address byte, is passed down from the network level protocol, the data link must accomplish the following tasks in order.

1. Compute the frame check.
2. Stuff bits.
3. Add the Begin and End flags.

At the receiver, these tasks are reversed.

1. Find flags to isolate message while removing superfluous 0's.
2. Compute and compare framecheck.

Before discussing the error-check process, let us consider an example implementation of receiver task 1.

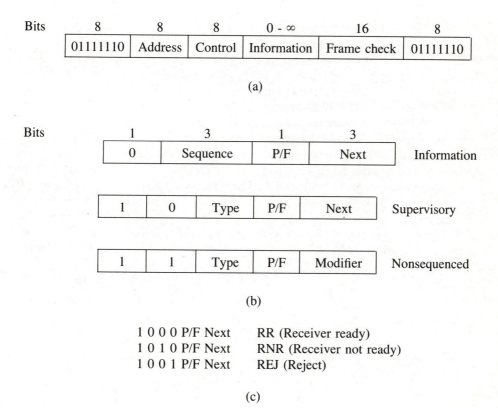

Figure 12.18. HDLC.

Example 12.4

Suppose that the level-1 protocol passes a serial stream of bits on line x to the level 2-hardware implementation shown in Fig. 12.19. The MICBUS arbitrator functions exactly as the one in Fig. 11.8. The midpoint of each data bit is marked by a negative transition on line **strobe**, which also serves as the syncrhonizing clock in level 1. Frames including the address and control field will be no more than 256 bytes long. A received frame will be left by task 1 in locations 0000 to 00FF of the memory of the 8-bit microprocessor. Write a partial AHPL control sequence that will accomplish task 1 of level 2.

Solution

When looking for the beginning of a new HDLC message, the receiver will continuously shift received bits into a register, R, of the same length as the flag (8 bits), and on receipt of each bit compare the register contents with the flag. A simple AHPL sequence for this purpose is given here.

1 $\rightarrow (\overline{strobe})/(1)$.
2 $R * \overline{strobe} \leftarrow x, R[0:6]$;
   $\rightarrow (strobe)/(2)$.
3 $\rightarrow (\overline{R[0]} \wedge (\wedge/R[1:6]) \wedge \overline{R[7]})/(1)$.

Detection of the flag not only identifies the beginning of the message, but it establishes bit synchronization. That is, when control passes to step 4, the next bit to be accepted will be the first bit of the frame to be passed to level 3.

First, however, superfluous 0's must be deleted. Once these 0's are removed from each successive string of 8 bits, that segment of the message is stored in memory. The register **ADDRCNT**, which counts through the memory addresses, is intitialized at step 4. The register **BITCNT**, which marks the end of each 8-bit unit, will be continuously incremented each time an original message bit is shifted into register R. The register **ONES** will contain a continuous count of the number of consecutive 1's that have appeared on line x since the last 0. If the register **ONES** contains 101, indicating five consecutive 1's, a 0 on line x is not shifted into the receive register R. Each time a superfulous 0 is deleted, the register **ONES** is reset to 0. If **ONES** reaches

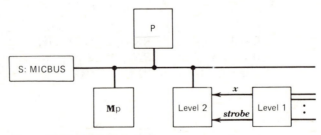

Figure 12.19. HDLC receiver.

six, a real END character has been encountered. The critical activity is found in step 8 following a check for a negative transition on line *strobe* by steps 6 and 7.

4	$BITCNT \leftarrow 3 \top 0$; $ADDRCNT \leftarrow 16 \top 0$:
5	$ONES \leftarrow 3 \top 0$.
6	$\rightarrow (\overline{strobe})/(6)$.
7	$\rightarrow (strobe)/\underline{(7)}$.
8	$BITCNT * (\overline{\overline{x}} \wedge ONES[0] \wedge ONES[2]) \leftarrow INC(BITCNT)$;
	$R * (\overline{x} \wedge ONES[0] \wedge ONES[2]) \leftarrow x, R[0{:}6]$;
	$ONES \leftarrow (INC(ONES) \,!\, 3 \top 0) * (x, \overline{x})$;
	$\rightarrow (\wedge/(ONES[0{:}1], \overline{x}))/(12)$.
9	$\rightarrow (\vee/BITCNT)/(6)$.
10	$micbusreq = 1$;
	$\rightarrow (\overline{micbusgrant})/(10)$.
11	$MICDATA = R$; $MICADDR = ADDRCNT$; $buswrite = 1$;
	$ADDRNCT \leftarrow INC(ADDRCNT)$;
	$\rightarrow (6)$.
12	"continue"

Each time a new 8-bit byte has been received in *R,* it is written in memory at the address specified by *ADDRCNT.* If the message did not contain an integral number of bytes, some of the flag bits may be in the last memory location, which is marked for task 2 of level 2 by the final contents of *ADDRCNT.* ∎

So far, we have implemented a limited error-control capability using a parity bit in each character. In the tape transport example of Section 11.6, the error-detection capability is enhanced somewhat through the computation of longitudinal as well as lateral parity. Very often, errors occur in bursts in a communications medium. Combinations of lateral and longitudinal parity detection schemes are easily defeated by various combinations of burst errors. The following paragraph considers a method that is not as vulnerable to bursts of errors.

In an HDLC frame, the frame-check bits are a cyclic redundancy check. That is, they are determined at the time of transmission by implementation of polynomial division (polynomials in the algebraic field containing two elements, 0 and 1) using a shift register and exclusive-OR gates. The 16-frame-check bits are the remainder from this division process. The same division process is repeated at the receiver. The message is considered to be error free if the remainders are the same. This process can be demonstrated to detect bursts of erroneous bits up to 16 bits in length. Mathematical justification of this approach to error correction is well documented elsewhere [1, 8, 9]. We shall confine our treatment to the following example, which illustrates the generation of a coded message using the polynomial

$$P(x) = 1 + x^2 + x^{15} + x^{16} \tag{12.6}$$

that has been established as a standard for generation of 16-bit CRCs within the United States.

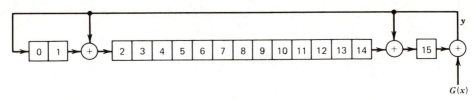

Figure 12.20. Division by $1 + x^2 + x^{15} + x^{16}$.

Division mod-2 by the polynomial given by Eq. 12.6 is implemented by a shift register of the form given in Fig. 12.20. The frame-check bits will be left in the shift register following the division. Input $G(x)$ is the sequence of message bits taken as a polynomial of order k where $k + 1$ is the number of bits in the message. The bit applied to the exclusive-OR gate during the first clock period of the division is considered to be the coefficient of x^k and so on.

Because the division process at the sending and receiving ends are the same, it would be quite feasible to continue task 2 at the receiving end by dividing the catenation of the 256 bytes, left in memory by task 1, by $P(x)$. We choose a somewhat simpler example to allow you to focus on the frame-check generation process.

Example 12.5

Write an AHPL sequence that will sequentially output on line *zout* a message contained in a 64-bit register **MESSAGE**[64] and simultaneously generate a 16-bit frame cyclic redundancy check vector to be stored in a register **CRCREG**[16]. The polynomial $P(X)$ given in equation 12.6 will control the CRC-generation process. The CRC vector is to be transmitted immediately following the message.

Solution
One additional register, **CNT**[6], will be required to count the 64 message bits. The polynomial notation is compatible with the left to right indexing convention for registers used in AHPL. **CRCREG** will be essentially a left to right shift register with a few bits determined in a more complicated fashion as dictated by $P(X)$.

for x^0 **CRCREG**[0] ← **MESSAGE**[63] $\oplus$ **CRCREG**[15]
for X^2 **CRCREG**[2] ← **MESSAGE**[63] $\oplus$ **CRCREG**[15] $\oplus$ **CRCREG**[1]
for X^{15} **CRCREG**[15] ← **MESSAGE**[63] $\oplus$ **CRCREG**[15] $\oplus$ **CRCREG**[14]

Therefore

1   **CNT** ← 6T0; **CRCREG** ← 16T0.
2   *zout* = **MESSAGE**[63]; y = **MESSAGE**[63] $\oplus$ **CRCREG**[15];
     MESSAGE ← 0, **MESSAGE**[0 : 62]; **CNT** ← INC(**CNT**);
     CRCREG ← y, **CRCREG**[0], **CRCREG**[1] $\oplus$ y, **CRCREG**[2:13],
                                         $y \oplus$ **CRCREG**[14];

     → ($\overline{\wedge\text{CNT}}$)/(2).

3      $CNT \leftarrow$ INC(CNT); $CRCREG \leftarrow 0, CRCREG[0:14]$;
       $zout = CRCREG[15]$;
       $\rightarrow \overline{(/\backslash CNT[2:5])}/(3)$.   ∎

12.9   Fault-Tolerant Memory

In the previous section, we considered briefly the mechanism for detecting errors and facilitating retransmission in digital communications. Similar mechanisms are required in dealing with errors that arise in computer memories. With the ever-increasing density of devices in RAM ICs and the increasing capacity of complete memory systems, it has become necessary to operate these random access memory systems in an error-tolerant mode. That is, failure in a small number or scattered memory elements in a system may not result in immediate shut down and maintainance of that system. Although errors in RAMs are often the result of permanent failure, errors arising in magnetic tape and magnetic disk systems are usually caused by transient noise during the write or read process, much the same as are errors in communications systems.

The treatment of errors in tape and disk memories must differ in one important respect from treatment of errors in communications systems. Eventually, a message in a communications system can be recovered by retransmission. If noise causes errors in the process of reading a file from a tape or disk, the file can be recovered by rereading. Uncorrectable errors may occur in the process of writing to a tape or disk. Unless the file is read back and the errors detected before the file disappears from the system RAM, information will be lost. Decisions on whether to read after writing are passed up to the operating system and often from there to the user.

For reasons just discussed, providing additional redundancy such that errors can be corrected rather than merely detected becomes even more attractive for SRAMs and sequential memories than for communications systems. The combination of longitudinal and lateral parity checks, as illustrated for the tape transport in Section 11.6, offers a simple method of correction of single-bit errors. If a parity error is identified in a single byte and the longitudinal parity is wrong for one row, the single erroneous bit is uniquely identified and can be complemented. More sophisticated error-correction methods are based on cyclic redudancy check polynomials similar to, but often of higher order than, the one given in equation 12.6. A consideration of multiple-bit error-correction requires considerably more depth of insight into the algebra of polynomials than was needed in the previous section. We defer this treatment to any of several books that have been written on this single subject.

Errors in random access memories may be caused by permanent failures. That is, the output of a particular memory element may be *stuck-at-1* or *stuck-at-0*. An error of this type will be classified as a *hard error*. That is, it will be repeated each time that particular memory element is accessed. For various reasons (e.g., noise) errors that are not reproducible do occur in RAMs. Such errors will be termed *soft errors*. In between are errors that appear hard for a time and then disappear. This phenomena might occur in a device that was fabricated at the very edge of the design specifications. The device might be sensitive to temperatures within the normal operating range and, in time, it may fail permanently. Such errors are sometimes called *firm errors,* but when observed they may be lumped with hard errors for purposes of the following discussion.

Ordinarily, single-bit errors can only be detected but not corrected, if the single redunancy mechanism is a simple parity bit. This is true for soft errors in RAMs as well. Interestingly, single-bit hard errors may actually be corrected using one parity bit by a process called *double complementing.* Suppose a memory, whose ouput data bus is 8 bits, actually internally implements 9 bits per word including a parity bit to establish overall even parity. To simplify the discussion, we use asynchronous control of the memory bus so that a read will require two clock periods in the absence of error. A partial AHPL model of the memory follows, where **DR** is the 9-bit internal memory data register and **DBUS** the 8-bit data bus. Although ODDPARITY = EVENPARITY, when these two combinational logic units have the same arguments, note that in the description that follows ODDPARITY has an 8-bit argument and EVENPARITY a 9-bit argument.

1   **DR** * *read* $\leftarrow$ **RAM** * DCD(**ADBUS**);
      DR * *write* $\leftarrow$ **DBUS**, ODDPARITY (**DBUS**);
      $\rightarrow$ ((read$\setminus$/*write*), *read*, *write*)/(1,2,6).

2   **DBUS** = **DR**[0:7] * EVENPARITY(**DR**);
      RAM * (DCD(**ADBUS**) $\wedge$ $\overline{\text{EVENPARITY}(\textbf{DR})}$)$\leftarrow$**DR**;
      ack = EVENPARITY(**DR**);
      $\rightarrow$ (*read*/$\overline{\text{EVENPARITY}(\textbf{DR})}$, $\overline{read}$, *read*/$\overline{\text{EVENPARITY}(\textbf{DR})}$)/(2,1,3).

3   **DR** $\leftarrow$ $\overline{\textbf{RAM}}$ * DCD(**ADBUS**).

4   **DR** $\leftarrow$ $\overline{\textbf{DR}}$; **RAM** * DCD(**ADBUS**) $\leftarrow$ $\overline{\textbf{DR}}$;
      softerror $\leftarrow$ EVENPARITY($\overline{\textbf{DR}}$).

5   *ack* = 1; **DBUS** = **DR**[0:7];
      $\rightarrow$ (*read*, $\overline{read}$)/(5,1).

If the data byte is read from memory without a single-bit error, its availability on the data bus during the second clock period will be indicated by a signal on line **ack**. The sequence of events that result, if a hard error is detected, are depicted in Fig. 12.21, given that the data word 111010110 has been addressed. The figure suggests that the correct data word is actually stored but that the output of memory element [4] is stuck-at-0. The result would be no different if the input to the memory element were stuck-at-0. Notice that, after execution of step 1, parity over the 9 bits in **DR** is odd, indicating an error. That the error is in bit 4 of the memory word is evident to the reader, but at this point it is unknown to the memory control sequence. The complement of the erroneous word is written back into the same memory location by step 2. This complemented word is read back into **DR** by step 3. It can be seen that the effect of the stuck-at-0 again turns up in **DR**[4]. What is now in **DR** is the complement of the original data word. The correct bits were complemented, and bit

After step	Addressed word	DR	
"previous write"	111010110		
1	111010110	111000110	— Parity bit / — Hard error
2	000111001	111000110	
3	000111001	000101001	
4	111010110	111010110	— Corrected

Figure 12.21. Correction of hard error with one parity bit.

4 was again read back as the complement of the correct bit. Step 4 complements **DR** again, and step 5 places the resultant correct data byte on **DBUS**.

Now suppose the error is soft and is, therefore, not repeated in the second read accomplished by step 3. In this case, the word in **DR** after step 3 will be 000111001, and there is no indication of which of the original data bits was in error. The soft error cannot be corrected, but it is detected by the simple fact that the word read back in step 3 will have even parity and is recorded by the last of the three statements in step 4.

If randomly distributed hard errors are the major concern, multiple-bit correction may be of interest. You will recall that minimum-distance-3 *Hamming codes* can be used to correct single-bit errors. (By minimum-distance-3, it is meant that each character in the code must differ from every other character in the code by at least 3 bits.) If one more overall parity check bit is added, 2-bit errors may also be detected in communications applications. Providing that no more than one error is soft, it is possible to correct errors in up to 2 bits of a word read from RAM, using codes similar to the one just described, together with the double complement mechanism introduced earlier.

To demonstrate this, we must resort to an example. First, we choose a memory with a data bus of 16 bits. If k is the number of information bits and r the number of parity check bits, it can be easily shown (see, e.g., Ref. 17) that Eq. 12.7 must be satisfied for minimum-distance-3 Hamming type codes.

$$k < 2^r - 1 - r \tag{12.7}$$

Therefore, $r = 5$. Adding one additional check bit, the equivalent of an overall parity bit, results in a 22-bit code with the properties claimed in the preceding paragraph. Codes with greater redundancy than 22 bits for 16 information bits are unlikely to be used in random access memories.

Having decided that 22 bits will be used, considerable freedom remains in constructing what is usually called a *modified Hamming code*. Let us use the code described by the parity check matrix given in Eq. 12.8, in which the c diagonal indicates the C portion of the array. When H, C is used in a computation, c will be 1.

$$\text{H, C} = \begin{bmatrix} 0\,0\,0\,0\,0\,0\,0\,0\,0\,0\,1\,1\,1\,1\,1\,1\,c\,0\,0\,0\,0\,0 \\ 0\,0\,0\,0\,1\,1\,1\,1\,1\,1\,0\,0\,0\,0\,0\,0\,0\,c\,0\,0\,0\,0 \\ 0\,1\,1\,1\,0\,0\,0\,1\,1\,1\,0\,0\,0\,1\,1\,1\,0\,0\,c\,0\,0\,0 \\ 1\,0\,1\,1\,0\,1\,1\,0\,0\,1\,0\,1\,1\,0\,0\,1\,0\,0\,0\,c\,0\,0 \\ 1\,1\,0\,1\,1\,0\,1\,0\,1\,0\,1\,0\,1\,0\,1\,0\,0\,0\,0\,0\,c\,0 \\ 1\,1\,1\,0\,1\,1\,0\,1\,0\,0\,1\,1\,0\,1\,0\,0\,0\,0\,0\,0\,0\,c \end{bmatrix} \qquad (12.8)$$

Suppose the 16 information bits are given by the vector I[16]. Then a code word is defined by $W = I$, CH[0:5], where the elements of CH are given by Eq. 12.9.

$$CH = \oplus / (\text{H} \wedge I\,!\,I\,!\,I\,!\,I\,!\,I\,!\,I)) \qquad (12.9)$$

This is just the hardware implementation of the modulo-2 matrix multiplication

$$CH = \text{H} \cdot I^t \qquad (12.10)$$

The word W is written in memory. The *syndrome* of a 22-bit word R read back from memory is defined by the modulo-2 computation in Eq. 12.11 (with c = 1).

$$\text{SYNDR} = (\text{H, C}) \cdot R^t \qquad (12.11)$$

If $R = W$, the syndrome is 0,0,0,0,0,0. For a single-bit error in $R[j]$, the syndrome is the transpose of (H, C)[j]. Note that each bit of SYNDR is merely an odd-parity computation over those bits of R corresponding to 1's in a row of H, C. The error in $R[j]$ will affect parity only in those rows in which (H, C)[j] = 1. Once the syndrome is computed, it uniquely identifies the single erroneous bit, which can then be corrected. This will be so whether the error is hard or soft.

A bit of the syndrome as computed in Eq. 12.11 will be 1, if the parity computed from that row is incorrect.

Definition 12.1: The weight, w, of a syndrome is defined as the number of 1's in the syndrome.

Interestingly, the syndrome will contain an odd number of 1's (w odd) for any single-bit error, because each column of H, C contains an odd number of 1's. In contrast, double-bit errors will always result in an even number of 1's (not 0) in the syndrome. You may verify this by considering the overlap of the 1's in the various pairs of columns of H, C. If both erroneous bits are included in the parity computation for a row, the result is left unchanged. If only one erroneous bit is included, the expected parity will be reversed. Armed with this information, a strategy may be worked out for correcting double-bit errors using the double-complement method.

Fig. 12.22 is a flowchart showing the procedure for correcting memory errors based on the code just defined. The flowchart is entered by reading a 22-bit word, R, from RAM and obtaining the syndrome from the combinational logic implementation of Eq. 12.11. From point A of the chart there are four alternative actions depending on the weight of the syndrome. If $w = 0$, there are no single- or double-bit errors, so the information word, I, is connected immediately to the data bus. If $w = 1$ or 3 and the syndrome matches one of the columns, this column identifies the erroneous bit in R. This bit is corrected, and the resulting data word is connected to the data bus. Should $w = 5$, more than 2 bits are in error. This fact is logged before the probable bad word is connected to the data bus. It should be emphasized that instances of errors in 3 or more bits will usually result in the same syndromes a 1- or 2-bit errors and will go undetected. Memory chips are, of course, tested before they are incorporated in systems. It is anticipated that memory boards will be good when installed and will be retired for maintainance when a history of 1- and 2-bit errors have been recorded. The probability is that numerous single-bit error conditions will be recorded before a failure in 3 or more bits of the same word occurs.

When $w = 2$, 4, or 6, a double-bit error is assumed. The double complement process begins at point B in the chart. The 22-bit data word is complemented and then rewritten at the same address. It is read back, complemented again, and the syndrome is recomputed. From point C there are three possibilities. If both the errors were hard, $w = 0$, indicating that they have already been corrected. If $w = 1$ or 3, only one error remains. The other error was hard and has already been corrected. The new syndrome uniquely identifies the soft error bit, which is then corrected. If w is again even, the result is logged as two soft errors that cannot be corrected.

Example 12.6

Suppose an information vector $I = 11111111,00000000$ is written in memory together with 6 check bits. In the process of reading the 22-bit word back, a hard error appears in bit-0 and a soft error in bit-1. Compute check bits and syndromes, and detail the error correction process.

Solution:
For the first check bit, we have

$$CH[0] = \oplus / (H\langle 0\rangle \wedge I)$$
$$= \oplus / (00000000,00111111) \wedge (11111111,00000000) = 0.$$

Similarly, $CH[1:5] = (0, 0, 1, 1, 0)$
Therefore, $W = 11111111,00000000,000110$
and the read back word is

$$R = 00111111,00000000,000110.$$

The computation of the syndrome begins with ANDing R with each of the rows of H, C. That is,

$$H,C \wedge (R!R!R!R!R!R) = \begin{bmatrix} 0\ 0\ 0\ 0\ 0\ 0\ 0\ 0\ 0\ 0\ 0\ 0\ 0\ 0\ 0\ 0\ 0\ 0\ 0\ 0\ 0\ 0 \\ 0\ 0\ 0\ 0\ 1\ 1\ 1\ 1\ 0\ 0\ 0\ 0\ 0\ 0\ 0\ 0\ 0\ 0\ 0\ 0\ 0\ 0 \\ 0\ 0\ 1\ 1\ 0\ 0\ 0\ 1\ 0\ 0\ 0\ 0\ 0\ 0\ 0\ 0\ 0\ 0\ 0\ 0\ 0\ 0 \\ 0\ 0\ 1\ 1\ 0\ 1\ 1\ 0\ 0\ 0\ 0\ 0\ 0\ 0\ 0\ 0\ 0\ 0\ 1\ 0\ 0 \\ 0\ 0\ 0\ 1\ 1\ 0\ 1\ 0\ 0\ 0\ 0\ 0\ 0\ 0\ 0\ 0\ 0\ 0\ 0\ 0\ 1\ 0 \\ 0\ 0\ 1\ 0\ 1\ 1\ 0\ 1\ 0\ 0\ 0\ 0\ 0\ 0\ 0\ 0\ 0\ 0\ 0\ 0\ 0\ 0 \end{bmatrix}$$

Completing the computation of the syndrome by exclusive-ORing all the bits in each of the rows yields

$$\text{SYNDR} = (0, 0, 1, 1, 0, 0)$$

The weight $w = 2$, indicating a 2-bit error. The double complement process is, therefore, executed. Because bit-0 is a hard error, the read back word is now after complementing

$$R' = 10111111,00000000,000110.$$

Only the first column of this array changes to

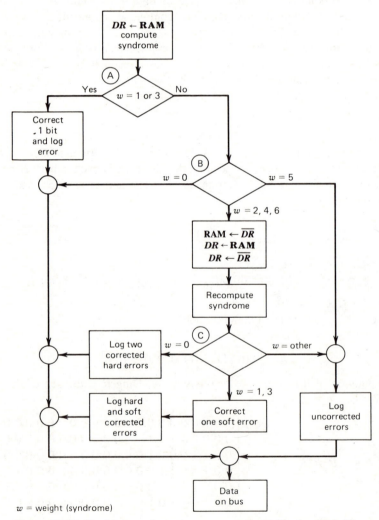

Figure 12.22. Double-complement error correction with six check bits.

The last 3 bits of the syndrome calculation are reversed, so

$$\text{SYNDR}' = (0, 0, 1, 0, 1, 1).$$

Now it is known that bit-1 was a soft error. This bit is corrected, and the correct word R'' [0:15] = 11111111,00000000 is placed on the data bus. ■

Typically, the error logging referred to in Fig. 12.22 will be accomplished by the memory controller itself in a special section of memory reserved for the operating system. Each entry will probably require two 16-bit words and must include at least the address and type of error. The log is accessible to the operating system and can be passed on to the user for input in maintainance decisions. Error-management techniques of the type just discussed will probably not be used in conservatively designed microcomputer systems. In larger systems where memory speed is pushed to the limit of component specifications, errors become more likely, and some form of error management will probably be implemented. The process just described probably represents the limit of complexity in error-correction coding for RAMs. Eq. 12.7 suggests that a 32-bit word can be encoded using only one additional check bit.

Problems

12.1 Suppose that for some reason it has become necessary to interface a keyboard (a coded keyboard as found with any CRT terminal or personal computer) to communicate at 300 baud with a modem independent of any other device. Simplify and adapt the module SERIALRT in Section 12.5 to satisfy this function in the most economical way. For example, the receive section of the module may be deleted and it should function only at the single baud rate. The output of the keyboard will consist of the vector *KEYDATA*[8] on which an ASCII coded character will appear each time the line *datavalid* is 1. A completely responsive handshake is to be implemented using line *accept*, the only input to the keyboard. Ignore clock synchronization issues.

12.2 A more economical redesign of the module SERIALRT that will function only at 1200 baud but still in the asynchronous unclocked mode is to be developed. Simplify the declaration portion of the module description as much as possible. Modify only the receive portion of the control sequence accordingly.

12.3   Suppose that it is desired to place a baud rate converter on a transmitted data line so that the bit rate format within each asynchronous character is converted from 300 baud to 1200 baud. The line is the ouput of a DTE and the input to a modem. There can, of course, be no actual change in the character transmission rate. Write a complete AHPL module description of the baud rate converter. Let the transmitted data input line be labelled *tdataold* and the transmitted data output be labelled *tdatanew*. Assume a 10-MHz clock driving the baud rate converter and ignore clock synchronization issues.

12.4   Suppose that a special communications channel of 32-kHz bandwidth is available through the telephone company. Assume that the modulation scheme used will permit data transmission at a rate equal to 25% of the maximum predicted by Shannon's equation for $S/N = 1000$. Suppose that an 8-bit parallel responsive (three-line handshake) approach is also under consideration. Which approach will permit transmission at the highest data rate over very long distances? Assuming a delay of 6 μsec/km on the responsive control lines, for what distance would the maximum data rate for the two transmission schemes be exactly the same?

12.5   Revise the AHPL module description of the printer terminal in Example 12.1 so that it will function at 30 characters/sec. Consistent with Fig. 12.5, assume that the bits are clocked by an external clock generated within the DCE. Let this signal be available on line *dd*. This clock should make it possible to eliminate the 13-bit counter.

12.6   Assume that an external 9600-baud synchronizing clock is available for synchronizing the bits for the module SERIALRT. This signal will appear on input line *dd*. Revise the AHPL description of only the transmit portion of the module so that it will function at 9600 baud with external synchronization.

12.7   Add to the declarations of the module CONCENTRATOR in Section 12.6 those elements necessary in a description of DMA output. Define the bits of *CMD*, allow RIC to specify DMA to each of the eight **DOB** output arrays. Take the approach that the control sequence will branch to separate short sequences to provide DMA loading of the eight separate arrays.

(a)   Write sufficient control sequence to describe the loading of **DOB** 0.

(b)   Write a control sequence that will be active in parallel with that of part (a) and that will service all eight output arrays, sending bytes whenever possible to the corresponding SERIALRTs. Characters cannot be taken from an output array when DMA is in progress for that array.

12.8 Add declarations as necessary and write the program control portion of the description of the module CONCENTRATOR.

12.9 Suppose an alphanumeric CRT has an array of 16 control registers, **CTREG**$\langle 16 \rangle$ [8]; a transmit data register, **TDR**; and a receive data register, **RDR**. The status of **TDR** and **RDR** are indicated by memory elements, **tfull** and **rfull**, respectively. Write a partial AHPL description of a DTE that includes three registers and provides for asynchronous RS-232 communications with a modem at 1200 baud. The DTE will only be able to transmit characters from **TDR**. Similarly, the normal receive mode calls for moving each received character to **RDR**. However, any two received characters immediately preceded by an escape character are to be treated uniquely. The first of these two characters is a pointer to a byte of **CTREG**. The second is control information to be written in that byte of **CTREG**. The effect of an escape lasts for only the next two characters. With the exception of the third character following an escape (1B hex), the normal receive mode resumes and this character is placed in **RDR**. Assume that receive overrun is not possible. Neglect framing errors and parity. Assume the existence of, but do not write, the parallel control sequence that will process data and interact with this sequence through **rfull** and **tfull**. A 1200-baud bit synchronizing clock is connected to input line **dd**.

12.10 The start of header (SOH), start of text (STX), and end of text (ETX) are 01, 02, and 03 in ASCII. SYN is 16 hex. Suppose the message given in Fig. P12.10 is passed to the data link level to be formatted in BISYNC. With the exception of the BCC block, modify and add to the message to form a message suitable to pass to the physical protocol level. For convenience, some characters are shown in alphanumeric form and others in hexadecimal. The commas are for clarification and are not part of the message.

01,A,A,A,03,B,B,B,B,B,02,N,U,M,B,E,R,S,00,85,17,85,03,L,A,S,T,03
Fig. P12.10.

12.11 Assume that the following sequence of bits comprises the address, control, and information fields of a short message. Accomplish all functions of the transmitter HDLC data-link-level protocol by generating the complete message that will be passed to the physical level. Ignore the spaces.

11110000 00010011 11111111 11110011

12.12 Assume that all messages received by the data-link level of the HDLC receiver, whose AHPL description is partially given in Section 12.8, contain an integral number of bytes once "stuffed" 0's are deleted. Write the AHPL description of the portion of the module that will compute the 16-bit frame check for the received message and compare it with the received frame check. Recall that the message is stored in the first 256 bytes of the microprocessor RAM and that **ADDRCNT** will be pointing at the byte immediately following the received frame check.

12.13   If a soft error is generated in the process of reading from a random access memory, the correct byte may be obtained simply by repeating the read and rechecking parity.

(a)   Rewrite the partial AHPL description given in Section 12.9 so that a reread of the addressed word to correct a soft error will be accomplished, if a parity error is observed prior to the double-complement process for correcting a hard error.

(b)   Will the procedure just described be successful, if the soft error was generated when the word was originally written in memory?

12.14   Write an AHPL statement representing the hardware implementation of Eq. 12.11

12.15   Construct a matrix for H, C similar to that given in Eq. 12.8 for syndrome calculation in a code for 32-bit data words with 7 check bits.

12.16   Use Eq. 12.9 to compute the check bits for the data word 1111000011110000. Write the word **W**, which will be written in memory. Suppose when read back, bits **R**[2] and **R**[3] are changed by hard errors. Compute the resulting syndrome. Determine the word **R'** returned by the double-complementing process of Fig. 12.22. Compute the new syndrome.

12.17   Suppose a triple-bit error appears in bits **R**[0:2] of the 16-bit data word given in Problem 12.16. Determine the syndrome for this error condition.

(a)   What will be the outcome of the double-complement process of Fig. 12.22 for this error condition?

(b)   Suppose an even more elaborate error management scheme is employed in which the most recent entry in the error log for a given address is made available from an associative memory when an error indication again appears for that same address. Now what determination could be made, if the prior error entry for this address were a hard double-bit error in bits **R**[1:2]?

12.18   Write an AHPL description of the error-correction process described by Fig. 12.22.

12.19   Determine a triple-bit error (indicate the 3 error bits) that will result in a syndrome of $w = 5$ computed from Eq. 12.11. Code words are generated using Eq. 12.9. What will be the outcome if this error is encountered by the error-correction procedure of Fig. 12.22.

12.20 Write a partial AHPL control sequence describing a hardware mechanism for stuffing bits to eliminate strings of six or more consecutive 0's. Assume that the frame-check field has already been added to the message. The sequence must be compatible with the restoring mechanism described by Example 12.4.

References

1. N. Abramson and F. F. Kuo. *Computer Communications Networks*, Prentice–Hall, Englewood Cliffs, N.J., 1973.
2. J. L. Eisenbies, "Conventions for Digital Data Communications Link Design," *IBM Syst. J.*, 6(4), 1967, pp. 267–302.
3. E. L. Lohse, ed., "Proposed USA Standard, Data Communications Control Procedures for the USA Standard Code for Information Interchange," *Commun. ACM*, 12(3), 1969, pp. 166–178.
4. Publications of the ANSI Standards Committee on Data Processing, *Technical Committee X353 on Data Communications*, Business Manufacturers Association, New York.
5. C. E. Shannon, "The Mathematical Theory of Communication," *Bell System Technical Journal*, July and Oct. 1948.
6. L. N. Holzman and W. J. Lawless, "Data Set 203 A New High Speed Voiceband MODEM," *Computer*, Sept./Oct. 1970, pp. 24–30.
7. D. W. Davies and D. L. A. Barber, *Communications Networks for Computers*, Wiley, London, 1973.
8. J. E. McNamara, *Technical Aspects of Data Communications*, Digital Equipment Corp., Maynard, Mass., 1977.
9. D. Davies, D. Barber, W. Price, and C. Solomondies, *Computer Networks and Their Protocols*, Wiley, New York, 1979.
10. A. L. Scherr, "A Perspective on Communications and Computing," *IBM Syst. J.*, 22(1,2), 1983, pp. 5–9.
11. *Data Communications Network Interfacing and Protocols*, IEEE, New York, 1981.
12. J. W. Conrad, "Character Oriented Data Link Control Protocols," *IEEE Trans. on Communications*, April 1980, pp. 445–454.
13. D. E. Carlson, "Bit Oriented Data Link Control Procedures," *IEEE Trans. on Communications*, April 1980, pp. 455–467.
14. J. W. Cotton, "Technologies for Local Area Networks," *Computer Networks*, Nov. 1980, pp. 197–208.
15. R. M. Metcalfe and D. R. Boggs, "Ethernet: Distributed Packet Switching for Local Computer Networks," *Communications of the ACM*, July 1976, pp. 395–404.
16. A. S. Tannenbaum, "Network Protocols," *Computing Surveys*, Dec. 1981, pp. 453–459.
17. S. Lin and D. J. Costello, *Error Control Coding*, Prentice–Hall, Englewood Cliffs, N.J., 1983.
18. B. Nelson, "Effortless Error Management," *Computer Design*, Feb., 1982, pp. 163–168.

Memory Approaches for Large Systems

13.1 Overview

In this chapter, we shall turn our attention to large machines that are designed to accomplish many computations per unit time and as much computation as possible per unit cost. Many large computer systems are operated in either the batch-processing or the time-sharing mode. In both situations, a queue of programs awaiting execution is always present at the input terminals to the system. Thus the computer system takes on many of the characteristics of a production process. The goal becomes to maximize the number of jobs (weighted of course by their complexity) that are inputted to the system and executed per unit of time. A measure of accomplishment of this goal is called the machine's *throughput*.

The raw material of the production process is programs rather than parts of an automobile to be assembled together. Programs as contrasted to sets of automobile parts are conceived and constructed independently by many different persons, with little thought given to the convenience of the production process. Some of the largest installations can afford the luxury of assigning different types of jobs to different machines. Other batch-oriented installations attempt to improve throughput by spacing jobs in time, according to memory requirements or other apparent features that provide information as to job type. It is, of course, impossible to anticipate the requirements of a program completely until it is executed. In general, it is the same flexibility that makes the computer program so very useful that renders it so hard to treat as a production item. Perhaps more than any other one feature, it is the conditional branch

467

instruction that limits the applicability of mass production techniques on program execution.

There are two obvious approaches to improving a machine's throughput. The speed with which the central processor can perform arithmetic can be increased. It is also possible to increase the speed at which data can be moved about in the machine. This includes input/output rates and memory access times. In general, an efficient machine represents a balance between the two capabilities. For example, it would be wasteful of computation capability to use an extremely fast central processor with a slow random access memory and a minimum input/output capability. When a central processor is forced to stand idle for significant periods of time because the system I/O is unable to deliver programs or carry off results fast enough, we say the system is *I/O bound*. Because batch-processing facilities must handle many small programs and many I/O-oriented data processing assignments, such systems usually operate I/O bound.

Memory organization is often the determining factor with respect to the speed at which data can be moved about within a computer system. This chapter is thus devoted to memory organization whereas Chapter 17 is concerned with other approaches to increasing machine throughput.

In Fig. 13.1 we see a block diagram of a computer system that will allow us to outline the data flow problem in more detail. Here we classify the major subunits of a computer system into three sections according to response time. A memory unit is included in each section. As mentioned in Chapter 3, the capacity and speeds of the three memory units vary inversely. The high-speed memory in block 3 has the smallest capacity whereas the mass memories of block 1 are slowest. The random access memory is intermediate in both categories. The set of memories of differing characteristics may be termed a *memory hierarchy*. In some systems, it is possible to divide the hierarchy into more than three blocks. For example, the mass memory is assumed to include both magnetic disk and magnetic tape memories, which have different speeds and capacities. Three blocks are convenient for this discussion, however.

The high-speed memory may consist of a few data registers, as will be discussed

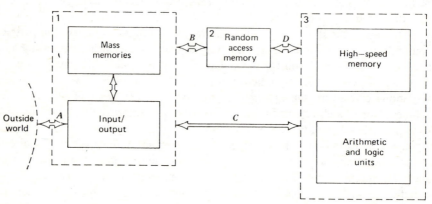

Figure 13.1. Data flow.

in Section 13.2, or a larger number of registers capable of accommodating instructions or data, such as the *scratch-pad* or *cache memory* discussed in Section 13.4. In the latter case, it may take on many of the characteristics of the random access memory. Reading and writing in the memory in block 3 may be accomplished in a single clock period. It is likely that considerations such as LSI chip area and power requirements will always place a cost premium on the components of the high-speed memory. One would, therefore, expect to find in most systems a slower, cheaper, and larger capacity RAM, as shown in block 2, regardless of the organization of the high-speed memory.

Block 3 is organized so as to attempt both to minimize the cost per computation and to maximize the number of computations per unit time. Both these parameters will be optimized for sequences of operations carried on entirely within block 3. Unfortunately, such utopian situations will be highly temporary in most real-world job environments. The overall system throughput must depend on the flow of information along paths *B, C,* and *D* in Fig. 13.1. Ideally, path *C* will be used only rarely, so as to avoid slowing block 3 to the data rates achievable by the devices in block 1. Thus data flow will normally be along the path *ABD* when the system is operating routinely in the batch mode.

Clearly, data flow along path *A* will occur simultaneously with other system functions without interfering in any way. This is possible primarily because the system demands the right to accept programs from users and to furnish results at its own convenience. Many organizations have been devised that will relieve the central processor in block 3 of the responsibility of data flow on path *B*. One of these will be discussed in Section 13.5. Thus jobs can be placed in a queue in the random access memory to be executed in order by the central processor, with the results independently removed after execution. This procedure is, of course, complicated by programs that demand large shares of the RAM or use auxiliary storage.

With independent control, data flow along path *B* will depend on the capacity of block 1 to provide data and the capacity of block 3 to execute programs. The cost per computation will be lowest when these capacities are matched. A quantitative model of this relation may be found in Hellerman [1]. The more common situation finds the capacity of block 1 to provide programs and data less than the capacity of block 3. We have already referred to this situation as I/O bound.

Path *D* is intimately involved in program execution. The high-speed memory of block 3 may contain both instructions and data so that short sequences may be executed entirely within block 3. When a branch to an instruction in the RAM of block 2 occurs, however, it often becomes necessary to replace a sequence of instructions in the high-speed memory in as little time as possible, without requiring block 3 to wait. Similarly, it may be possible to transfer arrays of data from the RAM to the high-speed memory at a data rate exceeding the maximum of the access rate for individual words in the RAM.

If the size of the user program exceeds the size of the RAM (or the portion of RAM assigned to that program) of block 2 of Fig. 13.1, it becomes necessary periodically to move portions of the program between the RAM and the direct access storage device of block 1 in Fig. 13.1. The typical programmer does not like to bother with such details and would prefer a larger RAM, even though the average response time of this RAM might be slower. The illusion of a larger RAM can indeed be provided by modifying the hardware to permit the operating system to replace unused blocks of words in the RAM with relevant information from the DAS device as the user addresses data in a large nonexistent RAM. This concept, termed *virtual memory,* will be discussed in Section 13.5.

Implementation of both the scratch pad and the virtual memory depend on the employment of a small *associative memory*. This concept will be introduced in Section 13.3 to provide background for the scratch pad and virtual memory discussions of Sections 13.4 and 13.5. Equally fundamental and more widely used than the associative memory is the push-down stack, which will be discussed in the next section.

In Section 13.6, we shall consider a method of organizing the random access memory so that the reading and writing of individually addressed words may be overlapped. Not only will this increase the effective data rate, but this same organization will permit communication with the memory by more than one processor. As with each of the topics of this chapter, the approach of Section 13.6 may be included in a system design at the option of the designer. The designer must decide whether the performance improvement to be expected from the inclusion of one of these features is sufficient to justify the cost.

13.2   A Third Dimension for AHPL

The AHPL that formed the basis of the previous edition of this book and that has been presented so far in this edition is called AHPL II. Several software tools, including a function-level simulator and a hardware compiler, have been developed to support AHPL II. As we have seen, this language has been sufficient to support the exploration of all the fundamental concepts of digital systems. Its effectiveness as a design tool comes into question only when one turns to large systems containing numerous repetitions of the same structures. In an array processor, for example, it would be helpful to declare a MODULE and interconnect *n* copies using a compact syntax as opposed to repetition of the almost identical module description *n* times.

In this chapter, we shall need a third index variable (a third dimension) in a combinational logic unit description to be presented in Section 13.6. In Section 13.10, we shall confront a system that could be expressed either as an array of modules or using a set of two-dimensional memory arrays. In either case, convenient description will require a third index variable and a syntax for selective and repetitive interconnections. The greatest value of formalizing a third dimension in AHPL is conciseness and clarity in the introduction of the memory array concepts of this chapter. Software implementations of these extensions of AHPL will not be available to most readers. With the help of a modern editor program, the reader should be able to translate a description like those given herein to a bulkier representation in AHPL II.

An appropriate syntax for repetitive and selective interconnections of combinational logic units has already been introduced in Chapter 5. To satisfy the needs of this chapter, we add the following features to the existing AHPL II.

1. A third index variable in addition to the row and column indices.
2. Declaration of sets of
    a. MODULES
    b. CLUNITS
    c. Arrays of memory elements
    d. CTERMS
    to be indexed by the third index variable.
3. A new construct called a STRUCTURE representing a network of connected modules and combinational logic units.
4. Implicit assignment of the index value of a module to each input and output line of that module.
5. Notation for selection of vectors declared in separate sets according to 2c*(used only in Section 13.10).

We shall not name the version of AHPL resulting from the incorporation of these features into AHPL II. A generalization of this language has been implemented and identified in the literature [7] as AHPL III. (The implemented version of AHPL III allows structures within structures and more than one additional index variable.)

Selection on the basis of the index variables of AHPL II is expressed by superscripts and subscripts or the brackets $\langle \rangle$ and [ ] in the implemented version. No further variation of either of these notations is available. We, therefore, introduce the notation

$$\text{ITEMS\_I}$$

to indicate the Ith member of a set, ITEMS. ITEMS could have been declared as a set of modules, a set of CLUNITS, or as a set of memory element arrays.

The declaration statement

$$\text{MEMORY: } \mathbf{M}\_0{:}3\langle 1024 \rangle\ [16]$$

declares the existence of four copies of an array of memory elements with 1024 rows and 16 columns. When used as here, the third index variable is much the same as a third dimension. In the following declaration of a set of modules within a structure, the new notation provides for the only index variable used.

$$\text{MODULES: PROC\_0{:}15} <: \text{PROCESSOR}$$

In this chapter, we shall use only a single structure that will include the entire system of interest. The syntax for a structure description is depicted in Fig. 13.2, where keywords are capitalized.

The last of the foregoing listed features provides for uniquely identifying the input/output lines of a particular module, several copies of which might appear in the same structure. It also permits the use of the combinational logic unit notation of Chapter 5 in the interconnection of these lines. Suppose, for example, x is declared as an input of a module, PROCESSOR. If an instance of PROCESSOR, PROC_I, is included in a structure, the corresponding input will be identified as x_I. This convention requires that no more than one set of a particular module type be declared

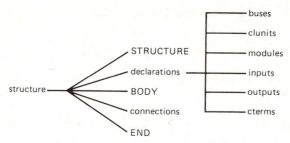

Figure 13.2. Syntax of a structure.

and that distinct identifiers of I/O lines be used in the various modules that might be incorporated into a structure.

When a set of modules is declared, buses may be declared in these modules indexed according to module numbers. Connection of such buses or any set of separately declared buses may be accomplished using the bidirectional connection operator, : = :. Writing the statement

$$ABUS := BBUS$$

within the body of a structure results in permanently joining these two buses into a single bus.

Example 13.1

Write an AHPL description of the structure depicted in Fig. 13.3. Each PROC__I is an instance of a module, PROCESSOR, the description of which begins as follows.

> MODULE: PROCESSOR.
>> INPUTS: x.
>> OUTPUTS: y.
>> COMBUSES: $IOBUS[8]$.

Solution:

Notice that all four instances of the *IOBUS* and the *SBUS* are effectively joined as a single bus. Thus, if any bus line is 1, the corresponding line of all four buses will be 1. For this purpose, we use the bidirectional connection operator just defined.

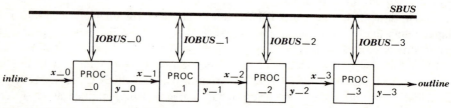

Figure 13.3. Example structure.

```
STRUCTURE: EXAMPLE.
    MODULES: PROC__0:3 <: PROCESSOR.
    BUSES: SBUS.
    INPUTS: inline.
    OUTPUTS: outline.
    BODY
        FOR I = 0 TO 3
            CONSTRUCT SBUS := : IOBUS__I;
            IF I > 0 THEN x__I = y__I-1
            ELSE x__I = inline
            FI;
        ROF;
        outline = y__3.
    END.
```

So far, we have only mechanisms for selective connection from rows of an array and for selecting a row from a two-dimensional array to be the target of a transfer. To meet the formal description challenge of Section 13.10, we shall need a conditional target selection mechanism and a conditional connection notation for the third dimension for which notation has just been introduced. Also needed in this chapter is the mechanism for selecting individual memory elements from a vector. We shall introduce both notations as the final topic in this section. The application of both forms of conditional notation will be limited to within module descriptions.

We shall use the double asterisk for both the left and right side conditional with respect to the dimension denoted by the underline. Suppose, for example, that we have declared a set of memory data registers

$$\text{MEMORY: } MD\_\_0:7[32]$$

each perhaps associated with a different memory. The third dimension is only a convenience for the memory data registers (although a necessity for the associated memories), but clarity will be added to a discussion if arrays and associated registers can be similarly indexed. Although nowhere implemented, the following transfer and connection notations will be considered as part of our descriptive AHPL throughout the remainder of the book.

$$(MD\_\_0:7) ** \text{DCD}(REG[0:2]) \leftarrow DBUS \tag{13.1}$$

$$DBUS = (MD\_\_0:7) ** \text{DCD}(REG[0:2]) \tag{13.2}$$

In Eq. 13.1, one of the registers, **MD**, is selected as a target of the transfer, depending on which of the bits in the condition vector is 1. Eq. 13.2 connects one of these registers to the **DBUS**. In both cases, the effect would be the same if the **MD** registers were row catenated in an array and the analogous single asterisk notation was used.

For denoting the selection of individual memory elements from a vector, we use an encircled asterisk. Expression 13.3 specifies that $X[0]$, $X[1]$, or $X[2]$ is connected to a single bit bus, depending on which one if any of **a**, **b**, or **c** is 1.

$$busbit = X \circledast (a, b, c) \tag{13.3}$$

Similarly, in Expression 13.4, memory elements $Y[0]$, $Y[1]$, or $Y[2]$ can be the target of the single bit transfer, depending on which of a, b, or c is 1.

$$Y \circledast (a, b, c) \leftarrow x \tag{13.4}$$

13.3 Associative Memory

In the next two sections, we shall encounter a need to allow the scratch-pad memory and the virtual memory to function without direction from a user program. In both cases, making these functions *transparent* to the programmer will require the use of an *associative* or *content-addressable* memory. In an associative memory, a data word is not obtained by supplying an address that specifies the location of that data word in memory. Instead, an identifying descriptor is provided to memory. The memory is then searched until an exact match is found between the submitted descriptor and a descriptor associated with a data word. When a match is found, the corresponding data word becomes the desired memory output. A descriptor may be part of each data word, or the descriptors may be stored separately. The human mind is often thought of as an associative memory. As a person dwells on a particular thought, related thoughts seem to flow from memory into his consciousness.

An associative memory might be organized so that many data words will be associated with one descriptor. Here, each descriptor will be unique, so that only one output data word will be obtained at each memory reference. The memory search in an associative memory may be sequential or the input descriptor may attempt to match all stored descriptors simultaneously. A sequential search would be prohibitively slow in an associative memory intended for use in a high-speed processor. If the search is parallel, the large amount of combinational logic required will necessarily limit the size of an associative memory. Prior to 1970, logic costs made a combinational associative memory out of the question.

Sequential search associative memories are useful at the applications level in, for example, information retrieval systems. As a hardware component to be designed into more complex hardware systems, we are primarily interested in the combinational search associative memory. Let us now consider the design of a combinational search associative memory with 2^n words, each with m data bits. The cost of the combinational logic involved will typically place an upper limit on n of about 10 or 12.

Consider the organization depicted in Fig. 13.4. The data are arranged in an array **AM** of 2^n m-bit words. In addition, there is an array **AA** containing 2^n descriptors r bits in length. One r-bit descriptor will correspond to each word in **AM**. We shall insist that each word in **AM** have a unique descriptor so that $n < r$. In a typical application, 2^n might be the number of words in a scratch pad and 2^r might be the number of words in the main RAM. Thus n might be 8 while r might be 18.

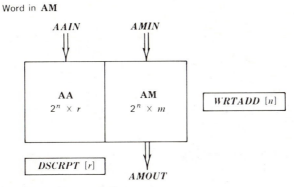

Figure 13.4. Associative memory.

Information can be stored in **AA** and **AM** from the vectors of input lines *AAIN* and *AMIN*. The address in both arrays of a data word and descriptor to be written is specified by the contents of the *n*-bit register *WRTADD*. Data are to be read from **AM** associatively. That is, the word in **AM** corresponding to the descriptor in **AA**, if any, that exactly matches the contents of the *r*-bit register, *DSCRPT*, will appear on the vector of output lines *AMOUT*.

Individual read and write operations can be expressed as single AHPL steps. It must be possible to replace the contents of a location in both **AA** and **AM** addressed by *WRTADD*. This write operation, effectively on a RAM with word length $r + m$, is expressed by Eq. 13.5.

$$\textbf{AA,AM} * \text{DCD } (\textbf{\textit{WRTADD}}) \leftarrow \textbf{\textit{AAIN, AMIN}} \tag{13.5}$$

We must also be able to both read and write associatively in **AM**, as expressed by Eq. 13.6.

$$\textbf{\textit{AMOUT}} = \text{BUSFN } (\textbf{AM}; \text{ASSOC } (\textbf{AA}; \textbf{\textit{DSCRPT}})) \tag{13.6}$$
$$\textbf{AM} * \text{ASSOC } (\textbf{AA}; \textbf{\textit{DSCRPT}}) \leftarrow \textbf{\textit{AMIN}}$$

The vector *AMOUT* is continuously available and may be clocked into a register to complete a read operation; BUSFN is the standard combinational logic unit developed in Chapter 5. The word lines are generated by the combinational logic unit ASSOC rather than by a decode as in a standard RAM. The ASSOC unit has 2^n outputs, one corresponding to each word of **AA** and **AM**. A bit of ASSOC[i] is 1 if and only if the corresponding word **AA** exactly matches the contents of the register *DSCRPT*. If there is no match, all 2^n outputs of ASSOC are 0. Each of the 2^n output functions of ASSOC are independent so that the unit may be represented in AHPL as follows, with one connection statement repeated 2^n times.

CLUNIT: ASSOC(X; **AA**) $\{n,r\}$.
INPUTS: $X[r]$; $\textbf{AA}\langle 2 \uparrow n \rangle [r]$.
OUTPUTS: *TERMOUT*$[2 \uparrow n]$.

BODY

> FOR I = 0 TO $(2 \uparrow n) - 1$ CONSTRUCT
>   ***TERMOUT***[I] = $\overline{\bigvee/(X \oplus \mathbf{AA}\langle I \rangle)}$
> ROF.

END.

Clearly, ***TERMOUT***[i] = 1 if and only if ***DSCRPT***[j] = $\mathbf{AA}\langle i \rangle$ [j] for all j.

13.4   Cache Memories

We use the term *cache* to refer to a high-speed memory that is not in itself of sufficient size to satisfy the RAM requirements in the system in which it is used. There are several ways in which a cache memory, sometimes called a "scratch pad," can be organized. Some of these approaches will be discussed in this section. The portion of Fig. 13.1 that depicts path D between the large RAM and the cache is reproduced in Fig. 13.5a. The simplest example of scratch-pad memory organization is the addressable register array that was discussed in Chapter 6. The use of these arrays depends on using multiaddress instructions with a small number of address bits to specify each argument. Thus the size of register arrays is limited.

If both a larger register array and the RAM are referenced by single-address instructions, the burden of when to store data in the RAM and when to use the register array is placed on the programmer. In this section, we shall consider alternative organizations in which decisions relating the two types of storage are made at the hardware level.

However the cache is organized, the goal is to make the average access time for words requested by the central processor as near as possible to the access time of the cache itself. This bound on the average access time can never be actually achieved, as the central processor will invariably request some items not stored in the cache from the larger RAM. The slowing effect of references to the RAM may be lessened in the following three obvious ways. Point 3 will be the topic of Sections 13.9 and 13.10.

1. Keep the ratio of RAM references to cache references as small as possible.
2. Overlap references to RAM with other central processor activities. Anticipate requirements for items from RAM in advance.
3. Organize the RAM so that blocks of a few words can be transferred to the cache at an increased average data transfer rate.

The three points are not independent. A certain anticipation of information requirements as well as the multiple use of items placed in the cache are implied if sequences of items are to be profitably obtained from the RAM at an increased transfer rate.

In this section, we are primarily concerned with point 1. Each time a word is

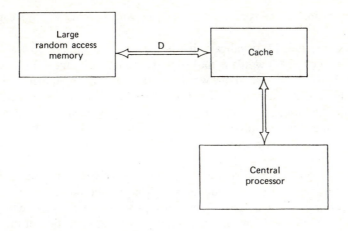

(a)

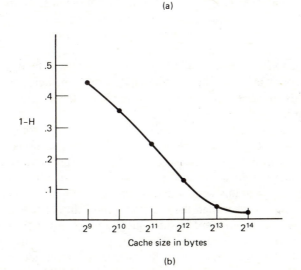

Cache size in bytes

(b)

Figure 13.5. (a) Cache memory. (b) Typical "miss ratios."

requested from memory, the cache is tried first. The *hit ratio* defined by Eq. 13.7 is the measure of success with respect to point 1.

$$H = \text{hit ratio} = \frac{\text{number of words found in cache}}{\text{number of memory accesses}} \qquad (13.7)$$

Sometimes the *miss ratio* given by $1 - H$ will be referred to, instead. Clearly, the miss ratio is reduced as the size of the cache is increased. We may assume that the cost per bit of the cache is considerably greater than that of the RAM. Fig. 13.5b indicates that, as the cache is increased in size, the point of diminishing returns on the cost-performance curve is reached for a cache with significantly less capacity than the RAM.

Empirical studies [2,3] indicate that Fig. 13.5b is relatively accurate if a block of four consecutive 32-bit words is moved to the cache each time a miss occurs. This is a sensible approach because, if one word is requested from RAM, there is a significant probability that subsequent memory locations will be accessed in the immediate future. The instruction look-ahead feature, to be discussed in Chapter 17, is based on this observation. Problems remain as to how large a block to transfer in the event of a miss, where to put the information in the cache, and how to inform the central processor of its new location.

These problems are best solved by organizing the cache in a manner so that it is completely transparent to the programmer. That is, the programmer may assume that he is working with the large RAM only. To the programmer, every memory reference will seem to be to the RAM. The only external indication of the cache will be the shorter than predicted average execution time for programs. To make the cache transparent, we shall organize it as an associative memory.

For convenience, we shall detail the design of a relatively small, 256-word, associative cache memory. We assume that access to this cache is synchronous, requiring only one period of the fast CPU clock. This cache will be operated in conjunction with a 256K-word asynchronous random access memory, which requires several clock periods for access. The registers required for the implementation of this memory are shown in Fig. 13.6.

In addition to the matrix **AM**, which constitutes the data storage, there is an additional 256-row matrix, **AA**. Each word stored in **AM** is also stored in the RAM. The address of **AM**$\langle i \rangle$ in the RAM is stored in **AA**$\langle i \rangle$. A word retrieved from RAM in response to a request from the central processor is also stored in the associative memory. The probability that this word will be requested again in the immediate future by the processor is much higher than the expected probability of request of a typical word in RAM. When the same word is subsequently requested from the associative memory, it will be obtained in only one clock period. Fig. 13.5b suggests hit ratios of up to 95%. Thus the associative memory can provide a considerable speed improvement. Of the remaining hardware in Fig. 13.6, **DSCRPT** and **AMD** are the address register and data register, respectively, for the associative memory. The registers **MA** and **MD** serve these functions in the RAM.

Because the 256-word memory will fill up quickly, it is necessary to provide a mechanism by which words that have not recently been accessed may be replaced. Keeping track of the history of accesses and deciding which word in **AA**, **AM** to replace is the task of a replacement algorithm. Four possible approaches to the design of the *replacement algorithm* are listed here, each permitting a variety of implementations.

1. Least frequently used
2. Least recently used
3. Not recently used
4. Random

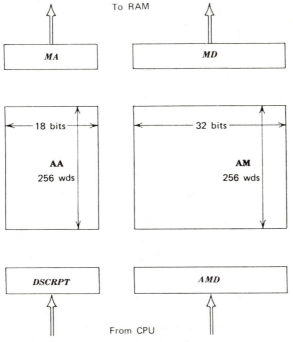

Figure 13.6. Associative scratch pad.

The *least frequently used* algorithm will probably lead to a minimal *miss ratio,* (i.e., the percentage of words addressed that are not found in the scratch-pad memory). Implementing this algorithm would require keeping track of a long history of accesses and performing several computations and comparisons each time it becomes necessary to replace a word in **AA,AM**. More easily implemented is the *least recently used,* algorithm, which simply means that each time a word is replaced in **AA,AM** the word to be replaced will be that word in **AA,AM** that has been accessed less recently than all the other words in the scratch pad. The third algorithm is an approximation of *least-recently-used* that might require less additional hardware. In this case, the word replaced might not actually be the least recently used but would at least be a word that has not been used for some time. The easiest to implement replacement algorithm is to select at random the word to be replaced. Implementation of the random algorithm requires only that a register sufficiently long to identify a word in cache be incremented every access to memory. When a "miss" occurs, the counter will point at the word to be replaced. Studies have shown that this simple random mechanism achieves a hit ratio almost as high as approximations of the least-recently-used algorithm.

One implementation of the least-recently-used algorithm is depicted in Fig. 13.7. Once the cache in Fig. 13.7 has been in operation for a period of time, the least recently used word in the cache and its address in RAM will occupy the last row of **AA,AM** and the most recently used word and address will occupy the top row. The remaining words will also be arranged in order of usage from top to bottom. Maintaining

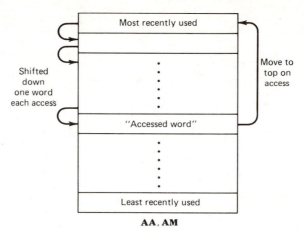

Figure 13.7. Implementation of least recently used algorithm.

this order, as words are continuously accessed from the cache, requires that each accessed word be moved from its former location to the top of **AA,AM** and at the same time all words above this location be shifted down one position. Figure 13.7 includes arrows depicting this operation. If a word not in the cache is obtained from RAM, its corresponding address and the data word are placed in the first row of **AA,AM** while each of the words in the cache are shifted down one position. The least recently used word will disappear from the cache but must be returned to the RAM at the addressed indicated by the corresponding row in **AA**.

There are many possible approaches to designing control for the associative memory. Since only one clock period is required to access the associative memory itself, we shall let this be accomplished by the primary CPU control sequence. If an access to the RAM is required, control for this function is the responsibility of a simultaneously active associative memory control sequence. Within the control sequence for the CPU, the following three steps must be inserted whenever it is desired to read from memory.

1   *DSCRPT* ← "desired address".
2   *AMD* ∗ (∨/ASSOC(**AA**; *DSCRPT*)) ← BUSFN(**AM**; ASSOC(**AA**; *DSCRPT*));
       AA⟨0⟩ ∗ (∨/ASSOC(**AA**; *DSCRPT*)) ← BUSFN(**AA**; ASSOC(**AA**; *DSCRPT*));
       AM⟨0⟩ ∗ (∨/ASSOC(**AA**; *DSCRPT*)) ← BUSFN(**AM**; ASSOC(**AA**; *DSCRPT*));
       AA⟨1:255⟩ ∗ ABOVE(ASSOC[1:255] (**AA**; *DSCRPT*)) ← **AA**⟨0:254⟩;
       AM⟨1:255⟩ ∗ ABOVE(ASSOC[1:255] (**AA**; *DSCRPT*)) ← **AM**⟨0:254⟩;
       → (∨/ASSOC(**AA**; *DSCRPT*))/(4).
3   *readram* = 1;
       → (*complete*)/(3).
4   "next CPU step"

The address of the desired word is first placed in ***DSCRPT***, where it is compared to each word in **AA**. If there is an address match, the corresponding data word from **AM** is placed in ***AMD*** at step 2. If a word is found, control passes directly from step 2 to the next CPU step. Thus a word from the associative memory is retrieved in only one clock period. If the desired word is not in the cache, a read request signal is sent to the RAM control module on line ***readram***.

If the desired word is in the scratch-pad, the appropriate rows must be shifted, as suggested in Figure 13.7. This is accomplished by the last four transfer statements in step 2. If any of the bits of ASSOC(**AA**; ***DSCRPT***) is 1, **AA**⟨0⟩ and **AM**⟨0⟩ will be replaced by the accessed word. The combinational logic unit, ABOVE, has 255 inputs and 255 outputs. ABOVE(X) may be described informally as follows:

If $X[i] = 1$, then ABOVE[j] $= 1$ for all $j \le i$. It is assumed that no more than one bit of X will be 1.

Using this definition of ABOVE, we see that each row of **AA**,**AM** above the accessed word is clocked in step 2. When clocked, a row becomes the target of a transfer from the row immediately above. Writing a formal combinational logic unit description for ABOVE(X) will be left as a problem for the reader.

When it is desired to write in memory, the following sequence is inserted.

1   ***DSCRPT*** ← "desired address";
       AMD ← "data to write".
2   **AA**⟨0⟩ ∗ (⋁/ASSOC(**AA**; ***DSCRPT***)) ← ***DSCRPT***;
       AM⟨0⟩ ∗ (⋁/ASSOC(**AA**; ***DSCRPT***)) ← ***AMD***;
       AA⟨1:255⟩ ∗ ABOVE(ASSOC[1:255] (**AA**; ***DSCRPT***)) ← **AA**⟨0:254⟩;
       AM⟨1:255⟩ ∗ ABOVE(ASSOC[1:255] (**AA**; ***DSCRPT***)) ← **AM**⟨0:254⟩;
       → (⋁/ASSOC(**AA**; ***DSCRPT***))/(4).
3   ***writeram*** = 1;
       → ($\overline{complete}$)/(3).
4   "next CPU step"

If the address to which the data is to be written matches a row of **AA**, the data and address are written in the first rows of **AM** and **AA**; and the rows of **AA**,**AM** above the row of **AA** that matched ***DSCRPT*** are shifted down one row. If the address is not in **AA**, a ***writeram*** signal is sent to the memory control module. In these two sequences, the combinational logic function ASSOC behaves as discussed in the previous section.

If a desired address is not found in the associative memory, control passes to the memory control module, which facilitates communications between the associative memory and the slower asynchronous RAM. A reference to RAM will cause the CPU to wait a much longer period of time than if the address had been found in **AA**. The interface between the associative memory and the RAM is illustrated in Fig. 13.8. The memory control is separate from the CPU control, but both are capable of controlling data transfers within the associative memory. To satisfy the conventions set forth in Chapter 9 completely, the CPU and memory control sequences would be included in the same module together with the data registers in the associative memory

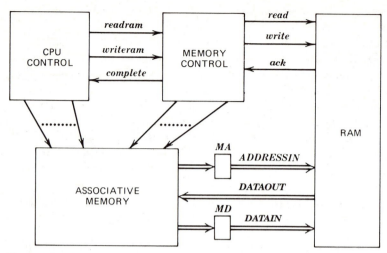

Figure 13.8. Associative memory/RAM interface.

that both control. We have already discussed the impact of the associative memory on the CPU control sequence. For convenience, we provide here a separately numbered description of the memory control sequence including declaration of registers in the associative memory.

MODULE:	MEMORY CONTROL.
INPUTS:	*readram*; *writeram*; *DATAOUT*[32]; *DSCRPT*[18]; *ack*.
OUTPUTS:	*complete*; *DATAIN*[32]; *ADDRESSIN*[18]; *read*; *write*.
MEMORY:	*AMD*[32]; *MA*[18]; *AA*⟨256⟩ [18]; *AM*⟨256⟩ [32]; *MD*[32].

1   $\rightarrow \overline{(readram \lor writeram)}/(1)$.
2   $MA \leftarrow AA⟨255⟩$;
    $MD \leftarrow AM⟨255⟩$.
3   *write* = 1;
    $\rightarrow (\overline{ack})/(3)$.

The receipt of either a ***readram*** or a ***writeram*** signal indicates that a space must be found in the associative scratch pad for a new data word. According to our implementation of the least-recently-used algorithm, this space will be the last row of **AA,AM**. In the case of ***writeram***, the new data word is already in **AMD**. For ***readram***, the word will eventually come from the RAM. The address stored in the last row of **AA** is transferred to **MA**, and the data word from the last row of **AM** is transferred to **MD**.

Control separates at step 4 so that a word can be obtained from the RAM to satisfy a read request. In the case of a write, the data are already waiting in **AMD** to be placed in the associative memory. The address is placed in **MA** at step 5, and the word is obtained from memory and placed in **AMD** by step 6.

4   → (*ack*, $\overline{ack}$/*readram*, $\overline{ack}$/*writeram*)/(4, 5, 7).
5   *MA ← DSCRPT*.
6   *read* = 1;
         AMD * *ack ← DATAOUT*;
         → ($\overline{ack}$)/(6).
7   **AA**:⟨0⟩ ← *DSCRPT*;
         AM⟨0⟩ ← *AMD*;
         AA⟨1:255⟩ ← **AA**⟨0:254⟩;
         AM⟨1:255⟩ ← **AM**⟨0:254⟩;
         complete = 1.
8   → (*readram* ∨ *writeram*, $\overline{(readram \vee writeram)}$)/(8,1).
ENDSEQUENCE
         CONTROLRESET(1);
         ADDRESSIN = *MA*; *DATAIN* = *MD*.
END.

Control converges at step 7 for the read and write operations. The word to be placed in the associative memory and its RAM address are now available in *AMD* and *DSCRPT*, respectively. Step 7 places these vectors in the top row of **AA,AM** while the rows of this array are simultaneously shifted down one position. As expected, the last row that has already been written in RAM now disappears from **AA,AM**. A complete signal is now returned to the CPU. For a read, the desired word remains in *AMD* for use by the CPU control. For a write, the word will not be placed in the RAM until it is later removed from the associative memory.

Not included in this control module is a sequence to sweep the entire associative memory into the RAM. Such a command might be helpful to the operating system at the completion of the program.

13.5   Virtual Memory

Somewhat analogous to the associative scratch pad is *virtual memory*. Although the scratch pad is included to shorten the effective access time of memory references, virtual memory is an organizational technique for increasing the apparent size of the random access memory. That is, the number of random access addresses available to the programmer is substantially greater than the number of locations in the physical RAM. These additional data are actually stored in a direct access storage device (DAS). The actual location of a particular data word is transparent to the programmer. Hence the term, *virtual memory*. To be of any value, the virtual memory control must operate so as to make the probability large that a piece of data will be residing in RAM when it is requested.

In Chapter 3, we observed that identifying and retrieving data files from DAS, particularly a magnetic disk, was usually a software function. If a word in the virtual memory, but not currently in the RAM, is addressed by an individual instruction, this fact must be noted by the hardware control sequence; also, provision must be made to transfer control to a software routine that will obtain this word and the entire *page* of data, in which it resides, from the DAS. This implies a very close coordination of hardware control sequences and software routines, as was the case in interrupt processing in Chapter 10. In fact, in our example of a virtual memory implementation, we shall rely on an interrupt to initiate a software search for a page of data.

A typical virtual memory will be organized into pages of data words with between 2^8 and 2^{12} words in each page. Since the object of the virtual memory is to provide a very large memory of apparently individually addressable words, one would expect to find at least 2^{10} pages in a virtual memory. A virtual memory consisting of 2^{12} pages of 2^{12} words each is depicted in Fig. 13.9a. Each word in the virtual memory is assigned a 24-bit address, called a *virtual address*. This address will consist of 12 bits specifying the *virtual page number* and 12 bits specifying the address within the page, *the page address*. Each memory address instruction must contain 24 address bits so as to specify precisely the location of each operand in the virtual memory.

No practical random access memory large enough to store the entire contents of the virtual memory of Fig. 13.9a exists. Typically, only a small subset of the virtual

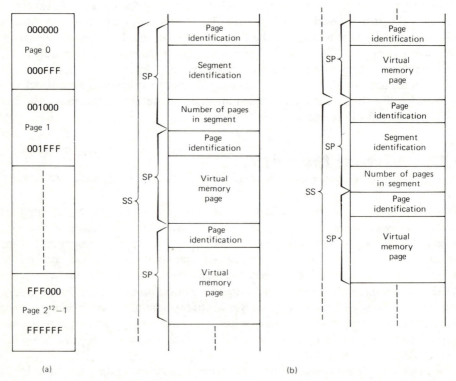

Figure 13.9 Typical virtual memory. (*a*) Virtual memory. (*b*) Storage of virtual memory in DAS.

memory pages, perhaps 64 pages, are actually stored in RAM. The remaining pages must be stored in DAS. You will recall that individual records were usually obtained from a track on a magnetic disk by a software search process. If the DAS is organized to support a virtual memory, the *DAS page* labelled SP in Fig. 13.9b will replace the record as the smallest addressable unit of data in the DAS. Thus each DAS page will consist of a virtual memory page and a page identifier to permit it to be located by search.

DAS must also be organized into files that constitute individual user programs or user-specified data structures. A file will usually include several records. The storage of each file must include identifying data as well as some form of password to prevent unauthorized use or alteration of the files. In a DAS device organized to support a virtual memory, the term *segment,* labelled SS in Fig. 13.9, is typically used in place of a file. A segment will consist of a variable number of DAS pages, up to a system-specified maximum, headed by a segment identification page containing the identifying data mentioned earlier and the number of pages to be expected in the segment. Segments are manipulated by the operating system. The special hardware control sequences necessary to identify missing pages in the RAM will not be cognizant of any partitioning of the virtual memory into segments. Since we shall not attempt to design an operating system in this section, it will not be necessary to structure the segment identification page in more detail.

The operating system together with pertinent tables must be stored continuously in RAM. Since this information must not be removed from the RAM to make room for missing pages, the RAM will be typically organized as illustrated in Fig. 13.10. It is assumed that each page contains 2^{12} words as in the virtual memory pages of Fig. 13.9 so that a page from virtual memory can be stored in each page of RAM. The RAM of Fig. 13.10 consists of 64 pages, or a total of 2^{18} words. We have arbitrarily set aside eight RAM pages or $1/8$ of the total memory for storage of the operating system and related tables. Therefore, only 56 pages of memory are available for storage of user pages from the virtual memory. Of the 2^{12} virtual memory pages, only those currently in use will be stored in the RAM. Others must be obtained from DAS as needed, replacing pages in RAM with the longest histories of disuse. The first three locations in RAM will be used by the hardware to inform the operating system of the number of a needed page that is missing from the RAM and the number of the page that has had the least recent use and can be deleted from the RAM.

Also shown in Fig. 13.10 are a 32-bit instruction register and a 24-bit program counter. The least-significant 12 bits of each specify the *page address,* that is, the address of a word within a 2^{12}-word page. The next 12 bits in each case specify a *page number* in virtual memory. Together, these 24 bits are the virtual address. If a particular page of the virtual memory is stored in RAM, it may be located by reference to the small *associative memory,* **RPAG.** When a virtual memory page number is connected to the bus **DSCRPTBUS,** the output of the associative memory is the corresponding 6-bit RAM page number. The catenation of these 6 bits with the page address specifies the location of a desired word in RAM. The first eight pages of RAM must always contain the operating system that cannot be removed to DAS. For the purpose of memory reference commands within the operating system, these RAM

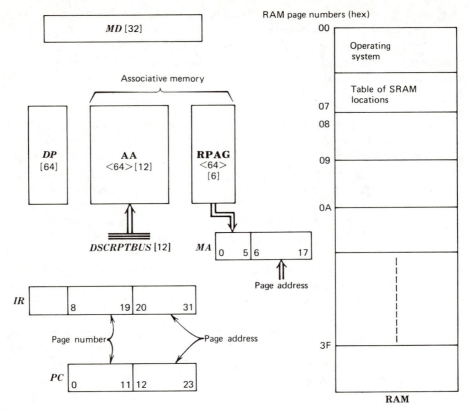

Figure 13.10. RAM organization for virtual memory.

pages will be assumed to correspond to the first eight pages of virtual memory. Therefore, the first eight rows of **AA** will contain binary equivalent of the fixed values 000 to 007 (hex) while the first eight rows of **RPAG** will be 00 to 07. Since the first eight pages will never be removed from RAM, the first eight rows of **AA,RPAG** will not be included in the implementation of the least recently used algorithm. Thus **(AA,RPAG)** ⟨8⟩ will represent the most recently used page unless this page was one of the eight system pages. Otherwise, the replacement algorithm will be implemented in much the same way as for the scratch pad by shifting the rows of **AA,RPAG** with each access to the RAM.

The register *DP*, shown in Fig. 13.10, represents another distinction between the replacement process for the virtual memory and that of the scratch pad in Section 13.4. *DP* is a register of *dirty page* bits, one for each of the pages in RAM or each of the rows in **AA,RPAG**. A *dirty page* is a graphic term for a page that has had new data written on it during its current residence period in RAM. If the least recently used page is a dirty page, when it is removed from the RAM, it must be copied back into DAS. There will be no need to take the time to copy a page back to DAS, if it

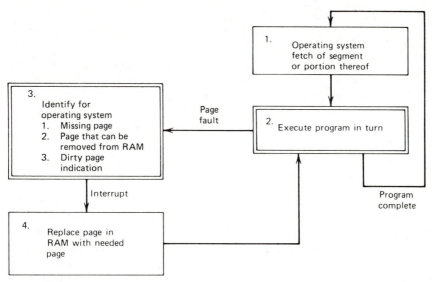

Figure 13.11. Management of virtual memory.

is a *clean page;* that is, if it contains exactly the same data as when it was placed in the RAM. If page *i* in the RAM is dirty, $DP[i] = 1$.

A flowchart illustrating the functions involved in executing a program in a virtual memory system is shown in Fig. 13.11. The process is shown as beginning with an operating system fetch from DAS of a segment of pages containing a user program. Only a portion of the segment will be retrieved, if the segment exceeds the 56 pages available in RAM or if the program must share the RAM with other programs. The treatment of a segment by the operating system will depend in part on control information supplied by the user.

The implementation of block 2 of Fig. 13.11 with virtual memory will require some special features in the hardware control sequence. Block 3 is entirely a hardware function, while blocks 1 and 4 can be accomplished by software using ordinarily available assembly language instructions. As part of block 2, the following sequence must be included at each read from virtual memory in the CPU control sequence.

R1   ***DSCRPTBUS*** = "virtual page number";
         MA ← BUSFN(**RPAG**; ASSOC(**AA**; ***DSCRPTBUS***)), "page address";
         MD * $\overline{\vee/\text{ASSOC}(\mathbf{AA};\ \mathbf{\textit{DSCRPTBUS}})}$ ← 20⊤0, "virtual page number";
         → ($\overline{\vee/\text{ASSOC}(\mathbf{AA};\ \mathbf{\textit{DSCRPTBUS}})}$)/(100).

R2   ***DSCRPTBUS*** = "virtual page number";
         MD ← BUSFN(**M**; DCD(***MA***));
         AA⟨8⟩ * ($\vee$/ASSOC[8:63](**AA**; ***DSCRPTBUS***))
                     ← BUSFN(**AA**; ASSOC(**AA**; ***DSCRPTBUS***));

RPAG⟨8⟩ * (⋁/ASSOC[8:63](**AA**; *DSCRPTBUS*))

$\qquad\qquad$ ← BUSFN(**RPAG**; ASSOC(**AA**; *DSCRPTBUS)));*

DP[8] * (⋁/ASSOC[8:63](**AA**; *DSCRPTBUS*))

$\qquad\qquad\qquad$ ← *DP* * ASSOC(**AA**; *DSCRPTBUS*);

AA⟨9:63⟩ * ABOVE(ASSOC[9:63](**AA**; *DSCRPTBUS*)) ← **AA**⟨8:62⟩;

RPAG⟨9:63⟩ * ABOVE(ASSOC[9:63](**AA**; *DSCRPTBUS*)) ←

$\qquad\qquad\qquad\qquad\qquad\qquad$ **RPAG**⟨8:62⟩;

DP[9:63] ⊛ ABOVE(ASSOC[9:63](**AA**; *DSCRPTBUS*)) ←

$\qquad\qquad\qquad\qquad\qquad\qquad\qquad$ *DP*[8:62].

R3   "next CPU step"

The first step connects the page number from *PC* or *IR* as appropriate to *DSCRPTBUS*. If any output of ASSOC(**AA**; *DSCRPTBUS*) is 1, 6 bits from **RPAG** catenated with the page address from the appropriate source are placed in *MA*. Control then passes to step R2, where the desired word is read from the RAM. If ⋁/ASSOC = 0, indicating a missing page, then the page number is placed in the last 12 bits of *MD;* and control branches to step 100, where the implementation of block 3 of Fig. 13.11 begins.

If the page is not a system page but is nonetheless found in RAM (⋁/AS-SOC[8:63] = 1), then the page number for that page must be moved up to row (**AA,RPAG**)⟨8⟩, which must represent the most recently used word. At the same time, the rows of (**AA,RPAG**)⟨8:63⟩ above the vacated row are shifted down. This implementation of the replacement algorithm is similar to that used in the previous section for the scratch pad. Here a similar manipulation is also done on the "dirty page" vector. This activity, required by the replacement algorithm, is accomplished by the last six transfer statements in step R2.

The following very similar pair of steps will be inserted in the main control sequence wherever it is necessary to effect a write to RAM.

W1   *DSCRPTBUS* = "virtual page number";

$\qquad$ *MA* ← BUSFN(**RPAG**; ASSOC(**AA**; *DSCRPTBUS*)), "page

$\qquad\qquad\qquad\qquad\qquad\qquad\qquad\qquad\qquad\qquad$ address";

$\qquad$ *MD* * ($\overline{\text{⋁/ASSOC}}$(**AA**; *DSCRPTBUS*) ← 20⊤0, "virtual page

$\qquad\qquad\qquad\qquad\qquad\qquad\qquad\qquad\qquad\qquad$ number";

$\qquad$ → ($\overline{\text{⋁/ASSOC}}$(**AA**; *DSCRPTBUS*))/(100).

W2   *DSCRPTBUS* = "virtual page number";

$\qquad$ **M** * DCD(*MA*) ← *MD;*

$\qquad$ **AA**⟨8⟩ * (⋁/ASSOC[8:63](**AA**; *DSCRPTBUS*))

$\qquad\qquad\qquad\qquad$ ← BUSFN(**AA**; ASSOC(**AA**; *DSCRPTBUS*));

$\qquad$ **RPAG**⟨8⟩ * (⋁/ASSOC[8:63](**AA**; *DSCRPTBUS*))

$\qquad\qquad\qquad\qquad$ ← BUSFN(**RPAG**; ASSOC(**AA**; *DSCRPTBUS*));

$\qquad$ **AA**⟨9:63⟩ * ABOVE(ASSOC[9:63](**AA**; *DSCRPTBUS*)) ←

$\qquad\qquad\qquad\qquad\qquad\qquad\qquad\qquad$ **AA**⟨8:62⟩;

TABLE 13.1

Eventual RAM location	Information	Source
000000	Number of missing virtual page	$MD[20:31]$
000001	Virtual page to be moved from RAM	**AA** $\langle 63 \rangle$
000002	FFFFFFFF (hex) to indicate dirty page	$DP[63]$

$$\textbf{RPAG}\langle 9:63 \rangle * \text{ABOVE} (\ \text{ASSOC}[9:63](\textbf{AA};\ \textit{DSCRPTBUS})) \leftarrow$$
$$\textbf{RPAG}\langle 8:62 \rangle;$$
$$\textit{DP}[9:63] \circledast \text{ABOVE}(\ \text{ASSOC}[9:63](\textbf{AA};\ \textit{DSCRPTBUS})) \leftarrow$$
$$\textit{DP}[8:62];$$
$$\textit{DP}[8] \leftarrow 1.$$

The last line of W2 updates the dirty-page bit corresponding to the page just written on and is unique to the write operation. Also, the second line of W2 differs from R2 to permit the actual write in memory. It is assumed that the data have already been placed in *MD*. We note that *MD* is affected by steps R1 and W1 only in the event of a missing page. In this case, execution of the instruction has been interrupted and will be restarted once the missing page is obtained. Thus there is no conflict in the use of *MD*.

Table 13.1 lists the information that must be provided to the operating system to retrieve a missing page and indicates where this information is to be found. It is the function of the sequence beginning at step 100 to obtain or store the appropriate page numbers and the dirty page indication in these first three locations of RAM. The number of the missing page is already in *MD,* so that step 100 merely places address 00 in *MA* and step 101 writes the missing page number in RAM. Step 102 increments *MA* and places the number of the virtual page to be moved from RAM in *MD,* so that it can be written in location 000001 by step 103. The page to be replaced is the one corresponding to the last entry in **AA,RPAG**. The corresponding virtual page number from **AA**$\langle 63 \rangle$ is, therefore, placed in *MD*. At the same time, the page number of the new page to be placed in RAM is transferred from *MD* to **AA**$\langle 63 \rangle$.

Location 000002 will be used to pass to the operating system an indication of whether or not the page to be replaced in RAM is a dirty page. If the page is clean, considerable time will be saved by the operating system in that it will be able to merely overwrite the page in RAM without first transferring it back to disk. All 1's in location 000002 will indicate a dirty page; otherwise the word will contain all 0's. At the same time the page number is loaded in RAM by step 103, the dirty page indication is placed in *MD*. This third word is moved to RAM by step 104, and an interrupt is issued to alert the operating system to the page fault.

100	$MA \leftarrow 18\top 0.$
101	$M * \text{DCD}(MA) \leftarrow MD.$

102     $MA \leftarrow \text{INC}(MA)$;
        $MD \leftarrow 20 \top 0,\ \mathbf{AA}\langle 63 \rangle$;
        $\mathbf{AA}\langle 63 \rangle \leftarrow MD[20{:}31]$.

103     $M * \text{DCD}(MA) \leftarrow \underline{MD};\ MA \leftarrow \text{INC}(MA)$;
        $MD \leftarrow DP[63] \wedge 32 \top 0$.

104     $M * \text{DCD}(MA) \leftarrow \underline{MD};\ DP[8{:}63] \leftarrow 0,\ DP[8{:}62]$;
        $(\mathbf{AA},\ \mathbf{RPAG})\langle 8{:}63 \rangle \leftarrow (\mathbf{AA},\mathbf{RPAG})\langle 63 \rangle\ !\ (\mathbf{AA},\mathbf{RPAG})\langle 8{:}62 \rangle$;
        interrupt $= 1$; "set status for interrupt".

With the generation of the interrupt, further responsibility for exchanging pages in RAM is passed to the operating system software. This function can be accomplished using ordinarily available assembly language instructions. The new virtual page number (missing page) is now stored in **AA.** Therefore, this number must be used in addressing the RAM page to be rewritten, both in removing old information and replacing it with new. The virtual page number of the page to be removed is used only to identify the DAS page to be updated. The data in the virtual page to be placed in DAS will probably be quite different from the old data that it will replace. This page in virtual memory has not changed since it was copied into RAM at an earlier exchange.

13.6   Table Lookup of Page Numbers

In the previous section, we saw an implementation of virtual memory based on a fully associative search. There are other ways to provide for locating a particular virtual page in the random access memory and for identifying page faults. One such alternative approach is a table lookup in a table of RAM page numbers. A complete table lookup requires a table containing as many words as there are pages of virtual memory. Each virtual page will map one-to-one onto a location in the table. Given a reasonable number of virtual pages, the table itself may be located in the primary RAM. In this case, each memory reference will be slowed by the necessity of accessing the RAM twice. If the table is stored in a smaller, faster RAM, the process can be speeded up somewhat.

The first bit of each word, called a *tagword,* in the page number table will be a flag bit. The remaining bits will be the number of a page in the RAM. If the flag bit of a word is 1, the corresponding virtual page is currently residing in RAM at the location given by the page-number field. If the flag is 0, the virtual page is not in RAM, and the page-number field has no significance. A page table for a virtual memory consisting of 4096 pages and a primary storage of 64 pages is depicted in Fig. 13.12. The virtual address of a word desired by the CPU is shown in hexadecimal. The flag of the addressed tagword is 1, so the corresponding virtual page is page number 1C in RAM.

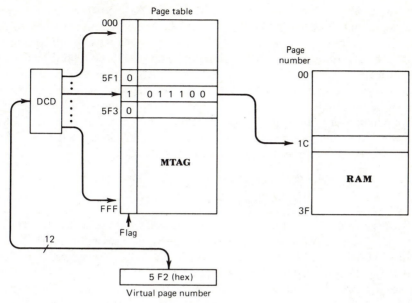

Figure 13.12. Table lookup of tagwords.

Example 13.2

Express in AHPL the steps associated with a read operation in a CPU supported by a virtual memory configured as given in Fig. 13.12. Assume that each page contains 4096 words. Let the table of tagwords be stored in a special memory array called **MTAG**⟨4096⟩[7]. Disregard the replacement algorithm.

Solution

R1   ***LKUPBUS*** = "virtual page number";
      MA ← $\overline{\text{BUSFN[1:6]}}$(**MTAG;** DCD(***LKUPBUS***)), "page address";
      MD ∗ $\overline{\text{BUSFN[0](MTAG; DCD(}}$***LKUPBUS***)) ← 20 ⊤ 0,
                                                      "virtual page number";
      → $\overline{(\text{BUSFN[0](}}$***MTAG; DCD(LKUPBUS)***)))/(100).
R2   ***MD*** ← BUSFN(**M;** DCD(***MA***)).

To facilitate comparison, these steps have been written in a form similar to the steps R1 and R2 of the fully associative virtual memory implementation of Section 13.5. The clock for ***MD*** and the possible branch to the page-fault steps is now controlled by the flag bit of the addressed word of **MTAG**. ∎

Of interest is an approximate comparison of the gate count of the read from tagword table in Example 13.2 with that of the combinational logic unit ASSOC in

Section 13.5, since memory dimensions are the same for the two cases. The combinational logic unit ASSOC for **AA**⟨64⟩[12] will be composed primarily of 768 EXCLUSIVE-OR gates or 3 × 768 = 2304 NAND gates. **AA, RPAG** will contain 1152 memory elements. Implementation of a clocked memory **MTAG**⟨4096⟩[7] will consist of 28,672 memory elements and a like number of AND gates to gate the memory element outputs together with 4096 AND gates for the final stage of the decoder. Letting Nv be the number of bits in a virtual page number, and Np the number of bits in a page number for primary RAM, results in the more general expressions 13.8 and 13.9 in which a memory element is weighted as two gates. As in Example 13.2, this comparison does not consider the replacement algorithm.

$$\text{Fully associative cost} = 2^{Np} \times (5Nv + Np) \qquad (13.8)$$

$$\text{Table lookup cost} = 2^{Nv} \times (3Np + 4) \qquad (13.9)$$

Because $Np < Nv$, the fully associative approach would seem always to be most economical, given the cost assumptions which led to Eqs. 13.8 and 13.9. If a memory cell in the **MTAG** could be more economically implemented, as suggested in Chapter 3, or if the table could itself be stored in a protected area of main RAM, then the table lookup approach might be cost competitive. Inclusion of the table of tagwords in RAM would imply two memory accesses for each instruction or data word actually obtained. The penalty might be alleviated somewhat by inclusion of a special cache memory that would store only the tagwords for the most recently used virtual pages. This technique will be explored in Section 13.8.

13.7   Set-Associative Virtual Memory

Where a large number of pages are involved, the fully associative approach to virtual memory implementation could imply a very large amount of combinational logic. For some design constraints, this could prove prohibitive in terms of either cost or required VLSI chip area. As discussed in the last section, the table lookup of tagwords would only be less costly than the fully associative approach if the memory medium for the table is the system RAM or some other RAM package whose access time would be longer than a clock period of a fast CPU. Typically, fully associative will be at one end of any spectrum of design choices as the fastest, but most costly. The table lookup will be at the other end as the slowest.

Are there alternatives for virtual memory implementation between these extremes? One approach to this question might be "How can the associative search be modified to reduce the amount of combinational logic required?" Is it possible to get by with an associative search over fewer page numbers than the total number of pages in RAM? The answer to the latter question is "yes," simply restricting those *page slots* (a page slot is a space in RAM that will accommodate a virtual page) in which a given virtual page can be placed.

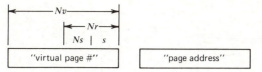

Figure 13.13 Address fields for set-associative memory.

We begin to explore a strategy for restricting the placement of virtual pages in RAM page slots by examining Fig. 13.13, which depicts the bits of a virtual address. Of primary interest are the most significant Nv bits, which specify the virtual page number. Let us divide these bits into three separate fields. The rightmost field will contain s bits. The middle field will contain Ns bits. We restrict the choice of s and Ns such that Eq. 13.10 is satisfied where $2 \uparrow Nr$ is the number of virtual pages that can be stored in RAM.

$$Nr = Ns + s \qquad (13.10)$$

The leftmost field in Fig. 13.13 thus contains $Nv - Nr$ bits.

The virtual memory can be visualized as composed of $2 \uparrow (Nv - Nr)$ *images* of the available space for page slots in RAM. Fig. 13.14 depicts these $2 \uparrow (Nv - Nr)$ sections of virtual memory, each of which includes exactly $2 \uparrow Nr$ pages. Now let us divide the page slots in RAM into $2 \uparrow Ns$ sets of $2 \uparrow s$ pages each. At the same time, let us also visualize that each of the $2 \uparrow (Nv - Nr)$ images of RAM in the virtual memory is similarly divided into $2 \uparrow Ns$ sets of $2 \uparrow s$ pages. All this is depicted in Fig. 13.14.

Now let us enforce the restriction that only those pages from set 0 in any of the $2 \uparrow (Nv - Nr)$ blocks in the virtual memory may be stored in the set 0 area of RAM. Similarly, only pages from the set 1 area of virtual memory may be stored in the set 1 area of RAM and so on. The implementation of the associative search for a virtual page in RAM may be modified to take advantage of these stated restrictions on the storage of a virtual page. The hope would be that a more economical realization could be achieved. The result may be termed a *set-associative* virtual memory.

It might be asked why the Ns bits that identify a particular image of the RAM space in virtual memory are not the most significant bits of the virtual page number. If this were the case, it would be impossible to put a contiguous block of $2 \uparrow Nr$ pages or for that matter any contiguous block of more than $2 \uparrow s$ pages in RAM at one time. This would make it very awkward for an operating system to place more than $2 \uparrow s$ pages of a user program in RAM at one time. This could be an intolerable restriction, particularly if there were fewer than Ns users at a given time. The model of Fig. 13.14 would permit a single-user program to occupy the entire user area of RAM, if so desired.

Because virtual pages are restricted in their location in RAM, the location of the corresponding virtual page numbers are similarly restricted in **AA.** That is, the page numbers for any set 0 area of virtual memory may be found only in the first $2 \uparrow s$

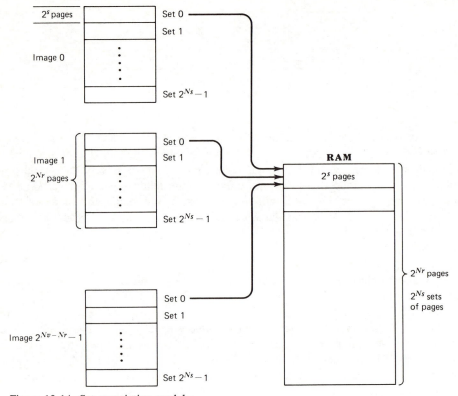

Figure 13.14. Set-associative model.

words of **AA** and so on. When a particular virtual page is referenced, the page number on *DSCRPTBUS* will be known to be in only one set area of **AA.** The *Ns* field of bits specifies the set number, and this field on the *DSCRPTBUS* may be used to find that set for associative matching against the rest of the bits on *DSCRPTBUS,* as depicted in Fig. 13.15. Thus the process of finding a page in virtual memory becomes a combination of memory lookup and associative match. This will be illustrated in Example 13.3.

To express the implementation of the fetch of a set of rows from a memory requires an extension of the combinational logic unit BUSFN. The output of the combinational logic unit EXTBUSFN, described as follows, is a set of m/n rows from an arbitrary **ARRAY** of m rows. To use this in the set-associative memory description, we shall merely let $m = 2 \uparrow Nr$ and $n = 2 \uparrow Ns$. Writing this description is made much easier with the use of the multiple-copy notation introduced in Section 13.2. We are thus able to divide **ARRAY** into n sets of m/n rows in the declaration of CTERMS.

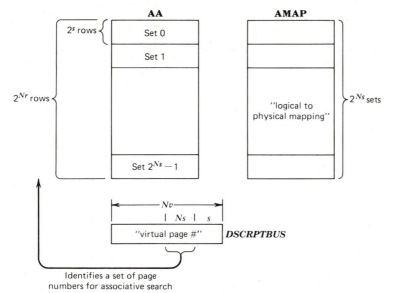

Figure 13.15. Sets of page numbers.

CLUNIT: EXTBUSFN(**ARRAY**; *VECTOR*) {m} {n} {r}.

  INPUTS: **ARRAY**$\langle m\rangle$[r]; *VECTOR*[n].

  OUTPUTS: **TERMOUT**$\langle m/n\rangle$[r].

CTERMS: **SELECT__0**:$n-1\langle m/n\rangle$ [r]; **ORSEL__0**:$n-1\langle m/n\rangle$ [r].

BODY

  FOR I $= 0$ TO $n-1$ CONSTRUCT

      SELECT__I $=$ **ARRAY**$\langle(m/n)*\langle I:(m/n)*I+m/n-1\rangle\rangle \;\wedge$

                                                    VECTOR[I];

      IF I $= 0$

              ORSEL__I $=$ **SELECT__I**

      ELSE

              ORSEL__I $=$ (**ORSEL__I**-1) $\bigvee$ **SELECT__I**

      FI;

  ROF;

  TERMOUT $=$ **ORSEL__**$n-1$.

END.

Notice that the array **RPAG,** which in Section 13.5 located pages in RAM, has been relabelled **AMAP.** The use of EXTBUSFN to fetch a set of rows from **AA, AMAP** will preclude the implementation of the least recently used replacement algorithm employed in Section 13.5. Row-to-row shifting is incompatible with fetching by address. Let us ignore the replacement algorithm and assume the rows of **AMAP** are fixed. Now **AMAP** can be a ROM containing a fixed mapping of the $2 \uparrow Nr$ virtual pages currently residing in RAM onto their actual RAM locations. This mapping is usually called a *logical-to-physical mapping*. The simplest possible mapping would use the row numbers of **AA, AMAP** as the RAM page numbers. In this case, a ROM would not actually be required (see Problem 13.12). The following example includes **AMAP** to allow maximum generality.

Example 13.3

Write in AHPL a virtual read statement for a 4096-page set-associative virtual memory. As in previous examples, each page will consist of 4096 32-bit words. The virtual memory will be divided into eight sets of pages ($Ns = 3$). The RAM, $M\langle 2 \uparrow 18\rangle[32]$ will accommodate 64 pages. Supply the appropriate declaration statements for any combinational logic units used. Ignore the replacement algorithm.

Solution

As in Section 13.5, an array, $AA\langle 64\rangle[12]$, would store the page numbers of the pages currently in RAM. However, as suggested previously and depicted in Fig. 13.16, bits *DSCRPTBUS*[6:8] do not actually need to be matched associatively with the corresponding bits of the page number. These bits identify the set of page numbers and are used to reference this set from **AA.** Thus the dimensions of our set associative **AA** will be $AA\langle 64\rangle[9]$. When a row from a set of page numbers is matched by *DSCRPTBUS,* the corresponding row from **AMAP** must be available to locate that page in RAM. Thus EXTBUSFN will operate on an **AA,AMAP** whose width is 15.

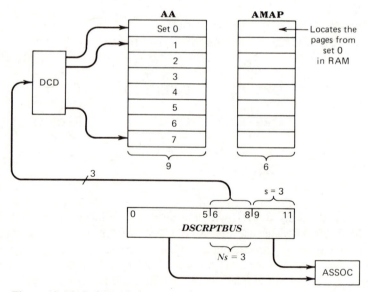

Figure 13.16. Set-associative example.

From $2 \uparrow Nr = 64$ we get $Nr = 6$ and $s = Nr - Ns = 3$. Thus a set of $2 \uparrow s$ $= 8$ page numbers must be read from **AA** to set up the associative matching process. The parameter n in the combinational logic unit EXTBUSFN, used to route a set of page numbers from **AA,** is $2 \uparrow Ns$. The dimensions of the output of EXTBUSFN are the same as a set of rows from **AA,AMAP,** namely, $\langle 8 \rangle [15]$. Therefore, we may declare the appropriate copy of EXTBUSFN as follows. For convenience, a label statement may also be included to shorten the description.

CLUNITS: EXTBUSFN1$\langle 8 \rangle [15]$ $\langle$: EXTBUSFN {64} {8} {15}.
LABEL: **SETFN**$\langle 8 \rangle [15]$ = EXTBUSFN1(**AA,AMAP;**
              DCD(*DSCRPTBUS*[6:8])).
LABEL: *DSCRPT* = *DSCRPTBUS*[0:5], *DSCRPTBUS*[9:11].

The array **SETFN** represents the set of partial page numbers together with the corresponding logical-to-physical mapping information fetched from **AA,AMAP.** The existence of the desired page in RAM will be determined by associatively matching this array with bits 0:5 and 9:11 of *DSCRPTBUS.* For compactness and clarity, the catenation of these bits has been labelled *DSCRPT.* We are now ready to express the read steps as follows.

R1 *DSCRPTBUS* = "virtual page number";
  MA ← BUSFN(**SETFN**[9:14]; ASSOC(**SETFN**[0:8];*DSCRPT*)),
                     "page address";
  MD ∗ $\overline{\bigvee/\text{ASSOC}(\textbf{SETFN}[0:8]; \textit{DSCRPT})}$ ← 20 ⊤ 0,
                 "virtual page number";
  → ($\overline{\bigvee/\text{ASSOC}(\textbf{SETFN}[0:8]; \textit{DSCRPT})}$)/(100).
R2 *MD* ← BUSFN(**M**; DCD(*MA*)).   ■

Calculation of the number of gates in a set-associative implementation as contrasted to fully associative will be left as a problem for the reader. If **AA** is treated as a clocked memory with BUSFN with the same family of logic elements as the ASSOC logic, the savings might seem too small to justify living with the constraints of the set-associative model. Choice of a set-associative approach would have to depend on the form of VLSI realization and the partition of the system among IC packages. If **AA** were implemented as a one-transistor per bit RAM, as discussed in Chapter 3, a set-associative model might be a reasonable approach.

13.8 Cache and Virtual Memory Combinations

So far in this chapter, we have explored associative cache memories and a variety of approaches to virtual memory implementation. In this section, we are going to consider a complete memory system that will include virtual memory and, out of necessity, more than one cache. For maximum clarity, we will pursue a particular example with certain numerical values for the memory parameters. These numbers will force certain design decisions. An interesting additional study might involve the determination of cross-over points for such design decisions as the values of the memory parameters are increased. We leave these problems to the interested reader.

Let us consider a computer system with, like RIC, a 32-bit word-length, a memory addressable only to the individual 32-bit word, but a virtual address space specified by 32 address bits. The RAM is to include a maximum of $2 \uparrow 20$ 32-bit words. Each page is to consist of 256 words. Therefore, the RAM will contain up to $2 \uparrow 12$ or 4096 pages. At the outset, we assume that a fully associative approach to identifying the presence and location of a virtual page among the 4096 pages of RAM is prohibitive to implement with available IC packages. We also reject the lack of flexibility of the set-associative approach for purposes of this example.

We seem to be left only with the use of tagwords, one for each page of virtual memory. Wow! There are $2 \uparrow 24$ such pages, but only $2 \uparrow 20$ words in the RAM. In this case, tagwords are only a viable approach if these words can be considered as stored in virtual memory. Even then, there would be $2 \uparrow 16$ virtual pages of such tagwords. One option would be to treat a virtual page containing tagwords just like any other virtual page. Of course, each such virtual page of tagwords would have its own tagword, which would be stored in some other virtual page. Consider the dilemma suggested by Fig. 13.17, which begins when a virtual address of a memory word required by the executing process is presented to the memory system. For convenience, we refer to this address as a *process virtual address* or PVA.

If the system actually arrived at step i, the desired word would be obtained after $k + 1$ memory fetches and after no more than k page swaps by the operating system. Although this observation alone makes the approach prohibitive should k be much greater than 3 or 4, it is unduly optimistic since the procedure will never actually reach step i. Instead, as is evident from inspection of the first four steps, no tagword ever becomes available, since no tagword can be fetched until some predecessor tagword has indicated its presence or nonpresence in RAM.

This dilemma could be bypassed by constraining the operating system to swap a page of tagwords into RAM without proof that the page was not already in RAM. A less wasteful option that we shall pursue here is to store all *tagwords of tagword pages* in RAM. Without further enhancement, the procedure in Fig. 13.17 would then simplify to that of Fig. 13.18.

For our example, it is necessary to assure that all tagwords of pages of tagwords can feasibly be stored in RAM. As mentioned previously, there are altogether $2 \uparrow 24$ tagwords of virtual memory pages. There are $2 \uparrow 16$ pages of tagwords and, therefore, $2 \uparrow 16$ tagwords of these tagword pages. The size of the RAM was set at $2 \uparrow 20$ words, so the tagwords of tagword pages will occupy only one-sixteenth of the total RAM capacity. This may seem large, but it is required if we are unwilling to implement the fully associative option.

Once again for clarity, let us choose the simplest possible "logical-to-physical mapping" of virtual page numbers into addresses of tagwords. First, we assign pages

1. present PVA to memory system.
2. identify virtual address of tagword 1 (of page including PVA).
3. identify virtual address of tagword 2 (of page containing tag-word 1).
4. identify virtual address of tagword 3 (of page containing tag-word 2)

.
.
.

i. fetch tagword k
   IF page containing tagword k-1 in RAM
        THEN fetch tagword k-1
        ELSE swap page and fetch
             tagword k-1
   IF page containing tagword k-2 in RAM
        THEN fetch tagword k-2
        ELSE swap page and fetch
             tagword k-2

.
.
.

   fetch contents of PVA

Figure 13.17. Tracing a PVA through tagwords.

1. present PVA to memory system
2. identify virtual address of tagword 1 (of page including PVA)
3. identify RAM address of tagword 2 (of page containing tag-word 1)
4. fetch tagword 2 from RAM
   IF page containing tagword 1 in RAM
        THEN fetch tagword 1
        ELSE swap page and fetch
             tagword 1
   IF page including PVA is in RAM
        THEN fetch contents of PVA
        ELSE swap page and fetch
             contents of PVA

Figure 13.18. Tracing a PVA with tagwords of tagword pages in RAM.

of tagwords to the first $2 \uparrow 16$ pages ($2 \uparrow 24$ locations) of virtual memory. This leads to the mapping of a PVA to the virtual address of the tagword for the page containing that PVA as given in Fig. 13.19a. Similarly, we assign the tagwords of tagword pages to the first $2 \uparrow 16$ locations in RAM. This leads to the mapping of the page number of a tagword page to the RAM address of the tagword of that page of tagwords, as shown in Fig. 13.19b. Figure 13.19c shows the RAM space assigned to tagwords of tagword pages. As usual, address values are in hexadecimal, but bit numbers are in decimal.

The procedure in Fig. 13.18 indicates that at least three memory references and perhaps as many as two page swaps will be required before the desired data word is obtained. The likelihood of page swaps is a function of the operating system and the programs in memory, and is not under control of the hardware. Three unavoidable memory referenecs for each memory word obtained by the executing process is discouraging. Therefore, let us look into the prospect of adding cache memory. In fact, let us include three separate caches. By adding a cache of data and instruction words from the executing program with virtual addresses in the associative array will eliminate all three references to RAM in the case of a cache hit. Including a cache of tagwords from virtual memory will reduce the number of memory references to one in the event of a hit of this cache. This cache is much like a set-associative virtual memory

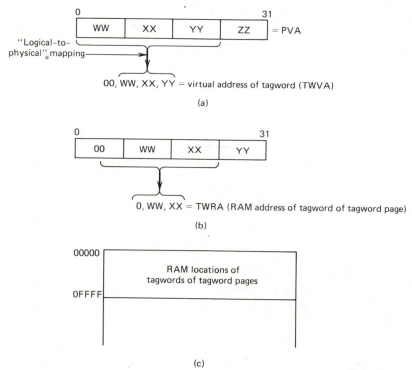

Figure 13.19. Tagword mappings.

implementation except that this cache will have substantially fewer entries than there are pages in RAM so that a miss of this cache will not necessarily imply a *page fault* for the PVA. Third, we add a cache of tagwords (of tagword pages) from the first $2 \uparrow 16$ RAM locations. Here the associative array will contain RAM addresses. A hit of this cache will reduce the number of memory references to two.

Fig. 13.20 illustrates the three levels of cache memories together with their relations to the RAM and the virtual memory. As shown, 256 pages of RAM in the address space 10000 to 1FFFF have been allocated to the storage of pages of tagwords from virtual memory. For convenience, we will refer to the desired tagword from virtual memory as VTW. The virtual address of this tagword has been referred to as TWVA. A desired RAM tagword in the space 00000 to 0FFFF will be referred to by RTW with address TWRA.

In Fig. 13.21, we see the hardware procedure that responds to each read from memory request. We have assumed that the page numbers are always the least significant bits of the tagwords. The use of the other bits need not concern us here. The only transfer specified from a cache is that of the desired process word into **MD**. Otherwise, the timing associated with cache references is not specified. It may be assumed that the time required for a cache reference is much less than for a read from RAM. Fig. 13.21 does not address the details of whether the cache reference is realized in combinational logic or the number of clock periods required by a RAM reference. Notice that the procedure either terminates after obtaining a word for the executing

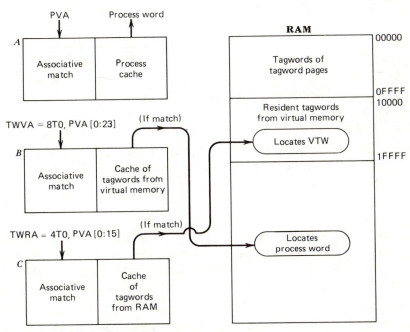

Figure 13.20. Multiple cache and RAM for virtual memory system.

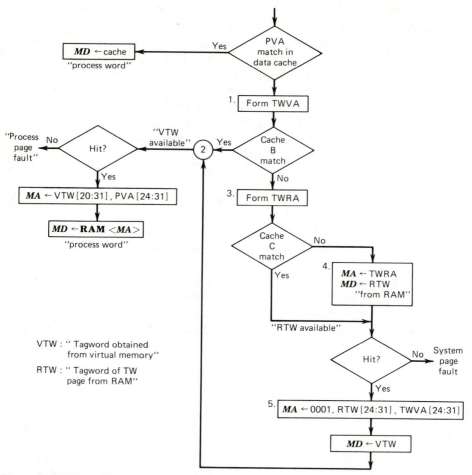

Figure 13.21. Response to a read request.

process or after a page fault has been determined by inspection of a tagword. In the latter case, the hardware procedure will resume from the point of the page fault once a page swap has been accomplished by the operating system.

Example 13.4

Suppose the executing user process desires the word at address PVA = ABCDEF11 (hex). Neither the data word nor either level of tagword are in a cache, but the data word itself is in RAM at location DDD11 (hex). Compute tagword addresses as required, and trace the process of locating this word in RAM.

Solution

First the PVA is associatively compared against the addresses in the data cache without success. Next, from the logical to physical mapping of Fig. 13.19a, the address of the tagword of the data is computed as follows.

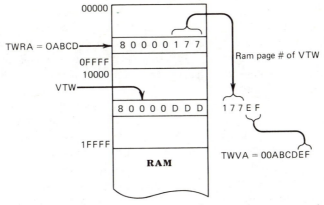

Figure 13.22. Locating a process word.

$$\text{PVA} = \underbrace{\text{ABCDEF}}11$$

$$\text{address of VTW} = \text{TWVA} = 00\overbrace{\text{ABCDEF}}$$

This address will be matched unsuccessfully against the contents of cache B. As specified by block 3 of the flowchart in Fig. 13.21, the next step is to compute the TWRA according to the mapping of Fig. 13.19b.

$$\text{page number of TWVA} = \underline{00\text{ABCD}}$$

$$\text{TWRA} = 0\text{ABCD}$$

Once again, the TWRA will not match an address in cache C. As shown in Fig. 13.22, the TWRA is now used to fetch from RAM the RTW, which is found to be 80000177 (hex). Because bit-0, the tag bit, is 1, the tagword of the page containing the VTW is in RAM within page 177. The address EF within the page in RAM is the same as the last 8 bits of the TWVA, the virtual address of the desired tagword. Found at location 177EF is the VTW or the tagword of the page containing the data. The VTW must be 80000DDD, because we were told in advance that the data would be found in RAM at location DDD11.   ■

13.9 Multiple-Memory Banks

The speed at which a random access memory may be operated is limited by physical considerations. The situation is only slightly more complex for a large semiconductor RAM. Once the cost per bit to be allowed for such a memory is fixed by design decision, the available technologies are constrained and a limit on the operating speed is the result.

There will always be applications of a random access memory in which its overall performance cannot be improved beyond a point dictated by the basic read and write times. There are circumstances, however, when the need for information from two consecutive memory locations becomes known at one time. It is possible to organize a slow random access memory so that several such memory references can be handled almost simultaneously. We shall first accomplish this by dividing the memory into several independent banks. The method of assigning addresses to these banks is called *interleaving*.

A memory consisting of 16 interleaved banks is partially depicted in Fig. 13.23. The complete memory contains 2^{20} words, 2^{16} in each bank. The assignment of memory addresses is shown in hexadecimal in the figure. Notice that the first overall address, 00000, is found in **M__0**, whereas the next address, 00001, is found in **M__1**, with 00002 in **M__2**, and so forth. Thus the first 16 addresses are distributed over the 16 banks, the second 16 are similarly distributed, and so forth. This is interleaving.

A sophisticated central processor will often find it advantageous to obtain the contents of several consecutive addresses from memory simultaneously. Typically, this information will be transferred to a scratch-pad memory. You will see more clearly how these blocks of data may be used in the next section.

It should be apparent that the memory in Fig. 13.23 can be in the process of retrieving up to 16 consecutive data words simultaneously. The feasibility of this set up depends on a disparity between the access time of the individual memory banks

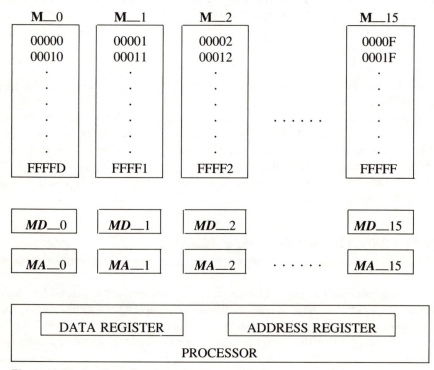

Figure 13.23. Interleaved memory banks.

and the basic clock period of the central processor. Suppose, for example, that MOS memories will access times of 500 nsec are used while the clock period is 20 nsec. Thus, as many as 25 high-speed register transfers could be accomplished while a word was obtained from a memory bank.

Suppose that the processor in Fig. 13.23 becomes aware of a need to read data from several consecutive memory addresses. It begins by placing the first address in the processor address register shown. It can place a second address in this register while the master memory controller routes the first address to the memory address register of the appropriate memory bank. This process can continue until an address in the processor address register is found to be located in a memory bank that is busy servicing a prior request. In the case of the transfer of a very long block of data, the memory controller will begin transferring data into the processor data register at the same time new addresses are routed to other memory banks.

The writing of the control sequence for the memory in Fig. 13.23 will be left as a problem for the reader. In the next section, a control sequence will be written for a somewhat more complicated situation.

An alternative approach to 16 interleaved banks would be organizing the memory with words equal in length to 16 processor words. When a block of processor words are requested, a long word is read from memory and broken into segments as it is transferred to the processor. For several reasons (left to your insight), this approach is less flexible than is interleaving.

13.10   Interleaved Banks with Multiple Entry Points

Once the decision has been made to include multiple-memory banks in a system, an additional advantage accrues: the memory can be accessed simultaneously from more than one entry point. These entry points may be connected to separate processors in a multiprocessing situation. Alternatively, they can be regarded as DMA points to speed up I/O operations and accomplish this in parallel with the execution of other programs. In this section, we shall construct a control sequence for a four-bank memory with four entry points. This sequence should serve to illustrate problems that will occur in other complex multipath data routing situations.

Our basic configuration will consist of four separate memory banks, as illustrated in Fig. 13.24. Each bank has a separate memory data register and memory address register as shown. Any of the four memory banks may communicate with any of four entry points through the respective communications address register, *CA,* and communications data register, *CD.* The memory unit and the processors are operated from the same clock source. Thus a processor can place a word in its *CA* register in one clock period, and this word may be taken from the register in the next clock period by memory control. The data communications process may take place in either direction through a *CD* register.

Two flip-flops, *r* (*r*_0 to *r*_3) and *w,* are associated with each *CA* register for

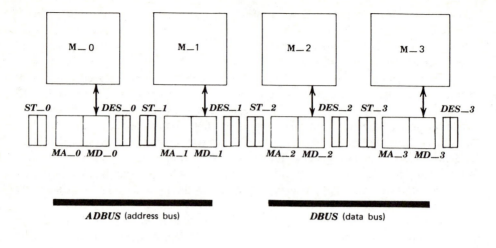

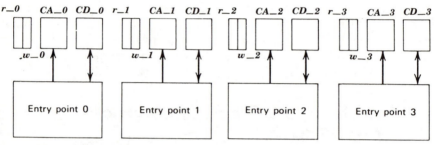

Figure 13.24. Memory layout.

control purposes. If the corresponding *r* flip-flop is set to 1, a read is being requested. If $w = 1$, a word to be written in memory is waiting in the communications data register with the address in the corresponding address register. If $r = w = 0$, the address and data communications registers are available to the entry point control unit. This indicates to the processor that it must take the next action.

The transfer of addresses between the *CA* and *MA* registers is accomplished by way of the bus *ADBUS*. Data are routed between the memory data registers and the *CD* registers by way of the *DBUS*. Data may pass through the *DBUS* in both directions.

Some provision must be made for keeping track of which entry point is currently served by a given memory bank so that word read out can be routed to the proper *CD* register. As the time required to access memory or to write in memory is many clock periods, it is possible for all four memory banks to be simultaneously in the process of retrieving four separate data words for the same entry point. Therefore, we include a 2-bit register *DES* with each memory bank element to identify the entry point that will receive the word, if any, currently being read from the memory bank. Also associated with each bank is a 2-bit status register, *ST*. If $ST = 00$, the bank is inactive. The status register will be 01 whenever a write or read operation is in progress.

If *ST* = 10, the bank has just completed a read operation; and the data is waiting in the memory data register.

The hardware associated with a typical memory bank **M__0** is detailed in Fig. 13.25a. The hardware associated with a typical entry point is given in Fig. 13.25b. Notice in particular that the communications address register, *CA__2*, contains 18 bits while the memory address register has space for only 16 bits. The two least significant bits in *CA__2* indicate the number of the bank containing the requested data while the most significant 16 bits specify the address within the bank. Thus each bank contains the data for every fourth address, as illustrated in Fig. 13.26, where the addresses are listed in hexadecimal.

If the other three entry points are not requesting data at a given time, one processor can supply four consecutive addresses to the four memory banks in only two clock periods per address. We make the assumption that if an entry point requests four words to be read from memory, this point will be ready to receive the words as they become available. Otherwise, the data words may not be transferred to *CD* in the same order as requested. In general, the control sequencers must in some way keep track of the requests for data that they have made. In particular, a processor must not attempt to write in a bank if a read request is outstanding.

We are now ready to begin consideration of the control sequence for our multibank memory. Control of this unit may be thought of as managing traffic through the address and data buses. To avoid slowing the process unnecessarily, we must permit simultaneous transfers on the two buses. As depicted in Fig. 13.27, the control sequence is divided into two sections. The first part of the sequence will accept a new

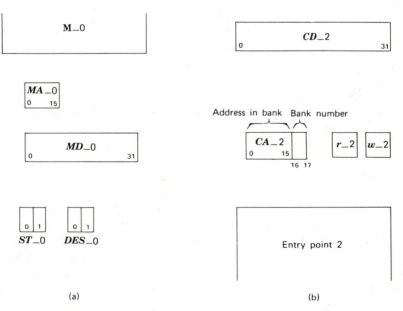

Figure 13.25. Typical memory bank and communications hardware.

00000	00001	00002	00003
00004	00005	00006	00007
00008	00009	0000A	0000B
.	.	.	.
.	.	.	.
.	. .	.	.
.	.	.	.
.	.	.	.
.	.		.
3FFFC	3FFFD	3FFFE	3FFFF

M__0   **M__1**   **M__2**   **M__3**

Figure 13.26. Address distribution.

READ request and simultaneously deliver the data from a completed READ. The upper left path in Fig. 13.27 specifies the interrogation of each entry point for a possible READ request. The first request encountered is set up by passing the address to the appropriate memory bank through the *ADBUS*. At the same time, a word may be returned to an entry point through the *DBUS*. Control for the latter activity is depicted in the upper right path of Fig. 13.27.

Following the processing of no more than one read request and one data return, control converges to permit a search for a possible WRITE request. We represent control convergence in the flowchart by the hardware symbol for this operation. Only the first WRITE request encountered is set up by the lower sequence in Fig. 13.27. Write requests are considered separately, since both data and an address must be passed to a memory bank. This ties up both buses, precluding any parallel transfer.

You may notice a priority system built into the flowchart in which the lower-numbered entry points and memory banks enjoy highest priority. It may even appear that repeated requests from the high-priority units will be honored, effectively causing the low-priority units to be ignored. This will not be the case. The actual read and write times for the memory banks are much longer than the time required for several passes through the bus control sequence. Each transfer of address or data between processor and memory bank takes only one clock period.

The following is a partial AHPL description of the interleaved multiple-entry-point memory. Here we include the controller in the same module as the entry points and the memory banks. We are, therefore, forced to cite the existence of essentially repeated code with comments. A description including two sets of four identical modules and a separate control module might take better advantage of the extended AHPL notation to provide a complete, but compact, description. The following approach has the advantage of focusing on all aspects of the function of the bus control process. Also not included here, but required in a complete description, would be a description of the setting of flip-flops *r* and *w* by the processes requiring memory access.

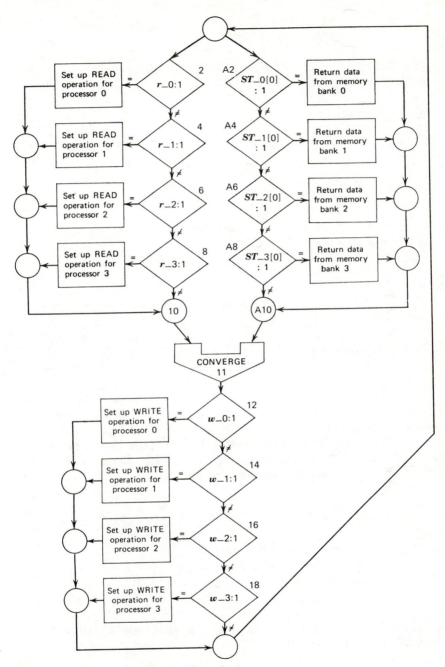

Figure 13.27. Bus control for interleaved memory.

MEMORY: M__0:3⟨2 ↑ 16⟩[32]; ST__0:3[2]; MA__0:3[16];
                        MD__0:3[32]; DES__0:3[2].

MEMORY: r__0:3; w__0:3; CA__0:3[18]; CD__0:3[32].
BUSES: $ADBUS$[16]; $DBUS$[32].
OUTPUTS: $dataready$__0:3.
1   → (2,A2).
2   NO DELAY
          → ($\overline{r\_0}$ ∨ (∨/(DCD(CA__0 [16:17]) ∧
             (∨/ST__0, ∨/ST__1, ∨/ST__2, ∨/ST__3))))/(4).
3   NO DELAY
          (DES__0:3) ** DCD(CA__0[16:17]) ← 0,0;
          (ST__0:3) ** DCD(CA__0[16:17]) ← 0,1;
          r__0 ← 0; $ADBUS$ = CA__0[0:15];
          $read$__0:3 = DCD(CA__0[16:17]);
          (MA__0:3) ** DCD(CA__0[16:17]) ← $ADBUS;$
          → (10).

"There will be similar pairs of steps 4,5; 6,7; and 8,9 for entry points 1, 2, and 3, respectively."

10   NO DELAY
         → (11).

If a read request by entry point 0 is encountered at step 2 and the bank addressed by CA__0[16:17] is inactive, step 3 causes the appropriate status changes and connects the $ADBUS$ for the transfer of the address from CA__0 to the appropriate memory address register as specified by CA__0[16:17]. Step 3 also carries out the address transfer and sends a read request to the appropriate bank. Similar pairs of steps are required to respond to the other three entry points.

A2   NO DELAY
         → ($\overline{ST\_0[0]}$)/(A4).
A3   NO DELAY
         ST__0 ← 0,0; $DBUS$ = MD__0;
         (CD__0:3) ** DCD(DES__0) ← $DBUS;$
         $dataready$__0:3 = DCD (DES__0);
         → (A10).

"There will be similar pairs of steps A4,A5; A6,A7 and A8,A9 for memory banks 1, 2, and 3, respectively."

A10   NO DELAY
         → (11).
11   CONVERGE(10, A10).

The concurrent steps for returning data from memory bank 0 are given by steps A2 and A3. Similar pairs of steps are required for each memory bank. The entry point that will be the target of the transfer from the **DBUS** is specified by **DES**_0. Step A3 establishes bus connections, returns the status of the memory bank to idle, transmits the data to the appropriate communications data register, and announces this fact with a *dataready* signal.

Following convergence, the entry points are checked for write requests, and these requests are serviced as required by steps 12 through 19.

12   NO DELAY
       $\rightarrow$ (**w**_0 $\vee$ ($\vee$/(DCD(**CA**_0[16:17]) $\wedge$
            ($\vee$/**ST**_0, $\vee$/**ST**_1, $\vee$/**ST**_2, $\vee$/**ST**_3))))/(14).

13   NO DELAY
       (**ST**_0:3) ** DCD(**CA**_0[16:17]) $\leftarrow$ 0,1:
       w_0 $\leftarrow$ 0; **DBUS** = **CD**_0;
       ADBUS = **CA**_0[0:15];
       (**MA**_0:3) ** DCD(**CA**_0[16:17]) $\leftarrow$ **ADBUS;**
       (**MD**_0:3) ** DCD(**CA**_0[16:17]) $\leftarrow$ **DBUS;**
       write_0:3 = DCD(**CA**_0[16:17]);
       $\rightarrow$ (20).

"There will be similar pairs of steps 14,15; 16,17; and 18,19 for entry points 1, 2, and 3, respectively."

20   NO DELAY
       $\rightarrow$ (1).

The preceding is not necessarily the fastest or most efficient solution. A pass through the sequence will require at most two clock periods. If the memory read-write cycle is 50 to 100 times the clock period (a possibility), the two clock period service time is not significant. If the read-write cycle is 10 or fewer clock periods, this delay may become significant. Clearly, a speed improvement could be realized by replacing the buses with direct transfers. Further improvement might be realized by eliminating the transfers altogether in favor of combinational logic routing of addresses. The result, of course, would be a formidable combinational logic network.

The hardware configuration just discussed was made as general as possible to illustrate the techniques involved. If certain of the entry points can be satisfied with lower-grade service, various less costly approaches can be used. When a larger number of memory banks are interleaved, a saving could be realized by advancing addresses from address register to address register in shift register fashion until a match of bank identification bits is obtained. Data could be shifted out in the same fashion. The number of variations of such schemes is almost endless.

Problems

13.1   Write a single combinational logic unit description that combines AS-SOC, as given in Section 13.3, and BUSFN. The arguments of the combinational logic unit are to be $AA\langle 2 \uparrow n\rangle[m]$ and $X[r]$, where $r < m$. The output vector is to be $AA\langle I\rangle[r:m-1]$, if $X = AA\langle I\rangle[r]$. If there is no match, the output may be all 0's.

13.2   Consider an approximation of the least recently used algorithm that does not require the extensive shifting logic implied by the approach in Section 13.4. Assign a 3-bit counter to each word in the scratch-pad memory. Each time a word in the scratch-pad memory is referenced or a new word is placed there from RAM, the value of the respective counter may be set to 1,1,1. The values of all other counters are to be decremented by 1 if greater than 0. Assume the existence of a combinational logic unit DECZ (establish the proper arguments) that will simultaneously decrement all but one row of the array of counters. The word to be replaced in RAM should be chosen in some psuedorandom fashion from the words corresponding to counters that are 0. Modify the scratch-pad memory read and write operations and the memory control module of Section 13.4 to implement this replacement algorithm.

13.3   An associative scratch-pad memory for a computer TRIC using a pseudorandom replacement algorithm is to be designed. The array containing addresses for associative matching is $AA\langle 256\rangle[20]$. The corresponding data array is $AM\langle 256\rangle[32]$. A counter, $RCNT[256]$, is to be declared to provide for implementing the replacement algorithm. This counter is to be incremented once each memory reference. Whenever it is necessary to replace a word in the cache, the word addressed by $RCNT$ will be replaced.
   (a)   How many words are addressable by TRIC?
   (b)   When an addressed word is found in cache, it is to be placed in the data register declared as AMD. Modify the four steps of the typical CPU cache read sequence of Section 13.4 to conform to the TRIC pseudorandom replacement algorithm.
   (c)   When a miss of the cache occurs, a control level is sent to memory control sequence. Modify the MEMORY CONTROL module as given in Section 13.4 to conform to the TRIC pseudorandom replacement algorithm.

13.4   Comparison of replacement algorithms is highly program dependent. The following contrived process provides one comparison between the least recently used (LRU) algorithm and a random replacement algorithm. Suppose a cache contains 256 words and during the execution of the contrived program each word, which is the object of a memory reference and is, therfore, moved to the cache, will be referenced exactly one more time before it is removed from the cache by the LRU algorithm. (That is every word will be used exactly twice per placement in cache.) More specifically, assume that each word will be referenced for the second time precisely as it has been shifted down to the center of the cache by the implementation of the LRU algorithm given in Section 13.4.

(a) Compute the hit ratio for this process with the least recently used algorithm.

(b) Let the process remain exactly as just described, but now let the replacement algorithm be random. Compute the hit ratio for this algorithm and compare it with that from part (a). (*Hint:* Some words will be replaced in the cache before they can be referenced a second time.)

13.5 Modify the AHPL descriptions in Section 13.4 to save a clock period each time a memory reference fails to hit a word in cache. The readram or writeram signal is to be issued in step 2, but the reference to RAM is to be aborted in the event of a hit.

13.6 Modify the scratch-pad memory read and write operations and the memory control module of Section 13.4 to include a mechanism so that only dirty words (words that have been modified by write operations) are returned to the RAM from the scratch pad.

13.7 Combine the control sequences of Section 13.4 so that all memory references are handled by a memory control sequencer. All memory references in the main control sequence will require a transfer of control to this unit. Write this sequence in AHPL. Discuss the advantages and disadvantages of the approach.

13.8 Write a formal combinational logic unit description for the combinational logic unit ABOVE used in the read and write to scratch-pad memory steps given in Section 13.4.

13.9 The first eight pages of the RAM in Fig. 13.10 will never be replaced by pages from virtual memory. The first eight vectors in the arrays **AA** and **RPAG** serve only to identify the locations of these pages, which are never moved. Modify the main control unit sequences labelled R1 and R2 and W1 and W2 so that reference to these pages is identified and the least significant 6 bits of the page number are shifted directly into $MA[0:5]$ without reference to **RPAG.** This would permit the number of rows in **AA** and **RPAG** to be reduced to 56 and would eliminate one-eighth of the logic in ASSOC(**AA;** *DSCRPTBUS*).

13.10 In step 101 of the sequence that identifies the missing virtual page (see Table 13.1) for the operating system, the missing page number is placed in $MD[20:31]$ by step 101 and loaded into the least significant 12 bits of the RAM location 0 by step 102. What benefit would result from placing this number instead in $MD[8:19]$ and storing it in the corresponding bit positions in location 0?

13.11 Consider the tag store as suggested by Fig. 13.12.
  (a) Write in AHPL the WRITE in memory steps W1 and W2 similar to the read steps of Example 13.2 but with the addition of the following feature. Add a dirty-page bit as the leftmost bit of each word of the tag store and manipulate this bit properly in the description.
  (b) Suggest a method for implementing the LRU replacement algorithm in conjunction with this table lookup of tagwords as illustrated by Fig. 13.12. How would a random algorithm be implemented? Which approach would you recommend?

13.12 If the counter approach of Problem 13.2 is used as the implementation of the virtual memory replacement algorithm, **RPAG** as given in Fig. 13.10 serves only to encode 1 of 64 code words (only one of the 64 terminals represented by ASSOC(**AA;** *DSCRPTBUS*) will be 1) to form $MA[0:5]$. This vector must be decoded later by the RAM decoder. Write a combinational logic unit description for the elimination of **RPAG.** The decoder will have as inputs ASSOC(**AA;** *DSCRPTBUS*) and $MA[6:17]$.

13.13 Write an AHPL control sequence that will sweep the entire contents of the associative scratch pad of Section 13.4 into RAM.

13.14 Rewrite the AHPL solution of Example 13.3, including declarations, for the revised parameters $Ns = 2$ and $s = 4$.

13.15 A certain set-associative virtual memory has $2 \uparrow 20$ 32-bit words. The RAM can accommodate $2 \uparrow 14$ words. A page will consist of 64 words. The number of pages per set is 8 (i.e. $s = 3$). The table lookup portion of the set-associative process will use the combinational logic unit EXTBUSFN, which is given in Section 13.7.
  (a) Determine Nv, Nr, and Ns.
  (b) Write a declaration of the appropriate instance of EXTBUSFN required by the parameters specified for this virtual memory implementation. Call the instance EXBUSFN1. Write a label statement for an array, **SETFN,** that will be a shortened representation of EXBUSFN1.
  (c) Write the read statements R1 and R2 similar to those given in Example 13.3 for this virtual memory implementation.

13.16   A triple-cache virtual memory system as described in Section 13.8 has
2 ↑ 32 words of virtual memory and 2 ↑ 20 words of RAM. As described,
there are 256 words per page and tagwords of virtual pages occupy the
first 2 ↑ 16 pages of virtual memory. Tagwords of these tagword pages
permanently occupy the first 2 ↑ 8 pages of RAM.

(a)   Suppose that the process virtual address of a word desired from
memory is FEDCBA01. Compute the virtual address of the tagword
(TWVA) of the page containing this data word.

(b)   If the data word were in cache, for what would the address computed in part (a) be used?

(c)   Would it be considered a page fault if no word with
PVA = FEDCBA01 were in the cache (yes or no)?

(d)   Assume that the TWVA computed in part (a) does not match an
address in the cache of first-level tagwords. Compute the RAM
address (TWRA) of the tagword of the corresponding page of
tagwords.

(e)   In what two places might the tagword addressed by the TWRA
computed in part (d) be found? Which is tried first? Why?

(f)   Suppose that the tagword whose address was computed in part (a)
is found in RAM at location 166BA. Indicate the contents of the
word in RAM at the address TWRA computed in part (d). Some
bits may be "don't cares."

(g)   Describe the situation if the hex contents of RAM location 166BA
is each of the following. If the desired data is in RAM, give the
complete address. (X = hex "don't care")

1. 8XXXXBDD   2. 0XXXXBDD

13.17   Write an AHPL description of an implementation of the hardware portion
of the virtual memory/cache combination described by the flowchart of
Fig. 13.21. Declare hardware as required. Assume that cache memory
data registers are to be used, and that the system clock is sufficiently
fast that one clock period is allocated to obtaining a word from a cache
memory, all of which are located within the CPU module. Assume that
the access time of the main RAM is about five clock periods but that
the RAM is a separate module from the CPU. The RAM and the CPU
are connected by buses, *DBUS* and *ADDRBUS*. The timing of RAM
CPU interchanges will be controlled by two-line responsive signalling.

13.18   Rewrite AHPL steps 2 and 3 of Section 13.10 so that all four entry
points will be processed by these two steps. Provide a priority mechanism
to select only one of the entry points that might be requesting service.
It may be necessary to provide a combinational logic unit similar to
BUSFN that, together with DCD, will select one of *CA__0:3*. If so,
write a combinational logic unit description of this unit.

13.19 Write a control sequence that will manage access to the 16-bank memory of Fig. 13.23 from a single entry point.

13.20 Consider a machine whose slow, large capacity RAM is arranged in blocks of 16 words. Each time a request is made for one of the words in a block, the entire block is read into the memory data register in one operation. Suppose that a single central processor will request words from this memory at a rate exceeding the reciprocal of the read time of this memory. Often the requests will be for data from consecutive memory locations and hence can be serviced at an increased rate. Write a control sequence for this memory so that it will satisfy as nearly as possible the needs of the mentioned central processor. Define control and data registers as needed.

13.21 Compare the efficiencies of the memory of Problem 13.20 and the multiple-bank arrangement of Fig. 13.23. Form a conjecture as to their respective abilities to satify the requests of a processor that may request data at a rate four times the reciprocal of the memory cycle time. How might hard data be obtained to substantiate this conjecture? Supply some details.

13.22 The associative memory controller of Section 13.4 requests only one word at a time from the RAM. Modify the control sequence so that each request for a word in RAM will cause the three succeeding words to be placed in the associative memory as well. Assume that the associative memory is dealing with an interleaved multibank RAM so that these transfers can take place approximately in parallel. What effect will this modification have on the "hit ratio"?

References

1. H. Hellerman, *Digital System Principles,* 2nd ed., McGraw–Hill, New York, 1973.
2. R. M. Meade, "How a Cache Memory Enhances a Computer's Performance," *Electronics,* Jan. 1972, pp. 58–62.
3. R. M. Meade, "Design Approaches for Cache Memory Control," *Computer Design,* Jan. 1971, p. 87.
4. R. M. Jones, "Factors Affecting the Efficiency of a Virtual Memory," *IEEE Trans. Computers,* Nov. 1969, p. 1004.
5. "The Multics Virtual Memory," *Honeywell Information Systems REPORT 1L02, 1L12,* Phoenix, 1972.
6. "Control Data 7600 Computer System," *Reference Manual,* Publication No. 60258200.
7. F. J. Hill, "Structure Specification With a Procedural Hardware Description Language," *IEEE Trans. Computers,* Feb. 1981, pp. 157–161.
8. R. Matick, *Computer Storage Systems and Technology,* Wiley Interscience, New York, 1977.

9. A. E. Bell, "Optical Data Storage Technology Status and Prospects," *Computer Design,* Jan. 1983, pp. 133–144.

10. D. P. Siewiorek, C. G. Bell, and A. Newell, *Computer Structures: Principals and Examples,* McGraw–Hill, New York, 1982.

11. J. K. Iliffe, *Advanced Computer Design,* Prentice–Hall, Englewood Cliffs, N.J., 1982.

12. *VAX Architecture Handbook,* Digital Equipment Corp., Maynard, Mass., 1981.

14 High-Speed Addition

14.1 Introduction

One of the main concerns of the computer designer is obtaining the highest possible operating speed, subject to various technical and economic constraints. As we have seen, the adder plays a central role in the operation of the computer, and is thus a major factor in determining the overall speed of most machines. As a result, the design of high-speed adders has been the subject of exhaustive study from the very beginning of the computer era.

Over the years, a number of fast adders have been developed, but today the majority of fast-adder designs use some version of the *carry look-ahead* principle. The carry look-ahead adder was first described by Weinberger and Smith [1] in 1956. The design was further refined in the design of the *Stretch* computer; this version was described by MacSorley [2] in a 1961 article that is the basic reference on the subject. Flores (1963) [3] presented the first description in a textbook, and his description is probably the most complete to date.

A particular problem of notation arises in describing adders. It is standard practice in articles on adders to number the bit positions starting with the least-significant-digit (lsd) position as bit 0, the next most significant as bit 1, and so on. However, as we have seen, the practice in numbering registers is exactly the opposite, the most-significant-digit (msd) position being bit 0. The former convention is convenient from the point of view of keeping the equations simple, since we start writing equations with the lsd position. If we adopt the latter convention, in a ρ-bit adder the lsd is bit $(\rho-1)$, the next digit is bit $(\rho-2)$, and so on, which makes for very cumbersome notation.

519

To keep things as simple as possible while remaining consistent with the register notation, throughout this chapter we shall discuss a fixed-length adder of 64 bits, from bit 0 (msd) through bit 63 (lsd). You should have no trouble adapting the equations to adders of any other length, and we believe that the slight loss of generality will be more than compensated for by the advantages of a consistent system of notation.

14.2 Ripple-Carry Adder

The simplest form of parallel adder is the ripple-carry adder, which consists of full-adders connected as shown in Fig. 14.1. The combinational logic subroutine generating this adder was presented in Section 7.7, but we wish to analyze it in detail at this time to set the stage for the discussion to follow. The adder combines an addend and an augend, A and B, to develop a sum S. A given full adder, in the jth bit position, receives the jth bits of the addend and augend, A_j and B_j, together with a carry-in from the next least significant digit, C_{j+1}, and produces the sum bit S_j and the carry-out C_j. The truth table for a full adder is shown in Fig. 14.2, and the equations for the sum and carry bits are given in Eqs. 14.1 and 14.2.

$$S_j = (A_j \wedge \overline{B}_j \wedge \overline{C}_{j+1}) \vee (\overline{A}_j \wedge B_j \wedge C_{j+1})$$
$$\vee (\overline{A}_j \wedge B_j \wedge \overline{C}_{j+1}) \vee (A_j \wedge B_j \wedge C_{j+1}) \tag{14.1}$$

$$C_j = (A_j \wedge B_j) \vee (A_j \wedge C_{j+1}) \vee (B_j \wedge C_{j+1}) \tag{14.2}$$

Note that these equations are written in the second-order, sum-of-products form; so that there are two levels of gating (AND-OR) between the input and output. If we let the delay through a single level of gating by Δt, then the delay in a single state is $2\Delta t$, which is the minimum possible. We assume that all bits of the addend and augend arrive at the same time, but each individual adder cannot develop its sum until $2\Delta t$ after it receives the carry from the previous stage. Further, if the addend bit is 1 and the augend bit 0 (or vice versa), the carry-out will not be developed until $2\Delta t$ after the arrival of the carry-in. In the worst possible case, the carry may have to propagate

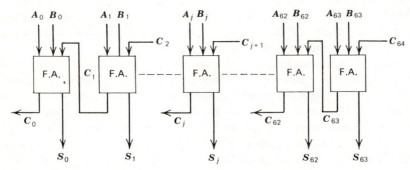

Figure 14.1. Basic ripple-carry adder.

A_j	B_j	C_{j+1}	S_j	C_j
0	0	0	0	0
0	0	1	1	0
0	1	0	1	0
0	1	1	0	1
1	0	0	1	0
1	0	1	0	1
1	1	0	0	1
1	1	1	1	1

Figure 14.2. Truth table for a full adder.

("ripple-through") the adder from one end to the other, with a delay of $2\Delta t$ in each stage and a total delay of $2\rho\Delta t$ for the whole adder. The worst case will rarely occur; if the addend and augend bits are both 0 or both 1, then the output carry is independent of the input carry. But we must allow for the worst case. Thus, for a 64-bit adder, we must allow $128\Delta t$ for addition; and even with very fast electronics, this can be an intolerable delay. As a result, the ripple-carry adder will generally be found only in small, inexpensive computers.

14.3   The Minimum-Delay Adder

A basic theorem of Boolean algebra states that any Boolean function, no matter how complex, can be realized in a second-order (sum-of-products or product-of-sums) form. All the bits of the addend and augend are assumed to be available simultaneously so that there would seem to be no theoretical reason why we cannot develop a second-order equation for each sum bit and eliminate the delays of carry propagation. Let us investigate this possibility for the 64-bit adder.

For the lsd position we have

$$S_{63} = (A_{63} \wedge \overline{B}_{63} \wedge \overline{C}_{64}) \vee (\overline{A}_{63} \wedge B_{63} \wedge \overline{C}_{64})$$
$$\vee (\overline{A}_{63} \wedge \overline{B}_{63} \wedge C_{64}) \vee (A_{63} \wedge B_{63} \wedge C_{64}) \tag{14.3}$$

and

$$C_{63} = (A_{63} \wedge B_{63}) \vee (A_{63} \wedge C_{64}) \vee (B_{63} \wedge C_{64}) \tag{14.4}$$

For the next stage we have

$$S_{62} = (A_{62} \wedge \overline{B}_{62} \wedge \overline{C}_{63}) \vee (\overline{A}_{62} \wedge B_{62} \wedge \overline{C}_{63})$$
$$\vee (\overline{A}_{62} \wedge \overline{B}_{62} \wedge C_{63}) \vee (A_{62} \wedge B_{62} \wedge C_{63}) \tag{14.5}$$

Substituting Eq. 14.4 into Eq. 14.5 to eliminate the propagated carry,[1] we have

---

[1] The input carry to the first stage, C_{64}, is used in complement arithmetic and is assumed to be available at the same time as the addend and augend.

$$S_{62} = (A_{62} \wedge B_{62} \wedge A_{63} \wedge B_{63}) \vee (A_{62} \wedge B_{62} \wedge A_{63} \wedge C_{64})$$

$$\vee (A_{62} \wedge B_{62} \wedge B_{63} \wedge C_{64})$$

$$\vee (A_{62} \wedge \overline{B}_{62} \wedge \overline{A}_{63} \wedge \overline{B}_{63}) \vee (A_{62} \wedge \overline{B}_{62} \wedge \overline{A}_{63} \wedge \overline{C}_{64})$$

$$\vee (A_{62} \wedge \overline{B}_{62} \wedge \overline{B}_{63} \wedge \overline{C}_{64})$$

$$\vee (\overline{A}_{62} \wedge \overline{B}_{62} \wedge A_{63} \wedge B_{63}) \vee (\overline{A}_{62} \wedge \overline{B}_{62} \wedge A_{63} \wedge C_{64})$$

$$\vee (\overline{A}_{62} \wedge \overline{B}_{62} \wedge B_{63} \wedge C_{64})$$

$$\vee (\overline{A}_{62} \wedge B_{62} \wedge \overline{A}_{63} \wedge \overline{B}_{63}) \vee (\overline{A}_{62} \wedge B_{62} \wedge \overline{A}_{63} \wedge \overline{C}_{64})$$

$$\vee (\overline{A}_{62} \wedge B_{62} \wedge \overline{B}_{63} \wedge \overline{C}_{64}) \tag{14.6}$$

Here we have a second-order equation exclusively in terms of the original inputs to the adder; so S_{62} will be developed with the same delay as S_{63}. However, Eq. 14.3 requires only 4 three-input AND gates whereas Eq. 14.6 requires 12 four-input AND gates. If we carry the same process on further, we find that S_{61} requires 4 four-input and 24 five-input gates, and S_{60} requires 4 four-input, 8 five-input, and 48 six-input AND gates. It is obvious that the number and size of gates very rapidly becomes totally impractical: S_0 would require approximately 10^{20} gates!

14.4   The Carry Look-Ahead Principle

We have seen that the ripple-carry adder is too slow and the minimum-delay adder impractical; therefore, we look for something in between. In one sense, we need to find a way to factor the equations of the minimum-delay adder into groupings of practical size. There are an infinite number of ways of factoring the equations, and many have been tried; but the most successful designs all use the *carry look-ahead* principle.

We begin by taking a slightly different approach to the implementation of the individual full adder. Notice from Fig. 14.2 that if $A_j = B_j = 0$, then $C_j = 0$ regardless of the value of C_{j+1}. Similarly, if $A_j = B_j = 1$, then $C_j = 1$ regardless of C_{j+1}. If $A_j \neq B_j$, then the carry-out C_j is the same as the carry-in C_{j+1}. In the latter case, we say that the carry propagates through stage j. When the carry-out stage j is a 1 regardless of the carry-in, we say that stage j is a *generate* stage. This interpretation of an adder stage is given in Fig. 14.3.

Stage j is a generate stage if and only if G_j as defined by Eq. 14.7 is 1:

$$G_j = A_j \wedge B_j \tag{14.7}$$

Stage j is a propagate stage if and only if P_j as defined by Eq. 14.8 is 1:

$$P_j = A_j \oplus B_j = (A_j \wedge \overline{B}_j) \vee (\overline{A}_j \wedge B_j) \tag{14.8}$$

A_j	B_j	C_j	
0	0	0	
0	1	C_{j+1}	Propagate stage
1	0	C_{j+1}	Propagate stage
1	1	1	Generate stage

Figure 14.3. Carry propagation.

From Fig. 14.3 we observe that we have a carry-out stage whenever $G_j = 1$ or when $P_j = 1$ and there is a carry into stage j. This yields Eq. 14.10 as an expression for C_j.

$$C_j = (A_j \wedge B_j) \vee (((A_j \wedge \overline{B}_j) \vee (\overline{A}_j \wedge B_j)) \wedge C_{j+1}) \qquad (14.9)$$

$$C_j = G_j \vee (P_j \wedge C_{j+1}) \qquad (14.10)$$

It is also possible to express the sum S_j as a function of G_j, P_j, and C_{j+1}. This is most easily accomplished by algebraic manipulation of the basic expression for S_j.

$$S_j = (A_j \wedge \overline{B}_j \wedge \overline{C}_{j+1}) \vee (\overline{A}_j \wedge B_j \wedge \overline{C}_{j+1}) \vee (\overline{A}_j \wedge \overline{B}_j \wedge C_{j+1})$$

$$\vee (A_j \wedge B_j \wedge C_{j+1}) \qquad (14.11)$$

$$= (((A_j \wedge B_j) \vee (\overline{A}_j \wedge \overline{B}_j)) \wedge C_{j+1}) \vee (((A_j \wedge \overline{B}_j)$$

$$\vee (\overline{A}_j \wedge B_j)) \wedge \overline{C}_{j+1})$$

$$S_j = (\overline{P}_j \wedge C_{j+1}) \vee (P_j \wedge \overline{C}_{j+1}) \qquad (14.12)$$

Equations 14.12 and 14.10 are certainly simpler in form than the original sum and carry equations, but it is not yet evident what effect they will have on the speed or complexity of the circuit. For this purpose, let us now apply these equations to the design of the 64-bit adder starting as usual with the lsd position:

$$S_{63} = (\overline{P}_{63} \wedge C_{64}) \vee (P_{63} \wedge \overline{C}_{64})$$

$$S_{62} = (\overline{P}_{62} \wedge C_{63}) \vee (P_{62} \wedge \overline{C}_{63})$$

$$S_{61} = (\overline{P}_{61} \wedge C_{62}) \vee (P_{61} \wedge \overline{C}_{62})$$

$$S_{60} = (\overline{P}_{60} \wedge C_{61}) \vee (P_{60} \wedge \overline{C}_{61}) \qquad (14.13)$$

The sum equations obviously all have the same form, so that we shall implement them with a special form of full-adder circuit, as shown in Fig. 14.4. For later convenience, we shall divide this circuit into two sections, the *PG section* and the *SUM section*, as shown.

The carry-in terms to the sum circuits will be developed as shown in the following equations.

High–speed addition/14

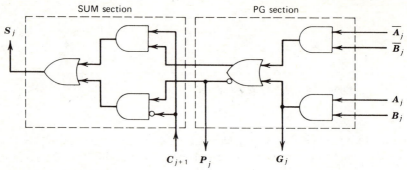

Figure 14.4. Full-adder circuit.

$$C_{63} = G_{63} \vee (P_{63} \wedge C_{64}) \tag{14.14}$$

$$C_{62} = G_{62} \vee (P_{62} \wedge C_{63})$$

$$= G_{62} \vee (P_{62} \wedge G_{63}) \vee (P_{62} \wedge P_{63} \wedge C_{64}) \tag{14.15}$$

$$C_{61} = G_{61} \vee (P_{61} \wedge C_{62})$$

$$= G_{61} \vee (P_{61} \wedge G_{62}) \vee (P_{61} \wedge P_{62} \wedge G_{63})$$

$$\vee (P_{61} \wedge P_{62} \wedge P_{63} \wedge C_{64}) \tag{14.16}$$

These three equations are implemented in the carry look-ahead (CLA) unit, shown in Fig. 14.5. (This unit also implements some additional equations, which will be discussed shortly.) Since the CLA unit may be used with any set of four bit-positions, we have used generalized subscripts in Fig. 14.5. For implementation of the preceding equations, $j = 63$.

The interconnection of the CLA unit with the adder units for bits 60 through 63 is shown in Fig. 14.6. Noting that each unit (SUM, PG, CLA) is a second-order circuit, we can analyze the propagation delays. Let us consider the worst case, a carry generated in bit 63 and propagated through to bit 60. The carry is generated in PG_{63} with a delay of $2\Delta t$, propagated through the CLA to C_{61} in $2\Delta t$, and propagated through SUM_{60} to develop S_{60} in $2\Delta t$, for a total delay of $6\Delta t$. This compares with a delay of $8\Delta t$ for ripple-carry through 4 bits. This is only a minor improvement; but this is just the beginning of the design, as we shall see.

If we examine Eqs. 14.14, 14.15, and 14.16, we see that they are iterative in form; there is no reason why we could not continue the same process to write equations for C_{60}, C_{59}, and so forth. These equations would also be second-order, so the CLA unit could be extended to cover more bits, with no increase in delay. However, as we increase the number of bits, the size and number of gates also increases: C_{61} requires four input gates, C_{60} would require five input gates, C_{59} would require six input gates;

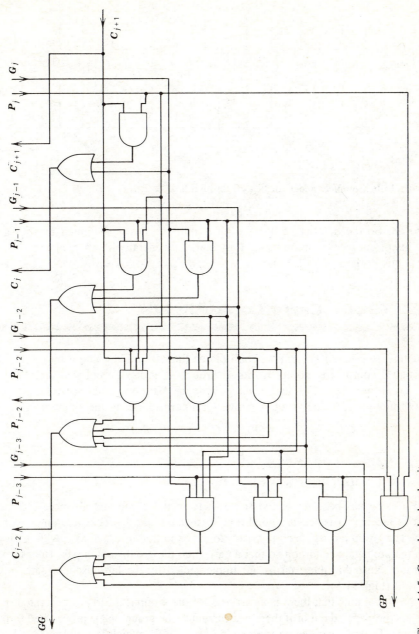

Figure 14.5. Carry look-ahead unit.

525

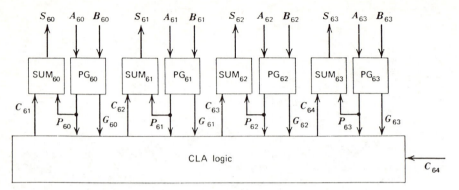

Figure 14.6. Complete adder for bits 60 through 63.

and so on. So the number of bits the CLA unit can cover is limited by the fan-in capability of our gates. Circuit technology makes it generally impractical to go beyond about 8 bits in the basic CLA unit.

14.5 Group Carry Look-Ahead

As the next step in our design, we shall divide the 64-bit adder into 4-bit groups, bits 0 through 3 comprising group 0, bits 4 through 7, group 1, and so forth. We then define *group generate, GG,* and *group propagate, GP,* terms, as shown for group 15 (bits 60 through 63). The group generate term corresponds to the situation

$$GG_{15} = G_{60} \lor (P_{60} \land G_{61}) \lor (P_{60} \land P_{61} \land G_{62})$$

$$\lor (P_{60} \land P_{61} \land P_{62} \land G_{63}) \tag{14.17}$$

$$GP_{15} = P_{60} \land P_{61} \land P_{62} \land P_{63} \tag{14.18}$$

where a carry has been generated somewhere in the group and all more-significant positions are in the propagate condition so that the carry propagates on out of the group. The group propagate corresponds to the condition in which all bits in the group are in the propagate condition so that a carry into the group should pass right through the group. Note that these terms are implemented by the leftmost five gates in the CLA unit (Fig. 14.5).

Next, we note that there is a carry-out of the group if a carry is generated in the group and propagated out or if there is a carry into the group that is propagated through the group. Thus we can define the *group carry, GC_{15},* which is equal to C_{60}, by the following equation.

$$C_{60} = GC_{15} = GG_{15} \lor (GP_{15} \land GC_{16}) \tag{14.19}$$

where $GC_{16} = C_{64}$, the carry into the group. In a similar fashion, we can develop equations for the group carries from succeeding 4-bit groups.

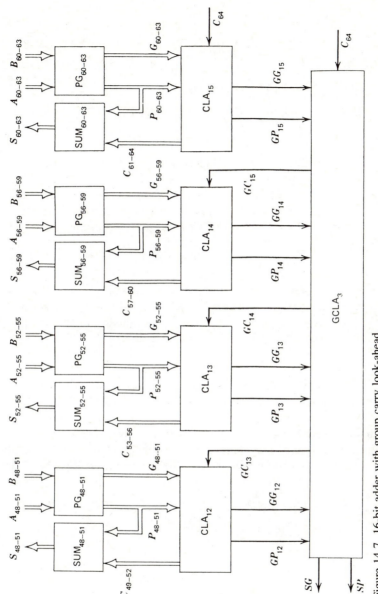

Figure 14.7. 16-bit adder with group carry look-ahead.

$$C_{56} = GC_{14} = GG_{14} \vee (GP_{14} \wedge GC_{15})$$

$$= GG_{14} \vee (GP_{14} \wedge GG_{15}) \vee (GP_{14} \wedge GP_{15} \wedge GC_{16}) \quad (14.20)$$

and

$$C_{52} = GC_{13} = GG_{13} \vee (GP_{13} \wedge GC_{14})$$

$$= GG_{13} \vee (GP_{13} \wedge GG_{14}) \vee (GP_{13} \wedge GP_{14} \wedge GG_{15})$$

$$\vee (GP_{13} \wedge GP_{14} \wedge GP_{15} \wedge GC_{16}) \quad (14.21)$$

Except for the names of the variables, Eqs. 14.19, 14.20, and 14.21 are seen to be identical to Eqs. 14.14, 14.15, and 14.16. Thus the group carry terms can be developed by the same type of CLA circuit as used for the ordinary carries (Eq. 14.5). The interconnection of adders and CLA units for bits 48 through 63 is shown in Fig. 14.7. (The group carry unit is labelled GCLA for purposes of identification but is the same circuit as the CLA units.)

Now let us consider the delay for these 16 bits, again considering the worst case. The carry is generated in PG_{63} in $2\Delta t$, propagates through CLA_{15} To Develop GG_{15} in $2\Delta t$, through $GCLA_3$ to develop GC_{13} in $2\Delta t$ and through CLA_{12} to develop C_{48} in $2\Delta t$. Thus the carry propagation delay in Fig. 14.7 is $10\Delta t$ compared to $32\Delta t$ for 16 bits of a ripple-carry adder. We are now beginning to see some significant improvements in delay times, but we are not done yet.

14.6 Section Carry Look-Ahead

We now divide the 64-bit adder into four 16-bit sections and define *section generate, SG,* and *section propagate, SP,* terms, in a manner exactly analogous to the group terms. These equations will be seen to have the same form as Eqs. 14.17 and 14.18 for the group generate and propagate terms. Thus the

$$SG_3 = GG_{12} \vee (GP_{12} \wedge GG_{13}) \vee (GP_{12} \wedge GP_{13} \wedge GG_{14})$$

$$\vee (GP_{12} \wedge GP_{13} \wedge GP_{14} \wedge GG_{15}) \quad (14.22)$$

and

$$SP_3 = GP_{12} \wedge GP_{13} \wedge GP_{14} \wedge GP_{15} \quad (14.23)$$

five leftmost gates of Fig. 14.5 will form SG and SP terms when the inputs are GG and GP terms. The SG and SP outputs from GCLA are shown in Fig. 14.7.

We now develop equations for *section carry-out* in the same manner as for the group carry-outs. These equations are seen to have the same form as

$$C_{48} = GC_{12} = SC_3 = SG_3 \vee (SP_3 \wedge SC_4) \quad (14.24)$$

$$C_{32} = GC_8 = SC_2 = SG_2 \vee (SP_2 \wedge SC_3)$$

$$= SG_2 \vee (SP_2 \wedge SG_3) \vee (SP_2 \wedge SP_3 \wedge SC_4) \quad (14.25)$$

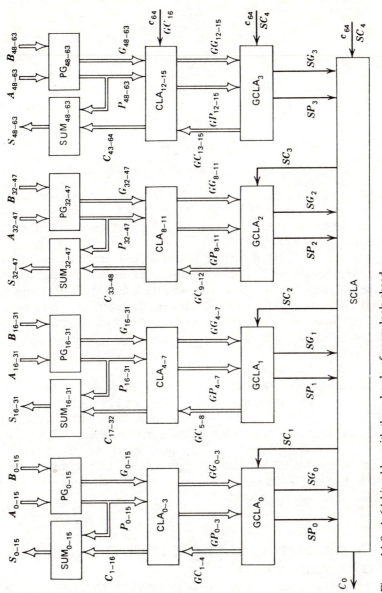

Figure 14.8. A 64-bit adder with three levels of carry look-ahead.

$$C_{16} = GC_4 = SC_1 = SG_1 \vee (SP_1 \wedge SC_2)$$

$$= SG_1 \vee (SP_1 \wedge SG_2) \vee (SP_1 \wedge SP_2 \wedge SG_3)$$

$$\vee (SP_1 \wedge SP_2 \wedge SP_3 \wedge SC_4) \tag{14.26}$$

those for the original CLA unit so that the same form of circuit can be used again, with one small change. Since there will be no further levels of look-ahead, the final output carry, C_0, must be developed. To develop this term,

$$C_0 = SG_0 \vee (SP_0 \wedge SG_1) \vee (SP_0 \wedge SP_1 \wedge SG_2) \vee (SP_0 \wedge SP_1$$

$$\wedge SP_2 \wedge SG_3) \vee (SP_0 \wedge SP_1 \wedge SP_2 \wedge SP_3 \wedge SC_4) \tag{14.27}$$

connect a SC_4 input to the gate in Fig. 14.5 that develops GP, and connect the output of this gate to the OR gate that develops GG in Fig. 14.5; this gate will now develop C_0. The complete block diagram of the 64-bit adder with three levels of carry look-ahead is shown in Fig. 14.8.

Applying the same sort of analysis as before, you should be able to convince yourself that the worst case delay through this adder would be $14\Delta t$, compared to $128\Delta t$ for the 64-bit ripple-carry adder. Thus we have achieved about 9:1 improvement in speed, certainly a worthwhile accomplishment. However, we must also consider the cost of this speed improvement. An exact cost analysis would depend on the hardware chosen, but a good measure of the cost of a logic circuit is the total number of gate terminals (inputs and outputs), since this number will generally be proportional to the total number of active devices.

The full adder of Fig. 14.4 has 22 terminals, giving a total of 1408 for 64-bits. The CLA unit of Fig. 14.5 has 56 terminals, and there are 21 CLA units in the complete adder of Fig. 14.8. If we include the two extra inputs in the SCLA required for C_0, this gives a grand total of 2586 terminals for the complete adder. The cost of a ripple-carry adder will depend on the full-adder configuration chosen. The simplest circuit known to the authors has 27 terminals, giving a total of 1728 terminals for 64 bits. Thus, for less than a 50% increase in cost, we have achieved about a 9:1 increase in speed, a remarkable speed/cost trade-off.

14.7 Combinational Logic Unit Description of Look-Ahead

We have now completed our discussion of the principles of the carry look-ahead adder, but have actually provided only samples from the description of its combinational logic. The structure of this adder is highly iterative and is, therefore, well suited to description as an AHPL combinational logic unit. Because of its overall complexity, the carry look-ahead adder is easily the most complicated example of a combinational logic unit description that we will have seen to this point.

If the number of pairs of inputs to the look-ahead unit is 4, the number of bits in a carry look-ahead adder must be given by $K \times 4^r$, where r is an integer and $K < 4$. One is unlikely to see anything but 16-, 32-, and 64-bit carry look-ahead adders in the future, so little would be gained by taking on the additional complexity associated with a generic description of such an adder. In this section, we shall look at 16- and 64-bit descriptions. First, let us develop descriptions of the necessary building blocks.

Example 14.1

Write separate combinational logic unit descriptions of the propagate and generate section and the sum section of the full adder given in Fig. 14.4.

Solution
In the following description, PROPGEN[0] is the generate bit and PROPGEN[1] is the propagate bit.

> CLUNIT: PROPGEN($x; y$).
>   INPUTS: $x; y$.
>   OUTPUTS: *TERMOUT* [2].
>   BODY
>   *TERMOUT*[0] $= x \wedge y;$
>   *TERMOUT*[1] $= x \wedge \bar{y} \vee \bar{x} \wedge y.$
>   END.

The sum unit, n of which will form the last two logic levels of an n-bit carry look-ahead adder, follows.

> CLUNIT: SUM($prop; cin$).
>   INPUTS: $prop; cin$.
>   OUTPUTS: *termout*.
>   BODY
> $termout = prop \wedge \overline{cin} \vee \overline{prop} \wedge cin.$
>   END. ∎

In previous discussions, a one-dimensional vector has always been regarded as a row. No transpose operator has been required. In the following example, it is necessary to catenate a transposed column with a row. The most recent implementation of the AHPL hardware compiler demands that an explicit transpose function be used in this case. For this purpose, a primitive function, TRANS(**ARRAY**), is recognized by the compiler. No logic gates are generated by a processing of this function. Wires are merely rearranged. This function may be used only within combinational logic unit descriptions.

Example 14.2

Write a combinational logic unit description of the carry look-ahead unit given in Fig. 14.9.

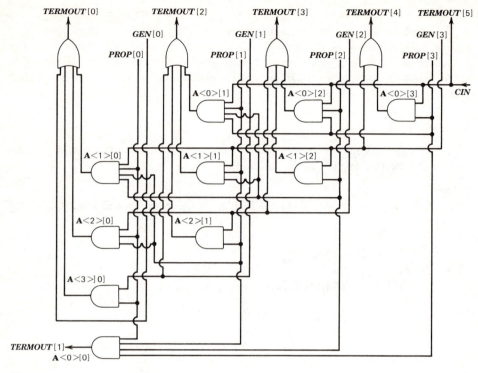

Figure 14.9. Relabelled carry look-ahead unit.

Solution

There is little repetition in Fig. 14.9, so the description is complicated and perhaps somewhat less revealing than the figure itself. The outputs of the AND gates shown in the figure are declared as an array of cterms, $A\langle 4\rangle[4]$. A structured AHPL description is given as follows. For this example, a gate-by-gate or row-by-row implementation might be more straightforward. This approach is left as a problem for the reader.

```
CLUNIT:      CLA(GEN; PROP; cin).
  INPUTS:    GEN[4]; PROP[4]; cin.
  OUTPUTS:   TERMOUT[6].
  CTERMS:    A⟨4⟩[4]; CYSRC[4].
  BODY
      CYSRC = GEN[1:3],cin;
      FOR J = 0 TO 3 CONSTRUCT
          FOR I = 0 TO 3 − J CONSTRUCT
              IF I = 0 THEN
                  IF J = 0 THEN
                      A⟨J⟩[I] = ∧/PROP
                  ELSE
```

$$A\langle J\rangle[I] = \bigwedge/(CYSRC[3 - J], PROP[I{:}3 - J])$$
        FI
     ELSE
$$A\langle J\rangle[I] = \bigwedge/(CYSRC[3 - J], PROP[I{:}3 - J])$$
        FI
    ROF
  ROF;
$TERMOUT[0] = \bigvee/(GEN[0], A\langle 1{:}3\rangle[0])$;
$TERMOUT[1] = A\langle 0\rangle[0]$;
FOR J = 0 TO 2 CONSTRUCT
    $TERMOUT[4 - J] = \bigvee/(\text{TRANS}(A\langle 0{:}J\rangle[3 - J]), CYSRC[2 - J])$
ROF;
$TERMOUT[5] = CYSRC[3]$.
  END.   ■

We are now in a position to consider overall descriptions of the look-ahead adders.

Example 14.3

Write a combinational logic unit description of a 16-bit carry look-ahead adder making use of as many copies as necessary of the combinational logic units developed in Examples 14.1 and 14.2.

Solution
The following will describe the 16-bit adder given in Fig. 14.7, except that the input bits will be numbered from 0 through 15 and so forth. Note that the first level of look-ahead and the group look-ahead units are all described by the combinational logic unit, CLA, as given in Example 14.2. For clarity, the first-level look-ahead units are declared as LA and the group look-ahead unit as GLA. Both are instances of CLA. Note that four copies of LA and only one of GLA are generated by the description. The description begins with the generation of 16 copies of the PG unit and concludes with the generation of the 17 output bits, 16 of which are the outputs of copies of the clunit, SUM. The carry-in to the adder unit, $C[16]$, is assumed to be 0.

```
CLUNIT:     ADDLA16(X; Y).
  INPUTS:     X[16]; Y[16].
  OUTPUTS:    TERMOUT[17].
  CLUNITS:    LA[6] <: CLA; GLA[6] <: CLA;
              PG[2] <: PROPGEN; SUMBIT <: SUM.
  CTERMS:     G[16]; P[16]; C[17]; GG[4]; GP[4]; GC[5].
  BODY
    FOR I = 0 TO 15 CONSTRUCT
      G[I], P[I] = PG(X[I]; Y[I])
    ROF;
```

```
    FOR I = 0 TO 3 CONSTRUCT
      GG[I], GP[I], C[4*I+1: 4*I+4] =
                              LA(G[4*I:4*I+3]; P[4*I:4*I+3]; GC[I+1])
    ROF;
    GC[1:4] = GLA[2:5](GG; GP; 0);
    TERMOUT[0] = GLA[0](GG; GP; 0);
    FOR I = 0 TO 15 CONSTRUCT
      TERMOUT[I+1] = SUMBIT(P[I]; C[I+1])
    ROF.
  END.                                                                    ∎
```

Only three additional lines of code and a few modifications are required to transform the 16-bit adder description into a 64-bit version.

Example 14.4

Write an AHPL description of a 64-bit carry look-ahead adder.

Solution

Now we have 16 LA units, four GLAs, and a section carry look-ahead unit called SLA. Now the most significant output bit comes from the SLA unit.

```
    CLUNIT:      ADDLA64(X; Y).
     INPUTS:     X[64]; Y[64].
     OUTPUTS:    TERMOUT[65].
     CLUNITS:    LA[6] <: CLA; GLA[6] <: CLA; SLA[6] <: CLA;
                 PG[2] <: PROPGEN; SUMBIT <: SUM.
     CTERMS:     G[64]; P[64]; C[65]; GG[16]; GP[16]; GC[17];
                 SG[4]; SP[4]; SC[5].
    BODY
        FOR I = 0 TO 63 CONSTRUCT
          G[I], P[I] = PG(X[I]; Y[I])
        ROF;
        FOR I = 0 TO 15 CONSTRUCT
          GG[I], GP[I], C[4*I+1: 4*I+4] =
                              LA(G[4*I:4*I+3]; P[4*I:4*I+3]; GC[I+1])
        ROF;
        FOR I = 0 TO 3 CONSTRUCT
          GC[4*I+1: 4*I+4] =
                      GLA[2:5] (GG[4*I: 4*I+3]; GP[4*I: 4*I+3]; SC[I + 1]);
          SG[I], SP[I] = GLA[0:1] (GG[4*I: 4*I+3]; GP[4*I: 4*I+3];
                                                                   SC[I+1])
        ROF;
        SC[1:4] = SLA[2:5](SG; SP; 0);
        TERMOUT[0] = SLA[0](SG; SP; 0);
        FOR I = 0 TO 63 CONSTRUCT
          TERMOUT[I+1] = SUMBIT(P[I]; C[I+1])
```

ROF.
END. ∎

In Section 5.7, it was noted that combinational logic unit descriptions need not be written in an order such that all inputs to a gate are generated in statements appearing before the statement generating that gate. The statements were not so ordered in Example 14.4. It may be observed from Fig. 14.8 that outputs from the look-ahead units go both backward and forward in the logic structure. A description ordered from input to output could be worked out, but separate specification of almost every gate would be required. If the instances of CLA are to be invoked as units, no such ordering is possible. A function-level simulation of the description in Example 14.4 must provide for multiple passes through the network each clock period. When all network values are the same for two consecutive clock periods, the simulation of the network is concluded for that clock period.

14.8   The Carry Completion Adder

Another type of adder that applies a completely different approach deserves some comment. We have noted that the worst case, the carry propagating from one end of the adder to the other, will occur only with certain combinations of operands. In most cases, there will be stages in either the *generate* or the *no propagate* condition every few bits, so that any given carry is likely to propagate through only a few stages. It has been shown [4] that the average maximum carry length for a 64-bit adder is about 7 bits. Thus the *average* time for addition in a ripple-carry adder would be about $14\Delta t$, the same as for the full CLA adder designed in previous sections.

In the carry completion adder, circuitry is added to detect when all carries have fully propagated and issue a completion signal. On receipt of the completion signal, the computer can then go on to the next step without waiting to allow time for the rare worst case. A carry completion adder of typical design [3] has a cost about halfway between that of the ripple-carry and the CLA adders. This type of adder has been used in a few machines but has not met with much acceptance. The main problem is that it is difficult to make effective use of the time "saved" by the carry completion adder. If the add time is fixed, we can schedule other activities to be going on at the same time. But if the add times may vary over a range of 64:1, it becomes very difficult to synchronize other operations with the adder.

14.9   Summary

The carry look-ahead adder has been considered in detail for two reasons: First, it is probably the most popular form of fast adder; second, it is a classic example of the ingenious application of logic design to the problem of obtaining increased speed at minimum cost.

The validity of the first reason may change with time due to developments in device technology. However, it is interesting to note that the carry look-ahead principle, which was first applied to vacuum-tube circuits, has also been applied to integrated circuits, resulting in CLA adders nearly a thousand times faster than the original vacuum-tube versions. A design principle that has remained viable while component speeds have increased by several orders of magnitude has certainly demonstrated some intrinsic validity.

On the other hand, as basic logic speeds continue to increase, the ordinary ripple-carry adder may become so fast compared to other system components, such as memory, that the CLA adder will be less attractive economically. But whatever the future may bring for the CLA adder, the logic design principles it illustrates will remain important. The careful analysis of the arithmetic process and the resultant factoring of the equations into iterative forms are basic ideas that will remain applicable to any technology.

Problems

14.1 Rewrite the combinational logic unit description of the propagate generate unit of Example 14.2, simplifying it as much as possible. Rather than relying on a two-dimensional array of CTERMS, describe rows of gates or even individual gates in separate statements, if this will simplify the description.

14.2 Write a combinational logic unit description of a 32-bit carry look-ahead adder.

14.3 Manually carry out an iterative function-level simulation of the 16-bit adder of Example 14.3. Add the hexidecimal numbers 0F0F and 0444. Record the values of $C[0:15]$, $P[15]$, $G[0:15]$, $GC[0:3]$, $GP[0:3]$, and $GG[0:3]$ each iteration. How many iterations are necessary before stability is achieved?

References

1. A. Weinberger and J. L. Smith, "The Logical Design of a One-Micro-second Adder Using One-Megacycle Circuitry," *IRE Trans. Elec. Computers,* Vol. EC-5, No. 2, June 1956, pp. 65–73.
2. O. L. MacSorley, "High-Speed Arithmetic in Binary Computers," *Proc. IRE,* Vol. 49, No. 1, Jan. 1961, pp. 67–91.
3. I. FLores, *The Logic of Computer Arithmetic,* Prentice–Hall, Englewood Cliffs, N.J., 1963, Chaps. 4, 5, and 6.
4. H. C. Hendrickson, "Fast High-Accuracy Binary Parallel Addition," *IRE Trans. Elec. Computers,* Vol. EC-9, No. 4, Dec. 1960, pp. 469–479.

15 Multiplication and Division

15.1   Signed Multiplication

In Chapter 6, the multiplication of negative numbers in complement form was accomplished by first determining the sign of the product, converting the operands to magnitude form, and then carrying out the multiplication. For numbers stored in one's-complement form, this conversion can be accomplished by merely reading the operand bits from the complement side of each flip-flop in the respective register. Thus, for one's-complement machines, sign and magnitude provide a satisfactory approach to multiplication.

In the two's-complement system, the process of complementing requires extra addition cycles, which may be considered to consume time unnecessarily. Recall that in Chapter 6 multiplication was initiated with the multiplicand in the MD register and the multiplier in the AC register. As the multiplication progressed, the multiplier was first transferred to MQ and the product was gradually formed in AC and shifted, least-significant bit first, into the MQ register. At the conclusion of this operation, the product is found spanning AC and MQ.

We now propose to carry out multiplication in the same manner without first converting the operands to magnitude form. Thus MD and MQ may contain two's-complement numbers. As we shall see, it will be necessary to modify the hardware program slightly. Our goal in doing so will be to accomplish any corrections in the same time intervals as the basic shift and add operations.

We see in Fig. 15.1 a tabulation of the possible contents of MD and MQ. We let a and b represent the respective numerical values, which may be either positive or

a	*b*	⊥ *MQ**	⊥ *MD*	**Desired Result** ⊥ (*AC, MQ*)
+	+	a	b	ab
+	−	a	$2^n - |b|$	$2^{2n} - a \cdot |b|$
−	+	$2^n - |a|$	b	$2^{2n} - |a| \cdot b$
−	−	$2^n - |a|$	$2^n - |b|$	$|a| \cdot |b|$

*The operator ⊥ converts a binary vector into a decimal integer. It is the inverse of the AHPL operator T.

Figure 15.1.

negative. If both a and b are positive, then two's complement and signed-magnitude multiplication are identical. As we shall see, the program to be specified for two's-complement multiplication will reduce to the program of Chapter 6 for this case.

Now consider the second case; the multiplier is still positive but the multiplicand is negative so that the product should be negative. Recall that the basic multiplication process consists of repeated cycles of adding the multiplicand to partial products in *AC,* followed by right shifts of the new partial product. If we add a negative multiplicand in the proper complement form to negative partial products in the proper complement form, the result will be a negative product in the proper complement form.

We already know that complement addition works, so that the only special precaution we must observe is to see that the shifting process produces a proper complement. Assume that the number y is loaded into an n-bit *AC* register, that is,

$$\perp AC = y$$

If we shift this number one place right, the effect is to reduce the value by 2^{-1}, that is,

$$\perp (0, AC [0: n - 2]) = 2^{-1} \times y$$

The correct complement form for the negative value of the shifted quantity would be a binary vector such that

$$\perp AC = 2^n - 2^{-1}y$$

Now suppose that the complement of y, $2^n - y$, has been stored in *AC* and is shifted one place right. The result is

$$\perp (0, AC[0: n - 2]) = 2^{-1}(2^n - y) = 2^{n-1} - 2^{-1}y$$

which is not the correct complement of the shifted number. To correct it, we must add 2^{n-1}, which gives

$$2^{n-1} - 2^{-1}y + 2^{n-1} = 2^n - 2^{-1}y$$

that is, a 1 is inserted in the vacated most-significant-digit position.

In summary, for both cases in which the multiplier is positive, we add the multiplicand and shift, the only difference being that a 0 is inserted in the vacated position for positive multiplicand and a 1 for negative multiplicand. This is equivalent to saying that the inserted bit is equal to the multiplicand sign; therefore, the desired shifting can be accomplished by the statement

$$AC, MQ \leftarrow MD[0], AC, MQ[0: n - 2]$$

Next we consider the situation in which the multiplier is negative. When this occurs, both the multiplier and multiplicand are complemented, thus giving the proper sign for the product. The complementation can be accomplished without lengthening the multiplication process. Recall that in the routine of Chapter 6 the multiplier is inspected 1 bit at a time to determine whether the multiplicand is to be added to the current partial product. We also recall that a bit-by-bit algorithm for taking the two's-complement of a number was discussed in Chapter 2. The bits of the number are examined and corrected sequentially from right to left. Until a 1 is encountered, 0's are left unchanged. The first 1 from the right is also left unchanged, but all remaining bits are complemented. We shall use this complementing process for each bit of the multiplier as that bit is used to control addition of the multiplicand to the partial product.

With a negative multiplier, the sign of the product will be the opposite of the sign of the multiplicand. Thus, if the multiplicand is positive, it must be complemented to the negative form before adding in order to produce a negative product, and vice versa for a negative multiplicand. Noting that an alternate procedure for taking the two's-complement is to take the logical complement (one's-complement) and add 1 in the least-significant-digit position, we see that the multiplicand can be complemented as it is added to the partial product. We need only gate the complement of *MD* to the adder and insert a 1 on the input carry line. Finally, the proper shifting algorithm must be followed, inserting 0 when a positive product is to be developed and 1 when the product is to be negative.

On the basis of this discussion, we can now set up a flowchart for the complete signed multiplication procedure, as shown in Fig. 15.2. For convenience, we shall assume 18-bit registers and shall assume that we start with the multiplier in *AC* and the multiplicand in *MD.*

Steps 1 and 2 check for zero operands, in which case steps 18 and 19 set the product to zero and exit:

1     $\rightarrow (\overline{\vee/AC})/(19)$
2     $\rightarrow (\vee/MD)/(18)$

Step 3 stores the multiplier sign in the link and transfers the multiplier to *MQ*. The storage of the multiplier sign is required because the shifting will move the sign into a different position of *MQ* after every cycle. Step 4 clears *AC* and the multiplication counter, *MC:*

3   *cff* $\leftarrow AC[0]$; *MQ* $\leftarrow AC$.
4   *AC* $\leftarrow 18 \top 0$; *MC* $\leftarrow 5 \top 0$.

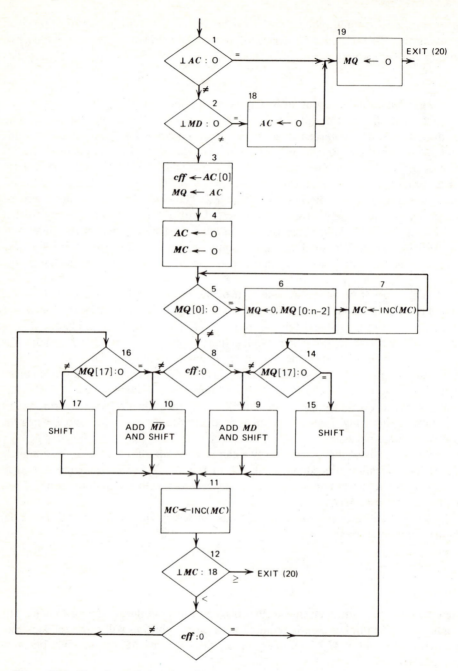

Figure 15.2. Flowchart of signed multiplication.

Step 5 commences the actual multiplication by checking the least-significant digit of the multiplier. As long as the multiplier bits remain 0, the product is to remain 0, regardless of the ultimate sign of the product. Thus we remain in the steps 5, 6, 7 loop, shifting only the multiplier, until the first 1 of the multiplier is encountered:

5     $\rightarrow (MQ[17])/(8)$.
6     $MQ \leftarrow 0, MQ[0:16]$.
7     $MC \leftarrow \text{INC}(MC)$.
      $\rightarrow (5)$

Step 8 checks the sign of the multiplier to determine whether the true or complemented contents of *MD* should be added. For a positive multiplier, step 9 adds the true contents of *MD* to *AC* and shifts right, inserting *MD*[0] in the vacated position. For a negative multiplier, step 10 *adds* the complement of the contents of *MD* and shifts right, inserting $\overline{MD}$[0] in the vacated position:

8     $\rightarrow (cff)/(10)$.
9     $AC, MQ \leftarrow MD[0], \text{ADD}(AC; MD; 0), MQ[0:16]$;
      $\rightarrow (11)$.
10    $AC, MQ \leftarrow \overline{MD}[0], \text{ADD}(AC; \overline{MD}; 1), MQ[0:16]$.

Whichever addition was made, step 11 increments the multiplication counter and step 12 checks to see if the multiplication is complete. If not, step 13 checks the multiplier sign, branching to step 14 for positive multiplier, to step 16 for negative multiplier. Step 8, which also checks the multiplier sign, is encountered only on the first 1 in the multiplier, which must be treated differently from succeeding 1's for negative multipliers.

11    $MC \leftarrow \text{INC}(MC)$.
12    $\rightarrow (MC[0] \wedge MC[3])/(20)$.
13    $\rightarrow (cff)/(16)$.

For positive multipliers, step 14 checks the current least significant bit of the multiplier, branching to step 15 for a shift if it is 0 and to step 9 for add-and-shift if it is 1. Step 16 makes a similar check for negative multipliers, branching to step 17 for a shift for a 1 bit or to step 10 for add-and-shift for a 0-bit

14    $\rightarrow (MQ[17])/(9)$.
15    $AC, MQ \leftarrow MD[0], AC, MQ[0:16]$;
      $\rightarrow (11)$.
16    $\rightarrow (\overline{MQ[17]})/(10)$.
17    $AC, MQ \leftarrow \overline{MD}[0], AC, MQ[0:16]$;
      $\rightarrow (11)$.
18    $AC \leftarrow 18 \top 0$.
19    $MQ \leftarrow 18 \top 0$.

After each shift or add-and-shift, control returns to step 11 to increment *MC* and check for completion. Steps 18 and 19 set the product to 0 for zero operands as determined in steps 1 and 2.

15.2 Multiplication Speed-Up—Carry-Save

The time-saving offered by the technique discussed in the last section is relatively small. At best, it eliminates two additions required for complementing; since there may be *n* additions required for an *n*-bit multiplier, this is a minor saving. It is often included, since it requires little extra hardware. To make any significant reductions in multiplication time, we must reduce either the number of additions or the addition time. If multiplication is to be provided, we shall almost certainly use a fast adder, such as the CLA adder discussed in the last chapter; but the necessity for *n* complete additions will still make multiplication relatively slow. Many techniques for multiplication speed-up have been proposed, most of which are discussed in Flores [1]. We shall consider only a few of the more significant and representative techniques.

Certainly, the best method of speed-up, in terms of cost/performance ratio, is the *carry-save* technique. This technique provides very significant increases in speed with relatively little extra hardware, and there are few multipliers of any size that do not include this feature in some form. The basic notion of carry-save is simple. The addition process may be visualized as developing a set of sum and carry bits, shifting of the carry bits right, and updating the sum and carry bits. The process continues until the carry has been formed and shifted $n - 1$ times. This is actually a synchronous interpretation of the usual carry propagation process. Now, suppose a series of numbers is to be added together, one at a time. Since addition is associative, the process is not changed if the next argument is added at the same time as the shifted carry. The process continues, with a new carry word formed and shifted with each addition, until the list of numbers to be added is exhausted. From that point, the carry is allowed to propagate normally through $n - 1$ stages to complete the arithmetic.

Multiplication is an example of the process just described, with the *i*th argument consisting of the multiplicand shifted $i - 1$ bits to the left if the *i*th bit of the multiplier is 1. Otherwise, the *i*th entry is 0. The process is illustrated for a simple example, in Fig. 15.3. The process consists of four steps of additions to the partial product, followed by a fifth step, representing completion of the carry propagation. In this figure we have shown the computer form of the process, with the relative left shift of the carry-save word, *CS,* and the multiplicand actually provided by a right shift of the partial product. The *CS* word is shown boxed for emphasis, and the space in the *AC, MQ* word indicates the boundary between partial product and the shifted remainder of the multiplier.

In analyzing the example, note that the contents of the *AC, MQ* registers, in each step prior to the last, do not represent the binary sum of the three inputs but rather represent the bit-by-bit exclusive ORing of the three input vectors. For example, at step 2,

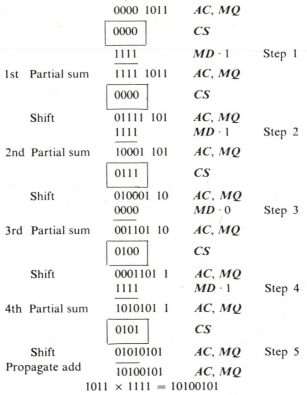

Figure 15.3. Example of carry-save multiplication.

$$(1, 0, 0, 0, 1) = (1, 1, 1, 1, 0) \oplus (0, 0, 0, 0, 0) \oplus (0, 1, 1, 1, 1)$$

and the carry bits 0111 are shifted and added in step 3. You should follow the process step by step; and if necessary, check by carrying out the multiplication in the usual manner.

In most computers, the same adder is used for multiplication as for all other operations involving addition so that provision must be made to modify this adder when carry-save is to be implemented. If we assume an 18-bit ripple-carry adder, the configuration for carry-save would be as shown in Fig. 15.4. The output-carry from each stage, instead of going directly to the input-carry line of the next stage, is stored in a position of the *CS* register. On the next cycle, this stored carry will become the input-carry to the same stage. In might seem that each stage of the *CS* register should provide the input-carry to the next stage to the left, until we recall that the partial sum is shifted to the right before the next cycle, providing the logical equivalent of a left shift of the carries. A two-level switching network on each carry-input can be added so that the same adder can function as given in Fig. 14.1 or Fig. 15.4, depending on the value of a single control signal.

The basic control program for the carry-save multiplication can now be written.

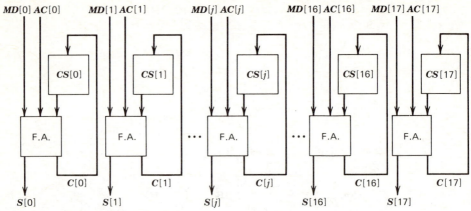

Figure 15.4. Ripple-carry adder converted to carry-save adder.

Note that steps 2 and 3, representing formation of the carries and partial sums, occur simultaneously and are written on separate lines solely for clarity. Also note that circuitry of the adder would require gating to convert from a conventional adder to a carry-save adder, and the complete program would probably include the setting and clearing of some sort of indicator to control this gating.

> 1 $MC \leftarrow 5 \top 0; CS \leftarrow 18 \top 0$.
> 2 $AC \leftarrow AC \oplus CS \oplus (MD \wedge MQ[17])$.
> 3 $CS \leftarrow (CS \wedge AC) \vee (CS \wedge (MD \wedge MQ[17]))$
> $$\vee (AC \wedge (MD \wedge MQ[17])).$$
> 4 $AC, MQ \leftarrow 0, AC, MQ[0:16]$.
> 5 $MC \leftarrow \mathrm{INC}(MC)$.
> 6 $\rightarrow (MC[0] \wedge MC[3])/(2)$.
> 7 $AC \leftarrow \mathrm{ADD}(AC; CS)$.

This considers the multiplication of magnitudes only. We leave it as an exercise for you to modify the signed multiplication routine to incorporate carry-save. Carry-save can be used with virtually any type of adder or other type of speed-up method.

15.3 Multiple-Bit Speed-Up Techniques

So far, we have assumed that only one multiplier bit is to be handled each cycle. By carrying out multiplication for several bits at a time, the number of cycles can be reduced. This will reduce the overall multiply time if extra hardware is provided to process multiple bits in the same time as single bits. First, we must provide for multiple shifts in the same time as single shifts; second, we must provide means of adding multiples of the multiplicand in a single addition cycle.

The simplest multiple-bit techniques is *shifting over 0s*. We inspect two or more of the multiplier bits. If they are all 0, we make a multiple shift over the corresponding number of bits. The speed advantage of this technique depends on the statistical likelihood that strings of 0s of various lengths may occur. The technique is fairly simple and frequently used.

A closely related technique is *shifting over 1s*. Assume that we have three 1s in a row in the multiplier. Essentially, this requires adding seven times the multiplicand, which can be accomplished by *subtracting* the multiplicand, shifting three places—which multiplies by eight—and then adding the multiplicand. Since this method requires two addition cycles, there must be at least three consecutive 1s before it is worth doing; it is therefore less popular than shifting over 0s.

Next let us consider the handling of arbitrary pairs of multiplier bits. If at a given step the least-significant-multiplier bits are 00, a 2-bit shift is carried out. It the bits are 01, the multiplicand is added and then a 2-bit shift is made. If the bits are 10, there are two possible techniques. The first is to revert to the single-bit method, that is, make a single shift to take care of the 0 and then pair the 1 with the next bit in the multiplier for the next cycle. Alternatively, we can shift the multiplicand one position to the left as it enters the adder—thus mutliplying it by two—and then make a 2-bit shift of the sum. If the bits are 11, there are also two possibilities. We can add, shift once, and pair the second 1 with the next multiplier bit. Or we can provide a special register, *TR*, in which we store three times the multiplicand at the start of the multiplication cycle. Then when 11 occurs, we add *TR* to the partial product and shift twice. Note that the use of *TR* and the use of multiplicand shifting will require the addition of an extra bit position to *AC* and the adder.

A control sequence for bit-pair multiplication, using *TR* and multiplicand shifting, follows. Note in step 4 that there are two separate shifts indicated. There is a two-bit shift of the catenation of the adder output and the *MQ* register, and a shift of the multiplicand as it is gated to the adder, indicated by the use of (0, *MD*) or (*MD*, 0) as an adder argument.

1    $AC \leftarrow MD, 0.$
2    $TR \leftarrow ADD(AC; (0, MD)).$
3    $MC \leftarrow 5 \top 0; \textbf{\textit{cff}}, AC \leftarrow 20 \top 0.$
4    $\textbf{\textit{cff}}, AC, MQ \leftarrow (\ (0, 0, lf, AC, MQ[0:15])$
$!(0, 0, ADD(AC; (0, MD)), MQ[0:15]$
$!(0, 0, ADD(AC; (MD, 0)), MQ[0:15]$
$!(0, 0, ADD(AC; TR), MQ[0:15]$
$*(MQ[16] \wedge (\overline{MQ[17]}), (MQ[16] \wedge MQ[17]),$
$(\overline{MQ[16]} \wedge (\overline{MQ[17]}), (\overline{MQ[16]} \wedge (MQ[17])).$
5    $MC \leftarrow INC(MC).$
6    $\rightarrow (\overline{MC[1]} \wedge MC[4])/(4).$

An alternate scheme for handling bit-pairs, known as *ternary* multiplication, is discussed by Flores [1].

Groups of 3 multiplier bits can be handled by techniques quite similar to those

Multiplier Bits	Action
0 0 0	Triple shift
0 0 1	Add *MD*, triple shift
0 1 0	Add 2 × *MD*, triple shift
0 1 1	Add *TR*, triple shift
1 0 0	Add 4 × *MD*, triple shift
1 0 1	Add *MD*, double shift
1 1 0	Add 2 × *TR*, triple shift
1 1 1	Add *TR*, double shift

Figure 15.5. Bit-triplet multiplication.

already discussed. In the table of Fig. 15.5 are listed the actions taken for various bit combinations. We see that this method requires the capability for both single and double shifts of *MD,* and single shifts of *TR*. For bit triplets 101 and 111, we revert to bit-pair methods, letting the third bit form part of the next triplet. Alternatively, we could provide special registers for storing $5 \times (\perp MD)$ and $7 \times (\perp MD)$.

One might expect to achieve further improvement by handling more than 3 bits at a time. However, extending this approach directly would imply the use of a large number of registers to store the products of the multiplicand and various prime numbers. To compute the contents of these registers serially prior to the multiplication would tend to negate any speed advantage that might be obtained. At some point one would expect a decrease in speed with the consideration of additional bits.

Alternatively, the multibit partial products could be expressed as a combinational logic subroutine. These products could then be added to the contents of *AC, MQ,* employing carry-save. Each addition of an r-bit partial product would be followed by a shift of r-bits. This approach will be considered in Section 15.5. Until recently, such lavish use of combinational logic would have been prohibitively expensive. With the continuing decrease in cost of large-scale integrated circuits, such approaches are becoming practical. The limiting case is a completely combinational-logic multiplier.

15.4   Speed Analysis

Before proceeding further, it will be instructive to derive some expressions that will allow us to compare the speed of various multiplier configurations. To carry out this analysis, it is necessary to make some assumptions regarding the speed of various operations relative to the basic clock rate of the computer. Let σ represent the propagation delay through two levels of logic. The time required to change the contents of a register will then be on the order to 2σ to 4σ, depending on the logic family used. To allow time for logical operations during transfer and some tolerance for stray delays, the clock period might typically be set to $\tau_c = 8\sigma$. As we saw in the last chapter, the carry propagation time for a very fast adder might be $\tau_p = 7\sigma$. On this basis, we shall assume that a shift operation requires one clock period, an add-and-shift operation, two clock periods.

First, let us consider bit-by-bit multiplication without carry-save. If the multiplier bit is 0, we shift in one clock period; if it is 1, we add and shift in two clock periods. The probabilities of a multiplier bit being 1 or 0 are both 0.5. Therefore, the average time for accomplishing multiplication is given by Eq. 15.1:

$$T_1 = 0.5N\tau_c + 0.5N(2\tau_c) = 1.5N\tau_c = 12N\sigma \tag{15.1}$$

where N is the word length. Becoming slightly more general, suppose that a slower adder were employed, requiring k clock periods to complete an addition. In this case, Eq. 15.1 takes the form of Eq. 15.2:

$$T_1 = 0.5N\tau_c + 0.5N(k\tau_c) = \frac{N\tau_c}{2} \times (1 + k) \tag{15.2}$$

If carry-save is employed, the partial-add requires a delay of only σ so that each cycle except the last requires only one clock period for a partial-add and shift. Thus the time for an N-bit multiplication is given by Eq. 15.3:

$$T_2 = (N - 1)\tau_c + k\tau_c = (N - 1 + k)\tau_c \tag{15.3}$$

For $k = 2$, we have $T_2 = (N + 1)\tau_c$, which approaches $2/3 T_1$ for large N. For a slower adder ($k > 2$), the improvement achieved by carry-save is more noticeable.

Consider next the bit-pair process described in the previous section. Let us assume that $k = 2$ and carry-save is not employed. Thus $N/2$ cycles will be required. Since an addition is required in all but the case in which both multiplier bits are 0, three quarters of the cycles will require two clock periods while one quarter will require one period. Therefore, the average bit-pair multiplication time is given by Eq. 15.4.

$$T_3 = \frac{N}{2} [0.75(2\tau_c) + 0.25\tau_c] + 2\tau_c = (0.875N + 2)\tau_c \tag{15.4}$$

The $2\tau_c$ on the right accounts for the addition time necessary to compute the contents of the **TR** register. If bit-pairs and carry-save are used, only one clock period is required for all but the last of the $N/2$ shift cycles. For this case, we express the multiplication time in Eq. 15.5.

$$T_4 = \left(\frac{N}{2} - 1\right)\tau_c + 2\tau_c + 2\tau_c$$
$$= \left(\frac{N}{2} + 3\right)\tau_c \tag{15.5}$$

For bit-triplets with carry-save, the average multiplication time is given by Eq. 15.6.

$$T_5 = \left(\frac{N}{2.75} + 3\right)\tau_c \tag{15.6}$$

Multiplication Scheme	Multiplication Time	Time for $N = 64$
Bit-by-bit	$1.5N\tau_c$	$96\tau_c$
Bit-by-bit with carry-save	$(N + 1)\tau_c$	$65\tau_c$
Bit-pairs	$(0.875N \times 2)\tau_c$	$58\tau_c$
Bit-pairs with carry-save	$\left(\dfrac{N}{2} + 3\right)\tau_c$	$35\tau_c$
Bit-triplets with carry-save	$\left(\dfrac{N}{2.75} + 3\right)\tau_c$	$26\tau_c$

Figure 15.6. Multiplication times for two clock periods per addition ($2\tau_0$).

The derivation of this expression will be left as an exercise. The various expressions for multiplication times are summarized in the table in Fig. 15.6.

15.5 Large, Fast Parallel Multipliers

For a large, fast machine with a heavy investment in memory and peripheral equipment, an additional investment in logic circuitry to speed up arithmetic and increase the machine's throughput is usually considered money well spent. The time for multiplication can be decreased from the level discussed in the previous sections by decreasing the number of intermediate storage times required. This must be accomplished while holding the propagation time preceding each storage time to a minimum.

Consider the "paper-and-pencil" multiplication of two 4-bit binary numbers, shown here as a specific example and in general terms. The P terms represent the bit-by-bit partial products, that is, $P_{33} = X_3 \wedge Y_3$, $P_{23} = X_2 \wedge Y_3$, $P_{32} = X_3 \wedge Y_2$, and so forth. The multiplication process can be divided into two parts, the development of the array of partial products and the summation of these partial products.

$$
\begin{array}{ll}
1011 & X_0 X_1 X_2 X_3 \\
1101 & Y_0 Y_1 Y_2 Y_3 \\
\hline
1011 & P_{03} P_{13} P_{23} P_{33} \\
0000 & P_{02} P_{12} P_{22} P_{32} \\
1011 & P_{01} P_{11} P_{21} P_{31} \\
1011 & P_{00} P_{10} P_{20} P_{30} \\
\hline
10001111 & Z_0 Z_1 Z_2 Z_3 Z_4 Z_5 Z_6 Z_7
\end{array}
$$

The array of partial products can be developed in the time of a single gate delay, $\sigma/2$, by an array of N^2 AND gates for the multiplication of two N-bit numbers. With all N^2 partial product terms available simultaneously, the addition of these terms can then be carried out in a single combinational logic adder, with no intermediate storage. The speed of the addition is limited primarily by adder complexity considered to be economically feasible.

The most straightforward multiple-operand adder is the combinational carry-saver adder shown in Fig. 15.7. This circuit consists of an array of full adders. In the top row of adders, the first two rows of partial products are partially added. The sums and carries from this addition are combined with the third row of partial products in the second row of adders. These sums and carries are in turn combined with the last row of partial products in the third row of adders. The last row of adders ripple the carries through to complete the addition. Note that the worst case for carry propagation would be through a path of six adders, for a delay of 6σ. The complete multiplication, including formation of the partial product in an array of 16 AND gates, summation of the partial products, and shifting or storage of the product, can thus be completed in $2\tau_c$. This compares with a time of $5\tau_c$ for the sequential carry-save multiplier for 4 bits.

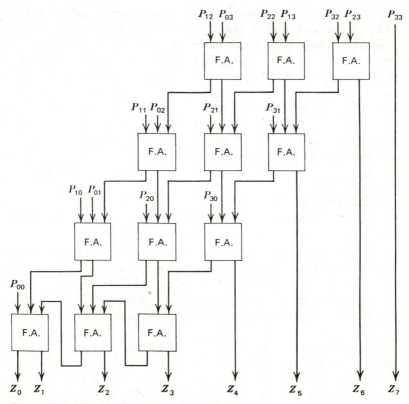

Figure 15.7. Four-bit, four-operand combinational carry-save adder.

This basic technique can be extended to any number of bits, with an additional delay of 2σ for each additional bit. The general relationship is

$$\tau_p = 2(N - 1)\sigma$$

Thus, assuming $\tau_c = 8\sigma$, as before, the time for a 64-bit multiplication would be $16\tau_c$, compared with a low of $26\tau_c$ for the methods previously discussed. Also note that this assumes ripple-carry for completion of the addition. The use of carry look-ahead in the last stage would reduce the time to $9\tau_c$.

Although this approach can theoretically be extended to any number of bits, the cost may become prohibitive for large numbers of bits, even with large-scale integrated circuits. For 64 bits, this technique requires an array of 4096 AND gates and an array of 4032 full adders for the ripple-carry version. As an alternative, we could use a combination of combinational and sequential techniques. In one large machine, using 48-bit words, the multiplier is divided in half. The multiplicand is first multiplied by the lower half of the multiplier, using a 24×48 array of AND gates to form the partial products and an array of adders to form 72-bit partial-sum and partial-carry terms, which are saved in registers. The same arrays are then used to multiply the multiplicand by the upper half of the multiplier, forming two more 72-bit partial-sum and partial-carry terms. The four partial terms are then added in a 4×96 carry-save adder to form two 96-bit partial-sum and partial-carry terms, which are then added in a 96-bit carry look-ahead adder to form the complete product. Depending on the exact form of the adder arrays, the time for this technique would be about $12\tau_c$.

There are many other possible ways of reducing multiplication time. If we consider the complexity of the operation, it is hardly surprising that a tremendous variety of techniques has been used, and many more will doubtless be developed in the future. We have tried here to indicate the basic ideas behind some of the more popular techniques, not to provide an exhaustive survey. Further, no general evaluation of the various techniques is practical, since so much depends on the characteristics of the system in which the multiplier is being used.

15.6 Division

In most computers, division is a considerably slower operation than is multiplication. Its logical nature is such that it does not lend itself to speed-up as well as multiplication does; and it occurs less frequently than does multiplication in the general mix of problems, so that slow speed can be better tolerated. In the machine using the complex 48-bit multiplication scheme described earlier, division takes four times as long as multiplication.

The basic technique of division is the comparison, or trial-and-error, method. In decimal division, we compare the divisor to the dividend or current partial remainder, estimate how many times it "fits," and then check the estimate by multiplying the divisor by the quotient digit and subtracting the resultant product from the partial remainder. If it does not "fit," we make a new estimate; hence the name "trial-and-error."

Binary division is considerably simpler, since the quotient bit is either 0 or 1. If the divisor is smaller than the partial remainder, the quotient bit is 1 and we subtract; if it is larger, the quotient bit is 0 and we do not subtract. An example of "paper-and-pencil" binary division of two 7-bit (including sign) numbers is shown in Fig. 15.8.

Consideration of this example indicates several special problems of division. First, placement of the binary point in the quotient requires not only knowledge of the position of the binary point in the divisor and dividend, but also some information as to the relative magnitudes of the two operands. For example, both divisor and dividend can be fractional (binary point to the left, as in Fig. 15.8); but if the divisor is smaller than the dividend, the quotient will not be fractional. It is usual to assume both operands fractional and to require that the divisor be larger than the dividend, thus ensuring a fractional quotient. Provisions to ensure this condition may be included in either the hardware or the software of the machine. We shall assume that this condition is met in the remainder of this chapter.

In the manual technique, we determine whether or not to subtract by a visual comparison of the shifted divisor and partial remainder. Unfortunately, the usual method of comparing the magnitudes of two numbers in a computer is to subtract one from the other and note the sign of the result. Thus we must subtract on every cycle. Further, since a negative difference will be indicated by a carry-out of the most-significant-digit position, we must allow time for the carry to propagate all the way through; so carry-save is ruled out.

In the manual technique, we shift the divisor right to make it smaller than the partial remainder. In a computer, since the adder is fixed in position relative to the registers, we accomplish the same result by shifting the partial remainder left. As we do so, we shift the quotient into the *MQ* register. Figure 15.9 illustrates the computer implementation of division for the same example as Fig. 15.8

The process starts with the divisor in *MD,* the dividend in *AC*, and the *MQ* register cleared. In the following we shall assume positive operands and shall write the AHPL statements for 18-bit division as we describe the process. Since the divisor is known to be larger than the dividend, step 1 shifts *AC*, *MQ* and enters the sign bit of the quotient (0 for this example) in the vacated position.

```
                0.101110
     0.011010)0.010011
             −011010          Divisor larger than dividend, shift
             ──────
              001100          Subtract, enter 1
              011010          Shift divisor, enter 0
             −011010          Shift divisor
             ──────
              010110          Subtract, enter 1
             −011010          Shift divisor
             ──────
              010010          Subtract, enter 1
             −011010          Shift divisor
             ──────
              001010          Subtract, enter 1
              011010          Shift divisor, enter 0
```

Figure 15.8. Binary division by trial-and-error method.

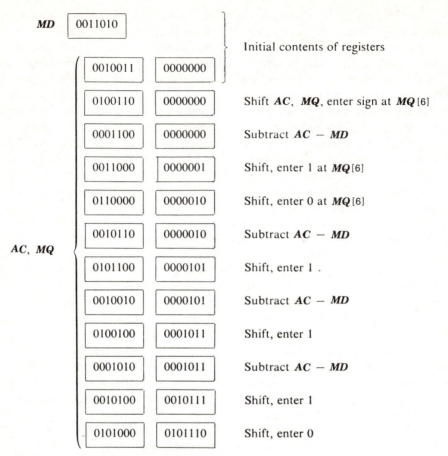

Figure 15.9. Computer division by trial-and-error method.

1      $AC, MQ \leftarrow AC[1{:}17], MQ, 0; MC \leftarrow 5 \top 0.$

Step 2 examines the result of a trial subtraction. Note that we have to make a subtraction in any case; but the subtraction is "completed," in the sense of entering the result into *AC*, only if the difference is positive, that is, the divisor "fits" into the partial remainder. Note that the subtraction is accomplished by using the logical (one's) complement of *MD* and injecting a 1 on the input-carry line.

2      $\rightarrow (\text{ADD}[0](AC; \overline{MD};\ 1))/(5).$

Step 3 enters the difference into *AC*, and step 4 shifts *AC, MQ*, entering a 1 into *MQ*. These two steps can be combined, but we have shown them separate for clarity. At step 5, if the subtraction did not work, *AC, MQ* is shifted, with a 0 entered in *MQ*.

3    $AC \leftarrow ADD[1:18](AC; \overline{MD}; 1)$.
4    $AC, MQ \leftarrow AC[1:17], MQ, 1$.
     $\rightarrow$ (6).
5    $AC, MQ \leftarrow AC[1:17], MQ, 0$.

Step 6 increments the multiplication counter, MC, which we assume was set to 0 at the start; step 7 checks to see if the division is complete. At the finish, the quotient is in MQ and the remainder in AC. The designer may add a step to switch their positions if it is desired that all arithmetic operations terminate with the answer in AC. In this discussion, we have considered only positive operands. We shall leave it as an exercise for you to devise procedures for handling negative operands.

6    $MC \leftarrow INC(MC)$.
7    $\rightarrow (MC[0] \wedge MC[4])/(2)$.
8   EXIT

As we mentioned earlier, it is relatively difficult to increase the speed of division significantly, but we might indicate the general nature of a few techniques that have been used. One technique is known as *nonperforming* division. The basic idea is to find some faster method of comparing the magnitudes of two numbers than subtracting them. One possibility is to use some type of carry-completion adder, in which a change in the sign of the difference can be detected in less time than it takes to complete the subtraction; or one might provide a combinational circuit for comparing the magnitudes of two numbers. With the increasing availability of large-scale integrated circuits, this last approach may be the most attractive.

The concept of shifting over 0's can be applied to division, but practical application requires that the divisor be normalized. For example, if the divisor is 0.1xxxxxxxxx and the dividend is 0.00001xxx, we can see that four shifts will be required before a subtraction can possibly be successful. Thus we can shift four places and enter four 0's in the quotient before trying a subtraction. On the other hand, if there were leading 0's in the divisor, it would be more difficult to determine how many shifts should be made.

Shifting over 1's and other multibit techniques, analogous to those used in multiplication, are possible; but they are so complex that their practicality is questionable. The interested reader is referred to Flores [1] for a full discussion.

15.7 Summary

Our goal in this chapter has been to suggest some of the problems and options available in the implementation of multiplication and division. We have not attempted to provide all the information that may be required to make a design decision. You will, we hope, have gained sufficient insight to consider in more detail the various aspects of multiplication and division as the need arises. As before, we have used AHPL as much as possible so that you will retain the confidence that you can fill in the details of a hardware realization in a straightforward way.

We have restricted ourselves to fixed-point arithmetic. Floating point is the topic of the next chapter. As we shall see, however, most of the material of this chapter is applicable to floating point. It is only necessary to add a few registers for handling the exponents and some additional control logic.

Problems

15.1 Suppose that a special-purpose computer is to be designed that will be called on frequently to compute x^3 in fixed point. The number x may be positive or two's-complement. Write an AHPl routine for accomplishing this operation. The sign should be developed directly as part of the multiplication operation, as discussed in Section 15.1. Assume an 18-bit word length.

15.2 Rewrite the carry-save routine of Section 15.2 to allow for two's-complement multipliers and multiplicands.

15.3 Improve the AHPL routine of Section 15.2 by adding a hardware capability to detect strings of 0's in the multiplier and providing for a multiple shift of that number of bits in AC.

15.4 Refer to the time for bit-by-bit multiplication with carry-save given in Fig. 15.6. Develop a similar expression valid where the capability for shifting over unlimited strings of 0's is provided. Assume that only one clock period is required to shift over a string. Suppose that the hardware could not detect strings longer than 5 bits. How would this affect your expression?

15.5 Compile a table similar to Fig. 15.5 for bit-quadruplet multiplication. How many multiple multiplier registers would you recommend? What would be the average number of bits handled in a cycle by this scheme?

15.6 Develop an expression for the multiplication time of a multiplier using bit-triplets without carry-save.

15.7 Modify the AHPL routine for elementary division in Section 15.6 to allow for negative arguments.

15.8 Write an AHPL routine for division that allows for shifting over strings of 0's. Assume that both divisor and dividend are positive.

References

1. I. Flores, *The Logic of Computer Arithmetic,* Prentice–Hall, Englewood Cliffs, N.J., 1963.
2. Y. Chu, *Digital Computer Design Fundamentals,* McGraw–Hill, New York, 1962.
3. A. Habibi and P. A. Wintz, "Fast Multipliers," *IEEETEC,* Vol. C-19, Feb. 1970, pp. 153–157.
4. S. D. Pezaris, "A 40-ns 17-Bit by 17-Bit Array Multiplier," *IEEETEC,* Vol. C-20, April 1971, pp. 442–448.
5. E. L. Braun, *Digital Computer Design,* Academic Press, New York, 1963.
6. H. Ling, "High-Speed Computer Multiplication Using a Multiple-Bit Decoding Algorithm," *IEEETEC,* Vol. C-19, Aug. 1970, pp. 706–710.
7. J. K. Iliffe, *Advanced Computer Design,* Prentice–Hall, Englewood Cliffs, N.J., 1982.
8. G. Wolrich, et al., "A High Performance Floating Point Coprocessor," *IEEE Journal on Solid State Circuits,* October 1984, pp. 690–696.
9. J. C. Kalb, et al., "The Microvax II System," *Digital Technical Journal,* No. 2, March 1986.

16 Floating-Point Arithmetic

16.1 Introduction

Floating-point notation is the computer equivalent of the familiar scientific notation. For example, rather than write the speed of light as

$$300,000,000 \text{ m/sec}$$

we generally write

$$3 \times 10^8 \text{ m/sec}$$

or the FORTRAN equivalent

$$3.0E08$$

Virtually all high-level programming languages provide for this type of notation, and provision for handling numbers in this form can be included either in the software (the compiler) or in the hardware. We are concerned in this chapter with the hardware procedures for handling numbers in this form.

All our discussions of computer arithmetic up to now have assumed *fixed-point* operation.[1] The radix (decimal or binary) point is not physically present in a computer register, but its assumed position clearly must be known. When we add two numbers together, such as

---

[1]This should not be confused with the *fixed format* (F format) of FORTRAN, which concerns only the form of the numbers for input-output.

$$36.81$$

$$+\,1.041$$

$$37.851$$

the decimal points must be aligned, whatever the length of the numbers. When we add the contents of two registers, the corresponding bit positions are combined; therefore, we must assume the same position for the radix point in both registers for the results to have any meaning.

A common practice in computers is to assume the radix point immediately to the left of the most significant digit, as was done for the division process in Chapter 15. The chief reason for this practice is to preserve alignment of the radix point in multiplication and division. For example, consider multiplication in a computer with three-digit decimal registers. Multiplication inherently produces a double-length product;

$$0.361$$

$$\times\,0.483$$

$$0.174363$$

but because our registers are only three digits, we can retain only the three most significant digits. We note that the decimal point in the product is in the correct position, to the left of the msd. With any other position of the decimal point in the multiplier and multiplicand, the decimal point of the product would be in the wrong position.

Not all numbers are fractions, so how can we use a fixed-point computer? The answer is that, at input, each number must have a scale factor assigned to it to convert it to a fraction. Thus 531 will have a scale factor of 1000 assigned and will enter the machine at 0.531 in one word, with the scale factor of 1000 in another word. Each time numbers are to be arithmetically processed, the software must compare the scale factors to determine how the numbers are to be combined and to determine the scale factor of the result. All this manipulation exacts a significant price in the speed of operation, as a single scaled addition, for example, will require many steps, rather than the execution of a single ADD command.

In a machine with *floating-point* capability, numbers will have to be similarly converted on input to a form of a fraction times an exponent, but the result will be stored as a single floating-point word and the adjustments of exponents (scale factors) during arithmetic operations will be automatically handled by the hardware. The net results are basically the same, but the speed of execution is greatly increased, typically by several orders of magnitude. The extra hardware naturally increases the cost of the machine, but the increased execution speed usually justifies the extra cost. Floating point is virtually standard on mainframe computers and is available as an option in all but the smallest computers. Even 16-bit micros often offer a floating-point option.

Another important reason for floating point is the increased range of the computer. Consider a fixed-point computer with 32-bit word length. With 1 bit reserved for the sign, the range of numbers that can be represented is $\pm 2^{31}$, which is approximately $\pm 2 \times 10^9$. Although this seems very large, there are many classes of problems for which it is inadequate. For example, in electronic circuit problems we frequently deal with resistance in megohms (10^6) and capacitance in picofarads (10^{-12}), a range of values of 10^{18}, too large for a 32-bit fixed-point machine.

In floating point, each data word A is divided into two parts, the *significand* and the *exponent*. If A stores a positive floating-point variable *a,* then *a* is given by

$$a = \perp AS \times 2^{\perp AE}$$

where AS and AE are the significand and exponent, respectively. In a typical 32-bit machine, the significand might be 24 bits including sign, and the exponent 8 bits. Now the range of numbers that can be represented is

$$\pm 2^{23} \times 2^{2^8} = \pm 2^{23} \times 2^{256} \approx \pm 10^{88}$$

The increase in range has a cost in accuracy, since we have lost 8 bits of precision, or about two decimal digits. However, 23 bits still provide about 7 decimal digits of accuracy, adequate for most problems. In addition, most machines with floating-point arithmetic also provide fixed-point arithmetic for greater accuracy and may also provide double-precision arithmetic for even greater accuracy.

16.2 Notation and Format

If we are to design a floating-point system, the first step is to specify the format. How many bits will be used for exponent and significand, and how will they be arranged in the floating-point word? Until about 1980, there were no standards at all in this area. Every manufacturer of floating-point hardware had a different format, each claiming special advantages over every other format. This lack of standardization had relatively little impact on users, since floating-point hardware was available only in large mainframe computers, which invariably came with proprietary software supplied by the manufacturer. The user saw the computer only through this software, so the details of internal organization were of little importance. The advent of the microprocessor has changed the whole situation. More and more, computers are built by firms that supply hardware only, and the software is supplied by independent companies whose success is often dependent on writing truly portable software that will run on a variety of machines from different manufacturers.

The demand for portable software has in turn led to a demand for standardization on certain hardware features. It became evident that standards for computer arithmetic were needed, so a working group was formed in 1978 under the sponsorship of the IEEE Computer Society to develop such standards. The membership of this working group included representatives of virtually every major software and hardware firm in the United States as well as several major universities. The result of their efforts is IEEE Standard 754 for Binary Floating Point Arithmetic. This standard represents more than 5 years of effort and a good deal of controversy. There is no room here to recount the various arguments pro and con with regard to various aspects of the standard. The interested reader is encouraged to consult the references cited at the end of the chapter. It is enough to note that the standard has been widely and rapidly adopted throughout the industry. The standard is very complex, and we do not have the space here to treat it completely, but everything we discuss in this chapter will be consistent with this standard.

The IEEE standard specifies two standard word lengths, single-precision 32 bits and double-precision 64 bits. We will consider only the 32-bit word length; the 64-bit length involves no new concepts, just more bits for greater precision and range. The floating-point word is divided into three sections, as specified in the standard.

2.2. Binary floating-point number. A bit-string characterized by three components, a sign, a signed exponent, and a significand. Its numerical value, if any, is the signed product of its significand and 2 raised to the power of the exponent.

This statement is not sufficient to define a unique floating-point representation of a given number since nothing has been said about the location of the binary point. For example (in decimal)

$$4.61 \times 10^2 = 0.461 \times 10^3 = 0.0461 \times 10^4$$

These three forms all represent the same number, but all have different significands and exponents. To eliminate this ambiguity, the IEEE standard specifies that significands will be in a form analogous to the leftmost form just presented, with 1 bit to the left of the binary point.

2.5. Significand. That component of a binary floating-point number which consists of an explicit or implicit leading bit to the left of its binary point and a fraction field to the right of the binary point.

Except for two special cases to be considered later, the leading bit to the left of the binary point will always be 1, that is, the significand will be of the form

$$1.fffff \ldots fffff$$

where the "f's" represent the *fraction* portion of the significand. Since the leading bit is always 1, there is no need to include it when floating-point words are transmitted from one module to another in the computer system. The standard form for floating-point words for transmission within a system will be as shown in Fig. 16.1. The sign will be represented by a single bit in the usual manner, the exponent will have 8 bits, and the fraction will have 23 bits, with the leading 1-bit being implied. When the

Figure 16.1. Standard floating-point format.

floating-point word is processed within the ALU, the fraction will be converted to the actual significand by adding the leading bit.

The separation of the fraction and its sign may seem awkward, but this arrangement offers several advantages. First, the leading bit is usually the sign bit and hardware is often set up for special manipulation of this bit in sign determination. Similarly, the rightmost bit position is set up for receiving the input carry for complement arithmetic. Third, in terms of the overall magnitude, the exponent is more significant than the fraction, so that placing the exponent to the left of the fraction facilitates magnitude comparisons by the same algorithms as for fixed-point numbers.

Next consider the matter of exponent representation. Since both positive and negative exponents must be represented, the most obvious choice would be to use standard 2's complement notation, with the exponent sign in the bit-1 position. Although this may seem obvious, the handling of signed numbers in the exponent creates some problems, and the IEEE standard uses *biased exponent* notation, in which a positive constant is added to each exponent as the floating-point word is formed, so that internally all exponents are positive. With the 8-bit exponent, 2^7 is added to each exponent, so that exponents range (in hex) from 00 to FF, with 10 corresponding to a true exponent value of 0. There are at least two major reasons for the use of biased exponents. One is that the absence of negative exponents may provide some simplification in exponent arithmetic.

The second factor relates to the manner in which 0 is represented in floating-point format. Formally, 0 times anything is 0, so that the exponent associated with a 0 significand is apparently arbitrary. However, with the convention stated, that there is always an implied leading bit of 1, there is no such thing as a 0 significand. To solve this difficulty, the IEEE standard specifies that 0 shall be assigned the smallest possible exponent, that is, 00 (hex) along with a 0 fraction. Whenever both the exponent and the fraction are all 0's, the implied significand bit is assumed to be 0, so that 0 has the same representation in floating point as in fixed-point numbers, all 0's. This is one of the exceptions mentioned earlier to the rule that the implied leading significand bit is always 1.

There are some other problems related to the means of representing certain special cases. One of these is overflow. As we have discussed earlier, overflow occurs when the result of a computation produces a result too large to be represented in the machine. Even with floating point, this can occur. For example, if we multiply two numbers with exponents of $+120$, the result will be a product exponent of $+240$, too large to be represented with an 8-bit exponent. Another special case is division by 0, resulting in infinity as the result. Yet another special case is an undefined operation, such as division 0/0 or multiplication $0 \times \infty$. The situations are quite different. If a result occurs that is defined but just too large to be represented, the situation can be dealt with by software scaling of the operands, but no amount of scaling can deal with an infinite or undefined result. Thus, a means must be provided to differentiate between these situations. In the IEEE standard, an overflow will result in setting the *eof* (exponent overflow) flag. The other two cases are indicated by the largest possible exponent (FF in hex). If the exponent = FF and the fraction is nonzero, an undefined operation was attempted. Such a result is symbolized by NaN (not a number). If the exponent $=$ FF and the fraction is 0, the result is infinity (symbolized in the standard by ∞).

Another special problem in floating-point systems is *underflow*—results too small to be represented in the system notation. This can occur in fixed-point systems, but it is usually dealt with by round off. For example, suppose we have a decimal system of only three digits accuracy and we wish to perform the multiplication

$$0.002 \times 0.003 = 0.000006$$

When this answer is rounded off to three digits, the answer is clearly 0, unless we have floating point. Then the process produces the result

$$2.00 \times 10^{-3} \times 3.00 \times 10^{-3} = 6.00 \times 10^{-6}$$

unless the product exponent is less than the minimum possible in the floating-point system. In that case, we have underflow.

The seemingly obvious solution is the same as suggested for fixed-point systems, when underflow occurs, set the result to 0. For reasons that would require another chapter to explain (see Ref. 3), this is not an entirely acceptable solution. Since the exponent 00 (hex) has been set aside to represent 0, the smallest "legal" exponent is 01, corresponding to a power of -126. However, the IEEE standard provides for *gradual underflow*, in which numbers in the range between 2^{-126} and 2^{-127} will be represented by an exponent of 00 with a nonzero fraction, the leading implied bit being assumed to be 0. Numbers in this form are referred to as *denormalized* in contrast to numbers with the usual implied leading bit of 1, which are considered *normalized*. Results less than 2^{-127} but greater than 0 will be indicated by setting the result to 0 and setting the underflow flag, *euf.* Complicated? Yes, very, but floating-point arithmetic is complicated. When considering only a single computation, all these fine points may seem unimportant. But we have to realize that computers often perform thousands, even millions, of cumulative calculations and errors that may be individually insignificant but that can accumulate to produce meaningless results. The preceding discussion can be summarized in Fig. 16.2, showing the significance of various forms in the IEEE floating-point system. You should note line "3" of this figure very carefully. This states that significands in floating-point notation are in signed-magnitude form, not 2's complement. This fact must be considered most carefully as we design the arithmetic processing unit.

Let X be a 32-bit floating-point number divided into three components: s, a 1-bit sign; e an 8-bit exponent; f, a 23-bit fraction. Then the value v of X is defined as follows.

1. If $e =$ FF and $f \neq 0$, then $v =$ NaN.
2. If $e =$ FF and $f = 0$, then $v = \infty$.
3. If $0 < e <$ FF, then $v = (-1)^s \, 2^{e-127} \, (1,f)$
4. If $e = 0$ and $f \neq 0$, then $v = (-1)^s \, 2^{-126} \, (0,f)$
5. If $e = 0$ and $f = 0$, then $v = 0$.

Figure 16.2. Numeric significance of floating-point representations.

16.3   Floating-Point Addition and Subtraction

In this section, we shall develop an AHPL routine for handling floating-point addition and subtraction. The emphasis will be on presenting an understandable treatment of the arithmetic operations without worrying about details of the hardware configuration. The existence of necessary registers, data paths, and combinational logic circuits will be assumed. In the last section of the chapter, a specific hardware configuration will be developed. In these analyses, the two input operands will be *A* and *B,* and the result will be *C.* It will be assumed that the numbers will be converted to extended form on entry to the floating-point unit; that is, the fraction will be converted to the significand by catenating the leading 1 bit, unless the exponent is 00, in which case the leading bit will be 0. Thus, within the floating-point unit, the operand *A* will be made up of the catenation of its three components,

$$A \;=\; as,AE,AS,$$

the 1-bit sign, *as,* the 8-bit exponent, *AE,* and the 24-bit significand, *AS.*

For addition and subtraction, the exponents must be equal before the significands can be added or subtracted. For example if $A = 1.111010 \times 2^7$ and $B = 1.101010 \times 2^5$, then *B* must be converted to 0.011010×2^7 before the significands can be combined. Thus, the first steps are to compare the exponents and shift the significand having the smaller exponent right a number of places equal to the difference between the exponents.

Note that significant digits will be lost from the number shifted; and if the difference between exponents is equal to or larger than the number of digits in the significand, the smaller number will be shifted right out. In the example here, if $B = 1.101010 \times 2^0$, then after shifting to equalize exponents, $B = 0.000000 \times 2^7$. Thus, if the difference between exponents is equal to or larger than the number of digits in the significand, the answer is taken as equal to the larger operand.

After exponent equalization, the significands are added or subtracted in the usual fashion. If the result is negative, it is complemented to restore it to the signed-magnitude form. If the result overflows, the result significand is shifted one place right and the exponent is increased by one. If the result exponent is $+127$, the overflow flag is set.

If there is no significand overflow, a check is made to see if the result is normalized. If not, the result is shifted left until a nonzero digit appears in the msd position, decreasing the result exponent by one for each shift. In the event of an all-zero result, the postnormalization step should be skipped. After normalization, a check for underflow is required.

The complete flowchart for the process is shown in Fig. 16.3. At step 1 we compare the exponents using the CMPR function, where CMPR[0] = 1 if *AE* > *BE,* CMPR[1] = 1 if *AE* = *BE,* and CMPR[2] = 1 if *AE* < *BE.* For *AE* > *BE,* step 2 subtracts *BE* from *AE.* Step 3 then checks to see if the difference is greater than or equal to 24, the number of bits in the significand, in which case step 4 sets the result equal to *A.*

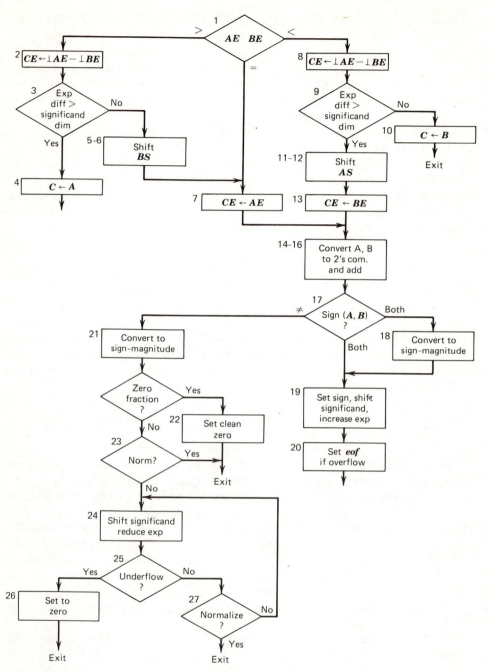

Figure 16.3. Flowchart of floating-point addition and subtraction.

1    $\rightarrow$ (CMPR(**AE;BE**))/(2, 7, 8).
2   **CE** $\leftarrow$ ADD[1:8](**AE;$\overline{BE}$**; 1).
3    $\rightarrow$ (CMPR(**AE**; 8 $\top$ 24))/(4,4,5).
4   **C** $\leftarrow$ **A;**
     $\rightarrow$ (28).
5   **BS** $\leftarrow$ 0,**BS**[1:22]; **CE** $\leftarrow$ DEC(**CE**).
6    $\rightarrow$ ($\vee$/**CE**)/(5).
7   **CE** $\leftarrow$ **AE;**
     $\rightarrow$ (14).

Next, the significand **BS,** corresponding to the smaller exponent, is shifted right at step 5 and the exponent difference is decremented for each shift. Step 6 checks to determine if the exponent difference has been reduced to zero, looping back to step 5 if it has not. When the shifting is complete, step 7 sets the sum exponent equal to the larger operand exponent. Step 1 also branches to step 7 for the case of zero exponent difference, since the result exponent is equal to either **AE** or **BE** for that case.

For the case where **BE** is larger than **AE,** step 8 subtracts **AE** from **BE,** and steps 9 through 13 repeat the function of steps 2 through 7, for the case in which **BE** is the larger exponent.

8   **CE** $\leftarrow$ ADD[1:8]($\overline{AE}$; **BE;** 1).
9    $\rightarrow$ (CMPR(**BE;**8 $\top$ 24)/(10,10,11).
10   **C** $\leftarrow$ **B;**
     $\rightarrow$ (28).
11   **AS** $\leftarrow$ 0, **AS**[0:22]; **CE** $\leftarrow$ DEC(**CE**).
12   $\rightarrow$ ($\vee$/**CE**)/(11).
13   **CE** $\leftarrow$ **BE.**

If the exponent difference is less than 24, the significands must be added or subtracted. It is assumed that a flag *subf* was set during the instruction decode phase if the operation is subtraction. Since both addition and subtraction must be accommodated, the use of 2's complement arithmetic is appropriate, which will require conversion of operands from signed-magnitude to 2's complement form. For either addition or subtraction, a negative *A* operand (an addend or the minuend) is converted to 2's complement form by complementing the significand, in step 14. For addition, the second operand is similarly complemented if it is negative. For the subtrahend in subtraction, it is not just a matter of changing notations, the number must be negated. For a negative number, all that is needed is to change the sign bit; for a positive number, both the sign bit and the significand must be complemented. All adjustments to the *B* operand are accomplished in step 15.

At step 16, the significands are added, with *cfp* denoting the carry flag that receives the output carry from the 25-bit adder, after which we check for overflow. With the significand representation used, addition of like-signed numbers will always result in significand overflow. Two numbers of the form 1.xxx . . . xx are being added, so the sum bits to the left of the binary point have to be 10 or 11; that is, there will always be an overflow of one bit. Step 17 checks the signs, branching to step 20 for unlike signs, to 19 for two positive operands, and to 18 for two negative operands. Step 18 converts the negative sum back to signed magnitude form, and step 19 shifts the result-significand one place right and increments the sum exponent. Step 20 sets the *eof* flag if the incremented result exponent is $+127$, and exits.

14     $AS * as \leftarrow \text{ADD}[1{:}23](\overline{AS}; 0; 1).$

15     $BS * (bs \oplus subf) \leftarrow \text{ADD}[1{:}23](\overline{BS}; 0; 1);$
       $bs * subf \leftarrow bs.$

16     $cfp,cs,CS \leftarrow \text{ADD}((as,AS);(bs,BS)).$

17     $\rightarrow (as \oplus bs,\ as \wedge bs,\ \overline{as} \wedge \overline{bs})/(20,18,19).$

18     $cs,CS \leftarrow \text{ADD}[1{:}24](\overline{cs},\overline{CS}; 0\ ;1).$

19     $cs,CS \leftarrow cfp,cs,CS[0{:}22];\ CE \leftarrow \text{INC}(CE).$

20     $euf * (\wedge/CE) \leftarrow 1;$
       $\rightarrow (28).$

At step 21, a negative answer is converted back to signed magnitude form. If the result fraction is zero, step 22 sets CE to zero to provide the correct representation for a zero result and exits. Step 23 checks to see if the answer is already normalized and exits in that case.

Step 24 starts the normalizing sequence by shifting the significand one place left and decrementing the result exponent. Step 25 checks for zero exponent, indicating underflow, in which event step 26 sets the result to zero, sets the underflow flag, and exits. Step 27 checks to determine if the significand is normalized, returning to step 24 if it is not, and exiting if it is.

21     $CS * cs \leftarrow \text{ADD}(\overline{CS}; 0\ ; 1).$

22     $CE * (\overline{\vee/CS[1{:}23]}) \leftarrow 8 \top 0;$
       $\rightarrow (\vee/CS[1{:}23])/(28).$

23     $\rightarrow (CS[0])/(28).$

24     $CS \leftarrow CS[0{:}22],0;\ CE \leftarrow \text{DEC}(CE).$

25     $\rightarrow (\vee/CE)/(27).$

26     $CS \leftarrow 24 \top 0;$
       $\rightarrow (28).$

27     $\rightarrow (\overline{CS[0]})/(24).$

28   exit to convert result to truncated form for transmission.

This sequence completely implements floating-point addition and subtraction in accordance with the IEEE standard except that gradual underflow has not been included. This will be left as an exercise for the reader.

16.4   Floating-Point Multiplication and Division

For floating-point multiplication, we add the exponents and multiply the significands. The significand multiplication may be done by any of the methods discussed in the previous chapter, and thus may be fairly simple or quite complex. In other respects, the signed magnitude format of the significands tends to simplify multiplication, as there is no need to complement operands.

A flowchart for floating multiplication is shown in Fig. 16.4. Step 1 checks for either operand equal to zero and sets the product to zero in that case at step 2.

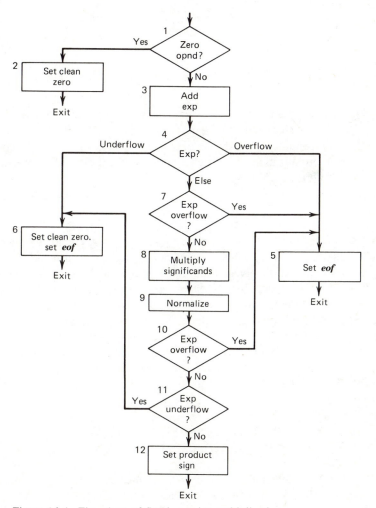

Figure 16.4. Flowchart of floating-point multiplication.

1     $\rightarrow ((\vee/AS) \wedge (\vee/BS))/C3).$

2     $C \leftarrow 32 \top 0;$

      $\rightarrow (13).$

Step 3 adds the exponents, and step 4 checks for overflow or underflow. We shall leave it to you to verify that exponent overflow (result exponent greater than $+127$) is indicated by $cs = CE[0] = 1$, and exponent underflow (result exponent less than -127) is indicated by $cs = CE[0] = 0$. In the event of overflow, step 5 sets the overflow flag, *eof,* and exits. In the event of underflow, step 6 sets C to all 0's and *euf* to 1.

3     $cs,CE \leftarrow \text{ADD}(AE; BE; 0).$

4     $\rightarrow (cs \wedge CE[0], \overline{cs} \wedge \overline{CE[0]}, cs \oplus CE[0])/(5,6,7).$

5     $eof \leftarrow 1;$

      $\rightarrow (13).$

6     $C \leftarrow 32 \top 0; euf \leftarrow 1;$

      $\rightarrow (13).$

If the sequence has reached this point, the result exponent is in the range $+127$ to -127. Recall that an exponent of $+127$ is overflow in the IEEE notation, so step 7 checks for this condition. We do not, however, check for the -127 condition at this time, since normalization after significand multiplication could move the product exponent back into the legal range.

7     $\rightarrow (\wedge/CE)/(5).$

Step 8 carries out the significand multiplication using techniques such as those discussed in the last chapter, which we indicate by a functional notation, although a lengthy sequence may be involved. Multiplication normally produces a double-length result, 48 bits for 24-bit significands. Step 8 saves only 25 bits of the product, with *cs* used temporarily to hold the twenty-fifth bit of the product, to preserve significance in the event of normalization. Since the operands are in the form 1.xx . . . xx, the product will be in the form xx.xx . . . . xx. If the two digits to the left of the binary point are 11 or 10, we normalize by taking the upper 24 bits as the product significand and incrementing the produce exponent, effectively shifting the significand one place right. If the digits to the left of the exponent are 01, we simply discard the leading 0 of the significand.

8     $CS,cs \leftarrow \text{MULT}[1:24](AS; BS).$

9     $CE * CS[0] \leftarrow \text{INC}(CE); CS * CS[0] \leftarrow CS[1:23],cs.$

Step 10 makes another check for overflow, since the exponent increment at step 9 might increase the exponent to $+127$. In a similar manner, step 11 checks for underflow, indicated if the exponent is a -127. Finally, assuming everything is in order, step 12 sets the product sign.

10     $\rightarrow (\wedge/CE)/(5)$.
11     $\rightarrow (\vee/CE)/(6)$.
12     $cs \leftarrow as \oplus bs$.
13   exit to develop output with truncated significand

Division is very similar. The exponents are subtracted and the significands divided. A zero divisor leads to an ∞ overflow, a zero dividend to a zero quotient. We shall leave the writing of a sequence for floating-point division as an exercise for you.

16.5 Hardware Organization for Floating-Point Arithmetic

In the previous sections, the exact hardware configurations were not specified. Separate registers were assumed for all operands and results, and no separate MQ register was specified for multiplication. In practice, the register layout for floating-point operations is generally quite similar to that for fixed-point operations in the same machine.

In view of the complexity of the floating-point processes, it is hardly surprising that there are many different hardware implementations, even though all may adhere to the IEEE standards. In large mainframe machines, where floating point is usually standard, an integrated ALU for both fixed-point and floating-point operations is the usual arrangement. As a general rule, the same registers and the ALU used for fixed-point or integer arithmetic will also be used for significand arithmetic, while separate registers and logic will be provided for exponent arithmetic. Such an arrangement will require that floating-point words be split up, or *unpacked,* with one portion of each word going to the significand section, the other to the exponent section.

A very common arrangement in smaller systems, particularly those based on microprocessors, is to provide a separate *coprocessor* to carry out the more complex arithmetic operations. The primary reason for such arrangements is not that there is any inherent logical advantage, but simply the fact that there are very real limits to the complexity of a processor that can be realized on a single VLSI chip. In such realizations, arithmetic operations on the primary CPU chip will usually be limited to integer addition and subtraction. More complex operations, such as multiplication and division and floating-point arithmetic, will be provided by programming in the system software. Such an approach, while entirely workable, does exact a severe penalty in operating speed. To avoid this speed penalty, most microprocessor families include arithmetic coprocessors that implement the more complex arithmetic processes in hardware, eliminating the need for complex software implementation of these processes. The net result in most cases is a dramatic increase in processing speed, usually well worth the extra cost.

An arithmetic coprocessor is basically a separate CPU on the system bus, with its own registers, logic, and control unit, capable of receiving data and a limited subset of the system instruction set from the primary CPU and returning results. It is not capable of operating independently of the primary CPU, which is responsible for fetching instructions and determining which should be sent to the arithmetic coprocessor.

Figure 16.5 shows the internal organization of an arithmetic coprocessor in which multiplication and division are accomplished by the conventional add-and-shift techniques using an **AC-MQ** pair. The exponent I/O register provides a bidirectional path between the system data bus and the exponent processing unit for the exponent portions of the floating-point words, **DBUS**[1:8]. Similarly, the significand I/O register provides a 24-bit path for the sign bits and fraction portions of the floating-point words, **DBUS**[0],**DBUS**[9:31]. The exponent ALU section includes the ADD function, INC and DEC, and CMPR functions, and logic for detecting special conditions, such as minimum or maximum exponents. The significand ALU includes ADD and various logic functions for sign processing and detection of special conditions. The shift logic could be included in the ALU, but has been shown separately to emphasize the importance of shifting in normalization and the multiplication and division operations.

Figure 16.5 shows only the registers, logic, and data paths directly involved in operand processing. The arithmetic unit would also include a control unit, a register to receive instructions from the primary CPU, and various status flags, such as *euf* and *eof.*

It should be emphasized that the separation of floating-point processing hardware into a separate module has no inherent advantages. It is an approach used only when technologic limitations make it impossible to incorporate all the processing functions into a single module. The separation of functions into a separate coprocessor module

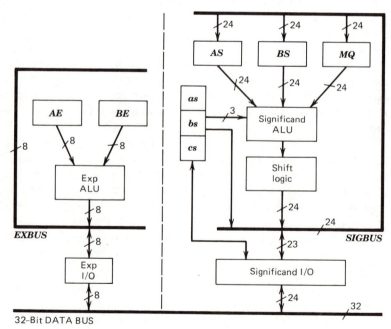

Figure 16.5. Basic block diagram of floating-point coprocessor.

introduces all the intermodule signalling problems discussed in Chapters 9 and 10, requiring signal protocols and delays to allow for signal propagation, all of which take time. For example, in the 78132 arithmetic coprocessor for the DEC Micro-Vax II system, floating-point add requires 1.8 μsec, of which 1.1 μsec is required for signalling protocols, only 0.7 μsec for the actual addition. It is safe to assume that separate arithmetic coprocessors will disappear as soon as the technology makes it possible to incorporate the various functions into a single integrated CPU chip.

Problems

16.1 The sequence for floating-point addition in Section 16.3 does not include provision for gradual underflow as specified by the IEEE standard. Modify the sequence as required to incorporate gradual underflow.

16.2 Modify the multiply sequence of Section 16.4 to incorporate the basic add-and-shift multiply algorithm of Chapter 6, assuming the hardware configuration of Fig. 16.5.

16.3 The multiply sequence of Section 16.4 incorporates neither the gradual underflow nor the undefined operation (NaN) provisions of the IEEE standard. Assuming the only undefined operation for multiplication is 0 × ∞, modify the sequence of Section 16.4 to incorporate these features of the IEEE standard.

16.4 In Section 16.4, it is stated that exponent overflow will be indicated by $cs = CE[0] = 1$ and that exponent underflow will be indicated by $cs = CE[0] = 0$. Show that this is true.

16.5 Write a sequence for floating-point division, representing the actual division algorithm by a combinational logic notation, as was done for multiplication in Section 16.4. Include provision for gradual underflow, infinite result of division by 0, and undefined operation for 0/0 or ∞/∞.

References

1. D. Stevenson, et al., "A Proposed Standard for Binary Floating-Point Arithmetic," *Computer*, Vol. 14, No. 3, March 1981, pp. 51–62.
2. W. J. Cody, "Analysis of Proposals for the Floating-Point Standard," *Computer*, Vol. 14, No. 3, March 1981.
3. J. T. Coonen, "Underflow and Demoralized Numbers," *Computer*, Vol. 14, No. 3, March 1981, pp. 63–68.
4. J. T. Coonen, "An Implementation Guide to a Proposed Standard for Floating-Point Arithmetic," *Computer*, Vol. 13, No. 1, Jan. 1980, pp. 75–87.

5. W. R. Bidermann, et al., "The MicroVAX 78132 Floating Point Chip," *Digital Technical Journal,* No. 2, March 1986, pp. 24–36.

6. G. Wolrich, et al., "A High Performance Floating Point Coprocessor," *IEEE J. of Solid State Circuits,* Vol. SC-19, No. 5, Oct. 1984, pp. 690–696.

7. I. Flores, *The Logic of Computer Arithmetic,* Prentice–Hall, Englewood Cliff, N.J., 1963, Chaps. 15, 16.

8. K. Hwang, *Computer Arithmetic,* Wiley, New York, 1979, Chaps. 9, 10.

17 Increasing CPU Capability

17.1   Introduction

In Chapter 13, we introduced the concept of throughput. We saw in that chapter that throughput could be improved by organizing the main memory and supplementary memories so as to minimize the time used up in retrieving data and instructions from memory. Throughput is also a function of the speed in which operations can be accomplished within the CPU. The speed of all computer functions can be increased by increasing component speed. In Chapters 14, 15, and 16, we saw that the speed of arithmetic operations could be increased up to a point by using more complex logic. Component speeds are limited by the state of the art, and a point of diminishing returns is always reached in speeding up individual arithmetic operations. In this chapter, we shall be concerned with further increasing computer throughput by organizational innovation.

In Sections 17.2 and 17.3, we shall investigate organizational innovations aimed at increasing the number of computations per unit time that can be performed by a central processor. In general, we shall try to organize machines so that more than one computation can be accomplished simultaneously or in parallel. We shall find that it is impossible to separate computation and data movement, thus, there will be considerable interrelation between this chapter and Chapter 13.

Section 17.4 will introduce the reduced instruction set, "RISC," concept. The chapter concludes with a descriptive section on large special-purpose computer organizations. These machines operate very efficiently on a particular class of complex computational problems.

573

17.2   Instruction Look-Ahead

The savings achieved by minimizing the number of storage references during instruction execution can never seem quite satisfying as long as a reference to memory is required by the fetch phase of each instruction. If a scratch-pad memory is not used, one might attempt to reduce the number of fetch cycles that require reference to the main RAM by allowing short sequences of instructions to be stored in high-speed electronic registers. If the number of *look-ahead* registers is sufficiently large, short loops in the program can be traversed entirely within the look-ahead unit. If a cache memory with an access time equivalent to the look-ahead registers is used, the same saving may be achieved by looping with the cache memory. This assumes block transfers into the cache. As the buffer memory may in some cases be quite large, the likelihood of storing a complete loop within the cache is great.

Thus, if a cache is used, a very large number of registers within the look-ahead unit would be redundant. There is further advantage in a look-ahead unit with a few registers, however. The time consumed by the memory references may be approximately cut in half by overlapping the fetch and execution phases. That is, while one instruction is being executed, the next instruction can be fetched, placed in the instruction register, and readied for execution. This approach would be particularly advantageous in places where more than one word from memory are required to form an instruction.

Rather than adding the look-ahead feature to RIC, let us consider a 32-bit machine with a 24-bit address similar to RIC but differing in the following respects. All instructions are 32-bit instructions. In addition to absolute (not branch-relative) conditional jump instructions, there are "skip" instructions, some of which simply call for the skipping of the next instruction as a function of a variety of data conditions. Another possible skip instruction could be ISZ (increment and skip if 0), which would fetch an argument from memory, increment it, replace it in memory, and then skip the next instruction if the result is 0. To simplify our treatment of look-ahead as much as possible, we postulate two functions, f and g. Both are functions of the current instruction and a complex set of data conditions. The function f will be 1 if the instruction is skip and the skip condition is satisfied. The function g is to be 1 if the condition associated with a specified conditional jump is 1. The third function JMP ("instruction") $= 1$, if the current instruction is any type of conditional jump. The only addressing modes applicable to jump instructions are direct and indirect. If the mode is indirect, $IR[7] = 1$.

Because execution of jumps and skips will result in the requirement to fetch up to three instructions simultaneously, the interleaved memory bank of Section 13.10 can be used effectively. For simplicity, let us suppose that the entire memory space is implemented in RAM. That is, each of the four banks will contain $2 \uparrow 22$ 32-bit words. Only two of the four entry points will be used. No scratch pad will be included in the design.

Given this configuration, the principal payoff of the look-ahead unit to be discussed will be simultaneous fetch and execution memory references approximately 75% of the time. On the average, 25% of the data addresses will be found in the same bank as the instruction addresses. The resulting design will be the most elementary form of a look-ahead unit, but it should serve as an introduction to some of the awkward problems that are created when look-ahead is included in a design.

Other than the memory, the only registers added to facilitate look-ahead are shown in Fig. 17.1. The instruction register *IR1* contains the instruction under execution whereas *IR2* and *IR3* are provided for the next two instructions in sequence. If at the beginning of the control sequence the special flip-flop *sh* (short) contains a 0, the registers *IR1* and *IR2* contain the next two instructions in order. If *sh* = 1, only *IR1* contains the proper instruction. These two situations are illustrated in Fig. 17.1a and 17.1b. We shall see that *sh* will be 1 following a jump or skip instruction.

The control sequence will cause the instruction in *IR1* to be executed while at the same time causing the next two instructions to be placed in *IR2* and *IR3*. The program counter will contain the address of the next instruction to be obtained from memory, whether this instruction is to be placed in *IR2* or *IR3*. The first step separates control for jump instructions. In effect, the execution of jump and determination of the next instruction are the same operation.

$$1 \quad \rightarrow (\text{JMP}(IR1) \wedge \text{g}, \text{JMP}(IR1) \wedge \bar{\text{g}}, \overline{\text{JMP}(IR1)})/(17,3,2).$$
$$2 \quad \text{NO DELAY}$$
$$\rightarrow (A3,3).$$
A3—AX Execution
$$AX + 1 \rightarrow (11).$$

Step 2 causes control to diverge to accomplish execution and fetch simultaneously. The A sequence executes all but the conditional skips at the end of the ISZ instruction and in the last event time of operate instructions. The execution sequence uses memory communications registers. *CA1* and *CD1*.

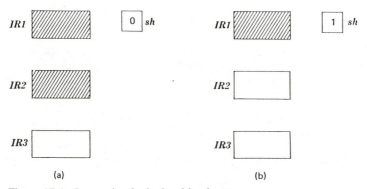

Figure 17.1. Instruction look-ahead hardware.

3      $CAO,ro \leftarrow PC$, 1;
         $\rightarrow (\overline{sh})/(9)$.
4      $PC \leftarrow$ INC(PC).
5      $\rightarrow (ro)/(5)$.
6      $CAO,ro \leftarrow PC$, 1.
7      $\rightarrow (\overline{dataready})/(7)$.
8      $IR2, wo \leftarrow CDO$, O.
9      $\rightarrow (\overline{dataready})/(9)$.
10     $IR3 \leftarrow CDO$.
11   CONVERGE (AX + 1, 10).

Step 3 provides the memory communications register with the address of the next instruction. If $sh = 0$, control branches to step 9 to wait for the remaining instruction to be retrieved. This instruction is subsequently placed in $IR3$. If $sh = 1$, the program counter is incremented and control circulates in a loop until CAO is free to accept another address. The second address is supplied at step 6. Control then waits for both instructions, placing the first in $IR2$ and the second in $IR3$. Notice that at step 8 only wo is reset to 0, since the processor does not know whether the second address has as yet been accepted by memory from CAO. There is no danger of saddling memory with a dummy read operation, however, as only one memory bank is addressed.

Control converges at step 11 to permit completion of any possible skip operation. We leave the combinational logic determining the skip operation to you. We merely use the function f, which is to be 1 if and only if any sort of skip instruction is called for *and* the skip condition is satisfied.

12     $\rightarrow (\overline{f})/(14)$.
13     $IR1,IR2,sh \leftarrow IR2,IR3$, 1;
        $\rightarrow(15)$.
14     $sh \leftarrow 0$.
15     $IR1,IR2 \leftarrow IR2,IR3$.

If $f = 1$, the instructions are advanced in the look-ahead unit at step 13 and sh is set to 1. If $f = 0$, sh is cleared to 0. At step 15, the instructions are advanced for all cases. Thus the instructions were advanced twice in the case of a skip.

16     $PC \leftarrow$ INC(PC);
        $\rightarrow(1)$.

Prior to step 16, the PC is always set at the last instruction already entered in the look-ahead unit. After PC is incremented at step 16, it contains the address of the next instruction to be obtained from memory.

Control branched at step 1 to step 17 for separate execution of the jump instructions. Indirect addressing is possible, and is provided for by steps 19, 20, and 21.

Step 22 completes the jump operation by placing the new instruction in **IR1** and setting **sh** to 1. As the address of this instruction has alredy been inserted in **PC**, the situation is the same as at step 15 following a skip instruction. This completes the discussion of the elementary look-ahead unit.

17   $CAO \leftarrow IR[8:31]$; $PC \leftarrow IR[8:31]$; $ro \leftarrow 1$.
18   $\rightarrow (\overline{dataready})/(18)$.
19   $(\overline{IR1}[7])/(22)$.
20   $CAO \leftarrow CDO[8:31]$; $PC \leftarrow CDO[8:31]$; $ro \leftarrow 1$;
21   $\rightarrow (\overline{dataready})/(21)$.
22   $IR1 \leftarrow CDO$; $sh \leftarrow 1$; $PC \leftarrow INC (PC)$;
     $\rightarrow (1)$.

If a scratch-pad memory is included in a computer, the actual execution of certain longer instructions will be more time-consuming than the instruction fetch or the data fetch operation. In this case, further advantage would be realized by overlapping the execution phases of several instructions. This approach would considerably complicate the design of the look-ahead unit. Some instructions use as arguments the result computed by the immediately previous instructions. Other sequences of instructions are independent. It would be the responsibility of the look-ahead unit to distinguish these two situations and to allow the execution of instructions only after the required arguments become available. Further complication is introduced by conditional branch instructions. These will either terminate a sequence of overlapping instructions or possibly cause partially computed results to be discarded.

The foregoing example should have made clear the fact that the design of a control sequence for even an elementary look-ahead unit is quite involved. The difficulties involved in handling jump and skip instructions were apparent. As we shall note in the next section, the handling of these instructions in a more sophisticated look-ahead unit requires a very powerful memory organization.

17.3   Execution Overlap

So far, we have limited our discussion of throughput improvement to speeding up the movement of data. If many of these innovations are included in the design of a machine, the execution of instructions by the central processor can become the bottleneck. A preferable situation would have the data movement and computation capabilities approximately matched. In this section, we begin our discussion of organizational techniques for speeding up instruction execution.

The notion of operating a computer like an assembly line with an unending series of instructions in various stages of completion has intrigued designers for many years. The instruction look-ahead problem, as discussed in the past section, and the hardware costs involved acted to keep the idea on the shelf during the early history of computing. With the advent of LSI, this concept has been reexamined and in some cases put into practice. Our goal in this section will be to define the reservation control and routing system for a computer featuring simultaneous execution of instructions. Once again, our system is only intended to suggest one possible approach. We begin by considering an example of overlap within a single *functional unit*.

Example 17.1

Design a multiplication unit capable of an average execution rate of one 18-bit multiplication per clock period, which will complete a given multiplication operation in three clock periods.

Solution

You will recall from Chapter 14 that many approaches to multiplication are possible, some requiring considerable combinational logic. We propose here a simple approach that satisfies the problem statement. No claim is made that this is a particularly efficient approach in terms of the cost of the combinational logic required. This method is illustrated in Fig. 17.2.

The multiplier is shown as composed of six strings of 3 bits each. The first step of the multiplication process computes, in parallel, six partial products by performing multiplication of each 3-bit segment times the multiplicand, *MTND*. Each product consists of 36-bits, with the significant bits of each partial product vector shifted left 3 bits (multiplied by 8) from those of the product immediately preceding. Those memory elements in the 36-bit products that always contain 0's would not be included in the actual physical implementation.

The second step of the operation will consist of adding *P1* ,*P2*, and *P3* to form *SUM1* and adding *P4*,*P5*, and *P6* to form *SUM2*. The last step consists of merely adding *SUM1* and *SUM2*. Two very fast adders are assumed, which can perform the additions in a single clock period. Note that a complete carry propagation must be provided for each step. Once again, we point out that quite likely breaking the process up in some other manner might permit a shorter carry propagation. The approach here was chosen for reasons of simplicity.

The registers required are illustrated in Fig. 17.3. The multiplier is stored in the register *MLTR*. Five control flip-flops, *c1, c2, c3, c4,* and *c5,* are included to control

| *MTND* | Multiplicand |
| *A, B, C, D, E, F* | Multiplier in 3-bit segments |

$$P1 = (36)\top(\perp MTND \times \perp F)$$
$$P2 = (36)\top(\perp MTND \times 8 \times \perp E)$$
$$P3 = (36)\top(\perp MTND \times 64 \times \perp D) \quad \text{36-bit partial products}$$
$$P4 \qquad\qquad \text{etc.}$$
$$P5$$
$$P6$$

PROD

Figure 17.2. Multiplication in six segments.

the flow of information through the multiplier. The values of **c1** and **c5** are supplied externally whereas **c2, c3,** and **c4** are under control of the multiplier control unit. Also, **c1** = 1 indicates the presence of arguments in **MTND** and **MLTR**; **c2** = 1 indicates that a set of six partial products are stored; **c3** = 1 indicates the existence of numbers in **SUM1** and **SUM2**; **c4** = 1 indicates the existence of a product in **PROD**; and **c5** = 1 indicates that the present stored product will remain in **PROD** after the next clock period.

1 $PROD * (\overline{c4 \wedge c5}) \leftarrow$ ADD(**SUM1; SUM2**);
  $(SUM1, SUM2) * (\overline{c3 \wedge c4 \wedge c5}) \leftarrow$ (ADD3(**P1; P2; P3**), ADD3(**P4; P5; P6**));
  $(P1, P2, P3, P4, P5, P6) * (\overline{c2 \wedge c3 \wedge c4 \wedge c5}) \leftarrow$ TIMES(**MTND; MLTR**);
  $c4, c3, c2 \leftarrow c3 \vee (c4 \wedge c5), c2 \vee (c3 \wedge c4 \wedge c5), c1 \vee (c2 \wedge c3 \wedge c4 \wedge c5)$;
  $\rightarrow (1)$.

The multiplication control routine consists of a single step as shown. As discussed in Chapter 7, the control unit might consist of only combinational logic connected directly to the clock. At every clock period in which arguments are entered in **MTND** and **MLTR,** a 1 is entered in **c1**. With each clock pulse, the contents of the registers at each level in Fig. 17.3 are replaced by more nearly completed results in the next lower level of registers. An exception occurs if the external reservation control indicates, by inserting a 1 in **c5**, that the result currently in **PROD** will not be removed during a given step. In this case, information will be advanced within the multiplication unit only insofar as empty registers exist within the unit. ∎

Execution overlap is facilitated by programming so that many consecutive instructions specify the same operation on different arguments. This is the assumption in the CDC STAR (see Section 17.5). Under these circumstances, execution overlap is referred to as *pipelining*. We shall find it convenient to refer to the array of registers containing arguments on which computation is in various stages of completion as *pipelines*.

Let us assume that a particular computer has only two arithmetic functional units, multiplication and division, which require more than one clock period for execution.

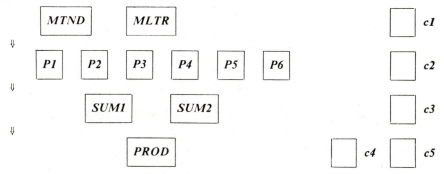

Figure 17.3. Registers for multiplication.

Execution overlap for multiplication is as discussed in the foregoing example. The division unit will accept arguments every 4 clock periods while requiring 12 clock periods to complete a given computation. Several additional logic units that require only one clock period for execution also exist within the machine.

Consider the look-ahead and reservation control unit required to manage this setup. Space will not permit complete development of this design, but we shall attempt to illustrate some of the complications involved. Let us assume that the machine under discussion has at least 10 general-purpose data registers. These are labeled a through j, as shown in Fig. 17.4a. In Fig. 17.4b, we see 10 arbitrary operations strung together to form an assembly language program. Although written in a distortion of APL, each step corresponds to a plausible assembly language operation. The lettered arguments refer to numerical values stored in the general-purpose data registers while three arguments are identified by their location in RAM. These three arguments may or may not be in the associative memory.

We assume that following a branch operation, the 10 instructions of Fig. 17.4 were placed in the look-ahead unit. From the point of view of the look-ahead unit, we have the unusual good fortune of only 1 branch instruction out of 10 instructions. Let us proceed to identify the tasks that must be accomplished by the look-ahead unit during each time period. We assume that nothing has previously been done for any of these instructions. The pipelines are empty, and so forth.

During step 1, arguments f and g must be entered into the division pipeline. They must somehow be tagged so that the result will be recognized later. An identifier must in some way be associated with register e so that this register will not be used as an argument for the next 12 clock periods. Memory references must be initiated for the three arguments stored in RAM. The instructions must be shifted ahead in the look-ahead unit with a memory reference initiated to replace instruction 10. These last operations, which must be repeated each step, will not be mentioned again.

Instructions 2 and 3 are conveniently executed in one step each. At steps 4 and 5, two sets of arguments are entered into the multiplication pipeline. If the data word in memory location 353432 was in the associative memory, all but the register **PROD** of the multiplication pipeline would be filled at step 6.

1. $e \leftarrow f \div g$
2. $a \leftarrow g + b$
3. $a \leftarrow a + c$
4. $c \leftarrow a \times d$
5. $d \leftarrow b \times d$
6. $b \leftarrow a \times (\mathbf{RAM}\langle 353432\rangle)$
7. $g \leftarrow d \times a$
8. $\rightarrow (c < \mathbf{RAM}\langle 353433\rangle)/(\mathbf{RAM}\langle 357777\rangle)$
9. $h \leftarrow e \times c$
10. $b \leftarrow g \div a$

a	f
b	g
c	h
d	i
e	j

(a) Data registers   (b)

Figure 17.4. APL-like assembly language program.

At first glance, it would appear that a multiplication pipeline will be completely filled at step 7. However, the look-ahead unit must observe that the argument d is tagged and that the new value has not yet emerged from the multiplication pipeline. The control unit must wait two clock periods before instruction 7 can be initiated.

In the meantime, look-ahead control advances to step 8. Conveniently, the new value of c emerges from the multiplication pipeline at this step so that it may be compared with the contents of memory location 353433 if available. If c is smaller, a new string of instructions must be placed in the look-ahead unit while the instuctions prior to 8 are completed.

If c is larger, instruction 9 may be initiated. Depending on holdups in prior instructions, the new value of e may or may not have emerged from the division pipeline. Also at step 9, instruction 7 may be initiated as the argument d is now available.

Clearly, the design of a control unit able to keep track of all the details discussed here would be a formidable task; also many of the details, particularly those involving new instructions being entered in the look-ahead unit, were not even mentioned.

The foregoing discussion reflected an attempt to handle one instruction per time step. If we consider all that must be done, it would be difficult indeed to realize this goal in the actual design of a look-ahead unit. Nonetheless, it is necessary if one processor is to have any chance of keeping up with the multiplication pipeline. Given the achievement of the goal of one instruction per time step, it is doubtful that one processor could have more than one computation in the pipeline often enough to be worth the cost of the multiplication unit. Filling the pipelines would require an extremely cooperative programmer or compiler.

Given the possibility of multiprocessing, execution overlap may be viewed in a different light. This is the topic of the next section.

17.4 Reduced Instruction Set Machines

The acronym RISC has recently been applied to a class of machines with a much smaller instruction set than the superminicomputers of the 1980s or even the first generation 16- and 32-bit microprocessors. One argument has been that the decoding of a complex instruction set adds significant delay in each clock period of instruction execution. You might verify this by analyzing the timing of critical steps in the byte interval instruction stream machine of Section 6.11 following the procedure of Section 7.4.

The argument in favor of an elaborate instruction set is, of course, that fewer instructions are required to implement a algorithm. If the overall execution time is shorter even though more instructions are executed for a given task, the advantage would fall to the RISC machine. At this writing, computer systems based on RISC processors are entering the marketplace. Preliminary studies have predicted that these machines can be competitive in certain classes of applications, in particular computer-aided engineering work stations.

Reducing the instruction set of a single chip processor will, among other advantages, decrease the chip area requird for instruction decoding. This chip area will typically be used for an on-chip instruction cache and two or more large arrays of data registers. Because of decreased execution time for all instructions operating only on data from the on-chip arrays, the chips can be driven at relatively higher clock rates. Off-chip memory would necessarily be asynchronous to this clock so that the hit ratio in the instruction cache and relative requirements for off-chip data would have significant impact on overall performance. A RISC will probably be most competitive where data management can be left up to the programmer in contrast to using one or more data caches. This would be most feasible in applications where a limited number of software products would be used repeatedly by all customers. Again, an example is the engineering work station.

The programming of some RISC architectures somewhat resembles microprogramming. That is, each instruction is separated into fields that control activities at separate points in the data paths. RISC programming and microprogramming differ in that RISC instructions are found in the primary address space rather than in a separate ROM or RAM. One such approach [8] incorporates a set of at least five ECL chips to maximize execution speed.

17.5 Parallel Processing

In the examples of Chapter 11, we observed that more than one processor could be designed into a system. So far, processors other than the CPU have been relegated to special tasks such as input-output processing with easily manageable interaction with the CPU. In this seciton, we shall consider briefly the possibility of processors of equal status working simultaneously on the same user program. This situation is usually called *parallel processing*. In one category of parallel processors, each processing element executes instructions from a single instruction stream but on different data. In the second category, the processors execute from individual instruction streams but work together on the same user problem.

First, let us consider the multiple-instruction stream approach. In Section 17.3, it was implied that to justify the cost of highly combinational arithmetic functional units, that these units must be kept reasonably busy. This implies an overall increase in the rate of execution of instructions within the CPU. In the case of the multiplication unit of Section 17.3, satisfactory utilization may mean only intermittent occurrences of more than one computation in the pipeline. The notion of continuously full pipelines within a general-purpose computing system may be wishful thinking.

The look-ahead unit, touched on in the previous section, represents an effort to increase the utilization rate of functional units. There it was assumed that only one program was in the process of execution at a given time. Relaxing this assumption leads to a multiple instruction stream. That is, let us postulate a set of n separate control units, each executing a separate program in central memory. Such a system is illustrated in Fig. 17.5. The processors share the items requiring the heaviest in-

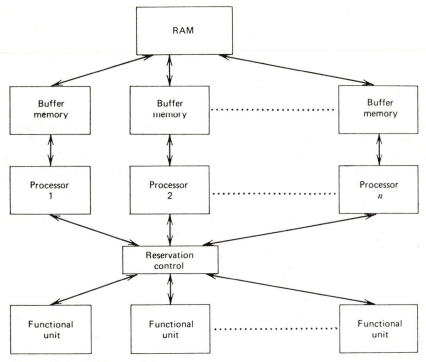

Figure 17.5. Multiprocessing.

vestment: the very large random access memory, peripheral equipments, and certain highly combinational functional units. The several processors should have less trouble keeping the pipelines filled than would a single look-ahead unit.

The advantage of the system in Fig. 17.5 is efficiency. The obvious disadvantage is that it is so large, and therefore so expensive, as to limit its use. In Fig. 17.5, the question might arise as to why the RAM is shared, rather than providing a separate smaller RAM for each processor. The reason is greater flexibility. If certain processors use less than their share of memory, this memory is available to a larger program that may be in the process of execution by another processor. Certain programs may even require the entire large memory. Although this situation would idle all but one processor, it still might be more economical than a frequent shuffling of overlays in a smaller memory.

Dedicating the entire configuration of Fig. 17.5 to a single program raises the question "Why can't all the processors work in parallel on the same program?" Clearly, if a program is serial in nature, that is, if most program steps depend on results of immediately preceding steps, it is not possible for more than one processor to work on the problem at a given time. But perhaps many problems are not all that serial. Perhaps they just look that way after being reduced to program form. Which problems can be formulated for parallel processing given the latitude to change even the numerical techniques or models used? Which, if any, programs written in the usual manner in a high-level language could be compiled for parallel processing? How difficult would be the writing of such a compiler? These are questions that we cannot answer but that must be faced by a designer contemplating a system relying on parallel processing for efficiency.

One more feature of Fig. 17.5, the reservation control block, merits further consideration. The interaction of more than one separate control unit has been encountered in the text. In most cases, this was a limited cooperative interaction between a processor and a supporting peripheral equipment. In Fig. 17.5, the processors are completely independent and competitive. That, at some point in time, two processors will attempt to supply arguments to one functional unit simultaneously, is unavoidable. At the minimum, some priorty network must be included. More likely, the reservation control will be a separate control unit similar to the memory bank control of Section 13.10.

The reservation contol cannot afford the luxury of sequential searching for requests, as was the case in the memory control. It must complete service of each request for a functional unit in only one or two clock periods. In the process, it must determine the priority of conflicting requests, check availability of the function unit, and tag arguments so that results may be returned to the correct processor. Simultaneous with servicing requests, it must return computed results. Again, no more than one or two clock periods can be allowed for this operation. Space limitations preclude presentation of the design of the reservation control. The design of a stripped-down version will be left as a problem for you.

The forerunner of most single instruction stream parallel processors was the ILLIAC IV. Although not installed on campus, it was the fourth in a series of computers developed at the University of Illinois. In its day, ILLIAC IV was a one-of-a-kind machine. With the advent of VLSI, array processors resembling this machine are finally becoming marketable products [10,14]. ILLIAC IV was designed as a very large multispecial-purpose machine. That is, it was intended for use for a variety of problems that consume extremely large amounts of time on ordinary computers. Not all programs can be run efficiently on ILLIAC IV, however.

A simplified hardware layout of one of four identical quadrants of ILLIAC IV is shown in Fig. 17.6. The disk memory and the Burroughs 6500 computer used for I/O communications are actually shared by all four quadrants. The quadrants can work independently or they can be joined together in a single array for large problems.

The 64 processing elements are actually independent arithmetic units. The basic clock period is 80 nsec. The use of emitter-coupled logic permits addition to be accomplished in three clock periods. The carry-save multiplication requires five clock periods. These figures are for 64-bit operations within each individual processing element (P.E.). The processing element memories are constructed using thin film technology to permit an access time of 120 nsec. You will note the close match achieved between the addition time and the memory access time.

The distinguishing feature of the ILLIAC IV organization is that the 64 processing elements do not possess individual control units. All P.E.s are under control of the single control unit shown. This feature constrains their operations such that all P.E.s must simultaneously execute the same operation on different data. The only local

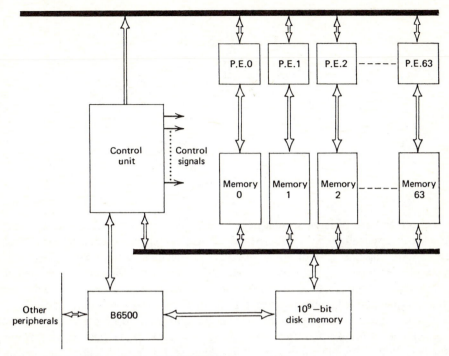

Figure 17.6. One quadrant of ILLIAC IV.

control available to the individual P.E.s is an 8-bit register, **RGM,** which stores the results of tests and specifies whether the P.E. will actually execute or will ignore an instruction issued by the control unit. The control unit depicted in Fig. 17.6 includes arithmetic and indexing capability, two 64-word buffer memories for accepting blocks of instructions from the P.E. memories, and broadcast registers to supply identical data items to all processing elements.

A principal advantage of the ILLIAC IV organization is necessarily the economy achieved in the sharing of a single control unit by 64 processing elements. An additional advantage in some applications is the fast transfer of information between operating registers in individual P.E.s. Interconnections between the P.E.s are provided so that they may be arranged in a two-dimensional (8 × 8) array or a 64-element linear array. Actual realization of these advantages depends on keeping the processing elements busy. If contol signals are disabled by all but a few processors, most of the time, then ILLIAC IV is operating very inefficiently indeed. Achieving a high P.E. utilization rate requires careful choice of problems and careful programming. Among the problems that seem suited to ILLIAC IV are matrix algebra, partial differential equations including hydrodynamic flow and weather modeling, linear programming, multiple target tracking, and logic simulation for test sequence generation in LSI circuits.

The foregoing discussion has necessarily been brief. For details, refer to Refs. 4 and 5. The notion of an array of processing elements under control of a single control unit is interesting and worth including.

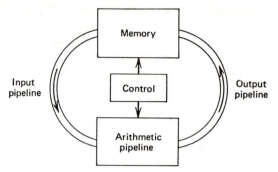

Figure 17.7. Pipeline processor.

Another form of large special-purpose computer seems to be suited to the very same set of applications as is ILLIAC IV. These are super pipeline machines. The CDC STAR was the first of these machines to become operational. The pipeline processor, illustrated figuratively in Fig. 17.7, gains its advantage by starting the retrieval of subsequent sets of operands, each located in memory adjacent to the first, before the first result has been returned to memory. To take maximum advantage of the pipeline concept, data on which similar operations are to be performed must be arranged in adjacent locations in memory. Thus, such sets of identical operations must actually exist in the applications algorithm as they will, to a sufficient extent, in those applications pointed out in the foregoing discussion of ILLIAC IV.

The arithmetic unit of Fig. 17.7 is arranged to perform arithmetic in pipeline form (see Section 17.7). In the special-purpose pipeline processor the memory read and write operations are also overlapped in pipeline form. Thus retrieval, arithmetic, and storage operations are performed in step as data move around the loop in Fig. 17.7. In most cases, all data in the pipeline must be subject to the same arithmetic operation. As an exception, the CDS STAR can perform the inner or dot product of two vectors as their elements pass through the piepleine in pairs.

Problems

17.1   Step 12 of Section 17.2 uses a Boolean function, f, to control whether or not a skip is to be executed. Write a Boolean algebraic expression for f.

17.2   Consider a look-ahead unit similar to the unit discussed in Section 17.3, but containing a block of 16 instruction registers, so that small loops can be contained with the unit. Assume that the instructions are replaced as a block after the last one is executed, or a jump out of the block. Write an AHPL control sequence for this look-ahead unit. Assume a 16-bank RAM but no scratch pad. Execution of the first instruction in a new block should begin as soon as it is received from memory.

17.3 Write the control sequence for the reservation control in Fig. 17.5. Assume that each request for a functional unit must be accomplished in no more than two clock periods.

17.4 Lay out a minicomputer version of ILLIAC IV. Assume that a single contol unit will contol eight processors, each possessing the approximate capability of RIC. Status flip-flops and a routing network must be included. Assume the processors to be arranged in a line.

Specify all registers required in the processors and the controller. Define a complete list of commands for the system. Include commands for routing data between the control memory and the individual processor memories. Also include commands providing for the testing and setting of status bits.

References

1. J. O. Murphy and R. M. Wade, "The IBM 360/195 in a World of Mixed Jobstreams," *Datamation*, Apr. 1970, p. 72.
2. J. E. Thorton, *Design of a Computer, The CDC 6600,* Scott Foresman, Glenview, Ill., 1970.
3. T. C. Chen, "Parallelism, Pipelining and Computer Efficiency," *Computer Design*, Jan. 1971, p. 69.
4. G. H. Barnes, et al., "The ILLIAC IV Computer," *IEEE Trans. Computers*, Aug. 1968, p. 746.
5. D. E. McIntyre, "An Introduction to the ILLIAC IV Computer," *Datamation*, Apr., 1970.
6. W. R. Graham, "The Parallel and the Pipeline Computers," *Datamation*, Apr. 1970, p. 68.
7. "Control Data 7600 Computer System," *Reference Manual*, Publication No. 60258200.
8. B. Case, "Building Blocks Yield Fast 32-bit RISC Machines," *Computer Design*, July 1985.
9. D. P. Siewiorek, C. G. Bell, and A. Newell, *Computer Structures: Principles and Examples*, McGraw–Hill, New York, 1982.
10. P. Alexander, "Array Processor Design Concepts," *Computer Design*, Dec. 1981, pp. 163–174.
11. *MC68000 16-Bit Microcessor User Manual*, 3rd ed. Prentice–Hall, Englewood Cliffs, N.J., 1982.
12. J. K. Iliffe, *Advanced Computer Design*, Prentice–Hall, Englewood Cliffs, N.J., 1982.
13. *VAX Architectue Handbook*, Digital Equipment Corp., Maynard, Mass., 1981.
14. J. F. Burns, "Greater Throughput with Multiple Array Processors," *Computer Design*, Sept. 1981, pp. 207–212.

Description of the Representative Instructional Computer (RIC)

In Part I of this appendix, we have assembled together all the steps of the RIC control sequence from Chapter 6 and all the interrupt processing steps presented in Section 10.3 so that you will be able to refer to a single description of RIC. The following cannot be considered a complete module description because declarations have been omitted and because those portions of the descriptions not provided in the text are not included. To avoid confusion, the control sequence in Part I has not been modified to incorporate the slow direct addressing mode presented in Section 10.8. The modified steps 4 through 19 supporting this addressing mode are provided separately in Part II.

Part I Description of the RIC Module

1A	$\rightarrow (\overline{irq \wedge ief}, irq \wedge ief\,)/(1, 200)$.	
1	$MA \leftarrow PC; shf \leftarrow 0$.	
2	$ADBUS = MA; MD \leftarrow DBUS; read = 1; PC \leftarrow INC(PC)$.	
3	$IR \leftarrow MD$.	
4	$\rightarrow (IR[4])/(50)$.	"16-bit instructions"
5	NO <u>DELAY</u>	" branch instructions "
	$\rightarrow (\overline{IR[0] \wedge IR[1] \wedge IR[2] \wedge IR[3]})/(30)$.	
6	NO <u>DELAY</u>	
	$\rightarrow (IR[5])/(8)$.	
7	$MD[0{:}7] \leftarrow \overline{8 \top 0} \wedge MD[8]$;	"sign extension"
	$\rightarrow (22)$.	

8   NO DELAY
      $\rightarrow$ (IR[7])/(11).

9   *MA* ← *MD*[8:31].

10   *ADBUS = MA; MD ← DBUS; read* = 1.

11   *MA* ← (*MD*[8:31] ! ADD(*MD*[8:31]; *IX*)) * (*IR*[6], *IR*[6]).

12   NO DELAY
      $\rightarrow$ ($\bigwedge$/*IR*[1:3])/(14).

13   *PC ← MA;*
      $\rightarrow$ (1).

14   NO DELAY
      $\rightarrow$ ($\bigwedge$/*IR*[0:2])/(16).

15   *IR*[8:31] ← *MA;*   "to JSR"
      $\rightarrow$ (32).

16   NO DELAY
      $\rightarrow$ (*IR*[1] $\wedge$ *IR*[2])/(19).

17   *MD ← AC.*

18   *write* = 1; *ADBUS = MA; DBUS = MD;*
      $\rightarrow$ (1).

19   *ADBUS = MA; MD ← DBUS; read* = 1;
      $\rightarrow$ ($\overline{IR[0]}$ $\wedge$ *IR*[1])/(22).

20   *MD ← (INC(MD)* ! DEC(*MD*)) * ($\overline{IR[3]}$, *IR*[3]);
      zff ← $\bigvee$ /*OBUS; nff* ← *OBUS*[0].

21   *write* = 1; *ADBUS = MA; DBUS = MD;*
      $\rightarrow$ (1).

22   *ABUS* = ($\overline{MD}$! *MD*) * ((($\overline{IR[0]}$ $\wedge$ $\overline{IR[1]}$) $\wedge$ $\overline{(\overline{IR[2]} \vee IR[3])}$),
       ((*IR*[0] $\wedge$ *IR*[1]) $\wedge$ (*IR*[2] $\underline{\vee}$ *IR*[3])));
   BBUS = AC; cin = (*cff* $\wedge$ $\overline{IR[3]}$) $\vee$ (*IR*[1] $\wedge$ *IR*[3]);
   OBUS = (ADD[1:32] (*ABUS; BBUS; cin*) ! (*ABUS* $\wedge$ *BBUS*)
     ! ($\overline{ABUS}$ $\vee$ *BBUS*) ! (*ABUS* $\oplus$ *BBUS*) ! *ABUS*)
      * (($\overline{IR[0]}$ $\wedge$ $\overline{(IR[2]} \vee IR[3]))$,
     (*IR*[0] $\wedge$ $\overline{IR[3]}$), ($\overline{IR[0]}$ $\wedge$ $\overline{IR[2]}$ $\wedge$ *IR*[3]),
     (*IR*[0] $\wedge$ *IR*[2] $\wedge$ *IR*[3]), (*IR*[0] $\wedge$ *IR*[2] $\wedge$ $\overline{IR[3]}$));
   AC * ($\overline{IR[2] \wedge IR[3]}$) ← *OBUS;*
   cff * ($\overline{IR[0]}$ $\wedge$ ($\overline{IR[2]}$ $\vee$ *IR*[3])) ← ADD[0] (*ABUS; BBUS; cin*);
   zff ← $\bigvee$ /*OBUS; nff* ← *OBUS*[0];
   vff * ($\overline{IR[0]}$ $\wedge$ ($\overline{IR[2]}$ $\vee$ *IR*[3])) ←
     (*ABUS*[0] $\wedge$ *BBUS*[0] $\wedge$ $\overline{ADD[1](ABUS; BBUS; cin)}$)
     $\vee$ ($\overline{ABUS[0]}$ $\wedge$ $\overline{BBUS[0]}$ $\wedge$ ADD[1] (*ABUS; BBUS; cin*));
      $\rightarrow$ (1).

30   $\rightarrow$ (($\bigvee$/(*IR*[7:15] $\wedge$ (C, $\overline{C}$,Z, $\overline{Z}$,N, $\overline{N}$,V, $\overline{V}$, N $\oplus$ V))) $\oplus$ *IR*[6])/(1).

31   NO DELAY
      $\rightarrow$ (*IR*[5])/(35).

32   *MA* ← DEC(*SP*); *SP* ← DEC(*SP*).

33   *MD* ← 8 $\top$ 0, *PC.*

34   *ADBUS* = *MA; DBUS* = *MD; write* = 1.

35   *ABUS* = (16 ⊤ 0, *IR*[16:31] ! 16 ⊤ 0, *IR*[16:31] ! 8 ⊤ 0,
      IR[8:31])) ∗ ($\overline{IR}$[0] ∧ ($\overline{IR}$[16], *IR*[16]), *IR*[0]);
    BBUS = 8 ⊤ 0, *PC; cin* = 0;   " accomodate JSR "
    OBUS = (*ABUS* ! ADD[1:32](*ABUS; BBUS; cin*)) ∗ (*IR*[0], *IR*[0]);
    PC ← *OBUS*[8:31];
    → (1).

50   → (*IR*[0] ∧ *IR*[1])/(70).   "other 16-bit"

51   NO DELAY
    → (*IR*[1] ∧ *IR*[2])/(60).   "shift/rotate"

52   *BBUS*[8:31] ← (*AC*[8:31] ! *IX* ! *SP*) ∗
      (*IR*[12], (*IR*[12] ∧ *IR*[13]), (*IR*[12] ∧ *IR*[13]));
    BBUS[0:7] = (8 ⊤ 0 ! *AC*[0:7]) ∗ (*IR*[12], *IR*[12]);
    ABUS[0:27] = (28 ⊤ 0 ! 28 ⊤ 0) ∗ (*IR*[12], *IR*[12]));
    ABUS[28:31] = *IR*[12:15];
    OBUS = (*ABUS* ! *BBUS*) ∗ (*IR*[10], *IR*[10]);
    MD ← *OBUS*.

53   *ABUS* = (*MD* ! *MD*) ∗ ((($\overline{IR}$[0] ∧ *IR*[1]) ∧ ($\overline{IR}$[2] ∨ *IR*[3])),
      ((*IR*[0] ∧ *IR*[1]) ∧ (*IR*[2] ∨ *IR*[3])));
    BBUS = (*AC* ! 8 ⊤ 0, *IX* ! 8 ⊤ 0, *SP*) ∗
      ($\overline{IR}$[6], (*IR*[6] ∧ $\overline{IR}$[7]), (*IR*[6] ∧ *IR*[7]));
    cin = (*cff* ∧ $\overline{IR}$[3]) ∨ ($\overline{IR}$[1] ∧ *IR*[3]);
    OBUS = (ADD[1:32](*ABUS; BBUS; cin*) ! (*ABUS* ∧ *BBUS*)
      ! (*ABUS* ∨ *BBUS*) ! (*ABUS* ⊕ *BBUS*) ! *ABUS*)
      ∗ (($\overline{IR}$[0] ∧ (*IR*[2] ∨ *IR*[3])),
      (*IR*[0] ∧ *IR*[3]), (*IR*[0] ∧ $\overline{IR}$[2] ∧ $\overline{IR}$[3]),
      (*IR*[0] ∧ *IR*[2] ∧ *IR*[3]), (*IR*[0] ∧ *IR*[2] ∧ $\overline{IR}$[3]));
    AC ∗ (($\overline{IR}$[2] ∧ $\overline{IR}$[3]) ∧ $\overline{IR}$[6]) ← *OBUS*;
    (*IX* ! *SP*) ∗ (($\overline{IR}$[2] ∧ $\overline{IR}$[3]) ∧ *IR*[6] ∧ ($\overline{IR}$[7], *IR*[7]))
      ← *OBUS*[8:31];
    cff ∗ ($\overline{IR}$[0] ∧ ($\overline{IR}$[2] ∨ *IR*[3])) ← ADD[0](*ABUS; BBUS; cin*);
    zff ← ∨/*OBUS; nff* ← *OBUS*[0];
    vff ∗ (*IR*[0] ∧ ($\overline{IR}$[2] ∨ *IR*[3])) ←
      ($\overline{ABUS}$[0] ∧ $\overline{BBUS}$[0] ∧ ADD[1](*ABUS; BBUS; cin*))
      ∨ (*ABUS*[0] ∧ *BBUS*[0] ∧ $\overline{\text{ADD}[1](ABUS; BBUS; cin)}$));
    → (100).

60   *SHC* ← DEC(*IR*[11:15]).

61   *AC*[0] ← (*AC*[0] ! *AC*[1] ! *AC*[31] ! *cff* ! 0) ∗
      ((*IR*[5] ∧ *IR*[6] ∧ *IR*[10]), *IR*[10],
      ($\overline{IR}$[5] ∧ *IR*[6] ∧ *IR*[10]), (*IR*[5] ∧ $\overline{IR}$[6] ∧ *IR*[10]),
      (*IR*[5] ∧ *IR*[6] ∧ *IR*[10]));
    AC[1:30] ← (*AC*[0:29] ! *AC*[2:31]) ∗ (*IR*[10], *IR*[10]);
    AC[31] ← (*AC*[30] ! *AC*[0] ! *cff* ! 0) ∗
      (*IR*[10], (*IR*[5] ∧ *IR*[6] ∧ $\overline{IR}$[10]),

$(IR[5] \land \overline{IR[6]} \land \overline{IR[10]}), (\overline{IR[5]} \land \overline{IR[10]}));$

$cff * (IR[5] \land IR[6]) \leftarrow (AC[31] ! AC[0]) * (IR[10], \overline{IR[10]});$

$SHC \leftarrow DEC(SHC);$

$\rightarrow (\bigvee /SHC, \overline{\bigvee /SHC})/(61, 100).$

70   NO DELAY

$\rightarrow (DCD(IR[2:3]))/(71, 110, 130, 170).$

71   NO DELAY

$\rightarrow (\bigvee /IR[6:9])/(100).$

72   DEAD END.

100   NO DELAY

$\rightarrow (shf)/(1).$

101    $IR[0:15] \leftarrow IR[16:31]; shf \leftarrow 1;$

$\rightarrow (50).$

130    $\rightarrow (DCD(IR[6:7]))/(131, 140, 150, 160).$

131    $cff \leftarrow IR[9];$

$\rightarrow (100).$

140    $\rightarrow (IR[9])/(144).$

141    $SP \leftarrow DEC(SP); MA \leftarrow DEC(SP).$

142    $MD \leftarrow AC.$

143    $ADBUS = MA; DBUS = MD; write = 1;$

$\rightarrow (100).$

144    $MA \leftarrow SP.$

145    $ADBUS = MA; MD \leftarrow DBUS; read = 1; SP \leftarrow INC(SP).$

146    $AC * IR[8] \leftarrow MD;$

$PC * IR[8] \leftarrow MD[8:31];$

$\rightarrow (100).$

200    $ief \leftarrow 0.$

201    $SP \leftarrow DEC(SP).$

202    $MA \leftarrow SP; MD \leftarrow 8 \top 0, PC; SP \leftarrow DEC(SP).$

203    $ADBUS = MA; DBUS = MD; write = 1;$

$MA \leftarrow SP; MD \leftarrow 24 \top 0, SR; SP \leftarrow DEC(SP).$

204    $ADBUS = MA; DBUS = MD; write = 1;$

$MA \leftarrow SP; MD \leftarrow AC.$

205    $ADBUS = MA; DBUS = MD; write = 1.$

206    $ADBUS = 24 \top 0; MD \leftarrow DBUS; read = 1.$

207    $PC \leftarrow MD[8:31];$

$\rightarrow (1A).$

210    $ief \leftarrow 1.$

211    $MA \leftarrow SP; SP \leftarrow INC(SP).$

212    $ADBUS = MA; MD \leftarrow DBUS; read = 1;$

$MA \leftarrow SP; SP \leftarrow INC(SP).$

213    $ADBUS = MA; MD \leftarrow DBUS; read = 1;$

$AC \leftarrow MD; MA \leftarrow SP; SP \leftarrow INC(SP).$

214    $ADBUS = MA; MD \leftarrow DBUS; read = 1;$

$SR \leftarrow MD[24:31].$

215     $PC \leftarrow MD[8:31]$;
        $\rightarrow$ (1A).

Part II Modified Steps for Slow Direct Addressing

5   NO $\underline{DELAY}$ " branch instructions"
        $\rightarrow$ ($IR[0] \wedge IR[1] \wedge IR[2] \wedge IR[3]$)/(30).
6   NO $\underline{DELAY}$
        $\rightarrow$ ($IR[5]$, $\underline{IR[5]} \wedge IR[6]$, $IR[5] \wedge IR[6]$)/(8, 7, 7A).
7       $MD[0:7] \leftarrow 8 \top 0 \wedge MD[8]$;
        $\rightarrow$ (22).
7A $MA \leftarrow MD[8:31]$;
        $\rightarrow$ (16).
16   NO $\underline{DELAY}$
        $\rightarrow$ ($IR[1] \wedge IR[2]$)/(19).
17      $MD \leftarrow AC$.
18      $write = 1$; $ADBUS = MA$; $DBUS = MD$;
        $\rightarrow$ ($IR[5]$, $\underline{IR[5]} \wedge ack$, $IR[5] \wedge ack$)/(1, 18A, 18).
18A $\rightarrow$ (ack, ack)/(18A, 1).
19      $ADBUS = MA$; $MD \leftarrow DBUS$; $\underline{read} = 1$;
        $\rightarrow$ ($IR[5]$, $IR[5] \wedge ack$, $IR[5] \wedge ack$)/(19B, 19A, 19).
19A $\rightarrow$ (ack)/(19A).
19B   NO $\underline{DELAY}$
        $\rightarrow$ ($IR[0] \wedge IR[1]$)/(22).

Index